WISCONSIN

THOMAS HUHTI

Contents

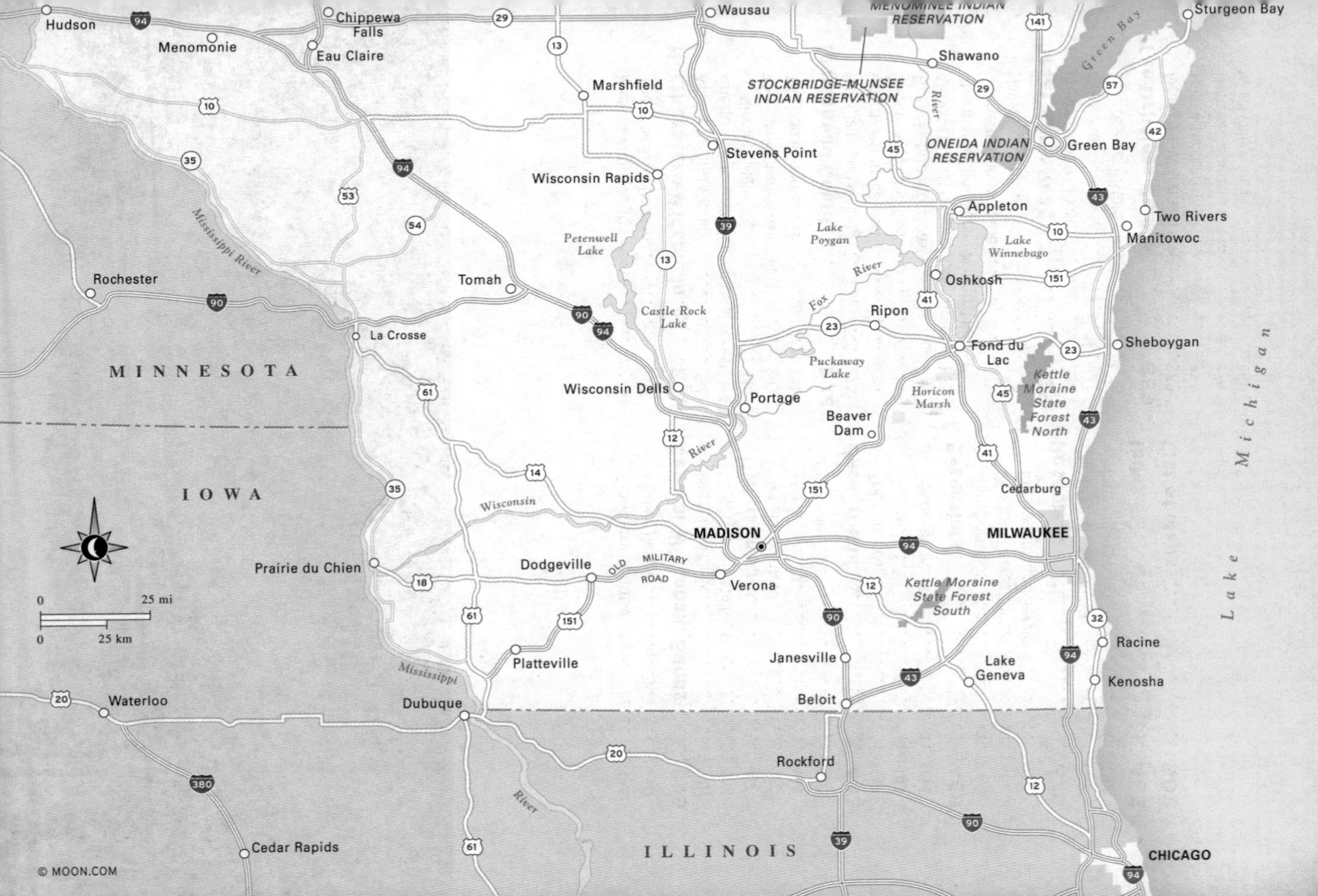

Hudson
Chippewa Falls
Wausau
MENOMINEE INDIAN RESERVATION
Sturgeon Bay
Menomonie
Eau Claire
Shawano
Green Bay
Marshfield
STOCKBRIDGE-MUNSEE INDIAN RESERVATION
River
ONEIDA INDIAN RESERVATION
Green Bay
Stevens Point
Wisconsin Rapids
Appleton
Two Rivers
Mississippi River
Petenwell Lake
Lake Poygan
Lake Winnebago
Manitowoc
Rochester
Tomah
River
Oshkosh
Fox
Castle Rock Lake
Ripon
La Crosse
Fond du Lac
Sheboygan
MINNESOTA
Puckaway Lake
Kettle Moraine State Forest North
Wisconsin Dells
Portage
Horicon Marsh
Beaver Dam
River
Cedarburg
IOWA
Wisconsin
Lake Michigan
MADISON
MILWAUKEE
Prairie du Chien
Dodgeville
OLD MILITARY ROAD
Verona
Kettle Moraine State Forest South
0 25 mi
0 25 km
Platteville
Janesville
Racine
Lake Geneva
Mississippi
Kenosha
Waterloo
Dubuque
Beloit
Rockford
River
Cedar Rapids
ILLINOIS
CHICAGO
© MOON.COM

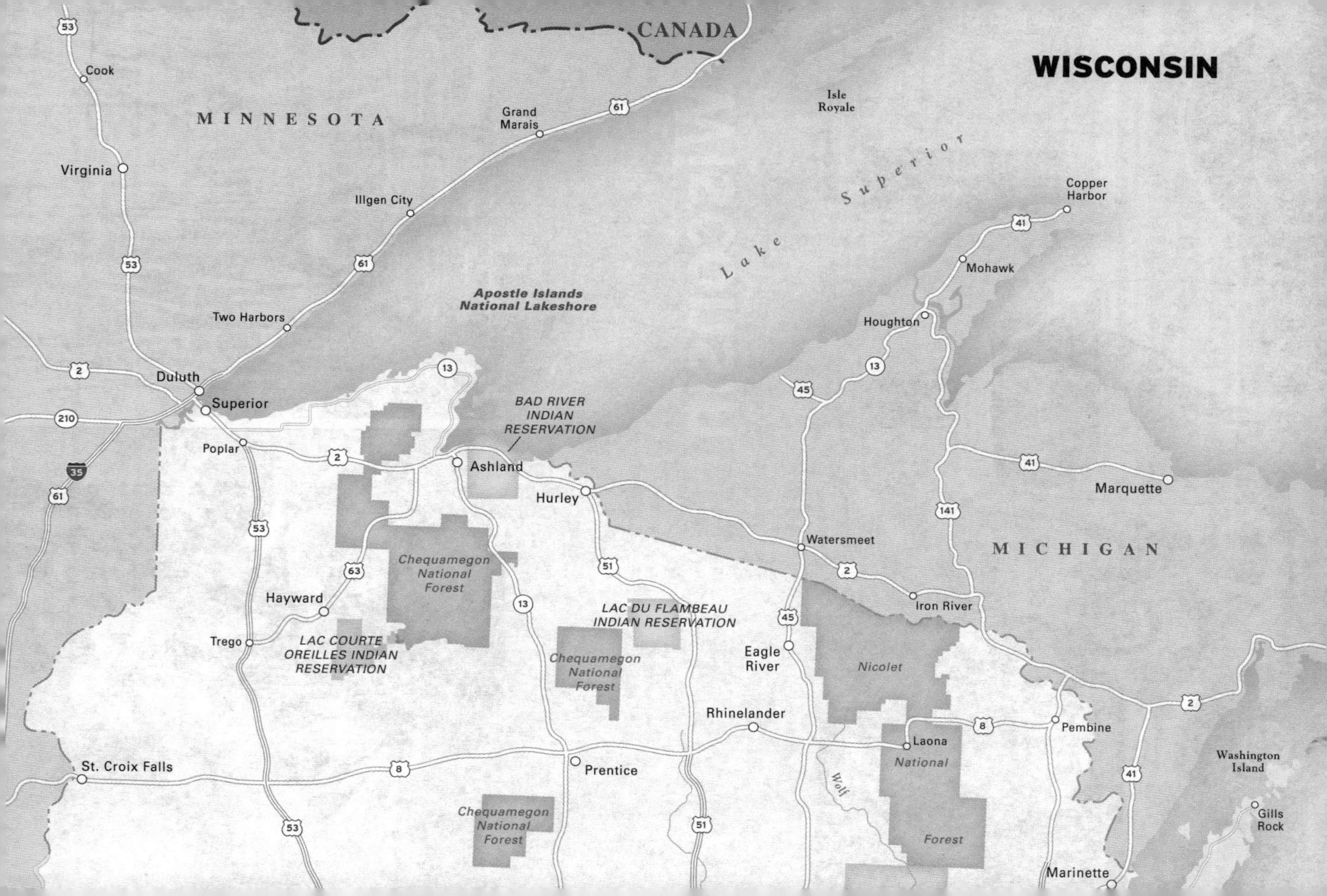
WISCONSIN
CANADA
MINNESOTA
MICHIGAN
Lake Superior
Isle Royale
Apostle Islands National Lakeshore
BAD RIVER INDIAN RESERVATION
LAC DU FLAMBEAU INDIAN RESERVATION
LAC COURTE OREILLES INDIAN RESERVATION
Chequamegon National Forest
Chequamegon National Forest
Chequamegon National Forest
Nicolet National Forest
Wolf
Cook
Virginia
Grand Marais
Illgen City
Two Harbors
Duluth
Superior
Poplar
Ashland
Hurley
Hayward
Trego
Copper Harbor
Mohawk
Houghton
Marquette
Watersmeet
Iron River
Eagle River
Rhinelander
Laona
Pembine
Prentice
St. Croix Falls
Washington Island
Gills Rock
Marinette
53
61
2
210
35
13
63
51
45
41
141
8

DISCOVER

Wisconsin

For generations, bumper stickers proclaimed "Escape to Wisconsin." The Department of Tourism later shelved this for other "genius" PR slogans, but so overwhelmingly opposed were the citizenry that the state chambers of commerce resurrected it. Succinctly Wisconsin: a retreat, a sojourn, a mental breather—a genuine escape.

Heck, even onetime Badger John Muir had it figured out in the 19th century when he proclaimed *Oh, that glorious Wisconsin wilderness!* That still holds true today for the hordes coming into the state pulling boats, bikes, kayaks, and canoes, all for that chance of bucolic splendor.

Wisconsin also isn't what you might think it is; it's even better. Wisconsin is truly Midwestern. It is generally content to remain in the middle on most things—except such important issues as livability quotients, at which it tends to excel. It's one of the top five most livable states in the nation. It's also the Midwest's overall most popular travel destination. And it boasts the planet's most diverse glacial topography, the United States' middle section's most amazing cataracts, and an immense North Woods region—so big that its national forest has

Clockwise from top left: hiking in Devil's Lake State Park; crabapple blossoms in spring; sublime views from the steeple at Holy Hill; superb views from Trempealeau Mountain; sandhill cranes; roadside stop in Door County

two names. Oh, and recreation? We're tops (or thereabouts) in bicycling, cross-country skiing, snowmobiling, fishing, and scenic hiking trails.

Indeed, Wisconsin puts the lie to all those clichés about flyover land, cow-flop redolence, hayseeds, corn-fed . . . you get the picture.

Folks come for a visit or to attend university and genuinely miss it when they leave. In fact, many come back. I've met more than a few who came for a visit decades ago and loved it so much that they return, often to the same cabin on a lake, every single year.

This has as much to do with the people of Wisconsin who, I'm happy to report, are the type who will chat you up and consider you a friend only five minutes after they meet you.

If this makes us rubes, then we'll happily plead guilty.

Clockwise from top left: relaxing on Lake Geneva; rock formation on Basswood Island; cow statue in New Glarus; jogging in the University of Wisconsin Arboretum

New

10 TOP EXPERIENCES

1 **Get Out on the Water:** Every vehicle in Wisconsin seems to be either towing a boat or lugging a canoe on the way to a watery escape from routine. Choose your destination: a stream, a lake, or the mighty Mississippi (page 28).

2 **Pick Door County Cherries:** Plan your own cherry harvest or snap a photo of the flowering orchards (page 140).

3 **Say "Cheese!":** Wisconsin produces over 650 varietals and makes one-quarter of U.S. cheese. Learn why Badger State denizens wear foam cheese heads with pride (page 29)!

^
^
^

4 **Grab a Beer:** Head to Milwaukee to find out how the "Beer City" earned its nickname at one of the many micro- or mega-breweries (page 43).

5 Follow Frank Lloyd Wright: The native architect shaped the natural beauty of the state into numerous famed buildings (page 24).

6 Root for the Packers: You don't need to bleed green and gold to get swept up in the Green Bay Packers fandom. Tour Lambeau Field, make the pilgrimage to the Hall of Fame, or watch a practice (page 201).

7 Feast at a Fish Fry: Given the 15,000 lakes, it's no wonder that fish is a mainstay here. A Friday night is simply not a Friday night without a fish fry (page 61).

>>>

8 Go Snowmobiling: What better place to rush along the frozen landscape than where snowmobiles were first invented (page 254)?

<<<

9 Take the Great River Road Trip: Explore one of the most precious, undeveloped areas of the state along the famed road that parallels the Mississippi (page 329).

>>>

10 **Enjoy Thrills and Spills:** You just haven't "done" Wisconsin without a trip to one of the boisterous Wisconsin Dells Waterparks (page 402).

Planning Your Trip

Where to Go

Milwaukee

The low-key residents are proud of their cultural, educational, and architectural gems along Milwaukee's fabulous **lakefront.** The wonderfully preserved **ethnic neighborhoods** and **Historic Third Ward** offer the state's best urban trekking tours. See what beer hath wrought at the sublime **Pabst Mansion.** Yet that lakefront beckons—hop aboard a **fishing charter.** Meander along the **spectacular bike paths.** And don't forget the names that made Milwaukee famous: the gargantuan **Miller Brewing** and **Harley-Davidson.**

Madison

The Mad City, also known as Madtown or the island surrounded by reality, is a vibrant and fetching city among a quartet of jewellike lakes, upon one of which sits eye-catching **Monona Terrace.** There's push and pull with the state government, represented by the grand **State Capitol,** and the **University of Wisconsin.** But most residents are nature lovers; you'll find no better chances to walk amid native state flora than at the UW's **Arboretum** and the **Olbrich Botanical Gardens.**

Southeastern Wisconsin

This true gateway region welcomes many travelers from Chicago. Extraordinary museums and parks await in **Kenosha** and **Racine,** the latter also home to much Wisconsin native **Frank Lloyd Wright's** architecture. Take the smaller roads and discover the **Geneva Lake** area. A crucial North American migration flyway with literally millions of birds is **Horicon Marsh.**

Door County

Jutting into Lake Michigan, the geographic "thumb" of Wisconsin offers the sublimest collection of **state parks** in the Midwest and the highest concentration of **lighthouses** of any U.S. county. How about **picturesque towns** right out of 19th-century postcards? Off the northern tip lies **Washington Island,** an isolated community where time seems not to matter. Beyond is another island, **Rock Island State Park,** the most superb camping spot in the state.

East-Central Waters

These waterways truly made the state, welcoming legions of immigrants and floating timber for paper mills of the **Fox Cities,** dominated by the enormous **Lake Winnebago.** To the west are such picturesque resort lands you'll run out of digital storage space, as well as the wild and wonderful **Wolf River.** No visit to Wisconsin would be complete without a pilgrimage to one of the NFL's most sacred institutions: **Lambeau Field,** home of the **Green Bay Packers.**

Northeastern Wisconsin

Find one of the world's highest concentrations of **lakes** and two of the Midwest's grandest rivers, the **Peshtigo River** and the **Turtle-Flambeau Flowage.** Marinette and Iron County **waterfalls** offer the most scenic drive in the region. Sleds have always ruled in northern Wisconsin, and the mecca is **Snowmobile Central** near the **Eagle River Chain of Lakes.**

Indianhead Country

Hydrophiles adore the **St. Croix National Scenic Riverway.** Anglers battle lunker muskies near **Hayward.** From preciously anachronistic Bayfield, head to the magnificent **Apostle Islands National Lakeshore.** Everyone should trace the Lake Superior coast along **Highway**

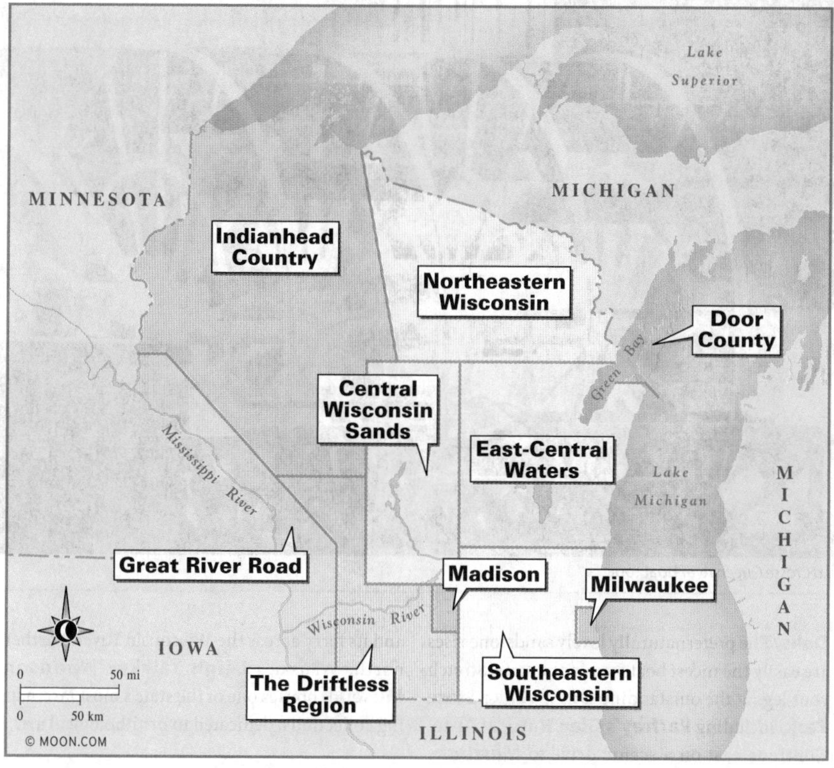

13—the most scenic drive in the state, bar none. **Pattison State Park** offers the best glimpse at the region's superb waterfalls, but don't forsake Superior's hardest-working **harbor** in the country.

Great River Road

For 200 miles, find untouristed river towns: **Alma,** funky **Trempealeau,** or **Cassville,** where eagles soar and one of the nation's last river ferries chugs across the Mississippi River. See the commanding view at **Granddad's Bluff** in La Crosse. At **Wyalusing State Park,** a ridgetop hike offers lovely views of the confluence of the Wisconsin and Mississippi Rivers. No better example of what sprang from enterprising settler souls exists than Prairie du Chien's **Villa Louis.**

The Driftless Region

This, the largest unglaciated region in the northern Midwest, is where the land gets ambitious. **Spring Green** was the home of Frank Lloyd Wright. Nearby is the architectural opposite, **The House on the Rock.** Roll through **Mineral Point,** very nearly still a 19th-century Cornish village, and **New Glarus,** a slice of Switzerland. Water lovers head for **Lower Wisconsin State Riverway** and, particularly, the Kickapoo River, which meanders through the twists and turns of the **Kickapoo Valley Reserve.** The **Elroy-Sparta State Recreational Trail** is the original U.S. rail-to-trail cycling route.

Central Wisconsin Sands

Central Wisconsin has the state's number-one family attraction—water park-heavy **Wisconsin**

La Crosse Queen river boat tour

Dells. The preternaturally lovely sandstone rises are easily the nicest boat tour in the state. Stretch your legs at the outstanding **Devil's Lake State Park,** including **Parfrey's Glen Natural Area.** Continue east on a scenic drive to **Merrimac** and its ferry across the Wisconsin River. Farther north, Wausau's **Leigh Yawkey Woodson Museum** houses one of the state's most fascinating collections, dedicated to ornithological art.

When to Go

Wisconsin is a **four-season** place with something for everyone in any season. Most visitors do come **between Memorial Day and Labor Day.** All accommodations, restaurants, and attractions will be open during this time; prices also rise significantly in more popular spots, and many lodgings will require a two- or three-night minimum stay. Another peak season is from **late September through late October,** when throngs arrive to witness fall's splendorous colors. Between Labor Day and late September you can often get great rates and, if cold weather comes early, great colors. Winter in general sees fewer visitors except for snowmobilers and skiers, and areas popular for those activities will not have lower rates. Other places may shut down entirely from November to April. Few people come in March and early April, as these months are grim, gray, muddy, and windy. Garrison Keillor said it best: March was intended by God "to show people who don't drink what a hangover feels like." Then again, it's dirt cheap to visit during this time.

Wisconsin Weekends

These itineraries can either be used as weekend getaways or combined for longer trips. Door County and the Wisconsin Dells are the most popular getaways in the state.

Milwaukee

Save this beer-centric city for a long weekend. After exploring Milwaukee, head to Door County or westward to the capital, Madison.

DAY 1

Driving to Milwaukee from Chicago, choose **Kenosha, Racine,** or a boat tour of **Geneva Lake** along the way. A drive through the **Kettle Moraine State Forest-Southern Unit** is a primer on glacial history right near a walk-through people's history at **Old World Wisconsin.** In Milwaukee, stay downtown in the historic **Pfister** or at **Brewhouse Suites** in the renovated **Pabst Brewery** just northwest of downtown.

DAY 2

The Milwaukee **lakefront** is a must. Tour **Miller Brewing** or the **Harley-Davidson Museum** and step into the unparalleled **Milwaukee Public Museum.** If you have time, go north to postcard-perfect **Cedarburg.**

Madison

After exploring Madison and Devil's Lake, you're so close to the Wisconsin Dells that you should try to combine the trips if you can.

DAY 1

In Madison, start with the architectural gems: Frank Lloyd Wright's **Monona Terrace** and, a few steps away, the magnificent **State Capitol.** Stroll the pedestrian-friendly State Street area to the **University of Wisconsin-Madison campus.** The **University of Wisconsin Arboretum** has the best urban trails anywhere, or visit the **Olbrich Botanical Gardens.** Downtown is the lovely **Mansion Hill Inn**.

DAY 2

Choose a longish drive northeast to the extraordinary **Horicon Marsh Wildlife Area** or a combination circus experience and workout in **Baraboo** and **Devil's Lake State Park.**

Monona Terrace

Rustic Road-Tripping

Travel media writers have consistently voted Wisconsin one of the United States' greatest road-touring states, in part because many rural roads, originally farm-to-market routes, seem to have changed little in a century and a half.

Wisconsin's Department of Transportation has highlighted 120 of the state's best back-roads trips with its **Rustic Roads designation.** Every Rustic Road in the state is guaranteed to offer an amazing palette of colors **mid-September-late October.** Each also has its own web page linked from the Department of Transportation (www.wisconsindot.gov) website's "Travel" menu.

- Near **Milwaukee,** Cedarburg is a lovely anachronism. From here, take Highway NN northwest five miles and then north a few more miles on Highway M, where signs to **Rustic Road 52** (seven miles) lead you past fieldstone buildings and ancient cabins before skirting a wetlands preserve.
- Heading for **East-Central Waters?** From Waupaca, go southwest on Highway 22 to the Yankee village of Rural, possibly the state's quaintest original. From here, **Rustic Roads 23 and 24** (three miles total) form a V shape around Hartman Creek State Park and take you three times over the Crystal River atop stone bridges, then past a spring-fed trout stream.
- In **Northeastern Wisconsin,** the Peshtigo River Parkway **(Rustic Road 32)** cannot be beat for river beauty and waterfalls. To get here, head to little Pembine at the junction of U.S. 141 and U.S. 8. Head west on U.S. 8 approximately nine miles to signs leading you south. This is a big one, 37 miles long, but you'll have plenty of places to stop and rest at state and county parks.
- Also in **Northeastern Wisconsin, Rustic Road 60** begins at Highway K, two miles south of Boulder Junction along Highway M. Coming from the south, take U.S. 51 from Minocqua and follow signs to Boulder Junction. Driving for 11 miles, you'll pass the remains of logging camps, cruise through tunnels of conifers and hardwoods, and find an extant sawmill at the eastern end.
- In **Southwestern Wisconsin, Rustic Road 31** starts in West Salem northeast of La Crosse at the exit off I-90 at Highway C, running to Highway 16. Head north on Highway 16 to Highway 108 and the **Mindoro Cut,** 20 miles of some of the loveliest roller-coaster driving imaginable. A massive project when undertaken around the turn of the 20th century, the road was cut into a ridge between the La Crosse and Black River Valleys by hand, one of the most ambitious hand-built roads in the United States when it was finished in 1906.

During the spring or fall migratory periods, visit **Horicon Marsh;** otherwise, Devil's Lake is a gem of a park.

Door County

Door County is easily reached from Milwaukee and Madison. It's also customary for Wisconsin football fans to pilgrimage to Green Bay and **Lambeau Field** on the way to Door County or on the way back.

You could substitute one of the days in Door County with a ferry ride to quiet, great for biking **Washington Island** and potentially another short ferry ride to **Rock Island State Park** to hike as far as you can get from the mainland.

DAY 1

First day—explore the bay side of the Door's sublime natural environment and grand food, lodging, and shopping. Must-sees for nature and recreation are **Potawatomi, Peninsula,** and **Newport State Parks.** Spend the night in Fish Creek for the food and shopping; top picks for lodging are the **White Gull Inn** or the **Whistling Swan.**

DAY 2

On your second day, explore the lakeside. Must-sees are hiking or kayaking at **Whitefish Dunes State Park** or **The Ridges Sanctuary** as well as the nation's densest county concentration of **lighthouses.** This is the more tranquil side of Door County, and some people spend their entire weekends on this side for that reason.

Wisconsin Dells

Following a riotous trip to the Dells, you could head southwest to explore the rivers of Wisconsin.

DAY 1

Pick a megaresort and let the waterslide fun commence. Make sure you do your homework; you can get some amazing deals. Top choice for a place with capital-E everything is the amazing **Kalahari Resort Convention Center** for

the Apostle Islands cruise

Following Frank Lloyd Wright

The famed architect Frank Lloyd Wright, a native Badger, melded the natural world into his architecture. In 1938, *Time* magazine called him "the greatest architect of the twentieth century." In 2019, two of his Wisconsin works—Taliesin in Spring Green and a private home in Madison—were added to UNESCO's World Heritage Sites.

Highlights of Wright's work in Wisconsin include:

- In Wauwatosa, west of Milwaukee, check out Wright's "little jewel," the **Annunciation Greek Orthodox Church.** You can also find examples of Wright's American-Built System in Milwaukee—homes designed to be affordable for those of average means. These are on West Burnham Street and Layton Boulevard, but they're privately owned and open to the public only on specific dates; check www.wrightinmilwaukee.org for more information.
- Wright's **SC Johnson Wax Building** in Racine helped *Time* make its grand claim.
- In Southeastern Wisconsin, stop off in the **Delavan Lake** area, where more and more Wright-designed homes can be seen from the outside but not toured.
- Wright's Madison masterwork, the **Monona Terrace Community and Convention Center,** has a view so sublime that even his detractors will be in awe. Then drive to Madison's west side to view his **First Unitarian Church,** recently named a National Historic Landmark. This was topped by the privately owned **Herbert and Katherine Jacobs House,** which in 2019 was named a UNESCO World Heritage Site.
- In the Wisconsin Dells, you can sleep in one of the only Frank Lloyd Wright-designed buildings available for rent—the **Seth Peterson Cottage.**

the Frank Lloyd Wright Visitor Center at Taliesin

- Along the Wisconsin River is the pilgrimage to Spring Green, home to **Taliesin,** Wright's home and studio and a UNESCO World Heritage Site. Have lunch at the Riverview Restaurant in the **Frank Lloyd Wright Visitor Center,** the only Wright-designed eatery anywhere. Driving through the area, you'll see "Wright-inspired" everything.

The state also has the **Frank Lloyd Wright Trail** (www.wrightinwisconson.org) marked along I-94 from Racine in Southeastern Wisconsin to Richland Center in south-central Wisconsin. The brown signs will lead you to highlights of his work.

Want more? Check out the numerous websites devoted to Wright, among them www.wrightinwisconsin.org, www.taliesinpreservation.org, and www.franklloydwright.org.

Devil's Doorway at Devil's Lake State Park

indoor and outdoor water parks, rooms, villas, and many other options.

DAY 2

See the real Dells of the Wisconsin River on the World War II-era **duck boat tour.** If you've had your fill of water, **Devil's Lake State Park** down the road offers superb hiking and, next door, fetching **Baraboo** is small-town quaint and has a grand circus museum, replete with outdoor shows.

The Northern Cap

From the Northern Cap, the Great North Woods are nearby.

DAY 1

Drive to **Bayfield** on a Friday and eat whitefish. Stay at the budget **Seagull Bay Motel,** or for a splurge, the **Old Rittenhouse Inn** cannot be beat for the historic lodgings and epicurean delights.

DAY 2

In the early morning either kayak the sea caves or cycle the rolling hills filled with apple orchards, then in the afternoon either take a shuttle to an island and hike or take the grand evening boat tour of the **Apostle Islands National Lakeshore** for amazing vistas.

DAY 3

Spend today driving the extraordinary Highway 13 along **Lake Superior** to **Superior** to see the big lakers (freight ships) and waterfalls.

Great North Woods

Combine the Northern Cap and the Great North Woods for a week of outdoor bliss.

DAY 1

Get a cabin, cottage, or resort room in **Hayward** in northwest Wisconsin, or in the northeast, in the **Minocqua area, Eagle River,** or **Boulder Junction.** Spend the day with a rowboat, canoe on the lake, or nap to the sound of lapping water.

Geologic Wonders

Wisconsin's landscape is so unusual that the topography is federally recognized as part of the Ice Age National Scientific Reserve. Wisconsinites assume that everyone knows what a "kame" or "kettle" is; let them explain it to you as you explore the lovely natural world of the state.

DOOR COUNTY

Start by exploring the bluffs of the **Niagara Escarpment** at **Potawatomi State Park** (also the beginning of the Ice Age National Scenic Trail) and **Peninsula State Park.**

EAST-CENTRAL WATERS

Drive along **Lake Winnebago** to the **Kettle Moraine State Forest-Northern Unit** scenic drive, designed to take you past every type of glacial topography. The **Henry Reuss Ice Age Interpretive Center** along this route is an absolute must for an explanation of the magnificent landscape.

CENTRAL WISCONSIN SANDS

The most famous sites in Wisconsin draw millions of people who may not even know the reason for the gorgeous scenery. **Devil's Lake State Park** has the state's best hiking trails atop glacial land. Take in the vistas of the Wisconsin River on a **Wisconsin Dells boat tour.**

SOUTHWESTERN WISCONSIN

North of the Wisconsin River and south of I-90, Wisconsin's **Coulee Country** is a landscape of undulating hills, crooked rivers, and the **largest unglaciated region** in the world. The landscape is extraordinary and puts the rest of the Midwest into perspective.

NORTHWEST WISCONSIN

St. Croix Falls and **Interstate State Park** are sites of interpretive centers explaining the state's postglacial natural history. You're in for stunning views of what awesome powers the glaciers had as they bulldozed south.

DAY 2

From Hayward, spend a day at the **National Freshwater Fishing Hall of Fame** and a **lumberjack show.** From Minocqua, take in the **Turtle-Flambeau Flowage.** If you're in Eagle River, spend your second day on a snowmobile in winter or fishing the amazing **Eagle River Chain of Lakes.**

Southwestern Wisconsin

From the Great North Woods, head south. Southwestern Wisconsin is also close to the Dells.

DAY 1

Camp at **Wildcat Mountain State Park** or stay at the extraordinary **Inn Serendipity Woods;** either canoe the extraordinary serpentine Kickapoo River or bike the original U.S. rail-to-trail path, the Elroy-Sparta State Recreational Trail.

DAY 2

Drive very slowly in the region, the **Coulee Range,** to wave at horse-drawn buggies of the Amish, and visit one of their amazing bakeries for great sustenance. The Amish should only be photographed with permission.

Door County Escape

It seems like such a tiny "thumb" on the map, so how could you possibly need a whole week? Trust me, you can easily spend a week here; lots of folks spend the whole summer.

Day 1

Start in **Sturgeon Bay,** learning about the history of shipping and shipbuilding at Maritime Museum and heading for Potawatomi State Park, and then visiting the town's lovely art center and museum.

Day 2

Head north to **Egg Harbor.** You'll be surprised that the short trip up the bay takes the entire morning. Unpack at a historic inn in **Fish Creek,** then unwind with a stroll through the historic downtown.

Day 3

The bulk of the day is spent exploring the **Peninsula State Park,** where you could easily spend a whole week. The sunset here is not to be missed. Continue up the coast, appreciating the vistas around Ephraim. Take in some ice cream at Wilson's before deciding where to lodge in **Sister Bay.**

Days 4-5

Take the awe-inspiring drive up and over the bluffs in **Ellison Bay** and the winding road to **Gills Rock.** Ride the ferry to **Washington Island** and find something comfortably rustic for your abode that night. Come morning, hop the ferry to this author's favorite Door retreat, **Rock Island State Park,** easily explored as a half-day trip.

kayaks at Peninsula State Park

Baileys Harbor

Day 6

Take the earliest ferry back to the mainland. Delve into the wilderness of **Newport State Park** before getting a lunch featuring Swedish pancakes in **Rowleys Bay.** Be careful of traffic, as most travelers will be racing to the next stop, the must-see **Moonlight Bay** area, home to the most splendid of the county's lighthouse sentinels and one of the country's most precious ecological preserves. **Baileys Harbor** makes an unassuming retreat.

Day 7

The final day's peregrinations begin with a casual drive down the lakeside to another happy place, **Whitefish Dunes State Park,** with gorgeous buttermilk dunes. Take it all in before you have to leave this beautiful place.

Get Out on the Water

Wisconsin, cartographically, can appear to be splattered with blue paint. Minnesota may claim to be the Land of 10,000 Lakes, but Wisconsinites love to point out they've got more than 15,000. This is what defines an Up North experience—days spent in a rented cottage lolling by the mom-and-pop resort's lake, which likely will be sparsely populated. Many visitors have three generations who visit the same lake year in and year out, using the same boat to catch (or not) dinner.

Rivers? Wisconsin's got a few to try out in its 84,000 miles of rivers and streams. Experience the Wisconsin River; nearly 300 miles of National Wild and Scenic Riverways; the Mighty Mississippi; and many other gems. Hands in this state are calloused from paddles just as much as from farming or factory work.

In short, the Wisconsin ethos involves a one-to-one relationship with water, and an experience with it in its myriad forms can help you understand the place and its people.

Canoeing

- Only have time for one? Make it canoeing the **Lower Wisconsin State Riverway,** west of Madison, in the Driftless Region, since it puts

Say Cheese: Sampling America's Dairyland

How could one come to Wisconsin and not learn more about moo juice and its uses? Check out www.wisconsincheese.com and their eye-poppingly detailed information on 120 **cheese factories** and **dairy operations** open for visits—or just head out and look for the hand-lettered signs saying "Fresh cheese curds today."

Only have time for one? Make it Green County, south of Madison, home to a number of operations and the only limburger cheese maker in the country. And try the limburger and onion sandwich at Baumgartner's in Monroe, the county seat. Then you can say you've truly done Wisconsin.

- Kids love to try their hand at churning butter and milking cows at **Old World Wisconsin** in Eagle.
- Bike the **Sugar River State Trail** from New Glarus, Wisconsin's Little Switzerland. Mile for mile, there are more cows here than anywhere in the state. The glacier-fed minerals in these soils are credited with producing the richest milk anywhere.
- Yes, but of course you actually want to *eat* this, right? So then, first of all northwest of Sheboygan in tiny Kiel is **Henning's Wisconsin Cheese,** notable for possibly being the last U.S. cheese maker to create enormous (up to 12,000 pounds!) wheels of cheese. If you can't find some kind of cheese you like here, well then you likely won't find it anywhere.
- If you are going to Kiel, you should then bop south 13 miles to Plymouth for its wondrous new **Cheese Counter and Dairy Heritage Center.** It may be hard to believe, but this little town is responsible for producing, storing, or shipping a significant percentage of U.S. cheese, and this new place tells you about it (and has great cheese-inspired food!).
- In the capital city, examine and sample the result of high-tech research in the dairy industry at the University of Wisconsin's **Babcock Hall Dairy Plant** in Madison. Cheese made on-site in the sandwiches (and the ice cream) can't be beat.
- Wisconsinites are addicted to cheese curds. Officially declared Wisconsin's "Cheese Curd Capital," **Ellsworth Cooperative Creamery** in Ellsworth along the Great River Road makes 160,000 pounds of fresh curds daily (starting at 11am). Better—if you can't find the time for a trip, loads of markets (and even convenience stores) sell their curds statewide.
- Wisconsin's cheese curd addiction is represented by a Wisconsin specialty—deep-fried cheese curds. Everyone and their grandmother insists they know who makes the best deep-fried cheese curd, and this was put to the ultimate test in a national survey in 2019, when **The Old Fashioned** in Madison came out on top. However, EatStreet deemed **Stone Arch Brewpub's** the best. Why not see for yourself?
- Ice cream is dandy, but Wisconsinites can't resist their frozen custard (egg yolk makes it denser and creamier). Milwaukee takes the crown here; seriously, Milwaukee is a bit loony about their custard. In fact, it's so prevalent that its custard drive-in stands inspired Big Al's Drive-In in the TV show *Happy Days* of the 1970s and '80s. You can't go wrong at any of their dozens of legendary spots, but **Leon's** takes the crown for this author since it seemingly has remained so focused on one thing—custard—since the 1940s.
- Having said that, you can get great frozen custard almost anywhere in the state at the Wisconsin original **Culver's.** (Just look for the blue oval sign!) It is—gasp!—fast food, but hang on a bit. First, it beat out the In-N-Out chain for its food (its butter burgers are amazing). Second, it actually does have healthful options such as steamed vegetables. Third, its company ethos results in amazingly friendly service. Finally, well, the custard is pretty darned good (www.culvers.com).

you in close proximity to endless other locations within a day trip.

- Canoeists have a few options for underrated canoe trails. My favorite is in northern Wisconsin some 25 miles from the Upper Peninsula of Michigan. The **Turtle-Flambeau Flowage** is rightfully called Wisconsin's version of the Boundary Waters. The **St. Croix**

National Scenic Riverway has sections of equally magnificent canoeing. Head to Trego, the headquarters in Northwestern Wisconsin, and judge for yourself.

Kayaking

- Kayakers will never, ever forget an experience at the otherworldly sea caves of **Apostle Islands National Lakeshore,** where Wisconsin runs up against Lake Superior. The sea caves of **Cave Point County Park** in Door County also draw flocks.

Rafting

- White-water rafting is sublime in Northeastern Wisconsin along the National Wild and Scenic **Wolf River** and the slightly more sedate **Peshtigo River.**

Scenic Boat Tours

- Not in the mood to work up a sweat? No problem, since scenic boat tours allow you to get out and about on the water. From picturesque Bayfield on Wisconsin's northern cap, take a sunset cruise to see the **Apostle Islands** or cruise out Green Bay onto Lake Michigan to see **Death's Door** (along with a good number of eye-catching lighthouses along the way).

Fishing

- And a by-the-way, fishing hasn't even come up, simply because it is such a religion here that is beyond the scope of this book to even scrape a thin layer. (And there is a greater than 50 percent chance that any Wisconsinite is going to have a fishing rod tucked into the canoe or kayak anyway.) That said, blue-ribbon trout streams are everywhere, but **muskie fishing** is the real draw, so head to **Hayward** in the northwest or **Boulder Junction** in the northeast and have a go!
- If you want a sailfish-style battle, equal numbers of fishers come here for lake trout or salmon fishing on **Lake Michigan** and, to a lesser extent, **Lake Superior.** From Kenosha near the Illinois border all the way to Door County you can hire a guide and boat in any community.

taking a break on the Wisconsin River

Family Fun

ice cream in Wisconsin

WISCONSIN DELLS

- This is the number-one family attraction in the Midwest, bar none. The small town was deliberately contrived for family fun and boisterous wet revelry in **Wisconsin Dells.** Soak in the country's most amazing lineup of gargantuan water parks like **Mt. Olympus** or go on a tour of the gorgeous river scenery.

MILWAUKEE

- Head to Milwaukee and let the kids go wild at the **Discovery World at Pier Wisconsin,** lauded as one of the best representations of interactive learning. They'll also go nuts for the zoomobiles, train rides, and skyway rides at the oft-imitated **Milwaukee County Zoo.**

MADISON

- Not to be outdone by Milwaukee, the **Madison Children's Museum** has been awarded the museum world's equivalent of a Pulitzer Prize. And the **Henry Vilas Zoo** isn't as big as Milwaukee's, but parents will love the admission cost—nada—along with the contiguous beach and playgrounds.

EAST-CENTRAL WATERS

- In Oshkosh, let the kids ogle the unbelievable **EAA AirVenture Museum** displays and try their escape skills at the **A.K.A. Houdini** exhibit at **History Museum at the Castle** in Appleton. Football-oriented adults adore **Lambeau Field,** home of the **Green Bay Packers,** and kids can emulate the Packer greats in its interactive zone by throwing the football and jumping into the stands. Downtown Green Bay also has one of the quaintest anachronisms in the state, the **Bay Beach Amusement Park,** where classic rides cost a quarter.

DOOR COUNTY

- **Door County** has plenty for kids to do: petting zoos, trail rides, beach dune climbing, hayrides, fruit picking, swimming, boating, biking, and more.

Milwaukee

It seems a cliché these days to bemoan the lack of appreciation for those Great Lakes (translation: Rust Belt) cities not called Chicago. Indeed, social media loves to tout Milwaukee as one of the most under-respected, much like Cleveland and other Great Lakes metropolises. Only, here it happens to be true. Milwaukee, a funky and unpretentious amalgamation of hardworking people, truly will surprise you.

For the record, even Milwaukeeans' Badger siblings down I-94 in Madison can't escape ingrained imagery of belching smokestacks and tannery effluvia, not wanting to admit that they picture Milwaukeeans as beer-and-bowling knuckleheads.

Milwaukee is decidedly more lunch box than bento box, but that's

Highlights

Look for ★ to find recommended sights, activities, dining, and lodging.

★ **Historic Third Ward and Riverwalk:** Milwaukee's most historic commercial district has shops, a farmers market, cafés, museums, and a cool Riverwalk (page 39).

★ **Milwaukee Art Museum:** This museum's stunning architecture has been trumpeted in international media—and don't forget the fantastic collections inside the building (page 41).

★ **Discovery World at Pier Wisconsin:** Learn through hands-on exhibits at this lakefront science and technology museum (page 41).

★ **Pabst Mansion:** The brewery family spared no expense showing off its riches. Ornate details and furnishings are the draw here (page 45).

★ **Milwaukee Public Museum:** This phenomenal museum pioneered the concept of walk-through exhibits; its massive scale may require a full day (page 45).

★ **Miller Brewing:** This megacomplex must be seen to be believed. It's a definite point of local pride (page 49).

★ **Harley-Davidson Museum:** Beer may have made Milwaukee famous, but its denizens are likely even prouder of their motorcycle heritage (page 49).

★ **Summerfest:** Otherwise known as the Big Gig, it's the granddaddy of festivals—an 11-day blowout of music, food, and fun (page 58).

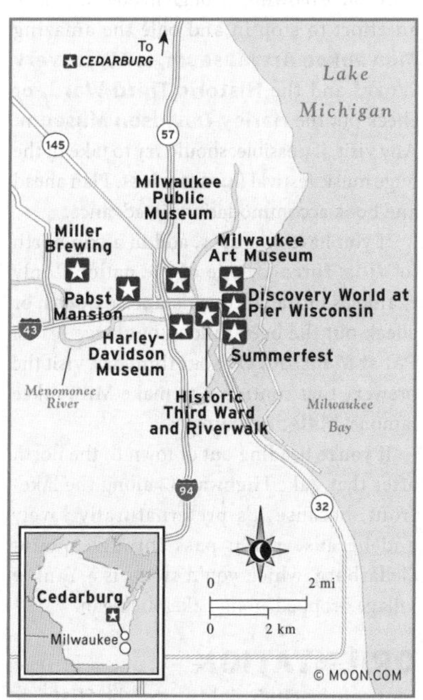

★ **Cedarburg:** To Milwaukee's north is a gem of an anachronism, a preserved village with lots of charm (page 72).

only one piece of this low-key, rootsy mosaic of 500,000 people. The lingua franca in the city's older neighborhoods is often a mother tongue peppered with accented English. In fact, you'll often hear people speak of *gemütlichkeit* (warmth, hospitality in German) in Milwaukee, and it's by no means hyperbole. Hey, the city even rates in the top 5 percent in the nation in terms of arts, attractions, and recreation.

PLANNING YOUR TIME

Milwaukee is great for a day, a weekend, or even a few days. Much of everything downtown is walkable (use the skywalks in winter). Even better, traffic on the interstates (newly upgraded, fantastically) is rarely that bad, and you've almost always got a nice lake or river view.

If you're blowing through in one day, make an effort to stop in and ogle the amazing **Milwaukee Art Museum,** see **Discovery World** and the **Historic Third Ward,** or check out the **Harley-Davidson Museum.** Any visit, if possible, should try to take in the huge music festival **Summerfest.** Plan ahead and book accommodations in advance.

If you have two days, add in a trip north to **Villa Terrace,** one of the nation's only examples of Italian Renaissance gardens, or check out the beer-funded opulence of the **Pabst Mansion.** On your third day, visit the brewery that continues to make Milwaukee famous, **Miller Brewing.**

If you're heading out of town to the north after that, take Highway 32 along the lakefront, because it's preternaturally lovely and because you'll pass through quaint Cedarburg, which you'd swear is a Yankee village dropped along Lake Michigan.

ORIENTATION

Most of the city's sights, save the **Historic Third Ward** or outlying sights, are concentrated in a rough square bounded by Highway 145 to the north, I-43 to the west, I-794 to the south, and Lake Michigan to the east. The Milwaukee River splits the square down the middle and separates the city into its east and west sections. The river is also the line of demarcation for street numbering: Wisconsin Avenue runs east to west to and from Lake Michigan; this main artery splits the downtown in two and always keeps me oriented. It is also a great midpoint to park and stroll from or return to and start over if you get lost.

Historic Districts

"Indeed, it is not easy to recall any busy city which combines more comfort, evidences of wealth and taste and refinement, and a certain domestic character, than this town on the bluffs," an impressed Easterner observed more than a century ago.

The unusually high concentration of magnesium and calcium in Milwaukee clay created the yellowish tint that gives much of the city's original architecture a distinctive flair. Factories produced top-quality bricks of such eye-catching light hues that the city became known as Cream City.

Historic Milwaukee Inc. (828 N. Broadway, 414/277-7795, www.historicmilwaukee.org) offers an astonishing number of guided expert strolling tours ($10).

YANKEE HILL

Yankee Hill makes other grand Milwaukee neighborhoods appear raffish. This grande dame enclave arose north of East Mason Street to East Ogden Avenue and west off the lakefront to North Jackson Street. Originally owned by Milwaukee's first resident, Solomon Juneau, this became the city's center of government, finance, and business.

JUNEAUTOWN

Today, both Water Street and Wisconsin Avenue competitively claim the title of most-happening area in the city. Original

Previous: scenic downtown Milwaukee; Miller Brewing; Harley-Davidson statue

architectural gems such as the **Milwaukee City Hall, Pabst Theater,** and **Iron Block** remain. **St. Mary's Church** (836 N. Broadway, at the corner of E. Kilbourn Ave. in Juneautown) is precisely the same age as Milwaukee. Made of Cream City brick in 1846, it is the oldest Catholic church in the city.

KILBOURNTOWN

Speculator Byron Kilbourn refused to align his bridges with Juneautown's, the consequence of which is apparent today, as the bridges are at an odd angle when they span the river. Other than North Old World 3rd Street, much of the architecture here has been razed for megaprojects. Highlights in Kilbourntown include the Germania Building on West Wells Street, once the site of a German-language publishing empire and notable for its carved lions and copper-clad domes (endearingly dubbed "Kaiser's Helmets"); the odd-shaped Milwaukee County Historical Center; the legendary Turner Hall; the Milwaukee Public Museum; and Milwaukee Public Library.

BRADY STREET

The newest gentrified neighborhood, Brady Street spans a land bridge connecting the Milwaukee River and Lake Michigan, originally Milwaukee's version of Little Italy. There's an appreciable quotient of hipsters and misunderstood geniuses lining coffeehouse windows.

BRONZEVILLE

Bronzeville, an African American cultural and entertainment center that has faded, has begun a Brady Street-style gentrification to make it hip and happening. The district runs from North 4th Street to North 7th Street.

WALKER'S POINT

Immediately north of the Allen-Bradley clock, between 1st and 2nd Streets on West National Avenue, is a stretch of Milwaukee that smacks of a Depression-era photo during the day, but by night becomes one of the city's most underappreciated tip-the-elbow neighborhoods. The shot-and-a-beer crowd now mingles with some serious restaurant action, a major LGBT influence, and even (gasp!) trendy nightclubs.

Walker's Point is also one of the most ethnically mixed neighborhoods in Milwaukee. German, Scandinavian, British, Welsh, Irish, Serb, Croatian, and Polish settlers came in originally, and Latinos and Southeast Asian immigrants have arrived more recently.

Activated in 1962, the **Allen-Bradley clock,** the second-largest four-faced clock in the world, according to *Guinness World Records* (it was first until 2010, when an enormous clock in Mecca, Saudi Arabia, dethroned it), has octagonal clock dials twice the size of those of Big Ben in London. The hour hands are 15 feet 9 inches long and weigh 490 pounds; the minute hands are 20 feet long and weigh 530 pounds. It's still crucial as a lake navigation marker.

NORTH POINT DISTRICT

Virtually all of the North Point District on the city's coastal bight is on the National Register of Historic Places. This longtime exclusive community lies west of North Lincoln Memorial Drive and south of East Park Place to East Woodstock Place.

East of here along the lakefront is **Lake Park,** designed by Frederick Law Olmsted, planner of New York City's Central Park and San Francisco's Golden Gate Park. At the top of North Avenue is the 1870s Victorian Gothic **North Point Lighthouse.**

WEST END

A case can be made that the West End rivals Yankee Hill's opulence. The area, bounded by North 27th Street, North 35th Street, West Wisconsin Avenue, and West Vliet Street, was the city's first residential suburb. Yankee bluebloods and prominent German American families competed in building the most opulent mansions. Highland Boulevard was at one time referred to as "Sauerkraut Boulevard." Highlights include the **Tripoli**

Milwaukee

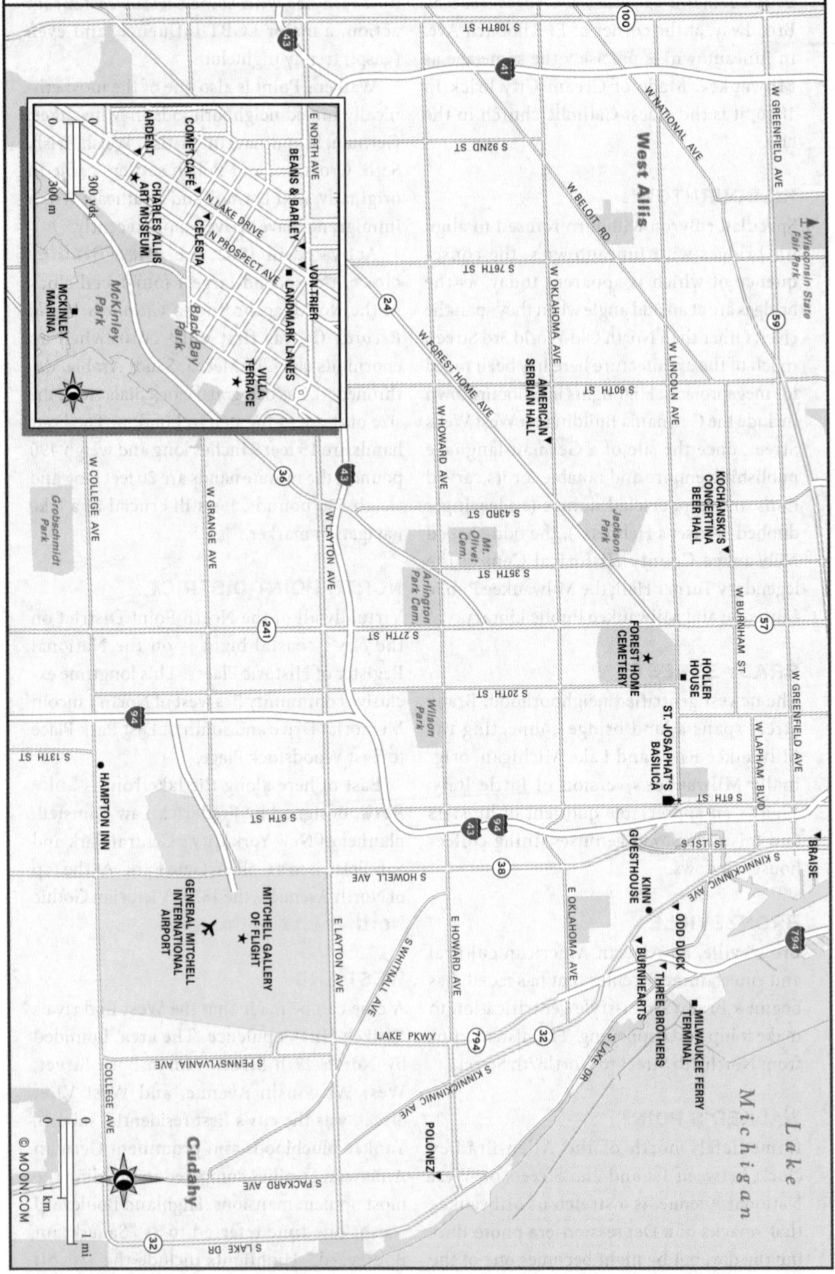
West Allis
Wisconsin State Fair Park
W GREENFIELD AVE
W NATIONAL AVE
S 108TH ST
S 92ND ST
W BELOIT RD
S 76TH ST
W OKLAHOMA AVE
W LINCOLN AVE
S 60TH ST
AMERICAN SERBIAN HALL
W FOREST HOME AVE
W HOWARD AVE
KOCHANSKI'S CONCERTINA BEER HALL
Jackson Park
S 43RD ST
Mt. Olivet Cem.
S 35TH ST
Arlington Park Cem.
W BURNHAM ST
S 27TH ST
FOREST HOME CEMETERY
HOLLER HOUSE
S 20TH ST
Wilson Park
ST. JOSAPHAT'S BASILICA
W LAPHAM BLVD
S 16TH ST
S 13TH ST
HAMPTON INN
S 6TH ST
S 1ST ST
BRAISE
S KINNICKINNIC AVE
KINN GUESTHOUSE
ODD DUCK
BURNHEARTS
THREE BROTHERS
MILWAUKEE FERRY TERMINAL
S HOWELL AVE
E OKLAHOMA AVE
E HOWARD AVE
MITCHELL GALLERY OF FLIGHT
GENERAL MITCHELL INTERNATIONAL AIRPORT
E LAYTON AVE
S WHITNALL AVE
LAKE PKWY
S LAKE DR
S PENNSYLVANIA AVE
COLLEGE AVE
POLONEZ
S PACKARD AVE
Cudahy
Lake Michigan
W COLLEGE AVE
Grobschmidt Park
W GRANGE AVE
W LAYTON AVE
E NORTH AVE
BEANS & BARLEY
COMET CAFÉ
ARDENT
N LAKE DRIVE
CHARLES ALLIS ART MUSEUM
CELESTA
N PROSPECT AVE
VON TRIER
LANDMARK LANES
McKinley Park
Back Bay Park
MCKINLEY MARINA
VILLA TERRACE
0 300 yds
0 300 m
0 1 mi
0 1 km
© MOON.COM

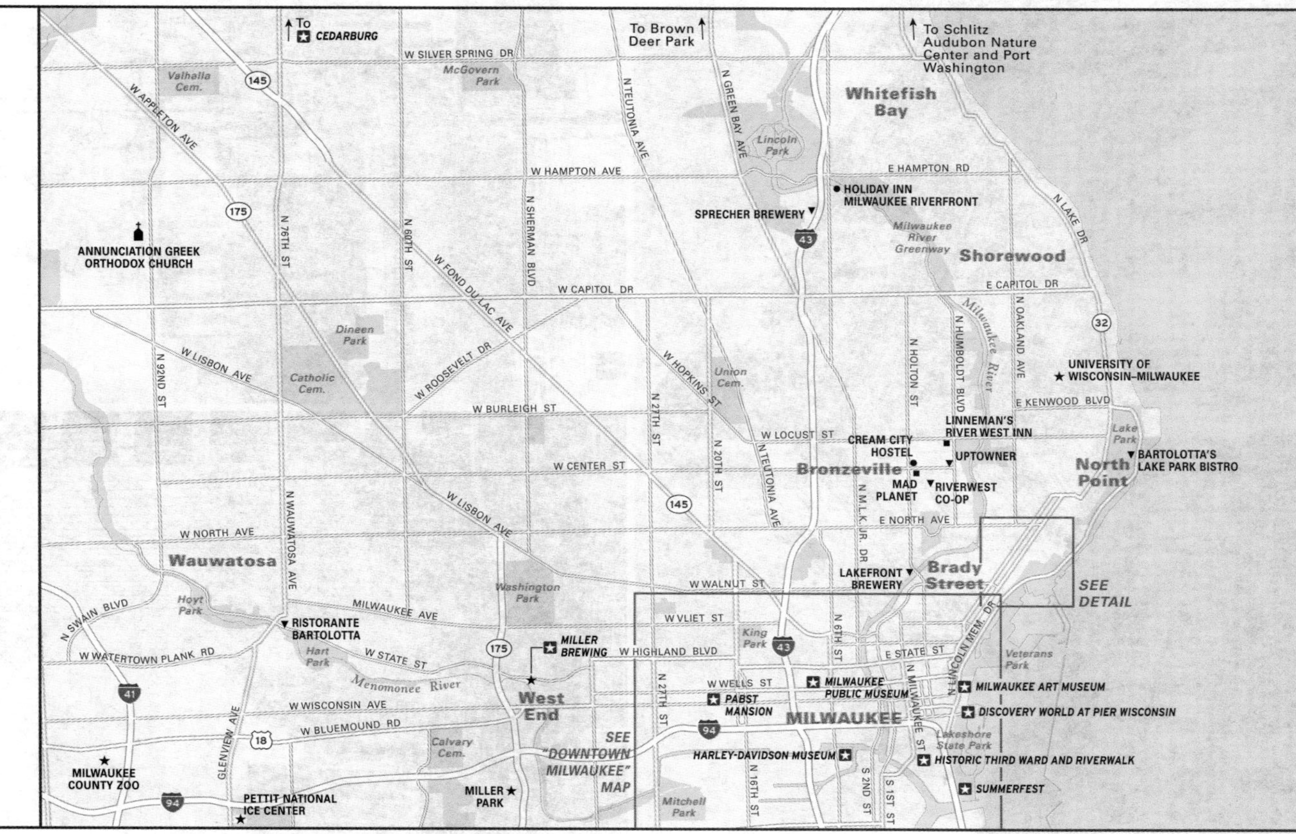
To CEDARBURG
To Brown Deer Park
To Schlitz Audubon Nature Center and Port Washington
W SILVER SPRING DR
McGovern Park
Valhalla Cem.
W APPLETON AVE
145
N TEUTONIA AVE
N GREEN BAY AVE
Whitefish Bay
Lincoln Park
W HAMPTON AVE
E HAMPTON RD
HOLIDAY INN MILWAUKEE RIVERFRONT
SPRECHER BREWERY
43
175
N 76TH ST
N 60TH ST
N SHERMAN BLVD
ANNUNCIATION GREEK ORTHODOX CHURCH
Milwaukee River Greenway
Shorewood
N LAKE DR
W FOND DU LAC AVE
W CAPITOL DR
E CAPITOL DR
32
Dineen Park
W ROOSEVELT DR
N HUMBOLDT BLVD
Milwaukee River
N OAKLAND AVE
W LISBON AVE
N 92ND ST
Catholic Cem.
W HOPKINS ST
Union Cem.
N HOLTON ST
UNIVERSITY OF WISCONSIN–MILWAUKEE
E KENWOOD BLVD
W BURLEIGH ST
N 27TH ST
LINNEMAN'S RIVER WEST INN
W LOCUST ST
Lake Park
CREAM CITY HOSTEL
UPTOWNER
BARTOLOTTA'S LAKE PARK BISTRO
W CENTER ST
N 20TH ST
Bronzeville
North Point
MAD PLANET
RIVERWEST CO-OP
W LISBON AVE
N M.L.K. JR. DR
E NORTH AVE
W NORTH AVE
N WAUWATOSA AVE
Wauwatosa
LAKEFRONT BREWERY
Brady Street
Washington Park
W WALNUT ST
SEE DETAIL
Hoyt Park
MILWAUKEE AVE
N SWAIN BLVD
RISTORANTE BARTOLOTTA
W VLIET ST
King Park
N 6TH ST
N LINCOLN MEM. DR
MILLER BREWING
W HIGHLAND BLVD
E STATE ST
Veterans Park
W WATERTOWN PLANK RD
Hart Park
W STATE ST
Menomonee River
41
West End
W WELLS ST
MILWAUKEE PUBLIC MUSEUM
MILWAUKEE ART MUSEUM
PABST MANSION
N MILWAUKEE ST
DISCOVERY WORLD AT PIER WISCONSIN
W WISCONSIN AVE
MILWAUKEE
W BLUEMOUND RD
18
94
SEE "DOWNTOWN MILWAUKEE" MAP
Lakeshore State Park
Calvary Cem.
HARLEY-DAVIDSON MUSEUM
HISTORIC THIRD WARD AND RIVERWALK
MILWAUKEE COUNTY ZOO
GLENVIEW AVE
Mitchell Park
N 16TH ST
S 2ND ST
S 1ST ST
SUMMERFEST
MILLER PARK
PETTIT NATIONAL ICE CENTER

1
2
3

Shrine Temple on West Wisconsin Avenue, **Central United Methodist Church** on North 25th Street, **Harley-Davidson's corporate headquarters,** and **Miller Brewing Company.**

Sights

Beware: Jaywalking is illegal, and the law is often enforced in Milwaukee. On the other hand, the police dole out equal numbers of tickets to drivers who don't give way to pedestrians.

A comprehensive skywalk system connects the Convention Center, the Federal Plaza, and the Shops at Grand Avenue. When it was built, one stretch over the Milwaukee River, called the Riverspan, was the only skywalk in the United States that bridged a navigable river.

Milwaukee Angels

Bless the city of Milwaukee for its angels. Not seraphim, but civic altruists officially called public service ambassadors (PSAs), they'll happily help with anything, seven days a week, sun or snow. On busy days, you may see them stationed at temporary kiosks. Otherwise, you're likely to encounter an angel as you walk the streets.

DOWNTOWN

★ Historic Third Ward and Riverwalk

In this conglomeration of 1890s buildings, antiques stores and art galleries is the norm among dozens of cafés, upscale shops, and a few longtime holdovers. It's also the fruit and vegetable district. A quick tour via http://historicthirdward.org before arrival may help you avoid confusion or getting lost in this area.

The unofficial "off-Broadway" area of the city, the Historic Third Ward has the **Broadway Theatre Center** (158 N. Broadway, 414/291-7800, www.cart.broadwaytheatrecenter.com), which smacks of an 18th-century European opera house; juxtaposed with that is a smaller experimental theater.

The well-regarded **Milwaukee Institute of Art and Design** (MIAD, 273 E. Erie St., 414/847-3200, www.miad.edu) is housed in an old terminal, rebuilt in the days after the 1892 Third Ward fire. Two galleries (10am-5pm Mon.-Sat., free), the **Brooks Stevens Gallery of Industrial Design** and the **Frederick Layton Gallery,** display student work.

The **Riverwalk** in the Third Ward includes the **Public Market** (414/336-1111, www.milwaukeepublicmarket.org, 10am-8pm Mon.-Fri., 8am-8pm Sat., 9am-6pm Sun.), a year-round farmers market, replete with anachronistic warehouse-style buildings and early-20th-century facades.

The Riverwalk's newest attraction is a statue of Arthur Fonzarelli, more commonly known as **The Fonz** from the TV show *Happy Days* (1974-1984), which was set in Milwaukee. Though some sniffed it was lowbrow and that serious art belonged there, the good-humored folks of Brewtown have taken to it with pride, and actor Henry Winkler occasionally stops by for selfies with fans.

Old World 3rd Street and Water Street

North of I-794 is another modestly gentrified zone along both sides of the Milwaukee River. To the east is **Water Street,** the happening mélange of microbreweries, sports pubs, dance clubs, restaurants, and cultural attractions. To the west is **Old World 3rd Street,** with more classic Milwaukee edifices, original old hotels and factories, the Fiserv Forum

1: Milwaukee's lovely Riverwalk **2:** Milwaukee's downtown **3:** classic Milwaukee architecture

Downtown Milwaukee

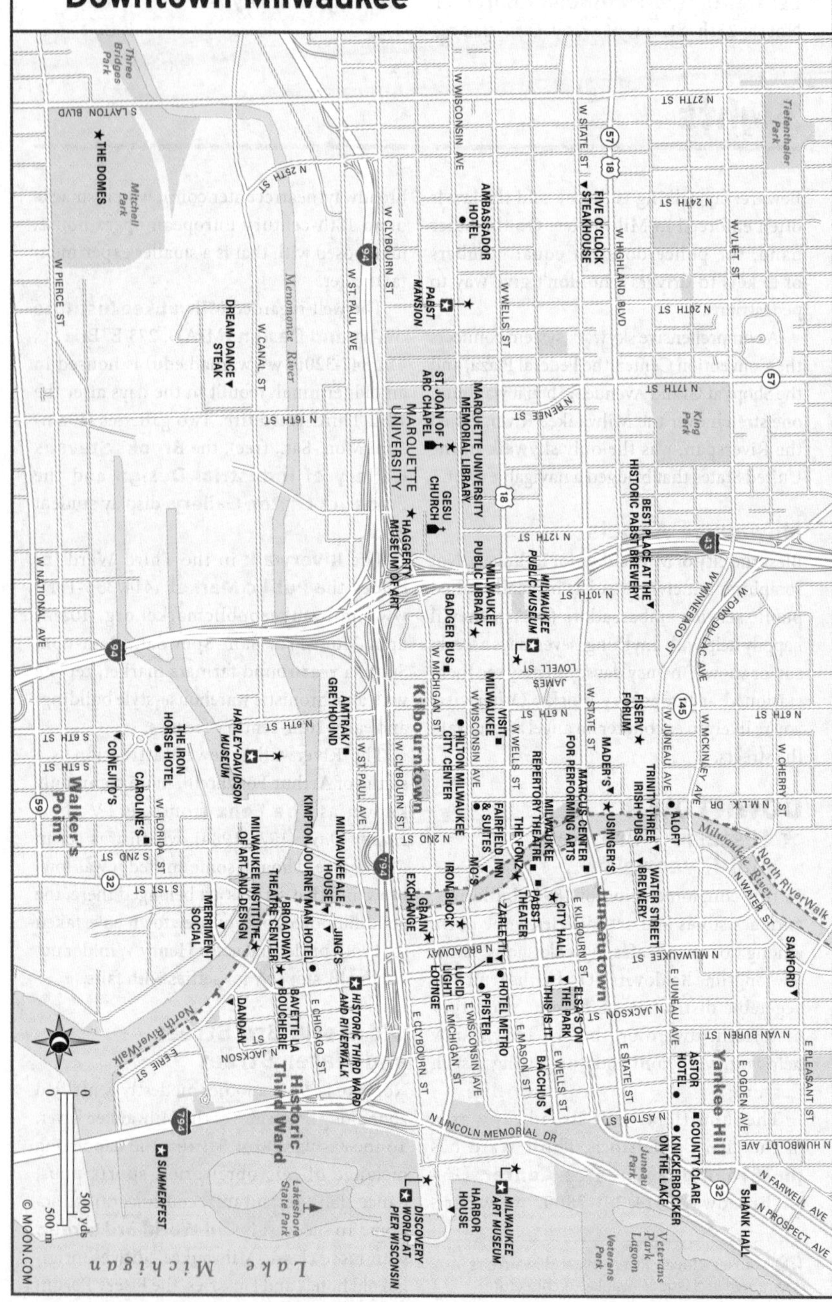

Weather Report

In every weather report, you'll hear the tagline "cooler" or "warmer near the lake." The Great Lakes establish their own microclimates and influence inland areas for miles. Look for the tear-shaped light atop the Wisconsin Gas Company building downtown: Gold means cold, red means warm, blue means no change, and any color flashing means precipitation is predicted.

district (the home of the NBA's Milwaukee Bucks), and a river walk.

Also along North Old World 3rd Street is **Usinger's** (1030 N. Old World 3rd St., 414/276-9100, www.usinger.com, 9am-5pm Mon.-Sat.), known as the Tiffany of sausage makers. In a city raised on *fleisch,* Usinger's has been carnivore heaven since 1880. Usinger's presence partially explains the occasional sweet scent downtown of woodsmoke mingling with the aroma of brewer's yeast. *Food & Wine* magazine has dubbed Usinger's bratwurst the best sausage in America.

Lakefront

Milwaukee sits on the deepest harbor on the western edge of Lake Michigan. For miles, the city rolls like a sideways wave along the lake. You can drive the entire lakefront on Highway 32 or bike most of it on separate county park bike paths. You pass nine beaches along the way.

South of the Milwaukee Art Museum and Discovery World at Pier Wisconsin is one of Wisconsin's newest state parks, **Lakeshore State Park,** a nearly 20-acre parcel of land adjacent to the Summerfest grounds, with beaches, fishing, and trails linking it to the rest of the state.

★ Milwaukee Art Museum

Among the best visual arts museums in the Midwest is the **Milwaukee Art Museum** (700 N. Art Museum Dr., 414/224-3200, www.mam.org, 10am-5pm daily, closed Mon. Labor Day to Memorial Day, $19). The museum has one of the United States' most important and extensive collections of German Expressionist art—not unimportant, given the city's Teutonic connections (the museum is ranked third in the world in German art). Other noteworthy exhibits include a panorama of Haitian art and the repository of materials on Frank Lloyd Wright's Prairie School of architecture. Some pieces date back as far as the 15th century. The permanent displays are impressively diverse, with old masters to Warhol through the Ashcan School. The Bradley Wing houses a world-renowned collection of modern masters.

In 2001, the museum was enhanced with a massive $50 million architectural feature by international designer Santiago Calatrava. It is, without exaggeration, breathtaking—don't miss it. The addition features a suspended pedestrian bridge linking it to downtown. Its gull-like wings can be raised or lowered to adjust the level of sunlight flooding the building. So important is this addition that *Time* magazine named it "building of the year" in 2001. It was even used as a set piece in *Transformers 3.* Weather permitting, the wings "open" at 10am, "flap" at noon, and close at 5pm.

In 2018 the museum finished a $34 million renovation to other fading areas of the complex, giving it 60 percent more space and allowing for it to display more of its holdings such as the Bradley Collection of Picasso and Kandinsky, among others, along with its stunning photography holdings.

★ Discovery World at Pier Wisconsin

An ultra-high-tech and fetchingly designed museum of every science, **Discovery World** (500 N. Harbor Dr., 414/765-9966, www.discoveryworld.org, 9am-4pm Tues.-Fri., 10am-5pm Sat.-Sun., $20 adults) is overwhelming in the best way. It has 120,000 square feet with 200 exhibits—including two massive aquariums, one freshwater and one saltwater— many of which are cutting-edge.

The freshwater education center is the best in the United States, and kids adore it.

Either moored outside or off on some research jaunt is the ***Denis Sullivan,*** a floating classroom. It's the only Great Lakes schooner re-creation in existence, and it also serves as the flagship of the United Nations Environment Program. From May to September you can generally take a public sail ($40), which is amazingly fun.

Local Architecture

A block from the Milwaukee Public Museum, the distinctive **Milwaukee Public Library** (814 W. Wisconsin Ave., 414/286-3000, free tours 11am Sat.) is an impressive 1895 edifice. You can find it by looking for the dome. Inside, a spacious rotunda displays well-preserved original old-world detail work, while graceful century-old design and ambient light predominate farther in; the staircase alone is worth a look.

In the 200 block of East Wells Street, **Milwaukee City Hall** (414/286-2266, 8am-4pm Mon.-Fri., free) is a navigational aid for first-timers, with its can't-miss-it Flemish Renaissance design, and also because many remember it from the TV sitcom *Laverne and Shirley* (1976-1983). Antechambers there display old-world artisanship. The 10-ton bell in the tower now rings only for special occasions, and it rocks the entire downtown when it does. Free tours are offered at noon the second and fourth Thursdays of the month, June to September.

On the southeast corner of Water Street and Wisconsin Avenue, the antebellum **Iron Block** is the only example of cast-iron architecture left in Milwaukee, and one of only three in the Midwest.

Wisconsin's onetime status as a leading world grain producer explains the lavish interiors of the **Grain Exchange** (225 E. Michigan St.). The three-story exchange was built in 1879 as the first centralized trading center in the United States; its atavistic Victorian opulence is shown in gold motifs and enormous paneled murals within the 10,000-square-foot room.

Breweries

Milwaukee was once home to dozens of breweries churning out the secret sauce of *gemütlichkeit*. The pungent malt scent can still pervade, and beer remains a cultural linchpin.

Schlitz, the "Beer that Made Milwaukee Famous," has made a reappearance, though it's not brewed in Milwaukee. Miller is the lone megabrewing holdout, though Milwaukeeans flipped their collective wig in 2008 when, after a merger with Coors, the corporate headquarters relocated to (oh, the betrayal!) Chicago. Worry not; the brewery itself isn't going anywhere.

Meanwhile, microbreweries and brewpubs are now everywhere. In fact, in one year six new microbreweries opened, which of course means this is but a thumbnail sketch.

Lakefront Brewery (1872 N. Commerce St., 414/372-8800, www.lakefrontbrewery.com, tours from noon daily, more frequently Sat.-Sun., from $9) has specialty beers such as pumpkin- and Door County cherry-flavored varieties. More impressive: it was the first brewery in the country to be certified organic and the first to produce gluten-free beer; they even convinced the government to change its definition of "beer" for this. Lakefront is generally voted best brewery tour by local media and citizen surveys. The brewery also has a boat dock and lies on the Riverwalk.

The brews at **Milwaukee Ale House** (233 N. Water St., 414/226-2336, www.ale-house.com, 11am-10pm Mon.-Thurs., 11am-1am Fri.-Sat., 11am-9pm Sun., $6-15) are among the best, and even better sipped at its great riverside location with double-decker biergarten. There's great live music here. This building was once a saddlery and, later, the home of the inventor of the Hula-Hoop.

North of here, you'll find Milwaukee's original brewpub at **Water Street Brewery** (1101 N. Water St., 414/272-1195, www.waterstreetbrewery.com, food served

TOP EXPERIENCE

Milwaukee Beer

A linguistic Rorschach test. Say Milwaukee and think what? Beer, of course. Yes, it still is the Brew City (or Brew Town) as it's been known for some 160 years. Wisconsin is famous for drinking beer, but part of this is because Milwaukee has always been so good at making beer. Even the major league baseball team is named the Brewers, after all!

Thus, when in Milwaukee, one simply must experience at least part of its beer culture.

stained glass window of the historic Pabst brand

- Milwaukee's brewing past meets present at industry leviathan **Miller Brewing**—the megabrewer that most people associate with Milwaukee today. Its enormous city-state-size complex showcases original 19th-century beer caves through up-to-the-minute brewing technology on its lengthy but worthwhile tours. It is truly a sight to behold.
- Pabst put Milwaukee on the national (and international) brewing map. Its fortunes waned but it has arisen phoenix-like again, and at the heart of the renaissance is **Best Place at the Historic Pabst Brewery.** The original Pabst complex (and it is a massive, multiblock place) is bit by bit being renovated into what is gradually becoming a kind of beer lover's theme park, including a taproom, brewery in an old church, chic hotel, short but wonderful tours, and—best of all—beer resurrected from recipes archived at the University of Wisconsin-Milwaukee.
- A nod goes to **Sprecher Brewery** in Glendale north of downtown for being a leader of Milwaukee's craft-brewing renaissance beginning in the 1980s. The enormous number of craft breweries in town owe a great deal to this brewer and its Special Amber; the brewery also happens to make a killer root beer.
- Of the myriad microbreweries and craft breweries—all worthy—hands-down the best all-around experience for beer lovers is at **Lakefront Brewery**. The brewers here are so serious that they forced the U.S. government to redefine beer when they became the first to produce their gluten-free beer. The lively-to-the-nth-degree restaurant and fish fry are perennially among the top draws in town. Best—the tours are equal parts hilarious irreverence and fascinating information.
- An easy way to take in Lakefront Brewery and several other craft breweries is a tour from the highly rated **Untapped Tours.** This small operation (which also has great city tours) has knowledgeable, friendly, and conscientious guides, and it is worth the money.
- Beer lovers should check out **Burnhearts** as it has among the best craft beer menus around and has been cited by *Draft* magazine as one of the top 100 U.S. beer bars. It also gets a nod for also being more than adept at mixed drinks if your friends are not beer lovers.
- For what a tavern (or "tap" as they were often known) used to be like, head to the longest-running drinking establishment in Milwaukee: **Uptowner.** This, the "Home of the Beautiful People," was an original "tied" house (since it was "tied" to the maker of Schlitz, the Beer that Made Milwaukee Famous) and today is essentially what it always was—a quiet corner place to chat, meet new people, and appreciate a cheap beer. Not chic, not trendy, not hopping—just a tippler's joint par excellence. And they still have Schlitz, natch.

1
2
3
4

11am-9pm Mon.-Sat., $5-15) with an amazing beer memorabilia collection comprising some 60,000 items.

In 2017 the brews of Pabst, once the sixth-largest and oldest U.S. brewer, made a reappearance at the erstwhile Pabst brewery, made from original recipes housed at the University of Wisconsin-Milwaukee. The former offices and interiors of the original Pabst Brewery have been rejuvenated into the **Best Place at the Historic Pabst Brewery** (901 W. Juneau Ave., 414/630-1609, http://bestplacemilwaukee.com), which has tours (2pm and 4pm Mon. and Wed.-Thurs., noon, 1pm, and 2pm Fri.-Sun., $8) and a cool tavern with classic Milwaukee beers on tap Thursday-Sunday. It is true Milwaukee. Even better: This is all but the beginning of rebuilding the site, including a new brewery in the former distribution center.

★ Pabst Mansion

The first stop for any historic architecture buff is the grandest of the grand: the **Pabst Mansion** (2000 W. Wisconsin Ave., 414/931-0808, www.pabstmansion.com, 10am-4pm Mon.-Sat., noon-4pm Sun. Mar.-Jan., $12 adults). Built between 1890 and 1893 of those legendary cream-colored bricks, it was the decadent digs of Captain Frederick Pabst, who slummed as a steamship pilot while awaiting his heirship to the Pabst fortune. The Flemish Renaissance mansion is staggering even by the baroque standards of the time: 37 rooms, 12 baths, 14 fireplaces, 20,000-plus feet of floor space, carved panels moved from Bavarian castles, priceless ironwork by Milwaukeean Cyril Colnik, and some of the finest woodwork ever seen. The room that eventually became the gift shop was designed to resemble St. Peter's Basilica.

★ Milwaukee Public Museum

Among the most respected nationally and number one nationwide in exhibits is the **Milwaukee Public Museum** (800 W. Wells St., 414/278-2702, www.mpm.edu, 9am-5pm Fri.-Wed., 9am-8pm Thurs., $17 adults). It initiated the concept of walk-through exhibits in 1882 and total habitat dioramas (with a muskrat ecosystem mock-up) in 1890. Today, its "Old Milwaukee" street life construct is quite possibly Milwaukee's most-visited tourist spot (the newish streetcar is a fave). The museum's multilevel walk-through Rain Forest of Costa Rica, featuring its own 20-foot cascade, wins kudos and awards on an annual basis. Among the catacombs of displays on archaeology, anthropology, geology, botany, ethnography, and more are its jewels of paleontology: the world's largest dinosaur skull and a 15-million-year-old shovel-tusk elephant skeleton obtained from the Beijing Natural History Museum. Intriguingly, the museum has announced a 10-year plan for an epic, $100 million new home (site to be determined); its design is to be enormous and among the most cutting-edge of museums worldwide.

The museum constantly reworks exhibits to allow some of its six million-plus pieces in storage to see the light of day. The **Live Butterfly Garden** has become the most popular exhibit with the general public (and especially with this author's relatives). The $17 million, six-story-high **Dome Theater and Planetarium**—Wisconsin's first IMAX theater—is a big deal, as it is the only place on earth to have the advanced Digistar 6 computer projection system.

Be sure to take walking shoes for all of this.

Marquette University

Though the university's namesake was not particularly enamored of the Great Lakes coastline, Jesuit **Marquette University** (Wisconsin Ave., 414/278-3178, www.marquette.edu) was founded in 1881 and named for the intrepid explorer Jacques Marquette. The university even has bone fragments purportedly from the Black Robe, Father Marquette himself.

The primary attraction is the **St. Joan**

1: Milwaukee Art Museum 2: Schlitz Audobon Nature Center 3: gateway to the Historic Third Ward 4: the opulent Pabst mansion

History of Beer City

King Gambrinus, the mythical Flemish king and purported inventor and patron of beer, would no doubt be pleased to call this city home—his statue lives in the back courtyard of the Best Place at the Historic Pabst Brewery.

THE BEGINNING

The first brewery in Milwaukee wasn't started by a German; Welshmen founded a lakefront brewery in 1840. Germans got into the act not much later, though, with Herman Reuthlisberger's brewery in Milwaukee, and in 1844 Jacob Best started the neighborhood Empire Brewery, which later became the first of the megabreweries, Pabst. The same year saw Milwaukee's first beer garden—that all-inclusive picnic and party zone with lovely flower gardens and promenades, so essential to German culture—two years before the city's charter was even approved. The next half decade saw the establishment of the progenitors of Milwaukee's hops heritage—in chronological order, Blatz, Schlitz, and the modern leviathan Miller.

THE RISE

Without question, the primary reason beer took off was massive immigration. Most influential were the waves of German immigrants, who earned Milwaukee the nickname "German Athens" by the 1880s. When the government levied a whiskey tax of $1 per barrel, tavern patrons immediately began asking for beer instead.

Another factor in Milwaukee's brewery success was its location; Wisconsin was a world agricultural player in herbs, hops among them. In addition, the availability of natural ice gave it an edge over other U.S. brewers. The Great Chicago Fire of 1871 also helped by devastating almost all of the competing breweries. Milwaukee became famous for beer production and consumption, and by

of Arc Chapel (generally 10am-4pm Mon.-Sat., noon-4pm Sun., may be closed weekends when school is out), an inspiring five-century-old relic from the Rhone River Valley of France. Transported stone by stone, along with another medieval chateau, it was reassembled on Long Island in 1927 by a railroad magnate; the French government put an end to cultural relocation after this. It was lovingly redone by some of the nation's premier historic architects and renovators and remains the only medieval structure in the Western Hemisphere where mass is said regularly. In a perhaps apocryphal story, Saint Joan is believed to have kissed one of the stones during the war between France and England, and that stone has been said to be colder than its surrounding neighbors ever since.

Another treasure of architecture here is the Brobdingnagian Gothic **Gesu Church,** built in 1894. The vertiginous heights of the spires are enough, but the gorgeous stained glass, in the shape of a rose divided into 14 petals, is equally memorable. Starting in summer 2012, the church underwent its first restoration—polishing the copper cherubs, sealing cracks—in some 120 years.

Also on campus is the **Haggerty Museum of Art** (530 N. 13th St., 414/288-1669, www.marquette.edu/haggerty, 10am-4:30pm Mon.-Sat., 10am-8pm Thurs., noon-5pm Sun., free). It is easily one of the city's most challenging galleries, and worth it for anyone jaded by excessive exposure to the old masters. It's multicultural and multimedia with a modernist bent. The most valuable piece is the series of more than 100 hand-colored Bible etchings by Marc Chagall.

One fascinating item at the **Marquette University Memorial Library** (1415 W. Wisconsin Ave., 414/288-7555) is the world-renowned J. R. R. Tolkien Collection, with more than 10,000 pages for *The Lord of the Rings* alone and thousands of other

the time of the Civil War, there was one bar for every 90 residents—and during the war, breweries again doubled their production. At one time there were nearly 600 breweries in the state. This led temperance crusader Carrie Nation to declare in 1902, "If there is any place that is hell on earth, it is Milwaukee. You say that beer made Milwaukee famous, but I say that it made it infamous."

The brewers' vast wealth allowed them to affect every major aspect of Milwaukee society and culture; ubiquitous still are the brewing family names affixed to philanthropic organizations, cultural institutions, and many buildings. So popular was Pabst beer that it could afford to place real blue ribbons on bottles by hand; so pervasive were the beers that Admiral Robert Peary found an empty Pabst bottle as he was nearing the North Pole.

THE DECLINE

After the industry's zenith, when there were perhaps 60 breweries, the number dwindled to only a dozen or so after the enactment of Prohibition, and today there is just one left, Miller. In the 1950s, Milwaukee could still claim to produce nearly 30 percent of the nation's beer; as of now, the number is less than 5 percent.

Microbreweries and brewpubs have inevitably cut into the megabrewery markets. And yet microbrews are a throwback of sorts. The first beer brewed in Milwaukee came from neighborhood brewers, most of which put out only a barrel a week, just enough for the local boys. As the major breweries gained wealth, they gobbled up large chunks of downtown land to create open-atrium beer gardens and smoky beer halls, in effect shutting out the smaller operators.

Most telling of all may be the deconstruction of yet another Wisconsin stereotype: Cheeseheads, despite being born clutching personalized steins, do not drink more beer per capita than other states—the top honor goes to Nevada. It isn't for lack of trying; *Forbes* once called Milwaukee "America's drunkest city."

documents; this collection is only open to academic researchers. Library hours vary by semester and are reduced in summer.

NORTH OF DOWNTOWN

Charles Allis Art Museum

Overlooking Lake Michigan, the **Charles Allis Art Museum** (1801 N. Prospect Ave., 414/278-8295, www.cavtmuseums.org, 1pm-5pm Wed.-Sun., $10 adults) is in a Tudor mansion built by the first president of Allis-Chalmers, a major city employer. It has a superb collection of world art, fine furniture, and nearly 1,000 objets d'art dating back as far as 500 BC and covering the entire world. The museum's upscale interiors feature Tiffany windows, silk wall coverings, and loads of marble.

Villa Terrace

Within walking distance of the Charles Allis Art Museum, the lavish 1923 Mediterranean Italian Renaissance **Villa Terrace** (2220 N. Terrace Ave., 414/271-3656, www.cavtmuseums.org, 1pm-5pm Wed. and Fri.-Sun., till 8pm Thurs., $10 adults) houses an eclectic collection of decorative arts, including art and handcrafted furniture from the 16th through the 20th centuries. A four-year garden renovation program involved the restoration of a variety of botanical collections, organically melding interiors and exteriors. It is now one of the country's only existing examples of Italian Renaissance garden art and design.

University of Wisconsin-Milwaukee

The **University of Wisconsin-Milwaukee** (UWM) is second in enrollment only to the main campus in Madison; it's well known for its civil engineering program. The **Golda Meir Library** (2311 E. Hartford Ave., 414/229-6282, www.uwm.edu, hours vary by semester, free) houses the **American Geographical Society Collection,** a priceless collection of more than half a million maps, atlases, logbooks, journals, globes, charts, and navigational aids. It includes what is reportedly the world's oldest known map, dating from the late 15th century.

Sprecher Brewery

Sprecher was one of the original Milwaukee microbrews and also makes killer root beer and cream soda. At the **Sprecher Brewery** (701 W. Glendale Ave., Glendale, 414/964-2739, www.sprecherbrewery.com, $8) you'll find one of the city's favorite microbrewery tours, given its oompah music in a heavily Bavarian-themed lager cellar. Tours (4pm Mon.-Fri., noon, 1pm, 2pm, and 3pm Sat.-Sun. year-round, reservation required) are offered, with occasional added tours in summer, though tour times and dates are subject to change.

Schlitz Audubon Nature Center

On the far north side of the city, in Bayside, **Schlitz Audubon Nature Center** (1111 E. Brown Deer Rd., 414/352-2880, www.sanc.org, 9am-5pm daily fall-spring, 9am-5pm Mon.-Thurs., 9am-8pm Fri.-Sun. summer, $8) abuts the edge of Lake Michigan on the grounds of an erstwhile Schlitz brewery horse pasture. A six-mile network of trails winds along the beach and through diverse prairies, woodlands, and wetlands. An observation tower with a parapet offers lake views. The interpretive center spent $5.5 million on many environmentally friendly features, such as capturing rainwater, using sustainable wood sourced from Aldo Leopold's homestead, solar power panels, and low-flow toilets.

SOUTH OF DOWNTOWN

St. Josaphat's Basilica

Just south of downtown, the first Polish basilica in North America is the city's **St. Josaphat's Basilica** (Lincoln Ave. at S. 6th St., 414/645-5623, tours after 10am Sunday mass, public welcome at masses). Parishioners built the structure out of salvaged rubble from the Chicago Federal Building. The capacious dome is modeled after St. Peter's in Rome; inside is a rather astonishing mélange of Polish iconography and hagiography, relics, stained glass, and wood carvings. It's open for visits 9am to 4pm, Monday to Saturday.

Beer Corner at Forest Home Cemetery

The only-in-Milwaukee award goes to **Forest Home Cemetery** (2405 W. Forest Home Ave.) and its designated sector of eye-catching monuments to the early Milwaukee brewing giants: Blatz, Pabst, Best, and Schlitz rest in peace beneath the handcrafted stones. Kooky or spooky, heritage is heritage. You can usually enter the cemetery until around 4pm Monday to Friday and on Saturday mornings.

Mitchell Gallery of Flight

Mitchell International Airport has the **Mitchell Gallery of Flight** (5300 S. Howell Ave., 414/747-4503, www.mitchellgallery.org, 8am-10pm daily, free), housing a number of aircraft, including a zeppelin. More appealing is the retrospective of the iconoclastic and innovative military aviation pioneer Billy Mitchell, a Beer City native.

Speaking of the airport, a unique, free way to kill time waiting for your plane to depart is to drive your rental car along Layton Avenue to near South Kansas Avenue, on the north side of Mitchell International Airport. You'll find a small, relatively unknown viewing area to watch planes take off and land.

Whitnall Park

One of the larger municipal parks in the United States at 600-plus acres, **Charles B. Whitnall Park** (5879 W. 92nd St., Hales Corners, 414/425-7303, free) is the cornerstone of Milwaukee County's enormous park system and of the state's Oak Leaf Birding Trail, which has 35 separate parks and forests to view crucial avian habitat. Lush landscaped gardens are found inside the park at

Boerner Botanical Gardens (414/425-1130, www.boernerbotanicalgardens.org, 8am-sunset daily late Apr.-mid-Oct., garden house 8am-7pm daily summer, hours significantly reduced early Apr. and mid-Oct.-mid-Nov., $7.50). The 1,000-acre arboretum surrounding the gardens includes the largest flowering crab apple orchard in the United States. The gardens are closed from late November through early April.

WEST OF DOWNTOWN

★ Miller Brewing

King of the hill is **Miller Brewing** (4251 W. State St., 414/931-2337, www.millercoors.com, tours 10:30am-3:30pm Mon.-Sat., tours Sun. seasonally, $10), technically called Molson Coors, but nobody says that. This slick, modern operation is the very antithesis of a neighborhood brewer. Frederic Miller apprenticed and served as a brewmaster at Hohenzollern Castle in Sigmaringen, Germany, before striking out for the United States in 1855 at age 28 and starting a small brewery. His original Plank Road Brewery, bought from the son of the Pabst progenitor and not to be confused with Miller's shrewdly named contemporary brewing operation, put out 300 barrels per year—no mean feat, but nothing stellar. Today, Miller is the second-largest brewery in the nation, with a total production of 45 million barrels a year; the warehouse is the size of five football fields. Hour-long tours take in the ultra-high-tech packaging center, the hangar-size shipping center, and, finally, the brewhouse. Tours end at the Caves Museum, a restored part of Miller's original brewery in which kegs of beer were cooled.

★ Harley-Davidson Museum

Harley-Davidson has created hog heaven—the **Harley-Davidson Museum** (Canal St. and S. 6th St., 877/436-8738, www.h-dmuseum.com, 9am-6pm Fri.-Wed., 9am-8pm Thurs. May-Sept., 10am-6pm Fri.-Wed., 10am-8pm Thurs. Oct.-Apr., $20 adults), a massive, 100,000-square-foot facility. This $30 million project, the mecca for Made in America, features an interactive museum and exhibits on the history, culture, and lifestyle engendered by the company and its slavishly devoted riders. Rooms are full of vintage vehicles; not surprisingly, Elvis's bike probably gets the most attention. In 2012, the newest permanent exhibit found its home: After the 2011 earthquake and tsunami in Japan, a Harley-Davidson floated to North America in a shipping container. The owner asked that it be

Miller Brewing

Hog Heaven

Beer may have made Milwaukee famous, but to some, Milwaukee-born **Harley-Davidson**—the bikes, the devoted riders, and the company—truly represents the ethos of Milwaukee: blue-collar tough, proud, and loyal.

THE COMPANY

William S. Harley and Arthur Davidson, boyhood friends in Milwaukee, were fascinated by the bicycle and German motorcycle craze around the turn of the 20th century. In 1903 they rigged a single-cylinder engine (the carburetor was a tin can) and leather-strap drive chain onto a thin bicycle frame—with no brakes. Thus began the first putterings of the company known for roaring.

The company incorporated in 1907, and within a decade became the largest motorcycle maker in the world. The Harley reputation for sound engineering and thus endurance—the first motorcycle lasted 100,000 miles—made them popular with the U.S. Postal Service and especially police departments. In the first Federation of American Motorcyclists endurance test, a hog scored above a perfect 1,000 points, leading to Harley dominance in motorcycle racing for decades. Constant innovations, such as the first clutch, fueled success.

During World War I Harley gained the U.S. government's devotion, and Harleys with sidecars equipped with machine guns pursued pesky Pancho Villa into Mexico in 1917. Europeans found a great enthusiasm for the machines after the Great War; within five years, 20 percent of the company's business was exported.

No motorcycle maker could claim the innovation or the zeal with which Harley-Davidson catered to its riders. Original dealers were instructed to employ the consumers in as much of the process as possible. Harley-Davidson open houses were legendary. *The Enthusiast,* the company's newsletter, is the longest-running continuously published motorcycle organ anywhere.

THE BIKES

The company hit eternal fame with the goofy-looking, radically designed Knucklehead in 1936, when a public initially dismayed by the bulging overhead valves (hence the name) soon appreciated its synthesis of art and engineering; it has been called the most perfect motorcycle ever made. The Sportster, introduced in 1957, also gets the nod from aficionados—it's called the Superbike. In the 1970s, the Super Glide—the *Easy Rider* low-rider's progenitor—single-hand-

placed here, untouched. The museum stays open 365 days a year, in true blue-collar style.

The best way to experience Harley otherwise is to be around for Harley riders' conventions, when literally 100,000 Harleys descend on the city to fete the metallic beasts. It's an indescribable experience to hear and feel thousands of Harleys roaring down I-94 toward Miller Park on their way to a Brewers game from the museum, when the Beer City becomes a tented Hog City for a glorious summerlong celebration.

Annunciation Greek Orthodox Church

"My little jewel—a miniature Santa Sophia" is how Frank Lloyd Wright described the final major work of his life, the **Annunciation Greek Orthodox Church** (9400 W. Congress St., Wauwatosa, 414/461-9400). Its imposing rondure is a landmark to Milwaukee architecture—a dramatic inverted bowl into which Wright incorporated symbolic golds and blues and the Greek cross. The blue-tiled dome rises 45 feet above the floor and spans 104 feet. Some find the whole place stunning; others think the outside looks like a UFO and the interior murals far too modern in style. Tours are not available.

Other Churches

The progressive **Central United Methodist**

edly rescued the company. The modern Softail and Tour Glides are considered by Harley-Davidson to be the best ever engineered.

Harley-Davidson

GOOD TIMES, BAD TIMES

By the 1940s, two-thirds of all U.S. bikes were Harley-Davidsons. By the 1950s, swelled by demand, Harley managed to push out its main competitor, Indian Motorcycle. But somewhere along the line, something happened. Harleys had been derisively dubbed "Hardly Ablesons" because of their tendency to break down—or so said owners of archrival Indian motorcycles.

When AMF (American Machine and Foundry) took control of the company in 1969, sales were plummeting. Whatever the cause, the morale of the workforce hit an all-time low, and things got so bad that manufacturing was doled out to separate factories around the country.

In 1981, a group of about 30 Harley employees bought the company back and virtually reinvented it. With top-of-the-line products, brilliant marketing, and a furious effort at regaining the trust of the consumer, Harley-Davidson moved steadily back into the market. By the late 1980s, the company was again profitable against Japanese bikes. The effects are manifest: There's a veritable renaissance of the Harley craze, an extensive waiting list for bikes (all 75,000 produced in a year are spoken for up to a year in advance), and Harley groups riding even the streets of Hong Kong. More than half of Harley owners are senior citizens, married, college educated, and have high incomes.

The contemporary Harley-Davidson headquarters sits very near the site of that shed workshop that cobbled together the first bike. The company remains firmly committed to its downtown location. It has programs encouraging employees to live in the neighborhood and is one of the most in-touch corporations in town. Its **Harley-Davidson Museum** cements it as a Milwaukee brand forever.

Church (639 N. 25th St., 414/344-1600, tours by appointment, free) is partially enclosed by earth and incorporates significant energy-saving and solar-energy measures (the tower holds solar panels).

It's not a church, but the **Tripoli Shrine Temple** (3000 W. Wisconsin Ave., 9am-4pm Mon.-Fri., free) is worth a look, if only for the architecture. It was built during the 1920s and was based on the Taj Mahal of India. The main dome is 30 feet in diameter and flanked by two smaller domes. Camels, lanterns, floral designs, and other works of art decorate the interiors. They don't offer tours per se, but you could ask. If nothing else, go for the awesome fish fry held from 4:30pm-8pm on Fridays.

Milwaukee County Zoo

Believe it or not, the innovative designs at the **Milwaukee County Zoo** (10001 W. Bluemound Rd., 414/771-3040, www.milwaukeezoo.org, 9:30am-2:30pm Mon.-Fri., 9:30am-4:30pm Sat.-Sun. Jan.-Feb. and Nov.-Dec., 9am-4:30pm daily Mar.-late May, 9am-5pm daily late May-Labor Day, 9am-4:30pm daily Labor Day-Oct. 31, $16.25 adults, $13.25 ages 3-12, under age 3 free, parking $12) have been mimicked nationally and internationally for the past five decades. In fact, they set the standard for what many today take for granted in zoological park settings. The animals' five global environments, grouped in specific continental areas with a system of moats, juxtapose predator and prey. Almost 5,000 specimens live here, many of them also on the endangered species list. Perennially popular are the polar bears and other aquatic leviathans viewable through subsurface windows. A century-old barn houses a dairy complex, giving visitors an educational look at milk production. Zoomobiles ($3) roll about the expansive grounds, and mini trains ($3) also chug around, while sky-chairs and zip lines run overhead. On occasion, you can even hop aboard an elephant or a spitting camel. Animal shows take place throughout the day.

The rides and animal shows have varied schedules. All rides and activities are extra. Admission is cheaper October-May.

The Domes

Though it's officially the **Mitchell Park Horticultural Conservatory** (524 S. Layton Blvd., 414/649-9800, www.countyparks.com, 9am-5pm Mon.-Fri., 9am-4pm Sat.-Sun., $7 adults), everybody knows this complex as **The Domes.** You'll know why once you take a gander at the conical, seven-story, 148-foot-tall glass-encased buildings. The capacious interiors, totaling about 15,000 square feet, are isolated into arid desert, traditional floral, and tropical rainforest biospheres. One is relandscaped up to half a dozen times annually. Outside, the conservatory, ringed with more sunken gardens, is the only structure of its type in the world.

Recreation

Milwaukee has been rated in the top 10 percent of like-size U.S. cities for recreational opportunities in and around the city. Don't forget, too, that the Beer City is major league: It supports three professional teams along with a minor league hockey team.

Looking for something more aerobic? Consider the city's more than 150 parks and parkways and 15,000 acres of green lands. Milwaukee has more park area per person than any metropolitan city in the United States, and has won a Gold Medal for Excellence from the National Recreation and Park Association. The place to inquire first is the **Milwaukee County Parks System** (414/257-6100, www.countyparks.com).

HIKING AND BIKING

The following is just a thumbnail sketch of what the county has to offer.

The **Oak Leaf Trail** is the diamond of all Milwaukee-area trails. With one name but comprising multiple loops, this beauty wends through all the parkways and major parks of the county, topping out at longer than 100 miles. The main section for most, though, is an easy loop around the lakefront. The trail begins along Lincoln Memorial Drive between Ogden Avenue and Locust Street. Signs from here point your way, though note that not all myriad loops are well marked (or even marked at all). The most popular trail is a 13-mile marked route, the **Milwaukee '76 Trail,** starting from O'Donnell Park and stretching along the lakefront to the Charles Allis Art Museum and through east-side historic districts. Since the Oak Leaf trailhead is along the lakefront, the best thing to do after huffing and puffing all day is finish by exploring the littoral scenery. At 2400 North Lincoln Memorial Drive is **Bradford Beach,** the city's most popular.

Henry Aaron State Trail, a new addition to the state's reputable system, is a six-mile path leading from the lakefront, through historic districts, and ending in the near-west suburbs, much of it following the Menomonee River.

Find great ski trails at a number of parks, including the Schlitz Audubon Nature Center, Whitnall Park, and, believe it or not, the zoo.

1: The Domes, otherwise known as the Mitchell Park Horticultural Conservatory 2: river tour boats in Milwaukee

1
2
PARKS

Bike and inline skate rentals and personal watercraft and kayaks are usually available along the lakefront at **Milwaukee Bike and Skate Rental** (414/273-1343, www.milwbikeskaterental.com) in Veterans Park. Just north of McKinley Marina, **Welker Water Sport Rentals** (414/630-5387) also rents personal watercraft and kayaks.

PADDLING

Not many cities offer paddling on a river and a lake, but Milwaukee is one of them. Rent a kayak or paddleboard and take your own tour via **Milwaukee Kayak** (318 S. Water St., 414/301-2240, milwaukeekayak.com, from $35 for 4 hours) on the south end of the Riverwalk.

CHARTER FISHING

Milwaukee leads the state in charter operations and salmonoids taken. On a scintillating summer day, the marina and harbor areas of Milwaukee appear to be discharging a benevolent whitewashed D-Day flotilla.

The **Convention and Visitors Bureau** (414/273-7222, www.visitmilwaukee.org) can provide more detailed information on specific charter operations. Investigating charter operators before sailing can save quite a lot of personality friction; the boats are not that big, and you are the one who'll have to sit out on the big lake with the skipper all day.

BOWLING

An apt local joke: Wisconsin's the only state where you can factor your bowling average into your SAT score. The city's 81 regulation bowling centers can take care of your bowling jones, but even better, a couple of neighborhood joints have old-style duckpin bowling. The **Holler House** (2042 W. Lincoln Ave., 414/647-9284) has the two oldest sanctioned bowling lanes (lanes 1 and 2) in the United States. A tradition of sorts here is to "donate" your bra to the rafters on your first visit. When city leaders cracked down on this for being a fire hazard, the outcry from around the country was so fierce that the tradition was given a sheepish pass again.

A true Milwaukee treasure is the long-standing **Koz's Mini Bowl** (2078 S. 7th St., 414/383-0560), with four 16-foot lanes and balls the size of oranges; the pin setters still make $0.50 a game, plus tips. An aside: Koz's was actually a World War II-era house of ill repute; the lanes were simply a cover to keep locals from asking questions.

ICE SKATING AND HOCKEY

The **Pettit National Ice Center** (500 S. 84th St., off I-94, 414/266-0100, www.thepettit.com) is the only one of its kind in the country and one of only five of its scope in the world. National and international competitions are held here regularly. The public can enjoy the 400-meter ovals and two Olympic-size hockey rinks ($7.50) when they're open.

GOLF

Milwaukee is often mentioned for its nearly 20 golf courses, all within a short drive. Most prominent in the near vicinity is **Brown Deer Park** (7835 N. Green Bay Rd., 414/352-8080), a great public course. **Whitnall** and **Oakwood Parks** also have excellent courses.

SPECTATOR SPORTS

Milwaukee remains something of an anomaly as the smallest of the small markets. And most markets of comparable size support just one major league franchise, not three, as Milwaukee does.

The Brew Crew

Miller Park, the stadium of the **Milwaukee Brewers** (tickets 414/902-4400, www.brewers.com), is absolutely magnificent. It has been described as the most perfect synthesis of retro and techno in the world. Baseball season runs early April-late September, and obtaining tickets is sometimes difficult, especially on weekends or whenever the archenemy Chicago Cubs come to town.

Milwaukee Bucks

Except for an occasional woeful hiccup season, the **Milwaukee Bucks** (414/276-4545, www.bucks.com) are generally a competitive team in the NBA Eastern Conference. Tickets are sometimes hit-or-miss, but unless a big-name opponent is in town, you can usually land them. The Bucks opened a new arena—Fiserv Forum—in 2018, part of an enormous entertainment district downtown. The professionalism of the staff matches the modernity of the arena.

Entertainment and Events

NIGHTLIFE

Milwaukee is no Austin, Texas, but there's a lot more music and nightlife than people realize. Then again, it's also the city where sheepshead (a native card game) tournaments might get equal billing with live music in the same bar. Milwaukee has more than 5,000 bars, which is in the top 10 cities per capita nationwide, so there's something out there for everyone (*Forbes* called it "America's drunkest city"). And it is the City of Festivals: Throw a dart at a calendar and you'll hit an enormous festival of some sort.

Stretching along the Milwaukee River, aptly named **Water Street** draws a preponderance of Marquette students and lots of downtown business types. If you want rowdy, come here. Nightlife varies from a brewpub to sports bars and dance clubs.

More and more shops, boutiques, and restaurants are moving into the **Walker's Point** neighborhood by the month. Nightspots vary from a pub with a sand volleyball court outside to a Teutonic watering hole, dark sippers' pubs, and a whole lot more. If you need it, you'll likely find it here.

Bar-restaurants all packed in the same area have given **North Jefferson Street** and environs the feel of a subdued scene, all in the ritzy section of town full of boutiques, galleries, and the like—the yin to Water Street's noisy yang.

Venues tend to come and go, but the ones included in this guide show staying power. The free weekly *Shepherd Express* gives a rundown of most of the clubs; the *Milwaukee Journal-Sentinel* is also fairly thorough.

Burgers, chicken on Monday, and a

North Water Street's nightlife anchors

noticeable amount of pork offerings in a casual environment may make **Elsa's on Park** (833 N. Jefferson St., 414/765-0615, www.elsas.com) seem average, but the rotating art and skillfully crafted cocktails elevate the place to something special.

Beer Halls, Brewpubs, and Taverns

The **Water Street Brewery** (1101 N. Water St., 414/272-1195, www.waterstreetbrewery.com, food served 11am-9pm Mon.-Sat., $5-15) is Milwaukee's original brewpub. The same people also run what is likely the hottest spot in the neighborhood, the **Trinity Three Irish Pubs** (125 E. Juneau Ave., 414/278-7033, http://trinitythreeirishpubs.com, 11am-close daily), which offers three different pubs in one venue. One even turns into a dance club at night.

The folks at **Kochanski's Concertina Beer Hall** (1920 S. 37th St., 414/837-6552, www.beer-hall.com) certainly have big shoes to fill, seeing as their place was the home of legendary Milwaukee polkameister Art Altenberg, who for decades ran this club to preserve live polka music. Many nights his heritage still lives on here, though it might be roots rock or alt country; guaranteed, every Wednesday night is traditional polka music. It's the real deal, and it's a hoot.

Along bopping North Farwell Avenue, **Von Trier** (2235 N. Farwell Ave., 414/272-1775) could pass for a German *bierhalle* with its long heavy wooden bench seating and summertime biergarten. New management wanted to upscale the place; the hue and cry batted that down. Even after a minor refreshing, it's lost none of its essence. Good German eats, too. West of here across the river, **Uptowner** (1032 E. Center St., 414/368-0809) has been a Milwaukee fave forever. In fact, it dates to 1884 as a Schlitz house. It darn near closed in 2015, but regulars saved it—proving it is a cornerstone.

Without question the best selection of craft beers is at the neighborhood bar-meets-beer genius **Burnhearts** (2599 S. Logan Ave., 414/294-0490). Even beer snobs will learn something in this low-key place.

Too many neighborhood taverns to count exist in Milwaukee, and everybody's got a different recommendation. The since-1908 **Wolski's** (1836 N. Pulaski St., Walker's Point, 414/276-8130) is a corner tavern that defines a Milwaukee tippler's joint. You're an unofficial Beer City denizen if you drive home with an "I closed Wolski's" bumper sticker on your car.

Join the Brew Crew

Not a baseball or even a sports fan? It matters not; a Brewers game is a cultural necessity. Consider the following:

TAILGATING

Nobody but nobody parties before a ball game like Wisconsinites, and Milwaukeeans (and Green Bay Packers fans) have perfected the pregame tailgate party. The requisite pregame attraction is the meal of beer, grilled brats, and potato salad, eaten while playing catch in the parking lot. *Guinness World Records* recognized the Brewers' erstwhile home, Milwaukee County Stadium, as the site of the world's largest tailgate party, while the new Miller Park has nearly double the party area. And the food inside the stadium is superb: Sports commentator emeritus Bob Costas has deemed the stadium's bratwurst tops in the major leagues.

THE SAUSAGE RACE

But brats alone are not the only reason to go to a game. The Brewers have the coolest stunt in pro sports: the **Sausage Race.** Grounds-crew members stick themselves into big clunky sausage outfits—a hot dog, a Polish sausage, an Italian sausage, a bratwurst, and a Mexican *chorizo*—and lumber around the field to a thrilling finish at home plate. It's so popular that opposing players beg for the opportunity to be a Milwaukee sausage for the day, and it's being copied by many teams now.

Dance Clubs

One with the most staying power locally is the live music and dance club **Mad Planet** (533 E. Center St., 414/263-4555, 9pm-2:30am Fri.-Sat., varies on weeknights), a perennial winner of local awards for best dance club. There are regular dance parties that always turn into a mix of all local subcultures; here, goths mix with punks. Get here early. Otherwise, dance clubs are notorious for changing. Currently the place to dress to the nines and see touring DJs is the **Lucid Light Lounge** (729 N. Milwaukee St., 414/431-5557).

Live Music

ROCK

Shank Hall (1434 N. Farwell Ave., 414/276-7288) offers a constant barrage of prominent local, regional, and national acts. It was once a stable, so the interior isn't exactly a delight when the lights come up. Another good spot for local rock or regional alternative acts and mostly college crowds includes the acoustically atrocious **Rave** (2401 W. Wisconsin Ave., 414/342-7283).

Many readers of local websites and other media have voted the live music at **Milwaukee Ale House** (233 N. Water St., 414/226-2336, www.ale-house.com, 11am-10pm Mon.-Thurs., 11am-1am Fri.-Sat., 11am-9pm Sun., $6-15) as tops.

Not here on a weekend? Fret not, for the **Cactus Club** (2496 S. Wentworth Ave., 414/897-0663) has music, often national acts, many weeknights.

BLUES AND R&B

It used to be all blues all the time at the **Up and Under Pub** (1216 E. Brady St., 414/276-2677); under new owners it's had a freshening-up and added a nice variety of rock, roots, and more.

The Riverwest neighborhood is a prime spot, and a small neighborhood tavern unconcerned with decor, **Linneman's River West Inn** (1001 E. Locust St., 414/263-9844), has blues and some folk.

JAZZ

Serious jazz fans should head for a local institution, **Caroline's** (401 S. 2nd St., 414/221-9444) in Walker's Point, where you go for the music and atmosphere, not necessarily the decor.

WORLD MUSIC AND ECLECTIC

International flavors, musical and otherwise, are on offer in a comfortable setting at **Nomad World Pub** (1401 E. Brady St., 414/224-8111), part coffee shop, part unpredictable drink-pouring bar where you can get betel nuts while listening to world beat music, sometimes live.

Regular Irish music, along with Irish fare, is available at **County Clare** (1234 N. Astor St., 414/272-5273), set in a retro guesthouse.

Nightclubs and Lounges

At **Landmark Lanes** (2220 N. Farwell Ave., 414/278-8770), in the bowels of the Oriental Landmark Theater, there's bowling (this is Milwaukee, after all), but mostly it's a happening young nightclub with three separate bars, pool tables, and dartboards. The place has been around forever, and it's great.

If you're looking for a more upscale place, try the **Hi-Hat Lounge** (E. Brady St. and Arlington St., 414/220-8090). With cool jazz wafting in the background, it's got a classy but not showy feel and an older, sophisticated crowd.

LGBTQ

Near North Jefferson Street is Wisconsin's oldest LGBT dance club, **This is it!** (418 E. Wells St., 414/278-9192); it's been expanded and is now equal parts neighborhood bar and dance spot. Plus it has *stiff* drinks.

THE ARTS

In Rand McNally's *Places Rated,* Milwaukee hit the top 5 percent of big cities for cultural attractions and the arts. Since the 1990s, more than $100 million has been poured into downtown arts districts. Per capita, Milwaukeeans donate more to the arts than any U.S. city besides Los Angeles. Four dozen cultural organizations, including 23 theater companies, call the city home.

Rundowns for all cultural activities can be found in the *Milwaukee Journal-Sentinel*. *Milwaukee Magazine* also has a comprehensive monthly compendium.

Cultural Centers

The **Pabst Theater** (144 E. Wells St., 414/286-3663, www.pabsttheater.org), an 1895 Victorian piece of opulence that today seems as ornate as ever, is a majestic draw in its own right. Free public tours are given at noon Saturday if show schedules don't conflict. It also continues to attract national acts of all kinds. The **Marcus Center for Performing Arts** (929 N. Water St., 414/273-7206, www.marcuscenter.org) has a regular season of theater, symphony, ballet, opera, children's theater, and touring specials. It is the home of the Milwaukee Symphony Orchestra, the Milwaukee Ballet Company, the Florentine Opera Company, and more.

Theater

The city has nearly two dozen theater companies performing in many locations. The **Skylight Music Theatre** (414/291-7800, www.skylightmusictheatre.org) and **Milwaukee Chamber Theatre** (414/276-8842, www.chamber-theatre.com) are residents of the lovely **Broadway Theatre Center** (158 N. Broadway, 414/291-7800) downtown. The Chamber Theatre's language-centered contemporary plays are always a challenge.

One of the nation's few African American professional theater groups is the **Hansberry-Sands Theatre Company,** which performs at the **Marcus Center** (929 N. Water St., 414/273-7121, www.marcuscenter.org).

The **Milwaukee Repertory Theater** (108 E. Wells St., 414/224-1761, www.milwaukeerep.com) is part of an international network of cooperating organizations and offers classical, contemporary, cabaret, and special performances September-May.

Music

The **Milwaukee Symphony Orchestra** (700 N. Water St., 414/291-6010, www.mso.org) is one of the nation's top orchestras. No less than *New Yorker* magazine, with a typical coastal undercurrent of surprise, described it as "virtuoso."

Dance

Milwaukee has a thriving modern dance culture; New York City companies make regular visits for performances in numerous sites around the city. Ranked among the top ballet companies in the country is the **Milwaukee Ballet Company** (504 W. National Ave., 414/643-7677, www.milwaukeeballet.org).

Milwaukee's modern **Ko-Thi Dance Company** (414/273-0676, www.ko-thi.org), committed to the preservation and performance of African and Caribbean arts, is also nationally renowned. Tremendously popular shows are held in spring and fall at the Pabst Theater.

FESTIVALS AND EVENTS

Bless Milwaukee for always featuring free events. Downtown, Pere Marquette Park has free **concerts** Wednesday evenings. Cathedral Square Park at Jefferson and Wells features free **live jazz** Thursday evenings. Virtually every county park has free summertime music, too. Check online for schedules (www.county.milwaukee.gov).

★ Summerfest

Summerfest (www.summerfest.com) is the granddaddy of all Midwestern festivals and the largest music festival in the world (says *Guinness World Records*). For 11 days in late June, top national musical acts as well as unknown college-radio mainstays perform on innumerable stages along the lakefront, drawing millions of music lovers and partiers. Agoraphobics need not even consider it. Shop around for discount coupons at grocery stores and assorted businesses, or consider a multiday pass, available at businesses all around town.

City of Festivals

Another term of endearment for Milwaukee is the City of Festivals, as you'll find a nearly infinite variety of celebrations here. Aside from Summerfest and its innate chaos, the festivals on this list are relatively headache-free. Unless otherwise specified, each of the following takes place at Henry W. Maier Festival Park, the Summerfest grounds.

JUNE

- **Summerfest:** This is the largest music festival in the world. For 11 days in late June, national and local acts perform on multiple stages along the lakefront, drawing millions of music lovers and partiers. During Summerfest, traffic will be a nightmare, and there are no tricks to avoid it. You'll also have to scrounge for a hotel room, even six months in advance.
- **Polish Fest** (414/529-2140, www.polishfest.org): America's largest Polish festival
- **Lakefront Festival of Arts** (Milwaukee Art Museum grounds, 414/224-3253, http://lfoa.mam.org, late June)

JULY

- **German Fest** (414/464-9444, www.germanfest.com): The largest multiday cultural festival in the country
- **Festa Italiana** (414/223-2808, www.festaitaliana.com)
- **Bastille Days** (Cathedral Square Park downtown, 414/271-1416, www.easttown.com)

AUGUST

- **Mexican Fiesta** (414/383-7066, www.mexicanfiesta.org)
- **Irish Fest** (414/476-3378, www.irishfest.com): Called by the Smithsonian the best celebration of Irish culture in the nation, it is certainly the largest.
- **Black Arts Fest MKE** (www.blackartsfestmke.com): A celebration of African and African American culture through art, music, food, and fun (with wonderful storytelling)
- **Wisconsin State Fair** (414/266-7000, www.wistatefair.com): West of downtown along I-94, this fair of fairs, second only to Summerfest in attendance, features carnivals, 500 exhibits, livestock shows, entertainment on 20 stages, and the world's greatest cream puffs.

SEPTEMBER

- **Indian Summer** (414/604-1000, www.indiansummer.org): The largest Native American festival in the United States
- **Oktoberfest** (Heidelberg Park, Glendale, west of downtown, 414/476-3378, www.oktoberfestmilwaukee.com, weekends starting in late Sept.): Milwaukee's downtown has a (free) Oktoberfest, but this has been the real deal for 60 years now

NOVEMBER

- **International Holiday Folk Fair** (Wisconsin State Fair Park, west of downtown, 414/225-6225, www.folkfair.org)

Shopping

There's more to shopping in Milwaukee than the requisite cheddar cheese foam-wedge hat and cheese-and-bratwurst gift packs (though these should, of course, be on your list).

NORTH OLD WORLD 3RD STREET

To the north, North Old World 3rd Street has mostly good restaurants but a few long-standing shops, the highlight of which has to be **Usinger's** (1030 N. Old World 3rd St., 414/276-9100, www.usinger.com, 8:30am-5pm Mon.-Sat.). Sausage as a souvenir—is that a Milwaukee gift or what?

OTHER SHOPPING DISTRICTS

The **Historic Third Ward, Jefferson Street,** and **East Brady Street** areas offer the most compelling strolls for shoppers. All are blocks-long areas of carefully updated old-world-style streets, filled with art and antiques galleries, specialty shops, and oodles of places to grab a cup of java or a quick bite in a chic setting to recharge the shopping batteries. East Brady Street has a high quotient of hipster misunderstood geniuses. Chic upscale boutiques are found along **North Broadway.**

Food

Gastronomically, you'll be surprised by Milwaukee. It's a pan-ethnic food heaven spanning the gamut from fish fries in cozy 120-year-old neighborhood taprooms to four-star prix fixe repasts in state-of-the-art gourmet restaurants. That is, no casseroles and meat-and-potatoes monotony here!

DOWNTOWN

Asian

First off, yes, yes, we all know Chinese food is better on the coasts. Yet after two decades of living in and traveling around China, this author was impressed by the cuisine at **Jing's** (207 E. Buffalo St., 414/271-7788, www.jingsmke.com, 4:30pm-9pm Sun.-Mon., 11:30am-9pm Tues.-Fri., noon-9pm Sat., $9-13), a pan-Cathay place but with a specialty in the east and southeast provinces—think sweeter rather than hotter. Ask for the special menu.

Dan Dan (360 E. Erie St., 414/488-8036, 11am-2pm and 5pm-10pm Mon.-Fri., 5pm-10pm Sat., 5pm-9pm Sun., $9-22) is run by two guys who say they have a Chinese soul with a Midwestern sensibility, which is spot-on. They have a great take on Sichuan cuisine.

Where else but Wisconsin would you find a wondrous dim sum cart alongside delectable Germanic rye spaetzle with chops? And of course, baked cheese curds (spicy ranch is amazing). The whimsical but real-deal **Merriment Social** (240 E. Pittsburgh Ave., 414/645-0240, dinner Mon.-Sat., brunch Sun., from $9), runs one of the best restaurants for creativity and execution.

Coffee and Tea

Those with a java fixation should head for the **Brady Street** area (www.bradystreet.org), where you'll find an inordinate number of coffee shops of every possible variety.

Fine Dining

Garnering a wall full of awards, feted by national media regularly, and definitely worthy of a splurge is the nouvelle cuisine done magnificently at ★ **Sanford** (1547 N. Jackson St., 414/276-9608, 5:30pm-9pm Mon.-Thurs., 5pm-10pm Fri.-Sat., $30-70), one of the state's

TOP EXPERIENCE

Friday Fish Fries

Cuisine experience number one in Wisconsin is a Friday-night fish fry. Its exact origins are unknown, but it's certainly no coincidence that in a state contiguous to two Great Lakes, featuring 15,000 glacial pools and undergoing waves of Catholic immigration (Catholics traditionally don't eat meat on Friday during Lent), people would specialize in a Friday-night fish-eating outing.

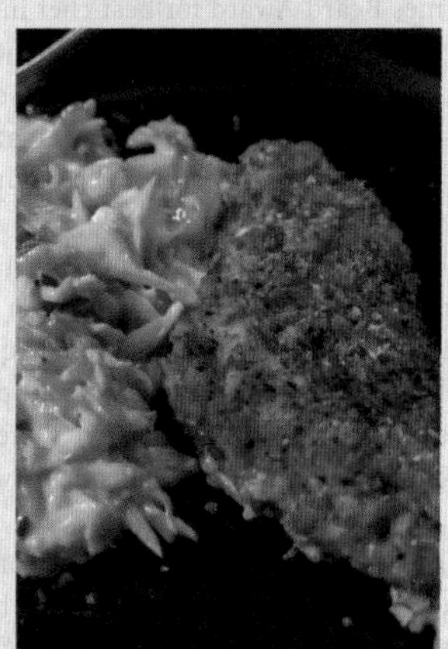

Friday fish fry!

Fish fries are myriad—it's so popular that even the local fast-food joints have them; Chinese, Mexican, and other ethnic restaurants get in on the act; and even Brewers games have offered them. More upscale places have them, too; however, they are generally not all you can eat and there is something weird about fine dining with a fish fry, to be honest.

Everybody has an opinion on who has the best fish fry, but, truthfully, how many ways can you deep-fry a perch or one of the other species variants—haddock, walleye pike, and cod? You can find broiled options at times. I've always preferred the ones in church basements, VFW Halls, and the like. Generally set up as smorgasbords and sometimes including platefuls of chicken too, the gluttonous feasts are served with slathered-on homemade tartar sauce and a relish tray or salad bar. The truly classic fish-fry joints are packed to the rafters by 5:30pm. Some even have century-old planks and hall-style seating. One reporter remarked recently in a fish-fry story that he got some cheese curds for dessert, and there is absolutely nothing more Wisconsin than that.

Consider yourself truly blessed if you get to experience a smelt fry. This longtime tavern tradition has pretty much disappeared; in the old days, smelt—milk-dipped, battered, and even pickled—were the thing.

For an only-in-Wisconsin eye-popping fish-fry experience, the **American Serbian Hall** serves *2,500 people* at a drive-through with a line down the street. However, for an *overall* experience, this author loves the fish fry on offer at the **Beer Hall** at Lakefront Brewery. Take the wonderful beer tour, but stay for the variety of fish, including smelt, as well as family-style seating, live polka music, and real-deal potato pancakes (necessary in my family).

Outside Milwaukee, your best bet is to kill two birds with one stone. The fish fry's twin as part of Wisconsin culinary heritage, a supper club provides the ambience of Wisconsin—the bartender will likely be your best friend as soon as you walk in—as well as the fish fry (not to mention cheese platters, natch).

To go completely over the top for fish fry, Wisconsin has rivals for "world's largest" fish fry. In June, Fond du Lac's **Walleye Weekend** brings umpteen thousands to have fried walleye (a fave for this author); in July Port Washington to the southeast follows it up with the "world's largest outdoor fish fry" at **Fish Day.**

For fish fries in Milwaukee not in this book, www.onmilwaukee.com and www.jsonline.com (search for "fish fries") are two good sites to peruse the many available options.

most original and respected innovators of cuisine. *Gourmet* magazine has more than once named it one of the United States' top 50 restaurants. The chef-owner was once awarded the James Beard Award for best chef in the Midwest. The attentive service, attention to detail, and superb execution of seasonal dishes remain excellent. It is simply amazing how consistently wonderful this restaurant has been.

Bacchus (925 E. Wells St., 414/765-1166, 5:30pm-9pm Mon.-Thurs., 5:30pm-10pm Fri., 5pm-10pm Sat., $11-22) rivals Sanford in quality but is the antithesis of stuffy. Small-plate menus feature artisanal cheeses, and there are excellent vegetarian options. It has a top wine menu, as well.

Billing itself as dedicated to Wisconsin heritage cuisine—sausage to dairy to ham hocks—**Ardent** (1751 N. Farwell Ave., 414/897-7022, dinner Wed.-Sat., $11-29) is a relaxed place with challenging fare done exquisitely. The farm boy-turned-chef was the only 2016 James Beard Award finalist in the state (his second time as a finalist), and he repeated in 2017. He uses beef from the family farm.

Something you'd never expect: How about a remarkable meal in a Milwaukee casino? The elegant and creative fare at Potawatomi Bingo Casino's **Dream Dance Steak** (1721 W. Canal St., 414/847-7883, www.paysbig.com/dining, 5pm-9pm Tues.-Thurs., 5pm-10pm Fri.-Sat., $26-39) is worth the trip even for the non-slots players.

The casino has other restaurants that make foodies woozy, including **RuYi** (414/847-7335, www.paysbig.com/dining, 11am-midnight Sun.-Thurs., 11am-2am Fri.-Sat., $13-35) with pan-Asian cuisine.

Locavore

Sustainably raised, locally sourced meats in a butcher shop sprang into a cozy restaurant at **Bavette La Boucherie** (330 E. Menomonee St., 414/273-3375, 11am-5pm Mon.-Tues., till 9pm Wed.-Sat., from $15). Find excellent cheese and charcuterie plates. The proprietor was a James Beard Award finalist.

Fish Fries

In Milwaukee, you'll find fish fries everywhere, even at the chain fast-food drive-throughs. Dozens of neighborhood taverns and bars still line up the plank seating and picnic tables with plastic coverings on Friday nights. Or head for a Catholic church; Milwaukee's got 275 parishes, so you'll find a good one. I would go for Lakefront Brewery, where its restaurant, **Beer Hall** (1872 N. Commerce St., 414/273-8300, www.lakefrontbrewery.com, 4pm-9pm Fri., $11-15), has a wondrous Friday fish fry. Expect loads of varieties, including smelt, walleye, and perch. You can even get real-deal tater pancakes, like the old days, and rollicking polka music. It's great fun.

Italian

The casual but wondrous **Zarletti** (741 N. Milwaukee St., 414/225-0000, lunch Mon.-Fri., dinner Mon.-Sat., $9-21) may feature seasonal squash ravioli, or homemade ricotta gnocchi with lamb ragu, but the highlight may be the proprietor's mother's baking!

German

Rollicking, boisterous, and full of lederhosen, **Mader's** (1037 N. Old World 3rd St., 414/271-3377, 11:30am-9pm Mon.-Thurs., 11am-10pm Fri.-Sat., 10:30am-9pm Sun., $18-24) has held its position as *the* German restaurant for the masses since 1902. Purists sometimes cringe at the over-the-top atmosphere (it's packed to the rafters with German knickknacks, not to mention tour buses idling outside), but the cheeriness is indomitable. Try the *knudel* (which doesn't taste as if it came out of a box), Rheinischer sauerbraten, oxtail soup, or Bavarian-style pork shank. Mader's also serves a Viennese brunch on Sunday.

1: the old Pabst Brewery, now one of the state's coolest taverns **2:** American Serbian Hall, the king of Milwaukee fish fries

1

2

Seafood

Harbor House (550 N. Harbor Dr., 414/395-4900, lunch and dinner daily, $17-50), just north of Discovery World, has fare that changes with the season, but whether it's dreamy lobster potpie or pan-seared Great Lakes walleye, it's outstanding, as are the sublime water and city views.

Steak Houses and Supper Clubs

In the meat-and-potatoes Midwest, it's hard for a steak place to stand out, but **Mo's: A Place for Steaks** (720 N. Plankinton Ave., 414/272-0720, 5pm-11pm Mon.-Sat., $18-55) and its aged marbled Wagyu steaks do. Sit in the leather chairs, listen to the piano, and salivate. Also appreciate the superlative service.

Vegetarian and Health Food

This author's favorite centrally located place is definitely the vegan **On the Bus** (Milwaukee Public Market, 414/204-8585, 10am-8pm Mon.-Fri., 8am-7pm Sat., 10am-6pm Sun., $4-8), especially for its homemade seitan and acai bowls (psst—awesome ice cream, too).

Northeast of downtown you'll find not a veggie restaurant per se but a slow-food movement follower: **Comet Café** (1947 N. Farwell Ave., 414/273-7677, 10am-10pm Mon.-Fri., 9am-10pm Sat.-Sun., $6-12). Your carnivore friend can have the traditional mom (well, Milwaukee mom, anyway) meat loaf with beer gravy, while your vegan friend can have the vegan Salisbury steak.

Not far away from here is "otherworldly vegan" (their words—and close) at **Celesta** (1978 N. Farwell Ave., 414/251-3030, 11am-10pm Tues.-Sat., 11am-2pm Sun., $6-11). Call it global vegan with a lot made in-house. This carnivore loved the buffalo burger.

NORTH OF DOWNTOWN

Coffee

The **Fuel Cafe** (818 E. Center St., 7am-6pm Mon.-Fri., 8am-6pm Sat.-Sun.) is exceedingly young, hip, and alternative. Here you'll find cribbage players and riot grrls. The decor is mismatched rummage sale furniture with an arty flair. The service bills itself as lousy, but it isn't, and there's a great menu of coffee drinks, bakery items, salads, sandwiches, and even Pop-Tarts. Try the Kevorkian Krush: three shots of espresso and mocha. It's vegan-friendly.

Custard

Frozen custard is an absolute must of a Milwaukee cultural experience; the dozens of Milwaukee family custard stands were the inspiration for Big Al's Drive-In on the TV show *Happy Days* of the 1970s and '80s. An informal poll of 20 Milwaukeeans resulted in a dozen different recommendations for where to experience frozen custard. Most often mentioned (but you really can't go wrong anywhere): **Kopp's** (5373 N. Port Washington Rd., 414/961-2006, www.kopps.com, 10:30am-11pm daily), which does custard so seriously that it has a flavor-of-the-day hotline.

Fine Dining

Opened by a prominent local restaurateur and housed in an exquisitely restored century-old park pavilion, **Bartolotta's Lake Park Bistro** (3133 E. Newberry Blvd., 414/962-6300, 11am-9pm Mon.-Fri., 11am-2pm and 5pm-10pm Sat., 10am-2pm and 5pm-9pm Sun., $7-12) has managed to remain rock solid as a dining highlight. Its rustic French cuisine (buttressing pan-European choices) is superb, and if nothing else, the view from the drive along the lake is worth the time. A popular Sunday brunch spot, its interiors are airy, offering plenty of privacy between tables.

Soul Food

Mr. Perkins (2001 W. Atkinson Ave., 414/447-6660, 7am-1pm Wed.-Thurs. and Sat., 3am-7pm Fri., 11am-3pm Sun., from $5) is the place to go for soul food, with tons of down-home specialties like collard greens, catfish, chitterlings, and turkey necks. This place has been *it* since the 1960s!

Vegetarian and Health Food

A longtime standby for a low-key and decidedly body-friendly meal is **Beans and Barley** (1901 E. North Ave., 414/278-7878, 8am-9pm daily, from $4). Very much a hip—though low-priced—eatery, it's housed in what smacks of an old grocery store warehouse encased in glass walls from an attached grocery and small bar. Everything from straight-up diner food to creative vegetarian is on the menu, with Indian and Southwestern options, as well as juices and smoothies.

SOUTH OF DOWNTOWN

Custard

The south side has perhaps the most legendary custard in the city. An institution since the early 1940s is **Leon's** (3131 S. 27th St., 414/383-1784, 11am-midnight daily); it's got the best neon. The **Nite Owl Drive-In** (830 E. Layton Ave., 414/483-2524, 11am-6pm, Tues.-Sat. closed winter) has been dishing up ice cream and doling out burgers by the same family for a half-century; even Elvis loved to eat here. It's worth noting that they'll close early if they sell out of burgers (it happens).

Fish Fries

For the most one-of-a-kind fish fry anywhere, head for ★ **American Serbian Hall** (53rd St. and Oklahoma Ave., 414/545-6030, www.americanserbhall.com, 11:30am-9pm Fri., $10), recognized as the largest in the nation. On Friday night, this hall serves more than a ton of Icelandic-style or Serbian baked fish to more than 2,500 people (make that two tons of fish on Good Friday). The operation got so big that a drive-through has been added, which serves an additional 1,200 patrons. Cars back up for miles, while next to the complex, waiting patrons, many chatting in Serbian, engage in fun-spirited boccie ball games.

Locavore

Well-respected is the New American ★ **Braise** (1101 S. 2nd St., 414/212-8843, dinner Tues.-Sat., $17-30), which absolutely lives the "eat local" and "sustainable" mantra. Small plates and butcher-board items are all locally sourced and beg to be shared. This place is absolutely top-notch. The chef was a James Beard Award finalist.

Not far behind Braise is **Odd Duck** (2352 S. Kinnickinnic Ave., 414/763-5881, dinner daily, from $18) for its international small plates done fantastically with local ingredients.

Mexican

Milwaukee's southeast side is a haven for unpretentious authentic Mexican eateries; some Mexican grocers have lunch counters in the back or sell delectable tamales ready for takeout. **Conejito's** (539 W. Virginia St., 414/278-9106, www.conejitos-place.com, 11am-midnight daily, from $4) is a neighborhood bar-restaurant with authentic atmosphere and real-deal Mexican food (served on, wonderfully, paper plates).

Polish

Polonez (4016 S. Packard Ave., St. Francis, 414/482-0080, 11am-3pm Tues.-Thurs., 5pm-9pm Tues.-Sat., 11am-8pm Sun., $5-17) is a longtime Milwaukee favorite that has transformed geographically and atmospherically into a white-tableclothed fine-dining (but very casual in feeling) experience. The pierogi and cutlets are phenomenal, as is the very good *czarnina* (a raisin soup with duck stock, duck blood, and fruits). Seven soups are available daily. The Sunday brunch is unrivaled.

Serbian

Enjoy top-notch Serbian food in a delightful old-world atmosphere at ★ **Three Brothers** (2414 S. St. Clair St., Bay View, 414/481-7530, dinner 5pm-10pm Tues.-Sat., from $11). The 1897 turreted brick corner house, an original Schlitz brewery beer parlor, was turned into a restaurant by the present owner's father, a Serbian wine merchant. Not much has changed. The high ceilings, original wood, semi-dusty bottles on the bar, murals, and mismatched tables and chairs remain. Only a new floor and a bit of wall paint have been added recently. All of it is charming. The food is heavy on pork and chicken, with lots of *paprikash* and stuffed cabbage. The signature entrée is *burek*, a filled phyllo-dough concoction the size of a radial tire; you'll wait half an hour for this one. The restaurateur's daughter has also added vegetarian options. The restaurant is difficult to find, and you'll likely wind up asking for directions from a horseshoe club outside a local tavern.

Vegetarian Indian

With rock-bottom pricing (most of the many choices are under $7), outstanding takeout, and mesmerizing smells, you can't beat local unknown **Bombay Sweets** (3401 S. 13th St., 414/383-3553, 10am-10pm daily).

WEST OF DOWNTOWN

Italian

The name Bartolotta seems to be omnipresent in Wauwatosa. **Ristorante Bartolotta** (7616 W. State St., Wauwatosa, 414/771-7910, 5:30pm-9pm Mon.-Thurs., 5pm-10pm Fri.-Sat., 5:30pm-8pm Sun., $16-28) is a warm and friendly eatery run by a legendary Milwaukee restaurateur, and it's definitely worth the trip.

Steak Houses

Five O'Clock Steakhouse (2416 W. State St., 414/342-3553, 5:30pm-9:30pm Tues.-Sat., $19-32) has been around forever and is so popular that you absolutely need a reservation. It has the largest portions in town, all simmered in the eatery's legendary meat juice, and old-fashioned touches such as relish trays, though some have opined that its quality doesn't always match its legendary tradition.

Some locals say the best steaks aren't even in Milwaukee but in Wauwatosa at **Mr. B's, a Bartolotta Steak House** (17700 W. Capitol Dr., Wauwatosa, 262/790-7005, 5:30pm-9:30pm Mon.-Thurs., 5:30pm-10pm Fri.-Sat., 5-8pm Sun., $16-37), run by one of Milwaukee's most successful restaurateurs. The steaks are grilled over hardwoods; Italian entrées are also available.

Vegetarian

Loads of restaurants in Milwaukee can accommodate vegetarians, but we all know that generally means a couple of pasta entrées or something done the same way, only they don't throw in the meat. **Café Manna** (3815 N. Brookfield Rd., Brookfield, 262/790-2340, www.cafemanna.com, 11am-9pm Tues.-Sat., 9am-2pm Sun., $6-15) is a favorite vegetarian restaurant (it's also vegan-friendly) far west of downtown in Brookfield, but worth the drive. Try the Indian beet burger—that's right.

Accommodations

Most travelers will find lodging in downtown Milwaukee much better than they may have expected, given the historic grace of many buildings. A good trick is to check the **Milwaukee Convention and Visitors Bureau**'s website (www.visitmilwaukee.org) for frequent package deals at local hotels, even in peak seasons.

Note that all rates given are merely the lowest average price. Weekends in summer can be extremely expensive at some hotels, so check around.

DOWNTOWN

Downtown Milwaukee is full of aging anachronisms, some wearier than others. One hint: Given Wisconsin's winter, you may want to note whether the lodging is linked via the downtown **skywalk system.**

$100-150

Assume this category will be closer to $150 on weekends or during festivals. About the lowest price is at the **Fairfield Inn & Suites** (710 N. Old World 3rd St., 414/224-8400, $117-219), which gives you bang for your buck with new renovations and a cool warehouse lobby.

The next place to check is the 1920 art deco **Astor Hotel** (924 E. Juneau St., 414/271-4220 or 800/558-0200, www.theastorhotel.com, from $117), which must have the record for most consistently hit-or-miss reviews with travelers but is cheap for the location. It has character, including the original fixtures. The staff are always pleasant, but do check a few rooms.

Aloft (1230 N. Old World 3rd St., 414/226-0122, www.aloftmilwaukeedowntown.com, $129-299) is a minimalist boutique and very trendy. The high ceilings and windows exhibit wonderful design, but keep in mind it caters to a very boisterous crowd. No one disputes the friendliness of the staff, however.

The historic apartment-condo building housing **Knickerbocker on the Lake** (1028 E. Juneau Ave., 414/276-8500, www.knickerbockeronthelake.com, $150) overlooks Lake Michigan in a great location, on a bluff just northeast of the funky Brady Street area. The lobby sports original marble floors and vaulted ceilings; some rooms have smashing deck views, fireplaces, or other extras. You get old (real keys in original doors) with new (tasteful lighting and fresh beds). Some find it too anachronistically funky; others say that's part of the charm.

Over $150

The **Hilton Milwaukee City Center** (509 W. Wisconsin Ave., 414/271-7250 or 855/605-0316, www.hiltonmilwaukee.com, from $189) is perhaps the best example of restored charm downtown with a recent $19 million upgrade. This incarnation features limestone ashlar, pink granite, and buff terra-cotta; it's Milwaukee's sole Roaring '20s art deco-style hotel, right down to the geometric marble motifs in the lobby. Love the skywalk to keep you warm in winter but more so Millie, the house dog!

Generating lots of well-earned buzz is ★ **Hotel Metro** (411 E. Mason St., 414/272-1937, www.hotelmetro.com, $219), an upscale but cute boutique hotel in an erstwhile art deco office building. Glass sinks from Wisconsin's Kohler Company are among the noticeable design highlights in the 65 oversize suites (up to 450 square feet!), replete with steeping tubs or whirlpool baths; downstairs is a chic sceney bar. The art deco stylings include environmentally friendly bamboo-wood floorings and wood from sustainable forests. If that weren't enough, at the time of writing it was finishing up a massive refreshing. Hotel Metro offers guests the use of one of their cruiser bicycles to get around town. It's also got a nice bistro.

A few minutes' walk south, **Kimpton Journeyman Hotel** (310 E. Chicago St., 414/291-3970, www.journeymanhotel.com.com, $220) is one of the city's newest (and best) hotels, with up-to-the-minute stylings and amenities (yoga mats for guests) but a nod to the past (shuffleboard in the bar). Best, it's the closest to the Summerfest grounds, a ten-minute walk.

The impressive all-suite boutique hotel **Brewhouse Suites** (1215 N. 10th St., 414/810-3350, brewhousesuites.com, $269) is housed in the defunct Pabst Brewery; its lovely five-story atrium with brewing kettles is wonderful, as is the cream city brick. Think all-green, sustainably built, steampunk-influenced suites.

The granddaddy of Milwaukee hotels, referred to as the "Grand Hotel," is the ★ **Pfister** (424 E. Wisconsin Ave., 414/273-8222 or 800/558-8222, www.thepfisterhotel.com, $274 d), built in 1893. This upscale behemoth oozes Victorian grandeur. The overwhelming lobby, filled with displays of 19th-century art, is of such ornate intricacy that the hotel organizes regular tours. Its state-of-the-art recreation facility outshines most health clubs. The laundry list of attractive features and service accolades could fill a phone book. Then again, many believe that the Pfister is spectrally inhabited.

NORTH OF DOWNTOWN

Milwaukee finally has a hostel. The **Cream City Hostel** (500 Center St., 414/510-2181, www.creamcityhostel.com, from $28), just north of downtown in the Riverwest neighborhood, is a lovely and well-run place in what was a 1920s bank. The large backyard is great. A variety of room options are available, including private rooms. Given that this dirt-cheap option is quite close to downtown, you can bet reservations far in advance are necessary.

Most lodging choices to the north otherwise are found off I-43 along Port Washington Road. Best overall rooms and location are at the **Holiday Inn Milwaukee Riverfront** (4700 N. Port Washington Rd., 414/962-6040 or 877/854-5095, www.himilwaukee.com, $111), which underwent an $8 million renovation to give even more rooms river views. The excellent restaurant has an even better river view. It has consistently friendly staff.

SOUTH OF DOWNTOWN

If you've got an early-morning flight or are just looking for something cheap close to downtown, head south. At least two dozen lodgings are scattered around, most along South Howell Avenue, West Layton Avenue, and South 13th Street, and all but one are neon-light chain options: an amazingly well-run **Hampton Inn** (1200 W. College Ave., 414/762-4240, $109).

Over $150

Any hotel that aims to mingle business suits with biker leathers and boots is going to raise a few eyebrows, but **The Iron Horse Hotel** (500 W. Florida St., 414/373-4766 or 888/543-4766, www.theironhorsehotel.com, from $300) is a success at it. It's a biker boutique hotel, appropriately a stone's throw from the Harley-Davidson Museum. Its loft-style rooms are loaded to the gills with chic-but-tough design, with everything geared toward someone waltzing in with biker boots or their work laptop (or both).

Decidedly cheaper but no less worthy is **Kinn Guesthouse** (2535 S. Kinnickinnic Ave., 888/546-6021, www.kinnmke.com, $175), open only on weekends year-round in Bay View, which calls itself a "hand-curated micro-hotel," translated as chic guesthouse with a lovely shared full kitchen and living area in a historic building of cream city brick

the Brewhouse Suites, a chic steampunk-influenced boutique hotel

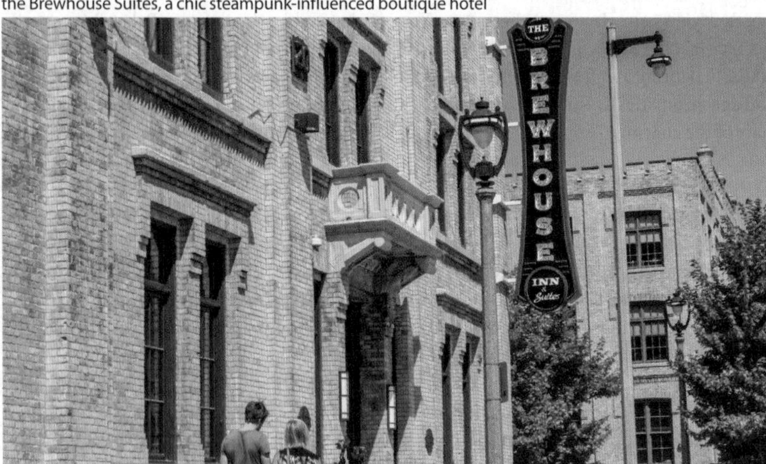

and original wood floors and trim. This garners well-earned raves.

WEST OF DOWNTOWN

Follow the interstates in any direction for most chain options. Resurrected from the doldrums (and helping the neighborhood do the same) is the **Ambassador Hotel** (2308 W. Wisconsin Ave., 414/342-8400 or 877/935-2189, www.ambassadormilwaukee.com, $129), just outside the western fringes of downtown. Inside a remodeled 1927 art deco structure, this place is historic meets state-of-the-art. You'll love sipping a Prohibition-era cocktail in the Gin Rickey restaurant, one of three on-site recently renovated to the 1920s era. Its only drawback is the location: not close enough to downtown to walk. Also, be careful you're contacting the hotel, not the inn across the street.

There's a hostel in an 1890s farmhouse not too far away in Kettle Moraine State Forest in Eagle, called **Hi-Eagle Home Hostel** (Hwy. 58, Eagle, 262/495-8794, www.eaglehostel.com, $30), but it's open only on weekends year-round.

CAMPING

The best public camping is half an hour west via I-94 and south on Highway 67 in **Kettle Moraine State Forest** (262/646-3025, reservations at 888/947-2757, www.wisconsin.goingtocamp.com, year-round, from $25 nonresidents); follow the signs for the Kettle Moraine Scenic Drive. It's very popular and often fully booked, so reserve early.

The nearest private campground is southwest of Milwaukee along I-43 in Mukwonago at **Country View Campground** (S110 W26400 Craig Ave., Mukwonago, 414/662-3654, mid-Apr.-mid-Oct., $25). Country View offers a pool, a playground, hot showers, and supplies.

Information and Services

VISITOR INFORMATION

Visit Milwaukee (400 W. Wisconsin Ave., 414/273-7222 or 800/554-1448, www.visitmilwaukee.org, 8am-5pm Mon.-Fri., 9am-2pm Sat., 10am-3pm Sun. summer, 8am-5pm Mon.-Fri. fall-spring) is in the convention center.

The local sales tax totals 5.6 percent. You'll pay a 9 percent tax on hotel rooms in addition to the sales tax, 3 percent on car rentals, and a 0.5 percent tax on food and beverage purchases.

MEDIA

The ***Milwaukee Journal-Sentinel*** is a morning daily. Fans of alternative views pick up weekly copies of the free ***Shepherd Express,*** which is also a good source of local arts and nightlife info. The local monthly repository of everything Milwaukee is ***Milwaukee Magazine.*** For online help, check www.onmilwaukee.com, generally the best of the half-dozen or so online guides.

Listen to the eclectic, student-run **WMSE** at 91.7 FM. The local standby has always been **WTMJ** (620 AM) for news and talk radio.

Transportation

GETTING THERE

Air

General Mitchell International Airport (5300 S. Howell Ave., 414/747-5300, www.mitchellairport.com) is southeast of downtown, near Cudahy. It's best reached by traveling I-94 south and following the signs. From downtown, head south on 6th Street North; it leads to Highway 38 (Howell Ave.). Nearly 40 cities have direct flights to Milwaukee; more than 220 flights depart each day.

Milwaukee County Transit System **buses** run to the airport; almost any bus can start you on your way if you ask the driver for transfer help. A taxi from downtown costs $20 and takes 20 minutes. Airport limousines cost half that.

For questions about these services, call the airport's **ground transportation hotline** (414/747-5308).

Car

From the west, I-94 is Milwaukee's primary thoroughfare. I-894 skirts the southern and western fringes north to south, and I-43 meets I-94 at the Marquette interchange downtown and then heads north toward Door County.

Driving to Milwaukee from Chicago (via I-94 and I-43, 100 miles) takes two hours without traffic. From Minneapolis (via I-94, 382 miles), the drive takes seven hours. From Door County (via Hwy. 57 and I-43, 154 miles), it takes 2.5 hours.

Bus

Greyhound (414/272-2156 or 800/231-2222, www.greyhound.com) operates at the **Intermodal Station** (433 W. St. Paul Ave.). Buses leave up to a dozen times daily for Chicago; buses also go to Minneapolis, Madison, and certain points in central Wisconsin. A few other intercity coaches offer services but have inconsistent schedules.

Up the street from the Intermodal Station is the **Badger Bus** (635 N. James Lovell St., 414/276-7490, www.badgerbus.com). Buses leave this location for Madison nine times daily. Badger Bus also serves Mitchell Field International Airport and Minneapolis-St. Paul when universities are in session.

Discount bus service **MegaBus** (877/462-6342, http://us.megabus.com) runs from near the Intermodal Station in Milwaukee to Chicago (about $18) as well as Minneapolis. There are no ticket offices, terminals, or sometimes service, so it is imperative to check the website for pickup information.

Train

Amtrak operates more than half a dozen trains daily to Chicago. Trains to Minneapolis run once daily. Amtrak operates at the **Intermodal Station** (433 W. St. Paul Ave., 414/271-9037, www.amtrak.com), which also houses Greyhound.

Boat

High-speed ferry service from Milwaukee to Muskegon, Michigan, is available from **Lake Express** (866/914-1010, www.lake-express.com). Three round-trips make the zippy 2.5-hour run across the lake, leaving the **Milwaukee Ferry Terminal** (2330 S. Lincoln Memorial Dr.), in the south-side neighborhood of Bay View, at 6am, 12:30pm, and 7pm daily May-October. Round-trip rates ($161 adults, $45 under age 17, $198 cars) are not cheap, but the service is outstanding.

GETTING AROUND

Car

Many highway upgrades are ongoing, so driving in Milwaukee requires patience. At least parking is generally available unless there is a major event going on downtown.

Every major rental car agency is represented at Mitchell International Airport, and many have offices throughout the city. There is a 3 percent tax on car rentals.

Taxi

Taxis are all metered and have a drop fare of around $3 for the first mile and about $1.50 for each additional mile. **American United Taxicab** (414/220-5010) is the state's largest operation and uses GPS-aided navigation.

Bus

The **Milwaukee County Transit System** (414/344-6711, www.ridemcts.com) operates loads of buses. You can save 25 percent by buying a 10-pack of tickets.

Streetcar

A new $24-million streetcar called **The Hop** (https://thehopmke.com, $1) started in 2018, but it serves only the Third Ward and not much else as far as tourists are concerned.

Organized Tours

Increasingly popular are Milwaukee River (and occasionally Lake Michigan harbor) cabin cruiser tours, some also offering dining cruises.

The venerable ***Iroquois*** boat tours of **Milwaukee Boat Lines** (414/294-9450, www.mkeboat.com, usually from noon-4pm daily June-Aug., $20 adults) depart from the Clybourn Street Bridge on the west bank of the Milwaukee River and offer scenic narrated tours. Sporadic evening tours are also offered June-September.

At the Municipal Pier, south of the Milwaukee Art Museum, the replica 19th-century schooner ***Denis Sullivan*** (414/276-7700, www.discoveryworld.org) is Wisconsin through and through, with all lumber culled from northern Wisconsin forests; it is more than 130 feet long with three 95-foot native white pine masts. Technically it's a floating classroom, part of the new nonprofit Pier Wisconsin project, but its pricey tours ($50-55 adults, $25 children) are available to anyone interested in maritime history and ecology. They're also jaw-droppingly spectacular, not to mention better-than-any-book educational. Sailing schedules vary by season and year.

A wonderful and easy way to take in Lakefront Brewery and several other up-and-coming Milwaukee craft breweries is the Saturday tour from **Untapped Tours** (414/698-8058, untappedtours.com, 1pm, $55). This small operation (the owner will likely be your guide) has friendly and solicitous service, and everyone raves about it. (They also have excellent city tours.) Tours leave from Company Brewing (735 E. Center St.).

Vicinity of Milwaukee

TEN CHIMNEYS

A mere 15-minute drive west of downtown Milwaukee, close to Waukesha, is "Broadway's Retreat" in the Midwest: **Ten Chimneys** (S43 W31575 Depot Rd., Genesee Depot, 262/968-4161, www.tenchimneys.org), the former home of the Great White Way's legendary Alfred Lunt and Lynn Fontaine. From its creation as a haven for artists in the 1920s, it welcomed legions of actors, writers, singers, and film stars, all seeking spiritual rejuvenation in a bucolic retreat. Having fallen into disrepair, it was nearly razed before an extraordinary renovation effort saved it. Inside, the exquisite detailing and furnishings are almost an afterthought, so caught up are visitors by mementos sent to Fontaine and Lunt from Helen Hayes, Noël Coward, and Charlie Chaplin, among others. The sublime 18-room main house sits perched above 60 acres of rolling moraine topography; nearby are a "quaint" eight-room cottage and a Swedish-style log cabin, as well as a dozen other buildings. Not simply a memorial to a bygone era, Ten

Chimneys is a living artists' retreat again. It sponsors workshops, collaborations, teacher-training programs, and public classes.

Tours (main house tour $30, full estate tour $35) are available, but don't visit without calling ahead; officially it's open to the public 10am-2:30pm Tuesday-Saturday, noon-2:30pm Sunday May-October, but if a special event is taking place, you may not get in.

★ CEDARBURG

What candy-facade original-13-colony spots such as Williamsburg are to the East Coast, Cedarburg is to Wisconsin. It's been seemingly preserved in a vacuum thanks to local residents who successfully fought off wholesale architectural devastation from an invasion of Milwaukeeans looking for an easy commute. About half an hour north of downtown Milwaukee, Cedarburg was originally populated by German and a few British immigrants, who hacked a community out of a forest and built numerous mills along Cedar Creek, which bisects the tiny community. It had the only worsted wool mill and factory in what was then considered the West. Those mills, and more than 100 other original Cream City-brick buildings, have been painstakingly restored into the state's most concentrated stretch of antiques dealers, shops, galleries, bed-and-breakfasts, and proper little restaurants.

The heart and soul of the town is **Cedar Creek Settlement** (www.cedarcreeksettlement.com), an antebellum foundation mill once the village's center of activity but now a several-blocks-long hodgepodge of shops, restaurants, and galleries. The **Cedar Creek Winery** (N70 W6340 Bridge Rd., 262/377-8020, www.cedarcreekwinery.com, 10am-5pm daily with added hours in peak times) is also on the premises; tours take in the aging cellars. West of Washington Road, the main drag, Portland Road features one of the original structures in Cedarburg, the enormous five-story **Cedarburg Mill,** now home to a pet store. Along Riveredge Drive is the **Brewery Works** (W62 N718 Riveredge Dr., 262/377-8230, 1pm-4pm Wed.-Sun.), a restored 1840s brewery housing the **Ozaukee County Art Center.**

Three miles north of town is the last extant **covered bridge** in the state, dating from 1876; to get here, head to the Highway 143/60 junction on Washington Avenue. This is an excellent bike tour. Southeast of Cedarburg via Hamilton Road is the original settlement of **Hamilton,** with another picturesque creek-side mill.

The local **visitors center** (Columbia Rd., 262/377-5856, www.cedarburg.org) is very friendly and useful staffers will point you in the right direction. A small **general store museum** is also in the complex.

For food, you can get classic Wisconsin German tavern fare or casually upscale cuisine. It's a chichi name and menu at **Cream and Crepe Café** (Cedar Creek Settlement, 262/377-0900, 10am-8pm Tues.-Sat., 10am-5pm Sun.-Mon., $4-10), but the crepes are delectable, as is the creek-side dining area.

Galioto's Twelve21 (1221 Wauwatosa Rd., 262/377-8085, www.galiotostwelve21.com, dinner Tues.-Sun., $8-26) is a smashing eatery housed in a classic Wisconsin country tavern. The superb renovation features original beams and flickering flames in an original fireplace. The well-done dishes focus on creative comfort food. The pork chops are legendary.

Gorgeous lodging options exist; nobody comes here to stay in a motel. The **Stagecoach Inn and Weber Haus Annex** (W61 N520 Washington Ave., 262/375-0208 or 888/375-0208, www.stagecoach-inn-wi.com, from $125) is a historic inn and pub on the old Milwaukee-Green Bay stagecoach line. Find nine lovely rooms in the main inn and three in a restored 1847 frame building across the street, where you can stroll in a private garden. Rumors say a benign, black-garbed apparition wafts through the inn.

1: Washington House Inn **2:** Cream and Crepe Café **3:** Cedarburg's wonderful covered bridge

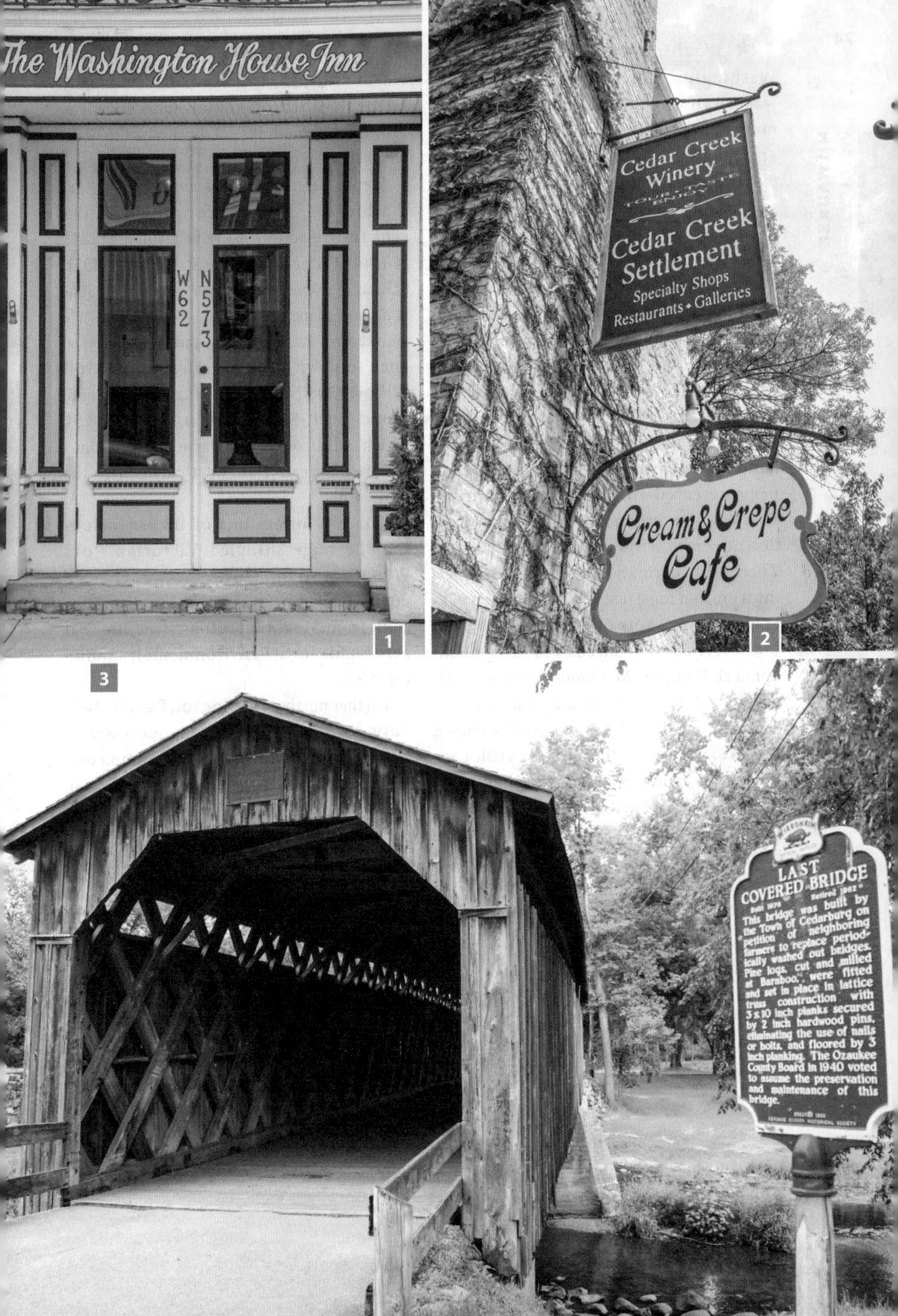

The Washington House Inn
W62
N573
Cedar Creek Winery
Cedar Creek Settlement
Specialty Shops
Restaurants • Galleries
Cream & Crepe Cafe
LAST COVERED BRIDGE
Retired 1962
This bridge was built by the Town of Cedarburg on petition of neighboring farmers to replace periodically washed out bridges. Pine logs, cut and milled at Baraboo, were fitted and set in place in lattice truss construction with 3 x 10 inch planks secured by 2 inch hardwood pins, eliminating the use of nails or bolts, and floored by 3 inch planking. The Ozaukee County Board in 1940 voted to assume the preservation and maintenance of this bridge.
1
2
3

★ **Washington House** (W62 N573 Washington Ave., 800/554-4717, http://washingtonhouseinn.com, from $189) may be even better than Stagecoach. It's an amazing combination of classic and cutting-edge modern with outstanding service.

PORT WASHINGTON

Forty minutes north of Milwaukee is Port Washington, a littoral Lake Michigan community that put itself into the history books with its quixotic anti-Civil War draft riots, when mobs took over the courthouse and trained a cannon on the lakefront until the army showed up and quelled the disturbance. Part Great Lakes fishing town and part preserved antebellum anachronism, Port Washington is known for its enormous downtown **marina** and fishing charters. There are historic structures and even a new museum, but most just stroll along the breakers, snapping shots of **Port Washington Light** (311 Johnson St., 262/284-7240, noon-4pm Fri.-Sun., late May-mid-Oct., $5), an art deco lighthouse that's now a historical museum. Along Grand Avenue, what's known as **Pebble House,** the site of a visitor information center, was painstakingly built of stones scavenged from beaches along the lake. Franklin Street, dominated by the thrusting spire of St. Mary's Church and various castellated building tops, rates as one of the most small-town-like of any of the Lake Michigan coastal towns.

Port Washington claims to hold the **world's largest outdoor fish fry** annually on the third Saturday of July (also known as Fish Day), though it's got a couple of in-state rivals for that title.

Plenty of good food is available in Port Washington. Every place will have a decent fish selection. **Bernie's Fine Meats Market** (119 N. Franklin St., 262/284-4511, 9:30am-5:30pm Mon.-Fri., 9:30am-4pm Sat.) is a good place to scout out Wisconsin-style smoked meats, especially sausage varieties. For a sit-down meal, you can't beat **Twisted Willow** (308 N. Franklin St., 262/268-7600, dinner Tues.-Sat., lunch Fri.-Sun., $11-25), which pulls from its own farm for its luscious American creative-comfort cuisine (try the pork loin).

The city offers lots of B&Bs, including the huge shingled Victorian **Port Washington Inn** (308 W. Washington St., 262/284-5583, www.port-washington-inn.com, from $159), a gorgeous structure that gets kudos for its environmentally sound practices.

Farther north is **Harrington Beach State Park** (262/285-3015, reservations 888/947-2757, www.wisconsin.goingtocamp.com, reservation fee $8, from $23 nonresidents), unknown outside the Milwaukee area. It's got great lake and limestone bluff views, an abandoned limestone quarry and quarry lake, and hiking trails, some a bit treacherous. Reserve campsites in advance since it's popular on weekends and holidays.

Madison

A Wisconsin governor's aide once quipped,

"Madison is 60 square miles surrounded by reality." The quote has become a proud bumper-sticker slogan in the city.

Madison has always been progressive and a bit loony, which is why so many love it. Much of the rest of the state's stereotype of Madison is of outdated, self-centered radicals.

It loves to recall its leftist hot-spot days of protest (which erupt now and then still), but the salad days of revolution are not always so apparent. The student population rarely raises a fuss anymore, unless to over-celebrate University of Wisconsin (UW) sports teams' championships or holidays in beer-soaked student bacchanalia. Financial institutions are rather more conspicuous than cubbyhole progressive action

Highlights

Look for ★ to find recommended sights, activities, dining, and lodging.

★ **Wisconsin State Capitol:** Stand in awe of the largest state capitol in the country—then go inside and be blown away by the art and handcrafted interiors (page 78).

★ **Monona Terrace Community and Convention Center:** This striking white building designed by Frank Lloyd Wright has a lovely rooftop garden (page 78).

★ **University of Wisconsin-Madison Campus:** You'll find a weekend's worth of museums, gorgeous lakeside trails, and the Memorial Union—a beautiful indoor/outdoor student center that sits on Lake Mendota (page 82).

★ **University of Wisconsin Arboretum:** Take a guided tour or an evening walk here and get a glimpse of what Wisconsin looked like in its virgin form (page 83).

★ **Olbrich Botanical Gardens:** These 16 magnificent gardens include a tropical forest conservatory, a traditional English garden, and a serenity garden of cottonwood and cherry trees next to a gorgeous Thai pavilion (page 83).

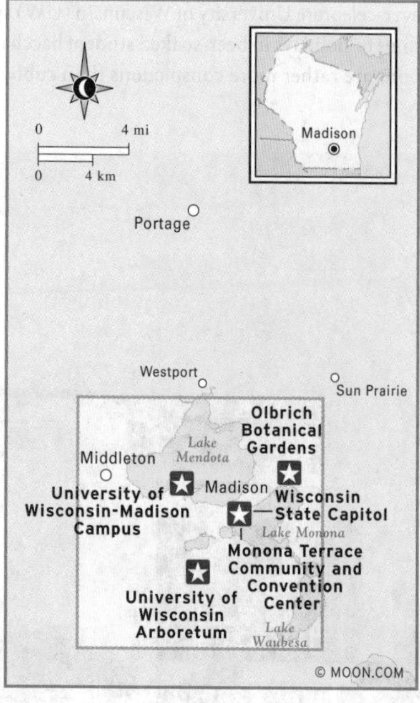

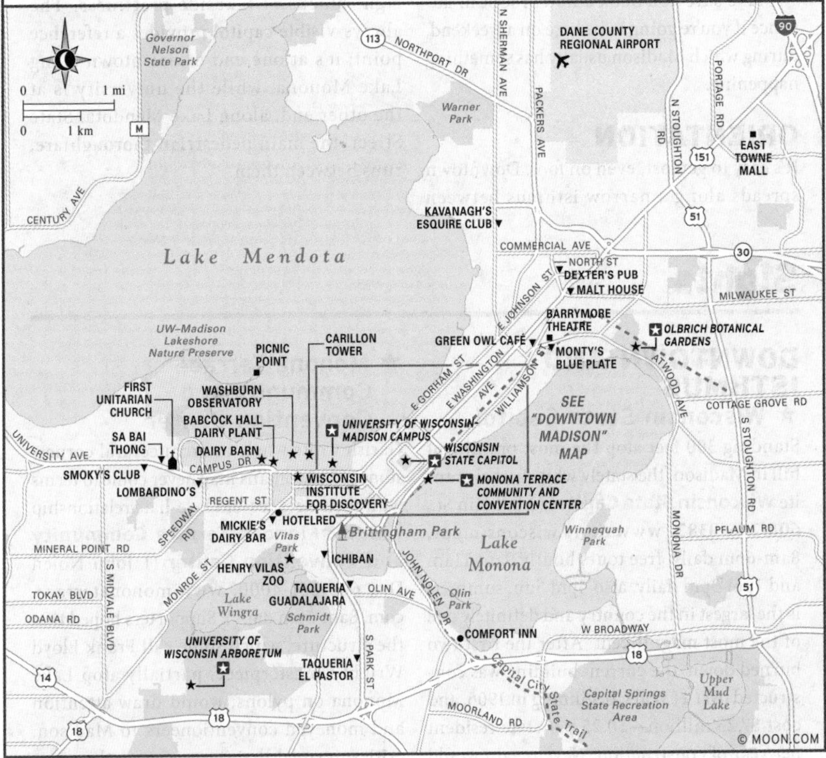

storefronts, and corpulent lobbyists seem to outnumber radicals. Octogenarian progressives and aging hippies mingle with legions of corporate and capitol yuppies.

Madison is a lovely town, sited erratically on an isthmus between two lakes, and was named by *Money* magazine as the best place to live in the United States; it would later repeat the honor. Everyone agrees it's a wonderful place. The student body omnipresence is a given—everyone in Madison is considered a de facto student anyway. It remains the "Madtown," the "Mad City," an agreeable, engaging, oddball mix.

Perhaps the best way to explain the Mad City: Madison is populated by droves of people who came for college and never left.

PLANNING YOUR TIME

The Mad City makes for a fabulous weekend. Base yourself downtown and spend the first day walking between **Lakes Monona and Mendota:** from the **Monona Terrace** to the **capitol** to the **University of Wisconsin** via State Street. Visit the **University of Wisconsin Arboretum** and the **Olbrich Botanical Gardens** on the second day. If you only have a day, any one of these sites makes a good stop, and you'll also find much better

Previous: Frank Lloyd Wright's Monona Terrace Community and Convention Center; the capitol building; the Madison Museum of Contemporary Art

food in downtown Madison than anywhere on the highways.

Make sure you book a hotel room in advance if you're going to be here on a weekend, during which Madison usually has something happening.

ORIENTATION

It's easy to get lost, even on foot. Downtown spreads along a narrow isthmus between two large lakes, which makes for difficult navigation, although you're always within eight blocks of lakeside prettiness. The always-visible capitol provides a reference point; it's at one end of downtown along Lake Monona, while the university is at the other end, along Lake Mendota. State Street, the main pedestrian thoroughfare, runs between them.

Sights

DOWNTOWN AND ISTHMUS

★ Wisconsin State Capitol

Standing 300 feet atop the most prominent hill in Madison, the stately white bethel granite **Wisconsin State Capitol** (2 E. Main St., 608/266-0382, www.tours.wisconsin.gov, 8am-6pm daily, free tours hourly 9am-11am and 1pm-3pm daily, also 4pm Sun. summer) is the largest in the country and definitely one of the most magnificent. After the first two burned down, the current building was constructed over 11 years, beginning in 1906, and cost $7.25 million—$0.25 per state resident per year of construction. Never again would something like this be possible on the public nickel. From afar it resembles the Capitol Building in Washington DC; thus, Hollywood occasionally uses it as a stand-in. The powers that be in DC took this as a sign of homage, but then realized plans were to build Wisconsin's capitol taller than DC's. So ours had to be shorter, though its volume is greater (holds more beer). The interior features 43 different types of stone from eight states and six foreign countries, including semiprecious marble that is unobtainable today. The mosaics, imported and domestic hand-carved furniture, massive murals, and hand-stenciling make the building priceless. If you don't arrive in time for a tour, the observation deck is also generally open in summer, with superb views.

★ Monona Terrace Community and Convention Center

Garish white whale or architectural cornerstone? Madisonians may never come to terms with their decades-old love-hate relationship with the **Monona Terrace Community and Convention Center** (1 John Nolen Dr., 608/261-4000, www.mononaterrace.com, 8am-5pm daily). Supporters hoped that the structure, which some call Frank Lloyd Wright's masterpiece, partially atop Lake Monona on pylons, would draw attention and moneyed conventioneers to Madison; critics moaned that it was yet another civic white elephant.

Wright's hoped-for design included much more than was finally constructed, and only three years after it opened, it already required repairs—typical of many Frank Lloyd Wright buildings. But even opponents admit that nothing like it exists in a city of comparative size.

The rooftop has a garden area (8am-10pm Sun.-Thurs., 8am-midnight Fri.-Sat. summer, Fri.-Sun. other times). Guided tours (1pm daily, $5) are available. Free concerts are offered often during summer.

State Street and Museum Mile

Bookended by the capitol on one end and the university on the other, State Street is a quasi-pedestrian mall full of shops, boutiques,

Downtown Madison

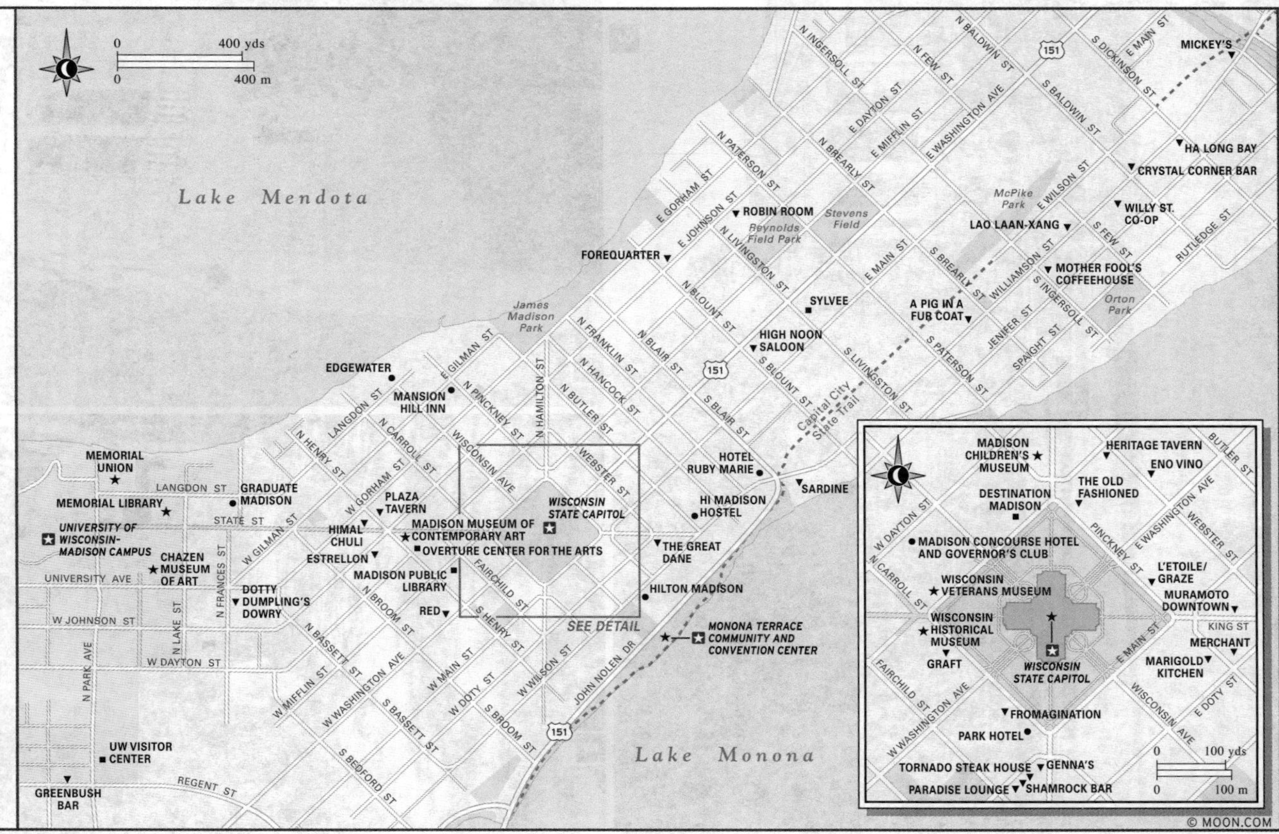

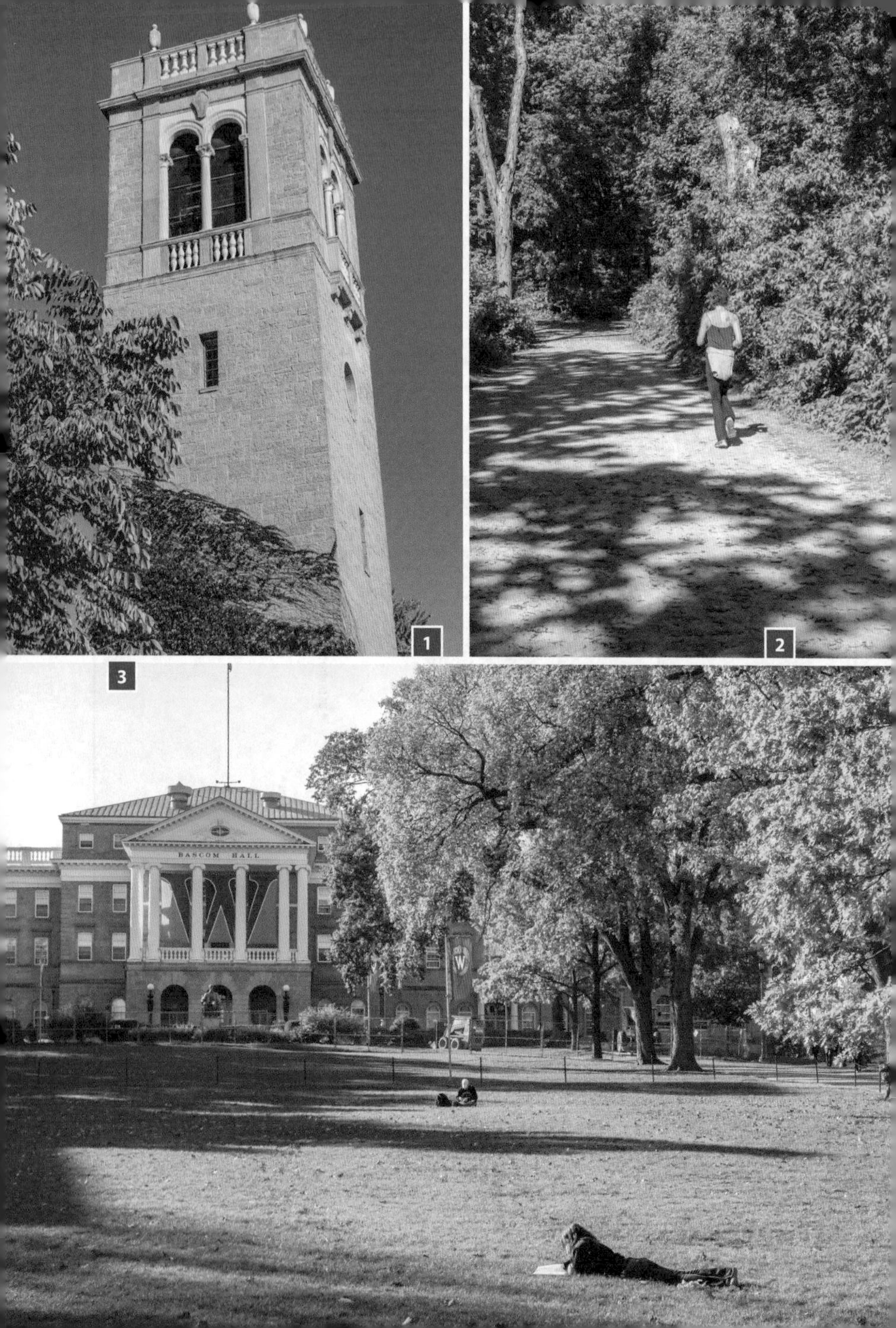
1
2
3
BASCOM HALL

coffeehouses, restaurants, bookstores, museums, cultural centers, and much of the downtown's character. People-watching along these seven blocks is a long-standing tradition.

The **Madison Arts District** takes up the 100 block of State Street, along with a few blocks on either side of it, for a zone of galleries, art spaces, museums, and performance venues. It was brought about by the amazingly generous donation of $50 million by a local Madtown philanthropist. This being Madison, it didn't come without vocal opponents. Did Madison really need an upscale arts venue? Unbelievably, the original plans called for gutting the memorable Oscar Mayer Theater inside the Civic Center. These were later scaled back, but not enough for some.

Six museums and a couple of other highlights lie along State Street and Capitol Square. On the State Street corner of Capitol Square, the **Wisconsin Historical Museum** (30 N. Carroll St., 608/264-6555, www.historicalmuseum.wisconsinhistory.org, 9am-4pm Tues.-Sat., tours 2pm Sat., $5 suggested) lets you stroll through commendable, challenging permanent multimedia exhibits that detail the state's geological, Native American, and European settlement history. This museum also has the best bookstore for Wisconsin titles.

Kitty-corner from the historical museum, the **Wisconsin Veterans Museum** (30 W. Mifflin St., 608/267-1799, www.wisvetsmuseum.com, 9am-4:30pm Mon.-Sat. plus noon-4pm Sun. Apr.-Sept., free) has two impressive main galleries of exhibits, dioramas, and extensive holdings tracing Wisconsin's involvement in wars from the Civil War to the Persian Gulf conflict. Main attractions are the mock-ups of battles and cool aircraft hovering overhead. Children will love the submarine periscope sticking out of the gallery's roof, which allows for a true panoramic view of downtown Madison.

The kid-centric **Madison Children's Museum** (100 N. Hamilton St., 608/256-6445, www.madisonchildrensmuseum.org, 9:30am-5pm daily Memorial Day-Labor Day, 9:30am-5pm Tues.-Sun. Labor Day-Memorial Day, $9) two blocks east, is housed in an old triangular corner edifice and features state-of-the-art and cutting-edge displays. Visiting the rooftop alone is worth the admission cost. This being Madison, the construction materials were all recycled and earth-friendly. The Huffington Post rated it one of America's top eight "uncommonly cool" places, and in 2018 *Reader's Digest* named it one of the ten best in the U.S.

One block nearer to the university from the historical society museum is the distinctive Madison Civic Center and, within it, the **Madison Museum of Contemporary Art** (211 State St., 608/257-0158, www.mmoca.org, noon-5pm Tues.-Thurs. and Sun., noon-8pm Fri., 10am-8pm Sat., free). The prominent gallery window always attracts the attention of passersby, most staring quizzically at the art or, occasionally, the performance artist trapped inside. The small galleries are interspersed on three floors of the civic center complex and feature contemporary art. A good gift shop is here.

As State Street runs its final block and melds with the Library Mall, walk past the bookstore and a church and then bear left down a cul-de-sac. The **Chazen Museum of Art** (800 University Ave., 608/263-2246, http://chazen.wisc.edu, 9am-5pm Tues.-Wed. and Fri., 9am-9pm Thurs., 11am-5pm Sat.-Sun., free) contains almost 16,000 holdings, the oldest dating from 2300 BC. The open, airy museum finished off a massive $43-million renovation and jolted returning visitors with something new: modern art in all its forms to supplement its better-known ancient Egyptian and Greek porcelain, Roman coins, Japanese ceramics, Indian figurines, Russian icons, early European and American art, and moody Renaissance church art, among many others.

1: Carillon Tower on UW-Madison campus
2: a lovely stroll at Picnic Point **3:** relaxing in front of Bascom Hall on campus

★ University of Wisconsin-Madison Campus

Bascom Hill, on the other end of State Street, affords a view similar to the one from the State Capitol rises. Crowning this is Bascom Hall, one of the original buildings of the **University of Wisconsin-Madison,** established in 1848; the tiered hill is a favorite sack-out spot for students between classes. From a handful of students and wild animals in 1848, the university has grown to 1,000 acres and more than 50,000 students and faculty; it is a world-renowned institution and has always imbued the fabric of the community more than even the state government has.

The nucleus of campus is **Memorial Union** (800 Langdon St., visitor center 608/265-3000, www.union.wisc.edu, 8am-10pm daily). Perched beside Lake Mendota, it's a must-stop for any visitor. If you have only one night in the Mad City, you'll never forget relaxing by the lakeside on the **Union Terrace,** sipping a refreshment in one of the legendary Union rays-of-the-sun metal chairs as the sun lazily sets.

There are two other **visitor information centers** at **Union South** (21 N. Park St., 608/890-3000, 8am-10pm daily) and the **Wisconsin Institute for Discovery** (330 N. Orchard St., 608/316-4300, 7am-6pm weekdays, 9am-3pm Sat.).

Not far from Bascom Hall is **Carillon Tower,** with 56 bells and sporadic Sunday afternoon performances. Up the hill from the tower is **Washburn Observatory** (1401 Observatory Dr., 608/262-3071, www.astro.wisc.edu, from 9pm 1st and 3rd Wed. Apr.-mid-June and Aug.-Oct., from 9pm Wed. mid-June-July, from 7:30pm Wed. Nov.-Mar.), one of the first observatories to use radio astronomy. It was also renovated to restore its historic charm. Note that it's open only if skies are at least 75 percent clear. If for nothing else, hike up to the observatory to drink in the views of Lake Mendota. Walk along Observatory Drive and follow its seemingly endless gardens.

This is the Dairy State, after all, so when you need to refuel, the **Babcock Hall Dairy Plant** (1605 Linden Dr., 608/262-3045, www.babcockdairyplant.wisc.edu, 7:30am-5:30pm Mon.-Fri., 11am-4pm Sat.) is where you can get an up close look at the creation of UW's famed ice cream; the department also makes cheese and other dairy-related products. My personal fave is the legendary fudge-bottom pie, but don't walk away without an ice cream cone. Biotechnology is a new addition to the agricultural campus, but the aesthetics of the **Dairy Barn** (1915 Linden Dr.) aren't to be missed. Designed in 1898 by a UW professor, its cylindrical style became a world standard. Tours focusing on the university's crucial role in Midwestern agriculture, biotechnology, and veterinary science can be arranged through the information centers (608/263-2400, http://visit.wisc.edu).

Where State Street ends and the university begins stands the **Memorial Library** (728 State St., 608/262-3193, http://library.wisc.edu, hours vary). Ranking in the top five nationwide for its collection of more than five million volumes, it also has a few rare books. A plan to add floors to the library raised a hullabaloo, since the addition would have blocked the view of the capitol. In 2018, a new plan was developed to be more accessible to the general public, which would be wonderful.

Bus lines, many of them free within campus areas, serve just about everything. For general campus information, call 608/262-2400.

A lakeshore path runs from the popular terrace of the Memorial Union, bypassing dormitories, boathouses, beaches, and playing fields, and winds up at yet another of the university's gorgeous natural areas—**Picnic Point.** This narrow promontory jutting into Lake Mendota is split by a screened gravel path and is popular with hikers, joggers, and bikers. You can walk to the tip in under 20 minutes; along the way there are offshoot roads and trails as well as fire-pit picnic sites. The views of the city merit the stroll. However, it is mosquito central, so be prepared.

OUTSIDE DOWNTOWN

Henry Vilas Zoo

Still, delightfully free to enter is **Henry Vilas Zoo** (702 S. Randall Ave., 608/266-4732, www.vilaszoo.org, 9:30am-5pm daily, free). For a city of Madison's size, the array of 800 wild animals, representing almost 200 species, is quite impressive, with constantly expanding facilities, especially for big cats and primates. The Herpetarium and Discovery Center offer hands-on entertainment for kids; they can also get free rides and various entertainment Sunday mornings in summer.

★ University of Wisconsin Arboretum

It's definitely a Madison thing. Nice day and need some exercise? Head to the **University of Wisconsin Arboretum** (1207 Seminole Hwy., 608/263-7888, www.arboretum.wisc.edu, 7am-10pm daily, free), one of the most expansive and heavily researched of its kind in the nation and, as of 2019, on the National Register of Historic Places. Its 1,260 acres include stretches of natural communities from wetland to mixed-grass prairie; the restoration work on some is unique—designed to resemble Wisconsin and the Upper Midwest before European settlement. More than 300 species of native plants grow on the prairies, some of which are the world's oldest restored tallgrass prairie and the site of the first experiments, in the 1940s, on the use of fire in forest management. The deciduous forests include one virgin stand dating to the time of European settlement in the lower half of the state. Flower lovers the world over come here to sit beneath the fragrant lilac stands. Best of all are the more than 20 miles of trails and fire lanes. Note that no bicycles, inline skates, or pets are allowed.

The **McKay Center** (608/263-7888, 9:30am-4pm Mon.-Fri., 12:30pm-4pm Sat.-Sun.) is a solar-heated visitors center plunked in the middle of the arboretum, surrounded by 50 acres of ornamental gardens and shrubs. It has free guided tours at 1pm most Sundays, along with lovely evening walks once per month.

First Unitarian Church

One structure Frank Lloyd Wright designed that attracts many viewers is the **First Unitarian Church** (900 University Bay Dr.), distinctive for its acclivitous triangles but more so for its sublime new 21,000-square-foot $9 million extension, adding some graceful rondure to the original angular geometry, not to mention a host of cutting-edge design and construction implementations such as geothermal heating, mowing-free landscaping, and high-tech glass.

★ Olbrich Botanical Gardens

Along Madison's east side, the treasured **Olbrich Botanical Gardens** (3330 Atwood Ave., 608/246-4550, www.olbrich.org, gardens 9am-8pm daily Apr.-Aug., 9am-6pm Sept.-Oct., 9am-4pm Nov.-Mar., free; conservatory 10am-4pm daily, $2, free 10am-noon Wed. and Sat.) feature a tropical forest conservatory with a waterfall inside a 50-foot glass pyramid, along with a botanical education center and seemingly endless gardens covering almost 15 acres. Free concerts are held on Tuesday in summer.

A highlight for the center is a magnificent Thai-style pavilion, donated in part by the royal family of Thailand in recognition of the close relationship between the university and Thailand. Admission to the Thai pavilion is always free.

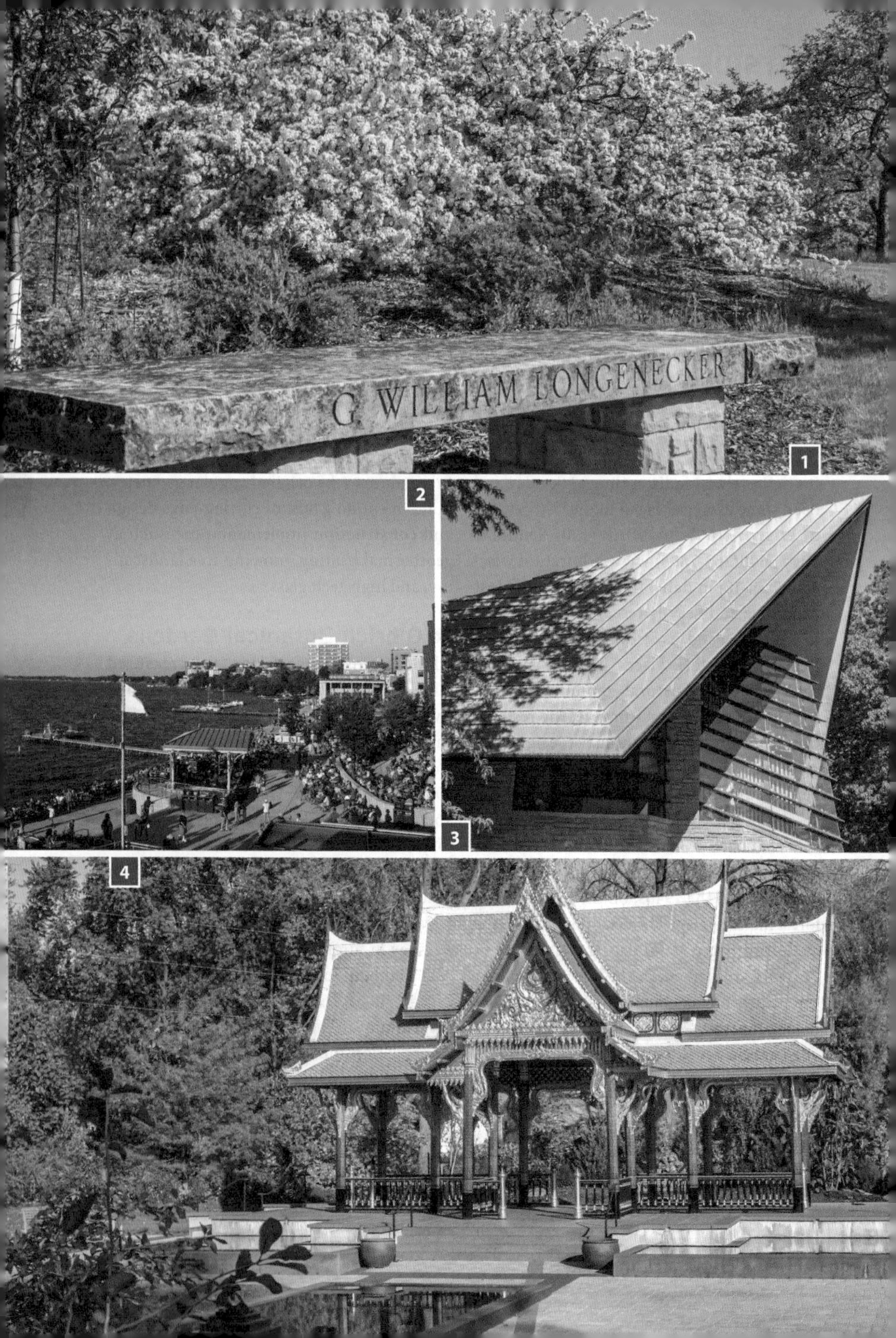
G WILLIAM LONGENECKER
1
2
3
4

Sports and Recreation

You may notice that Madisonians spend all their time jogging, biking, blading, skiing, or participating in some other cardiovascular exercise. In fact, this may be why *Outside* magazine has declared Madison a dream spot to live.

RECREATION

Biking and Hiking

No doubt about it, cycling is king in Madison. *Bicycling* magazine called Madison the fourth-best biking city in North America. Second only to Seattle in number of bikes per capita, Madison pedals virtually everywhere it goes. There are—quite seriously—bike traffic jams on certain routes in peak hours, since 10 percent of the citizenry commutes by bicycle. There are 25 miles of established pathway on trails and more than 110 miles of interconnected routes along city streets, bike paths, and parkways.

The most popular path is the **Lake Monona Loop,** easily accessible along John Nolen Drive, which passes the Monona Terrace Convention Center along the lake; it's about 12 miles long and runs through residential neighborhoods. A caveat: The route is marked much better if you go clockwise from the Monona Terrace, though the best lake views come if you start counterclockwise and double back when you hit residential streets.

Many head over to the UW Arboretum for a lovely ride, but note that the arboretum's unpaved trails are for walking only.

Here's an outstanding way to combine the two: the **Capital City State Trail** (trail pass required, $5 per day). You can reach it from the Lake Monona Loop where the lakeshore path bisects the Beltline Highway at Waunona Way; signs point along a spur underneath the overpass, 300 yards to the official trailhead. Follow this through Fitchburg and then turn right on bike-friendly Seminole Highway and continue to the entrance of the arboretum.

If you stay on the Capital City State Trail, it stretches west from Lake Monona all the way to Fitchburg, where it links with the existing **Military Ridge State Trail,** a grand journey you can take another 30 miles. The Fitchburg junction has other trails leading all the way to Illinois or down along Madison's southwest side back to the university.

The Madison segment of the Capital City State Trail is part of a visionary project dubbed E-Way, a corridor encompassing more than 3,200 acres for ecological, educational, and recreational use. It isn't just a trail—it's an established "necklace" of linked islands of educational and environmental importance.

A much easier ride is to start at the UW's Memorial Union, from where a path leads along Lake Mendota to **Picnic Point,** where the sunrises are gorgeous.

Machinery Row Bicycle (601 Williamson St., 608/442-5974, www.machineryrowbicycles.com) 100 yards east of Monona Terrace rents bikes starting at $30 per day. They also stock maps of city bicycle routes.

Find easy rentals in many places with **B-cycles** (www.madison.bcycle.com, $6 per day). Dozens of bike rental kiosks are scattered throughout the downtown. However, they're for commuters, so you need to reset the time at a station every 30 minutes to avoid surcharges.

Any cycling trail in the city is also open to hikers. The UW Arboretum has the most bucolic trails, some of them quite superb for an urban area.

Golf

An outstanding course is the University of Wisconsin golf center, **University Ridge**

1: quiet spot at the UW Arboretum **2:** Union Terrace on campus **3:** Frank Lloyd Wright's First Unitarian Church **4:** Thai pavilion at Olbrich Botanical Gardens

Golf Course (9002 Hwy. PD, 608/845-7700, www.universityridge.com), a championship par-72 course with the tightest slingshot fairways you'll find in town. Professional golf events take place here.

Canoeing and Water Sports

Canoeing magazines also rave about Madison. This comes as little surprise, since the city boasts four lakes, the larger two of which—**Lake Mendota** and **Lake Monona**—are connected by the **Yahara River,** a superb urban stream passing through locks and a series of smaller lakes. The Yahara connects to the Rock River, which flows through southern Wisconsin. Factoring in tributaries of the Rock leading westward to the Mississippi, technically you could paddle all the way to New Orleans.

Downtown, the UW Memorial Union rents canoes and kayaks. **Wingra Boats** (824 Knickerbocker St., 608/233-5332, www.madisonboats.com) rents boats, canoes, kayaks, and sailboats, and also gives lessons; find them at Vilas Park next to the Henry Vilas Zoo. Another location is at Brittingham Park on Monona Bay.

SPECTATOR SPORTS

The UW is what draws sports fans to Madison. The university is NCAA Division 1A in all sports, and the cardinal red-garbed citizenry is enthralled with the Badgers. Camp Randall Stadium on a football Saturday is an experience you'll not soon forget. If the opponent is a Big 10 foe, it will be impossible to get a ticket, but for early-season games, an occasional ticket may be available. The same goes for the six-time national champion hockey Badgers, who play at the Kohl Center, one of the best hockey facilities in the United States; the women's team has five national titles. The men's and women's basketball teams both regularly get to their respective tournaments. For information on ticket availability, call the **UW ticket office** (608/262-1440).

Entertainment and Events

NIGHTLIFE

The city's best nightlife is downtown and on the east side; cultural draws are all downtown. Check the free local paper ***Isthmus*** (www.isthmus.com) for club happenings.

Downtown

MEMORIAL UNION

It's free, open to all ages, and a local tradition: an alfresco music mélange on the **Memorial Union's outdoor terrace** (800 Langdon St., 608/265-3000, www.union.wisc.edu, Thurs.-Sat.). The place really gets bopping Friday and Saturday when the music cranks up and the beer starts flowing. During inclement weather, the event moves indoors to the cavernous Rathskeller. You have to have a UW ID and a valid driver's license to buy beer here; they're strict about it.

BARS AND PUBS

Madison is a drinking city in a drinking state. This is mostly thanks to the UW—it's pretty much always in the top 10 in the *Princeton Review* list of party schools, and the city leads in binge drinking.

The closer you are to the university, the greater the population of students in the raucous bars. Agoraphobics need not even consider venturing into them, but at least Madison's legendary drink specials keep things cheap. The Capitol Square area, a mere seven blocks from the university, has a much lower undergrad quotient; you'll be rubbing elbows with lots of suit-and-tie government types.

1: a bicycle trail roundabout **2:** the Capital City State Trail next to Lake Monona **3:** kayaking the Yahara River

Wisconsin Polka

Wisconsinites possess a genetic predisposition to polka, established by statute as the state's official dance. Given the state's heady 19th-century influx of Eastern and Central European immigrants—the highest concentration in the United States at the time—it's only natural that the peasant dance would take root here. Some cultural historians claim Wisconsin harbors more species of polka than anyplace else in the world. Polka music emanates from across the AM dial. At weddings, one polka per hour is an unwritten house minimum. You'll find polka at Brewers games, polka in the capitol building, even polka at church services. In Wisconsin, polka is king.

They aren't all the same. The Swiss did the polka step on the first beat of a bar, while the Austrians did it on the last half beat. The Dutch used a backward swing and omitted the hop, replacing it with only a slight rise or roll of the body. The Poles' polka stepped in measures of four, with the polka lead foot every second step. Czechs did it without a hop. Finns used a 4/4 rhythm and an abrupt heel step and added bits from their own baleful tango. Generally, polka couples turn right continuously without reversing and always move to the right.

The European elite considered it base, but Americans liked it from the get-go. Eastern and Central Europeans also gravitated to the South, where predominantly African American steps were incorporated. A large population of Europeans took their music to Texas and melded border flavors into the music called *conjunto*. Today, some country-western two-steps are being traded back and forth between country and polka camps.

And in Wisconsin, all forms have melded into one eclectic, happy dance. Wisconsin polka mainly originates from the Polish mazurka and the Dutch, Swiss, and Czech polkas.

It's mostly students at the well-lit and capacious **Plaza Tavern** (319 N. Henry St., 608/255-6592, www.theplazatavern.com) just off State Street at the corner of Johnson Street, known for its tangy burgers. Two floors of 20-somethings—the upper level looks for all the world like a house party—socialize at **Genna's** (105 W. Main St., 608/255-4770, www.gennaslounge.com) across from the capitol along West Main Street. A half block away is the dimly lit **Paradise Lounge** (119 W. Main St., 608/256-2263, http://thenewparadiselounge.com), once home only to serious hard-core drinkers but now a popular spot for anyone who likes loud music in dark bars. A few doors down is the **Shamrock Bar** (117 W. Main St., 608/259-8480), one of Madtown's gay bars.

Another string of bars—nay, sports bars—chock-full of students is found along Regent Street down from Camp Randall stadium. The hordes of students generally don't stray as far as the subdued **Greenbush Bar** (914 Regent St., 608/257-2874, www.greenbushbar.net), an excellent Italian neighborhood eatery in an old Italian workmen's club and *the* place in the area for a glass of wine or a scotch.

Beer lovers need go no further than **Malt House** (2609 E. Washington Ave., 608/204-6258), with nearly two dozen rotating domestic and international taps, along with over 100 bottled brands and 75 whiskeys. Its antebellum bar and low-key atmosphere away from the downtown din rate highly.

Best chance for a brandy old-fashioned (Wisconsin's real drink) done right comes at **Robin Room** (821 E. Johnson St., 608/284-7638), along with other mixed drinks in a funky, hip atmosphere.

Excellent views of Lake Mendota come from atop the Graduate Hotel (601 Langdon St., 608/257-6949) at **Camp Trippalindee**, a casual and irreverent watering hole and bistro with an Up North design and feel. They even have s'mores!

LIVE MUSIC

You can always find something at the **High Noon Saloon** (701A E. Washington Ave., 608/268-1112, http://www.high-noon.com), opened by a legendary Madison alt-club owner after her equally legendary previous alt-club burned down.

However, not far away, the **Sylvee** (25 S. Livingston St., 608/709-8157, http://www.thesylvee.com) is a brand-new, amazingly professional live music venue in a gentrifying area that overnight ramped up Madison's place in the Midwest music scene.

Near East Side

The near east side begins four or five blocks east of the capitol, downhill along East Wilson Street to the junction of six or seven roads at the cusp of Lake Monona. Here, legendary Williamson Street ("Willy Street") begins. Willy Street and its neighborhoods are a pleasant hodgepodge of students and families, with an up-and-coming array of restaurants, clubs, bars, and shops all recalling the 1960s salad days when these blocks were the hippy-fied enclaves of revolution and fighting the Man. The cornerstone is the **Crystal Corner Bar** (1302 Williamson St., 608/256-2953, http://thecrystalcornerbar.com) at the corner of South Baldwin and Willy Streets; this neon-lit bar is a hot roots rock, Cajun, R&B, and especially blues spot.

Up the road to the west is funky **Mother Fool's Coffeehouse** (1101 Williamson St., 608/259-1301, http://www.motherfools.com), with regular eclectic music, and a bit farther is **Plan B** (924 Williamson St., 608/692-1900, http://www.planbmadison.com), the hippest gay bar in town.

Continuing east of the Crystal, you'll find one of the greatest neighborhood bars in Madison: **Mickey's** (1524 Williamson St., 608/251-9964). It used to be famous for rock-bottom beer prices, coasters made from well-worn carpeting, and rum rats. It's been ever so slightly refreshed and now also has amazing food.

THEATER AND CLASSICAL MUSIC

A cornerstone of local culture is the **Overture Center for the Arts** (201 State St., 608/258-4141, www.overturecenter.com), home to several performing venues.

The popular **Madison Symphony Orchestra** (608/257-3734, http://www.madisonsymphony.org) performs a dozen or more times during the year at Overture Hall.

FESTIVALS AND EVENTS

Summer's biggie is the now-annual **Shake the Lake** choreographed fireworks display

the cornerstone of the Near East Side — the Crystal Corner Bar

the closest weekend to the Fourth of July. Later that month, the **Art Fair on the Square** is a huge draw—one of the largest events in the Midwest and one of the largest juried art fairs in the country.

October brings the world's largest dairy show, the **World Dairy Expo,** a big-time international event, with agriculturalists and scientists from all over the globe coming to check up on any new dairy industry progress; regular folks can get a lifetime of knowledge about dairy.

Free Events

Grab a picnic basket and head for the Capitol Square on Wednesday evenings for free concerts put on by the **Wisconsin Chamber Orchestra.** Though the weather is incessantly bad for these concerts, they are wildly popular. The **Memorial Union** (800 Langdon St., 608/265-3000, www.union.wisc.edu) at the UW is the most popular place to be Thursday-Saturday for its free concerts.

For family-themed freebies, always check the free local paper ***Isthmus*** (www.isthmus.com).

Food

Given a cosmopolitan-minded citizenry that apparently doesn't like to stay home and cook, you're sure to find something you like.

DOWNTOWN

Downtown Madison's dearth of *traditional* supper clubs is particularly galling. You'll find chic approximations, but they don't count. Madison has also never taken on the fish fry in a traditional, must-have way—one local media survey doesn't even have a "Favorite Fish Fry" category. There are some more traditional fish fries, just not downtown (well, see the Old Fashioned below, which is pretty good, albeit not all-you-can-eat).

Pan-Wisconsin

It's raucous inside, but the brats, cheeses, fish, and other pan-Wisconsin-produced fare at **The Old Fashioned** (23 N. Pinckney St., 608/310-4545, www.theoldfashioned.com, 7:30am-2am Mon.-Fri., 9am-2am Sat., 9am-10pm Sun., $7-28) is well worth a trip to find out what Wisconsinites eat. National media have sung praises about its cheese curds, which also win local best-of awards. Simply everyone goes here, so expect a wait at all times.

Steak Houses and Supper Clubs

Grazing vegetarians—a dominant sociopolitical force locally—must have been taken aback by the resurgence of the true carnivorous experience downtown: steak houses with true-blue 1950s martinis and slabs, exemplified by the **Tornado Steak House** (116 S. Hamilton St., 608/256-3570, www.tornadosteakhouse.com, 5:30pm-10pm daily, $17-36). This might be the best nouveau take on the old supper club in town. Steaks are the highlight, natch. Not a fan of intentional retro, but this one is *good*.

Burgers and Brewpubs

Dotty Dumpling's Dowry (317 N. Frances St., 608/259-0000, www.dottydumplingsdowry.com, 11am-10pm or later daily, $6) always wins local surveys for burgers, which really are sublime creations (if a bit pricey). Some Madison radicals frequent the place simply because the owner put up a pyrrhic battle against the city when it wanted to buy his former location for the city's new arts district.

The Great Dane (123 E. Doty St., 608/284-0000, www.greatdanepub.com, 11am-11pm daily, $7-16) is a brewpub occupying what was Madison's landmark Fess Hotel. The interior upstairs is fairly spacious,

Dane County Farmers Market

Madison's farmers market

Visiting friends in Madtown over the weekend? Don't sleep in on Saturday. No matter how hungover or workweek-weary you are, rise early for a stroll around the capitol at the **Dane County Farmers Market** (www.dcfm.org, Sat. Apr.-Oct.)—the largest of its kind in the United States—to pick up goat cheese, salmon, organic produce, and java. More than 200 farmers line Capitol Square to dispense everything you could possibly imagine.

A keyword is *organic,* though not exclusively. Everything, however, must be grown or raised in Wisconsin. The only-in-Madison juxtapositions include an organic herb farmer, a free-range-chicken vendor, a Hmong family selling vegetables, jugglers, local politicos pressing the flesh, and a panoply of political or social organizations of many bents. Add to this throngs of customers circling counterclockwise.

but it's best known for its great courtyard. The catacomb-like downstairs is a great place for moody drinking. The Great Dane has been ranked in the top 10 brewpubs in the nation in terms of beer consumption—no surprise in a university town in Wisconsin. The food is above basic pub grub, and the place has a billiards hall.

Breakfast

Finally, something other than greasy eggs at a casual place downtown: ★ **Marigold Kitchen** (118 S. Pinckney St., 608/661-5559, http://marigoldkitchen.com, 7am-10:30am and 11am-3pm Mon.-Fri., 7am-2pm Sat., 8am-2pm Sun., $4) does more than breakfast, but this is the best meal. This place is extremely understated, doing unique takes on breakfasts and lunch, with personalized sandwiches like you've never experienced. The Sunday brunch is outstanding.

Cafés and Bistros

The ★ **Heritage Tavern** (131 E. Mifflin St., 608/283-9500, www.heritagetavern.com, dinner Mon.-Sat., brunch Sat.-Sun., late-night food available, from $12) perhaps best represents Madison with its world-view menu, insistence on locally produced ingredients, and its equal welcome for carnivores and vegans. The chef-owner, a three-time James Beard Award semifinalist, has executed his farm-to-table gastropub ideal flawlessly, including raising his own heritage breed pigs. From simple but fantastic pub fare to a succulent lobster and rabbit dish, you'll get it all including, amazingly, the best deviled eggs you'll ever have and what many consider to be Madison's best brunch.

Not only will you find amazing Midwestern-inspired small plates at **Graft** (18 N. Carroll St., 608/229-8800, www.graftmadison.com, dinner Tues.-Sat., from $13), you can trust the wine list since the chef is a sommelier who has consulted for White House dinners.

Meat-centric but also handy with fruits and vegetables is **Forequarter** (708¼ E. Johnson St., 608/609-4717, www.forequartermadison.com, dinner Mon.-Sat., late-night food Thurs.-Sat., from $9), whose interiors smack of a chic hunting cabin. Better: the menu changes often. Its use of the whole animal may inspire you to try, well, the whole animal.

Theirs are not typical Midwest-farm family meatballs. The chef was a 2018 James Beard finalist for the Best Chef Midwest.

Merchant (121 S. Pinckney St., 608/259-9799, www.graftmadison.com, dinner daily, brunch Sun., from $12) admirably focuses on the dining experience, source to execution. They get major kudos for extending that to the craft of mixology.

Perhaps best views while eating are at **Eno Vino** (1 N. Webster St., 608/455-0663, dinner daily, from $12), perched atop the AC Hotel. It is tapas heavy and has a reputable wine list.

Custard and Ice Cream

Madison has caught the custard bug so prevalent in Milwaukee. Personal favorites include **Michael's Frozen Custard,** with lots of locations, and **Culver's,** found throughout southwestern Wisconsin (the latter's butter burgers are also something to write home about). However, you'll not find either one near downtown. On the UW campus, however, is **Babcock Hall,** with delectable batches of its own proprietary ice cream, also served at the Memorial Union.

Diners

The most classic downscale Madison breakfast place has to be **Mickie's Dairy Bar** (1511 Monroe St., 608/256-9476, breakfast/lunch Tues.-Sun.), with awesome breakfasts, luscious pancakes, and malts since the 1940s. The atmosphere is superb and the decor real, down to the aging napkin dispensers and anachronistic knickknacks everywhere. The café's name harks back to the establishment's days as one of the largest milk and bread retailers in the city. Try the Scrambler or the Frisbee-size flapjacks.

Quick Bites

Late spring through early autumn, buy a box from a food cart and sprawl on the mall at the university end of State Street or at the Capitol Square and munch with the ever-friendly squirrels. A local favorite food cart is **Banzo,** where you can get awesome falafel or a Philly cheesesteak; it's also got carts at the university and capitol ends of State Street. At the capitol end, at the corner of West Washington Avenue, is this author's favorite, **El Grito Taqueria.** Roasted chicken with tangerine adobo or braised lamb (all sustainably raised) tacos? Yes, please. Actually, you probably won't get this since the menu is ever changing, but it doesn't matter—you hadn't thought you needed it till you arrive here.

Head for the cheese lover's nirvana, **Fromagination** (12 S. Carroll St., 608/255-2430, www.fromagination.com), which has extraordinary artisanal cheeses and a few select sandwiches. It's well worth it if you know nada about *fromage*.

Fine Dining

If you're in town for only one night and want to eat somewhere special, ★ **L'Etoile** (1 S. Pinckney St., 608/251-0500, www.letoile-restaurant.com, 5:30pm-8:45pm Mon.-Fri., 5pm-9:45pm Sat., $20-35), on Capitol Square directly opposite the capitol, has creative regional fare that has garnered raves and placed the owners in the national cuisine spotlight—it was named one of the United States' top 50 restaurants by *Food & Wine* magazine. It is always a finalist for a James Beard Award, winning once. The restaurant in fact helped put the concepts of slow food and locavore into public consciousness decades ago; it also truly strives to reach that esoteric netherworld of the harmony of cuisine, art, and culture. Simply put, the menus are incredible gastronomic representations of the geography and ethos of this place. L'Etoile is highly recommended.

The owners of L'Etoile also have a wonderful locavore gastropub, **Graze** (1 S. Pinckney St., 608/251-2700, www.grazemadison.com, 11am-9pm Mon.-Thurs., 11am-10pm Fri., 9:30am-10pm Sat., 9:30am-3pm Sun., $11-21) a few steps south, with a delectable bakery,

1: outdoor coffee shop seating **2:** The Old Fashioned

1
2
THE OLD FASHIONED
Old Fashioned
Old Fashioned

creative light meals all day, and comfort food on Sunday.

Holding its own is **Sardine** (617 Williamson St., 608/441-1600, www.sardinemadison.com, dinner daily, brunch weekends, $6-20). It may not consider itself a fine-dining establishment, but the French-oriented cuisine, with excellent seafood as well, in a capacious lakeside (great views) dining room, is really something special.

To really escape the students, the best views in the city come at **Fresco** (211 State St., 608/663-7374, www.frescomadison.com, from $19), perched atop the Madison Museum of Contemporary Art. Sit in a chic sofa encased by glass with a panorama of the city; prices reflect the view. Go for the charcuterie and cheese board or brussel sprouts with bacon to start, and the pasta and seafood/meat, though limited, are expertly done.

Asian

Without question, among the best restaurants in town is always anything to do with the genius proprietor of ★ **Muramoto Downtown** (108 King St., 608/255-4343, www.downtown.muramoto.biz, 11:30am-2pm Mon.-Fri., 5pm-9pm Mon.-Fri., 5pm-9pm Sat., $8-16). Its cuisine is Japanese for the most part, but the proprietor himself claims to be too impatient to specialize, so you never know what you're going to get. The miso and Japanese whiskey cod is a great example of the treat you're in for.

The oddly named **Ichiban** (610 S. Park St., 608/819-8808, www.ichibanszechuan.com, lunch and dinner daily, from $6), has even better Sichuan-style food (especially its liberal use of *hua jiao*, a kind of peppercorn). The beef tendon and duck tongue are things most haven't tried but will love.

The Madison institution for Nepali cuisine has always been **Himal Chuli** (318 State St., 608/251-9225, 11am-8pm Mon.-Sat., noon-8pm Sun., from $7), a great little place with a menu that will never let you down.

Italian

The proprietor of **Naples 15** (15 N. Butler St., 608/250-6330, 5pm-10pm Mon.-Sat., $8-21) has to be the most joyful restaurateur in the city, and his infectious love for cooking shows in the food. From Neapolitan wood-fired pizzas to an amazing red snapper in "crazy water," it's all great.

Sushi

Red (316 W. Washington Ave., 608/294-1234, lunch weekdays, dinner daily, $8-21) often gets overlooked due to the aforementioned Muramoto restaurants in Madison, but make no mistake—this is real deal food in a chic, swank (perhaps edgy) environment. The presentation is outstanding, as well.

Spanish

A legendary local restaurateur's latest option, eagerly awaited by locals, is **Estrellon** (313 W. Johnson St., 608/251-2111, www.estrellonrestaurant.com, dinner Tues.-Sun., from $8), a wonderfully conceived choice heavy on locally sourced Spanish tapas and small plates, but along with other dishes that may surprise you.

NEAR EAST SIDE AND NORTH SIDE

Fish Fries

For what a fish fry meant to grandma and grandpa, head for **Kavanaugh's Esquire Club** (1025 N. Sherman Ave., 608/249-0193, www.esquireclubmadison.com, lunch Mon.-Sat., dinner daily, from $8). This 1940s institution is the real deal old-school style.

Worth a trip for local flavor is **Dexter's Pub** (301 N. St., 608/244-3535, 11am-10:30pm daily, $8-15), where the fish is wild-caught and/or sustainably harvested. Depending on the season, get excellent cod, walleye, and bluegill. Beer geeks also love the place, and there are vegan options.

Cafés

The best place to take guests when they show up unannounced on a Saturday morning for the farmers market is **Monty's Blue Plate** (2089 Atwood Ave., 608/244-8505, www.montysblueplatediner.com, breakfast/lunch/dinner daily, $5-11), an unpretentious creative diner on the near east side with deliciously art deco cool-blue interiors. You'll find the best synthesis of American meat and potatoes with trendy off-the-beaten-menu items. The chefs are equally adept with meat loaf, tofu, or scrambled egg Mediterranean surprise.

Small Plates

Madison may have the state's highest percentage of vegetarians, but let's not forget you're in the Midwest, so carnivores delight at **A Pig in a Fur Coat** (940 Williamson St., 608/316-3300, www.apiginafurcoat.com, 4pm-10pm Mon.-Thurs., 4pm-11pm Fri.-Sat., from $9). Where else are you going to get four-star-quality poutine and pork belly with Mediterranean influences in a funky, shared table atmosphere? I adore this place.

Southeast Asian

The food will clear your sinuses, but the spices don't dominate the wondrously simple but rich fare at **Lao Laan-Xang** (1146 Williamson St., 608/280-0104, www.llx-restaurant.com, lunch and dinner daily, $6-16), which has good specials. No less than the *New York Times* called this Madison's best.

If they're full, head two blocks east and you'll find the newer **Ha Long Bay** (1353 Williamson St., 608/255-2868, www.halongbaymadison.com, lunch and dinner daily, $6-15), a fusion of Vietnamese, Thai, and Lao cuisine. Go for anything—it's all done well. You will always wait.

Vegetarian and Health Food

Many restaurants have vegetarian-friendly food—vegan-friendly is another matter. You can grab a lunch to go from the **Willy St. Co-op** (1221 Williamson St., 608/251-6776, www.willystreet.coop, 8am-9pm daily), Madison's legendary fruits and nuts location.

Amazingly, in a city with an enormous percentage of vegetarians, only one restaurant is fully vegetarian. A five-minute drive east from the co-op is the **Green Owl Café** (1970 Atwood Ave., 608/285-5290, www.thegreenowlcafe.com, 11am-9pm Tues.-Sat., 11am-3pm Sun., $5-10), where you'll find only vegan and vegetarian dishes; the soups are worth the trip, as are the faux-meat sandwiches and vegan desserts.

WEST AND SOUTH OF DOWNTOWN

Italian

The decor can be a bit garish, with fountains and all, but Madisonians solidly support **Lombardino's** (2500 University Ave., 608/238-1922, www.lombardinos.com, 5pm-9pm Tues.-Thurs. and Sun., 5pm-10pm Fri.-Sat., $6-21), with a seasonally adjusted menu of freshly prepared high-quality Italian fare.

Mexican

Ask a local for Mexican food and they'll probably take you to **Taqueria Guadalajara** (1033 S. Park St., 608/441-9536, www.lataqueriaguadalajara.com, lunch and dinner daily, $4-12). The menu features a heart attack-inducing steak torta that is irresistible.

A couple of friends insist that **Taqueria El Pastor** (2010 S. Park St., 608/280-8898, www.pastorrestaurant.com, 10am-11pm daily, $3-9), a most unassuming little place, is better than Taqueria Guadalajara. Ask for the house specialties.

Steak Houses

Smoky's Club (3005 University Ave., 608/233-2120, www.smokysclub.com, 5pm-10pm Mon. and Wed.-Sat., $15-35) is one of a dying breed, a real charcoal place. The classic supper club-steak house, Smoky's is the type of place where the waitresses have been bustling for four decades and the bartender will remember your drink on your second visit. Big 10 sporting teams make pilgrimages here when they're in town. Some have opined that this place occasionally hasn't been worth the higher cost, according to some, but others absolutely swear by it.

Thai

Diminutive **Sa Bai Thong** (2840 University Ave., 608/238-3100, www.sabaithong.com, 11am-9pm or 10pm Mon.-Sat., 5pm-9pm Sun., $5-15) is among the best Thai restaurants in the state. Ensconced drearily in another strip mall on the near west side, its menu really isn't extensive, but the food is generally done to perfection. It's so popular that it recently expanded into the suite next door.

Accommodations

Always check ahead—football Saturdays and many UW events fill all the guest rooms in town.

DOWNTOWN

Under $50

Madison's **HI Madison Hostel** (141 S. Butler St., 608/441-0144, www.hiusa.org, $30), a year-round facility, is central, progressive, and very well run. Six-bed dorms and one- to three-person rooms fill in summer, so try to make reservations.

Over $150

You can get a decent view at the **Park Hotel** (22 S. Carroll St., 608/285-8000, www.parkhotelmadison.com, $180), opposite the magnificent capitol. An $8 million renovation gave it a sheen, and the responsiveness of staff and management make it good value (not to mentioned that view!).

Slightly cheaper and the opposite of cookie cutter is the unclassifiable **Hotel Ruby Marie** (524 E. Wilson St., 608/327-7829, www.rubymarie.com, from $160). Let's call it a boutique B&B, housed in an 1873 Victorian. Locals don't know about it, but visitors love it. Don't judge it by its exteriors, to be sure.

Madison's first official chic boutique hotel was **HotelRED** (1501 Monroe St., 608/819-8228, www.hotelred.com, $229), near the Camp Randall football stadium. This means lots of concrete and glass, minimalist design, and for cynics, an attempt to mimic trendy European or New York City boutique hotels. However, even with clearly heavy use, it comes off as fresh and appealing.

Equally comfortable and with killer views in some rooms is the **Hilton Madison** (9 E. Wilson St., 608/255-5100, http://www.hiltonmadison.com, $175), adjacent to the Monona Terrace. As of 2019, it was undergoing a complete renovation, so check it out.

A spiffy newer boutique hotel with European flair just off State Street is the **Graduate Madison** (601 Langdon St., 608/257-4391, www.graduatemadison.com, from $249). It's very distinctive, and more than one traveler has raved about the service.

The towering (for the Mad City, anyway) **Madison Concourse Hotel and Governor's Club** (1 W. Dayton St., 608/257-6000, www.concoursehotel.com, $250) certainly can boast some of the most reputable dining and sceney options in town.

It's stratospherically priced, but the ★ **Mansion Hill Inn** (424 N. Pinckney St., 608/255-0172, www.mansionhillinn.com, from $299), an opulent 1858 Romanesque Revival on the National Register of Historic Places, still draws raves. Set snugly along a quiet residential street close to downtown, this ornate piece of Victoriana features a distinctive gabled roof and wrought-iron railings encircling the etched sandstone facade. Inside, the opulence is breathtaking, with thrusting round-arched windows, ornate cornices, hand-carved marble, a spiral staircase, and a wraparound belvedere, all surrounded by Victorian gardens.

Gorgeous vistas of a more natural bent and sybaritic studios and suites are found

1: the Mansion Hill Inn, Madison's most opulent historic inn **2:** HI Madison Hostel **3:** fresh kettle corn

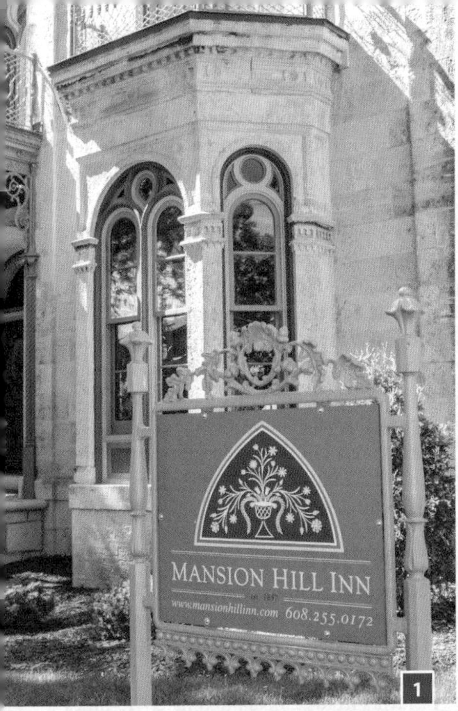

MANSION HILL INN
www.mansionhillinn.com 608.255.0172
1

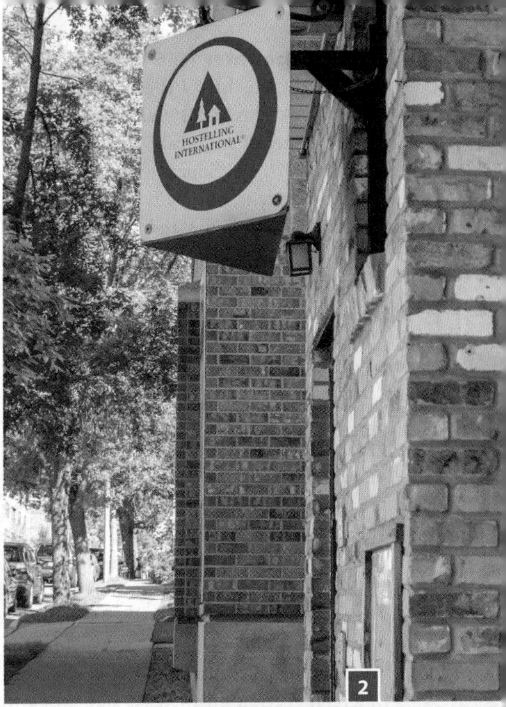

HOSTELLING INTERNATIONAL
2

3 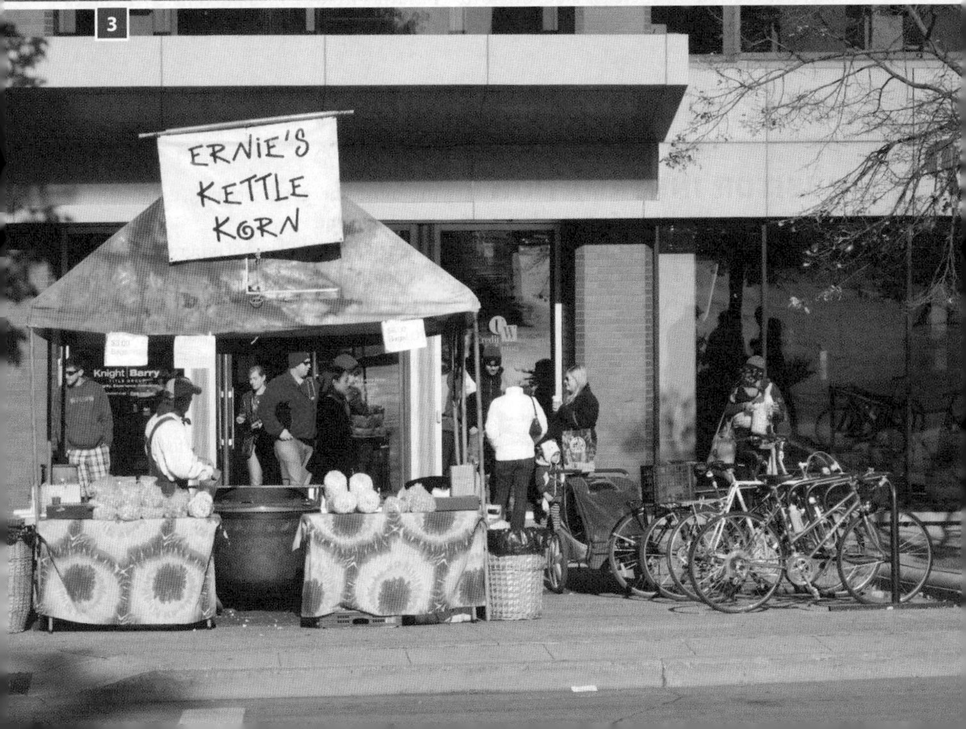
ERNIE'S
KETTLE
KORN

at the **Edgewater** (666 Wisconsin Ave., 608/535-8200, http://theedgewater.com, from $270). This historic lakefront hotel was at the center of a typical Madison hullabaloo for years: Developers wanted the city to help renovate it, but many locals protested it would be a glaring standout amid historic homes. The $100 million reconstruction (seriously) incorporates an acre of public access to the lakefront, with a park and skating rink, that didn't exist before. Inside is an amazing restoration of the art deco style with modern luxury.

BEYOND DOWNTOWN

Lodging zones made up mostly of chain or mom-and-pop operations are strung along the Beltline (U.S. 12, U.S. 14, U.S. 18, U.S. 151), the artery linking east and west Madison. Another concentration of motels is found at the junction of U.S. 151 and U.S. 51 and east along U.S. 151 (E. Washington Ave.) to East Towne Mall, the major commercial section on the east side. Stick to name brands.

$100-150

It ain't chic, but at only two miles to downtown and with prompt service and above average rooms, **Comfort Inn** (722 John Nolen Dr., 608/255-7400, from $110) is a chain that may be a steal in Madison.

The west side is home to tons of mall zones, and strung along the Beltline are dozens of motels and hotels. Families generally head directly for the **Holiday Inn Hotel and Suites-West** (1109 Fourier Dr., 608/826-0500, $175), as it's home to Madison's only full-fledged indoor water park. The kids go nuts on the waterslides or in the games room; parents relax in the grand piano bar. Some rooms have kitchenettes. Remember: this can be family cacophony.

CAMPING

The nearest public campground is **Lake Kegonsa State Park** (608/873-9695, reservations 888/947-2757, www.wisconsin.goingtocamp.com, reservation fee $8, nonresidents from $25), approximately 15 miles southeast off I-90 on Highway N.

Information and Services

VISITOR INFORMATION

The **Greater Madison Convention and Visitors Center** (22 E. Mifflin St., 608/255-2537 or 800/373-6376, www.visitmadison.com) is right on the Capitol Square.

MEDIA

The thin daily newspaper ***Wisconsin State Journal*** and its ***Capital Times*** partner (available online only)—are at www.madison.com. Check for the free weekly ***Isthmus*** (www.isthmus.com); Madisonians dutifully trek to java shops for a scone and a folded *Isthmus* with their lattes. A civic watchdog, it's got the most energetic writing, especially in entertainment.

A delightful mélange of progressivism, professionalism, at times near-anarchy, and great music, **WORT** (89.9 FM) is a local community-sponsored station. There's nothing else like it in town.

INTERNET ACCESS

Virtually all the downtown coffee shops have wireless Internet access. The **public library** (201 W. Mifflin St., 608/266-6300, www.madisonpubliclibrary.org) has free Internet terminals—but count on a wait.

Transportation

GETTING THERE

Air

The **Dane County Regional Airport** (MSN, 4000 International Ln., 608/246-3391) has direct flights daily to 19 U.S. cities. A taxi from the airport to downtown costs minimum $18.

Car

Getting to Madison from Milwaukee (via I-94, 75 miles) takes just over an hour. From Chicago (via I-90, 148 miles), the drive takes 2.5 hours. From Minneapolis (via I-94, 273 miles), it takes 4.5 hours. From Door County (via Hwy. 57, U.S. 41, and U.S. 151, 183 miles), it takes 3.5 hours. From Wisconsin Dells (via I-90/94, 60 miles), it takes one hour.

Bus

Greyhound (800/231-2222, www.greyhound.com) has lost its Madison terminal and is stopping near the Chazen Museum of Art (800 University Ave.). It has no ticket-dispensing options, so you have to preorder your ticket online.

Badger Bus (877/292-8259, www.badgerbus.com) has departures to Milwaukee ($22) 4:30am-7pm daily, some via Milwaukee's Mitchell International Airport. The terminus is the UW Memorial Union. Badger Bus has service to Minneapolis when the university is in session; these will probably leave from the Chazen Museum of Art.

For Chicago, also head to the UW Memorial Union, where the **Van Galder** bus (608/257-8983 or 800/747-0994, govangalder.com) leaves up to 12 times 1am-9pm daily for Chicago's O'Hare Airport (one-way $30); some continue to downtown Chicago (one-way $31) or Midway Airport.

GETTING AROUND

Car

Given the skewed topography, traffic can be maddeningly circuitous. Always keep an eye on the capitol. Also keep in mind that east and west in street names are approximations—it's actually closer to northeast and southwest. All east-west streets use the capitol as the dividing point.

The main thoroughfare down the throat of

fishing on Lake Monona

the isthmus is East Washington Avenue (U.S. 151); it leads directly to, and then around, the massive state capitol, which is connected to the university by State Street, which cannot be driven on, so take Wisconsin Avenue north of the capitol to Gorham Street and follow that to the university.

The main artery between east and west Madison is the white-knuckled swells of the Beltline—U.S. 12/14 and U.S. 151/18. It's unlikely you'll be able to avoid the Beltline altogether; just avoid rush-hour peaks. A Windy City denizen has described it as "the only place where Madison traffic ever rivals Chicago's."

Unlike in Milwaukee, drivers don't follow the rules regarding right-of-way and full stops; drive carefully.

Taxi

Numerous taxi services operate in Madison. The most common choice is **Badger Cab** (608/256-5566), since it operates a shared-ride (cheaper) service. If that's not an option, **Madison Taxi** (608/258-7458) and **Union Cab** (608/242-2000) are both reliable.

Bus

Madison's **Metro Transit** (608/266-4466, www.cityofmadison.com/metro) runs buses 6am-10pm or 11pm daily, although the hours vary by line. You can always head to Capitol Square, around which spins just about every bus downtown.

Mad Driving

Most Madisonians are among the politest folks you'll ever meet (Wisconsin actually scored second highest in the country in an Oxford University study), but while driving, pedaling, or walking, we simply do not pay attention to anyone else. Bicyclists will fly through a stop sign in front of you, and pedestrians will walk against red lights.

In Madison, the issue is hypocrisy mixed with self-righteousness. We honestly believe we're Mr. and Ms. Polite, yet when riding our bikes, stop signs just don't apply to us. We may growl at you to stop at a stop sign on your bike, but we don't have to use our turn signals, or give a pedestrian right-of-way in our car. Even the cops never give me and my dog the right-of-way.

Some advice for driving in Madison: Always assume there is a bicycle in your blind spot; this includes opening your door after parking. Second, anywhere near State Street, pedestrians will waltz right out in front of your car.

Organized Tours

A couple of places offer water tours of Madison lakes, including **Betty Lou Cruises** (608/246-3138, www.bettyloucruises.com, Thurs.-Sun. summer, $27-57), which has dining and sightseeing trips.

Southeastern Wisconsin

In Southeastern Wisconsin, you'll find prairies,

lakes, farms—and most of Wisconsin's people. Over 150 years ago, steamships laden with European immigrants landed at Milwaukee and the southern ports, where about 90 percent of Wisconsinites live today.

This region is worth visiting. Yes, the trees have long since been felled, replaced by agricultural tracts on the fecund glacial till, and its population centers have unfairly been labeled the Rust Belt. Yet within a short bike trip, you can find bustling city life, multiethnic neighborhoods, gorgeous vistas from an enormous expanse of coastline, and, yes, classic pastoral dairy land.

Highlights

Look for ★ to find recommended sights, activities, dining, and lodging.

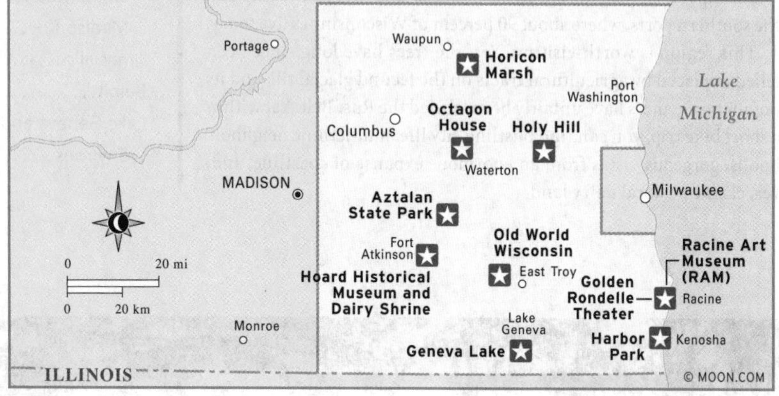

★ **HarborPark:** Kenosha's lovely lakefront park has a few great museums, including the important Kenosha Public Museum, home to the Schaeffer Mammoth (page 104).

★ **Racine Art Museum (RAM):** The retro-chic RAM holds the United States' most superlative collections of folk arts (page 108).

★ **Golden Rondelle Theater:** This distinctive architectural landmark premiered at the 1964 New York World's Fair and was moved to Racine by Frank Lloyd Wright's team (page 109).

★ **Holy Hill:** Recharge your soul at this neo-Romanesque cathedral towering over surrounding forests, which are home to a section of the Ice Age Trail (page 113).

★ **Horicon Marsh:** Millions of birds take flight here on their epic migrations (page 114).

★ **Octagon House:** Watertown's one-of-a-kind behemoth was the site of the nation's first kindergarten (page 117).

★ **Old World Wisconsin:** Take a tour of the United States' most expansive collection of settler structures. More than 65 have been relocated here from around the state (page 119).

★ **Hoard Historical Museum and Dairy Shrine:** This museum traces every possible aspect of the state's fascinating dairy history (page 120).

★ **Aztalan State Park:** Lake Mills' isolated park gives visitors a look at early human history in North America as they stroll along a river past Native American stockades (page 121).

★ **Geneva Lake:** This tranquil resort area has outstanding old-time paddle-wheel tours and one of the loveliest lakeside strolls anywhere (page 126).

Southeastern Wisconsin

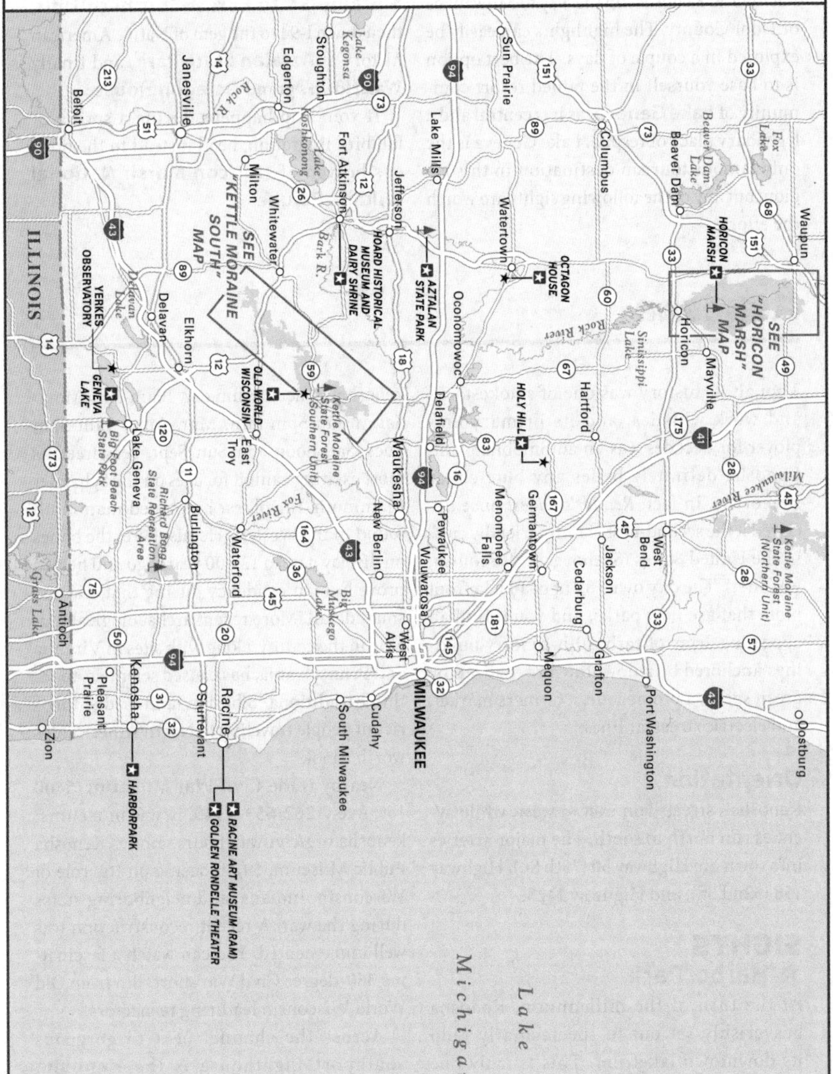

PLANNING YOUR TIME

This region is generally known for the cities of Racine and Kenosha, on the way to Milwaukee or Door County. The highlights can easily be explored in a couple of days. The best option is to base yourself in the famed resort community of **Lake Geneva,** as it is central and a legendary place of respite. Lake Geneva is the only famous tourism destination in this region, but any of the following sights are worth the effort.

Highway 67 is a lovely day drive north to **Old World Wisconsin** or the **Kettle Moraine State Forest-Southern Unit,** then down I-94 to the gem of Native American history at **Aztalan State Park,** and finally Watertown's grand **Octagon House.**

If your trip happens during a spring or fall bird migration, head instead to the birder's heaven of **Horicon Marsh National Wildlife Refuge.**

Kenosha

Though its history was one of smokestacks and work whistles, and its primary employer for decades was an automobile plant, Kenosha definitely belies any blue-collar stereotype. In fact, *Reader's Digest* once declared it the second-best "family-friendly city" in the United States (Sheboygan, Wisconsin, was first). The city owns 8 out of 10 lakefront plots that are now parks, and you'll find an appealing array of early-20th-century buildings anchored by a downtown revitalized by green space, a promenade, a farmers market, and electric streetcar lines.

Orientation

Kenosha's streets run east to west, while avenues run north to south. The major arteries into town are Highway 50 (75th St.), Highway 158 (52nd St.), and Highway 142S.

SIGHTS

★ HarborPark

At the turn of the millennium, Kenosha beaverishly set out to spectacularly redo its downtown lakefront. This is truly one of the freshest-looking Lake Michigan city stretches anywhere. The cornerstone is definitely the **Kenosha Public Museum** (56th St. at 1st Ave., 414/262-4140, www.kenoshapublicmuseum.org, 10am-5pm Mon.-Sat., noon-5pm Sun. Mar.-Aug., 9am-5pm Tues.-Sat., noon-5pm Sun. Sept.-Feb., free). Its most exciting exhibit focuses on the Schaeffer Mammoth, the oldest butchered mammoth found in the Western Hemisphere; the bones on display date to 12,000 years ago and helped prove human residency during that era—no small detail. More recent archaeological digging in the county, along with sites in Virginia and Pennsylvania, has caused scientists to rethink traditional Siberian land bridge theories of people traveling to North America. It's worth a look.

Nearby is the **Civil War Museum** (5400 1st Ave., 262/653-4140, www.museums.kenosha.org/civilwar, hours same as Kenosha Public Museum, $9), focusing on the role of Wisconsin, Indiana, and neighboring states during the war. A recent reconstruction was well implemented. You can watch a fascinating 360-degree Civil War short film from Old World Wisconsin featuring reenactors.

Across the channel next to gorgeous Southport Lighthouse is the **Kenosha History Center** (220 51st Place, 262/654-5770, www.kenoshahistorycenter.org, 10am-4:30pm Tues.-Fri., 10am-4pm Sat., noon-4pm Sun., free). The main museum here focuses

Previous: shoreside at Lake Geneva; Holy Hill; Old World Wisconsin

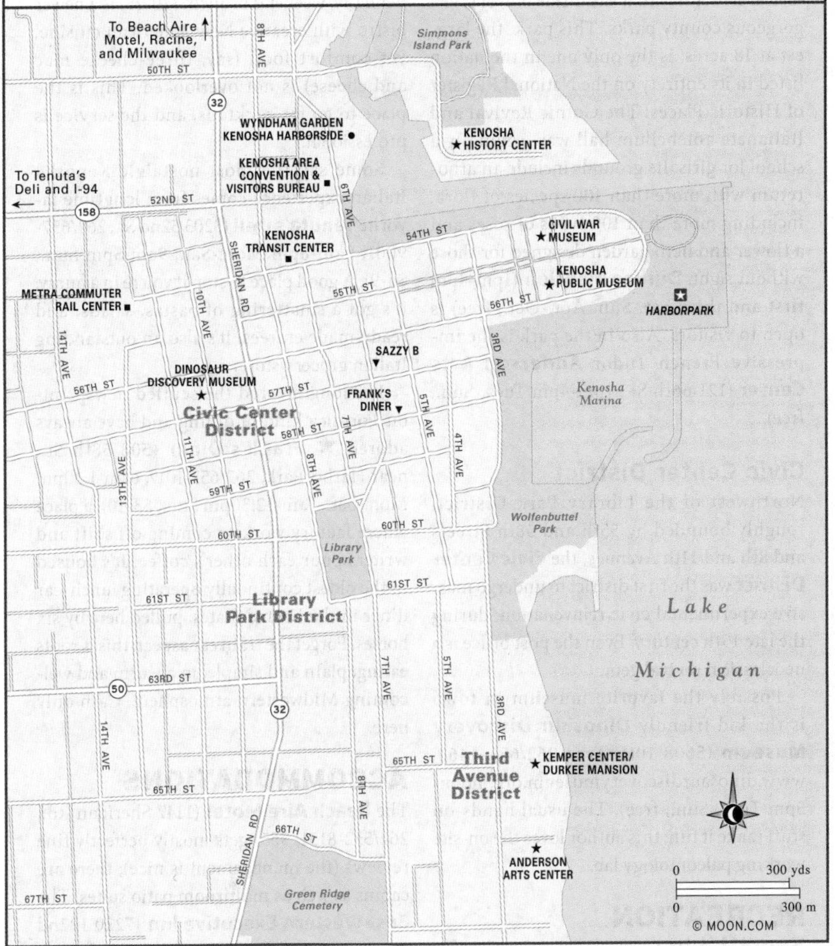

fascinatingly on the crucial role transportation—specifically auto manufacturing—played in the history of the city. A renovated lighthouse keeper's residence is nearby. Lighthouse tours (Thurs.-Sun. mid-May-Oct., $10) are available.

Library Park District

The **Library Park District,** bounded by 59th Street, 62nd Street, 6th Avenue, and Sheridan Road, was once the site of homes on the Underground Railroad, which are now marked by a plaque. Visitors can view the birthplace of Orson Welles at 6116 7th Avenue.

3rd Avenue District

East of the Library Park District and fronting the lake between 61st and 66th Streets, the **3rd Avenue District** is the most popular historic stroll, featuring most of the ornate mansions of wealthy early-20th-century residents.

Kemper Center (6501 3rd Ave.,

262/657-6005, www.kempercenter.com, park grounds open daily, free) is a complex of historical structures that sits inside one of seven gorgeous county parks. This park, the largest at 18 acres, is the only one in the nation listed in its entirety on the National Register of Historic Places. The Gothic Revival and Italianate antebellum hall was originally a school for girls. Its grounds include an arboretum with more than 100 species of flora, including more than 100 types of roses and a flower and herb garden designed for those without sight. **Durkee Mansion** (1pm-4pm first and third Sat.-Sun. Apr.-Oct., free) is open to visitors. Also in the park is the impressive French Tudor **Anderson Arts Center** (121 66th St., 1pm-4pm Tues.-Sun., free).

Civic Center District

Northwest of the Library Park District, roughly bounded by 55th and 58th Streets and 8th and 11th Avenues, the **Civic Center District** was the first district to undergo massive experimental civic rejuvenation, during the late 19th century. Even the post office is a neoclassical revival gem.

Possibly the favorite museum in town is the kid-friendly **Dinosaur Discovery Museum** (5608 10th Ave., 262/653-4460, www.dinosaurdiscoverymuseum.org, noon-5pm Tues.-Sun., free). The usual hands-on stuff make it fun; this author loves the on-site working paleontology lab.

RECREATION

Sportfishing

Most years, Kenosha sportfishing rates number one in the state in terms of fish caught per hour, especially trout and salmon. Here you'll find the greatest opportunities to catch coho salmon, rainbow trout, king salmon, brown trout, and lake trout. Contact the **Kenosha Charter Boat Association** (800/522-6699, www.kenoshacharterboat.com) for all details.

FOOD

Sazzy B (5523 6th Ave., 262/925-8499, dinner daily, weekend brunch, $10-25) is a newer bistro with creative New American cuisine, yet comfort food (say, three-cheese mac and cheese) is not overlooked. This is the place to go for cocktails, and the service is professional.

Some say the most nostalgic Kenosha Italian experience comes from longtime favorite **Tenuta's Deli** (3203 52nd St., 262/657-9001, 9am-8pm Mon.-Sat., 9am-5pm Sun., $4-9). A good place to stop if you're in a hurry, it's got a smattering of pastas, salads, and ready-made entrées. It's also an outstanding Italian grocery store.

I've long favored the scuffed newsprint-on-Formica kind of dining and have always adored ★ **Frank's Diner** (508 58th St., near HarborPark, 262/657-1017, 6am-1:30pm Mon.-Sat., 7am-12:30pm Sun., $3-10), a place where factory workers coming off shift and writers pour each other's coffee. It's housed in the oldest continually operating lunch-car diner in the United States, pulled here by six horses. Forget the train car aspect; this is roots eating, plain and simple, in a warm and welcoming Midwestern atmosphere. Cash only here.

ACCOMMODATIONS

The **Beach Aire Motel** (1147 Sheridan Rd., 262/552-8131, $65) gets mostly perfectly fine reviews (the management is nice); there are cabins as well as multiroom patio suites. The **Best Western Executive Inn** (7220 122nd Ave., 262/857-7699, $110) consistently garners high marks for its service. You'll get great views at the **Wyndham Garden Kenosha Harborside** (5125 6th Ave., 262/358-9566, from $199), right on the lake. This place refreshes constantly, as they did for this edition, and it's worth it to get a newer room.

1: HarborPark **2:** Kenosha's electric streetcar
3: Dinosaur Discovery Museum

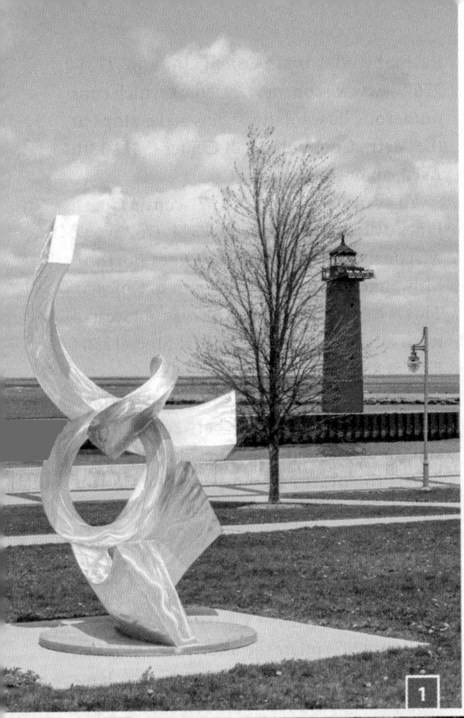

1

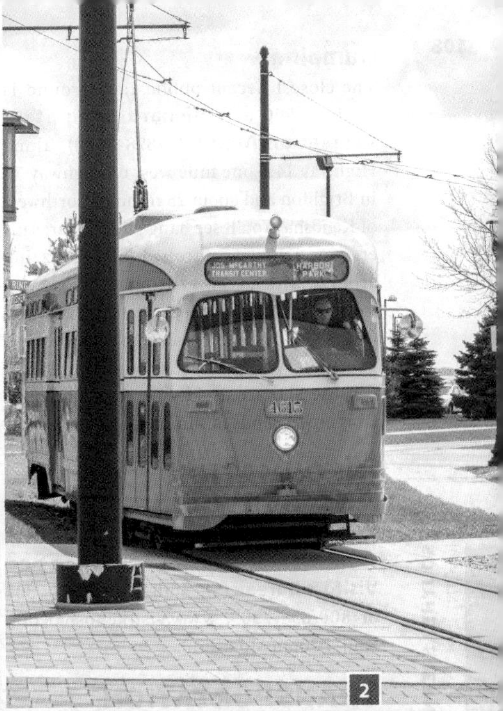
JOS McCARTHY TRANSIT CENTER
HARBOR PARK
4615

2

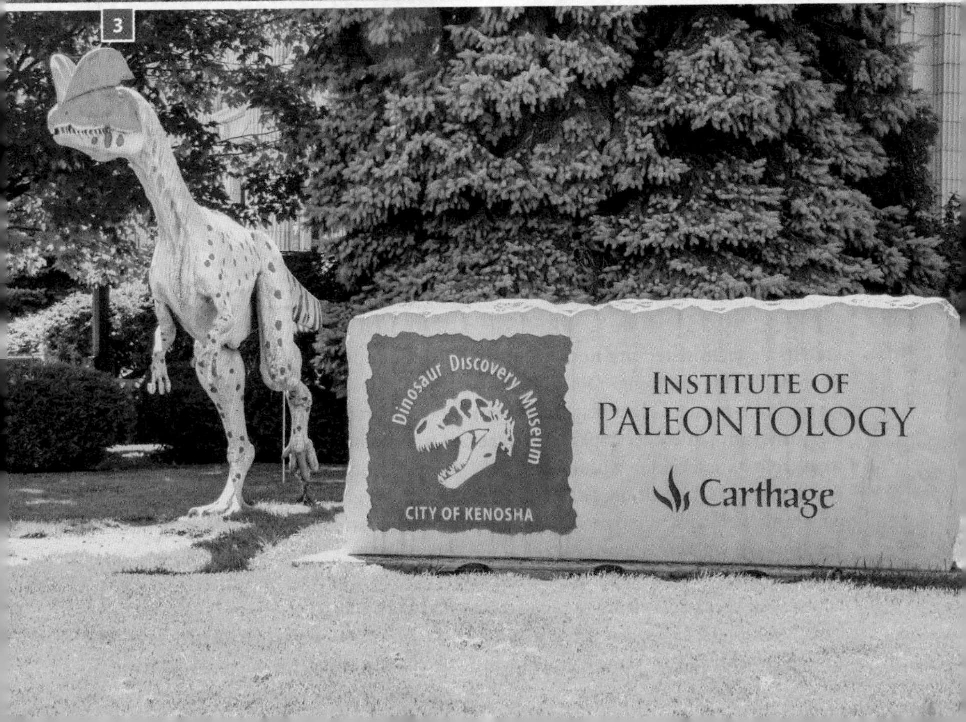
Dinosaur Discovery Museum
CITY OF KENOSHA
INSTITUTE OF PALEONTOLOGY
Carthage

3

Camping

The closest decent public campground is at the 4,500-acre **Richard Bong State Recreation Area** (262/878-5600), along Highway 142, one mile west of Highway 75 in Brighton and about 25 minutes northwest of Kenosha. You'll see hang gliders, parasailers, and remote-controlled planes buzzing around, which seems fitting, as it's named for a World War II flying ace. **Reservations** (888/947-2757, http://wisconsin.goingtocamp.com, reservation fee $8, nonresidents $23, day-use $11) are usually necessary on holidays or weekends in summer.

INFORMATION AND SERVICES

You'll encounter solicitous and chatty folks at the **Kenosha Area Convention and Visitors Bureau** (812 56th St., 262/654-7307 or 800/654-7309, www.visitkenosha.com, 8am-4:30pm Mon.-Fri.).

TRANSPORTATION

Getting There

Getting to Kenosha from Chicago (via I-94, 65 miles) takes just under 1.5 hours. From Milwaukee (via I-94, 40 miles), the drive takes 50 minutes. Getting to Kenosha from Racine is a 20-minute drive via pretty Highway 32.

Kenosha is connected to Milwaukee via Racine by **Wisconsin Coach Lines** (877/324-7767, www.wisconsincoach.com), which runs numerous buses daily. They make stops at the Metra Commuter Rail Center (5414 13th Ave.), among others.

You can also hop aboard Wisconsin Coach Lines' **Airport Express** (877/324-7767, www.wisconsincoach.com), which goes north to Milwaukee via Racine and south to Chicago. This is less ideal, since it stops way out west of town at the restaurant-bar Brat Stop (12304 75th St./Hwy. 50) on the interstate.

Metra (312/322-6777, www.metrarail.com) offers train service between Kenosha and Chicago's Madison Street Station. Trains depart the **Metra Commuter Rail Center** (5414 13th Ave., 262/653-0141) up to eight times daily.

Getting Around

The **Kenosha Transit Center** (724 54th St., 262/653-4287) offers the utterly cool **electric streetcar** (10:35am-6:15pm Sat.-Sun. Jan.-Feb., 10am-2pm Mon.-Fri., 10:30am-6:15pm Sat.-Sun. Mar., 11:05am-6:35pm Mon.-Fri., 10:35am-6:15pm Sat.-Sun. Apr.-Dec., adults $1) as a means of transportation about town. It rumbles through the downtown area to the Metra train station and back, through two of the historic districts, all in a matter of 15 minutes. An all-day pass ($2.50) is available.

Racine

Like its de facto sister city to the south of Kenosha, Racine (meaning "root" in French, for the knife-resistant plantlife of Root River that made early settlers decamp) suffers somewhat from its association with manufacturing. But the city lakefront, once a true-to-form ugly mill town with a horizon of gas tanks and brown sloughs, was mostly razed in the early 1990s and spruced up. Now it's full of landscaped parks and plenty of public boat launches, and the city sports the largest marina on Lake Michigan—more than 100 acres.

Ethnically, while in the early 20th century the city boasted the nation's most appreciable Bohemian influence, it is now known for its Danish contingent—it's got the largest Danish population outside Denmark—and West Racine is even referred to as "Kringleville" for the pastry produced in huge numbers by local bakeries.

SIGHTS

★ Racine Art Museum (RAM)

In the city center, the impressive **Racine Art**

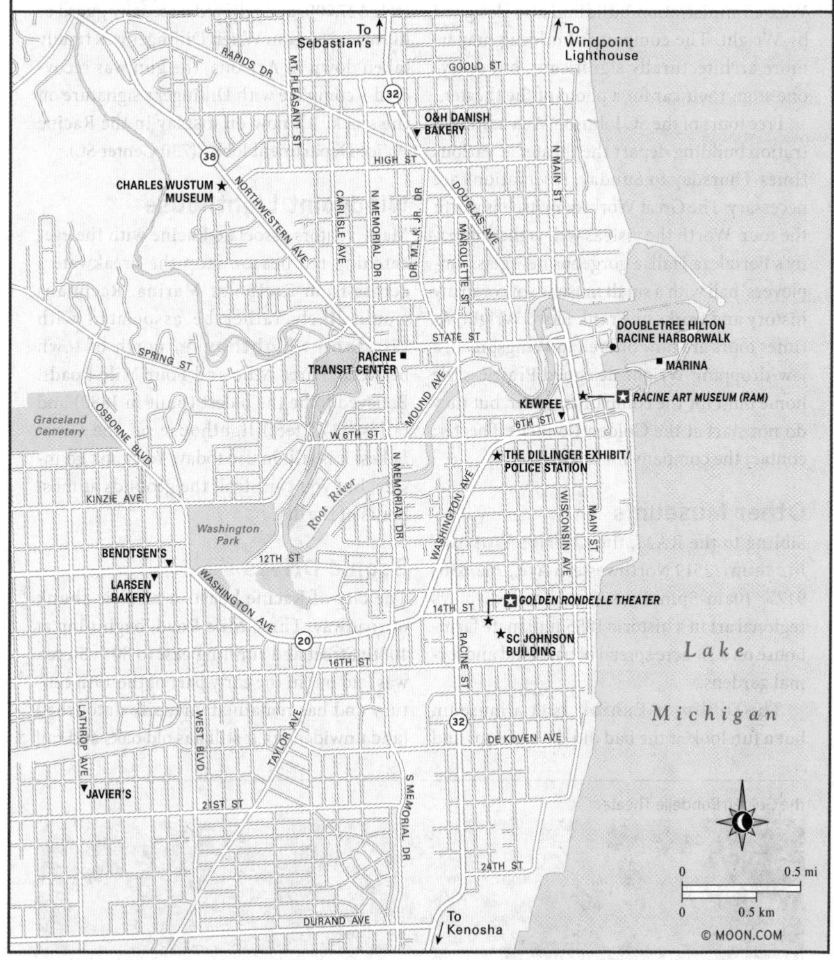

Museum (RAM, 441 Main St., 262/638-8300, www.ramart.org, 10am-5pm Tues.-Sat., noon-5pm Sun., $7), in a scintillatingly chic edifice meshed superbly with its 1860s structure, with little hyperbole, is one of the best in the Midwest. Holding one of the top three collections, more than 4,000 pieces, of Works Progress Administration (WPA) traditional arts and crafts, it is rivaled only by the Smithsonian and the American Craft Museum in New York. As an aside, this building, once a bank, was robbed by John Dillinger in 1933.

★ Golden Rondelle Theater

It's hard to miss the globular-shaped **Golden Rondelle Theater** (1525 Howe St., 262/631-2154), with its 90-foot arching columns, on the city's south side. The most distinctive of Racine's architectural landmarks, it was unveiled at the New York World's Fair in 1964-1965. Afterward, Taliesin Associate Architects was commissioned to bring the theater to Racine and incorporate it near the SC Johnson Wax administration building, also designed by Wright. The company's building may be more architecturally significant, but everyone stops their car for a photo of the theater.

Free tours of the SC Johnson Wax administration building depart the theater at various times Thursday to Sunday; reservations are necessary. The Great Workroom itself is worth the tour. Worth the visit as well is the company's Fortaleza Hall, a gorgeous new glass employees' hall with a small museum of company history and works by Frank Lloyd Wright. At times tours are now offered to Wingspread, a jaw-dropping Wright-designed Prairie-style home built for the company's leader, but they do not start at the Golden Rondelle Theater; contact the company for details.

Other Museums

Sibling to the RAM, the **Charles Wustum Museum** (2519 Northwestern Ave., 262/636-9177, 10am-5pm Tues.-Sat., free) displays regional art in a historic 1856 Italianate farmhouse on a 13-acre spread of parkland and formal gardens.

The **Dillinger Exhibit** isn't a museum but a fun look at the bad old days of cops and robbers. On November 20, 1933, four brazen robbers held up a downtown Racine bank, stole $27,700, and relieved a security guard of his machine gun. When Dillinger was finally taken down in Arizona, the gun was recovered—complete with Dillinger's signature on the stock. It's now on display in the Racine Police Department lobby (730 Center St.).

Windpoint Lighthouse

Many visitors associate Racine with the eye-catching red beacon atop the breakwaters across from Reefpoint Marina. Racinians would likely rather be associated with **Windpoint Lighthouse,** north of town between Three Mile and Four Mile Roads. Believed to be the oldest (built in 1880) and tallest (112 feet) lighthouse on the Great Lakes, it is still in use today. You can't go inside, but you can stroll the grounds at most hours of the day.

Scenic Drives

The city of Racine boasts a historic chunk of roadway. Three Mile Road, beginning at 108th Street and running east to 80th Street, was laid out in the early part of the 19th century and has remained virtually untouched (and unwidened). It still has old oaks and rail

the Golden Rondelle Theater

fences at its verges and makes for a beautiful drive.

State Rustic Roads are everywhere you look. One heads north of town along Honey Lake Road, Maple Lane, and Pleasant View Road to Highway D and Highway 83, passing along the way a woodland preserve, dairy farms, and marshes with muskrat houses. Backtrack to Highway DD and it picks up with another Rustic Road adjacent to the **Honey Creek Wildlife Area.** This route also passes the **Franklyn Hazelo Home** (34108 Oak Knoll Rd., not open to the public), which is on the National Register of Historic Places. Southeast of Burlington off Highway 142 via Brever Road or Wheatland Road, a Rustic Road passes under an expanse of oak and black walnut trees. Highlights include old barns, an old farmhouse, marshes, and lots of great fishing along the Fox River, accessible from Hoosier Creek Road.

Burlington

Burlington is about 25 miles west of Racine. For a town of only 8,900 people, it's sure got a bunch of liars: The home of the world-famous Burlington Liar's Club, it hosts an annual yarn- and fib-spinning festival and also distributes a brochure about the town's **Tall Tales Trail.** Burlington is the hometown of former Dallas Cowboys' quarterback Tony Romo. Also called Chocolate Town USA (there's a Nestlé plant here), Burlington has many streets named after candy bars and, of course, the **Chocolate Experience Museum** (Chamber of Commerce office, 113 E. Chestnut St., 262/763-6044, 9am-5pm Mon.-Fri., 10am-2pm Sat., free).

RECREATION

Charter Fishing

Racine has one of the most productive charter operations on Lake Michigan; it also has the largest marina on the Great Lakes. Six different species of salmon and trout cohabit near three reefs outside the harbor. In July 2010, a man caught a Wisconsin-record—and likely world-record—41.5-pound brown trout off Wind Point.

For more information, contact the **Fishing Charters of Racine** (http://fishracinewi.com).

ENTERTAINMENT AND EVENTS

On Memorial Day weekend, little Burlington whoops it up during **ChocolateFest** (www.chocolatefest.com).

Racine's **Fourth of July** celebration (www.realracine.com) is the largest in the state, replete with the longest parade in Wisconsin. If you're very lucky, it'll be a year when 19th-century mock clipper ships are sailing around.

The granddaddy of all events is mid-July's **Salmon-a-Rama** (www.salmon-o-rama.com), during which more than 4,000 anglers from 25 states land about 18 tons of fish and another 200,000 people crowd the lakefront for a huge blowout of a festival. It's the largest freshwater fishing festival in the world.

FOOD

Burgers

Not a greasy spoon per se, ★ **Kewpee** (520 Wisconsin Ave., 262/634-9601, 7am-6pm Mon.-Fri., 7am-5pm Sat., from $1) rates a nod as perhaps the best burger joint in southern Wisconsin. Devotees regularly come from as far away as the Windy City. Decades old (it started in 1927), this erstwhile teen hangout doesn't have much in the way of ambience now. It's as fast as fast grub gets, but you can't beat the burgers or malts. It's standing-room-only at lunchtime.

Kringle

Racine is still lovingly called Kringleville, for good reason. Almost all travelers leave town with white wax-paper bags stuffed with *kringle,* a flaky, ovoid kind of coffee cake filled with a variety of fruits and almond paste or pecans. Family bakeries vie annually for top honors of best *kringle,* and they still make it the old-world way, with some taking three days to prepare the dough alone. Aficionados say: (1) pecan *kringles* are best; and (2) always go for the thinnest slice on the plate, since it always has the most filling. Another Danish highlight is *aebleskiver*, a lovely spherical waffle.

O&H Danish Bakery (1841 Douglas Ave., 262/637-8895, 5:30am-6pm Mon.-Fri., 5am-5pm Sat.) does the most advertising and probably ships the most *kringles*, and President Obama did make a stop here in 2010. But most readers have opined that ★ **Larsen Bakery** (3311 Washington Ave., 262/633-4298, 6am-5:30pm Mon.-Fri., 6am-4:30pm Sat.) or ★ **Bendtsen's** (3200 Washington Ave., 262/633-0365, 5:30am-5:30pm Mon.-Sat.) have the best.

Bistros

Sebastian's (6025 Douglas Ave., 262/681-5465, 5pm-9pm Mon.-Sat., $6-18), just north of downtown, has long been a fine bistro. Cuisine varies by season; expect classics like bone-in rib eye done in varied styles, many using produce from its adjacent garden.

Mexican

Javier's (2815 Durand Ave., 262/598-9242, dinner Mon.-Sat., $6-18) is best described as fusion Mexican. There are wonderful Mexican standards, but you may also find baked chicken pasta or whatever else Javier thinks up. It also rates a mention for quite possibly being the friendliest eatery in the state.

ACCOMMODATIONS

The only over-the-water hotel on southern Lake Michigan is a goodie. The **Doubletree Hilton Racine Harborwalk** (223 Gaslight Circle, 262/632-7777, from $200) has rooms affording gorgeous lake views and suites with whirlpools on the balconies. Boaters can dock at slips, and the restaurant on-site is well regarded. Extras include 24-hour room service, in-room coffeemakers, airport transportation, and more.

INFORMATION AND SERVICES

The nonprofit tourism organization **Real Racine** (14015 Washington Ave., Sturtevant, 262/884-6400 or 800/272-2463, www.realracine.com, 9am-5pm daily mid-Apr.-Oct., 9am-5pm Mon.-Sat. Nov.-mid-Apr.) is just west of the Washington Avenue and I-94 interchange.

kringle, the local treat of Racine

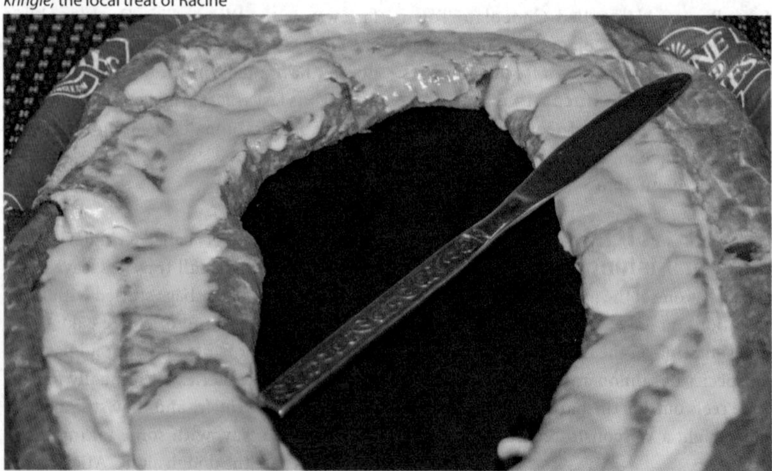

GETTING THERE

Car

From Kenosha, Racine is 20 minutes north via a picturesque drive along Highway 32. From Chicago (via I-94, 76 miles), the drive takes around 90 minutes. From Milwaukee (via I-94, 30 miles), it takes 40 minutes.

Train

There's no **Amtrak** (800/872-7245, www.amtrak.com) service directly to Racine, but trains do stop at **Sturtevant Station** (9900 Exploration Ct., Sturtevant), eight miles west. From there, you can hop on a Racine city bus. Chicago's Metra trains don't extend north to Racine, only running as far as Kenosha.

Bus

Airport Express (877/324-7767, www.wisconsincoach.com) makes stops in western Racine on its routes to and from Chicago's O'Hare Airport and Milwaukee's Mitchell International Airport. **Wisconsin Coach Lines** (877/324-7767, www.wisconsincoach.com) also stops in Racine on its run between Milwaukee and Kenosha. Buses stop at the **Racine Transit Center** (www.racinetransit.com) in the 1400 block of State Street.

From Milwaukee to Madison

★ HOLY HILL

Even recovering Roman Catholics might appreciate a side trip to **Holy Hill** (1525 Carmel Rd., Hubertus, 262/628-1838, www.holyhill.com), with its neo-Romanesque church dominating the skyline, simply because, as one visitor noted, there is nothing like the sound of Holy Hill's bells tolling through the Wisconsin countryside. In 1855, a disabled mendicant hermit experienced a cure atop the 1,340-foot bluff and established Holy Hill as a pilgrimage site. One of the church spires, 180 steps up, affords commanding views of variegated Kettle Moraine terrain and, on clear days, the downtown Milwaukee skyline. A $5 million-plus renovation replaced the roof with Vermont slate that matches the surrounding hills; the priceless interiors were painstakingly reappointed.

Then again, some say, get there while you can. The nearby town of Erin is showing every sign of becoming suburbia, so much so that Scenic America placed Holy Hill on its 10 Most Endangered Landscapes list.

Around the church are 400 heavily wooded acres crossed by the **National Ice Age Scenic Trail;** the grounds also contain a 0.5-mile trail and a grotto. The monastery has guest rooms and retreat facilities; reservations are required. There is also a cafeteria (Tues.-Sun. May-Nov.); the Sunday brunch is another nice reason to visit. To get there, head 30 miles north of Milwaukee via U.S. 41/45, then west on Highway 167.

HARTFORD

Little Hartford is a few miles north of Holy Hill via Highway 83. It's worthy of a stop just to see the art deco interiors and interesting pieces of auto history at the **Wisconsin Automotive Museum** (147 N. Rural St., 262/673-7999, wisconsinautomuseum.com, 10am-5pm Mon.-Sat., noon-5pm Sun. summer, shorter hours fall-spring, $10 adults). The museum displays include Wisconsin-produced Nash automobiles and high-caliber Kissels, which were built in Hartford from 1906 to 1931.

WEST BEND

The **Museum of Wisconsin Art** (300 S. 6th Ave., 262/334-9638, www.wisconsinart.org, 10am-5pm Tues.-Wed. and Fri.-Sun., 10am-8pm Thurs., $15) boasts a large holding of early-19th-century Wisconsin art. In addition to the works of Milwaukee-born German Carl von Marr, an antique dollhouse spans an entire room. This smashing $12 million renovation was designed by the same folks who brought you the lovely Discovery World complex in Milwaukee.

North of town on Highway 144 and Highway A is the awe-inspiring **Lizard Mound County Park** (2121 Hwy. A, 262/335-4400, daily Apr.-Nov., free), along with Aztalan State Park, one of the state's most important archaeological sites. The Mississippian people here predated the Aztalan people by perhaps 500 years and built amazingly detailed earthworks in geometric and animal forms.

★ HORICON MARSH

One of nine nodes of the **National Ice Age Reserve** (8am-3pm Mon.-Fri. and some Sat. mid-Apr.-mid-Sept.), the Horicon is divided into two parts: the **National Wildlife Refuge** in the north and the **Horicon Marsh Wildlife Area** in the southern tier of the greenery. Spreading over 32,000 acres, the marsh was formed by the Green Bay lobe of the Wisconsin Glacier beginning around 70,000 years ago. The result was a shallow glacial lake bed filled with silt—the largest freshwater marsh in North America, often called the "Little Everglades of the North." It's the largest cattail marsh in North America.

The marsh was populated originally by nomadic Paleo-Indians who hunted animals along the edge of the receding ice. Europeans showed up and began felling the region's deciduous forests. A dam was later built to facilitate floating timber logs on the Rock River and to create mill power. The water levels rose nine feet, resulting in the world's largest artificial lake. Around the time of the Civil War, far-thinking conservationists succeeded in having the dam removed and reconverting the marsh to wetland. It became a legendary sport-hunting paradise; private clubs removed whole wagonloads of birds after hunts.

Around the end of the 19th century, agricultural interests once again lobbied to drain the marsh and reestablish farming. What couldn't be drained off was going to be used for profit-rich muck farming or moist-soil

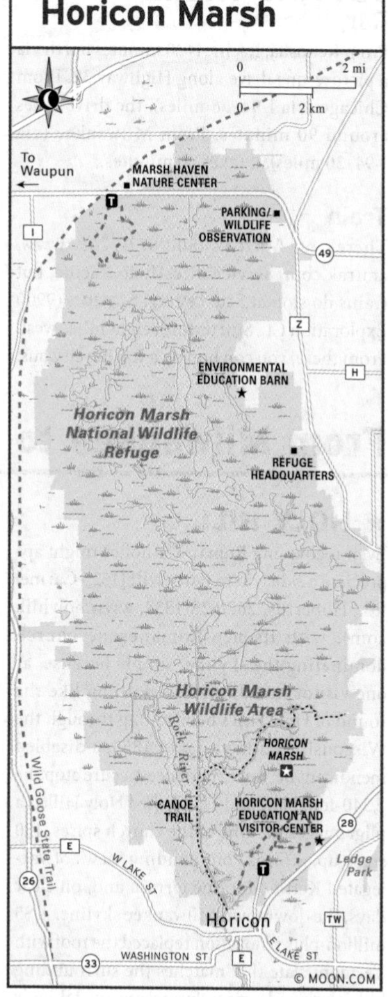

agriculture. The efforts failed, though the dikes the companies built still exist in a grid-like pattern today. Citizens' groups finally organized in the 1920s to call for legal designation of the marsh as a refuge. In 1927, the state legislature passed the law, which officially protects the lower one-third; the federal government maintains the upper two-thirds.

The marsh has a few Native American mounds along the east side, accessible by a driving route, as well as a four-mile-long island, an educational barn, and plenty of fishing, but birds are the big draw. Annually, more than one million migrating Canada geese, ducks, and other waterfowl take over the marsh in a histrionic and cacophonic invasion. Geese alone account for three-quarters of the arrivals.

The marsh has an established 30-mile-long **Wild Goose Parkway,** a drivable loop that takes in the whole of the marsh and offers some spectacular vistas. There are innumerable pull-offs with educational displays.

Wildlife

The deep marshes are flooded every year except during severe droughts; water levels can rise four feet—crucial for nesting waterfowl, especially diving ducks, grebes, and fish-eating fowl. The denser vegetation brings security in nesting, breeding, and rearing young. Even wild rice grows again in the great marsh.

Some of the more than 260 species of birds include mallards, blue-winged teals, coots, ruddy ducks, cormorants, herons, and terns. The marsh is the largest nesting area east of the Mississippi River for redhead ducks, almost 3,000 of which show up each year. Birds are most often spotted during spring and fall migrations. Rookeries—particularly one on **Cotton Island**—attract egrets, herons, and cormorants. In 1998, for the first time in more than 100 years, trumpeter swans returned to the marsh. No state has spent more time or money to bring trumpeter swans back to native areas, and after years of preparation, a dozen swans were released. The goal is to eventually have 20 nesting pairs.

What of those honking geese? They come from the watery tundra near Hudson Bay in northern Canada. Some begin arriving by mid-September, with a gradual increase through October and sometimes into November. Upon arrival, they establish a feeding pattern in surrounding fields, eating waste corn and grass. Picture-perfect mass take-offs occur right around sundown. The geese remain until dwindling temperatures freeze their water supply.

Marsh Haven Visitors Center

Three miles east of Waupun along Highway 49 is the marsh's **visitors center** (920/342-5818, noon-4pm Mon.-Fri., 9am-5pm Sat.-Sun., $2). It has a theater, art displays, exhibits on the natural history of the marsh—including a live display of birds—and trail access from the parking lot.

Marsh Headquarters

The **National Wildlife Refuge Headquarters** (Hwy. Z, 920/387-2658, 9am-4pm Mon.-Sun. Oct., reduced hours in other months, free) upgraded recently with a multimillion-dollar facility and has nearby hiking trails and a wildlife-viewing area. The **Horicon Marsh Education and Visitor Center** (920/387-7893, 9am-5pm Mon.-Fri., 10am-5pm Sat.-Sun.) is along Highway 28 and housed in a $5 million center. The Explorium (daily, $6) is a new 6,500-square-foot multimedia education center with a glacier you can stroll through (not to mention a huge woolly mammoth!). They also have restrooms available year-round, bless 'em.

Waupun

Even with a maximum-security prison casting a shadow over the town, Waupun somehow manages to maintain an attractive, if somewhat subdued, downtown. It was described by the old WPA Wisconsin guidebook as "almost oppressively pleasant." One of five life-size bronze statues in town, on Madison Street, is the first casting of James Earl Fraser's *End of the Trail,* part of a series commemorating the genocidal expansion of the frontier. Waupun has an access trail leading east to the **Wild Goose State Trail.**

Mayville

East of the marsh in the town of Mayville—whose city water has been judged as some of the best-tasting in the United States—is the **White Limestone School** (N. Main

1
2
3

St., 920/387-3474, www.mlsm.org, 1:30pm-4:30pm 1st and 3rd Sun. May-Oct., free), known mostly for its collection of rural Wisconsin photographs taken by Edgar Mueller. The local historical society operates the **Hollenstein Wagon and Carriage Factory** (11 N. German St., 920/387-5530, www.mayvillehistoricalsociety.org, 1:30pm-4:30pm 2nd and 4th Sun., free), an old factory that once produced wagons. Several wagons are on display.

One of the best inns in Wisconsin—for eating and sleeping—the ★ **Audubon Inn** (45 N. Main St., 920/387-5848, www.auduboninn.com, from $120) dates from 1897, and you'll feel you're in bygone days when you enter.

Recreation

The Horicon Marsh Wildlife Area, in the southern half of the marsh, has several established **canoe trails** through the wetlands, Mieske Bay, and along the east branch of the Rock River.

More than six miles of **hiking trails** are accessible on the south side of Highway 49. You also have access to the 30-mile-long **Wild Goose State Trail** (cyclists $5 pass).

Canoes can be rented at **Blue Heron Landing** (Hwy. 33 at the bridge, Horicon), which is also the place to get aboard a **pontoon boat tour** (12:30pm daily May-Sept., noon Sat.-Sun. Oct.-Apr. one hour, $14 adults) of the marsh with **Blue Heron Tours** (920/485-4663, www.horiconmarsh.com).

Tons of special events take place throughout the year. One of the best in North America is early May's **Bird Festival** (www.horiconmarshbirdclub.com).

COLUMBUS

Downtown Columbus has intriguing small-town architecture, the most significant example of which is the 1920 **Farmer and Merchants Union Bank** (159 W. James St., 920/623-4000, 8:30am-4pm Mon.-Fri., 8:30am-11am Sat., free), also called the **Jewel Box,** a lovely example of Louis Sullivan's Prairie School style and now a quasi-local museum full of banking and architectural objects upstairs.

1: Holy Hill 2: geese in Horicon Marsh 3: viewing platform in Horicon Marsh

WATERTOWN

Watertown justifies its name: It lies at the bifurcation of the Rock River as it wends through an oxbow bend in the valley.

Historically, Watertown was known for geese and its German residents. Watertown goose livers were the top of the pâté de foie gras line. The city exported up to 25 tons of the rich meat to eastern markets annually, and Watertown farmers perfected the art of "noodling"—force-feeding the geese with noodles to fatten them up. The local high school's team nickname is the Goslings—not exactly ferocious, but at least historically relevant.

The city had heavy immigration of enlightened freethinkers fleeing political and social persecution in 1848 Germany. Most notable was Carl Schurz, a political reformer who arrived in Watertown in 1855 and eventually left his mark on U.S. politics. His wife put the town on the map in contemporary terms; hers was the first kindergarten in the United States, which continues to be one of the city's primary tourism draws. Watertown was rumored at one time to be on the short list for state capital relocation.

★ Octagon House

The **Octagon House** (919 Charles St., 920/261-2796, docent-led tours 10am-4pm Wed.-Mon. Memorial Day-Labor Day, 11am-3pm Labor Day-Memorial Day, $9 adults) may be the most impressive house in the state. It is certainly the largest pre-Civil War family residence in the Midwest, with more than 8,000 square feet of floor space and 57 rooms, although only one fireplace. Built during the course of 13 years by John Richards—who owned three mills on the river below the vertiginous hill upon which the house sits—the house sports one of the nation's only cantilevered spiral staircases, a basswood and cherry

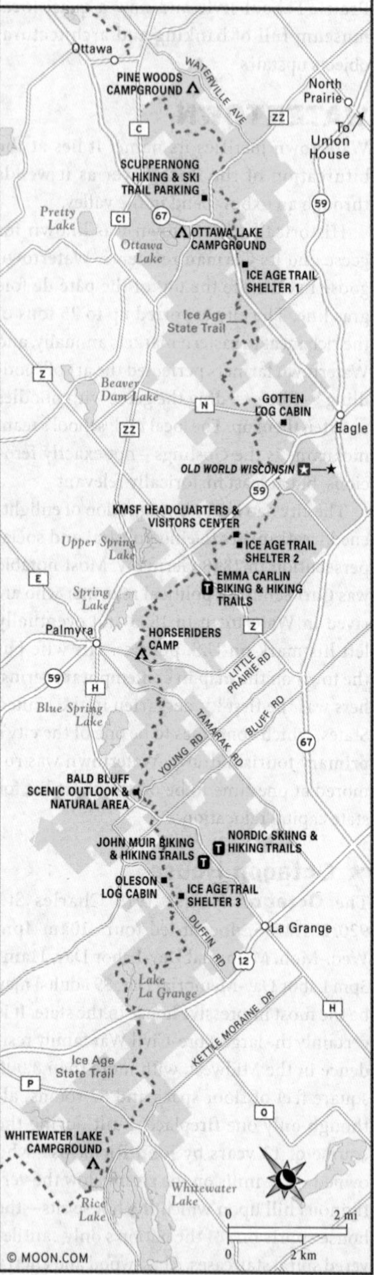

marvel that pirouettes 40 feet to the upper levels. It was so well built that reportedly not one of the stairs on the staircases creaks. Behind the house on the large grounds is the nation's first kindergarten.

OCONOMOWOC

That's "oh-KAHN-uh-muh-wahk" (sometimes that first syllable sounds like "uh"). It's the only city in the country with a name spelled with five o's, one in every odd-numbered position in the word. Oconomowoc is another trim, spread-out Victorian city, this one wound around Lac La Belle and Fowler Lake, with other lakes nearby.

Oconomowoc is primarily a strolling town; in the lobby of the **First Bank of Oconomowoc** (155 W. Wisconsin Ave., 262/569-9900), you'll find paintings of many of the homes in town.

Food

Purportedly the oldest dining establishment in Wisconsin is the ★ **Red Circle Inn** (N44 W33013 Watertown Plank Rd., 262/367-4883, www.redcircleinn.com, 4:30pm-9pm Mon.-Fri., 5pm-9:30pm Sat., $18-25), established in 1848. Enjoy gourmet American and some French country cuisine. You'll find it along Highway 16 east of Oconomowoc Lake at the junction with Highway C.

KETTLE MORAINE STATE FOREST-SOUTHERN UNIT

The Kettle Moraine State Forest-Southern Unit is sibling to the northern tier. Debate continues—and gets bristly at times—over plans to acquire sufficient private lands to link the two and the Ice Age National Scenic Trail, creating a green buffer against Lake Michigan suburban expansion and thus preventing the destruction of southern Wisconsin's glacial topography. The Wisconsin Department of Natural Resources (DNR) is planning to gradually add more than 15,000 acres over coming decades.

The state's oddball glacial heritage pops up everywhere—residual kames, eskers, and the eponymous kettles and moraines. Also within the forest are weather-beaten homestead log cabins, now one-eyed and decaying in the tall grass, and a handful of bluff-line panoramas taking in all the glacial geology. In 2002 the forest literally returned to life. Original prairie seeds dormant for 150 years bloomed again; the resurgence happened because the agricultural lands remained fallow for long enough. With time, the DNR hopes to bring back 5,000 acres of seeds this way, which would make it the largest natural prairie area east of the Mississippi River.

The **Kettle Moraine State Forest Headquarters** (S91 W39091 Hwy. 59, 262/594-6200, 9am-4pm Mon.-Sat., 11am-4pm Sun.) has detailed maps of the whole forest.

Recreation

Kettle Moraine is popular, so be prepared. The forest offers 160 miles of trails, some for hiking, some for biking, some for both; most are groomed for cross-country skiing in winter. The **National Ice Age Scenic Trail** cuts through the park from the **Pine Woods Campground** to **Rice Lake,** about 30 miles that's usually done in four segments. The rough but popular **John Muir Trails** boast incredible blooms of pasqueflowers in spring and some of the best biking—diverse, challenging, and designed specifically for mountain bikes. (Look at the twists and turns of the blue loop's southernmost point, stretching into a mature hardwood forest, and you'll see the outline of a squirrel.)

Camping

Primitive camping is allowed at three Adirondack backpacking shelters (free, registration required) along the Ice Age Trail. The forest also has four campgrounds, some with walk-in sites. There is also a fully accessible camping cabin. For tranquility, head directly to **Pine Woods Campground;** not only does it have the most isolated shaded campsites, but it also has 32 sites where radios are banned. You can also get to boat-in campsites; check at the ranger station.

Reservations (888/947-2757, http://wisconsin.goingtocamp.com, reservation fee $8, nonresidents $23, vehicles $11) are advised.

Food

★ **Union House** (S42 W31320 Hwy. 83, 262/968-4281, www.theunionhouse.com, dinner from 4:30pm Tues.-Sat., $17-32), in Genesee Depot, is impressive. There's great heartland fare buttressed by unique entrées such as quail and lots of other wild game.

Supplies and Rentals

La Grange General Store (N1242 Hwy. 59, 262/495-8600, www.backyardbikes.com, 9am-5pm Mon.-Thurs., 9am-6pm Fri.-Sat.) is a welcome little gem dispensing a luscious array of deli, café, and natural-food items. You can also get items such as buffalo burgers, organic chicken from Oconomowoc farms, and other meat from local producers. It also rents out mountain bikes and cross-country skis.

★ OLD WORLD WISCONSIN

Say "Eagle, Wisconsin," and even natives say, "Where?" But say, "Old World Wisconsin" and everybody's eyes light up. City-size **Old World Wisconsin** (Hwy. 67, 262/594-6301, www.oldworldwisconsin.wisconsinhistory.org, 10am-5pm daily summer, shorter hours May and Sept.-Nov., $20 adults), a 575-acre outdoor museum run by the state historical society, comprises more than 65 settler structures relocated from around the state and organized here into Polish, Danish, Norwegian, Yankee, Finnish, and two German homesteads. Its collection of original log and wood buildings is the largest in the United States and considered the best. Newer are the reconstructed buildings and a cemetery from Pleasant Ridge in Grant County in southwestern Wisconsin, five miles south of Lancaster; this was among Wisconsin's first African

American communities. The complex is so big that trams ($2) make a circuit continuously.

New proposals include relocating an original Wisconsin beerhouse here, constructing a Native American village, and even letting buffalo and elk roam the site. Note the lack of trees in some areas due to a terrifying tornado in 2010.

Very popular is the **Clausing Barn Restaurant,** an octagonal 1897 barn designed by a Mequon immigrant. It offers casual cafeteria-style dining with an emphasis on heritage cuisine.

FORT ATKINSON

Bisected by the Rock River, which flows sluggishly south and west of town into Lake Koshkonong, the town was hastily erected by soldiers during the 1832 Black Hawk War. Dairying truly put the town on the map. William Dempster Hoard, the patron saint of Wisconsin's dairy industry, began *Hoard's Dairyman,* a newsletter-cum-magazine, here in 1873. Fort Atkinson is a trim slice of Americana. It's been called by *Money* magazine one of the "hottest" small towns in the country.

★ Hoard Historical Museum and Dairy Shrine

No visit to America's Dairyland would be complete without a look at the **Hoard Historical Museum** (407 Merchants Ave., 920/563-7769, www.hoardmuseum.org, 9:30am-4:30pm Tues.-Sat. June-Labor Day, shorter hours Labor Day-May, free), housed in a Gothic Revival-mission oak-style mansion. The museum displays a restoration of the Dwight Foster House—the area's first frame house, built in 1841—along with two rooms of exhibits, the anchors of which are a 15,000-piece Native American artifact collection—so extensive the Smithsonian once eyed it—and a wealth of information on the Black Hawk War. Even Abe Lincoln, who traveled through the county in 1832 with the militia chasing Black Hawk, gets a fairly impressive exhibit.

The museum is also the site of the **Dairy Shrine,** an assemblage of audiovisual displays, dioramas, and artifacts tracing the history of Wisconsin dairying.

Food

A favorite place of mine in these parts is the ★ **Cafe Carpe** (18 S. Water St., 920/563-9391, www.cafecarpe.com, hours vary Tues.-Sat., $4-12), one of the best

experiencing Wisconsin's history at the the living museum of Old World Wisconsin

Lorine Niedecker's Poetry

Unknown to Wisconsinites—except in her hometown of Fort Atkinson—Lorine Niedecker has been included in no less than the *Norton Anthology* as one of the 20th century's most significant American poets. Her simplistic, haiku-like poetry celebrates life among common people and captures the ethos of the Wisconsin wilderness very well, perhaps more evocatively than any other writer in the canon of Wisconsin literature.

Lorine Niedecker was born in 1903 on her beloved Blackhawk Island, a peninsular marshy swale with a rustic collection of minor resorts and fishing families in shotgun shacks. Blackhawk Island's isolation and tough life—the river flooded, her father seined carp in scows, and her mother went deaf—caused her to leave Beloit College early.

Reading Louis Zukofsky's "Objectivist" issue of *Poetry* magazine in 1931 changed her profoundly. The objectivist doctrine of viewing a poem as a pure form through which the things of the world are seen without the ambiguity of feeling resonated deeply in her. Like those of other prominent Wisconsin writers—among them Zona Gale, John Muir, and Aldo Leopold—Niedecker's works were ecological in every sense. Her attention to the "condensory" (her word) called for using only words that contributed to a visual and aural presentation. Resolutely hermitic, Niedecker cloistered herself in her small hand-built cottage. This sense of isolation is fundamental to appreciating her passionately understated writing.

Niedecker never sold many books, but was not interested in teaching, so she supported herself by scrubbing floors at Fort Atkinson General Hospital, scriptwriting for WHA radio in Madison, and proofreading for *Hoard's Dairyman*. Her greatest work may have been as field editor for the classic Wisconsin guidebook—the 1942 WPA guide to the Badger State.

An unhappy first marriage ended in 1930. She remarried happily in 1961 and traveled widely throughout the Midwest for the first time. It was this travel that raised her poetry to another level; for the first time she wrote extended poems. Her output was prolific as she lived quietly on the island until her death in 1971.

What many consider her greatest poem, "Lake Superior," was included in the great *North Central*, published in 1968 in London, followed two years later by the classic *My Life by Water: Collected Poems 1936-68*.

casual eateries in the state. The food is a carefree, delicious blend of Midwestern diner and downscale café. But "the Carp" is even more famous as Wisconsin's best venue for folk music. Low-key and friendly, this is one place you'll want to revisit.

Jefferson

The next town north of Fort Atkinson (via Hwy. 26) is Jefferson, worth a visit for its natural beauty. The **Jefferson Marsh Wildlife and Natural Area,** east of Jefferson via Highway Y, is a 3,129-acre tamarack preserve—the state's largest—and a sanctuary for endangered egrets. It's even got effigy mounds.

★ AZTALAN STATE PARK

Aztalan State Park (920/648-8774), near I-94 and Lake Mills, is currently overlooked by most passing travelers, but when funding becomes available, the state has plans to upgrade facilities, reclaim surrounding farmland, add a chic new visitors center, and increase attendance by 700 percent. Visit now while it's still an isolated gem.

The park feels eerily historic; the Rock River silently rolls by, and the only sound audible is the wind shuffling through the leaves of the corn. One of the largest and most carefully researched archaeological sites in Wisconsin, Aztalan covers almost 175 acres and features remnant stockades and hiking trails snaking in and around the large burial mounds. Scientists theorize that this spot was a strategic northern endpoint, among the farthest north, of a Middle Mississippian culture whose influence stretched south to New Orleans and into Mexico. It rivals Illinois' better-known Cahokia. Scientists also believe it to be one of the only places where the Mississippians lived among late-Woodland Native Americans.

Lake Mills is an engaging small Victorian town. Encircling a central park, it has wide tree-lined avenues, mansions, and droopy willow trees. Visitors can enjoy Lake Mills' free Bartles Beach or, for a fee, Sandy Beach, on the other side of Rock Lake.

As an aside, there are those who believe that there are pyramids beneath the black surface of Rock Lake. This is no joke; universities have sent research teams. Allegedly these structures were produced by copper-mining expeditions from Asia and Europe several thousand years ago. Why they would halt mining and build pyramids hasn't been explained.

The less leisure-minded should head to the junction of Highway 89 and Highway A, a node for the **Glacial Drumlin Trail**, a 47-mile multipurpose recreation trail spanning from Waukesha (west of Milwaukee) to Cottage Grove east of Madison. The Lake Mills segment may be the most picturesque along the entire trail, with an old depot and trestle at the trailhead not far from Rock Lake. There's also a good wildlife area south of Lake Mills.

The community arguably has the best burgers in the state—butter-filled little heart-attack patties called sliders served all summer by the **American Legion** (129 S. Main St., Lake Mills, 920/648-5115) right downtown. Hours vary.

Janesville

General Motors bought out a local factory in 1919 and began Janesville's first assembly line. Within a decade, more than half of the city owed its economic fortunes to GM, until the shocking economic collapse of 2009 left its final GM plant shuttered. But blue-collar doesn't mean generic. You'd be amazed how trim and architecturally special the city can be—approximately one-fifth of all of Wisconsin's buildings on the National Register of Historic Places can be found in Janesville.

SIGHTS

Rotary Gardens

One slice of the city's 2,100 acres of park, the **Rotary Gardens** (1455 Palmer Dr., 608/752-3885, www.rotarybotanicalgardens.org, 9am-8pm daily mid-May-mid-Sept., less rest of year, $7) is spread over a dozen acres and encompasses several landscaping techniques—Japanese rock, English cottage, French, Italian, sunken, and perennial, all united by a theme of "Dialogue: World Peace Through Freedom." Across the street you'll find a segment of the Ice Age Trail.

Not far from Rotary Gardens is **Palmer Park** (2501 Palmer Dr.), a large green space with a wading pool, tennis courts, and the Camden Playground, the largest fully accessible playground in the United States.

Lincoln-Tallman House

The **Lincoln-Tallman House** (440 N. Jackson St., 608/752-4509, 10am-4pm daily June-Sept. and Dec., $10 adults), the 1855 home of a prominent abolitionist, is the only private residence in Wisconsin in which Abe Lincoln hung his hat. Architecture mavens have called it one of the finest of its kind in the country. Also here are the original horse barn and a Greek Revival stone house once used by servants.

A million-dollar-plus renovation added heating and air-conditioning to preserve the original decorations and interiors, including the bed in which Honest Abe slept. The house offers lots of special holiday tours.

Wisconsin Wagon Company

The Janesville-based **Wisconsin Wagon Company** (507 Laurel Ave., 608/754-0026, www.wisconsinwagon.com, tours by appointment, $5) makes replicas of wooden American Classic coaster wagons—an outstanding bit of Americana brought to life, since the original factory went out of production in 1934, and the Sears-Roebuck catalog was never the same.

GETTING THERE

Van Galder buses (608/752-5407) stop in Janesville en route to Madison and Chicago up to 10 times a day. The bus stops at 3120 North Pontiac Drive.

From Madison (via I-90, 42 miles), the drive to Janesville takes 50 minutes. From Beloit (via U.S. 51, 14 miles), it takes 24 minutes.

VICINITY OF JANESVILLE

Milton

At the junction of Highways 26 and 59 in tiny Milton is the **Milton House Museum** (608/868-7772, www.miltonhouse.org, 10am-4pm daily Memorial Day-Labor Day, 10am-4pm Tues.-Fri. Labor Day-Memorial Day, $8 adults), a 20-room hexagonal erstwhile stagecoach inn once used as part of the Underground Railroad—stone and earth tunnels still lie beneath it. It was purportedly the first building made from poured grout "concrete" in the United States. Also on the grounds are an 1837 log cabin, the terminus of the subterranean tunnel, and plenty of 19th-century artifacts.

Edgerton

In the fields surrounding Edgerton, you'd swear you were in North Carolina or Virginia by the odor of tobacco on the air. Edgerton is Wisconsin's "Tobacco City," and the **Tobacco Heritage Days** (608/347-4321, www.edgertontobaccoheritagedays.com) are held in mid-July. For a few years the festival dropped the *T* word due to concerns over political correctness, but now it's back to "tobacco." The tobacco-spitting contest, however, has been discontinued.

Lincoln-Tallman House

Beloit

Beloit lies along a wide expanse of the Rock River at its confluence at Turtle Creek. It is a lovely spot, explaining in part the migration of virtually the entire village of Colebrook, New Hampshire, to this town in 1837.

The city's founders erected the respected Beloit College, patterned after eastern religious seminaries, and a church before much of anything else, and landscaped the town around designs of a New England village with a square. It must have had a positive effect. In the rough-and-tumble 1840s, a traveler wrote of it as "an unusual community, amid shifting pioneer conditions already evincing character and solidity." Anthropologist Margaret Mead once called busy and vibrant Beloit "a microcosm of America."

SIGHTS

Beloit College

Founded on the Rock River's east bank as Beloit Seminary, **Beloit College** is the oldest college in Wisconsin. Its founding philosophy was to preserve eastern mores and culture in the heathen West—though it could pay its two professors only $600 a year "if they can raise it." The Middle College building, dating from 1847, is the oldest college building north of Chicago. Beloit College's Victorian Gothic **Logan Museum of Anthropology** (College St. and Bushnell St., 608/363-2677, www.beloit.edu/logan, 11am-4pm Tues.-Sun., free) is now one of the most respected museums in the state, with 250,000 artifacts from around the globe, including the most extensive Stone Age and Paleolithic collections outside Europe. There are those who believe, incidentally, that a certain Beloit College professor was the inspiration for Indiana Jones.

The **Wright Museum of Art** (Bushnell St. and Prospect St., 608/363-2677, www.beloit.edu/wright, 11am-4pm Tues.-Sat., closed during campus holidays, free) has permanent holdings, including American and European paintings and sculpture, Asian decorative arts, and graphics.

Hanchett-Bartlett Homestead

The limestone Greek Revival and Italianate mansion that is the **Hanchett-Bartlett Homestead** (2149 St. Lawrence Ave., 608/365-7835, 1pm-4pm Sat. June-Sept., donation $3 adults), built from locally quarried stone, sits on 15 acres and has been restored to period detail, with special attention to the original color schemes. A great limestone barn filled with farm implements sits on the property, along with a smokehouse nearby. A rural school has been relocated here, and the gray shed-planked **Beckman-Howe Mill** (608/365-1600), on the National Register of Historic Places and dating to the post-Civil War period, is a five-minute drive west on Highway H. The mill has been selected as one of the 10 most endangered historic sites in Wisconsin.

Side Trips

Tough-to-find little **Tiffany** lies northeast of Beloit on Highway S, but it's worth a search; it's got one of the most unusual **bridges** anywhere, a remnant five-arch iron truss span based on Roman architecture. Built by the Chicago and North Western Railway in 1869, the structure was modeled after a bridge in Compiegne, France. Each arch spans 50 feet with a 26-foot radius. To reach Tiffany, head east on Highway S from Shopiere and turn left onto Smith Road. You can really view the bridge only from the Smith Road iron truss bridge, built in 1890. Tiffany is a personal favorite, an anachronistic relic in the dewy midst of nowhere.

Back in **Shopiere,** check out the village's antique weight-driven timepiece adorned with four lion heads.

FOOD

Enjoy *huge* burgers and assorted "roadkill" at **Hanson's Bar & Grill** (615 E. Cranston Rd., 608/313-8797, from 11am daily, close time varies, $4-8) on the river along U.S. 51. It's also hands-down the best place to experience local flavor.

Domenico's (547 E. Grand Ave., 608/365-9489, 11am-11pm daily, $6-9) is the pizza joint of choice, with a good veggie pie. Also featured are Italian goodies such as chicken primavera, veal a'dominico, and lots of shrimp and seafood.

Equally traditional (as in, the chairs may be five decades old) and open for over seven decades is ★ **The Butterfly Club** (Hwy. K, east of town, 608/362-8577, 5pm-9:30pm Tues.-Sat., noon-8pm Sun., $9-23). Enjoy supper club dining on a patio and likely the best fish-fry around (Wed. and Fri.). You have to love getting fresh-baked cinnamon rolls with your meal. Live entertainment is featured on Friday and Saturday.

ACCOMMODATIONS

Given the proud architecture of Beloit, it's surprising that the city lacks a historic inn or B&B. A boutique hotel with dark, rough wood exteriors but chic bedding is the newish **Ironworks Hotel** (500 Pleasant St., 608/362-5500, www.irwonworkshotel.com, $209), right downtown. This attractive place has studio and one-bedroom suites with lots of extras. Many have opined it's worth the money.

INFORMATION

The **Beloit Visitor Center** (23 Eclipse Ctr., 608/365-4838, www.visitbeloit.com) is temporarily located at this address but has plans to relocate.

GETTING THERE

Van Galder buses (608/752-5407) stop in Beloit on the route between Madison and Chicago's O'Hare Airport and downtown Chicago. The 10 daily buses (each way) stop at the FasMart in South Beloit (15766 Manchester Rd.), at the junction of Highway 75 and U.S. 51.

Driving to Beloit from Janesville (via U.S. 51, 14 miles) takes 24 minutes. From Madison (via I-90, 50 miles), it takes 45 minutes. From Milwaukee (via I-43, 75 miles), it takes 75 minutes.

Ironworks Hotel

Lake Geneva and Environs

Of Wisconsin's three lakes regions, the southernmost playground is the gateway resort city of Lake Geneva, not to be confused with the lake itself, Geneva Lake.

Lake Geneva is visited by Windy City summertime refugees who'd prefer not to tackle the five-hour drive to the northern woods. About 60 percent of annual visitors call Chicago home. The Great Fire of 1871 cemented the city's status as a getaway when it became a retreat for Chicago's refugees. In the town and around the entire perimeter of the lake are eye-catching anachronistic residences, cautious development (a modicum of ersatz New England exists—it has been dubbed "Newport of the West"), a state park, and sites of historical interest.

Lake Geneva is one piece of the Geneva Lake area mosaic. Actually composed of four lakes—Delavan, Comus, Como, and Geneva—the area forms a rough triangle, with the city of Lake Geneva to the east, Delavan 10 miles to the west, and little Fontana to the south on the western cusp of Geneva Lake. Williams Bay is also included, along the northern perimeter of Geneva Lake. Lakeless little Elkhorn lies to the north, outside the immediate area.

★ GENEVA LAKE

With a surface area of 5,262 acres, 7.6 miles long by 2.1 miles wide, and a depth of 135 feet, Geneva Lake is one of the larger lakes in southern Wisconsin. Spring-fed, it was carved out by the Michigan glacier during the last glacial epoch. Today one can't help but love its loopy mix of restored Victorian and low-key resort structures, natural splendor, and, most of all, its accessibility to the public.

The coolest activity in southern Wisconsin? Lake Geneva residents still get their mail delivered by boat, just as in the 1930s. Visitors can also hop on the mail boat, the ***Walworth II*** (Riviera Docks, 262/248-6206 or 800/558-5911, www.cruiselakegeneva.com, $33 adults), in operation for more than 100 years, seven days a week in summer, albeit at a price.

Busy types with itchy feet absolutely insist the most fun is a 26-mile-long **footpath** that circles the lake via linked ancient Native American trails. It is truly remarkable, given that it has been a tourist haven for a century; the law actually requires its preservation. You can reach it at any park along the lakefront. Along the way, the path passes those same gargantuan palatial summer homes, a state park, and loads of natural beauty. The biggest draw is **Yerkes Observatory** (373 W. Geneva St., Williams Bay), which has the world's largest refractor telescope. The observatory, now obsolete, though lovely from the outside,

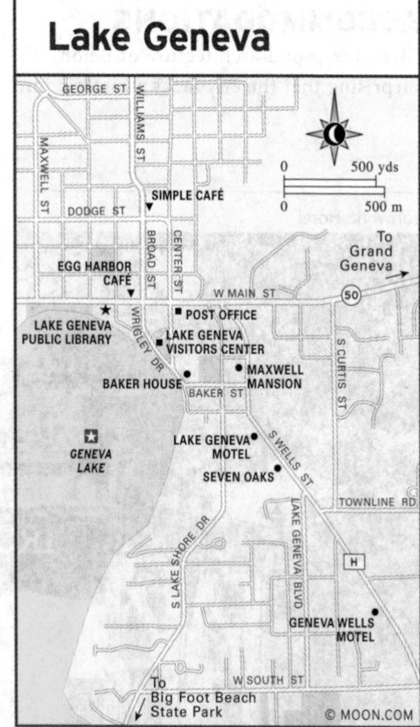

has been shopped around by its owner, the University of Chicago. One plan included—gulp—building a luxury resort around it, but that was quashed due to public outcry. No public tours are offered, but it's lovely to see in person from the outside.

Black Point Estate (262/248-1888, www.blackpointestate.com) has been called by one state historian the most perfect example of a summer mansion in the state. It underwent $1.2 million in renovations for all to enjoy. In order to see it, you have to arrive the way residents always did: by boat (10:30 daily May-Nov., also 12:30pm in peak periods, $39 pp, including tour). You'll need to climb about 100 stairs to scale the bluff.

The easiest and thus most popular way to experience the lake is on a tour in either a replica Mississippi paddle wheeler or lake steamer from **Geneva Lake Cruise Lines** (Riviera Docks, 262/248-6206 or 800/558-5911, www.cruiselakegeneva.com, $32-70 adults). Tours leave six times daily mid-June-early September, less frequently off-season. Full tours range from one hour up to just under three hours and include lunch, dinner, and Sunday brunch cruises. In peak summer season, boats seem to depart constantly. Other boats in the cruise line include genuine lake steamers, including one still using a steam engine from the early 1900s, the only large steamboat left in Wisconsin.

SIGHTS

For a great freebie, check out the **Lake Geneva Public Library** (918 W. Main St., 262/249-5299, 9am-8pm Mon.-Thurs., 9am-6pm Fri., 9am-1pm Sat.), which has comfy chairs and a four-star view of the lake. You can also peruse detailed county guidebooks on historical structures and local history. Beyond that, head immediately for **Big Foot Beach State Park** (262/248-2528, $10), where you'll find sublimely cool waters for dipping.

RECREATION

Boating

The Geneva Lake region has more marinas than you can imagine, including **Gordy's** (320 Lake Ave., 262/275-2163, www.gordysboats.com) in Fontana, with ski boats, ski schools, sailboats, and cruises.

Golf

The list of golf courses is the size of a small phone book. Noteworthy is **Geneva National** (1221 Geneva National Ave. S., 262/245-7010, www.genevanationalresort.com), four miles west of Lake Geneva town on Highway 50. Rated in the state's top 10 by *Golf Digest*, it's got championship courses designed by Arnold Palmer and Lee Trevino. Greens fees are high.

FOOD

Cafés

You'll want to visit the **Simple Cafe** (525 Broad St., 262/248-3556, breakfast and lunch daily, $6-14), though it's only open for breakfast and lunch. All ingredients are sourced locally, if possible. I will always ask for the Korean barbecue breakfast bowl. Alternately, the **Egg Harbor Cafe** (827 W. Main St., 262/248-1207, breakfast and lunch daily, $6-12) has similar hours and amazing food done with a conscience.

Fine Dining

If you're staying in the Grand Geneva Resort, there are a couple of the state's best-regarded restaurants, including the **Geneva Chophouse** (262/249-4788, 5:30pm-10pm daily, steaks from $32). Another restaurant of note is the **Grandview** (2009 S. Lake Shore Dr., 262/248-5680, open daily for breakfast/lunch/dinner, closed Mon. and Tues. during winter, from $9), which has a beautiful lakeside patio and is located at the Geneva Inn.

But you needn't head to a resort; in this town, if you throw a stick, you hit a bistro. At the handful in town, the food is great, but the service tends toward mediocre.

Steak Houses and Supper Clubs

An institution on the lake is the tavern

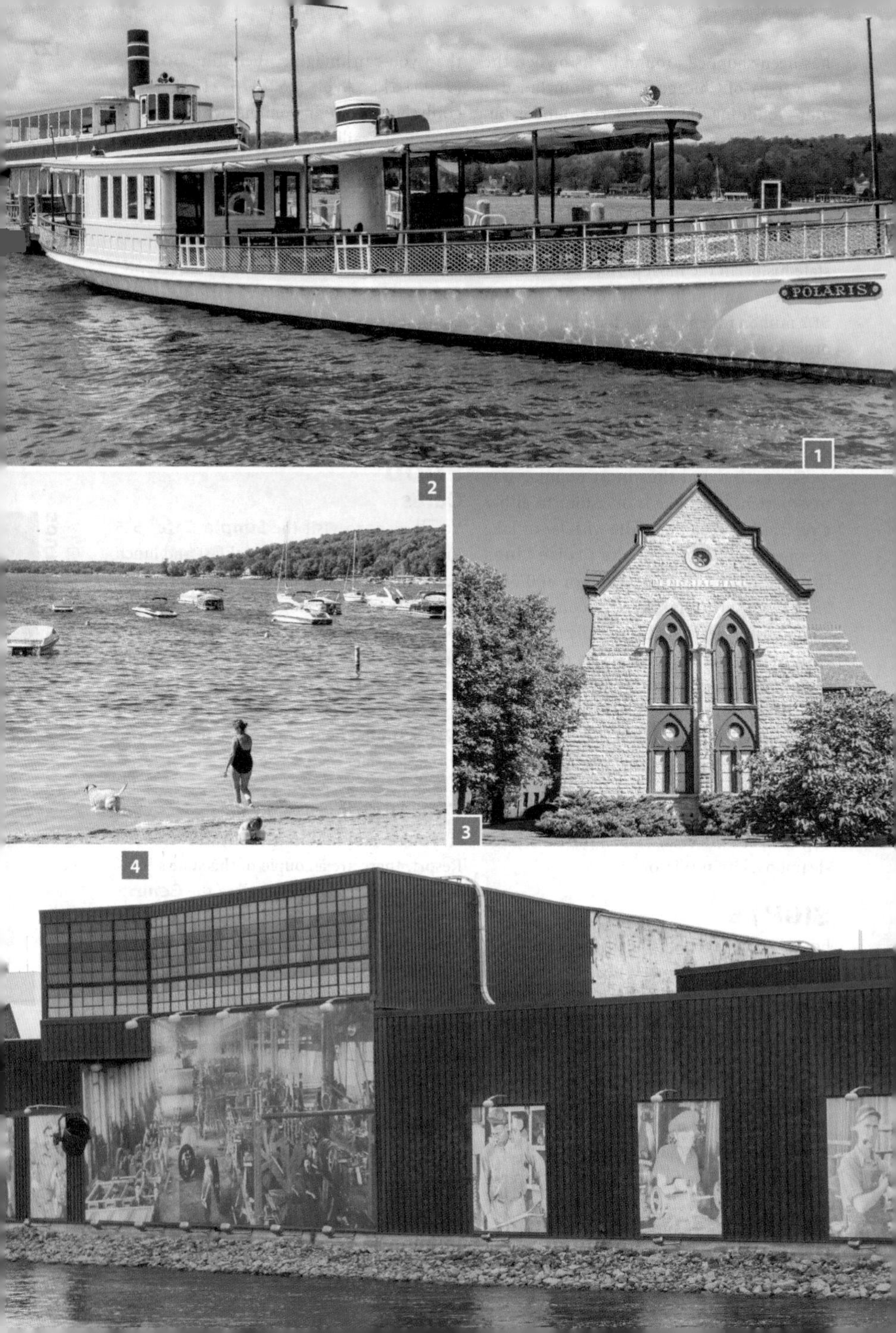
POLARIS
1
2
3
4

downstairs at **Chuck's** (352 Lake St., 262/275-3222, lunch and dinner daily, breakfast Sat.-Sun., from $7) on Lake Street in Fontana. The "seven-mile view" is legendary.

Worth a side trip just for the ambience is **Fitzgerald's Genoa Junction Restaurant** (727 Main St., 262/279-5200, 5pm-8:30pm Wed.-Thurs., 5pm-9pm Fri.-Sat., 3pm-8pm Sun., reduced hours in winter, $15) in Genoa City, approximately 10 minutes southeast of Lake Geneva. Housed in a historic octagon house, the supper club is famed for fish boils made with cod rather than whitefish, so the bone quotient is far lower. Otherwise, its barbecue ribs and chicken are renowned.

ACCOMMODATIONS

Dozens of motels, hotels, inns, bed-and-breakfasts, and resorts line Geneva Lake and fill downtown Lake Geneva town as well as the small communities surrounding the lake—you definitely need to call ahead for summer weekends.

$50-100

The only rooms that you *might* find under $100 are at the **Lake Geneva Motel** (524 S. Wells St., 262/248-3464, http://genevalakemotel.com, $99-149).

$100-150

Renovated from the inside out, the **Geneva Wells Motel** (1060 Wells St., 262/248-1809, http://genevawells.com, $109-150) has very helpful owners in addition to excellent rooms. The weekday rates are quite good.

Over $150

The **French Country Inn** (Hwy. 50 W., 262/374-5999, www.frenchcountryinn.com, $185-290) was partially constructed in Denmark and shipped stateside more than a century ago to serve as the Danish pavilion in the 1893 World's Fair; the house later did time as a Chicago rumrunner's joint during Prohibition. All rooms have TV and air-conditioning; some have fireplaces. Some have opined the rooms have become a bit worn, but I haven't seen it.

The **Maxwell Mansion** (421 Baker St., 262/248-9711, www.maxwellmansion1856.com, from $200) is an 1856 stable, dubbed an "urban barn," that offers an incredible feeling of history and luxury. It is actually paired with the ultimate of luxury downtown at **Baker House** (327 Wrigley Dr., 262/248-4700, www.bakerhouse1885.com, from $355), an equally historic B&B with amazing brunch and cuisine.

The multiple-diamond, multiple-starred ★ **Grand Geneva** (U.S. 12 and Hwy. 50, 262/248-8811 or 800/558-3417, www.grandgeneva.com, from $349) is worth every penny if the media is to be believed. A three-story lodge with more than 300 rooms, its amenities include indoor tennis, a 36-hole golf course, a driving range, boat and ski rentals on-site (a downhill ski mountain is adjacent), bicycles, skeet shooting, a recreation room, indoor exercise facilities, massage therapists, weights, whirlpools, a sauna, and a steam room. Its private landholdings include almost 1,500 acres of diverse meadow and forest, along with its own lake.

Many insist that the best of all isn't even a resort. At ★ **Seven Oaks** (682 Wells St., 262/248-4006, www.sevenoakslakegeneva.com, $269), there is a cottage layout with boutique hotel interiors, and guests universally adore this place as much for the caring, welcoming owners. It's a genuine retreat; many reports have used "amazing experience."

Camping

Just outside Lake Geneva, south along Highway 120, **Big Foot Beach State Park** (262/248-2528) features great swimming and picnicking. The short trails make for easy strolls and great cross-country skiing. It has too many campsites, however, for a 270-acre park. **Reservations** (888/947-2757, http://wisconsin.goingtocamp.com, reservation fee

1: boat on Geneva Lake **2:** Geneva Lake **3:** Logan Museum of Anthropology **4:** Beloit's downtown waterfront

$8) are available for sites (from $23 nonresidents, plus $11 per vehicle).

INFORMATION

The **Lake Geneva Chamber of Commerce** (201 Wrigley Dr., 262/248-4416 or 800/345-1020, www.visitlakegeneva.com) is well versed in helping tourists out.

VICINITY OF LAKE GENEVA

Elkhorn

This trim village on U.S. 12 northwest of Lake Geneva lies splayed around a somnolent tree-shaded square. It's sometimes called "Christmas Card Town"—and you'll know why if you show up anytime around Christmas. It's the kind of place where local businesses list their home phone numbers as well as their business phones. The oldest municipal band in the state, established in the 1840s, still plays on summer Friday evenings at Sunset Park. This seems singularly appropriate, because five primary industries of the town are related to the manufacture of musical instruments.

One rumor running rampant around Elkhorn concerns the existence of a large-eared, werewolf-type beast said to prowl the surrounding forests. During the last century, many sightings were reported; the local humane officer once even had a file labeled "Werewolf."

While in Elkhorn, don't miss **Watson's Wild West Museum** (signed off U.S. 12/67, 262/723-7505, www.watsonswildwest.weebly.com, 10am-5pm Mon.-Sat., 1pm-5pm Sun. May-Oct., $5 adults). This is the lifelong labor of love of the proprietor, who's got a serious Western obsession. Over 35 years his collection has grown to museum-worthy proportions. Branding irons seem to be a specialty, but there are also thousands of assorted knickknacks. The owner may even show up dressed like Wyatt Earp. Call first, since they might have a bus tour taking over the place. Admission includes a Wild West show.

Delavan

Delavan's two lakes are great reasons to visit—there is excellent fishing on Delavan Lake—but for nonfishers, Delavan is also home to a bit of clown history. For about 50 years in the 19th century, Delavan was the headquarters for most of the country's traveling circuses, including the prototype of P. T. Barnum's. Local cemeteries at the end of 7th Street are full of circus performers and workers dating from this time; **Tower Park** is chock-full of colorful circus memorials and statuary.

Visitors can wander about trails at the **arboretum** north of town along the shores of Lake Comus. Delavan Lake was once one of the most polluted in Wisconsin, heavily laden with phosphorous runoff; an aggressive rehabilitation campaign has turned it into one of the region's cleaner lakes, leading to the establishment of the **Turtle Valley Wildlife Area** just north of town. Restored from fallow farmland, these 18,000 acres are a good example of Wisconsin's aggressive wetlands restoration programs. Hike through dark peat and mint.

Door County

Hold your left hand up for a moment, palm out.

The thumb is, as the Depression-era WPA Wisconsin guidebook put it, "the spout...of the Wisconsin teakettle." That's the Door Peninsula. Today, Door County is being called the "Cape Cod of the Midwest," the "California of the North," and other silly likenings. Comparisons to Yankee seaside villages don't wholly miss the mark, although in spots the area seems just as much like chilled, stony Norwegian fjords.

Bays in all the colors of an artist's palette are surrounded by variegated shoreline: 250 miles (more than any other U.S. county) of alternately rocky beaches, craggy bluffs, blossom-choked orchards, bucolic heath, and meadows. Door County's established parkland acreage (state, county, and municipal) is staggering, considering its size.

Highlights

Look for ★ to find recommended sights, activities, dining, and lodging.

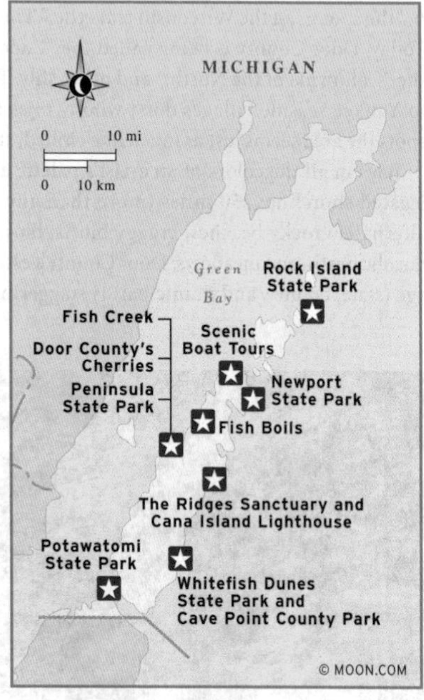

★ **Potawatomi State Park:** Hike the first miles of Wisconsin's epic 1,200-mile Ice Age Trail and overlook the historic waterways of the Door—all from a high perch atop the Niagara Escarpment (page 143).

★ **Whitefish Dunes State Park and Cave Point County Park:** Splendid dunes and critical habitat here were formed by the rough wave action. Hike to the beach and check out the dunes and wildlife and then visit Cave Point's eponymous caves (page 147).

★ **The Ridges Sanctuary and Cana Island Lighthouse:** This beloved sanctuary is a must for birders and wildlife lovers. It also leads to the grand, brilliantly white Cana Island Lighthouse (page 154).

★ **Scenic Boat Tours:** Take a scenic boat tour of Door County's incredible coastline in Fish Creek and Gills Rock (page 154).

★ **Newport State Park:** Find preserved wilderness in one of the Midwest's most traveled vacation destinations. Outdoor aficionados make pilgrimages for the pack-in campsites and off-road biking (page 157).

★ **Fish Creek:** Experience the "soul of Door County" by strolling through the village's historic buildings, taking a tour of a local winery, or seeing a play at the Northern Sky Theater (page 160).

★ **Door County's Cherries:** Whether you pick your own or taste them in a slice of warm pie, Door County's cherries are not to be missed, but the blooming season offers unrivaled beauty (page 140).

★ **Peninsula State Park:** Bike the Sunset Trail or kayak to Horseshoe Island in this picturesque park, which has visitor numbers rivaling Yellowstone (page 164).

★ **Fish Boils:** You haven't experienced Door County until you've attended a fish boil, preferably on a chilly fall evening (page 171).

★ **Rock Island State Park:** This unparalleled getaway spot is as far as you can get from anywhere else in Door County. The beachside campsites make this park one of the best escapes in the state (page 180).

Door County

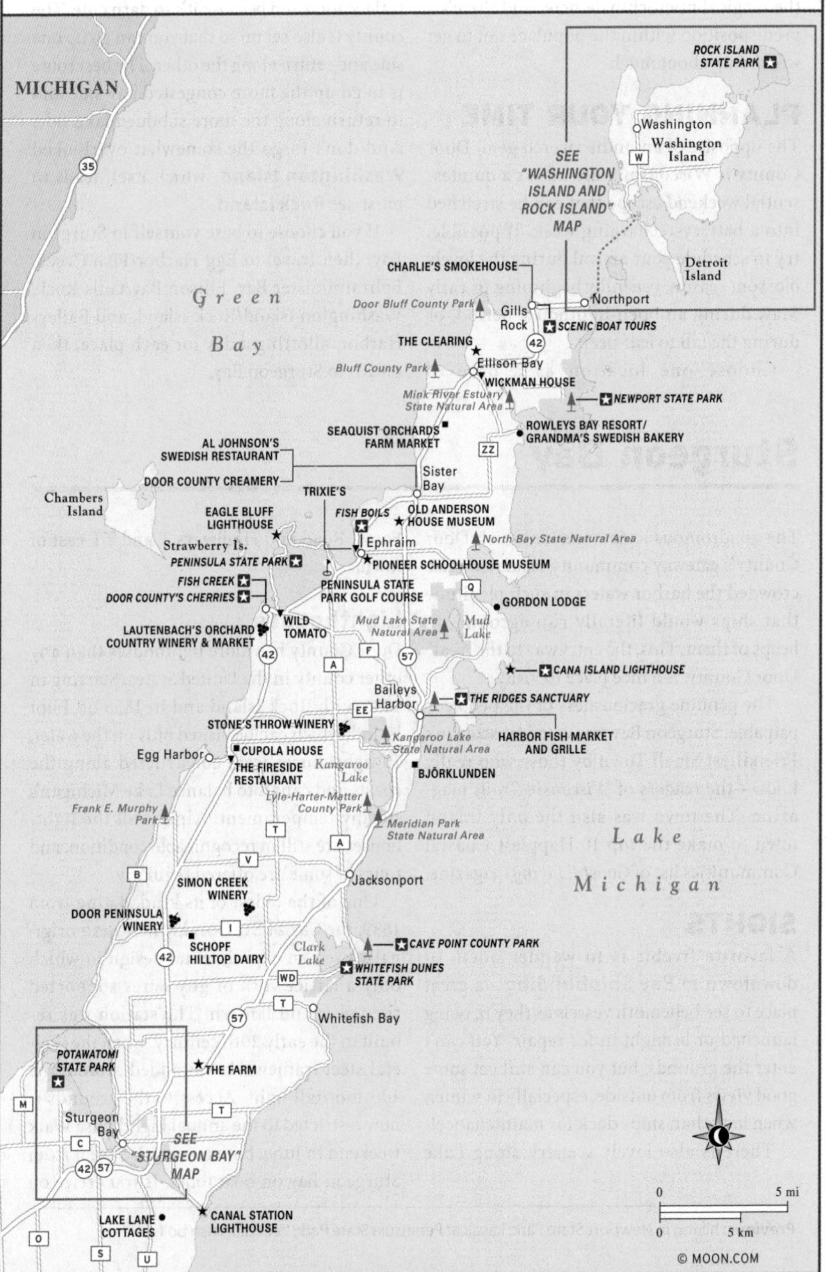

MICHIGAN
Green Bay
Lake Michigan
ROCK ISLAND STATE PARK
Washington
Washington Island
SEE "WASHINGTON ISLAND AND ROCK ISLAND" MAP
Detroit Island
Northport
CHARLIE'S SMOKEHOUSE
Door Bluff County Park
Gills Rock
SCENIC BOAT TOURS
THE CLEARING
Ellison Bay
Bluff County Park
WICKMAN HOUSE
Mink River Estuary State Natural Area
NEWPORT STATE PARK
SEAQUIST ORCHARDS FARM MARKET
ROWLEYS BAY RESORT/ GRANDMA'S SWEDISH BAKERY
AL JOHNSON'S SWEDISH RESTAURANT
DOOR COUNTY CREAMERY
Sister Bay
Chambers Island
TRIXIE'S
EAGLE BLUFF LIGHTHOUSE
FISH BOILS
OLD ANDERSON HOUSE MUSEUM
North Bay State Natural Area
Strawberry Is.
Ephraim
PENINSULA STATE PARK
PIONEER SCHOOLHOUSE MUSEUM
FISH CREEK
DOOR COUNTY'S CHERRIES
PENINSULA STATE PARK GOLF COURSE
GORDON LODGE
LAUTENBACH'S ORCHARD COUNTRY WINERY & MARKET
WILD TOMATO
Mud Lake State Natural Area
Mud Lake
CANA ISLAND LIGHTHOUSE
Baileys Harbor
THE RIDGES SANCTUARY
STONE'S THROW WINERY
HARBOR FISH MARKET AND GRILLE
Kangaroo Lake State Natural Area
Egg Harbor
CUPOLA HOUSE
THE FIRESIDE RESTAURANT
Kangaroo Lake
BJÖRKLUNDEN
Frank E. Murphy Park
Lyle-Harter-Matter County Park
Meridian Park State Natural Area
Jacksonport
SIMON CREEK WINERY
DOOR PENINSULA WINERY
SCHOPF HILLTOP DAIRY
Clark Lake
CAVE POINT COUNTY PARK
WHITEFISH DUNES STATE PARK
Whitefish Bay
POTAWATOMI STATE PARK
THE FARM
Sturgeon Bay
SEE "STURGEON BAY" MAP
LAKE LANE COTTAGES
CANAL STATION LIGHTHOUSE
35
42
57
W
ZZ
Q
F
A
EE
T
V
B
I
WD
M
C
O
S
U
0
5 mi
0
5 km
© MOON.COM

Generation upon generation of shipbuilders, fishers, and farmers have benefited from the magical microclimate here, and there's a predisposition within the populace not to get worked up about much.

PLANNING YOUR TIME

The opposite of an undiscovered gem, Door County *is* Wisconsin tourism. It's a quintessential weekend escape that can be stretched into a battery-recharging week. If possible, try to schedule your arrival during the lovely blossom season, *generally* beginning in early May, during an open-lighthouse period, or during the fall to leaf-peep.

Choose one location as a base of operations—**Sturgeon Bay,** for less driving time when leaving, or **Fish Creek,** for its central location and because it's so darn cute. The county is also set up so that you can go up one side and return along the other. The best route is to go up the more congested bay side and to return along the more subdued lake side. And don't forgo the somewhat overlooked **Washington Island,** which itself leads to must-see **Rock Island.**

If you choose to base yourself in Sturgeon Bay, then travel to Egg Harbor/Fish Creek, Ephraim/Sister Bay, Ellison Bay/Gills Rock, Washington Island/Rock Island, and Baileys Harbor, allotting a day for each place, then return to Sturgeon Bay.

Sturgeon Bay

The anadromous leviathans for which Door County's gateway community is named once crowded the harbor waters in such plenitude that ships would literally run aground on heaps of them. This, the entryway to the "real" Door County, is a nice place to visit.

The genuine graciousness of the people is palpable. Sturgeon Bay was voted Wisconsin's Friendliest Small Town by those who really know—the readers of *Wisconsin Trails* magazine. The town was also the only inland town to make the top 10 Happiest Coastal Communities list of *Coastal Living* magazine.

SIGHTS

A favorite freebie is to wander north of downtown to **Bay Shipbuilding**—a great place to see behemoth vessels as they're being launched or brought in for repair. You can't enter the grounds, but you can still get some good views from outside, especially in winter, when leviathan ships dock for maintenance!

There is also lovely scenery along Lake Forest Road and Highways T and TT east of town.

Lighthouses

Door County has more lighthouses than any other county in the United States. Starting in 1836 with Rock Island and in 1858 on Pilot Island, which can be visited only on the water, 10 lighthouses were constructed along the coasts and canals to balance Lake Michigan's stormy temperament. Almost all the lighthouses are still in recognizable condition, and tours of some are offered regularly.

One of the oldest of its kind, dating from 1899, the **Canal Station Lighthouse** originally used an experimental design in which only a latticework of guy wires supported the tower and lantern. The station was rebuilt in the early 20th century, when the skeletal steel framework was added around the 100-foot-tall light. Access to the grounds is now restricted to the annual Lighthouse Walk weekend in June, but you can also see it from Sturgeon Bay on boat tours. If you arrive on

Previous: hiking in Newport State Park; kayak at Peninsula State Park; Pelletier's fish boil

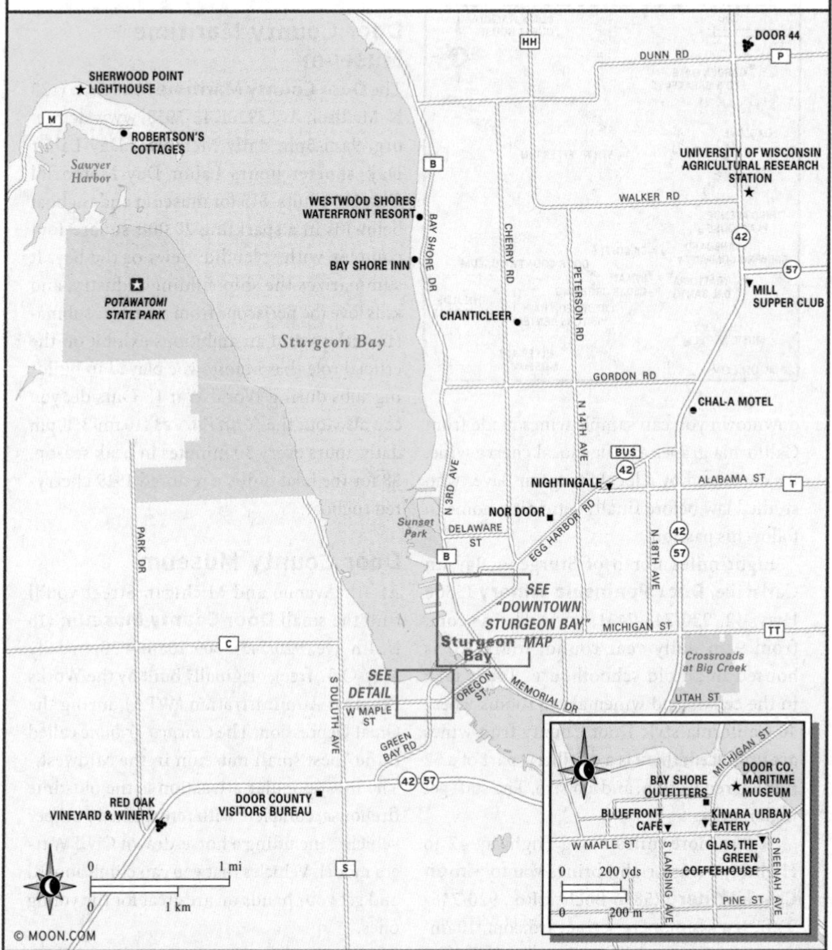

wheels, the north breakwater is accessible, but the views aren't great.

Access to the nearby **Sherwood Point Lighthouse** is similarly restricted.

Wineries

Given the county's proclivity for fruit production, perhaps it's not surprising that wineries have sprouted up around the region. Just northeast of town, **Door 44** (4020 Hwy. 42/57, 888/932-0044, 10am-6pm daily May-Oct., shorter hours Nov.-Apr.) is a large operation featuring many grapes from the Green Bay region and virtually all from the Midwest. It's so successful (and popular) that they've created a new winery near the same location. Go for the Bubbler sparkling!

Red Oak Vineyard & Winery (3017 Enterprise Rd., 920/743-7729, www.redoakvineyard.com,10:30am-5:30pm Sun.-Thurs., 9:30am-6pm Fri.-Sat., tasting $6) has no official tours, but at the tasting room

Downtown Sturgeon Bay

downtown you can sample wines made from California grapes and one local cherry wine. It's co-owned by a local Sturgeon Bayer who studied law before finally returning home to follow his passion.

Eight miles north of Sturgeon Bay, in Carlsville, **Door Peninsula Winery** (5806 Hwy. 42, 920/743-7431, www.dcwine.com, from 9am daily year-round, tours $3) is housed in an old schoolhouse. Tours take in the cellars and winemaking rooms where 40 California-style Door County fruit wines are produced; there is a distillery, part of a $2 million renovation, and a bistro. The staff get high marks.

A few more miles along Highway 42 to Highway I (turn right) brings you to **Simon Creek Winery** (5896 Bochek Rd., 920/746-9307, www.simoncreekvineyard.com, 10am-6pm Mon.-Sat. mid-May-late Oct., shorter hours Nov.-mid-May, free tours at 2pm), the county's largest winery. There's an added bonus of live music on Sunday afternoon. Try the Untouchable red or American gewürztraminer.

Since you're on Highway I, you can't help but notice the enormous Holstein at nearby **Schopf's Hilltop Dairy** (920/743-9779, http://dairyview.com, 10am-6pm daily, free tours), with a viewing area where you can watch them milk the cows. You can even milk Cookie the cow yourself. Schopf's is well reviewed by people with children.

Door County Maritime Museum

The **Door County Maritime Museum** (120 N. Madison Ave., 920/743-5958, www.dcmm.org, 9am-5pm daily Memorial Day-Labor Day, shorter hours Labor Day-Memorial Day, $10 adults, $15 for museum and tugboat below) is in a sparkling 20,000-square-foot complex with splendid views of the bay. It summarizes the shipbuilding industry, and kids love the periscope from a nuclear submarine; it's part of an ambitious exhibit on the crucial role that Manitowoc played in building subs during World War II. Outside, you can also tour the ***John Purves*** (10am-3:30pm daily, tours every 30 minutes in peak season, $8 for the boat only), a restored 1919 cherry-red tugboat.

Door County Museum

At 4th Avenue and Michigan Street you'll find the small **Door County Museum** (18 N. 4th Ave., 920/743-5809, 10am-4:30pm daily May-Oct., free), originally built by the Works Progress Administration (WPA) during the Great Depression. The *Chicago Tribune* called it the "best small museum in the Midwest." The most popular attraction is the old-time firehouse, complete with refurbished pumper vehicles, including a horse-drawn Civil War-era model. Vehicles that you can climb aboard and get your hands on are great for the young ones.

Miller Art Museum

The **Miller Art Museum** (107 S. 4th Ave., 920/746-0707, www.millerartmuseum.org, 10am-8pm Mon., 10am-5pm Tues.-Sat., free) is a fine art gallery in the Sturgeon Bay library. The top floor houses the permanent collection, with an emphasis on 20th-century Wisconsin artists. One room houses works of its namesake Gerhard Miller (1903-2003), the most famous Door County artist; he continued to paint until he was nearly 100.

Door County Driving Distances

TO THE DOOR

- Chicago–Sturgeon Bay: 231 miles (4.5 hours)
- Milwaukee–Sturgeon Bay: 145 miles (2.75 hours)
- Madison–Sturgeon Bay: 184 miles (3.75 hours)

WITHIN THE DOOR (LAKESIDE)

- Sturgeon Bay–Jacksonport: 15.4 miles
- Jacksonport–Baileys Harbor: 7 miles
- Baileys Harbor–Rowleys Bay: 15.5 miles
- Rowleys Bay–Gills Rock: 7.5 miles

WITHIN THE DOOR (BAYSIDE)

- Sturgeon Bay–Egg Harbor: 19 miles
- Egg Harbor–Fish Creek: 6 miles
- Fish Creek–Ephraim: 5 miles
- Ephraim–Sister Bay: 4.3 miles
- Sister Bay–Ellison Bay: 5.6 miles
- Ellison Bay–Gills Rock: 3.9 miles

The Farm

The Farm (N. Hwy. 57, 920/743-6666, www.thefarmindoorcounty.com, 9am-5pm daily Memorial Day-mid-Oct., $8.50 adults) bills itself as a living museum of rural America, and it lives up to that. Various old-style dwellings and structures dot 40 acres of an original homestead, and pioneer implements line the walls. The primary draw for families is the menagerie of farm animals—you can never get tired of milking a goat, can you? There are also nature trails and informative displays about the diverse ecology of the peninsula.

TOURS

A few resorts and lodges offer boat tours from their marinas; **Door County Fireboat Cruises** (120 N. Madison Ave., 920/495-6454, www.ridethefireboat.com, $25 adults) depart from the Maritime Museum and use a retired Chicago fireboat to chug along for two-hour cruises (10:30am and 12:30pm daily Memorial Day-Labor Day). The 10:30am tour travels through the Sturgeon Bay Ship Canal to Lake Michigan, while the 12:30pm tour travels out into Sturgeon Bay to Sherwood Point and past its lighthouse. In July-August these trips are on unless the wind is howling; in fact, these itineraries may even be reversed depending on weather. In May-June and September-October, call ahead to confirm.

RECREATION

Shore Fishing

The protected coves and harbors of the bay have made Sturgeon Bay one of the premier places in the Midwest for smallmouth bass fishing. In fact, BASS, a bass angling society, named Sturgeon Bay all the way north to Fish Creek as the top bass spot in the country. You

PURVES
CHICAGO FIRE BOAT
FRED A. BUSSE
1
2
MOTEL
ENTRANCE
3
4
No Vacancy

also have a good chance of catching the king of Wisconsin's fish, the walleye, along with northern pike, perch, and even a misplaced muskie or two.

Contact the **Wisconsin Department of Natural Resources** (DNR, 888/936-7463, http://dnr.wi.gov) for information on regulations and obtaining a license.

Charter Fishing

Sturgeon Bay's sportfishing charter fleet ranks high in the state in terms of the total salmon take, but that's in numbers only. When you consider the small population, the Door Peninsula is much more prolific. Around here, lunkers prevail. The Wisconsin DNR says Sturgeon Bay charters catch more fish per trip than any other north of Milwaukee, and a record 44.92-pound chinook salmon was landed by a 16-year-old off Sturgeon Bay near the legendary fishing spot called the Bank (as in bank reef); however, Algoma won't let you forget that it was from an Algoma charter boat.

Biking

Pick a direction, and you'll find grand bike touring. Head up the lakeside in the morning, starting from the Coast Guard Lighthouse (note that there can be lots of traffic on Highway T), and then head back along the bay in the afternoon. The **Ahnapee State Trail,** best suited for mountain bikes, although road bikes can handle it, starts just south of Sturgeon Bay and runs to Algoma. For off-road riding, head to Potawatomi State Park south of town.

Rentals

Outdoor recreation equipment that doesn't have an engine can be rented from several outfitters. Off the water and on wheels or skis, **Nor Door** (60 S. Madison Ave., 920/818-0803, bicycles average $25 per day) rents by the hour or day. On the water, **Bay Shore Outfitters** (59 N. Madison Ave., 920/818-0431, www.kayakdoorcounty.com) is downtown opposite the Maritime Museum and has kayak rentals (from $60 per day) as well as guided tours.

Boats, canoes, and other outdoor gear can be rented from **Door County Boat Rental** (920/746-6071, http://doorcountyboatrentals.com), with several locations in Sturgeon Bay—the most convenient at the **Maritime Museum** (120 N. Madison Ave.). Potawatomi State Park also has rentals, including kayaks. Rates run about $85 per hour for a WaveRunner.

ENTERTAINMENT

Sturgeon Bay is not a happening place when the sun goes down, but there are options. The **Third Avenue Playhouse** (239 N. 3rd Ave., 920/743-1760, www.thirdavenueplayhouse.com) has a year-round slate of theatrical and musical performances in a renovated movie house.

One consistently good place to catch live music is **GLAS, the Green Coffeehouse** (67 E. Maple St., 920/743-5575), with regular live music during the day that's not on a set schedule. In addition to good coffee and a lovely view of Sturgeon Bay's waters, there are food items available as well. The name, by the way, is Gaelic for "green"—they get asked a lot.

FOOD

For an old-school supper club, travelers adore **Nightingale** (1541 Egg Harbor Rd., 920/743-5593, dinner Mon.-Sat., $8-25), with an old-school interior and top-notch prime rib. **Donny's** (920/746-9460, 4-9pm daily) in the Glidden Lodge below is perhaps the most adored traditional local eatery.

Beer aficionados will love **Starboard Brewing Company** (151 N. 3rd Ave., 920/818-1062, 5-9pm Wed.-Thurs., noon-9pm Fri.-Sat., noon-6pm Sun., $9-25), a self-dubbed (and appropriate) "nano" brewery—specializing in quality, not quantity. Find Wisconsin cheeses and salmon along with board games and bumper pool.

Stop for java at **Kick Coffee** (148 N.

1: Door County Fireboat Cruises **2:** strolling the lift bridge in Sturgeon Bay **3:** Holiday Music Motel, a budget boutique venue with live music **4:** Reynolds House B&B

TOP EXPERIENCE

Cherry on Top

The cherry trees blossom in May and harvest season runs from mid-July to early August. The loveliness of endless blossoms is a sight to behold, but the *fragrance* of the place is equally astonishing—a living air freshener. Getting a photo of the blossoms and/or strolling through an orchard to pick your own cherries is *the* top Door County experience.

CHERRY BLOSSOMS (MID-MAY)

The bay side blooms first; the lake side follows a bit later. Here's a tip: the blossoms open south to north, so you can have a two- to three-week window to see cherry blossoms. Check online (www.doorcounty.com) for a blossom report and up-to-the-minute details on what is blooming and where.

The whole peninsula gets in on the act with special celebrations! They may not specifically *say* cherry festivals, but everyone knows that's why they're happening at the time. A good one to time your trip with is the **Door County Festival of Nature** in mid- to late-May.

A good way to see the best of the blossoms is with **guided tours**—via hiking, biking, or kayaking—through many natural areas, some of which aren't open to the public. They are organized out of The Ridges Sanctuary (920/839-2802, www.ridgessanctuary.org) near Baileys Harbor, and for most outings preregistration is a must as they're so popular.

HARVEST (LATE JULY - AUGUST)

The pick of the pick-your-own cherries during harvest season are south of Fish Creek at **Lautenbach's Orchard Country Winery & Market,** among the oldest and largest operations in Door County. Its summer harvest (read: cherry) **festival** in late July is a hoot, with complimentary food and beverages, horse-drawn wagon rides, and their famous cherry pit spitting contest. In early August is a lovely cherry festival in **Jacksonport.** Here you'll find features ethnic cuisine such as *kolaches* (a Central European fruit pastry) done up with cherries; true Wisconsin style are the cherry bratwurst. Lots of kid-centric events are here, as well.

Here are some south-to-north highlights to see blossoms and/or cherries (depending on the season). Everywhere you see cherries, you will find a business offering pick-your-own cherries and a jaw-dropping variety of cherry goods.

- South of Sturgeon Bay and north of Forestville when WI 42 crosses the aptly named **Cherry Lane** you'll find lovely orchards surrounding you.
- Leaving Sturgeon Bay headed north, ignore the crowds on WI 42 and follow **Highway HH** (north off 8th St.)—which is also listed as "Cherry Road" on some maps—to pass more fields of cherry orchards.
- Hop back on WI 42 to just south of Fish Creek for the next stop—**Lautenbach's Orchard Country Winery & Market,** a cornerstone of cherries in Door County. This is like the Disney of cherries, meant in the best way possible.
- North of Sister Bay along WI 42 is another amazingly large—over 1,000 acres—operation run by the fifth generation of farmers: **Seaquist Orchards Farm Market.** You can explore lovely little side roads surrounding the farm to take in all of the cherry trees.

YEAR-ROUND

Visiting outside of cherry season? Don't fret! Here are some ways to enjoy Wisconsin cherries....

- Try the cherry-stuffed french toast at Fish Creek's **White Gull Inn.** It was good enough to take first place in *Good Morning America*'s quest for the best breakfast in America.
- Buy a cherry pie, jam, or one of many other cherry souvenirs at **White Cottage Red Door** in Fish Creek or at **Seaquist Orchards** in Sister Bay.
- Sample a local cherry wine at **Red Oak Vineyard & Winery** in Sturgeon Bay.

3rd Ave., 920/746-1122, 7am-5pm Mon.-Sat, 7:30am-4pm Sun.), serving coffee by Milwaukee's Colectivo Roasters. You'll also find healthful foods, such as the walnut burger. It's tiny enough to have standing room only if you bring a family (there's a small garden out back in summer), but it's cozy and friendly.

Great coffee but even better burritos—for breakfast or late lunch—are at **5th & Jefferson** (232 N. 5th Ave., 920/746-1719, 7:30am-3pm daily, from $6), where the pulled pork is sublime and served with a smile.

Traditionalist (as in hash browns and eggs)? **Morning Glory** (7502 Hwy. 42, 920/743-5555, breakfast/lunch daily, from $7), south of town, has you covered. Ignore the gas station and low-rent diner exteriors, this place does good food—go for the chive wedges!

Another delicious food-on-the-fly option is the Indian cuisine at **Kinara Urban Eatery** (25 N. Madison Ave., 920/743-8772, lunch Mon.-Sat., from $6), inside a, yes, gas station. The owners are wondrous, and you can't beat the lamb!

West of the ship canal, ★ **Bluefront Café** (86 W. Maple St., 920/743-9218, lunch Tues.-Sun., $8-18) is a casually chic and energetic place that defines eclectic. It is Sturgeon Bay's eatery of choice when you need something cheery and fresh and often recommended by locals. You'll find locally caught panfried walleye next to a Vietnamese banh mi; try the fish tacos.

Solid northern Italian cuisine in a cozy but contemporary setting is right downtown at **Trattoria dal Santo** (117 N. 3rd Ave., 920/743-6100, http://dalsantosrestaurant.com, 5pm-9pm daily, $17-25). This wonderful place has been honing its cuisine for nearly two decades, and they've never overlooked anything in terms of atmosphere; the wine bar is also nice.

An epicurean mainstay is the **Inn at Cedar Crossing** (3rd Ave. and Louisiana St., 920/743-4200, 7:30am-9pm Sun.-Thurs., 7:30am-9:30pm Fri.-Sat., $8-32), featuring original decor but nicely updated for this edition, including pressed-tin ceilings, ornate glasswork, and a roaring fireplace in each dining room. The menu, heavy on fresh fish and seafood, emphasizes regional ingredients; go for the black bean chili.

ACCOMMODATIONS

Expect multiple-night minimum stays during peak season, and even year-round at some venues if your stay includes a Saturday night. Unless specified, all these accommodations are open year-round.

$50-100

A few of the cheapest motels might have high-season rates in the $75-85 range for a single in summer; these dip as low as $49 in non-peak seasons. However, most places cost much more.

Home away from home has always been ★ **Holiday Music Motel** (30 N. 1st Ave., 920/743-5571, www.holidaymusicmotel.com, $90, weekends $139). A group of local and national musicians, including Jackson Browne, once came here to write songs for a benefit for the Michigan Street Bridge. They loved the experience, and the place was for sale, so they bought it and rejuvenated it into a budget boutique venue. You likely won't need the recording studio (don't worry, it's quiet), but the rooms have fridges and new amenities. This is truly one of the most unique choices in Door County.

Lodging generally a few bucks cheaper can be found a couple of miles north of Sturgeon Bay along Highway 42/57 at a solid standby, the old-school but well-run **Chal-A Motel** (3910 Hwy. 42/57, 920/743-6788, Apr.-Nov., $90), where Wi-Fi is included and there's a fridge in every room—not to mention friendly owners.

Lots of folks come for cottage life, and all the higher-end resorts have isolated cottages strong on creature comforts. On the economical end, **Lake Lane Cottages** (5647 Lake Ln., 920/495-3343, www.lakelanecottages.com, $99, weekly $594) sleeps 2-4 people. It even has a tree house outside for the kids, and pets

Blooming Season

flowers and butterfly

Recently, *Forbes* named Door County number one for foliage photography. Indeed—little Door County. And it's not just fall colors. Everyone does those. What also makes Door County stand out is spring and early summer blooms of wildflowers, apples, and cherry trees.

Flowers show up in **early May.** If you have the chance to see them, do it—it's worth navigating the crowds. Cherry trees are lovely enough, but hey, their apple blossoms are pretty cool, too. And absolutely don't forget that a lot of other blossoms are out there! Much of the county's cutover land and agricultural pasture have been left to regrow wild. The county contains five state parks and the Ridges National Natural Landmark, a wildflower preserve with 13 species of endangered plants. (A personal favorite is the endangered dwarf lake iris, a lovely little purple thing that thrives at the **Ridges National Natural Landmark;** you can usually see it mid-May to mid-June, depending on when winter decides to leave. Heck, at the same time you can see the ram's head lady slipper orchid, one of 25 native orchids at the Ridges!) Door County is also making an effort to become one of the daffodil capitals of the world, planting more than 100,000 bulbs annually. Look for the white- and peach-colored daffodil—called "doorfodil" (seriously)—that was developed locally. **Door County Trolley** (8030 Hwy. 42, 920/868-1100, www.doorcountytrolley.com) has a very popular blossom tour ($67) on weekends during this time.

If you can't make it in May, fret not. June means the cherries have blossomed, but the rest of the flowers are in maximum color. Late July (at the earliest) is when you can start picking cherries (two months-ish after the bloom), but also head to Washington Island for amazing fields of lavender. August is the only time the purple gerardia blooms, and what a lovely flower it is. In September everyone takes a break but starts testing the air for dropping temperatures, which means it will soon be time for another gorgeous Door County pastime—fall leaf-peeping.

are welcome. It's southeast of Sturgeon Bay via Highway U (Clay Banks Rd.).

$100-150

Robertson's Cottages (4481 Cabots Point Rd., 920/743-5124, http://robertsoncottages.com, from $950 per week, daily rentals in low season) north of Potawatomi State Park costs a bit more but has island cottages and gets many multiple-decade repeat customers.

Amazing value given the quality and welcoming serve is at the **Garden Gate Bed & Breakfast** (434 N. 3rd Ave., 920/217-3093, http://doorcountybb.com, from $120). While the rooms may not be enormous (except the Lavender Room, which has a double whirlpool tub), they are modern and well-kept.

Ditching quotidian day jobs, the transplanted Milwaukeeans of **Whitefish Bay Farm B&B** (3831 Clark Lake Rd./Hwy. WD, 920/743-1560, www.whitefishbayfarm.com, $130), a 1908 farmhouse with four sunny rooms five miles north on Highway 57, now raise Corriedale sheep on a 75-acre sustainably run farm. With all that wool, the owners, accomplished weavers, give spinning and weaving demonstrations in their barn art gallery.

Over $150

At the ★ **Reynolds House B&B**

(111 S. 7th Ave., 920/493-1113, www.reynoldshousebandb.com, $160-200), the ersatz anachronism of spinning parasols is eschewed; it actually feels like a century ago in this antique-adorer's paradise. It emphasizes small but gorgeous guest rooms and superb service, and it was voted as having the best breakfast in the Midwest by the knowledgeable readers of *Midwest Living* magazine. Indeed, the proprietor is a gourmet. A special treat is the house dog!

More sheep grazing in a 30-acre orchard are a highlight of the restored farmhouse **Chanticleer** (4072 Hwy. HH N./Cherry Lane Rd., 920/746-0334, www.chanticleerguesthouse.com, $220-520). Find multilevel suites with 15-foot vaulted ceilings and private terraces, lofted suites with bisque pine ceilings and rafters, and an array of amenities in each. Notable extras include a solarium, a sauna, hiking trails, and a heated pool. Guests adore this place.

A wondrous proprietor awaits at the splendid **Black Walnut Guest House** (454 N. 7th Ave., 877/255-9568, www.blackwalnut-gh.com, from $180). The inn's relaxing guest rooms are entirely different from one another—choose one with a spiral staircase to a hot tub in a tower or another with a double-sided fireplace—and all are delightfully well-conceived. This guesthouse is highly recommended.

With a lodge that was once a 1920s dairy barn, the **Bay Shore Inn** (4205 Bay Shore Dr., 920/743-4551, www.bayshoreinn.net, from $200) has long been known as one of the most family-friendly resorts in the United States; it has three dozen luxurious apartment suites overlooking the bay as well as a private beach. Follow Highway B north from Sturgeon Bay.

Eminently gracious are the proprietors at ★ **Foxglove Inn** (344 N. 3rd Ave., 920/746-9192, www.foxglovedoorcounty.com, from $220). The inn's historically modern (no oxymoron) rooms are amazing, and the sister owners have a real knack for the trade. Guests have raved about this place, and for good reason.

The 1930s **Glidden Lodge** (4676 Glidden Dr., 920/746-3900 or 866/454-3336, www.gliddenlodge.com, $280-445) was the epitome of hedonistic delight in its time—a massive fieldstone main building offering stunning lake views. On the quiet side of the peninsula, it has a prime location. It is all suites, all with breathtaking lake views and magnificent sunrises. Follow Highway 57 north to Highway T and turn right to Glidden Drive.

INFORMATION

The **Sturgeon Bay Visitors Center** (36 S. 3rd Ave., 800/301-6695, www.sturgeonbay.net) is downtown. The **Door County Visitors Bureau** (1015 Green Bay Rd., 920/743-4456 or 800/527-3529, www.doorcounty.com), just south of town, has all the information you're likely to need. It has a 24-hour touch-screen information and reservations service. You'll find boatloads of local newspapers and other media.

GETTING THERE

Wait till you see the auto traffic on a peak weekend: Door County shares the American antipathy toward public transportation. People disembarking from a Greyhound bus evidently doesn't fit into the sunset postcard scene. There are no buses, no trains, and no ferries from points south.

★ POTAWATOMI STATE PARK

Unfolding along the western edge of Sturgeon Bay and flanked by Sherwood and Cabot Points, **Potawatomi State Park** (920/746-2890) is known for rolling birch-lined trails atop the limestone ridges scraped off the Niagara Escarpment. Indeed, the stone from here was carted off to build ports all around the Great Lakes. Islets rimmed in hues of blue and gray pepper the outlying reaches off the park (bring a polarizing filter for your camera on a sunny day). The geology of the park is significant enough that Potawatomi marks the eastern terminus of the Ice Age National Scenic Trail.

1
2
3
4

Shipbuilding History

Given its welcome promontory jutting into the water, 425 miles of shoreline, the safe haven of Green Bay, innumerable bights offering linked harbors, a plethora of native oak, and most important, a channel toward the outside world, it's no surprise that Door County became so important in shipbuilding.

As early as the 1830s, Manitowoc began to turn out oak sailing ships sturdy enough for the Great Lakes on the way to the St. Lawrence River; the crowning achievement was the Great Lakes schooner, a wooden ship with tight ends front and back that met below the water, a shallow draft, and a raisable centerboard, designed specifically to tackle Lake Michigan.

Meanwhile, to the north, Door County had newer shipyards that didn't have to go through later refitting to convert facilities to turn out steamships instead of clippers. Sturgeon Bay churned out ships in amazing numbers: The first left Sturgeon Bay shipyards in the mid-1850s, but it wasn't until the prime of the schooner days, in the mid-1860s, that the town really hit the big time. In the decade following the Civil War, perhaps two dozen famed ships were manufactured in the new shipyards.

Opened in the 1880s, the first major shipbuilder in Sturgeon Bay was Leathem and Smith, predominantly a ship repair facility. By World War I it had expanded its operations into a prosperous boat works and produced more tugboats than any other company. Now called Bay Shipbuilding, it is still the largest operator in Sturgeon Bay, comprising a number of Sturgeon Bay builders that can handle boats up to 1,100 feet long.

Many shipbuilders relocated here for the environment and the abundant resources. In 1896, Riebolt and Wolter moved an entire dry dock from Sheboygan. During the past 50 years, various corporate mergers have resulted in most of Sturgeon Bay's Michigan Street Bridge area becoming an arm of one or more subsidiaries of the same company. Despite the decline in shipping brought about by the advent of railroads and autos, 40 ships were constructed between 1970 and 1986.

Peterson Builders started just after the turn of the 20th century and constructed yachts, fishing tugs, and rowboats. Business boomed during the 1930s and World War II—24-hour operations cranked out subchasers and minesweepers. Today, shipbuilding output still includes military vessels (and yachts). Tours of shipbuilders are generally available during the first week of May through the **Sturgeon Bay Visitors Center** (36 S. 3rd Ave., 800/301-6695, www.sturgeonbay.net) or the **Door County Visitors Bureau** (1015 Green Bay Rd., 920/743-4456 or 800/527-3529, www.doorcounty.com). In winter, huge ships dock at the shipyards for maintenance, and it's also a great time to get a gander at some huge ships!

Sights

The great **Tower Trail** quickly ascends the ridges through thicker vegetation, leading to a 75-foot-tall **observation tower** with a belvedere vantage point of Michigan's Upper Peninsula, some 16 miles away, visible on a good day; come for sunset.

Beech trees, in this region found only close to Lake Michigan, are a highlight of the nature in the park. Otherwise, expect to see some 50 types of resident songbirds, plenty of hawks riding bluff wind currents, or deer staring quizzically at you from stands of sugar maples, basswood, and white and red pines.

For a quick road trip, head back toward Highway 42/57, turn right onto Highway C, and then right onto Highway M, which takes you all the way to the **Sherwood Point Lighthouse;** it's a bit difficult to spot. Built in 1883, it took a century before it was finally automated. The 38-foot-high structure guarding the bayside entrance to Sturgeon Bay was constructed with a 10-sided cast-iron light. Closed to the public, today the lighthouse and the old keeper's house are used as a retreat by the Coast Guard. It is open during

1: lovely sights from Potawatomi State Park's bluffs
2: shoreline at Potawatomi State Park
3: Potawatomi State Park **4:** kayaking at Potawatomi State Park

designated Lighthouse Festival times, generally in late May or early June. Check with the Door County Maritime Museum (www.dcmm.org) for official dates.

Recreation

HIKING

Almost 11 miles of trails wind through the park; you'll see hemlock, sugar maple, aspen, and birch trees in addition to the beech trees. The trails become nine miles of cross-country skiing trails in winter. Vertical gain is only around 150 feet, but the trails rise and fall a lot. Maps are available at the nature center.

The easiest trail is the 0.5-mile **Ancient Shores Trail,** which begins near the nature center; it's loaded with easy-to-understand signs pointing out geology and flora along the way.

The most popular trail is the 3.6-mile **Tower Trail,** which runs up and over ridges to the observation tower. The most popular trailheads are at the tower itself or at a nearby overlook (an old ski hill) on the main park road. In the southern half of the park, closer to the water, the 2.6-mile **Hemlock Trail** doesn't have the sweat-inducing climbing and passes the most popular recreation areas; access it at Parking Lot 2 in the picnic area.

The must-hike trail is the three-mile segment of the **Ice Age National Scenic Trail** that begins next to the observation tower and runs along the ridgeline above the water. It's only a small part of the epic trail's 1,000 miles, but this is where it starts.

BIKING

An eight-mile **off-road bicycle trail** also meanders through mostly grassy meadows and mildly challenging terrain. If you're a novice, go slowly. Bikes can be rented in the park. The trailhead is at Parking Lot 1 at the picnic area.

FISHING AND WATER ACTIVITIES

Fishing in the naturally protected bay is some of the best in the lower Door, especially for smallmouth bass. Canoes and kayaks are also rentable at the park. A large caveat: There is no sand beach in Potawatomi State Park, just lots of rocky shoreline.

CAMPING

Camping at the park's **Daisy Field Campground** (reservations 888/947-2757, www.wisconsin.goingtocamp.com, from $25 nonresidents, plus $8 reservation fee) is very popular, so reserve on the first day possible the winter before your trip. Even with 125 or more sites in two loops along the shoreline, it is always chock-full in summer. A camping cabin is available for disabled travelers in the south loop; it even has a stove, a microwave, and a fridge, along with air-conditioning. A park sticker is required in addition to the campsite fee. Showers are available in season in both loops.

The campground locations are wonderful, and you can get sites with splendid views, but they are very close to each other. Prime sites are numbers 54 or 104, as they're farthest from the madding crowd. Also consider the even-numbered sites 32-50, since they back up on the Niagara Escarpment and provide a bit of isolation.

Administrators take quiet hours seriously. Expect a ranger visit any time after 10pm if you are being too loud.

Getting There

There is no public transportation. Drive south of Sturgeon Bay to the bridge over the canal, head west, and then head immediately north—all roads lead to the park. It's also possible to take an obscenely expensive taxi ride from Green Bay.

Lakeside

Otherwise known as the "quiet side," this area shows less commercial development than the rest of the peninsula. The lakeshore side of the Door is a wonderland of pristine heath, healed cutover forest, rocky sea caves, some of Lake Michigan's finest beaches, biome preserves, picture-postcard lighthouses, and two of Wisconsin's best state parks.

The quick way into the area is Highway 57, branching off Highway 42 north of Sturgeon Bay. Farther off the beaten path, get right above the water along the coast starting southeast of Sturgeon Bay at the Sturgeon Bay Ship Canal North Pierhead Lighthouse. From here, an established State Rustic Road hugs the coastline all the way to Whitefish Dunes State Park, bypassing Portage and Whitefish Points and the Lilly Bay curve. Don't worry about getting lost once you find Highway T; there are no other roads.

★ WHITEFISH DUNES STATE PARK AND CAVE POINT COUNTY PARK

Some say **Whitefish Dunes State Park** (920/823-2400), eight miles northeast of Sturgeon Bay, is the most pleasant park in the state system. The beach is indisputably so, with miles of mocha-colored dunes sculpted into ridges by the prevailing winds. The contiguous **Cave Point County Park** is technically a separate park, but it's only a one-minute drive to the northeast from Whitefish Dunes, and there's also a trail connecting the two parks. It's best to visit them at the same time.

Plants and Animals

Stay off the dunes to protect the fragile plants and microscopic critters. Staying on the trail also avoids contact with the abundant poison ivy. Many of the grasses holding together the mounds are unique to this park, and once they're gone, the dunes will disappear; just take a look at the lifeless gashes created by motorcyclists before the park was established. The park is also the home of the Lake Huron locust, which lives only in Door County. The cooler prevailing winds mean that there is about one month's delay in flowers blooming compared to the bay side of the county. Rare and threatened plant species include dune goldenrod, dune thistle, dwarf lake iris, and sand reedgrass.

Large wildlife sightings are rare, other than an occasional white-tailed deer or red fox, but there have been occasional reports of black bears.

Recreation

HIKING

The dunes are among the highest on Lake Michigan. They were formed by numerous advances and retreats of ancient lakes, and later Lake Michigan, as well as countless storms. Sandbanks first closed off Clark Lake in what is now the mainland, and as vegetation took hold three millennia ago, wind deposits began piling up atop the sandbar. The result is a microcosm that couldn't occur on the bay side of the peninsula—a wide beach rising to forested dunes. The tallest, Old Baldy, stands 93 feet high.

Check out the nature center, where all trails start and where you can pick up trail maps, for its exhibits on the geology and anthropology of the area. A Native American village site (10am-4pm Sat.-Sun. summer) has been recreated just outside to illustrate life during one of the eight periods of human habitation.

There are nearly 15 miles of trails; thoughtfully, the park has a plasticized trail mat on the first hundred yards of all trails to both protect the ground and make it easier for you to trudge. Until you get to the dunes themselves, the park is completely flat. Plank-and-rope boardwalks off the trail allow beach

1
2
3

access on the 2.8-mile **Red Trail;** at the midpoint, it branches away from the water to link with longer trails through mixed hardwood, red pine, and oddball wooded dune areas. The beginning of the Red Trail is also the only place where you can ride a mountain bike. Continuing on the Red Trail to its southern end, hikers can reach the only climbable dune—Old Baldy, which offers panoramas of Lake Michigan and Clark Lake inland. From there, it's possible to connect to longer trails, including the **Yellow Trail,** which heads west for another 1.5 miles through a red pine plantation and wooded dune area that is very solitary, even for this park, and passing the 0.5-mile **Red Pine Trail** through more red pines and a 0.25-mile-long spur trail to Clark Lake.

If you want to start hiking from the other direction, starting from the nature center parking lot, the second-most popular trail after the one to Old Baldy is the 2.5-mile **Black Trail,** which heads northeast along the limestone bedrock of the Niagara Escarpment and leads to **Cave Point County Park,** likely the most photographed parkland in Door County. (If you want to visit Cave Point County Park but don't want to hike this trail, you can reach the park by driving about a minute to the north.) Along the way the trail joins up with an interpretive walk with an anthropomorphic brachiopod (a prehistoric clam-like creature) named Byron who explains the geology of the area.

Cave Point is a must-stop. From south to north in Whitefish Bay, the geology shifts from dunes to mixed sand and stone to, at Cave Point, exposed limestone ledges thrusting up to 50 feet above the water on the Niagara Escarpment, the bedrock of the peninsula. Some 425 million years ago, the Silurian Sea covered this entire region, and you can still find fossils in exposed rock. These ledges are on a bowl, the opposite side of which is Niagara Falls. Aeons of crashing waves have hewn caves and cenotes that show up as blowholes as the surf pounds and crashes, echoing like rolling thunder. The whole effect is not unlike the crumbled parapets of a timeworn castle. Sea kayakers have a field day exploring this small promontory. Straight-faced old-timers tell of a schooner that slammed into the rocks at Cave Point in 1881 (true). Laden with corn, the ship cracked like a nut and spilled its cargo (true), and within a few days, corn had mysteriously appeared in Green Bay, on the other side of the peninsula (hmm).

1: Red Trail at Whitefish Dunes State Park
2: kayaking around Cave Point 3: trail in Whitefish Dunes State Park

SWIMMING

Do not take swimming lightly here. The concave bend of Whitefish Bay focuses all the current, forming tough riptides. Predicting where these form is never entirely possible, and lifeguards are never on duty. If you do plan on swimming, practice extra caution and pay strict attention to all posted signs.

CAMPING

This park is for day use only, and camping is not allowed. It is great for picnicking, which can be done right atop the limestone ledges overlooking the lake, not to mention along the beaches.

JACKSONPORT

You can always tell those who have explored the bay side of the peninsula first and then backtracked through Sturgeon Bay to come back up this side. Generally, these are the people who race right through Jacksonport as if they didn't know it was there and then slam on the brakes to turn around to try to find what they missed.

At one time, Jacksonport rivaled Fish Creek as the epicenter of economic activity on the Door. Once the local lumber was depleted, Jacksonport's docks were relegated to fishing boats.

Sights

Somnolent Jacksonport hosts a few antiques

Calmer Near the Lake

Jacksonport is on the 45th parallel, exactly halfway between the equator and the North Pole, but the peninsula's climate is far more temperate than northern Wisconsin. The waters of Lake Michigan, legendary for their unpredictability, also even out the weather, keeping things cool in the summer and taking the bite out of winter's Alberta clippers.

Early weather reports from Door County show that the northern tip of the peninsula is generally a few degrees warmer than the southern end, although the difference between the bay side and the lake side is climatically more important. This partly explains why most Door residents live on the bay side: With Lake Michigan in a huff, blowing fog, spray, and mist, Green Bay, in the lee of 15 miles of limestone wind-block, remains sedate, if a bit cloudy.

Another oddity is "lake effect" snow: Much more snow falls at the lakeside than even a few miles inland, especially on the eastern shores of the Great Lakes. Green Bay is not large enough to produce the necessary conditions, so Door County receives some of the lowest amounts of precipitation in the state.

shops and gift cottages selling crafts from dozens of Door County artists. A lazy stretch of sand acts as a beach, and top-notch fun comes in the form of the sweets at the **Town Hall Bakery** (6225 Hwy. 57, 920/823-2116).

Festivals

The last community to be settled in the county, Jacksonport caught one of the waves of Germanic immigrants, and its annual **Maifest** (www.jacksonport.org) is among the larger shindigs held during the summer.

The Jacksonport Historical Society hosts a **Cherry Fest** (www.jacksonporthistoricalsociety.org) on the first Saturday in August every year. There are all kinds of cherry-related foods, historical displays, and arts and crafts.

Food and Accommodations

The supper club of choice is **Mr. G's** (5890 Hwy. 57, 920/823-2112, dinner Tues.-Sat., $6-14), with a ballroom that once had live entertainment.

Garnering rave reviews is the new **Island Fever** (6301 Hwy. 57, 920/823-2700, 11am-8pm Mon., Wed., and Sun., till 8:30pm Thurs., till 9pm Fri.-Sat., from $9). The "island" is less Jimmy Buffett than the owner's heritage from Washington Island. The menu does feature Caribbean, along with Mexican and, of course, local fish. Don't worry about the hodgepodge—it's all done well.

Right downtown is the pinnacle of Jacksonport's developmental ambition: the **Square Rigger Lodge and Cottages** (6332 Hwy. 57, 920/823-2404, www.squareriggerlodge.com, from $125). More than a dozen basic but comfortable modern motel and condo units overlook the water (some do not), and most have private balconies or patios. One- to three-bedroom cottages also line the waterfront. They have lively fish boils here nightly in July and August, four times a week September to June.

Rooms (spartan but decent) for about half the price can be found nearby at the **Innlet Motel** (6269 Hwy. 57, 920/823-2499, www.innlet-motel.com, from $85). This is also the home of **Mike's Port Pub** (920/823-2081, 11am-10pm daily, from $6) for some pretty good food, including breakfast. Try the Sandbox, a brat patty over hash browns and eggs.

BAILEYS HARBOR

Lake Michigan sportfishing is evident as you enter Baileys Harbor, with every inch of road chockablock with trucks and boat trailers

1: kayaking in Baileys Harbor **2:** Blacksmith Inn On the Shore **3:** the Cornerstone Pub **4:** rustic splendor in Baileys Harbor

1

2

and a glistening marina. It's a fitting legacy: In 1844 a Captain Bailey and his crew were foundering in a sudden squall when they came across this cove and took shelter. They were amazed to find a deep, well-isolated harbor and gorgeous stands of cedar backing the beach. So enthralled was the captain that he and the owner of the shipping company persuaded the U.S. government to construct a lighthouse at the harbor's entrance some years later, marking the first nonnative settlement in Door County. The harbor remains the only designated Harbor of Refuge on the peninsula's lake side.

Sights

Before you arrive, know that the sights are mostly south of Baileys Harbor, on the way from Cave Point County Park, just northeast of Whitefish Dunes State Park. South of town along Highway 57 at the southern end of Kangaroo Lake are two undiscovered gems—**Lyle-Harter-Matter County Park** and **Meridian Park State Natural Area,** which sandwich the highway and feature rough undeveloped trails past Niagara Escarpment rocks and one of the largest dunes in the county. As you sit here and munch your granola bar, you're halfway to the North Pole. If you're really looking to escape the crowds, even on a chaotic mid-July day, head north a few miles on Highway 57, then west two miles or so on Highway E to a trail spur leading toward **Kangaroo Lake,** a state wildlife area that's best explored on a canoe trip. It's beautiful and home to an impressive ecosystem; somehow the northern half of this lake has escaped development and is currently owned by the Nature Conservancy. The mesic open areas are rare in Wisconsin and home to a staggering list of threatened species, particularly the Hine's emerald dragonfly (this is one of only two breeding areas in the country). You'll never be disappointed by the waterfowl that call this place home, including the local black tern.

A bit south of town and along a splendid stretch of beach is a decidedly different kind of vacation, an educational seminar (from $1,000, including superb food, far less if you're staying off-site) at **Björklunden** (7590 Boynton Ln., 920/839-2216), more a relaxed soul-searching means of personal growth than a for-credit school experience, although it is the northern campus of Lawrence University in Appleton. Participants can live in a recently reconstructed Norwegian-style lodge built of local fieldstone and take courses in humanities and natural sciences. Some midweek seminars are cheaper. It's possible to stay at the lodge, which looks like a Viking ship, without taking courses if space is available. Travelers can also visit the **Boynton Chapel** (902/839-2216, tours given mid-June to late Aug. Mon. and Wed. 1pm-4pm, $5) built in a late 12th-century Norwegian *stavkirke* (stave church) style.

During the summer, the gardens of the estate host **Door Shakespeare** (920/839-1500, www.doorshakespeare.com), with evening performances Monday through Saturday.

In Baileys Harbor, take a simple stroll along one of the county's longest sand beaches at **Baileys Harbor Park.** The Town Hall—you can't miss it—has the local **visitors information center** (Hwy. 57 and Hwy. F, 920/839-2366, www.baileysharbor.com, daily summer and fall).

Recreation

SPORTFISHING

Chinook salmon and rainbow and brown trout are the quarry for local charter boats, and the fishing in Baileys Harbor is some of the best in the county. All charters will be met at the Baileys Harbor marina/town dock. Lilliputian Baileys Harbor (pop. 780) boasts a salmon harvest half the size of Milwaukee's. Plenty of local guides are available. The captain at **Lynn's Charter Fishing** (Baileys Harbor Yacht Club, 920/854-5109, http://lynnscharterfishing.com) has a PhD in zoology, has been guiding for many years, and runs an unequaled kayak fishing tour.

BOAT TOURS

One of the more intriguing options is to take a guided tour (generally 8am and/or 3pm daily, $59) of the local bays, including the legendary Cana Island Lighthouse, in a clear-bottomed kayak with **Lakeshore Adventures** (8113 Hwy. 57, 920/839-2055, http://lakeshore-adventures.com), which also rents virtually everything recreational.

Food

Door County wines get all the press, but suddenly craft brewing is not far behind. Newest are the whimsical overseers of the **Door County Brewing Company** (8099 Hwy. 57, 920/834-1515, www.doorcountybrewingco.com, 11am-10pm daily), housed in an erstwhile feed mill. They've got select all-season beers, the favorite being Polka King Porter. This place's music hall puts the hoot in hootenanny.

New bistros open regularly, but **Chives Door County** (8041 Hwy. 57, 920/839-2000, dinner Wed.-Mon. high season, from $8) remains the linchpin. It's a casual, but borderline fine-dining place whose goat cheese and chicken wonton or otherworldly New York strip could be anyone's mainstay. They have a food truck at the Door County Brewing Company, a genius idea.

★ **Harbor Fish Market and Grille** (8080 Hwy. 57, 920/839-9999, breakfast, lunch, and dinner daily, from $10), the local landmark, is a casually fine-dining place in a 120-year-old building with a wondrous atmosphere. All comers will be happy; try the lobster boil (Wed. and Fri.-Sun. summer, Fri.-Sun. off-season). There's great custard and espresso next door. You can sit outside with your pooch and order from the "doggie menu" for your best friend.

If you're old-school (or a Packers football fan), head immediately to **Cornerstone Pub** (8123 Hwy. 57, 920/839-2790, breakfast, lunch, and dinner daily May-Oct., shorter hours off-season, $6-16), which has solid comfort food (panfried perch since 1926) like its mammoth Foghorn burger; it's also pooch-friendly.

Accommodations

Baileys Harbor has a couple of basic, modestly priced motels. The **Sunset Motel and Cottages** (8404 Hwy. 57, 920/839-2218, www.baileysunsetmotelandcottages.com, from $80) is casual and rustic but comfortable, with friendly proprietors—the way things used to be everywhere in these parts. It's about 0.5 miles north of the Highway Q turnoff.

On the south side of town are above-average motel rooms and a lovely lakeshore setting at the **Beachfront Inn** (8040 Hwy. 57, 920/839-2345, www.beachfrontinn.net, from $170). In addition to a private beach, an indoor heated pool, and regular campfires, the inn gets many kudos for being so pet-friendly—they even have their own rescue dogs.

What may be the most enviably sited lodging in all of Door County is ★ **Gordon Lodge** (1420 Pine Dr., 920/839-2331, www.gordonlodge.com, $245-425). Spread across the tip of a promontory jutting into Lake Michigan's North Bay, the long-established Gordon Lodge sprouted in the 1920s as an offshoot of a popular Sturgeon Bay doctor's summer home. It has been updated just enough to be modern but not so much as to lose its rustic charm. The main lodge has a lake view, while villas with fireplaces creep out over the water. Some original cottages are set back and nestled under the pines, which also drape over fitness trails. The dining room is casually elegant, and the Top Deck lounge, originally a boathouse, is unsurpassed for after-dinner dancing. Go north out of town and follow Highway Q toward the lake to Pine Drive.

The **Blacksmith Inn On the Shore** (8152 Hwy. 57, 920/839-9222, www.theblacksmithinn.com, $255-305) is opulent and historic with stunning sunset views and no frilliness—and absolutely fabulous service. It's pricey in high season but a steal in less busy times.

★ THE RIDGES SANCTUARY AND CANA ISLAND LIGHTHOUSE

Baileys Harbor is sandwiched between the strategic safe harbor on Lake Michigan and Kangaroo Lake, the peninsula's largest inland body of water. Travelers are so preoccupied with these two sights that it's easy to miss the two large promontories jutting off the peninsula just north of town, forming **Moonlight Bay.** These two capes may be the state's most awesome natural landmarks and definitely have the most inspiring lighthouses.

North along Highway Q is a critical biotic reserve, **The Ridges Sanctuary** (Ridges Rd., 920/839-2802, www.ridgesanctuary.org, trails open daily, $5 adults), with 1,000 acres of boreal bog, swamp, dunes, and a complete assortment of wildflowers in their natural habitat. The eponymous series of ancient spiny sand ridges mark the advance of ancient and modern Lake Michigan. All 23 native Wisconsin orchids are found within the sanctuary, as are 13 endangered species of flora. The preserve was established in the 1930s by hard-core early ecologists, such as Jens Jensen, in one of the state's first environmental brouhahas, incited by a spat over plans for a trailer park. The U.S. Department of the Interior recognizes the site as one of the most ecologically precious in the region; it was the first National Natural Landmark in Wisconsin. Its new nature center has won energy and environmental design awards.

The famed **Baileys Harbor Range Lights** are a pair of small but powerful lighthouses—a shorter wooden octagonal one across the road on the beach, the other 900 feet inland—erected in 1869 by the Coast Guard. There are 20 miles of trails that are well worth the effort, including three easy trails, ranging from just under two miles to five miles, that snake through the tamarack and hardwood stands. Also on the grounds is a nature center, with some of the best educational programs in the state.

Continue on Ridges Road to additional sites deemed National Natural Landmarks by the Department of the Interior and dedicated by the Nature Conservancy. **Toft's Point** (also called Old Lighthouse Point) is along a great old dirt road that winds through barren sands with innumerable pullouts. A few trails can be found on the 600-plus acres that take up the whole of the promontory, which includes almost three miles of rocky beach shoreline.

To the north of the Ridges, the **Mud Lake Wildlife Area** is over 2,000 acres protecting the shallow lake and surrounding wetlands. In fact, its second-growth mesic ecosystem of white cedar, white spruce, and black ash is a rarity in Wisconsin. A prime waterfowl sanctuary, Mud Lake and its environs may be even more primeval and wild than the Ridges

☆ Scenic Boat Tours

One of the best views of Door County is of the shoreline. You'll see lighthouses, cliffs and caves, and islands, as well as hear about Door County's fascinating history.

STURGEON BAY

- **Door County Fireboat Cruises** (page 137) uses a retired Chicago fireboat to chug along for two-hour cruises onto Lake Michigan or Sturgeon Bay.

BAILEYS HARBOR

- **Lakeshore Adventures** (page 153) offers guided tours of the local bays, including the legendary Cana Island Lighthouse, in a clear-bottomed kayak.

FISH CREEK

- **Fish Creek Scenic Boat Tours** (page 160) is the easiest way to take in the views of Chambers Island.
- **Friendly Charters** (page 160) offers quiet tours of Fish Creek on their sailboat.

GILLS ROCK

- **Shoreline Resort** (page 173) has narrated boat tours of Death's Door as well as popular sunset cruises.

and are home to one of the few breeding spots of the threatened Hine's emerald dragonfly along with a lengthy list of waterfowl, including ospreys. Canoeing is also very popular, as Reibolts Creek connects the lake with Moonlight Bay.

On the southern promontory of Moonlight Bay is the one must-visit lighthouse on the peninsula that everyone photographs, the **Cana Island Lighthouse** (10am-5pm daily May-Oct., $12), accessible via Highway Q to Cana Island Drive to a narrow spit of gravel that may be under water, depending on when you get here. Note that this is a residential area, so go slowly—blind curves are everywhere—and don't park inappropriately if the parking area is full, which is not impossible. Impressively tall and magnificently white, the lighthouse is framed by white birch. One of the most crucial lighthouses in the county, it stands far off the coast on a wind-whipped landform. Built in 1870, it was considered a hardship station during storm season. North Bay is also the site of Marshall's Point, part of the **North Bay State Natural Area,** an isolated stretch of wildland completely surrounded by private development often touted as a potential state park for its remarkable microclimate and the fact that it's one of the last remaining stretches of undeveloped Lake Michigan coastline on the Door Peninsula. You'll find threatened and endangered species everywhere; most interesting is the fact that more than one million (of the local population estimate of up to 1.5 million) whitefish spawn in these waters.

ROWLEYS BAY

Out of Baileys Harbor, Highway 57 swoops back toward Sister Bay to Highway 42. The next lakeside community, Rowleys Bay, is mostly a massive and well-established resort and nearby campground, **Rowleys Bay Resort** (1041 Hwy. ZZ, 920/854-2385, www.rowleysbayresort.com, May-Oct., lodge or cottages $130-330). Originally a bare-bones fishing camp and later a rustic lodge, the city-state has transformed into what is certainly the most comprehensive operation on the upper Door Peninsula. From rustic-looking lodge rooms to plush suites and cottages of all sorts, somehow the place does it all and does it well. Rustically upscale two- and three-bedroom vacation villas are set on wooded or waterfront sites; some can house a dozen people comfortably, and all have whirlpool tubs and fireplaces.

The adjacent but unaffiliated **campground** (920/854-4818, www.wagontrailcampground.com, from $39 tents), in fact still called the Wagon Trail, spread over 200 acres along the bay, is really quite fastidious and professionally run; cabins and even yurts are available. Reservations are advised. (By the way, spend an extra $7 for a secluded tent site.)

Several miles of trails wend through the resort's acreage; one leads to Sand Bay Beach Park on Rowleys Bay, another to the Mink River estuary. On the bay, the resort's marina offers bicycles, canoes, kayaks, paddleboats, charter fishing boats, and scenic excursions.

The reason most people come to the resort, however, is ★ **Grandma's Swedish Bakery** (920/854-2385, daily May-Oct.), a magnet for anyone with a sweet tooth for 10 kinds of homemade bread, cardamom coffee cake, cherry pie, old-world bread pudding, and scads of muffins, cookies, and pastries. The specialty is Swedish sweets—*limpa* and *skorpa* (thinly sliced pecan rolls sprinkled with cinnamon sugar and dried in the oven).

Mink River Estuary State Natural Area

Stretching southeast from Ellison Bay to the edge of Newport State Park, the Mink River Estuary State Natural Area acts, by grace of the Nature Conservancy, to protect the river system as it empties into the bay through marsh and estuary. A crucial bird migratory site, the waters also act as a conduit for spawning fish. The topography of the 1,500 acres is astonishingly diverse and untouched; two threatened plant species—the dune thistle and dwarf lake iris—are found within the

1
2
3
Venture Kayaks

site's boundaries, and more than 200 species of birds pass through.

★ NEWPORT STATE PARK

Not everything is wild in Door County anymore, but the state's only designated wilderness park is here; the rough, isolated, backwoods **Newport State Park** (920/854-2500) constitutes half of the northern tip of the county, accessed from Highway 42 and stretching for almost 12 miles along the Lake Michigan coast through an established scientific reserve—a perfectly realized park.

A remarkable diversity of hardwoods and conifers, isolated wetlands, bogs, and even a few hidden coves along the lakeshore make the hiking appealing. Once an up-and-coming lumber village in the 1880s, the town decayed gradually as the stands of trees were depleted. Ghostly outlines of the foundations of buildings are still scattered in the underbrush.

Once wasted white pine cutover land, the inner confines of the park are now dense tracts of bog forest. The southern section of the park is an established scientific reserve on 140 acres of mixed hardwoods. The park's magnificent ecosystem draws one of the planet's highest concentrations of monarch butterflies, which make a mind-boggling trip from Mexico all the way here. Unfortunately, biologists have noted a dramatic drop-off in monarch numbers, attributed to pollution and logging.

And the best part: Even on a summer holiday weekend, few people visit the gorgeous beachfront here, probably because it requires a bit of walking. It is truly a secluded gem in a busy region. Its absolute isolation was one reason it was named an International Dark Sky Park in 2019.

Hiking

The park maintains nearly 40 miles of trails, along which you'll find wilderness campsites. A "rugged" rise here means 40 or 50 feet. Basic maps are available at the contact station. By far the most popular area of the park is the northern tier and trails leaving from the picnic area, including the **Europe Bay/Hotz Trail** (over 3 miles one-way) to Europe Lake, one of the largest of the county's inland lakes and a pristine sandy gem uncluttered by development. The trail runs through sandy forests to rocky beaches with great views of Porte des Mortes and the surrounding islands.

As you stroll the Europe Bay/Hotz Trail toward the lake, consider a quick jaunt toward a promontory called Lynd Point along **Lynd Point Trail** (1 mile one-way). Gravel Island, viewable from Lynd Point, is a national wildlife refuge.

In the southern section of the park, the picnic area also has access to the **Newport Trail** (a 5-mile loop), which heads west to Duck Bay on the eastern edge of the park; Spider Island, viewable from here, is another national wildlife refuge for nesting gulls. Along its western segment, the Newport Trail connects to the **Rowleys Bay Trail** (4 miles), which heads to the southern tip of the park at Varney Point and also passes most of the campsites. Both trails alternately pass through meadows, wooded areas, and along limestone headlands on the coast, mostly along old logging roads.

Biking

Mountain bikes are allowed on 17 miles of the park's trails; essentially, anywhere that hikers can go, bikers can also get to, but generally on a parallel trail. Bike camping is possible, although the park warns of porcupine damage to bikes parked overnight. The most conspicuous off-limits areas are the shoreline routes—it's too tempting for bikers to whip down onto the fragile sands.

Camping

The 16 sites are strictly walk-in; the shortest hike in is 0.5 miles, the longest nearly 4 miles. Two sites on Europe Lake are waterside, so canoes can land and camp. The Lake

1: gorgeous lighthouse at Cana Island **2:** classic lightouse of the Ridges Sanctuary **3:** kayak in Newport State Park

Michigan side has plenty of lakeside sites. Winter camping is outstanding here. Make your **reservations** (888/947-2757, www.wisconsin.goingtocamp.com, from $25 for nonresidents plus a $8 reservation fee) as early as possible.

Bayside

Highways 42 and 57 have been undergoing widening and straightening for years, and the debate over the project possibly exceeds the actual amount of work done. South of Sturgeon Bay, the road has already turned into multilane madness, and Highway 42 north of Sturgeon Bay is gradually approaching interstate highway capacity and speeds.

Highway 42 has perhaps the most intriguing history of any county road. Not your average farm-to-market remnant, it was hewn from a tundra-like wilderness in 1857 by starving millers and fishers who became desperate when winter arrived earlier than expected and froze their supply boats out of the harbor.

On the way to Egg Harbor from Sturgeon Bay, a great on-the-water side trip is along Highway B. Eventually, Highway B merges with Highway G around Horseshoe Bay and leads directly to Egg Harbor.

EGG HARBOR

There's something of a contrived (officially, "revitalized") feel to Egg Harbor on Highway 42. A couple of 19th-century structures have been redone with fresh facades, and there's more than a little new development, including a pseudo-Victorian strip mall that could have been plunked down in any city suburb or fringe sprawl in the country.

The name Egg Harbor isn't about an ovoid land configuration but comes from a legendary 1825 battle between vacationing rich folk. While rowing to shore in longboats, boredom apparently got the best of the well-to-do, who started throwing eggs from their picnic provisions at each other. Locals celebrate this event with occasional staged—and eminently delightful—egg throws. Thus, everything here is an "eggscape."

Sights

As you wind off Highway 42 and down the hillside into Egg Harbor, the first sight is perhaps the most picturesque **village park** in the county, with a small strand of smooth-stone and sand beach. There are lovely free concerts Thursday and Sunday in summer. A couple of miles farther south on Horseshoe Bay Road is an even better view of Horseshoe Bay and another very sandy beach at **Frank E. Murphy County Park.**

A noteworthy sight and a landmark for denizens of the Door is the Gothic Revival **Cupola House** (7836 Hwy. 42, 920/868-3941), a massive building constructed in 1871 by Levi Thorp, a local cordwood dealer and one of the wealthiest men in the county.

In Egg Harbor, **Harbor Ridge** (Harbor Ridge Ct. http://harborridgewinery.com, 920/868-4321) has as many soaps as wines (with delightful names), but they get kudos for their dedication to charities. An excellent cheese shop is adjacent.

Tours

Too tired to walk? **Door County Trolley** (8030 Hwy. 42, 920/868-1100, www.doorcountytrolley.com) has an array of historical, themed, culinary, and other fun tours ($22-67) on an old-fashioned streetcar. This is wildly popular and great fun.

Entertainment

Just east of Egg Harbor, a quaint old dairy barn now houses the **Birch Creek Music Center** (Hwy. E, 920/868-3763, www.birchcreek.org). The acoustics are extraordinary, considering that cows once lived here. Evening concerts by students and national names in the big barn are scheduled regularly, generally mid-July through Labor Day, and are something of a tradition in the area—the big band series is particularly popular, and percussion performances are the specialty.

Food

A favorite for a grab-and-go meal in the state is at **Macready Artisan Bread** (7836 Hwy. 42, 920/868-2233, http://macreadys.com, 9am-4pm Thurs.-Mon., from $5). The bread is sublime, and there are many varieties—including sweet potato bread. The proprietors are two of the nicest folks you will run into on your travels. Healthful vegetarian and vegan wraps and salads plus smoothies and coffee are at **Greens-N-Grains** (7821 Hwy. 42, 920/868-9999, 8am-5pm daily summer, from $5), which boasts almost 100 percent organic, local, and/or sustainably produced.

Shipwrecked (7791 Egg Harbor Rd., 920/868-2767, 11am-10pm daily, $10-28) has good pub grub but is better known as the county's only microbrewery; watch them brewing as you quaff, and try the cherry wheat ales. Al Capone supposedly loved to hang out with the lumberjacks here and used the subterranean caverns to hide from the law. Locals were worried a 2018 fire would take away all the charm, and while it's fresher now, it still has the ambience.

If you're skeptical about finding decent tapas in the Great Lakes region, rest assured that **Parador** (7829 Egg Harbor Rd., 920/868-2255, from 5pm daily, from $8) has fantastic Spanish cuisine in a comfortably small setting. As you're in the land of the Cheeseheads, be sure to try the Spanish mac and cheese.

Kids may prefer the **Log Den** (6626 Hwy. 42, 920/868-3888, lunch and dinner daily, brunch Sun., $8-25), just south of Egg Harbor on Highway 42, a 10,000-square-foot place that doesn't really feel immense. The name is no misnomer, as there is wood everywhere, much of it ornately, at times cheekily, carved into a menagerie of anthropomorphisms. The menu runs from great—and moderately priced—burgers and sandwiches to seafood. It's also a fun place to watch a Packers football game.

Carnivores will want to head directly to **Casey's BBQ & Smokehouse** (7855 Hwy. 42, 920/868-3038, http://caseysbbqandsmokehouse.com, 11am-9pm daily, $8-24), just about the perfect place to gorge on brisket or ribs after a long day of paddling or pedaling.

Shared-plate creative American cuisine sprang out of an artisanal cheese shop at **Glacier Ledge** (8103 Hwy. 42, 920/868-1333, 11am-8pm daily summer, less low seasons., $8-24), worth a trip for its casually upscale small plates. Do try the Door County raclette cheese—Daclette.

★ **The Fireside Restaurant** (11934 Hwy. 42, 920/854-7999, 4pm-9pm Tues.-Sat., $13-32) is that unique place that serves comfort food like its famed chicken and waffles along with creative concoctions with local ingredients (goat cheese grits) or venison Cajun style, all without feeling pretentious. This hasn't been around long, but it looks like a stayer.

Accommodations

Modest but clean lodgings—along with a nearby orchard—can be found at the budget-friendly **Cape Cod Motel** (7682 Hwy. 42, 920/868-3271, capecodmoteldoorcounty.com, from $90), where the proprietors are always helpful.

At the **Lullabi Inn** (7928 Egg Harbor Rd./Hwy. 42, 920/868-3135, www.lullabi-inn.com, from $140), on the north end of town, you can expect some renovated rooms and a welcoming atmosphere. Stay in small but clean doubles, or upgrade to an array of larger guest rooms and apartments.

Plenty of self-contained islands of luxury surround Egg Harbor. The least expensive guest rooms at the **Landing Resort** (7741 Hwy. 42, 920/868-3282, http://thelandingresort.com, from $190) are cramped but clean and well-appointed. Higher rates apply to the dizzying array of condo apartments. You can't beat a place that has been recommended by people for more than a generation. Ask for a room with the wood-side view.

One of the best-run resort complexes in the county, ★ **Newport Resort** (7888 Church St., 920/868-9900, www.newportresort.com, $190-279) has various one- and two-bedroom options, all with spectacular views. There are indoor and outdoor pools, a sauna, and lots of stuff for families, including a coin laundry.

You'll find award-winning guest rooms at **Ashbrooke Hotel** (7942 Egg Harbor Rd., 920/868-3113, www.ashbrooke.net, $249), with one- and two-bedroom suites done up in myriad styles, such as French country and wicker.

The service is superlative and the views equally spectacular from the villas at the **Bay Point Inn** (7933 Hwy. 42, 800/707-6660, http://baypointinn.com, from $249). The beds are amazingly soft, and the farm-to-table gourmet breakfasts are worth the price.

Coming into town on Highway 42, turn east onto Highway T for one mile to reach **Door County Cottages** (4355 Hwy. T, 920/868-2300, www.doorcountycottages.com, from $220 daily, $1,250-2,300 weekly). It has a reconstructed main cottage, lovingly put together from collected fieldstone. In fact, this place was green before green was in. Built into earthen berms with southern glassed exposure, two of the main retreats are very cozy. The sun-soaked two-bedroom cottage can sleep six and offers a combined kitchen-dining room-living area and a boardwalk to a Finnish wood sauna.

Information

The local community center has a small **Visitors Information Center** (920/868-3717, www.eggharbordoorcounty.org).

★ FISH CREEK

This graceful community offers visitors the anticipated coffee-table pictorials. It may be the soul of the county, but it's also just another Door County village with a small population. The most picturesque view in the county is along Highway 42 as it winds into the village from a casual bluff. The official village history describes the town's situation succinctly—"with its back to a rock and its face to the sea." A treasured stretch of road with a few hairpin turns, a roller-coaster drop, and suddenly you're in a trim and tidy Victorian hamlet that could have come from a Currier and Ives print. Fish Creek boasts the most thoroughly maintained pre-20th-century architecture on the peninsula, with about 40 historic structures.

Sights

Most visitors to Fish Creek simply stroll around to see the 19th-century architecture. The harbor area has remnants of the earliest cabins, and the remains of an 1855 cabin built by the founding Thorp brothers stands on the grounds of the modern Founders Square mélange of shops and restaurants in the village center; after a fire, they were rebuilt as closely as possible to the original designs. Another landmark structure is the notoriously haunted 1875 Greek Revival **Noble House** (Hwy. 42 and Main St., 920/868-2091, 10am-3pm Fri.-Sat. mid-May-mid-June, noon-5pm Tues.-Sun. mid-June-Labor Day, $5). The **Gibraltar Historical Association** (920/868-2091) provides **historic walking tours.**

Perhaps the most accessible winery in Door County, and one that focuses on the county, **Lautenbach's Orchard Country Winery & Market** (9197 Hwy. 42 S., 866/946-3263, www.orchardcountry.com, 10am-4pm Sun.-Thurs., 10am-5pm Fri.-Sat., $5 tours) is a favorite for everyone. The winery has award-winning county fruit wines, pick-your-own fruits, sleigh rides, and more. They hold a summer cherry festival with complimentary wine and food tastings and live music at the end of July.

Recreation

Without chartering a boat or flying your own plane, the easiest way to take in (but not actually step onto) **Chambers Island,** across the Strawberry Channel, is via **Fish Creek Scenic Boat Tours** (Clark Park, 920/421-4442, $40), which offers a variety of tours. You can take a quieter tour of Fish Creek twice daily with sailboat rides by **Friendly Charters** (920/256-9042, www.friendlycharters.com, from $45 pp), which also has several tour options.

Boat and bicycle rentals are available in town at **Nor Door Sport and Cyclery** (4007 Hwy. 42, 920/868-2275) near the entrance to Peninsula State Park. It is the place to get a hybrid bike, a mountain bike, or a single-speed cruiser ($25 per day average). Plenty of other equipment is also for rent. In winter, you can rent cross-country skis and even snowshoes and ice skates.

At **Edge of Park Bikes and Mopeds** (Park Entrance Rd., 920/868-3344), moped rental includes a state park access sticker.

Entertainment and Events

The country's oldest summer theater, the **Peninsula Players** (Peninsula Players Rd., off Hwy. 42 south of Fish Creek, 920/868-3287, www.peninsulaplayers.com) perform a Broadway plays and musicals in a gorgeous garden setting with bayside trails late June through mid-October, a tradition in its seventh decade. Reservations are advised. Relatively recent renovations to the theater include heated floors.

Less than half as old but with boatloads of attitude, the tongue-in-cheek **Northern Sky Theater** (920/854-6117, www.northernskytheater.com) is an acclaimed theater-and-song troupe, as likely to perform their own rollicking originals (*Cheeseheads: The Musical* and *Guys on Ice,* a paean to ice fishing) or a ghost story series as they are the works of the Bard. Performances (May-mid-Oct.) are held in Peninsula State Park and now include an autumn Town Hall Series, performed at venues around the county. Mixed with the zaniness is an admirable amount of history.

During August, professional musicians from across the country assemble in Fish Creek for the annual **Peninsula Music Festival** (920/854-4060, www.musicfestival.com), which offers Renaissance, Reformation, baroque, and chamber ensembles, along with an array of thematic material. Nationally known folk musicians and touring troupes appear at the **Door County Auditorium** (3926 Hwy. 42, 920/868-2728, www.dcauditorium.com); theater and dance performances are also held regularly.

Food

Road warriors with little time to spare: Coming into Fish Creek from the south, hit **Lautenbach's Orchard Country Winery & Market** (9197 Hwy. 42 S., 866/946-3263, www.orchardcountry.com, 10am-4pm Sun.-Thurs., 10am-5pm Fri.-Sat.) for some wine, then head up the road 0.5 miles to **White Cottage Red Door** (8813 Hwy. 42, 920/868-3667, 9am-6pm daily) to pick up cherry pie. Then go downtown to **Fish Creek Market** (4164 Hwy. 42, 920/868-3351, 9am-8pm Mon.-Sat, 9am-6pm Sun.) for some freshly baked bread and artisanal cheeses or other gourmet deli options. Find a spot on Green Bay and have a picnic. It's not necessarily the cheapest option, but it's an unbeatable experience.

As a sister of the excellent Chives in Baileys Harbor, **Barringer's** (1 N. Spruce St., 920/868-5445, dinner daily, $14-30) has good food genes. Solid supper club fare along with creative sides such as Asian fried brussels sprouts, all sourced locally, are savored in a chic black-and-white decor. It is off to a very good start.

The Cookery (Hwy. 42, 920/868-3634, breakfast, lunch, and dinner daily, $7-30), a sunny café with great healthy takes on standards, is a well-thought-out and well-run place despite often being packed. A rebuild was done with sustainability in mind, and the food comes from local producers as much as possible. Live music in summer/fall helps make the experience perfect.

Even picky foodies rave about the pizzas at ★ **Wild Tomato** (4023 Hwy. 42, 920/868-3095, 11am-10pm daily summer, lesser hours

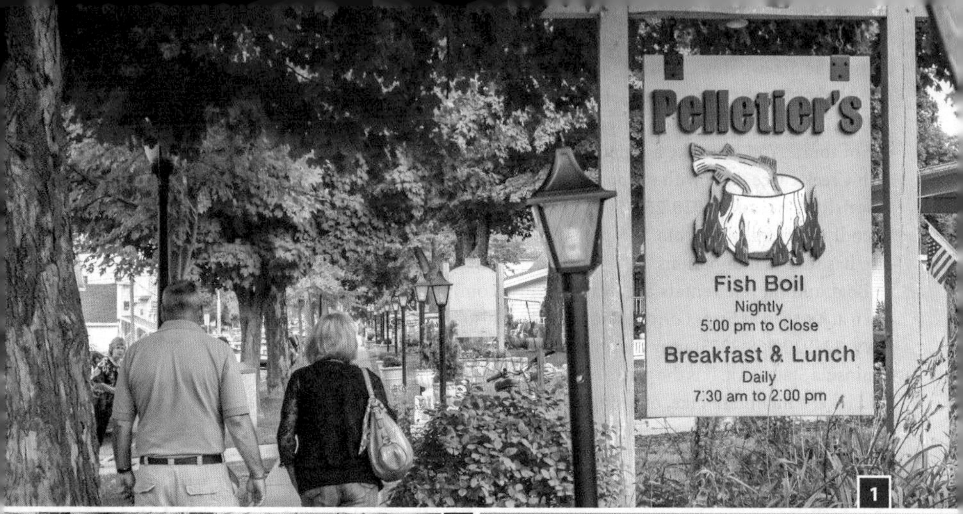

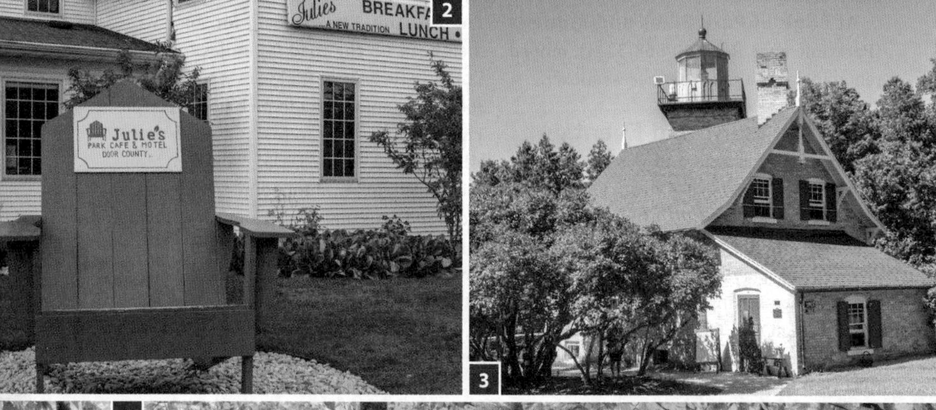

Pelletier's
Fish Boil
Nightly
5:00 pm to Close
Breakfast & Lunch
Daily
7:30 am to 2:00 pm
1

Julie's BREAKFA
A NEW TRADITION LUNCH
Julie's
PARK CAFE & MOTEL
DOOR COUNTY
2

3

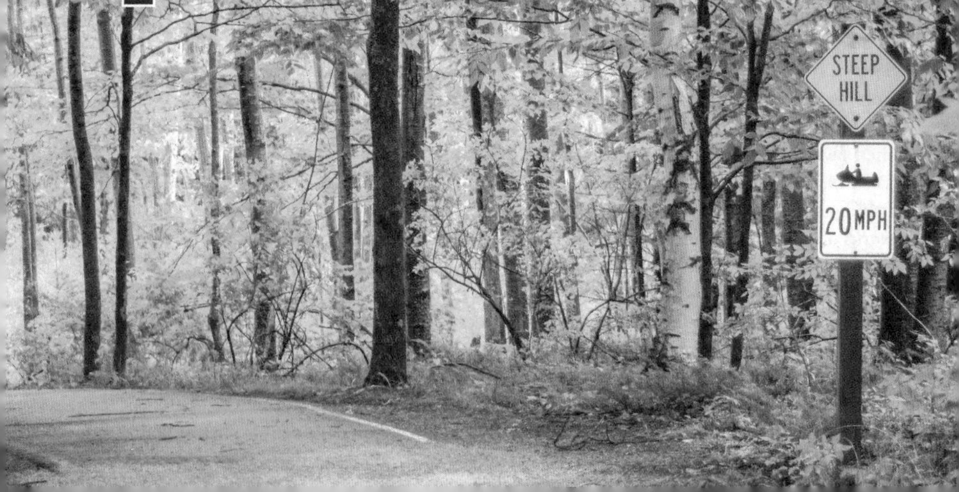

4
STEEP
HILL
20MPH

rest of year, $9-27). Even this author, no fan of tomato sauce and thus pizza, eats here regularly. Eat local, act local—it truly lives by social responsibility, as well.

Fish boils are a must, and Fish Creek's choice is the boisterous **Pelletier's** (Founder's Square, 920/868-3313, fish boils 5pm-7:30pm Sun.-Thurs., 5pm-8pm Fri.-Sat., fish boil $20). The fish boil is the best thing on the menu, but family-style meat-and-potatoes items are less expensive than at most other restaurants in town; this is also a great spot for a crowd of kids.

Resist the urge to balk at the words "fondue" and "Asian" in the same restaurant description: **Mr. Helsinki** (above the Fish Creek Market, Main St., 920/868-9898, 5pm-9:30pm daily, $7-22) is an international fusion bistro that specializes in everything from crepes to creative burgers and a lot of Asian tastes, and does it well, with nary a menu miss. It's a bit funky, irreverent, and a whole lot of something else.

The food at the almost-historic **Alexander's** (3667 Hwy. 42., 920/868-3532, dinner Tues.-Sat., brunch Sun., $14-30) can best be called an upscale supper club; the 1950s easy listening music is definitely so. The proprietor has four decades in Door County dining and takes care of the staff, and it shows.

It is extraordinary how consistent the ★ **White Gull Inn** (4225 Main St., 920/868-3517, www.whitegullinn.com, breakfast and lunch 7:30am-2:30pm and noon-2:30pm daily, dinner 5pm-8pm on varying weekdays, $14-25) has been despite absolute throngs coming for decades. The inn is *legendary* for its breakfast—*Good Morning America* even declared its cherry-stuffed french toast the best breakfast in the country. (In fact, they had to put in a new grill just for takeout french toast orders after the episode!) Dinner is lower-key and definitely for early birds. Note that dinner is served Saturday through Thursday only in the winter months and Monday, Tuesday, and Thursday in the summer months. The inn also hosts fantastic fish boils. In the summer, fish boils are offered on Wednesday and Friday-Sunday at 5:45pm, 7pm, and 8:15pm; in winter, only one fish boil is offered on Friday at 7pm.

The White Gull Inn gets much-deserved media attention for its dining, but for dinner, you may not be able to beat the ★ **Whistling Swan** (4192 Main St., 920/868-3442, www.whistlingswan.com, Tues.-Sat. 5pm-10pm, $18-36). Expect a gorgeous setting, gorgeous food impeccably done, and top-notch staff. The menu includes locally sourced, seasonal entrées with foraged produce, wild game, and local fish. This is a genuine treat.

Accommodations

Pet-friendly **Julie's** (4020 Hwy. 42, 920/868-2999, www.juliesmotel.com, from $120), a home-away-from-home near the state park, has rebuilt rooms for this edition, and includes nice touches such as LED lighting and insulating windows. The café breakfast rivals the pricier and better-known digs in town.

The wonderful **Main Street Motel** (4209 Hwy. 42, 920/868-2201, http://mainstreetmoteldc.com, from $129) is nothing ordinary. The solicitous, friendly proprietors offer very well-maintained themed guest rooms, but don't blanch at staying in the Teddy Bear Room, as the guest rooms and service rival any resort in terms of value—and it isn't kitschy. (Or stay in the Bicycle Room ... or Coffee Room.)

The **Juniper Inn** (9432 Maple Grove Rd., 920/839-2629, http://juniperinn.com, from $175) is a hidden gem, so travelers were worried when it was sold—not to worry, as the new proprietor is solicitous and it remains top-notch in every respect. Refreshingly modern with zero old stuff for the sake of old stuff, its four guest rooms offer something different, such as a gas fireplace, a private sitting room, and a deck with gorgeous views, and all share a lovely library.

Travel writers scour every inch of the peninsula annually, looking to scoop other

1: Pelletier's fish boil **2:** Julie's **3:** Eagle Bluff Lighthouse, Peninsula State Park **4:** Sunset Trail, Peninsula State Park

media outlets on an undiscovered gem, but they generally rehash the same old thing: the stately grace and charm of the ★ **White Gull Inn** (4255 Main St., 920/868-3517, www.whitegullinn.com, from $200). A proud old guesthouse since 1897, it's truly the grande dame of Door County, the longest-running inn in the county. Guest rooms—a couple with private porches—are anachronistic but still plush; a few cottages and guest rooms in a cliff house are also available. The dining room serves a spectacular array of continental, creative regional, and seafood cuisine in a country inn atmosphere that's not at all stuffy. And then there's that legendary boisterous fish boil, so popular that people swear they've made the return trip just to experience it. It's made extra special by the boil masters, who often preside over impromptu singing.

You'll find the most history of all at the **Thorp House Inn and Cottages** (4135 Bluff Rd., 920/868-2444, www.thorphouseinn.com, $179 rooms, $209 cottages), on land that once belonged to Freeman Thorp, nephew of Fish Creek's founding father. The inn is backed by the bluff overlooking the harbor. When Thorp perished in a 1903 shipwreck, his widow was forced to convert their new Victorian into a guesthouse. The B&B-style guest rooms at the inn and the great beach house feel anachronistic, and the cottages are quaint but modernized just enough that you can dock your iPod and access Wi-Fi.

A main rival to the White Gull Inn is the ★ **Whistling Swan** (4192 Main St., 920/868-3442, www.whistlingswan.com, $160-225), with the most dramatic local history—it was originally constructed across Green Bay in Marinette and skidded across the winter ice in 1907 to its present site. Five period guest rooms and two suites are available; the arched windows, fireplace, and high ceilings of the lobby are a draw for casual browsers in the shops on the main level. These rates are a steal in Door County.

Nightly rates of more than $350 may sound outrageous, but the villas at the **Little Sweden** (8984 Hwy. 42, 920/868-9950, http://little-sweden.com) timeshare property are absolutely enormous (the smallest two-bedroom is nearly 1,200 square feet). Guest rooms can sleep 4 to 10 people, the site is heavily wooded with good privacy, and you can access recreation options such as bicycles, golf, and more.

Information

The **Fish Creek Information Center** (4097 Hwy. 42, 920/868-2316 or 800/577-1880, www.visitfishcreek.com) is fully equipped to deal with your travel queries or last-minute needs.

★ PENINSULA STATE PARK

The park comprises 3,800 variegated acres stretching from the northern fringe of Fish Creek, past Strawberry Channel, past Eagle Bluff, past Nicolet Bay, and finally to Eagle Harbor and Ephraim, all of it magnificent. Deeded to the state in 1909, Peninsula is the second-oldest park in the state system and the most visited—it draws more visitors per year than Yellowstone National Park. Be advised that because it is so popular, a daily pass here is $2 more ($13 for out of state license plates) than other state parks.

The peninsula, rising 180 feet above the lake at Eagle Bluff, is a manifestation of the western edge of the Niagara Escarpment, here a steep and variegated series of headlands and reentrants. The ecosystem is unparalleled: Near Weborg Point in the southwest, the Peninsula White Cedar Forest Natural Area is a 53-acre stand of spruce, cedar, balsam, and hemlock along with the boggy residual tract of an ancient lake. The 80-acre Peninsula Beech Forest Natural Area is a primitive example of northern mixed hardwood; it's also a relatively uncommon stand of American beech. Within both natural areas are a few threatened species, including the vivid dwarf lake iris. Other rarities include gaywings, Indian paintbrush, blue-eyed grass, and downy gentian. Be sure to stay for the sunset.

Sights

A must-see is the **Eagle Bluff Lighthouse**

(920/421-3636), built during the Civil War by U.S. lighthouse crewmen as the second of the peninsula's lighthouses, a square tower about 45 feet tall attached to the keeper's house. It stands atop the bluff and can be seen for 15 miles; the views from its top stretch even farther. The prize assignment for lighthouse keepers on the peninsula, it had a commanding view and the best salary, the princely sum (for 1880) of $50 per month. Public interest prompted local historical societies to peel off 80 layers of paint and set to work refurbishing the lighthouse in the late 1950s. Tours ($8.50 adults) are given in early summer and autumn every 30 minutes 10am-4:30pm Monday-Friday, with shorter hours the rest of year.

Two 75-foot towers were erected at the park's inception and used as fire-spotting towers; one was later removed because of dry rot. **Eagle Tower** was built because so many people wanted to view a pair of long-term nesting eagles—the two for whom the bluff, the harbor, and the peninsula were eventually named. In 2015 the tower was closed due to structural decay, and money being what it is, it was thought rebuilding it wouldn't be feasible. Well, the hullabaloo that followed made it happen, resulting in a brand-new tower, the first wheelchair-accessible tower in the state!

Before going hiking, most visitors head to the **White Cedar Nature Center** (Bluff Rd., 920/854-5976, 10am-2pm daily Memorial Day-Labor Day, shorter hours Labor Day-Memorial Day) to walk a nature trail and view a host of exhibits covering the park's natural history.

Recreation

GOLF

Deemed one of the gems of Midwestern courses by the golf press, this 18-holer is in the eastern part of the park. It was built by a group of Ephraim businessmen in the early 1900s as a nine-hole course with sand greens. Tee-time **reservations** (920/854-5791, www.peninsulagolf.org) are required at this busy course. Make them as early as possible.

HIKING

More than 20 miles of hiking trails lace the park and the shores of the bays. After parking and checking out Eagle Tower in the northern section of the park, ambitious visitors can take **Minnehaha Trail** (easy, 0.5 miles) or **Sentinel Trail** (easy, 2-mile loop) for some grand hiking. Minnehaha also connects to the South Nicolet Bay campground (near site 844) and runs along the lakeshore with great bay vistas; Sentinel runs through stands of maple, birch, and red pine, and 0.5 miles is surfaced with gravel for accessibility. The moderately difficult 0.5-mile spur **Lone Pine Trail,** off Sentinel Trail, leads up a dolomite bluff and through beech and oak trees, at one point passing the trail's solitary pine tree, now fallen along the path. The toughest trail, but also the most rewarding, is **Eagle Trail,** skirting the harbor and a couple of natural springs for two miles and affording challenging scrambles over 200-foot bluffs; it's a workout, but you'll see lots of trilliums and thimbleberries.

In the north and west sections of the park, there are a couple of must-hike trails. In the north, so many people hiked from Nicolet Bay to Eagle Bluff Lighthouse through cool stands of trees that an easy 0.5-mile trail was blazed, now dubbed the **Trail Tramper's Delight Trail.**

At its halfway point, the Nicolet Bay Trail connects with two great trails, both moderately difficult. The two-mile **Hemlock Trail** rises up a modest bluff to great views of the Strawberry Islands, and the three-mile loop **Skyline Trail** rises up minor Sven's Bluff and past the remains of old homestead farms and fences, now decaying gracefully in the grasses and meadows.

BIKING

There are 15 miles of road and off-road bike trails; a state trail pass is required. What may be the most heavily used recreational trail—**Sunset Trail**—starts near the park entrance and roughly parallels Shore Road for nearly five miles through marsh and stands of hardwoods and conifers and along the lakeside perimeter of Nicolet Bay Beach, at which point lovely back roads lead back to the park entrance. At dusk it is definitely not misnamed. Remember that this trail is multiuse, meaning pedestrian and wheelchair traffic; wheels yield to heels.

Bicycle rentals ($25/day) are available at **Nicolet Beach Rentals** (920/854-9220) in the northern end of the park.

KAYAKING AND CANOEING

You won't forget a kayak or canoe trip to **Horseshoe Island,** which has its own one-mile trail. It is rugged and definitely isolated even though it's only a mile from Nicolet Bay. Kayakers and canoeists love Tennison Bay on the west side of the park due to its shallow draft. Kayak rentals ($50/day) are available from **Nicolet Beach Rentals** (920/854-9220) in the northern end of the park.

CAMPING

Camping was once allowed almost anywhere the ranger waved his hand and was either free or cost $0.50 per week. Today, the state's reservation system receives up to 5,500 applications for summer reservations in *January.* At last count there were 469 campsites in five sectors, and even though a handful are not reservable, it's almost impossible to get a site without a **reservation** (888/947-2757, www.wisconsin.goingtocamp.com, from $25 per site, $8 reservation fee), especially on Friday and Saturday.

Only one sector is open year-round. All sectors have showers, but a couple have no electrical hookups. Many people prefer **South Nicolet Bay** (143 sites) since it's large, has electrical hookups, and is closest to the sandy beach. You have to reserve early in January to get a waterside site. **North Nicolet Bay** campground (44 sites) is also not far from the beach but smaller and has no electricity. Early reservations are also a must to get a waterside site. The park's largest campground is **Tennison Bay** (188 sites); this is also the accessible campground. There is no beach nearby, however, and no waterside sites. **Weborg Point** (12 sites) and **Welcker's Point** (81 sites) fill up last. Given the small size, Weborg should be quieter, but the electrical hookups mean there is generator noise; it does have waterside sites. Welcker's Point, without electrical hookups, is quieter.

EPHRAIM

As the map tells it, five miles separate Fish Creek and Ephraim (pronounced EE-frum), but you'd hardly know it. On the way north, as you pass the north entrance of Peninsula State Park, a modest jumble of development appears and then vanishes, and shortly the fringes of beautiful Ephraim appear.

Another endlessly long Door County village along a vivid harbor, Ephraim isn't the oldest community in the county, nor are its structures the most historically distinguished, but aesthetically the community is the most perfectly preserved slice of Door County. The quaintness isn't accidental—for a while the village dictated, via social pressure, that all structures were to be whitewashed in proper fashion. The town is set along gorgeous Eagle Harbor. An enclave of pious fortitude, it was settled by Norwegian Moravians and named Ephraim, which means "doubly fruitful" in Hebrew.

Sights

The oldest church in the county, the **Moravian Church** (9970 Moravia St., 920/854-2804), built out of necessity when the village founder's living room no longer sufficed, was constructed in 1857 of cedar from the Upper Peninsula; local logs were too rough for such a sacred house. Tours ($5) of the church as well as museums below are offered at 1:30pm Thursday.

Also on Moravia Street are three other structures that operate as one museum (920/854-9688, 11am-4pm Mon.-Sat. mid-June-Aug., 11am-4pm Fri.-Sat. Sept.-Oct., $5 includes tour). The **Pioneer Schoolhouse Museum** (9998 Moravia St.) doubles as a repository of local history. Displays of local art in various media, from juried shows and chosen by local arts associations, are worth a look. The third historic structure along the street is the **Thomas Goodletson Cabin,** an 1857 original inside and out and one of the peninsula's first cabins. Down off the bluff are the **Anderson Barn and Store,** a ruddy barn built in 1870. During the summer, it's open for browsing; the prominent square silo is a rarity. Built in 1858 by Aslag Anderson, one of the original Scandinavian settlers, it sports old-time store items along with museum-like pieces.

Summertime **walking tours** of all the historic structures depart at 10:30am Tuesday-Friday (call to verify) from the Anderson Barn. Nice are the less-sweat-inducing 90-minute **tram tours** (11am Tues.-Sat., $10), a quick way to take in all the local history.

Recreation

South Shore Pier, in the heart of Ephraim village, has a large number of water-based recreation and tour opportunities. Hour-plus catamaran cruises (from $35), including a sunset cruise, depart up to seven times daily aboard the ***Stiletto*** (920/854-7245, www.stilettosailingcruises.com). Or rent your own pontoon boat, kayak, WaveRunner, paddleboat, or fishing boat from the **South Shore Pier** (920/854-4324). Other operations offer kayak and windsurfing lessons and rentals, and even parasail rides.

Festivals

The highlight of the entire year in Ephraim is the Scandinavian summer solstice celebration **Fyr Bal Festival.** Bonfires dot the shoreline and fish-boil cauldrons gurgle to commemorate the arrival of summer. A "Viking chieftain" is crowned and then blesses the ships and the harbor. The accompanying art fairs are less Norse in nature.

Food

Until 2016, Ephraim was the only municipality in Wisconsin that banned the sale of alcohol. In a state where drinking seems second only to Packer-backing, this lone dry town was an enormous anomaly, not to mention being as confusing as can be for tourists. However, a referendum was passed allowing the sale of beer and wine (only).

At **Good Eggs** (9820 Brookside Ln., 920/854-6621, 7am-1pm daily May-Oct., $5-9), set back along Highway 42, you can build your own omelet, wrap it up in a tortilla (try the cilantro), and dash. Or sit at their surfboard tables and relax with a view of the water.

However, if it's soup your soul needs, then absolutely head to the irreverent and awesome **Czarnuszka Soup Bar** (9922 Water St., 920/634-9649, 11am-5pm daily, $7-11). They have sandwiches too, but on a chilly day, potato chowder or—if you're lucky, the ethnic staple here of Belgian *booyah* (a stew)—will set all right in the world.

The **Old Post Office** (10040 Hwy. 42, 920/854-4034, breakfast and dinner daily, $5-10) in the Edgewater Resort has luscious Belgian waffles, but it really is known mostly for one of the biggest fish boils in the county, and it really is a favorite of this author. The presentation, the schticky (but wonderful) storytelling, the service—it just feels right here.

New-on-the-scene ★ **Trixie's** (9996 Pioneer Ln., 920/854-8008, lunch/dinner Mon.-Sat., $9-22) is worth a visit. It's hip but unpretentious and well-thought-out, from design to menu. They emphasize social responsibility in cuisine from, literally, the ground up; for example, they strive to work with female-owned vineyards. The Russian dumplings and flaming Greek cheese are worth the trip.

It's nearly a Door County law that you stop at **Wilson's** (9990 Water St., 920/854-2041, from 11am daily May-Oct.), an old-fashioned ice cream parlor in the heart of the village. Opened in 1906 and serving ever since, it has ice cream cones as big as bullhorns. Hanging out on the white-framed porch, you'll feel as if you're in a Norman Rockwell painting.

Accommodations

The **Eagle Harbor Inn** (9914 Hwy. 42, 920/854-2121, www.eagleharborinn.com, $119-275) is well reviewed. Some swear it's a better value than anywhere else in the region. The elegant nine-room inn, with two suites, is antique-strewn and offers a sumptuous country breakfast in the garden. The one- to three-bedroom cottages on nicely wooded grounds are also very appealing.

You won't find more charming hosts than those at the **Ephraim Motel** (10407 Hwy. 42, 920/854-5959, from $124); the guest rooms are worth the rates as well.

A longtime lodging cheap-sleep was gutted and recreated as the worthy **O'Malley's Inn** (10176 N. Water St., 920/854-7333, www.omalleysinn.com, $135), which didn't, thankfully, result in stratospheric rates. This is this author's new place. Part motel, part lodge, with even a log cabin, it's in a quiet wooded setting with hiking trails adjacent.

★ **Lodgings at Pioneer Lane** (9998 Pioneer Ln., 920/854-7656 or 800/588-3565, www.lodgingsatpioneerlane.com, from $199) has themed guest rooms. This might evoke images of embarrassing tackiness, but here it is impeccably executed, with kitchenettes, fireplaces, private porches or balconies, and superb details. The owners get rave reviews as well. It's north of Wilson's ice cream parlor, then right on Church Street.

Information

Ephraim's **Information Center** (920/854-4989, www.ephraim-doorcounty.com), is right along Highway 42. A 24-hour kiosk is there in season for last-minute motel seekers.

SISTER BAY

Sister Bay can get congested on a typical summer Saturday—symbolic of its status as the largest community north of Sturgeon Bay, even though the population is a mere 900. It's also the only spot north on the peninsula with a small shopping mall. Named for twin islands offshore, the bay—not offering quite the windbreak of Eagle Harbor—never got much notice from southbound steamers until Scandinavian settlers discovered the dense forestland in the surrounding hills and erected cabins in 1857.

Sights

Sister Bay's quaint **waterfront park** is the largest in the county at a third of a mile long, with one of the longest—and prettiest—stretches of beach around. Meaning: this is a good spot to get a bit of elbow room even in high season.

On the south edge of town is the **Old Anderson House Museum** (Hwy. 57 and Fieldcrest Rd., 920/854-7680, tours 10am-4pm Tues.-Sat. and holidays mid-May-mid-Oct., free), a restored house dating from 1895. The house was built in Marinette, Wisconsin, and dragged across the ice. Other area historical structures have also been relocated to this site.

Recreation

Bay Shore Outfitters (920/854-7598, www.kayakdoorcounty.com) at the waterfront has daily guided kayak tours along with rentals of cross-country skis, snowshoes, and bicycles. **Door County Boats** (10707 N. Bay Shore Dr., 920/421-4444, www.doorcountyboats.com) at the marina rents all sorts of water equipment, but its highlight is a slate of wonderful boat tours, including a worthy Death's Door cruise ($42). Their sunset music cruise is the opposite of the usual boozy and cringey—this one was a hoot and infectious for all.

Sister Bay has a local **dog park** (Woodcrest Rd., east of Hwy. 42 on Hwy. ZZ) to let the furry knuckleheads romp.

Festivals and Events

The waterfront park hosts the huge **Fall Festival** with a 900-square-foot outdoor stage. The park is the linchpin of a fine community network of parks that offer regular doses of free big band, jazz, country, and folk concerts—there is one every Wednesday in summer.

Food

For the "only in Wisconsin" file: The **Sister Bay Bowl and Supper Club** (504 Bay Shore Dr., 920/854-2841, lunch/dinner daily

1: Ephraim harbor **2:** a goat on the roof of Al Johnson's Swedish Restaurant **3:** Door County Creamery **4:** Sister Bay beachfront

1
2
3
4
DOOR COUNTY CREAMERY

Apr.-Jan.—closed the occasional Mon. Dec.-Jan.—Sat.-Sun. Feb.-Mar., from $5), right downtown, does have bowling, and it offers one of the better fish fries around—great if you're wearying of fish boils.

The **Base Camp Coffee House** (10904 Hwy. 42, 920/854-7894, 7:30am-2pm Sun.-Thurs., till 5pm Fri.-Sat., from $5) is hard to notice, as it's in the basement of an old church behind a clothing shop. It has a simple, special vibe. Besides coffee, you'll find ever-so-fresh sandwiches ($6), quiches, and a limited breakfast menu ($4-6).

Bier Zot Cafe (10677 N. Bay Shore Dr., 920/854-5070, lunch and dinner daily, $7-16) is a tiny gastropub specializing in Belgian beers (they have over 100). The service is phenomenal; do try the wild boar burger and my favorite, pork belly ramen.

For a great—no, otherworldly—treat, head for ★ **Door County Creamery** (10653 Hwy. 42, 920/854-3388, 10:30am-9pm, from $4), opened by lifers in the county's culinary industry. Try goat's milk gelato made daily (from their own goat farm). They've also got extraordinary handcrafted cheeses and use them to create sandwiches and salads.

Grasse's Grill (10663 N. Hwy. 42, 920/854-1125, breakfast/lunch daily, $5-16) is utterly unpretentious and friendly; it's run by a husband-and-wife team who obviously love food. Dishes include brisket hash and what may be their signature, the Hippie Breakfast—eggs with sweet potato, black bean, corn and cauliflower hash!

The most famous international eatery in the county, if not the state, is ★ **Al Johnson's Swedish Restaurant** (702 Hwy. 42, 920/854-2626, 6am-9pm daily, $8-18), where cars regularly screech to a halt when drivers see the legendary live goats munching the sod roof. The menu offers Swedish and American food. Pounds of Swedish meatballs are served nightly, and other favorites are the Swedish beefsteak sautéed in onions and lingonberry pancakes for breakfast. It's often standing room only, quite lively, and doesn't take reservations. Famous Al died in 2010, a great loss for the county.

On the north end of town, the **Waterfront** (10947 N. Hwy. 42, 920/854-5491, 5pm-9pm Tues.-Sun., $24-37) is run by a couple with three decades in the Door restaurant business; it is well-known for its seafood.

Two miles north of town, **Seaquist Orchards Farm Market** (11482 Hwy. 42, 920/854-4199, 9am-5pm daily) sells cherry pies as well as cherry jams, pie filling, salsa, vinaigrette, and more.

Accommodations

One of the cheapest motels on the Door is the pleasant **Village View** (10628 N. Bay Shore Dr., 715/896-4563, www.village-view.com, from $90), with clean and updated rooms and very friendly owners.

The helpful proprietors of **Coachlite Inn** (2544 Hwy. 42, 920/854-5503, http://coachliteinn.com, from $125) provide simple, well-kept guest rooms with fridges, and there's a nice whirlpool and hot tub room.

The guest rooms and breakfast area make the **Open Hearth Lodge** (2669 S. Hwy. 42, 920/854-4890, http://openhearthlodge.com, from $125) stand out. Indeed, the guest rooms are very well appointed, and they've done a nice job on the grounds as well; there's even enough room for a bit of hiking in the woods and meadow nearby. You'll also find a playground, an indoor pool, and fridges in every room. Guests have remarked at the welcoming staff and nice, unexpected extras here.

Also good is the rustic, century-old **Liberty Park Lodge** (Hwy. 42, north of Sister Bay, 920/854-2025, www.libertylodgesb.com, from $130). The main lodge has guest rooms dating back to the Door's tourism beginnings, now lovingly redone. Also available are Cape Cod-style woodland and shore cottages. Overall there is a rich balance of old and new, and for the price, you cannot beat it. Plus, they have rooms like the Johnny Cash Suite—how can you not go for that?

Forty-five large (up to 600 square feet) and

☆ Fish Boils

Just when travelers think they've come to understand Wisconsin's predilection for fish fries, Door County throws them a curveball with the fish boil, which is not at all the same thing.

Scandinavian immigrants came with their own recipes for fish soups and stews, but the fish boil likely came about for purely practical reasons. Door County had few cows or pigs but was rich in whitefish; the hardy potato and onion were also abundant.

The modern version is a different story. As some tell it, the proprietor of Ellison Bay's Viking Grill concocted the first modern fish boil back in the 1960s, ostensibly searching for something unique to serve at the restaurant. It was an immediate hit that snowballed into the de rigueur culinary experience of Door County. Whatever the historical genesis of the boil, it has become a cultural linchpin for the peninsula community.

A Door County fish boil requires only a couple things: a huge iron cauldron, sufficient firewood, and the ingredients—fish steaks, small potatoes, onions, and a lot of salt. Purists favor whitefish, but don't let that stop you from trying other varieties, such as trout.

Add salt to the water and bring to a boil (the salt raises the boiling temperature of the water and helps keep the fish from flaking apart in the water). Add potatoes and boil for 15 minutes. Add onions and boil another 4-5 minutes. Add the fish, which is often wrapped in cheesecloth to prevent it from falling apart, and boil for another 10 minutes. Now, here's the fun part: Right before the fish is done, use kerosene to jack up the flame to rocket-launch proportions. The kerosene induces a boil-over, which forces the oily top layers of water out of the cauldron, to be burned off in the fire. Drain the rest and slather it with butter. The requisite side dishes are coleslaw, dark breads, and this being Door County, cherry pie or cobbler for dessert.

Try one of the following places for a superb fish boil:

- **Square Rigger Lodge and Cottages** (6332 Hwy. 57, 920/823-2404, www.squareriggerlodge.com)
- **Old Post Office** (10040 Hwy. 42, 920/854-4034)
- **The Viking Grill** (12029 Hwy. 42, 920/854-2998)
- **White Gull Inn** (4225 Main St., 920/868-3517, www.whitegullinn.com)
- **Pelletier's** (Founder's Square, 920/868-3313)

attractive guest rooms are available at the ★ **Country House Resort** (2468 Sunnyside Rd., 920/854-4551 or 800/424-0041, www.countryhouseresort.com, $140-360). All feature fridges and private waterside balconies, and some have whirlpool tubs and other miscellaneous amenities. The grounds cover 16 heavily wooded acres with private nature trails and a 1,000-foot shoreline; for the price, this can't be beat. It's just south of the main drag, off Highway 42 and then toward the bay.

Like the county "used to be," and perhaps a steal for such updated old-school charm, **Little Sister Resort** (10620 Little Sister Hill Rd., 920/854-4013, www.littlesisterresort.com, from $185) is in a cedar forest south of Sister Bay off Highway 42 near a gorgeous bay. These very comfortable surroundings also cater to families. You'll need to brew some coffee and take a seat to go through the mind-boggling array of cabins and chalets, but this place is worth the money unless you're a solo traveler. The management is quite responsive.

Information

Sister Bay has a quaint **Visitor Information Center** (416 Gateway Dr., 920/854-2812, www.cometosisterbay.com) in a refurbished log schoolhouse.

ELLISON BAY

Plunked along the decline of a steep hill and hollow tunneling toward a yawning bay, Ellison Bay's facade isn't initially as spectacular as Ephraim's, the architecture isn't as quaint as Fish Creek's, and it's a fifth the size of Sister Bay. Nonetheless, there is something engaging about the place. It begins with what may be the best view from the highway in the whole county. Atop the 200-foot bluff on the south side of town, you can see clear to Gills Rock, farther up the peninsula. As recently as the 1930s, the town's commercial fishery led Wisconsin in tonnage—perhaps the reason a local restaurant is credited with creating the first fish boil.

Sights

Its name is often misinterpreted as representing the 130 lovely acres overlooking the northern fringe of Ellison Bay, but in fact, **The Clearing** (12171 Garrett Bay Rd., 920/854-4088, www.theclearing.org) refers to the metaphysical—"clarity of thought." A contemplative retreat for the study of art, natural science, and the humanities—philosophy is ever-popular—the school was the result of a lifetime's effort by famed landscape architect Jens Jensen.

The grounds contain a lodge, a library, a communal dining area, and cottages and dormitories for attendees. Summer classes are held May-October and last one week, though some day seminars are also offered. Meals are included. Lots of group work, outdoor exploration, campfires, and other traditional fare are the rule. Nonparticipants can visit and take free tours 1pm-3pm Saturday-Sunday mid-May-mid-October.

Ellison Bay has the grand **Bluff County Park,** three miles southwest of town along Highway 42. Nearly 100 wild acres atop 200-foot two-tiered rocky bluffs overlook the lake. Some cedar trees here are up to 260 years old, part of the Ellison Bluff State Natural Area incorporated into the park. Camping is not allowed here, but some rough trails wind through the area, although none go to the water. You'll find some lovely views.

Food

A popular fish boil spot has long been **The Viking Grill** (12029 Hwy. 42, 920/854-2998, 6am-9pm daily summer, 6am-7pm in other seasons, $4-15). The Viking is credited with filling that first iron cauldron with whitefish, potatoes, and onions, and brewing up a culinary tradition.

★ **Wickman House** (11976 Mink River Rd., east of Hwy. 42, 920/854-3305, 5pm-10pm Wed.-Mon. May-Mar., $12-30) is a Door County bistro worthy of an extra nickel or two. In an erstwhile lodge, it features as much sustainably raised local food as possible (including growing their own in an on-site garden) in a cheery, welcoming atmosphere. Take in one of their memorable harvest dinners.

Accommodations

The best places to stay are in the vicinity of Ellison Bay. The mom-and-pop (literally) **Hillside Inn** (11934 Hwy. 42, 920/854-2928, from $95) offers clean rooms and the proprietors busily making sure all is well. Up the rate scale, the impeccably well-run **Bayview Resort** (12030 Cedar Shore Rd., 920/854-2006, www.bayviewresortandharbor.com, from $195) offers everything from simple rooms up to suites for eight people. They even have a harbor.

Information

The smallest visitors center on the peninsula might be the closet-size **Ellison Bay Information Kiosk** (Hwy. 42, 920/854-5448, May-Oct.), across from The Viking Grill.

GILLS ROCK AND NORTHPORT

North of Ellison Bay, Highway 42 cuts east and then bends 90 degrees north again into the tightly packed fishing village of Gills Rock (pop. about 75). High atop 150-foot Table Bluff overlooking Hedgehog Harbor and across from Deathdoor Bluff, pleasant Gills Rock is as far as the road goes on the Door. Sleepy and quaint and known as the tip or top of the thumb, Gills Rock has the feel of an old tourist camp from the 1930s. A couple of miles farther east on Highway 42 is truly the end of the line, Northport. The highway leading to the ferry at Northport offers splendid scenery in fall.

Sights

DOOR COUNTY MARITIME MUSEUM

Door County's other maritime museum, an offshoot of Sturgeon Bay's, is on a dusty little side road in Gills Rock—the **Death's Door Maritime Museum** (12724 W. Wisconsin Bay Rd., 920/854-1844, www.dcmm.org, 10am-5pm daily May-Oct., $6 adults). This museum features gill nets and plenty of other old equipment related to the commercial fishing industry. The highlight is an old fishing tug, but in 2018 they unveiled a lovely new bronze sculpture honoring the maritime industry.

DOOR BLUFF HEADLANDS

Here you'll find the most solitude and best views of the bay at the largest park in the county, **Door Bluff Headlands,** comprising almost 200 acres of wild trails and woodland. That's over 7,000 feet of shoreline! Note that this park has deliberately been underdeveloped. The trails are rough and unmarked, and there are no established or safe trails to the water from the top. In 2019 a plan was unveiled to expand the park by nearly 50 percent but also to maintain its wild nature. Go off trail at your own risk. From Highway 42, take Cottage Road to Garrett Bay Road.

Recreation

FISHING

The Mariner (920/421-1578) is the go-to boat in Gills Rock for a fishing charter ($90 pp). Chinook salmon and German brown trout are the specialties, and the rates are reasonable; you fish virtually the entire time.

DIVING

Scuba divers come to Gills Rock for underwater archaeology. Beneath the surface of local waters lie more than 200 wrecks, and the Wisconsin Historical Society has ongoing "digs" on its Wisconsin Maritime Trails project. If you don't want to dive, the local visitors centers have maps of land-based information markers pointing out wreck sites from shore; visit the **Wisconsin Historical Society** (http://www.wisconsinshipwrecks.org) for more information. The **Shoreline Resort** (920/854-2606, www.theshorelineresort.com) has dive charters, but you must have your own gear and already be certified. The resort also offers daily narrated scenic boat tours (10am, 12:30 and 3:30pm, $42) of Death's Door.

FERRIES AND CRUISES TO WASHINGTON ISLAND

The most luxurious way to Washington Island is a narrated cruise aboard the ***Island Clipper*** (920/854-2972, www.islandclipper.com), a 65-foot cruiser specifically designed by a Sturgeon Bay boatbuilder for the Death's Door crossing. A basic crossing ($13 adults) is possible, as well as a crossing plus a Viking Train island tour ($25). In peak summer season there are five departures 10am-4pm daily.

Northport exists solely to accommodate the ferry line to Washington Island. The pier was built to escape the fierce prevailing winds on the Gills Rock side, and Northport has in fact eclipsed Gills Rock as a ferry departure point to Washington Island; it is almost always free of ice and saves precious crossing time.

Northport is the ferry to use to take a car to Washington Island. The **Washington Island Ferry** (920/847-2546 or 800/223-2094, www.wisferry.com) takes autos and passengers, and it connects with the Cherry Train tour of the island if you take the 9:45am or earlier crossing from Northport (11am from Gills Rock). The ferry runs frequently: in high season (July-late Aug.), 25 daily round-trips depart to and from the island beginning at 6:45am from the island, 7:30am from Northport (possibly no early trip on Sun.). Fewer trips depart in other seasons. In December-January there are only four trips per day; in February-March only one or two per day, and vehicle reservations are mandatory. In the off-season, call to check departure times. A car costs $26 (passengers not included), adults are $13.50, bicycles are $4, and motorcycles are $15; all prices are round-trip.

Food

The best food in Gills Rock is the grand smoked Lake Michigan fish at ★ **Charlie's Smokehouse** (12731 Hwy. 42, 920/854-2972, 9am-6pm daily May-Oct., 9am-5pm Sat., 12:30pm-4pm Sun. Nov.-Apr.), which has been doing it since 1932.

The **Shoreline Resort** (12747 Hwy. 42, 920/854-2900, www.theshorelineresort.com, lunch and dinner daily May-Oct., $7-22) is the other dining option, with good whitefish and basic hearty fare.

Accommodations

Prominent in Gills Rock, the **Shoreline Resort** (12747 Hwy. 42, 920/854-2900, www.theshorelineresort.com, $119) offers waterfront guest rooms with patios and a popular rooftop sundeck; the views are grand. Charter fishing tours and assorted sightseeing cruises (the sunset cruise is perennially popular) also leave the on-site marina. Shoreline also rents out bicycles.

Unheard-of **On the Rocks Cliffside Lodge** (849 Wisconsin Bay Rd., 920/854-4907, www.cliffsidelodge.com, Apr.-Nov., from $400) is possibly the most private Door County experience; you have to see it to believe it. This jewel is a massive 3,500-square-foot A-frame lodge with a fieldstone fireplace atop a 60-foot cliff. It was overwhelming enough for *National Geographic* to feature it. Rates start at $400 for two people, but it can accommodate up to 18 people ($780).

Washington Island and Rock Island

Rustic, time-locked Washington Island (an easy and safe ferry ride from the mainland across Death's Door) very nearly wasn't included as part of the Door, but in 1925 the U.S. Supreme Court ruled in Wisconsin's favor in a border dispute with Michigan. At issue were a number of the dozen or so islands in the Grand Traverse Chain, of which Washington and the surrounding islands are a part.

The island isn't like Michigan's candy-facade Mackinac Island, with historically garbed docents and fudge hawkers every few steps; Washington Island is populated by 650 permanent residents, and development is absolutely unobtrusive. The place has a pleasant weather-beaten seaside look to it rather than the sheen of a slick resort. This explains the island's perfectly apt advertising slogan: "North of the Tension Line."

WASHINGTON ISLAND

Sights

WASHINGTON ISLAND *STAVKIRKE*

Large-scale European settlement started in the early 1830s, when immigrants to Green Bay heard of trout the size of calves being taken from the waters around the island. The first nonnative fishers were Irish, but several thousand Icelanders took readily to the isolation and set down permanent roots. Their heritage is clearly manifested in the **Washington Island *Stavkirke*** (1763 Town Line Rd., 920/847-2179), a wooded stave church gradually built by island residents, one massive white pine log at a time, and by the proud Icelandic horses that roam certain island pastures.

ART AND NATURE CENTER

A mix of island natural and cultural history is displayed at the **Art and Nature Center** (1799 Main Rd., 920/847-2025, www.wianc.org, 10:30am-4:30pm Mon.-Sat.,

Washington Island and Rock Island

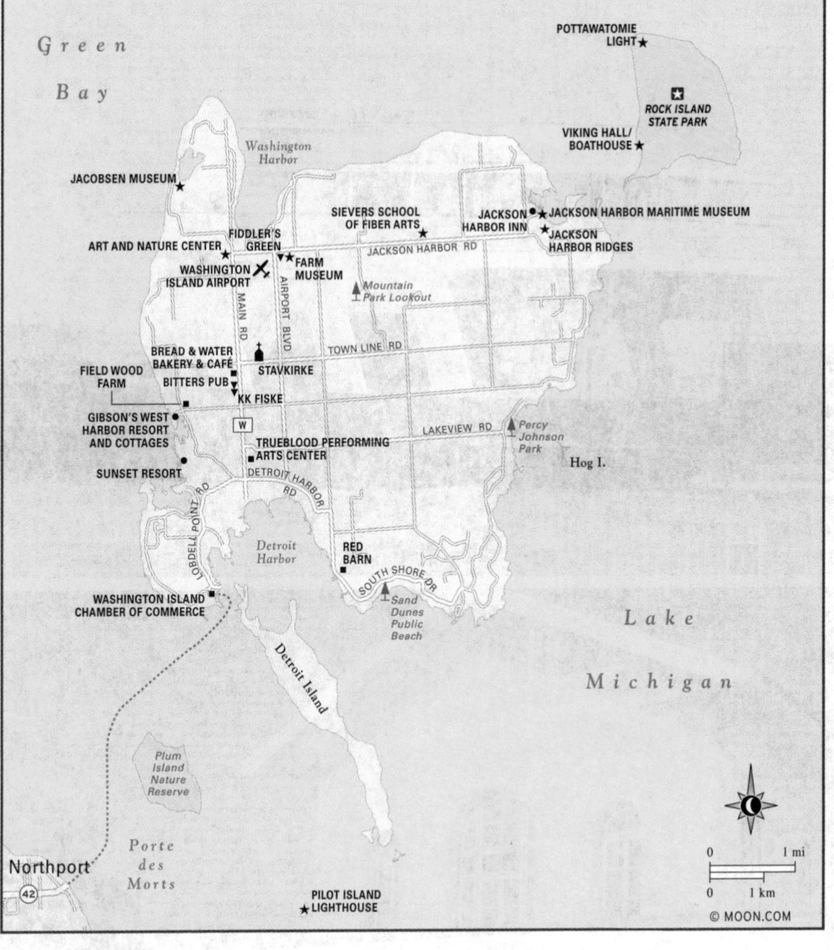

11am-4:30pm Sun. mid-June-mid-Sept., 11am-3pm daily in other seasons, $1 adults), at the corner of Main Road and Jackson Harbor Road, in an unassuming building resembling an old schoolhouse. Permanent artwork displays are housed within, and nature trails start from the rear. Art classes are offered, and regular musical events are held during a summer festival (the first two weeks of August).

MUSEUMS

The top stop for museum hoppers is the **Jackson Harbor Maritime Museum** (920/743-5958, 10am-4pm Mon.-Fri. Memorial Day-Oct., some weekends in summer, donation) at the east end of Jackson Harbor Road, opposite the ferry landing. The museum retains significant relics of the island's commercial fishing industry, which still operates out of secluded Jackson Harbor. You'll find a reconstructed fish shed, a couple

WASHINGTON
1
2

of icehouses, an old fisher's house, outdoor displays that include a Kahlenberg engine, an old Coast Guard boat, and remnants of a wreck. The museum is housed inside two fishing shacks. Most recently it's added a Fresnel lens from the Plum Island lighthouse.

The **Jacobsen Museum** (920/847-2213, 10am-4pm daily Memorial Day-mid-Oct., donation) is housed in a vertical log building once owned by early settler Jens Jacobsen on the south shore of Little Lake. Jacobsen collected a huge number of natural history artifacts, mostly Native American arrowheads and beads. Also inside are Danish scrollwork, maps, models of shipwrecks, fossils, and tools. There are unusual things lying out front, such as a massive ancient rudder from the steamer *Louisiana,* which ran aground here in 1913; ice cutters; and huge capstans for raising anchors.

The smallest museum is the **Farm Museum** (920/847-2156, hours vary June-Oct., free), a set of pioneer structures off Airport Road along Jackson Harbor Road. A pioneer log home, a double log barn and shed with a collection of hand tools, 15 pieces of horse-drawn machinery, a forge and blacksmith shop, a reconstructed stone building, and a popular petting zoo are on the grounds. Regularly scheduled farm activities are held for kids and families (Wed. July 5-mid-Aug.). The Thursday afternoon farmers market is wonderful!

SIEVERS SCHOOL OF FIBER ARTS

In its second decade, the **Sievers School of Fiber Arts** (Jackson Harbor Rd., 920/847-2264, www.sieversschool.com) is the most intriguing island highlight. It's less a school than a retreat into weaving, papermaking, spinning, basket weaving, batik, tapestry, drafting, Scandinavian wood carving, and a number of other classes in vanishing folk arts. On any given day, the solitude is accentuated by the thwack of looms or the whirring of spinning wheels. Classes are offered May-October, and weekend or one-week classes are available. A downtown consignment shop displays and sells the works created along with cherrywood looms.

1: the Washington Island 2: Rock Island's historic boathouse

Recreation

With 75 miles of paved roads, Washington Island was made for cycling. A weekend here is just about enough time to spin around the main perimeter and nose off on a few side roads. Much of the eastern lakeshore roadway is gravel, as is the main artery, Michigan Road, in the center of the island. Bicycles can be rented at the ferry dock, and trails are marked by green signs.

Field Wood Farms (W. Harbor Rd., 0.5 miles west of Main Rd., 920/847-2490) offers trail rides on descendants of original Icelandic stock horses—a rarity anywhere—and the oldest registered herd in the United States. Pony rides, riding instruction, and horse-drawn wagon rides are also available by appointment.

Fishing for 30-pound salmon is not unheard of in the sheltered waters around the island's bays; other big takes include perch, smallmouth black bass, rock bass, and especially northern pike, right in Detroit Harbor. A number of charter operators are available, including salmon and bass charters. Check the **Washington Island website** (www.washingtonisland.com) for current charters.

DUNES

No visit to the Maritime Museum is complete without a stroll on the nature trail through the ecosystem of the **Jackson Harbor Ridges,** a 90-acre State Scientific Reserve. The fragile mix of shore meadows, dunes, and boreal forest is not found anywhere else on the peninsula. Northern plant species such as the rare dwarf lake orchid and arctic primrose, along with white cedar, fir, and spruce, are found here. Part of the reserve was established with a Nature Conservancy tract. There is an isolated and generally underused beach adjacent to the reserve.

More great *Lawrence of Arabia* dunescapes are found across the island, southeast of Detroit Harbor along South Shore Drive at **Sand Dunes Public Beach.**

PARKS

The generally gravelly shoreline is rimmed with parks and beaches: **Schoolhouse Beach** in Washington Harbor, with tough and chilly swimming in a secluded setting (and extraordinarily smooth stones); the **Ridges** in Jackson Harbor; and **Percy Johnson Park** on the eastern side at the tip of Lakeview Road, offering vistas of Hog Island and a nesting sanctuary. None of the parks allow camping.

Inland are two interesting parks. A small picnic area and park are adjacent to the airport, and people head out with a lunchtime sandwich to watch the odd plane arrival. To get here, take Main Road north, then Town Line Road east to Airport Road. The most commanding views of all are at the 200-foot heights of **Mountain Park Lookout,** just about the center of the island.

Entertainment

The **Trueblood Performing Arts Center** (870 Main Rd., 920/847-2528) is an eye-catching, state-of-the-art theater (quite impressive for such a low-key place) with an enormous amount of offerings. The **Red Barn** (1474 S. Shore Dr., 920/847-3064), south of Gislason Beach along South Shore Drive, features a regular assortment of local talent—musicians or whoever else can be drummed up.

The **Art and Nature Center** (1799 Main Rd., 920/847-2025) offers a music festival during the first two weeks of August with concerts and other programs.

Food

An island delicacy is a "lawyer"—another name for the burbot, a mud-dwelling fish with barbels on its chin. To sample lawyers, **KK Fiske** (1177 Main Rd., 920/847-2121, breakfast, lunch, and dinner daily, from $6) is the place that specializes in them.

Delicious Icelandic pancakes and Norwegian *barkram pankaka*—cherry- and cream-filled pleasures—are the house specialties at breakfast at **Sunset Resort** (Old W. Harbor Rd., 920/847-2531, 8am-11am daily July-Aug., 8am-11am Sat.-Sun. June and Sept., $2-7). This local hot spot serves morning grub, including homemade breads. (They do have pleasant rooms, as well.)

You'll hear quite a bit about the potent bitters—a freeze-proof Scandinavian tradition still served in local pubs. If you can stomach a shot, you're in the club. The landmark ★ **Bitters Pub and Restaurant** (Main Rd., 920/847-2496, lunch and dinner from 11:30am daily) is in Nelsen's Hall, a century-old structure in the center of the island. Famed for its Bitters Club, initiated in 1899, it draws about 10,000 visitors annually. Bitters is the best elbow-rubbing option on the island; the restaurant is classic Americana—steaks, seafood, and chicken.

An exuberant and funky (and delightful) place, **Fiddlers Green** (1699 Jackson Harbor Rd., 920/847-2610, lunch/dinner daily, from $6), next to the Farm Museum, has a hodgepodge gastropub menu with tons of live music and lively banter, a real delight.

Accommodations

Washington Island features a patchwork of lodging options, stemming from its isolation. You'll find basic motels, intriguing and microscopic kiosk-cottages, spacious but threadbare cabins that look like deer-hunting shacks heated with oil furnaces, and even the odd resident's spare bedroom. Finding a room under $100 is generally no problem.

A really cheap sleep, **Gibson's West Harbor Resort and Cottages** (920/847-2225, http://gibsonswestharbor.com, from $40 s, $50 d, no cards), about halfway up the west shore from the ferry landing, is legendary and definitely the place to stay like it's the old days. They've got basic housekeeping cottages

The Man of the Rock

In 1910, Milwaukee inventor Chester H. Thordarson plunked down $5,725 for 775-acre Rock Island. Over the next 55 years, Thordarson gradually tamed the wilds and carefully transformed at least part of the island into his own private retreat.

Thordarson initially restored a few squat settlers' cabins while he pondered his masterpieces—a boathouse hewn meticulously from island limestone and, later, his grand mansion (it was never built), as well as gardens and other experiments in horticulture.

This was no simple exercise in a rich man's indulgence. As prescient as he was entrepreneurial (he made his fortune inventing more than 100 patentable devices), Thordarson developed only 30 acres of the island, with the full intent of leaving the remaining 745 as an experiment in ecological preservation. With a profound knowledge of the natural world, much of it the result of self-educated sweat, he spent the rest of his days analyzing the biological minutiae of his island. Because of this, in 1929 the University of Wisconsin gave him an honorary master of arts degree. The school also purchased his entire island library, containing one of the world's greatest collections of Scandinavian literature.

(about $100), but the coolest lodgings are the sleeping rooms—tiny but tidy—with shared baths above the main building, an erstwhile logging boardinghouse; they even have a five-person room for $65. There is absolutely nothing like it anywhere else.

A slight step up, the **Sunset Resort** (Old W. Harbor Rd., 920/847-2531, www.sunsetresortwi.com, $105) is a long-standing island getaway run by the fifth generation of the inn's original Norwegian founding family, who started the business in 1902. Cupped by spinneys of pine, the inn offers knotty pine cottages and one superb loft cabin. Guest rooms are simple but clean; impromptu campfires typify the family atmosphere. Breakfasts here are legendary.

On the far side of the island overlooking Rock Island is perhaps the nicest place on the island. **Jackson Harbor Inn** (920/847-2454, http://jacksonharborinn.com, $65-125) is meticulously kept by very friendly owners; you'll find several lovely guest rooms, all different, as well as a cottage. The inn is open Easter weekend through the end of October.

Information

The **Washington Island Chamber of Commerce** (920/847-2179, http://washingtonisland.com) has all the information you might want; it often has folks to greet you on the mainland side of the ferry.

Getting There

Ferry lines run to and from Washington Island via the "top of the thumb" (Gills Rock and Northport). Ferries have made the five-mile (30-minute) crossing somewhat ordinary, but it wasn't always so. Winter crossings used to be by horse-drawn sleigh or—unimaginably—car, but weather conditions could change the ice or eliminate it altogether within a relatively short period. Today, the ice freezes the crossing nearly solid for more than 100 days each year, but modern ferries can get through it. When ice floes pile up during extreme cold, the ferries either "back up" and try to make an end run, or "back down" and run right at the ice. At those times, ferry crossings are few and reservations are necessary to cross with an automobile.

The **Washington Island Ferry** (920/847-2546 or 800/223-2094, www.wisferry.com) takes autos and passengers, and it connects with the Cherry Train tour of the island if you take the 9:45am or earlier crossing from Northport (11am from Gills Rock). The ferry runs frequently; in high season (July-late Aug.), 25 daily round-trips depart to and from the island beginning at 6:45am from the island, 7:30am from Northport (no early trip on Sun.). Fewer trips depart in other seasons. In December-January there are only four trips per day; in February-March only one or two per day, and vehicle reservations are mandatory. In the off-season, call to check departure times. A car costs $26 (passengers not included), adults are $13.50, bicycles are $4, and motorcycles are $15; all prices are round-trip.

You could theoretically paddle a sea kayak from Northport all the way to Washington Island—and it has been done—but the currents and winds in the Porte des Mortes are deadly.

Getting Around

If you come without a car, bicycle and moped rentals await you at the dock. Otherwise, **Dor Cros Inn** (920/847-2126) rents bicycles ($15 for 2-4 hours, $20 per day; call before arrival). Taxi services come and go, so you can never be sure if one is available.

The main route is Main Road north to Jackson Harbor Road to Jackson Harbor (eight or so miles). After that, it depends where you want to go. A car is not absolutely necessary given the availability of rentals; in fact, the Gills Rock parking lot is generally full of parked cars from folks who go over for the day. This author has biked the circumference of the island in one day, but it was a long, sweaty day, and it didn't leave much time to explore Rock Island State Park.

A few tours and shuttles regularly depart from the ferry dock, linking with the ferries from Northport and Gills Rock. People rave about the **Cherry Train** (920/847-2546, www.cherrytrain.com, $16), essentially a Chevy Suburban pulling carriages, which offers four tours daily.

Head up Main Road from the ferry dock to **Bread & Water Lodging & Café** (1275 Main Rd., 920/847-2400, breadandwaterwi.com, 8am-3pm daily), where they have great food but more importantly where "kayak is spoken." The island has great kayaking, and this is the place to find a rental ($70/day); there's even a paddling museum. They've recently opened up lodge rooms (from $90) and farm accommodations (from $110).

★ ROCK ISLAND STATE PARK

Less than a mile from Washington Island's Jackson Harbor is one man's feudal estate turned overgrown state park. Getting to **Rock Island State Park** (920/847-2235), the most isolated state park in Wisconsin's system, necessitates two ferry rides. When you get here, it's a magnificent retreat: a small island, yes, but with delicious solitude, icy but gorgeous beaches, and the loveliest starry skies and sunrises in Wisconsin.

Native Americans lived in sporadic encampments along the island's south shore from 600 BC until the start of the 17th century. Around 1640, the Potawatomi people migrated here from Michigan; their allies, the Ottawa, Petun, and Huron people, followed in the 1650s, fleeing the threat of extermination at the hands of the Iroquois. The Potawatomi were visited in 1679 by René-Robert Cavelier, Sieur de La Salle, whose men built two houses, the remains of which are still visible amid the weed-choked brambles off the beach. Eventually, the French and the Potawatomi returned, establishing a trading post that lasted until 1730. Until the start of the 20th century, the island was alternately a base camp for fishers and the site of a solitary sawmill. Rock Island is thus arguably the true "door" to Wisconsin, and a ready-made one at that—the first rock on the way across the temperamental lake from Mackinac Island.

Note that water is available here, but that's all; you have to bring everything you'll need and pack it all out when you leave.

Plants and Animals

Here's why the isolated island is so great: There are no ticks, no pesky raccoons, no skunks, and no bears—no perils for backpackers. The worst thing is the rather pernicious fields of poison ivy (though these are usually well marked). There are white-tailed deer, lemmings, foxes, and a few other small mammals and amphibians. Plenty of nonpoisonous snakes can also be seen.

The northern hardwood forest is dominated

by sugar maples and American beeches; the eastern hemlock is gone. The perimeters have arbor vitae (white cedar) and small varieties of red maple and red and white pine.

Sights

Two of the most historically significant buildings in Wisconsin, according to the Department of the Interior, are Thordarson's massive limestone **Viking Hall** and **boathouse.** Patterned after historic Icelandic manors, the structures were cut, slab by slab, from Rock Island limestone by Icelandic artisans and workers and ferried over from Washington Island. Only the roof tiling isn't made from island material. That's a lot of rock, considering that the hall could hold more than 120 people. The hand-carved furniture, mullioned windows, and rosemaling detail, including runic inscriptions outlining Norse mythology, are magnificent.

The original name of Rock Island was Potawatomi Island, a moniker that lives on in one of the original lighthouses in Wisconsin, **Pottawatomie Light,** built in 1836. The original structure was swept from the cliffs by the surly lake soon after being built but was replaced. Unfortunately, it's not open to the public except for ranger-led tours. The area is accessible via a two-hour hike.

On the east side of the island are the remnants of a former fishing village and a historic water tower that's on the National Register of Historic Places. The village dwelling foundations lie in the midst of thickets and are tough to spot; there are also a few cemeteries not far from the campsites. These are the resting places of the children and families of lighthouse keepers and even Chief Chip-Pa-Ny, a Menominee leader.

Otherwise, the best thing to do is just skirt the shoreline and discover lake views from atop the bluffs, alternating at points with up to 0.5 miles of sandy beach or sand dunes. Near campsite 15, you'll pass some carvings etched into the bluff, made by Thordarson's bored workers.

Recreation

With more than 5,000 feet of beach, you can find somewhere to be alone, although the waters are chilly and currents are dangerous. At one time a sawmill buzzed the logs taken from the island; the wheel-rutted paths to the mill turned into rough roads. Thordarson let them grow over during his tenure on the island, but today they are a few miles of the park's 9.5 miles of hiking trails. The island is only about 900 acres, so you'll have plenty of time to cover it all if you're spending more than an afternoon. On a day trip, you can cover the perimeter on the 5.2-mile **Thordarson Loop Trail** in just under three hours. You'll see all the major sights and a magnificent view on the northeast side—on a clear day you can see all the way to Michigan's Upper Peninsula. For those less aerobically inclined, head for the **Algonquin Nature Trail Loop,** at most a one-hour hike. The other trails on the island are essentially shortcuts to cross the island and are all approximately one mile long.

No wheeled vehicles are allowed in the park. The dock does allow private mooring for a fee of $1 per foot.

CAMPING

The camping at Rock Island is absolutely splendid, with sites strung along a beachfront of sand and, closer to the pier, large stones. Many of the sites farthest from the main compound are fully isolated, almost scooped into dunes and thus fully protected from wind but with great views (site 13 is a favorite). The island has 40 primitive campsites, all reservable, with water and pit toilets: 35 to the southwest of the ferry landing, and another 5 isolated backpacker sites spread along the shore farther southeast. Two additional group campsites are also available. **Reservations** (888/947-2757, http://wisconsin.goingtocamp.com, $25 sites for nonresidents, plus $8 reservation fee) are a good idea in summer and fall, and essential on weekends during those times.

Note that the park is pack-in, pack-out, so plan wisely.

Firewood Bugs Us

Wisconsin now has quite strict restrictions on firewood due to the invasive insect called the emerald ash borer, which has been found in southern Wisconsin counties and is attempting to move northward. The name says it all—it has an emerald-colored coating on its back, and ash trees are its primary food. The larvae burrow under the bark and ravage the trees, most of which die within four years. Seven percent of Wisconsin's forests are ashes; it's even worse in cities, where 20 percent of trees are ashes.

The key for travelers is never to transport wood—including firewood for camping—from one location to another. The insect can only fly a mile or two, so its primary mode of expansion is unknowing humans and their wood. Out-of-state firewood and any wood from more than 25 miles away from any campground is strictly forbidden. Local wood is always available. Yes, it's more expensive, but for a few extra dollars you can help preserve Wisconsin's forestlands.

Getting There

If you're not kayaking over, the ***Karfi*** (920/847-2252) has regular service; the name means "seaworthy for coastal journeys" in Icelandic, so fear not. Boats depart Jackson Harbor on Washington Island daily from late May to mid-October, usually Columbus Day; the boat leaves hourly 10am-4:15pm daily in high season (late June-Aug.) with an extra trip at 6pm Friday. Round-trip tickets cost $11 adults and $14 for campers with gear requiring a cart. In the off-season you can arrange a boat, but it's expensive.

Private boats are permitted to dock at the pier, but a mooring fee ($1 per foot) is charged.

OTHER ISLANDS

Plum and Pilot Islands

Before the establishment of the lighthouse on Plum Island, more than 100 ships were wrecked on the shoals of the Door. In one year alone, Plum Island became the cemetery for 30 ships. Though safer than any U.S. highway today, it will never be stress-free; as recently as 1989 a ship was thrown aground by the currents. The U.S. Lighthouse Service established the **Pilot Island Lighthouse** in 1858. It stands atop what an early guidebook described as "little more than a rock in the heavy-pounding seas." Two brick structures stand on Pilot Island and are about the only things still visible. Once-dense vegetation has nearly been completely killed off, the island turned into a rocky field by the ubiquitous and odoriferous droppings of federally protected cormorants, which long ago found the island and stuck around.

Plum Island had to wait until 1897 to get its imposing 65-foot skeletal steel light, after which the number of wrecks at the Door dropped significantly. Plum Island—so-called for its plumb-center position in the straits—is home to an abandoned Coast Guard building on the northeast side, an old foghorn building on the southwest tip, and yet another decaying Cape Cod-style lightkeeper's residence near the range lights.

Neither island is accessible—unless your sea kayak runs into trouble—except on boat tours given during the **Festival of Blossoms** (late Apr.-early June), usually offered three times daily from Gills Rock.

Detroit Island

Steaming into Detroit Harbor on Washington Island, look to the starboard side. The island with the crab-claw bay is Detroit Island, one of the largest satellite islands surrounding Washington Island. Settlers built the first permanent structures on the island in the early 1830s and gradually forced the displacement of the resident Ottawa and Huronpeople who had been there for generations. The island was once an archaeological gem, but thieves have looted it. Today it is privately owned and not accessible.

East-Central Waters

These waters truly made the state of Wisconsin, serving as the site of the first permanent nonnative settlements and the state's timber-and-water commercial nucleus. When the Portage Canal linking the Upper Fox and Lower Wisconsin Rivers was completed, two of the most crucial waterways in the Great Lakes system were finally joined, allowing transport from the Atlantic Ocean all the way to the Gulf of Mexico. (The Fox River is one of the few rivers in North America that flows north.)

Today, you'll find picturesque lakeside resorts, quaint towns with excellent museums, and a rich blend of European heritage. And of course, the heart and soul of the region is the football mecca of Green Bay, home to the Packers.

Highlights

Look for ★ to find recommended sights, activities, dining, and lodging.

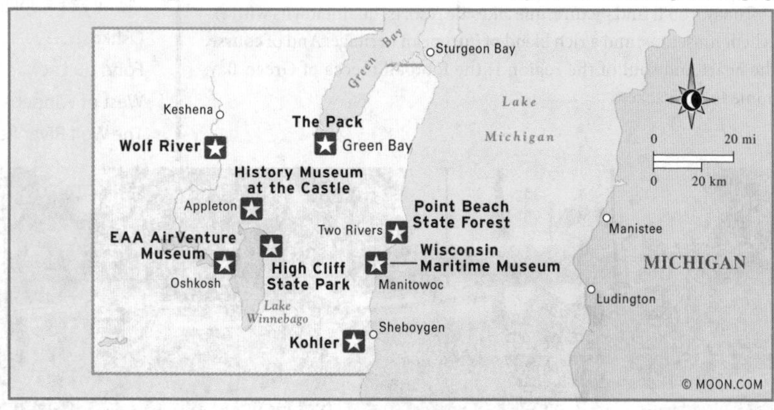

★ **Kohler:** The state's most incredible resort is located in this trim onetime factory town (page 189).

★ **Wisconsin Maritime Museum:** Learn about Manitowoc's shipbuilding; you can even clamber about a World War II submarine (page 196).

★ **Point Beach State Forest:** Relax along a grand lakeshore stretch of sandy beaches (page 199).

★ **The Pack:** Visit the home turf of Wisconsin's beloved Green Bay Packers at Lambeau Field (page 201).

★ **History Museum at the Castle:** Learn the secrets of the famed escape artist at the **A.K.A. Houdini** exhibit (page 211).

★ **High Cliff State Park:** It's worth a stop for its magnificent perch above Lake Winnebago (page 217).

★ **EAA AirVenture Museum:** The museum is fabulous, and the annual EAA AirVenture **Oshkosh fly-in** is jaw-droppingly amazing (page 218).

★ **Wolf River:** This natural beauty features dells, rapids, and misty cascades, and is the place for white-water rafting (page 230).

East-Central Waters

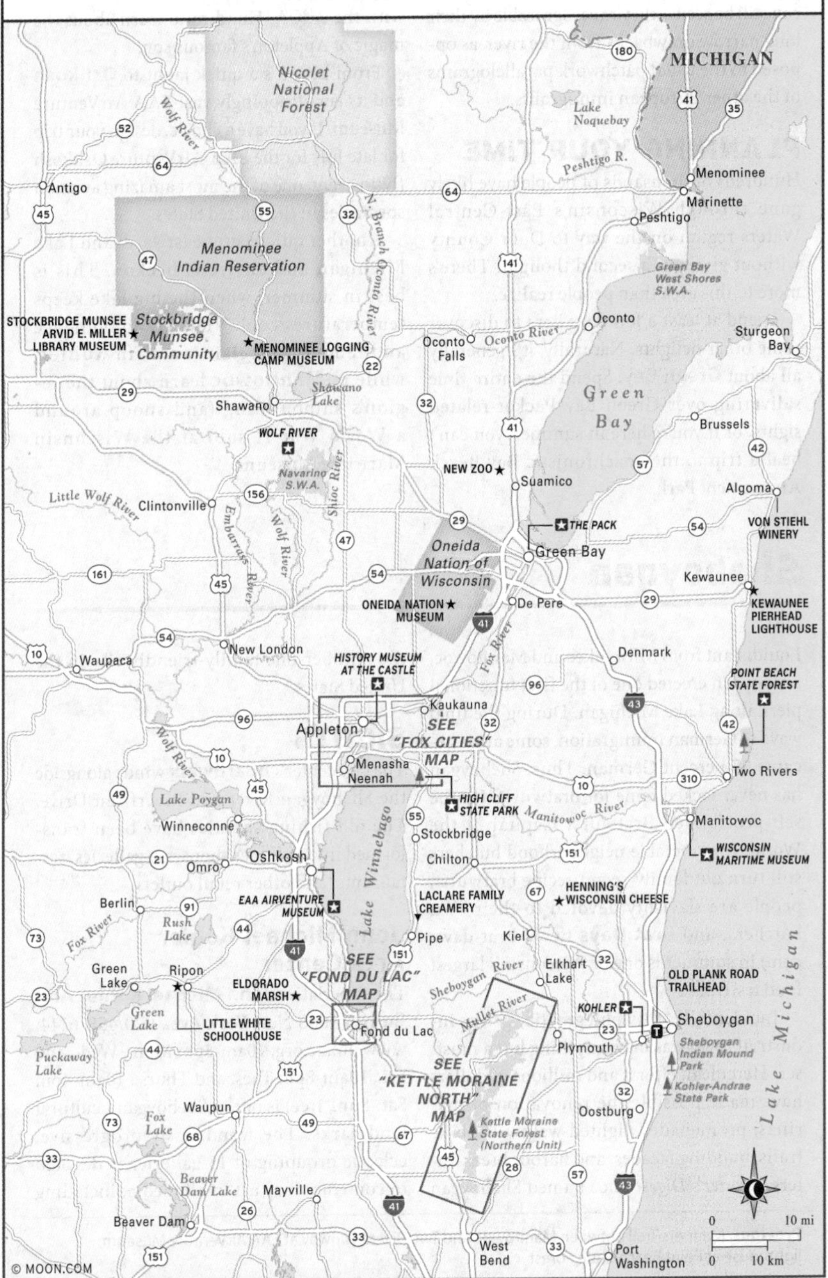

In addition to the locks, some of the only extant French-style agricultural developments can still be seen—they're recognizable by their long narrow drawbacks from the river, as opposed to the usual patchwork parallelograms of the other European immigrants.

PLANNING YOUR TIME

Hundreds of thousands of people have likely gone through Wisconsin's East-Central Waters region on the way to Door County without giving it a second thought. There's more to this area than people realize.

Spend at least a few days here to discover some other delights. Naturally, it's generally all about **Green Bay.** Spend the entire time salivating over Green Bay Packer-related sights, or if you're here in summer, you can't beat a trip to the anachronistic Bay Beach Amusement Park.

Or base yourself in the **Fox Cities,** usually Appleton, since they're so central, and start with the A.K.A. Houdini to learn about the magic of Appleton's famous son.

From here it's a quick jaunt to **Oshkosh** and its jaw-droppingly vast EAA AirVenture Museum. If you have a choice, design your trip for late July for the EAA AirVenture Oshkosh fly-in event, one of the most amazing aviation spectacles in the United States.

Another quick jaunt eastward, and Lake Michigan and environs beckon. This is best in summer, when the big lake keeps temperatures cool. View grand opulence and famous porcelain wares in **Kohler,** while in **Manitowoc** learn about the region's shipbuilding (and snoop around a World War II sub) at the Wisconsin Maritime Museum.

Sheboygan

Equidistant from Milwaukee and Manitowoc, Sheboygan erected one of the first functional piers along Lake Michigan. During the final wave of German immigration, some areas became 95 percent German. Thus, Sheboygan has never lacked fame for bratwurst. It's the self-proclaimed Bratwurst Capital of the World. Innumerable neighborhood butchers still turn out family-secret-recipe bratwurst, people are slavishly devoted to their own butchers, and **Brat Days** (www.brat-days.com) in summer is one of Wisconsin's largest food festivals.

Incidentally, this phlegmatic, gritty industrial town was once anything but a must-see. Herculean efforts and millions of dollars have made possible the renovation of marinas, promenades, lighted walkways, bike trails, building facades, and harbor breakwaters. *Reader's Digest* once named Sheboygan the number-one family-friendly city in the United States.

SIGHTS

The city center's **boardwalk** winds alongside the Sheboygan River and Riverfront Drive. The old fishing shanties have been transformed into antiques shops, art galleries, restaurants, and other retail outlets.

John Michael Kohler Arts Center

The superlative **John Michael Kohler Arts Center** (608 New York Ave., 920/458-6144, www.jmkac.org, 10am-5pm Mon., Wed., and Fri., 10am-8pm Tues. and Thurs., 10am-4pm Sat.-Sun., free) is one of Sheboygan's cultural landmarks. The wondrously progressive, eclectic grouping of 15 galleries is devoted to contemporary art in all media, including

Previous: Mariners Trail between Manitowoc and Two Rivers; runway at EAA AirVenture Museum; lighthouse at Point Beach State Forest

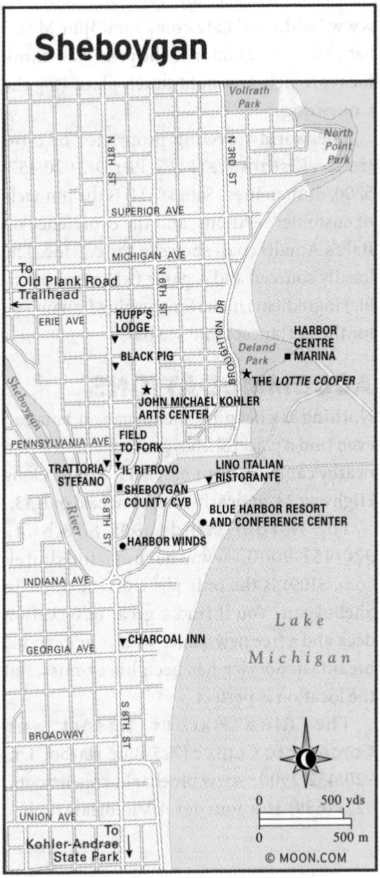

Sheboygan

galleries devoted to self-taught artists. The center has been nationally recognized for its unusually broad scope and its efforts to incorporate the community. This explains its consistent high ratings by industry groups nationwide.

The *Lottie Cooper*

One of 62 wrecks near Sheboygan, the ***Lottie Cooper,*** a three-masted lumber schooner, went down in a gale off the city on April 9, 1894, killing one. Including one of the longest salvaged keels of a Great Lakes wreck, the vessel now rests in Deland Park, near the North Pier.

RECREATION

Charter Fishing

The 300-slip **Harbor Centre Marina** (821 Broughton Dr., 920/458-6665, www.harborcentremarina.com) offers great fishing with about three dozen licensed skippers operating out of Sheboygan. Rates vary, but it's generally $350-500 for one to four people for a half-day charter, not including a tip or a Wisconsin fishing license.

Old Plank Road Trail

In 1843, the territorial legislature, hoping to effect permanent settlement in today's Sheboygan County region, began building the first plank road to reach all the way to Fond du Lac. Today, the **Old Plank Road Trail** is a paved 17-mile-long multipurpose recreation trail running from western Sheboygan to Greenbush and the Kettle Moraine State Forest's northern unit, and thus the Ice Age Trail, via Kohler and Plymouth. It's a lovely ride in spots.

FOOD

American

You want Wisconsin? Head to **Rupp's Lodge** (925 N. 8th St., 920/459-8155, 11am-2pm and 5pm-9pm Mon.-Fri., 4pm-9pm Sat.-Sun., $5-25), which has been around for six decades. Aged hand-cut steaks are the specialty, along with standard supper club fare. Through a glass partition, you get to watch the food being prepared in the kitchen. On Friday and Saturday nights, patrons join in sing-alongs at a piano.

At the casual yet upscale **Black Pig** (821 N. 8th St., 920/457-6565, www.eatblackpig.com, lunch and dinner Tues.-Sat., brunch Sun., $8-24) it's no surprise that the entire pig (organic and locally sourced) is on offer. (Worry not—several non-porcine dishes are available.) They call it creative comfort food, so go for their signature mac and cheese or beer-cheese soup.

Brats

To sample the "best of the wurst" you've got

myriad options. For me, it's the **Charcoal Inn** (1313 S. 8th St., 920/458-6988, 11am-7pm Tues.-Sat.; 1637 Greele Ave., 920/458-1147, 6am-2pm Tues.-Sat., $4-8), where they still fire up a fryer every morning to supplement their unpretentious Midwest fare. They also offer turkey brats, which some consider sacrilege, but heart-healthy is a good thing. Cash only here.

Italian

Sheboygan inexplicably has incredible Italian. Dishing up the best Italian is the mainstay, the ever-friendly ★ **Trattoria Stefano** (522 S. 8th St., 920/452-8455, 5pm-9pm Mon.-Thurs., 5pm-10pm Fri.-Sat., $12-28), a casually upscale place with a bright pastel and handmade-brick environment. For years this has been a foodie must-stop. For a more subdued Italian experience, across the street is another of the owner's ventures: **Il Ritrovo** (515 S. 8th St., 920/803-7516, www.ilritrovopizza.com, 11am-2pm and 5pm-9pm Mon.-Thurs., 11am-2pm and 5pm-10pm Fri., 11am-10pm Sat., $11-18), dinner with pizza good enough for Naples authorities to have certified it as OK. If that weren't enough, Stefano has also opened **Field to Fork** (511 S. 8th St., 920/694-0322, www.fieldtoforkcafe.com, 7am-3pm Mon.-Sat., $5-15) next door to the pizzeria—think locavore deli and light lunch place (try the Coney dog).

The world-traveling proprietor of **Lino Italian Ristorante** (422 S. Pier Dr., 920/457-5200, dinner Tues.-Sat., $8-24) is the pinnacle of customer relations, and the experience on Italy's Amalfi coast shows in the cuisine. The locally sourced and organic (whenever possible) ingredients make for amazing Italian—go for the puttanesca and sea bass.

ACCOMMODATIONS

Nothing is cheap in Sheboygan, if you can even find a place; Sheboygan lacks motels and nearby camping. Your best bet is to look along Highway 23, at nearly every exit east of I-43.

The **Harbor Winds** (905 S. 8th St., 920/452-9000, www.harborwindshotel.com, $109) is the only place on the water in Sheboygan. You'll find a great observation deck and a free newspaper with your included breakfast. Service has been hit-or-miss, but the location is perfect.

The **Blue Harbor Resort and Conference Center** (725 Blue Harbor Dr., 920/452-2900, www.blueharborresort.com, $229-689) is a four-level Victorian replica

the wreck of the *Lottie Cooper* in Sheboygan

with an indoor water park. The self-enclosed place boasts spas, fitness centers, two enormous restaurants, arcades, and more. Keep in mind that when you see "water park," it means occasionally chaotic family hordes.

INFORMATION

The **Sheboygan County Convention and Visitors Bureau** (712 Riverfront Dr., Ste. 101, 920/457-9497 or 800/457-9497, www.visitsheboygan.com) is along the boardwalk.

GETTING THERE

Driving to Sheboygan from Milwaukee (via I-43, 58 miles) takes one hour. From Door County (via Hwy. 57 and I-43, 100 miles) the drive takes one hour and 40 minutes.

Vicinity of Sheboygan

SHEBOYGAN INDIAN MOUND PARK

An archaic relic, **Sheboygan Indian Mound Park** (5000 S. 9th St., 920/459-3444, 5am-10pm, free), along the Black River region in south Sheboygan, is eerily impressive. The 18 Native American effigy mounds, in myriad geometric and animal shapes, date from AD 500. A beautiful nature trail runs along a creek.

KOHLER-ANDRAE STATE PARK

Kohler-Andrae State Park (1020 Beach Park Ln., 920/451-4080, 6am-11pm, day-use $11) may well be the best stretch of beach along Wisconsin's Lake Michigan shoreline. It includes two miles of windswept beach and a plank trail that meanders through the fragile Kohler Dunes Natural Area, one of the state's rarest habitats: an interdunal wetland. I've never failed to stumble upon white-tailed deer among the dunes. The chilly waters off the park are home to about 50 shipwrecks, a diver's paradise. Many of the recovered wrecks are on display at the Sanderling Center in the park.

Camping is superb, but it's virtually always full on weekends. **Reservations** (888/947-2757, http://wisconsins.goingtocamp.com, reservation fee $8, nonresidents from $25) are necessary.

★ KOHLER

A planned workers' community surrounding the operations of the Kohler Company, Kohler is trim and attractive. Kohler also houses the state's most incredible resort restaurant and puts on unforgettable factory tours.

The community is what one would hope to see in a land of opportunity. The scion of Kohler Company once said that a worker "deserves not only wages, but also roses as well" and set out to create a perfect (nay, utopic) worker environment. Barbershops, pubs, bowling alleys, gardens, even classrooms to teach civics and English—all were carefully laid out to show the immigrant workers that their new country was the best. Over a century later, the carefully preserved grounds are a fascinating mélange of production, posh getaway, and tourist attraction.

Sights

You never knew that bath and kitchen fixtures could be so fascinating. Believe it—the tours at the **Kohler Factory** and, to a lesser extent, **Kohler Design Center** (101 Upper Rd., 920/457-3699, www.us.kohler.com, 8am-5pm Mon.-Fri., 10am-4pm Sat.-Sun. and holidays, free) are must-sees. Old-world iron artisans form enormous cast-iron tubs from glass-like lava, and in the next area you get cutting-edge robotics; it's all quite amazing. The international manufacturer of bathroom fixtures showcases this in its 2.5-hour tour of the company's early factory and factory-town

Bratwurst: The Wisconsin Dish

Bratwurst, a Germanic legacy in Wisconsin, is the unofficial state dish. The brat (rhymes with "spot," not "spat") is pervasive. Supermarkets devote entire lengths of freezers to accommodate sausage makers. Many towns still have old butcher shops that string up homemade flavors.

THE IMMIGRANT EPICURE

Strictly speaking, the bratwurst is but one of hundreds of varieties of sausage, according to the official draconian German food laws. But sausage-making was done here before the Europeans arrived by the Native Americans, who had long stuffed deer intestines and hides with wild rice, grains, meats, offal, and herbs to produce pemmican, which is, technically, a sausage.

From the earliest settlement of the region, immigrants made their own sausage. Wisconsin's bratwurst, unlike some varieties, is almost always made from pork. The internal mixture was meat, fat, and seasonings, along with occasional starches such as rice and bread. Concoctions were, and remain, highly secret.

INFINITE VARIETIES

The Czech method includes a rice sausage and head cheese; the Norwegians make *sylte,* which is spiced and salted in brine. The main categories of Wisconsin sausage:

- **German:** The many German varieties are most often seasoned with marjoram, pepper, salt, caraway, and nutmeg.
- **Italian:** Sweeter and hotter; fennel gives it its trademark flavor.
- **Polish:** A garlic-heavy ring of two-inch-thick dark-pink bologna-esque sausage is traditionally steam-fried for dinner and then cut into sandwiches for leftovers and lunch boxes; Polish recipes often call for red cabbage and mustard sauces.

PREPARATION

Microwave a brat and you'll incur the wrath of any Wisconsinite. Frying one is OK, but traditionally, a brat must be grilled. Brats work best if you parboil them in beer and onions for 10 to 15 minutes before putting them on the grill. Sheboyganites absolutely cringe at parboiling, however. Another no-no is roughage crammed in the bun—lettuce, tomatoes, and so on; even sauerkraut, loved by Milwaukeeans, is barely tolerated by Sheboyganites.

Another option is to parboil brats briefly, sear them in butter in a frying pan, and set them aside. Pour two cups of dark beer into a frying pan and scrape out the residue. Combine a finely chopped onion, some beef stock, the juice of one lemon, and maybe a chopped green pepper. Put the brats

history, along with its wares in an incredible "Great Wall of China"—yes, a fascinating "wall" of porcelain is a must-see! Their Arts and Industry program is a wonderful look at how seemingly unconnected fields work synergistically. Tours of the factory itself are at 8:30am weekdays only and require advance registration. Find more information about the tour on the website.

Waelderhaus (House in the Woods, 1100 W. Riverside Dr., 920/453-2851, tours 2pm, 3pm, and 4pm daily except holidays, free), a dwelling based on homes from the mountainous Austrian Bregenzerwald region commissioned by a daughter of the Kohler founder, contains antique furnishings and highlights such as candle-reflected water-globe lighting.

Golf

Hands-down the best golf in Wisconsin—and some say the Midwest—is found in Kohler at **The American Club** (Highland Dr., 920/457-8000, www.destinationkohler.

bratwurst

back in and boil for 12 to 15 minutes. Remove the brats and place them on a hot grill. The sauce can be thickened with flour or cornstarch and poured over the top. A Cheesehead will stick the sauce in a bun along with the brat and mustard.

BRATS IN SHEBOYGAN

The place to go is **Miesfeld's Triangle Market** (4811 Venture Dr., 2 blocks north of the intersection of I-43 and Hwy. 42, 414/565-6328, 8am-5:30pm Mon.-Fri., 8am-3pm Sat.), where Chuck and the gang have been putting out national award-winning sausages—15 varieties have won 68 national awards—for as long as anyone can remember. The town has a celebratory fit of indulgent mayhem in August with Bratwurst Days. Some brat-related Sheboygan-specific tips:

- "double": You simply cannot eat just one brat.
- "fryer": Whatever thing you cook the brat on; Cheeseheads otherwise say "grill."
- "fry out": Used as both a noun and a verb.
- "hard roll": It looks like a hamburger bun but bigger and harder; sometimes called "sennel roll."

com) resort. There are two excellent options here: **Blackwolf Run** offers two PGA championship courses—one of them has been named the highest-rated gold medal course in the United States, according to *Golf* magazine. The preternaturally lovely courses of **Whistling Straits** (920/457-4446) are designed to favor the old seaside links courses of Britain; they even have sheep wandering around. In 2000 Whistling Straits unveiled its new Irish Course, a companion course to the first Straits course; among other things, it features some of the tallest sand dunes in the United States. It's all good enough for the PGA Championship to have been played here three times, as well as the 2020 Ryder Cup. Call 800/618-5535 for details.

Food and Accommodations

Easily Wisconsin's most breathtaking resort, ★ **The American Club** (Highland Dr., 920/457-8000, www.destinationkohler.com, $360-1,300) is the Midwest's only AAA five-diamond resort. The 1918 redbrick facade of an erstwhile workers' hostel and dormitory has been retained, along with the original carriage house, though both have been retrofitted. A full slate of recreation is offered, of note two championship Pete Dye golf courses, one of them considered one of the most perfect examples in the world of a shot-master's course. There's also a private 500-acre wildlife preserve to explore. If that's not enough, the seven dining rooms and restaurants include the state's best—the Immigrant Room (920/457-8000, 6-10pm Tues.-Sat., from $45), winner of the prestigious DiRoNA Award. Here, various rooms offer the ethnic cuisine and heritage of France, Holland, Germany, Scandinavia, and England. The food is created with regional Wisconsin ingredients. Jackets are required.

PLYMOUTH

Plymouth lies just west of Sheboygan and would definitely be on a National Register of Quaint Places—the aesthetics of its early Yankee settlements remain amazingly intact. Initially a solitary tavern-cum-stage stop, as all rail traffic passed through the little burg it eventually became the center of the cheese industry in eastern Wisconsin (the first Cheese Exchange was here). Today the city still produces, handles, stores, or otherwise deals with some 15 percent of U.S. cheese! This cheese history now lives on at the wondrous new **Cheese Counter and Dairy Heritage Center** (133 E. Mill St., 920/892-2012, 10am-4pm Mon.-Sat., free), a restored 1920s edifice that is both interactive museum and dairy-sampling eatery in which to indulge in glorious grilled cheese, mac and cheese, and anything else you could dream up. It's quite well done and a treat—literally—for families.

Food and Accommodations

Historic bed-and-breakfasts are everywhere you turn. A structure woodworkers will want to see is the **52 Stafford Irish Guest House** (52 Stafford St., 920/893-0552, www.52stafford.com, $120). The 19 guest rooms are decent, but the main attraction here is the food (Tues.-Sat. 5-9pm, from $12, open to non-guests). The limited but ambitious menu changes a lot; the signature meal is an Irish beef brisket basted in Guinness—it'll wow you. The rich woods, ornate stained glass, and original fixtures give the place a special atmosphere. Drop by Wednesday evenings for rousing Irish music.

If rousing isn't for you, ignore the strip-mall ambience and go for the fish at the delightful and unbelievably friendly and helpful Italian restaurant **Sweet Basil** (645 Walton Dr., 920/892-7572, www.sweetbasil-plymouth.com, dinner Mon.-Sat., $8-25).

ELKHART LAKE

Northwest of Sheboygan is one of the region's first resort areas, Elkhart Lake (www.elkhartlake.com), on the east side of the lake of the same name. In the early 20th century, well-to-do Chicagoans sought out the quiet getaway and, later, so did high-profile mobsters such as John Dillinger. Another major draw is the international speedway **Road America,** North America's longest natural road-racing course, along with a couple of subdued local museums.

Food and Accommodations

One of the most extraordinary meals of late has come at the newer ★ **Paddock Club** (61 S. Lake St., 920/876-3288, www.paddockclubelkhartlake.com, 4pm-close Tues.-Sun., $18-38). You'll find indescribably good New American cuisine in an erstwhile gangster hangout.

One of the oldest and most established lodgings, family-run since 1916, is **Siebkens** (284 S. Lake St., 920/876-2600, www.siebkens.com, $160-480), a turn-of-the-20th-century resort with two white-trimmed main buildings, open only in summer, and a year-round lake cottage. A nod to modernity is also available in the plush new condos. Take a look at all the options since there are many, and they vary a lot. The classic tavern and dining room (dinner daily, lunch Wed.-Mon., from

$9, open to non-guests) serve up regional fare on an old porch.

Much more upscale is the ★ **Osthoff Resort** (101 Osthoff Ave., 920/876-3366 or 855/876-3399, www.osthoff.com, $300-720), with lavish comfort and fine lake views. Lola's dining room (920/876-5840, lunch/dinner Mon.-Sat., brunch/lunch/dinner Sun., from $21, open to non-guests) and the Aspira spa are superb; there is a cooking school here. This is really a *wow* experience.

KIEL

Nobody else makes 'em like they do at the too-cool **Henning's Wisconsin Cheese** (20201 Point Creek Rd., 920/894-3032, www.henningscheese.com, 7am-4pm Mon.-Fri., 8am-noon Sat.), northeast of Sheboygan in little Kiel. They have an outstanding museum of cheese-making. You'll snap lots of images of the gigantic 12,000-pound wheels of cheddar cheese, this being the only place in the United States still producing them. This is not just touristy fun—this is a genuine, respected operation with regular awards in the U.S. and World Cheese Championships.

KETTLE MORAINE STATE FOREST-NORTHERN UNIT

A crash course in geology helps preface a trip through the 29,000 acres of the northern unit of the **Kettle Moraine State Forest** (262/626-2116). The **northern unit** was chosen as the site of the Henry Reuss Ice Age Interpretive Center—on the Ice Age National Scenic Trail—given its variegated topography of kettles, terminal moraines, kames, and eskers. Surrounded by suburban expansion, it somehow manages to hold 12 State Natural Areas inside its borders.

This northern swath of forest is the complement to its sibling southwest of Milwaukee. Supporters of the forest have always envisioned the two sections as parts of a larger forest, concatenate segments of lands acting

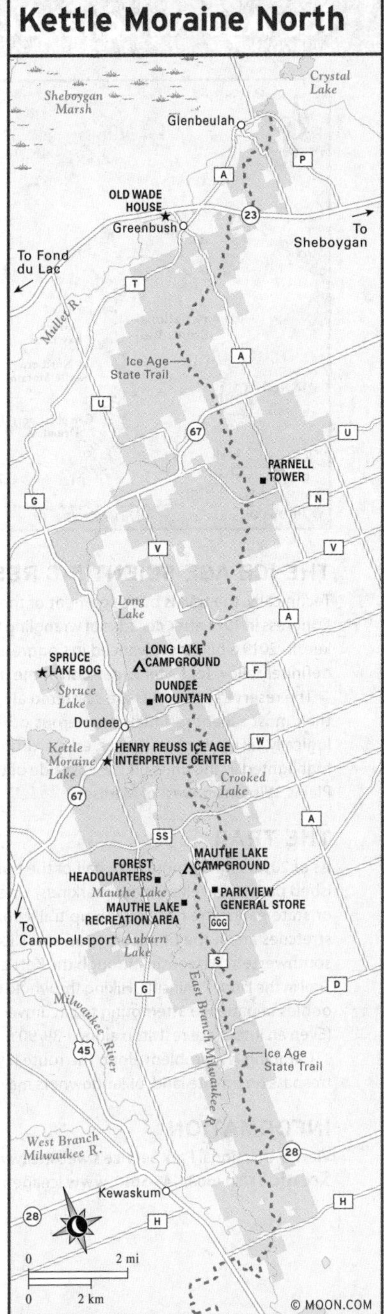

Ice Age National Scenic Trail

Glaciation affected all of the Upper Midwest, but nowhere is it more exposed than in Wisconsin. Southwestern Wisconsin's Driftless Area is also the only purely unglaciated region on the planet surrounded by glacial till.

Wisconsin's epic Ice Age National Scenic Trail is a 1,200-mile course skirting morainic topography left behind by the state's four glacial epochs. It's also an ongoing project, started in the 1950s and still being pieced together. When county chapters have finally cobbled together enough municipal, county, and state forestland with donated private land for right-of-ways, Potawatomi State Park in Door County will be linked with Interstate State Park on the St. Croix National Scenic Riverway via one continuous footpath.

THE ICE AGE SCIENTIFIC RESERVE

Technically, the trail is but a segment of the Ice Age National Scientific Reserve, established by Congress in 1971 after decades of wrangling by forward-thinking ecologist Ray Zillmer of Milwaukee. In 2019 a bill was advanced in Congress to raise the trail to national park status; this would definitely allow for faster expansion of the trail.

The reserve's nine units are scattered along the advance of the glacial periods and highlight their most salient residuals. Numerous other state and county parks, equally impressive geologically, fill in the gaps. Kames, eskers, drumlins, moraines, kettles, and all the glacial effects are highlighted in the units on the east side of the state. An interpretive center is planned for Cross Plains, Wisconsin, west of Madison.

THE TRAIL

As of 2019, slightly more than half of the trail had been finished (meaning that it is a clearly finished path with yellow blaze markings) whether by the National Park Service, county chapters, or state parks; the rest are link-up trails, roads, or even main streets. The longest established stretches are in the Chequamegon and Nicolet National Forests, along the Sugar River Trail in southwestern Wisconsin, through the Kettle Moraine State Forest, and along the Ahnapee State Trail in the Door Peninsula. Hiking the whole thing is possible, but it takes about three months and oodles of patience attempting to circumvent cityscapes where segments have not yet opened. (Even an interstate rest stop along I-39/90 north of Madison has a trail segment!)

Camping is a problem along the route if you're outside an established park or forest. Do not trespass on private land, or landowners may become resistant to completion of the trail.

INFORMATION

View the National Park Service's website (www.nps.gov/iatr) or contact the **Ice Age National Scenic Trail** (608/441-5610, www.iceagetrail.org) in Madison.

as an urban buffer zone along a 120-mile eco-corridor.

Henry Reuss Ice Age Interpretive Center

Along Highway 67 near the Highway G junction is the **Henry Reuss Ice Age Interpretive Center** (920/533-8322, 8:30am-4pm Mon.-Fri. and 9:30am-5pm Sat.-Sun. Apr.-Oct., shorter hours in winter). The back deck and short nature trail have outstanding vistas of the topography. The exhibits and documentary theater are well worth a stop. A self-guided 40-mile auto geology tour starts from the center.

Old Wade House and Wisconsin Jung Carriage Museum

Along Highway 23 in Greenbush the **Old Wade House** (Hwy. T, 920/526-3271, www.wadehouse.wisconsinhistory.org, 10am-4pm Mon.-Sat., 11am-4pm Sun. mid-May-mid-Oct., $12 adults) sits along the oak plank road that stretched from Sheboygan to Fond du Lac. The state historic site is a wondrous, detailed reconstruction of the 1848 original sawmill—note the post-and-beam work—one of few like it in the United States. Environmentally friendly construction was used, as in the original.

Perhaps the Wade House's biggest draw is the impressive **Wisconsin Jung Carriage Museum,** with the state's largest collection of hand- and horse-drawn vehicles, many rideable.

Scenic Drives

The forest offers a lovely scenic drive. As you cruise along highways that include official Rustic Roads, you'll trace the oldest geology in Wisconsin, a 10,000-year-old outwash of the last glacial period.

The scenic drive is linked in the south with other scenic back roads all the way to the southern unit, about 40 miles away. It's hard to get lost; just follow the acorn-shaped road signs. From Sheboygan Marsh in the north to Whitewater Lake in the southern unit, the road totals about 120 miles and passes through six counties.

Recreation

More than 140 miles of trails snake through the forest's narrow northern unit, including the highlight, the sublime 31-mile segment of the **Ice Age National Scenic Trail.** It runs the length of the park and connects with five other forest trails for plenty of hiking options. There are five shelters along the way. Backpackers must have permits ($18) to use shelters (generally easy to obtain, but plan very early for summer high season, especially weekends).

The best-known trail is the 11-mile **Zillmer Trail,** accessible via Highway SS; there's one tough ridge with a great vista. Some say the best view (1,300 feet above sea level, plus 60 feet of tower) is the one from **Parnell Tower,** two miles north of Highway 67 via Highway A.

Camping

In all, 400 campsites are available, lots of them reservable. Primitive shelter camping is possible along the Glacial Trail. **Mauthe Lake** also has a tepee for rent. **Reservations** (888/947-2757, http://wisconsingoingtocamp.com, reservation fee $8, nonresidents from $25, day-use $11) are not always necessary, but you should make them if possible.

Manitowoc and Two Rivers

These Lake Michigan quasi-sister cities were originally home to Ojibwa, Potawatomi, and Ottawa people. The tranquil harbors attracted fur traders, and by 1795, the Northwest Fur Company had built its post here. Under the Europeans the area prospered during the early decades of whitefish plunder and shipbuilding, an industry that still exists here.

MANITOWOC

This small bight was a port of call for weary Great Lakes travelers—the earliest ones in birch-bark canoes—heading for Chicago. Drive out into the countryside and you can still see smokehouses and bake ovens on early farmsteads, log threshing barns large enough to drive machinery through, split-rail fencing, and unique cantilever house designs.

An enormous fishing industry rose and then collapsed due to overfishing through injudicious use of drift nets and seines. The so-called Clipper City shifted to producing ships beginning in the 1800s, peaking around World War II, when Manitowoc's shipyard became one of the most important naval production facilities in the country.

★ Wisconsin Maritime Museum

At peak World War II production, Manitowoc eclipsed even major East Coast shipbuilding centers. Its legacy is remembered at the **Wisconsin Maritime Museum** (75 Maritime Dr., 920/684-0218, www.wisconsinmaritime.org, 9am-6pm daily July-Aug., less otherwise, closed Tues.-Wed. Nov.-mid-March, $15 includes access to the *Cobia*). Flanked by the USS *Cobia* submarine—a National Historic Landmark, one of 28 built here, and one reason Manitowoc is the only U.S. city with streets named after subs—the museum is an amazing agglomeration of Great Lakes and especially local maritime history. The gallery devoted to Wisconsin-built boats is very well done.

Other Sights

The **Rahr-West Art Museum** (610 N. 8th St. at Park St., 920/686-3090, www.

USS *Cobia* at the Wisconsin Maritime Museum

Manitowoc

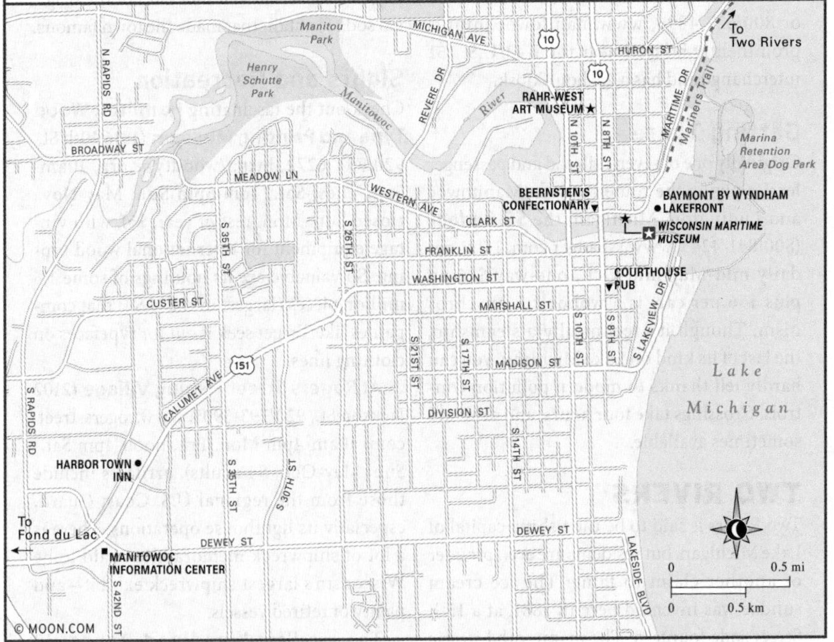

rahrwestartmuseum.org, 10am-4pm Tues.-Fri., 11am-4pm Sat.-Sun., free) is an 1891 Victorian with intricate woodworking and grand beamed ceilings housing one of the finer collections of decorative art in the Midwest. A tidbit: The brass ring in the street out front is where a piece of Sputnik struck in 1962.

Stretch your legs or ride your bike (no rentals are available locally) on the absolutely gorgeous **Mariners Trail,** a 12-mile-long paved recreation trail between Manitowoc and Two Rivers that follows the lakeshore.

Food

The boisterous **Courthouse Pub** (1001 S. 8th St., 920/686-1166, 11am-9pm Mon.-Sat., $5-15) handcrafts its own brews in a painstakingly restored 1860s Greek Revival. It has recently gone from slightly upscale pub grub to nearly gastropub in its fare, shocking more than a few locals, but it is still a mainstay. Their perch is recommended—not too heavy on the batter.

Chocolate fanatics and the dessert-minded should not miss **Beerntsen's Confectionary** (108 N. 8th St., 920/684-9616, https://beerntsens.com, 10am-10pm daily), a renowned local chocolatier for 50 years.

Accommodations

Most motels and hotels, including several chain operations, are clustered around the I-43/U.S. 151 interchange. The **Harbor Town Inn** (4004 Calumet Ave., 920/684-7841, www.harbortowninn.com, $90 s or d) has been very tastefully renovated and offers good value. There is a fitness center.

No luxury as such exists in town, but a solid midrange lodging has always been the **Baymont by Wyndham Lakefront** (101 Maritime Dr., 920/682-7000, $119), the only place right on the lake and adjacent to the maritime museum.

Information

The superb **Manitowoc Information Center** (4221 Calumet Ave., 920/683-4388 or 800/627-4896, www.manitowoc.info) is prominently housed near the I-43/U.S. 151 interchange and has a 24-hour kiosk.

Getting There

Originally one of seven railroad and passenger ferries plying the route between Manitowoc and Ludington, Michigan, the **SS *Badger*** (800/841-4243, www.ssbadger.com, 1-2 times daily mid-May-mid-Oct., one-way $76 pp plus $76 per car) is a wonderful anachronism. Though it's technically a steamship, the last of its kind on Lake Michigan, you can hardly tell thanks to modern pollution controls. Crossings take four hours, and deals are sometimes available.

TWO RIVERS

Two Rivers is said to be the fishing capital of Lake Michigan, but residents are even prouder of another claim to fame: The ice cream sundae was invented here in 1881, at a 15th Street soda fountain. The mammoth historic **Washington House Museum and Visitor Center** (17th St. and Jefferson St., 920/793-2490, 10am-8pm daily May-Oct., less rest of year, free), once an immigrant hotel, dance hall, and saloon, dispenses information as well as great ice cream at a mock-up of the original soda fountain that made the town famous.

Sights and Recreation

Check out the fascinating **Hamilton Wood Type and Printing Museum** (1816 10th St., 920/794-6272, http://woodtype.org, 10am-5pm Tues.-Sat., 1pm-5pm Sun. May-Nov., closed Sun.-Mon. rest of year, $5), with vintage equipment for international wood typing. So valuable are its holdings of some 1.5 million pieces (largest in the U.S.!) that companies like Target seek it out for typefaces on clothing lines.

At **Rogers Street Fishing Village** (2102 Jackson St., 920/793-5905, www.rogersstreet.com, 10am-4pm Mon.-Fri., noon-4pm Sat.-Sun. May-Oct., $4 adults), artifacts include those from the regional U.S. Coast Guard, especially its lighthouse operations. There is a lot of shipwreck memorabilia—said to be Wisconsin's largest shipwreck exhibit—and plenty of retired vessels.

The excellent **Woodland Dunes,** 10 miles west along Highway 310, are spiny mounds that were the littoral edges of a glacial lake.

Rogers Street Fishing Village

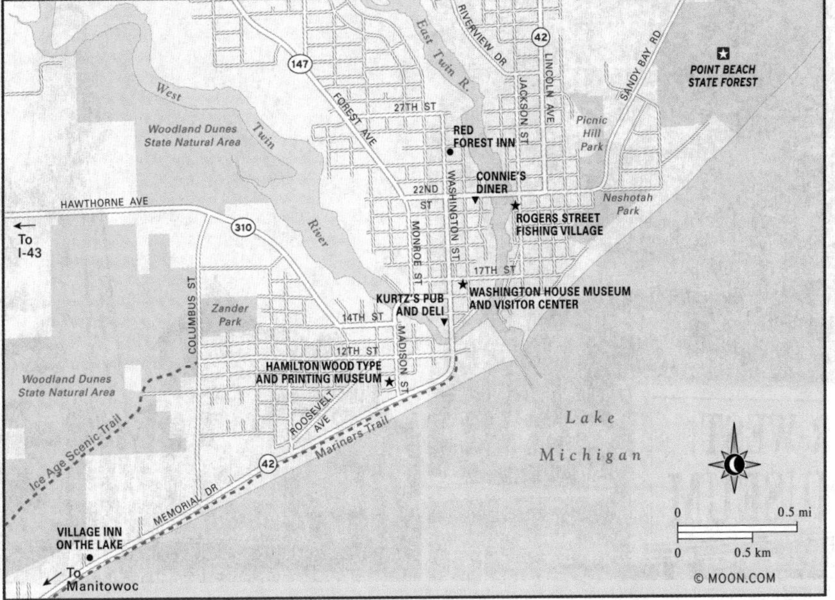

Food

Hole-in-the-wall **Connie's Diner** (1303 22nd St., 920/794-8500, 10:30am-8pm Mon.-Sat., from $3) used to be Phil Rohrer's, and when Rohrer sold it to an assistant, many locals blanched. It has since been redone in a 1950s style, and the stick-to-your-ribs comfort food hasn't declined. Try the mini burgers and raw fries.

One of the best-known restaurants in this region is **Kurtz's Pub and Deli** (1410 Washington St., 920/793-1222, 11am-10pm Mon.-Sat., $5-11). It was established in 1904 to serve the rollicking sailors hopping off Great Lakes steamers and clippers. Today it would be called an "upscale pub."

Don't forget the dessert tray at **Washington House Museum and Visitor Center** (17th St. and Jefferson St., 920/793-2490, 10am-8pm daily May-Oct., less rest of year)!

Accommodations

Farthest south toward Manitowoc, the **Village Inn on the Lake** (3310 Hwy. 42, 920/794-8818 or 800/551-4795, www.villageinnwi.com, $118) is a decent family-run operation. It's a two-level motel with RV sites, a coffee shop, and a minigolf course on the premises.

The **Red Forest Inn** (1421 25th St., 920/793-1794, www.reforestbb.com, $140) is well worth the money and gets raves for its delightful hosts. Ogle the lovely cross-beam ceilings of the 1907 buildings while you sample evening cheese plates.

★ POINT BEACH STATE FOREST

Just north of Two Rivers is the gorgeous **Point Beach State Forest** (920/794-7480), off Highway O, six miles east of town. You can't miss the **Rawley Point Lighthouse,** the majestic white lighthouse towering above the sandy pines. The wind-whipped 2,900 acres spread along latte-colored sandy beaches; the wicked shoals offshore have pulled plenty of

RAHR-WEST
ART MUSEUM
1
2
3

ships to their graves. The lighthouse is functional, but public access is irregular. The preserved ridges along the shoreline are residual effects of a glacial lake last seen retreating 5,500 years ago, one reason the entire forest is a State Scientific Area. One of Wisconsin's official **Rustic Roads** stretches along the park—Highway O, aka Sandy Bay Road.

Camping is possible, and **reservations** (888/947-2757, http://wisconsin.goingtocamp.com, reservation fee $8, nonresidents from $25, vehicles $11 per day) are advised.

One of nine Ice Age National Scientific Reserves in Wisconsin is the **Two Creeks** area, a few miles north of here. Two Creeks contains the remnants of a 12,000-year-old buried glacial forest.

DENMARK

Also a hop off the interstate on the way to Green Bay is the Danish enclave of Denmark, known previously as Copenhagen. There's lots of old Danish architecture downtown, and more cheese shops per capita than anywhere.

Green Bay

Not only colorful, *la baye verte* was a haven from the volatility of Lake Michigan. In 1669 New France, under Jesuit overview, established an official settlement—the first permanent settlement in what would be Wisconsin—at the mouth of the bay near the present-day suburb of De Pere.

The bay region's explorers and trappers found a wealth of beavers and new networks of inland waterways; the wilderness from here to the Fox River Valley produced more pelts than any other region in New France.

History and the current subtle gentrification notwithstanding, if there is one dominant cultural ethos underpinning the city, it is the beloved Green Bay Packers. *The Sporting News,* among many national media outlets, has rated the city the number-one sports fans of the National Football League, literally in a league of their own. The waiting list for season tickets is longer than a phone book in a midsize city; if you applied now, you'd get tickets in about 200 years. This is a city where 60,000 people pay just to watch the team practice.

1: Rahr-West Art Museum in Manitowoc 2: Rawley Point Lighthouse 3: The Mariner's Trail between Manitowoc and Two Rivers

Orientation

Cupping Green Bay and bisected by the Fox River, streets can sometimes be a confusing jumble. Always keep in mind which side of the river you're on, and when in doubt, head for Lake Michigan and start over.

TOP EXPERIENCE

★ THE PACK

One of the oldest professional football teams in the United States and the only community-owned team in professional sports, the **Green Bay Packers** (920/569-7500, www.packers.com) are it in this town. If nothing else, from outside check out renovated but still classic Lambeau Field; perhaps no stadium mixes tradition with modernity more than this national treasure. Fans care only that they can visit the stadium almost every day of the year. The atrium and its restaurants and shops are open 8am-10pm weekdays, 9am-10pm Sat., 10am-10pm Sun. except game days; you'd be surprised how many people are wandering around at 8:30am.

People often crowd the free twice-a-day practices during the Packers' late-summer **training camp,** held at the practice facility along Oneida Street across from Lambeau Field. Sometimes practices are held indoors in the team's state-of-the-art Hutson Practice

Green Bay

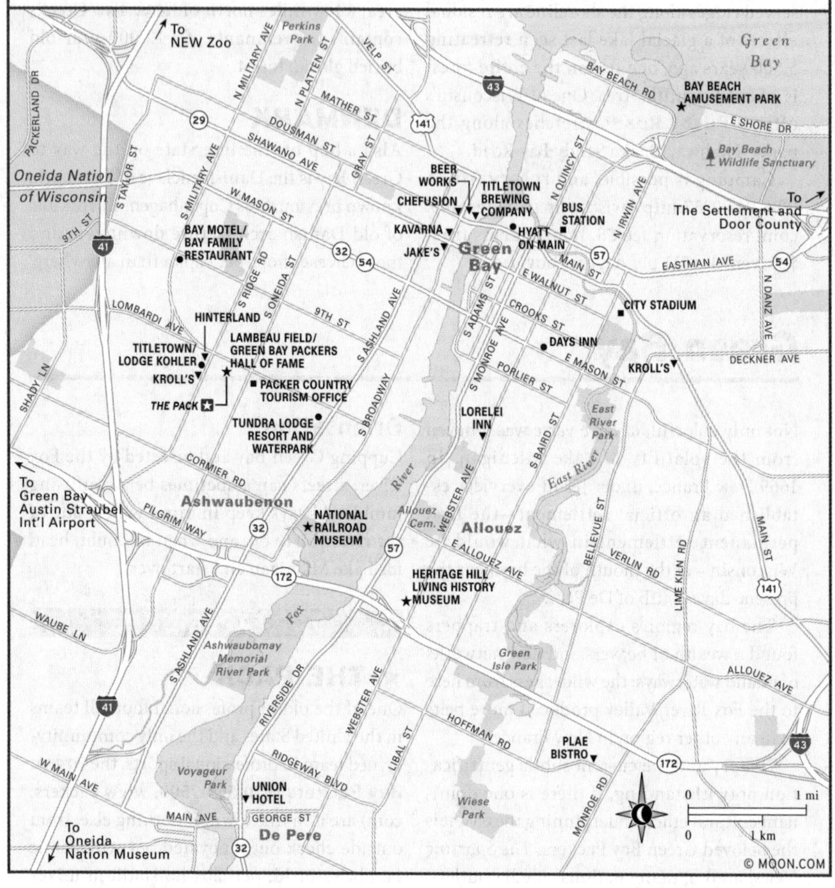

Facility. Practices begin in mid-July and run until preseason games begin in late August. In mid-July is the **Packer Hall of Fame Induction Ceremony,** a very big deal to Packers fans.

A perfect Packer Country day would start by watching some of the practice sessions; those standing along the fence line to watch are known as "railbirds," and it's a tradition for Packer players to ride local kids' bikes to and from the playing field. Offer your handkerchief to a weeping Packer fan who's come from afar to realize this dream.

Don't miss a **Lambeau Field** tour. Myriad tours exist; the more expensive the tour, the more things you see. As the price goes up, visitors explore virtually every corner of this local landmark (except, sadly, the Packers' locker room), including the press box, the visitors' locker room, the skyboxes, and even the field itself (though don't expect to be allowed to sprint downfield). Hour-long tours (920/569-7512, 9am or 10am-4pm daily on nongame days, starting at $15 adults) are given.

The number-one Packer destination is the Lambeau Field Atrium, home to the **Green**

Lombardi Time

When you visit Lambeau Field, pull out your mobile phone and check the time. Now look at the stadium clock outside. No, that isn't a mistake: The stadium's clock is intentionally set 15 minutes fast. That's because Vince Lombardi absolutely insisted that "on time" meant 15 minutes early, and hereabouts it's called "Lombardi Time."

Bay Packers Hall of Fame (920/569-7512, 9am-6pm Mon.-Sat., from 10am Sun., hours vary for home games, $15 adults). It's an orgy of fandom. Most fans weep at the life-size re-creation of the 1967 Ice Bowl—the defining moment in making the team the real "America's Team"; kids will have to push adults out of the way to go wild in the interactive zone.

In 2018 an actual Packer neighborhood was opened up across the street from Lambeau Field. **Titletown** is a gentrified family-friendly district of restaurants, a hotel, tubing hill, skating rink, football-themed playground, and even an entire football field for the kiddies to race around. You will always find something happening here!

By the way, it's virtually impossible to get face-value tickets to regular season Packers games, especially if the Pack's success continues; preseason games are another matter. Check http://packers.com for ticket information.

Other Packer Sights

A plaza has been dedicated at **City Stadium** (1415 E. Walnut St., behind Green Bay East High School), where the Packers played 1925-1956.

Believe it or not, in anti-Chicago Green Bay, there exists a Chicago Bears bar, the **Lorelei Inn** (1412 S. Webster St., 920/432-5921, www.lorelei-inn.com, Mon.-Sat.), originally owned by a Bears fan. You can expect good-natured ribbing. It's closed Sunday except when the Pack and the Bears clash.

For all things Packers, here are some good websites: www.packerseverywhere.com (done with the Packers' participation), www.packersnews.com, www.packerforum.com (a global fan site), www.packersbars.com (find a Packer bar wherever you are), www.jsonline.com (Milwaukee's newspaper covers the Packers), and www.greenbaypressgazette.com.

During training camp and on some game days, a cheery way to take in Packer sights is aboard the **Packer Heritage Trail Tour** (920/471-7951, http://packersheritagetrail.com, $30). It leaves from next to the **Convention and Visitors Bureau** (1901 S. Oneida St., across the street from Lambeau Field, 920/494-9507 or 888/867-3342, www.greenbay.com). The visitors bureau also has guides for the heritage trail for you to walk (or Segway, or whatever).

OTHER SIGHTS

Museums

The **National Railroad Museum** (2285 S. Broadway Ave., 920/437-7623, www.nationalrrmuseum.org, 9am-5pm Mon.-Sat., 11am-5pm Sun. Apr.-Dec., limited hours Jan.-Mar., $10 adults), with more than 80 railroad cars and locomotives, has a respected collection rivaling any in the nation. Available for close inspection is a personal favorite, the Big Boy, the world's largest steam locomotive. Train rides ($2) are also available, of course; a mile-long jaunt on a narrow-gauge railroad runs five times daily in summer.

Perhaps the most unusual state park in Wisconsin is **Heritage Hill Living History Museum** (2640 S. Webster Ave., 920/448-5150, www.heritagehillgb.org, 10am-4:30pm Mon.-Sat., noon-4:30pm Sun. Apr.-Oct., $10 adults). More than 25 historic buildings from around Wisconsin have been reconstructed at this 50-acre site—the buildings include mock-ups of the flimsy original sapling-and-bark dwellings of the Jesuits and some of the oldest extant buildings in Wisconsin. All areas are accessible via wagons.

1
2
3
LAMBEAU FIELD
SHOPKO GATE
TICKETS

Bay Beach Amusement Park

One of my favorites in Green Bay is the anachronistic (as in, since 1892) gathering of more than a dozen rides along the bay shoreline at the **Bay Beach Amusement Park** (1313 Bay Beach Rd., 920/391-3671, www.greenbaywi.gov/baybeach, 10am-9pm daily June-Aug., 10am-9pm Sat.-Sun. May and Sept.). The best part: Rides cost as little as $0.25. The Zippin Pippin roller coaster is Elvis Presley's favorite ride at an amusement park in Memphis; when the park bought it and put it in, attendance jumped by nearly 25 percent! Oh, and in 2019 they unveiled their newest—a 10-story Ferris wheel—still only 75 cents!

Bay Beach Wildlife Sanctuary

Up the road from the amusement park is the excellent **Bay Beach Wildlife Sanctuary** (1660 E. Shore Dr., 920/391-3671, www.baybeachwildlife.com, 8am-7:30pm daily Apr.-Sept., shorter hours Oct.-Mar., free), a 700-acre spread with exhibits on Wisconsin fauna, including the very popular timber wolf house.

NEW Zoo

The well-regarded **NEW Zoo** (4378 Reforestation Rd., 920/448-4466, www.newzoo.org, 9am-8pm daily June-Aug., shorter hours Sept.-May, $9 adults), eight miles north of Green Bay, allows the animals greater freedom to roam. Animal compounds include Prairie Grassland, Wisconsin Native, and International—you're as likely to see a Galápagos tortoise as you are a Wisconsin red fox. The zoo has constantly expanded and added many new exhibits, including a black-footed penguin zone. A children's area allows interactive experiences—who doesn't want to feed the giraffes?—and fun things like ziplining.

1: wolves at the Bay Beach Wildlife Sanctuary
2: family-friendly Titletown **3:** Lambeau Field, home of the Packers

Side Trips

West of Ashwaubenon is zany **Seymour,** which bills itself as the "Home of the Hamburger," purportedly invented here. The townsfolk fete their title with the annual **Burger Fest** the first Saturday in August; they try to fry a world-record burger (some three tons) annually. Just check out the enormous burger and Hamburger Charlie on Depot Street, west of Highway 55.

RECREATION

Trails

The **Fox River Trail** is a 14-mile multipurpose path stretching along the Fox Valley corridor to Greenleaf. The city is also the departure point for the **Mountain Bay Trail,** an eight-mile trail linking to trails west to Wausau.

FOOD

Don't forget that De Pere also has some fine eateries, especially the since-1918 **Union Hotel** (200 N. Broadway, 920/336-6131, lunch Mon.-Fri., dinner daily, $15-30), the most anachronistic environment (in a good way) you can find in the state. Service is outstanding and will probably include a visit from the owner, and the wine list is extraordinary.

Brewpubs

Green Bay's got a couple of lively brewpubs. Right downtown, at the west end of the Fox River Bridge along Highway 29, is **Titletown Brewing Company** (200 Dousman St., 920/437-2337, 11am-10pm daily, $8-15), with an above-average menu of creative fare. It's housed in a grand old depot with a soaring clock tower, making for great atmosphere. Two blocks west of here, Titletown also has a new Beer Works building (320 N. Broadway Ave.) with classic taproom and roof tap.

Virtually across the street from the main Titletown Brewing Company, the **Hinterland** (920/438-8050, lunch Sat., dinner Mon.-Sat., $8-18) has great beer and phenomenal food—even barramundi, wild boar, and the like. The food is professionally well made.

Titletown

It is always the same: Sunday morning at 11:59am, the network TV feed fades to black. Then, a still shot of the man, and slowly, with the melodrama of sports announcers, the voice-over: "The Man. Vincent T. Lombardi." Or, even more powerfully, "Titletown . . . " It incites goose bumps followed by the shaking of unwavering belief.

THE RELIGION

If there are any awards for professional sports fandom, the Green Bay Packers football team and its beloved legions win hands-down. One grizzled sportswriter wrote, "The Dallas Cowboys were only another football team; the Packers were a practicing religion."

The Packers are the only passively proselytizing franchise in all of professional sports. Hard-core travelers and football aficionados will find Packer bars and Packer fan clubs in every state in the Union and as far away as England. I've even found Packer faithful bellowing for Sunday satellite-dish equity as far away as Thailand.

EARLY YEARS

The Packers were founded in 1919 as one of the handful of teams that would eventually make up the National Football League (NFL). The team was born in the back room of the *Green Bay Press-Gazette,* where the cigar-chomping sports editor, George Calhoun, and legendary ex-Notre Damer Curly Lambeau agreed to found a local team. They convinced a local industry bigwig to supply a practice field and uniforms, thus obligating the team to call itself the Indian Packing Company Footballers. This was later shortened to the Packers. Going 10-1 its first season, the dynasty had begun.

After literally passing the hat in the crowd for the first season, the Packers, in need of finan-

Fish Fries

Local bar and grill **The Settlement** (3254 Bay Settlement Rd., from 11am daily, 920/465-8415, from $4) has a top-notch Friday fish fry featuring perch. It's as much a bar as a grill, but given the quality and portions of food, and the fact that they welcome you like a friend no matter who you are, it's a great local find.

Pizza

The best pizza in town is at **Jake's** (112 S. Broadway St., 920/437-5542, 4pm-10pm or later Tues.-Sun., $4-6). You'll have to wait up to half an hour for a seat at times, but it is well worth it.

Regional

If you really want to rub elbows with the locals, check out ★ **Kroll's,** the best family restaurant in town, with two locations. The more convenient one is on Main Street (1658 Main St., 920/468-4422, 10:30am-11pm daily, $4-11). The other (S. Ridge Rd., 920/497-1111), closer to Lambeau Field, is the older of the two and appears to have come straight out of a Hollywood movie set from the 1950s. They serve great walleye and perch along with legendary burgers. This Kroll's also features wall buzzers that customers can use to summon the waitstaff.

Kroll's competition is **Bay Family Restaurant** (Military Ave. and 9th St., 920/494-3441, breakfast, lunch, and dinner daily, $6-11). The Bay uses ingredients direct from family farms and serves homemade pies and piles of hash browns the size of encyclopedias. There are two other locations: 1245 East Mason Street and 1100 Radisson Street. All are open for three squares a day.

Fine Dining

Plae Bistro (1671 Hoffman Dr., 920/632-7065, lunch and dinner Mon.-Thurs., dinner Fri.-Sat., $13-45) has creative American cuisine—fish tacos as well as tenderloin—in

cial stability, hit on one of the most unusual money angles in sports. The community issued $5 nondividend public shares in the team; almost beyond logic, the citizens scooped up the stocks.

The only nonprofit, community-owned team in professional sports, the Packers have become a true anomaly: a small-market team with few fiscal constraints on finding and wooing talent. And they can never desert the town—if they try to move, the organization is dissolved and all money goes to a charitable foundation.

TITLETOWN'S TITLES

After the Packers beat their opponents in the first season, they became the first NFL team to win three consecutive NFL titles, and they did it twice—1929-1931 and 1965-1967. In all, they won 11 championships through 1968 and the Lombardi years. In fact, even though the Lombardi-led teams get all the glory, the teams of the early years were even more dominant, amassing a 34-5-2 record.

Then the well went dry. Before the 1990s brought in more forceful management, the Packers suffered through their longest drought ever between NFC Central Division Championships: 24 long, unbearable, embarrassing years. Still, the fans dutifully packed the stadium every Sunday; they always believed.

But after all those doormat decades, the Packers finally won the Super Bowl again in 1997, which began an always-in-the-playoffs run culminating in yet another notch in the Titletown belt on February 6, 2011, when the Packers defeated the Super Bowl-seasoned Pittsburgh Steelers 31-25 for their record 13th NFL championship and fourth Super Bowl title. The headline in the *Milwaukee Journal-Sentinel* said it all: "Titletown Again." A more apt quote often heard after the game was, "The Lombardi trophy is coming home."

a cozy atmosphere. The grilled apple or pear salad is divine.

Making a name for itself is the new **Chefusion** (307 N. Broadway Ave., 920/432-2300, dinner Tues.-Sat., $11-25). They say "eclectic" and, boy, does it fit. One area does casual small plates—the pork belly ramen is wondrous—while the other offers prix fixe fine dining. All is done well.

Vegetarian

Kavarna (143 N. Broadway, 920/430-3200, breakfast, lunch, and dinner daily, brunch Sat.-Sun., $5-10) is a coffee shop with a café complex rather than a restaurant, but the baked yam fries are worth a trip.

ACCOMMODATIONS

Don't expect to get lodging in Green Bay on a weekend when the Packers are playing at home. The visitors bureau website (www.greenbay.com) and the local lodging association (www.greenbaystays.com) have lodging links and deals.

Downtown

It has been possible to scare up a $100 room, though most are more, at the **Days Inn** (1125 E. Mason St., 920/430-7040, $100-189), which has a large number of amenities.

Upmarket digs are right nearby at the excellent **Hyatt on Main** (333 Main St., 920/432-1234, www.greenbay.hyatt.com, from $219). It's like a self-contained city with everything you need, with breakfast included in the morning.

Airport and Stadium

Where Lombardi Avenue swings around to Military Avenue is the step-up **Bay Motel** (1301 S. Military Ave., 920/494-3441, $60-90), where all rooms have free movies and some have minifridges.

Have a family? The only place to head is the **Tundra Lodge Resort and Waterpark**

(Lombardi Ave. and Ashland Ave., 920/405-8700, www.tundralodge.com, $180-399), close to Lambeau Field. Indoor and outdoor water parks let the kids work up a sweat; then let them gorge in the buffet-style restaurant. It's chaotic given all the families, but if you're with a brood, it's your spot.

Lodge Kohler (1950 S. Ridge Rd., 888/456-4537, www.lodgekohler.com, from $189) is a brand-new chic hotel in the new Titletown district (as in—you can see Lambeau Field from your room) with exquisite design and furnishings. (This is to be expected, as it uses fixtures from the Kohler Company; even the digital triple showerheads are state of the art!) It has had the expected growing pains of new hotels, but it is definitely not overpriced.

INFORMATION

The **Packer Country Tourism Office** (1901 S. Oneida St., 920/494-9507 or 888/867-3342, www.greenbay.com) is across the street from Lambeau Field. It covers Green Bay east to Two Rivers, Kewaunee, and Algoma.

The ***Green Bay Press-Gazette*** (www.greenbaypressgazette.com) is Wisconsin's oldest newspaper, started in 1833 as the *Green Bay Intelligencer.* It's a great source of local goings-on.

GETTING THERE

Air

Austin Straubel International Airport (GRB, 2077 Airport Dr., Ashwaubenon, 920/498-4800), in southwest Green Bay off Highway 172, has 50 flights daily to Chicago, Detroit, Minneapolis, Denver and Atlanta.

Car

Driving to Green Bay from Sturgeon Bay (via Hwy. 57, 45 miles) takes 50 minutes. From Milwaukee (via I-43, 118 miles), it takes two hours. From Madison (via U.S. 151 and U.S. 41, 135 miles), it takes 2.5 hours. From Minneapolis (via I-94 and Hwy. 29, 278 miles), it takes 4.5 hours. From Chicago (via I-94 and I-43, 208 miles), it takes 3.5 hours.

ONEIDA NATION

West of Green Bay are the 12 square miles of the **Oneida Indian Reservation.** Known as the People of the Standing Stone, the Oneida were members of the League of the Iroquois and once a protectorate of the Stockbridge-Munsee bands on the East Coast. They moved westward en masse (save for a small community still in New York) not long after the turn of the 18th century.

One of the only repositories of the history of the Oneida is the **Oneida Nation Museum** (W892 EE Rd., 920/869-2768, www.oneidanation.org/museum, 8:30am-4pm Tues., Thurs., Fri., till 6pm Wed., $2 adults, $1 children). Exhibits in the main hall focus on Oneida history and culture; a longhouse and stockade are outside, as well as a nice nature trail. The Oneida **powwow** takes place on or near the Fourth of July.

The Bottom of the Door

For many, Door County begins only when they have crossed the bridge spanning Sturgeon Bay's Lake Michigan canal; others claim that you're not in the county until Highway 42 and Highway 57 bifurcate into bayside and lakeside routes northeast of town. Still, Door County proper includes a chunk of 15 or more miles south of the ship channel, and the peninsula also includes underappreciated Kewaunee County, east of Green Bay.

Highway 57 leaves much to the imagination. More adventuresome travelers might attempt to find Highway A from Green Bay; it travels the same route but right along the lake. Bypassing Point Sable—once a boundary between Native American nations—the road offers views of a state wildlife area across the water. Farther up, you can see Vincent Point and, immediately after that, Red Banks. This byway continues through Benderville before linking with Highway 57 again before crossing the Kewaunee-Door County line into Belgian territory.

BRUSSELS AND VICINITY

Brussels and surrounding towns such as Champion, Euren, Maplewood, Rosiere, and Forestville constitute the country's largest Belgian immigrant settlement. The architecture of the region is so well preserved that more than 100 buildings make up Wisconsin's first rural National Historical Landmark. Right along Highway 57, the homes and Roman Catholic chapels show distinctive Belgian influences along with a lot of reddish-orange brick and split-cedar fencing. On alternating weekends through the summer, the villages still celebrate *Kermiss,* church mass during harvest season.

Brussels is the area's capital of sorts, with **Belgian Days** the first week of July—plenty of Belgian chicken, *booyah* (thick vegetable stock), *jute* (boiled cabbage), and tripe sausage. You'll find Belgian fare in a few places in Brussels, including **Marchants Food** (9674 Hwy. 57, 920/825-1244, 8am-8pm Mon.-Fri., 8am-6pm Sat., 8am-12:30pm Sun.), open daily for 50 years.

A quick side trip takes in lots of Belgian architecture. In Robinsville, 1.5 miles east of Champion along Highway K, sits the **shrine grotto,** a home and school for disabled children founded by a Belgian to whom the Virgin Mary is said to have appeared in 1858.

Not Belgian per se but north of Luxemburg, which is south of Brussels, near the junction of Highways A and C, is ★ **Joe Rouer's** (E1098 Hwy. X, Luxemburg, 920/866-2585), a classic bar with legendary burgers. The cheese curds are good as well.

North of Brussels along Highway C, the **St. Francis Xavier Church and Grotto Cemetery** is representative of Belgian rural construction; farmers contributed aesthetically pleasing stones from their fields to raise a grotto and crypt for the local reverend.

KEWAUNEE

Perched on a hillside overlooking a lovely historic harbor, Kewaunee was once bent on rivaling Chicago as the maritime center of the Great Lakes and likely could have given the Windy City a run for its money when an influx of immigrants descended after hearing rumors of a gold strike in the area. But Chicago had the rail while Kewaunee, despite its harbor, was isolated and became a minor port and lumber town.

Sights

Kewaunee is Wisconsin's Czech nerve center. Outlying villages show Czech and Bohemian heritage, and you may hear Czech spoken.

Everybody snaps a shot of the 1909 **Kewaunee Pierhead Lighthouse.** The structure consists today of a steel frame base and steel tower with a cast-iron octagonal lantern about 50 feet high.

At the harbor you can take a tour ($3) aboard a retired World War II tugboat with **Tug Ludington** (920/388-4317, 10am-4pm Sat.-Sun. summer, shorter hours in other seasons).

The central **Old Jail Museum** (Vliet St. and Dodge St., 920/388-4410, noon-4pm Thurs.-Sun. summer, $3) is near the courthouse in an old sheriff's home, part of which doubled as the jail, complete with gruesome dungeon cells. Statues of Father Marquette and solemn, pious Potawatomi are first on the tour, and you can visit the replica of the USS *Pueblo.* The ill-fated Navy ship, involved in an incident with North Korea in the 1950s, was built in Kewaunee during World War II.

Southwest of town in Montpelier township is a **Rustic Road** scenic drive involving parts of Hrabik, Cherneysville, Sleepy Hollow, and Pine Grove Roads. Close to here, south of Krok, is the only known Wisconsin rooftop windmill, a granddaddy of a historic structure.

At **Svoboda Industries,** along Highway 42 north of town, you'll see what is purportedly the world's largest grandfather clock, 39 feet tall.

The local **Visitors Information Center** (920/388-4822, www.kewaunee.org) is on Highway 42, north of downtown, near a great marsh walk.

Food

The local specialty is Czech and Bohemian food, including *kolace* (yeast buns with fruit filling) and *buhuite* ("BU-ta"—thin dough filled with seeds or fruit), sauerkraut rye bread, and *rohlik* (yeasty crescent-shaped rolls with caraway or poppy seeds). Near the bridge in town are a couple of places for great smoked fish.

Accommodations

The **Coho Motel** (705 Main St., 920/388-3565, http://cohomotel.com, $87) is an amazingly clean place for the cost.

ALGOMA

The whole drive along Highway 42 from Manitowoc to Algoma is spectacular—a resplendent, beach-hugging route. As you swoop into Algoma from the south, seemingly endless miles of wide, empty beach begin, both road and beach unencumbered by travelers. This freshly scrubbed little community of friendly folks resembles Door County.

The small town is known today mostly for its excellent sportfishing, and its marinas account for the state's most substantial sportfishing industry, with four state records. And there is, of course, a lovely lighthouse.

Sights

Von Stiehl Winery (115 Navarino St., 920/487-5208, www.vonstiehl.com, guided tours 9:30am-5:30pm daily July-Aug., shorter hours in other seasons, $4 adults) is the oldest licensed winery in Wisconsin, housed in what was once the Ahnapee Brewery, built in the 1850s and named after the local river. The three-foot-thick limestone walls provide a ready-made underground catacomb system. The house specialty is cherry wine; many other Wisconsin fruit wines are produced, all guarded by a patented system to prevent premature aging and light damage. Two doors down is the winery's Civil War-era **Ahnapee Brewery** (920/785-0822, hours vary), housed in an old garage, which features handcrafted beers and good cheer.

Algoma is also the southern terminus of the **Ahnapee State Trail** (daily trail pass $5), a section of the Ice Age National Scenic Trail stretching 18 miles partially along the Ahnapee River to the southern fringe of Sturgeon Bay. Another trail runs from Algoma to Casco.

Charter Fishing

Second in the state for fish taken, this is a prime place to smear on the zinc oxide and do some fishing. Early-season lake trout are generally plentiful in May, but June is Algoma's biggest month; rainbow trout and chinook salmon are everywhere. Steelhead and especially king salmon are added to the mix in July, and brown trout get big in August. September fishing is great.

Food

Several family restaurants and diners in town serve Belgian *booyah* and Belgian pie.

For espresso, coffee, tea, or light food—along with live music—in a trendy atmosphere, you can't beat the Mediterranean-influenced **Caffe Tlazo** (607 Hwy. 42, 920/487-7240, 6am-7pm Mon.-Fri., 7am-8pm Sat., 7am-3pm Sun. summer, lesser hours rest of year, from $5).

Fine dining in a low-rent bar atmosphere is at **Skaliwags** (312 Clark St., 920/487-8092, www.skaligwags.com, 4:30pm-10pm daily summer, $8-25), where there is Hawaiian-inspired seafood, pasta, and great steaks. The chef also operates a food truck in town.

For a picnic basket, **Bearcat's** (Hwy. 42 and Navarino St., 920/487-2372, 9am-5pm daily year-round) has great smoked fish for cheap prices.

Accommodations

A basic motel across the road from Lake Michigan is the **Scenic Shore Inn** (2221 Lake St., 920/487-3214, $79), with clean guest rooms and welcoming owners who have put a great deal of updating into the place. A smart new addition adds updated comfort.

Information and Services

The **Visitor Information Center** (Hwy. 42, 920/487-2041 or 800/498-4888, www.visitalgomawi.org) is on the south edge of Algoma along Highway 42.

Appleton

It has been called the Queen of the Fox Cities and the Princess of Paper Valley, although even locals might not know what you're talking about. Bisected by the Fox River, spread-out Appleton hardly seems paper-centered or industrial when you're in the gentrified downtown area.

One civic nucleus is well-respected Lawrence University, a small liberal arts college that was the state's first coed institution of higher education and also the first to initiate a postgraduate papermaking institute.

SIGHTS

★ History Museum at the Castle

Paper may be the city's raison d'être, but folks just can't get enough of that Houdini magic. Born Ehrich Weiss in Hungary in 1874, the enigmatic Harry Houdini spent most of his life in Appleton. The **History Museum at**

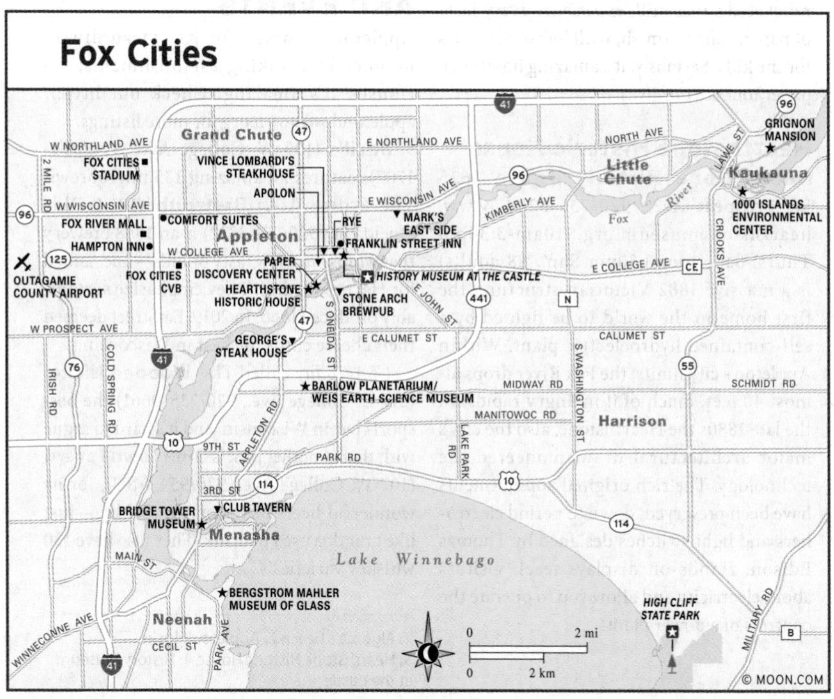

the Castle (330 E. College Ave., 920/735-9370 www.myhistorymuseum.org, 11am-4pm Tues.-Sun., closed holidays, adults $15) includes **A.K.A. Houdini,** the foremost collection of Houdini artifacts anywhere, including the Guiteau handcuffs, which bound President Garfield's assassin and from which the magician later escaped. The center has prepared a detailed walking tour of the city, marked with brass plaques, that takes in the sites of Houdini's childhood. Magic shows, hands-on exhibits, and more thrill kids and parents alike.

The museum also has rotating exhibits that detail everything from technology to, recently, the guitar.

Paper Discovery Center

Where else would the paper industry's hall of fame, the **Paper Discovery Center** (425 W. Water St., 920/749-3040, www.paperdiscoverycenter.org, 10am-4pm Mon.-Sat., $7), be but the Fox River Valley? In a renovated paper mill, experience every facet of paper, start to finish, with lots of activities for the kids. Seriously, it's amazing how much paper touches our lives.

Hearthstone Historic House

Hearthstone Historic House (625 W. Prospect Ave., 920/730-8204, www.hearthstonemuseum.org, 10am-3:30pm Thurs.-Sat., 1pm-3:30pm Sun., $8 adults) is a massive 1882 Victorian structure, the first home in the world to be lighted by a self-contained hydroelectric plant. Within Appleton's city limits, the Fox River drops almost 40 feet, much of it in angry rapids; in the late 1880s the Hearthstone, also the city's major architectural draw, pioneered the technology. The rich original appointments have been preserved, down to period electroliers and light switches designed by Thomas Edison. Hands-on displays teach visitors about electricity and allow you to operate the controls of a power plant.

Side Trips

Among the oldest paved trails in Wisconsin is hard-to-find number 53 on Wisconsin's Rustic Road system. Beginning in 1857, work was done on what today are Garrity, McCabe, Greiner, and Bodde Roads, northwest of Appleton along U.S. 41 at Highway JJ. Keep your eyes peeled for the signs—it's somewhat confusing. Along the way, you'll pass scenic double-arch bridges, a stone silo, and a wildlife conservation area.

SPORTS AND RECREATION

Spectator Sports

Fox Cities Stadium (2400 N. Casaloma Dr., 920/733-4152) is the home of the Wisconsin Timber Rattlers, a single-A minor league baseball franchise of the Milwaukee Brewers. It's typical family-friendly fun with zany promotions and dirt-cheap ticket prices.

ENTERTAINMENT AND EVENTS

Appleton is famed for its extraordinary number of drinking establishments; seriously, it's amazing. Check out http://appletondowntown.org for more listings.

Bazil's (109 W. College Ave., 920/954-1707) features an amazing 135 microbrews. The **Stone Arch Brewpub** (1004 Olde Oneida St., 920/751-3322) is an 1858 brewery that whips out a few tasty brands—one named for Harry Houdini. They emphasize sustainably produced food. In 2019, EatStreet deemed their cheese curds the best in Wisconsin.

USA Today called **The Wooden Nickel** (217 E. College Ave., 920/735-0661) the best sports bar in Wisconsin, and it's hard to argue with that. Another pick is **Olde Town Tavern** (107 W. College Ave., 920/954-0103), for its wonderful beers of yesteryear. Schlitz—just like grandpa used to drink. They also have 130 whiskey varieties!

1: Algoma's beach **2:** Appleton's locks
3: Hearthstone Historic House **4:** History Museum at the Castle

1

2

3

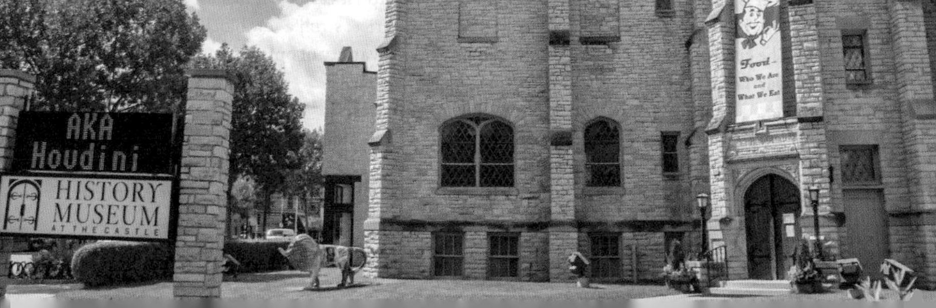
4
AKA
Houdini
HISTORY
MUSEUM
AT THE CASTLE
Food –
Who We Are
and
What We Eat

Joseph McCarthy

> I have in my hands a list of 205 names that were made known to the Secretary of State as being members of the Communist Party and who nevertheless are still working and shaping policy in the State Department.

These words, uttered by Senator Joseph McCarthy, a Fox Cities native, in Wheeling, West Virginia, in what became known as the 205 Speech, thrust him into the national political spotlight. Before his political fortunes waned, he dominated U.S. politics, electrified the nation, aided Tricky Dick Nixon, and inspired a new word, *McCarthyism*.

TAIL GUNNER JOE

After a lifelong struggle with education, McCarthy graduated from the law school at Marquette University and astonished everyone by winning an elected judgeship in 1938 through sheer grassroots flesh-pressing toil. He was not a widely respected judge, and he further infuriated opponents by stumping for higher office by exaggerating his military service in the South Pacific during World War II. Tail Gunner Joe was born.

THE JUNIOR SENATOR

McCarthy was swept up in the GOP wave of 1946 and made it to Washington DC, beating out a member of Wisconsin's La Follette dynasty. He incessantly angered the Senate with his intractable attitude, personal attacks, and rules violations. By 1949 the congressional leadership loathed him, and most assumed he was simply a lame-duck embarrassment.

What no one counted on was his shrewd prescience about the national paranoia over communism. In part, McCarthy concocted the Red Scare. He was once again reelected. His path culminated in his antics in the House Un-American Activities Committee, and McCarthyism was born.

By 1953 he had reached the zenith of his powers, attacking his peers and fending off censure attempts from his many Senate enemies. One charge finally stuck—a kickback scheme—and on December 2, 1954, he was officially censured, diminishing the junior senator from Wisconsin.

WISCONSIN AND MCCARTHY

Strident opposition to McCarthy was ever present throughout his time in office. The newspapers in Madison and Milwaukee lobbed many editorial shells to bring him down. "Joe Must Go" recall petitions collected almost half a million signatures statewide.

Ask Wisconsinites today about McCarthy, and they'll likely dodge the question or roll their eyes and shudder. There are still those who support him. Perhaps most tellingly, Appleton, his adopted hometown, removed his bust and all other McCarthy displays from the courthouse, while favorite resident Harry Houdini is celebrated with Houdini Plaza and a huge memorial sculpture of the man in the city center.

SHOPPING

Appleton is mall country, with so much mall space that bus tours make regular pilgrimages here. The city sported the nation's first indoor mall, partially demolished in 2006 for a new complex. The unity of the **Fox River Mall** (4301 W. Wisconsin Ave., 920/739-4100, www.foxrivermall.com), the state's second-largest indoor mall, is admirable, including the shops surrounding it.

FOOD

Downtown Appleton has an amazing array of eateries; stroll a few blocks and you'll find a wide variety of options.

Supper Club

For a wonderful supper club experience, **Mark's East Side** (1405 E. Wisconsin Ave., 920/733-3600, lunch and dinner Mon.-Sat., $10-25), which locals will always recommend, is a mainstay. In addition to steaks and seafood, there is a worthy selection of German cuisine and, of course, a great fish fry. Wait for your table at the comfy curved bar.

Mediterranean

One of the best dining experiences around is at ★ **Apolon** (207 N. Appleton St., 920/939-1122, 5pm-10pm Mon.-Sat., $9-20), a Hellenic-heavy pan-Mediterranean restaurant famed for its flaming cheese.

Bistro

Rye (308 W. College Ave., 920/380-4745, lunch and dinner Mon.-Sat., from $9) has garnered raves for its stylishly rustic atmosphere and creative, locally sourced cuisine, from steak to potato-weisswurst soup to grilled lamb. It's a wonderful new addition to the local scene.

Steaks

Open for 50 years and still going strong is **George's Steak House** (2208 S. Memorial Dr., 920/733-4939, lunch Fri., dinner Mon.-Sat., $9-30). It's strictly steaks and seafood, with piano music nightly.

This is Packerland, so a visit to **Vince Lombardi's Steakhouse** (333 W. College Ave., 920/380-9390, 4pm-10pm Mon.-Sat., 4pm-9pm Sun., $15-45) in the Radisson Paper Valley Hotel is a requisite for Packers football fans; the steaks are sublime.

ACCOMMODATIONS

The rates listed here will double during Experimental Aircraft Association (EAA) events in nearby Oshkosh. Most lodgings are west of downtown.

The Appleton **Hampton Inn** (350 Fox River Dr., 920/954-9211, $115) has been rated one of the top 10 Hampton Inns nationwide and gets rave reviews.

One of the largest recreation centers in the state is at the Appleton **Comfort Suites Comfort Dome** (3809 W. Wisconsin Ave., 920/730-3800, $120). Some guest rooms have kitchens and microwaves.

A few blocks north of the Avenue Mall is the 1897 Victorian **Franklin Street Inn** (318 E. Franklin St., 920/739-3702, www.franklinstreetinn.com, from $130). Original pocket doors, oak and maple hardwoods, and original chandeliers give one of the stateliest mansions in town a nice feel. Expect superlative service.

If you're planning to mall it at the Fox River Mall during your trip and need luxury, the **Grandstay Hotel & Suites** (300 Mall Dr., 920/993-1200, $125) is an amazing option for the money, with top-notch service and amenities for bargain prices.

Downtown, the best option for comfort is the European-style **CopperLeaf Boutique Hotel** (300 W. College Ave., 877/303-0303, www.copperleafhotel.com, from $145), a great deal considering the location, the freshness of the place, and amenities; guests rave about it.

INFORMATION AND SERVICES

The **Fox Cities Convention and Visitors Bureau** (3433 W. College Ave., 920/734-3358 or 800/236-6673, www.foxcities.org) is quite far west of downtown, but the staff are definitely helpful.

GETTING THERE

Air

The **Outagamie County Airport** (ATW, W6390 Challenger Dr., 920/832-5268, www.atwairport.com) is the fourth-busiest in Wisconsin, with around 60 flights daily to Chicago, Detroit, Minneapolis, Atlanta, Las Vegas, Phoenix, and several cities in Florida.

Car

Driving to Appleton from Green Bay (via U.S. 41, 30 miles) takes 40 minutes. From Madison (via U.S. 151 and U.S. 41, 105 miles), it takes two hours. From Sturgeon Bay (via Hwy. 57 and U.S. 41, 77 miles), it takes an hour and 20 minutes. From Milwaukee (via U.S. 41, 108 miles), it takes just under two hours. From Chicago (via I-94 and U.S. 41, 195 miles), it takes three hours.

Vicinity of Appleton

While Appleton may be the economic linchpin of the area, along Lake Winnebago's northwestern cap lie a dozen concatenate communities between Neenah and Kaukauna making up the Fox Cities region—part of but distinct from the Fox River Valley, which stretches along the Fox River-Lake Winnebago corridor and takes in all communities between Green Bay and Oshkosh. The smallest town is Combined Locks. All are based on the Fox River—one of the few rivers in North America that flows north. Together, the Fox Cities constitute the third-largest metropolitan area in the state (population 180,000), a statistic many Wisconsinites find surprising!

NEENAH-MENASHA

The twin cities of Neenah-Menasha are casually regarded as one entity, although they are governed separately. They share Doty Island, where Little Lake Butte des Mortes on the Fox River empties into Lake Winnebago.

Two Fox River channels flowing past the island and two minor promontories provided the water power that created both villages by the 1840s. Depressed industries gave way to papermaking, and within three decades Neenah-Menasha ruled the powerful Wisconsin papermaking region.

Bergstrom-Mahler Museum

This massive dwelling was once home to early area industrialist John Bergstrom. The highlight of the **Bergstrom-Mahler Museum of Glass** (165 N. Park Ave., 920/751-4658, www.bmmglass.com, 10am-4:30pm Tues.-Sat., 1pm-4:30pm Sun., free) is a world-renowned collection of paperweights, many dating from the French classic era (1845-1860). The glass menagerie, as the museum calls it, is made up of 2,100 exquisite pieces.

Downtown Neenah and Menasha Riverfront

The scenic, landscaped Fox River north channel sports more than 30 picturesque historic buildings, many straight neoclassical in design. The best view is from the still-hand-operated lock on the canal. A museum along Tayco Street, the **Bridge Tower Museum** (920/967-5155, by appointment, free), is in an 80-year-old bridge tender's tower and purportedly the smallest museum in the state.

Downtown Neenah's East Wisconsin Avenue gives the best glimpse of 19th-century opulence as well as great river vistas. The mansions along this stretch were part of the setting for Wisconsin native Edna Ferber's novel *Come and Get It*.

Menasha's **Kimberly Point Park,** at the confluence of Lake Winnebago and the Fox River, has a great lighthouse and some good views of the river. The big draw is the world-class **Barlow Planetarium** (1478 Midway Rd., 920/832-2848, www.uwosh.edu/barlow, public shows $8 adults), on the campus of UW-Fox Valley. It has virtual-reality exhibits and new public shows every week; reservations are not required.

Adjacent to the planetarium is the **Weis Earth Science Museum** (1478 Midway Rd., 920/832-2925, www.weismuseum.org, open daily, hours vary, $3), the official Wisconsin mineralogical museum. Learn about glaciers and the stunning sandstone formations of the state.

KAUKAUNA

The word *gran ka-ka-lin* is a French-Ojibwa pidgin hybrid describing the long portage once necessary to trek around the city's 50-foot cascades, which ultimately required five locks to tame. A bit more amusing: In 1793, the area's land was purchased—the first recognized deed in the state—for the princely sum of two barrels of rum.

Sights

The **Grignon Mansion** (1313 Augustine St., 920/766-6106, www.grignonmansion.org, noon-4pm Sat.-Sun. summer, $6) was built in 1838 by Augustin Grignon to replace the log shack lived in by rum-dealing city founder Dominique Ducharme. It has been thoroughly renovated, down to the hand-carved newel posts and imposing brick fireplaces, while the apple orchard still stands. Several of Kaukauna's legendary locks can be visited via the grounds. Call ahead to tour the mansion; walk-in visits are not possible.

Across the river at a bight is the aptly named **1000 Islands Environmental Center** (700 Dodge St., 920/766-4733, www.1000islandsenvironmentalcenter.org, 8am-4pm Tues.-Fri., 10am-3:30pm Sat., free), a vital stop on the Mississippi Flyway for waterfowl and predatory birds. A huge number of mounted animals are displayed, and live versions include plenty of native Wisconsin fauna, such as great blue herons, coots, and bitterns. The acreage also supports a stand of chinquapin oak, rare in the state. Great trails run along the Fox River here.

★ HIGH CLIFF STATE PARK

The vista from the sheer escarpment of **High Cliff State Park** (N7630 State Park Rd., off Hwy. 55, Sherwood, 920/989-1106, 6am-11pm daily year-round), on the northeastern edge of Lake Winnebago (12 miles southeast of Appleton), is truly sublime. The cliff is actually the western edge of the Niagara Escarpment, a jutting, bluff-like dolomite rise stretching almost 1,000 miles to the east, through Door County and beyond to Niagara Falls. From the top, almost 250 feet above the water, you can see all of the Fox River Valley—Appleton, Oshkosh, Neenah, Menasha, and Kaukauna. Perhaps we should do as Chief Redbird of the Ojibwa did; he loved to sit on the cliff and "listen" to the lake—his statue still does today.

High Cliff was founded on an old limestone quarrying and kiln operation. Junked equipment and structures still stand. Effigy mounds, 28 to 285 feet long, can be found along trails; they were built by unknown prehistoric Native Americans.

Recreation

The park maintains both a swimming beach and an 85-slip marina. Hikers have seven miles of somewhat steep trails to choose from, and cross-country skiers have access to four of those come winter. The **Lime-Kiln Trail** is just over two miles and runs from the lime kiln ruins to the lake and then up the east side of the escarpment. The longest trail is the mostly gentle **Red Bird Trail,** passing by the family campground; it goes by a tower with a commanding view of the lake.

Camping

The park's 1,200 acres have 112 fairly isolated campsites, most occupied early in the summer high season. **Reservations** (888/947-2757, http://wisconsin.goingtocamp.com, reservation fee $8, nonresidents from $25, day-use $11) are advised.

Oshkosh

Former President Jimmy Carter once said in a speech at the University of Wisconsin-Oshkosh campus, "I have never seen a more beautiful, clean, and attractive place." He was referring to this Fox River Valley city of 55,000—the one with the weird name. Situated on the western bight of Lake Winnebago and bisected by the Fox River, the city is often associated with bizarre airplanes. The annual Experimental Aircraft Association's Fly-In is the largest of its kind, a not-to-be-missed highlight of itinerant edgy aviation.

But it was lumber that built the town. By the end of the Civil War, about 35 factories were roaring. Hence, Oshkosh earned the moniker "Sawdust City." Excavations along Oshkosh riverbanks still reveal marbled layers of compacted sawdust.

This sawdust condemned the city to a painful series of conflagrations; an 1875 fire was so bad that the city—constructed in the cheap local timber—finally rebuilt with stone. Ironically, some of this stone came from Chicago, itself recently devastated by fire and rebuilt mostly with wood from Oshkosh sawmills.

★ EAA AIRVENTURE MUSEUM

The state has officially decreed the **EAA AirVenture Museum** (3000 Poberezny Rd., 920/426-4818, www.airventuremuseum.org, 10am-5pm daily, $12.50 adults) a state treasure, a consequence no doubt of the 800,000 or so visitors who converge on Oshkosh for the annual fly-in sponsored by the Experimental Aircraft Association (EAA). In one of the largest museums of its kind in the world, more than 250 airplanes of every possible type are displayed—aerobatic planes, home-built, racers, and more. Five theaters, numerous display galleries, and tons of multimedia exhibits make this well worth the admission. Kids of all ages adore the many hands-on exhibits in the Kidventure Gallery, including a g-force machine. The newest and most popular is an interactive F-22 simulator. Be there when flights are offered in old-timey planes, complete with the leather hat, goggles, and windblown hair. The museum is located off U.S. 41 at the Highway 44 exit, next to Wittman Regional Airport. Overall, this is perhaps the best money spent for family recreation in the region.

Oshkosh Fly-In

Oshkosh aviation pioneer Steve Wittman designed and built racing planes, one of which is on display at the Smithsonian. They were so impressive that he drew the attention of Orville Wright and other airplane aficionados. Soon after the EAA moved to Oshkosh, a tradition began: The gathering known as the **EAA AirVenture Oshkosh** (www.airventure.org), often referred to as the **Oshkosh Fly-In** or Airshow, is now a legendary jaw-dropping display of airplanes that draws hundreds of thousands of people from around the world.

It's a spectacle. The skies are filled with planes and pilots with an appetite for aviation the way it used to be done—strictly by the seat of the pants. Handmade and antique aircraft are the highlights, but lots of contemporary military aircraft are also on show. Thrilling air shows go on nonstop. In all, almost 12,000 aircraft and more than 750,000 people are on hand. Wear good walking shoes, a hat, and sunscreen and carry water.

The Fly-In is held at the end of July and possibly into the first week of August; it runs 8am-8pm daily. The air shows start at 3pm daily. For nonmembers, admission is $45 adults per day.

OTHER SIGHTS

Paine Art Center and Gardens

A lumber baron's Tudor Revival house, the

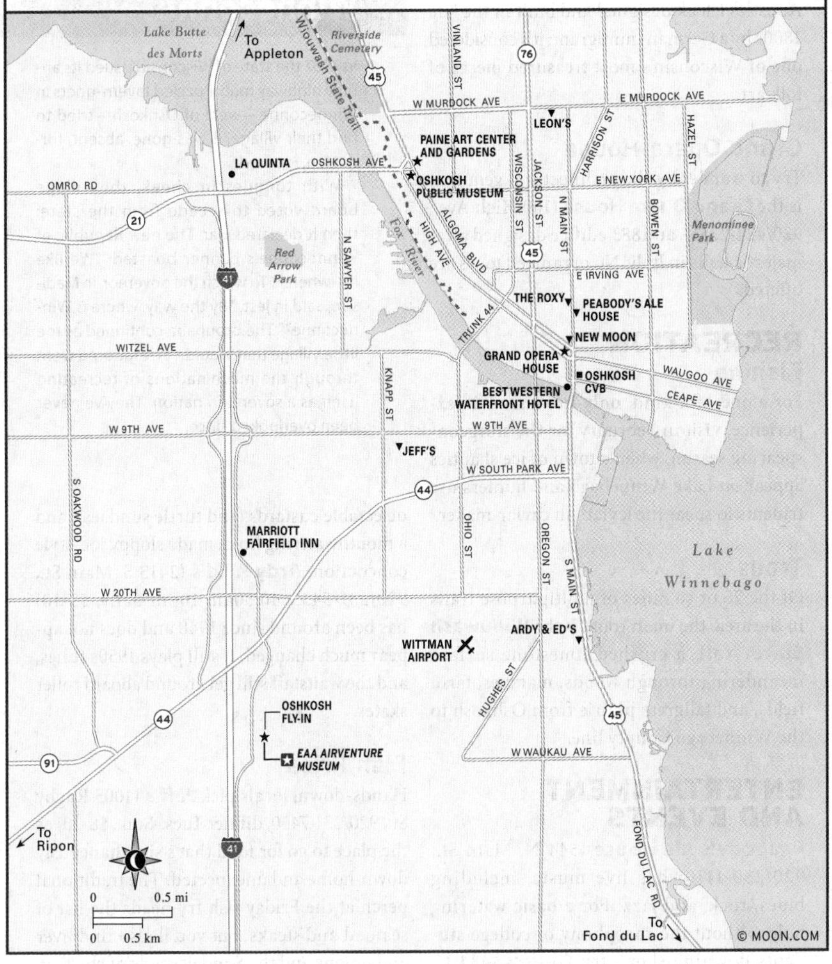

Paine Art Center and Gardens (1410 Algoma Blvd., 920/235-6903, http://thepaine.org, 10am-4pm Tues.-Sun. late June-late Sept., from 11am other periods Mar.-Nov., $9 adults) displays meticulously appointed rooms showcasing period furnishings and antiques, along with 19th-century French Barbizon and U.S. art. Outside are acres and acres of gardens; one, modeled after the Dutch Pond Garden at Hampton Court in England, features more than 100 varieties of roses. Legend has it the place is haunted, but the caretakers disavow any knowledge.

Oshkosh Public Museum

In a grand 1907 English-style home, the **Oshkosh Public Museum** (1331 Algoma Blvd., 920/236-5799, 10am-4:30pm Tues.-Sat., 1pm-4:30pm Sun., $8) is one of the best public museums you'll see in a town of this size. Permanent holdings range in subject from local and natural history, china, and pressed glass to Native American ethnology and archaeology. One highlight is an eight-foot-tall Apostles Clock designed and built in the late 1800s by a German immigrant; it's considered one of Wisconsin's most treasured pieces of folk art.

Grand Opera House

Try to wander by the architectural gem that is the **Grand Opera House** (100 High Ave., 920/424-2355), an 1883 edifice designed after majestic halls in Italy. No organized tours are offered.

RECREATION

Fishing

For a one-of-a-kind, only-in-Wisconsin experience, visit in February for the sturgeon-spearing season, when a town of ice shanties appear on Lake Winnebago and hunters use tridents to spear the leviathan caviar-maker.

Trails

Of the 75 or so miles of multipurpose trails in the area, the main route is the **Wiouwash State Trail,** a crushed limestone surface meandering through woods, marshes, farm fields, and tallgrass prairie from Oshkosh to the Winnebago County line.

ENTERTAINMENT AND EVENTS

Peabody's Ale House (544 N. Main St., 920/230-1110) has live music, including blues, rock, and jazz. For a basic watering hole without the cacophony of college students downing shots, try **Oblio's** (434 N. Main St., 920/426-1063). It has a pressed-tin ceiling, an antique wooden bar, and photos of old Oshkosh.

FOOD

Drive-Ins

Oshkosh has two classic drive-ins. **Leon's** (121 W. Murdock Ave., 920/231-7755, 11am-11pm Sun.-Thurs., 11am-midnight Fri.-Sat. summer) is a classic neon kind of place with delectable custards (and turtle sundaes!) and a mouthwatering homemade sloppy joe-style concoction. **Ardy & Ed's** (2413 S. Main St., 920/231-5455, 10:30am-10pm daily, $3-10) has been around since 1948 and does not appear much changed. It still plays 1950s tunes, and the waitstaff still get around aboard roller skates.

Fish Fries

Hands-down, locals pick **Jeff's** (1005 Rugby St., 920/231-7450, dinner Tues.-Sun., $8-20) as the place to go for food that's simultaneously down-home and unexpected. The traditional perch at the Friday fish fry heads the list of seafood and steaks, but you'll also find liver and onions and the Sunday staple of chicken.

Lighter Fare

Spacious but cozy, the **New Moon** (N. Main St. and Algoma Blvd., 920/232-0976, 7am-late daily, $3-6), in a renovated 1875 beauty, is the place for coffee or a light meal. Atypical sandwiches and creative soups emphasize local and state ingredients and products; it is also a good

The Republic of Winneconne

In 1967 the state of Wisconsin issued its annual highway map. Puzzled tavern-goers in Winneconne—west of Oshkosh—tried to find their village. It was gone, absent, forgotten, ignored.

With tongues in cheek, the village board voted to secede from the state; then it declared war. The new Republic of Winneconne's banner boasted: "We like it—where?" To which the governor, in Madison, said in jest, "By the way, where *is* Winneconne?" The brouhaha continued as the little village that wouldn't be ignored went through the machinations of recreating itself as a sovereign nation. They've never been overlooked since.

1: EAA AirVenture Museum **2:** Grand Opera House **3:** Ardy & Ed's, the best ice cream experience in the Fox Valley **4:** Oshkosh Public Museum

1
A020
GENERAL DELIVERY
2
RAND OPERA HOUSE
3
ICE COLD ROOT BEER ON DRAFT
SANDWICHES
TEMPTING SNACKS
BASKET LUNCHES
ICE CREAM TREATS
"Old Fashioned" FOUNTAIN FAVORITES
"The Friendly Place" Since 1948
4

stop for vegetarians. It also offers live music and poetry readings.

Supper Clubs

The Roxy (571 N. Main St., 920/231-1980, 11am-10pm Mon.-Sat., 8am-9pm Sun., $7-19) is an archetypal old-style Wisconsin supper club. Casual or formal, it's steaks and fresh fish; you can also get German specials on Tuesday.

ACCOMMODATIONS

All of the rates listed double during EAA events.

Downtown

A large centrally located hotel complex is the **Best Western Waterfront Hotel** (1 N. Main St., 920/230-1900, from $135), which gets high marks and consistent rave reports; it also has the largest number of amenities in town.

West

Most Oshkosh accommodations are spread along the highway interchanges of U.S. 41 west of town. The cheapest is the **La Quinta** (1886 Rath Ln., 920/233-4190, $85), northwest of town, which is a solid chain choice. The economical **Marriott Fairfield Inn** (1800 S. Koeller Rd., 920/233-8504 or 800/228-2800, $129) is off the 9th Street exit and offers a pool, a whirlpool tub, and a game room.

INFORMATION

The **Oshkosh Convention and Visitors Bureau** (at 100 N. Main St., 920/303-9200, www.visitoshkosh.com) is downtown.

GETTING THERE

By car, getting to Oshkosh from Appleton (via U.S. 41, 20 miles) takes 20 minutes. From Fond du Lac (20 miles, 30 minutes), take U.S. 45 rather than U.S. 41, since you can trace the shoreline of Lake Winnebago. From Milwaukee (via U.S. 41, 90 miles), it takes 90 minutes. From Madison (via U.S. 151 and U.S. 41, 86 miles), it takes 95 minutes.

Fond du Lac

Fond du Lac often refers to itself as "First on the Lake"—sort of a loose take on the French, which translates literally as "bottom" or "far end of the lake."

Despite its strategic location—at the base of a big lake and equidistant to the Fox-Wisconsin riverway—the town grew painfully slowly. Widely memorialized town father James Doty, later Wisconsin's first territorial governor, had the town platted in 1835.

Boomtown status effectively eluded Fond du Lac; the timber was too far north and receding fast. The local constabulary, the story goes, couldn't afford a pair of handcuffs. However, a plank road, laboriously laid down from Sheboygan, became a vital transportation route from the Lake Michigan coast.

SIGHTS

Galloway House and Village

The stately mid-Victorian Italianate villa **Galloway House** (336 Old Pioneer Rd., 920/922-1166, 11am-4pm Wed.-Sat., 1-4pm Sun. Memorial Day to Labor Day-Sept., $10 adults), originally finished in 1847, features 30 rooms, four fireplaces, and much Victorian opulence. Behind it is a turn-of-the-20th-century village containing 23 restored regional dwellings and structures, including the Blakely Museum, which holds an assortment of pioneer and early-20th-century Fond du Lac stuff, as well as an extensive private local Native American collection—even a mounted passenger pigeon.

St. Paul's Cathedral

The Episcopalian English Gothic stone **St.**

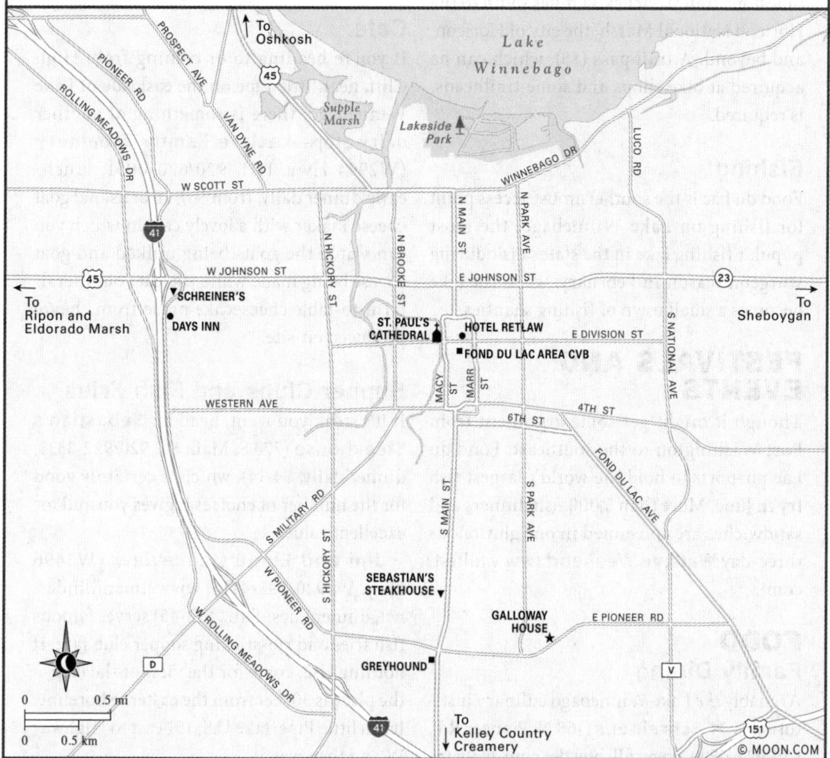

Paul's Cathedral (51 W. Division St., 920/921-3363, www.stpaulsepiscopalcathedral.org, $2) houses the Oberammergau unified collection, a priceless assemblage of wood carvings. Tours are by appointment.

Lakeside Park

One of the better municipal parks anywhere is the 400-acre **Lakeside Park** (555. N. Park Ave.). The eastern part's eye-frying-white sentinel lighthouse is probably Fond du Lac's most recognizable symbol. Nearby are landscaped islands, a deer park, a mini train, a harbor, and a marina. A carousel dating from the 1920s is one of the few wooden merry-go-rounds left in the state; it still runs on a simple two-gear clutch. All the horses are pegged—constructed wholly without nails.

Eldorado Marsh

Just a few miles west of Fond du Lac along Highway 23 and Highway C is a little-known canoeists' paradise, the 6,000-acre **Eldorado Marsh,** which subsumes the 1,500-acre shallow flowage marsh. Locals refer to it as the "Everglades of the North." I'm not sure if that's accurate, but it is a tranquil, solitary spot.

RECREATION

Biking

The city has a balanced system of rural trails, including the great **Ledge Lookout Ride,** 45 miles on the eastern shore of Lake Winnebago along the Niagara Escarpment. Better yet is the **Wild Goose State Trail,** of which Fond du Lac is the northern terminus. The screened limestone trail stretches 34 miles south to the Horicon National Marsh, the city of Horicon, and beyond. A trail pass ($5), which can be acquired at bike shops and some trailheads, is required.

Fishing

Fond du Lac is the southernmost access point for fishing on Lake Winnebago, the most popular fishing lake in the state. Visit during sturgeon season in February, when the lake becomes a small town of fishing shanties.

FESTIVALS AND EVENTS

Though it might get some argument from Port Washington to the southeast, Fond du Lac purports to hold the world's largest fish fry in June. More than 5,000 fish dinners and sandwiches are consumed in one gluttonous three-day **Walleye Weekend** (www.fdlfest.com).

FOOD

Family Dining

Arguably *the* Lake Winnebago culinary institution is ★ **Schreiner's** (168 N. Pioneer Rd., 920/922-0590, www.fdlchowder.com, 6:30am-2pm Tues.-Sun., $3-9), a hearty American-style family restaurant serving meals since 1938. The menu is broad, the servings copious, and the specials Midwestern. But the real highlight is the bread, made fresh on-site in the bakery. The New England clam chowder is also superb. It's so good it's in the restaurant's website name.

Ice Cream

Since the Civil War, the family of **Kelley Country Creamery** (W5215 Hwy. B, 920/923-1715, 11am-9pm daily summer, reduced hours fall-spring, from $4) has been a dairy mainstay in these parts. You'll love their ice cream, especially sitting on a porch looking at the cows the milk came from. This place is already packed by opening time the first day of the season they open! Head south on U.S. 41, then east on Highway B.

Café

If you're heading to or coming from High Cliff, near little Pipe on the east side of Lake Winnebago, there is something of another dairy stop—**Laclare Family Creamery** (W2994 Hwy. HH, 920/670-0051, lunch/early dinner daily, from $6), an artisanal goat cheese maker with a lovely café in which you can watch the goats being milked and goat cheese being made while you eat your literal-farm-to-table cheesecake made from chèvre produced on-site.

Supper Clubs and Fish Fries

If it's steak you want, head for **Sebastian's Steakhouse** (770 S. Main St., 920/922-3333, dinner daily, $4-14), which is certainly good for the number of choices it gives you and for excellent value.

Jim and Linda's Lakeview (W3496 Hwy. W, 920/795-4116, www.jimandlindas.net, dinner Tues.-Sun., $12-45) serves famous fish fries and rib-sticking supper club fare. If nothing else, come for the view of the lake—the place is 30 feet from the eastern shoreline. It's in little Pipe; take U.S. 151 east to Highway W and then west.

ACCOMMODATIONS

During EAA AirVenture Oshkosh, the rates quoted here double.

Cheapest on the west side is the **Days Inn** (107 N. Pioneer Rd., 920/923-6790, from $75), featuring a heated pool and a refreshing sense of on-the-ball-ness.

The full-service **Hotel Retlaw** (1 N. Main St., 833/473-8529, $149) had been absolutely and completely redone and just reopened at the time of research. Every historic element of the hotel has been restored to its Roaring '20s heyday. The interiors are gorgeous, and you won't want to leave the relaxation pool. Now, however, time will tell if they have been able to remove some possibly paranormal activity that has been reported for years!

Exploring Lake Winnebago

Lake Winnebago

Lake Winnebago dominates East-Central Wisconsin. At 10 miles across and 30 miles north to south, this shallow lake—once a glacial marsh—is among the largest freshwater lakes fully locked within one state. It totals 88 miles of shoreline and 138,000 surface acres formed more than 25,000 years ago by a lobe of the Wisconsin glacier.

The lake was always crucial to Native Americans as a part of the water transport system along the Fox and Wolf Rivers. The name purportedly comes from a linguistic mix-up—or deliberate pejorative snub—from the French, who dubbed the Native American community they discovered here the "stinkers" (an updated transliteration); "Stinking Water" was a natural follow-up.

Lake Winnebago today is heavily used by fishers and pleasure-crafters. In winter, up to 10,000 cars park on the frozen lake at any one time; if you're around in February, don't miss the annual throwback to the Pleistocene—the sturgeon-spearing season.

Drive east out of Fond du Lac via U.S. 151 to skirt the eastern shoreline along what locals call "the Ledge," the high, breathtaking rise above Deadwood Point. Along this route the small town of Pipe is home to an awesome 80-foot tower. Farther north is Calumet County Park, with six rare panther effigy mounds. At the entrance to the park, stop at The Fish Tale Inn to see the largest male sturgeon ever caught on the lake. An even better place to experience the lake is High Cliff State Park, along the northeastern edge.

INFORMATION

The **Fond du Lac Area Convention and Visitors Bureau** (23 S. Main St., 920/923-3010 or 800/937-9123, www.fdl.com) is well stocked with information.

GETTING THERE

Getting to Fond du Lac from Madison (via U.S. 151, 74 miles) takes 80 minutes. From Oshkosh (20 miles, 30 minutes), take U.S. 45 to trace the edge of Lake Winnebago. From Milwaukee (via U.S. 41, 67 miles), it takes just over an hour.

West of Winnebago

RIPON

One of the most picturesque small towns anywhere, winding Ripon has an oddball and fascinating heritage. Founded in 1844 by an organization called the Wisconsin Phalanx as an experiment in communal living, it was named Ceresco, after the Roman goddess of agriculture, and attempted to implement in pure form the democratic principles of French social progressive Charles Fourier. A decade later, it came to fame as the birthplace of the Republican Party. (This claim, incidentally, is hotly disputed by a few other communities in the United States, but hey, in 2004, the U.S. Senate passed a bill recognizing Ripon's status, and even the U.S. Postal Service commemorated it with a postmark.)

Later, Ripon became the birthplace of another political pioneer—Carrie Chapman Catt, one of the founders and first presidents of both the American Women's Suffrage Association and the League of Women Voters; it was under her leadership that the 19th Amendment to the Constitution was finally passed.

Little White Schoolhouse

Along the 300 block of Blackburn Street (Hwy. 44) stands the birthplace of the Republican Party, the **Little White Schoolhouse** (303 Blackburn St., 920/748-6764, www.littlewhiteschoolhouse.com, 10am-4pm daily June-Aug., 10am-4pm Sat.-Sun. spring and fall, free). This official national monument doesn't hold much more than a few mementos and photos (such as Eisenhower officially declaring this the birthplace); in fact, the interiors look like the schoolhouse that it was, but it's still fun to poke around in.

GREEN LAKE

Green Lake is approximately one-sixth the size of Ripon, but this tiny town pulls in tons of visitors for the eponymous 7,320-acre lake—the deepest in the state, if not the largest. In 1867, the first resort west of Niagara Falls was built here. When Chicagoans heard about it, the rush was on. Within three decades, upscale resorts had begun to dot the shores. Despite its granddaddy status, the guests are neither aloof nor so numerous that the small-town charm is obliterated.

Sights

Explore local history at an old **railroad depot** (10am-1pm on Sat. during summer, free) housing historic artifacts in Friday Park (along Mill St.); architecturally even more appealing are the historic 1910 **Thrasher Opera House** (506 Mill St.) and 1898 **Green Lake County Courthouse** (492 Hill St.).

Scenic Drives

Rustic Road 22, also known as White River Road, ends at Highway D, north of Princeton, but affords the experience of two original plank bridges and views of mostly Department of Natural Resources-protected wetlands. From Green Lake, head west along Highway 23 to Princeton, then north on Highway D.

Speaking of **Princeton,** do check out this little treasure. This time-locked little burg plunked along the Fox River and has plenty of anachronistic architecture, worthy galleries, and the state's largest weekly flea market (held on Saturdays from mid-Apr.-mid-Oct.). For ice cream and light foods, you can check out, let's see, a refurbished gas station or renovated general store.

Or how about a drive with an eco-bent? A number of miles west of the little town of Montello, then south on Highway F, takes you to **Muir Park and Fountain Lake Farm,** the boyhood home of John Muir as well as a birder's paradise. Many sandhill cranes can be seen here—the Fox River Unit of the Horicon National Wildlife Refuge is across the road. It's estimated that Marquette County alone

Birth of the Republican Party

By the early 1850s, the powers within the contemporary political parties were impotent, willfully ignorant, or hamstrung on both sides regarding the issue of slavery. Antislavery activists within the Whig Party in Ripon ultimately grew tired enough to call for action. In 1852, Alvan Earle Bovay visited Horace Greeley in New York City to discuss matters. The Whigs were waning, but what was next?

Senator Stephen Douglass of Illinois provided an opportunity for a minor revolution with his Kansas-Nebraska Bill; the proposal was to extend slavery beyond the perimeters of the earlier Missouri Compromise. Bovay immediately and quietly summoned 53 other voters back to Ripon to devise a battle plan for opposing the slavery proponents. Ripon had long been a nerve center of the abolitionist movement; so strong was its opposition, in fact, that the city was the site of what's known as "Booth's War," a guerrilla skirmish between Milwaukee abolitionist Sherman Booth, who helped escaped slaves along the Underground Railroad, and the federal authorities; local citizens helped Booth and frustrated the authorities for five years.

Bovay hoped to organize the abolitionists into a cohesive force to be called Republicans—"a good name . . . with charm and prestige," he said. His oratory was effective, and the Republican Party was born on March 20, 1854, in the Little White Schoolhouse in Ripon. The official declaration of its platform came two years later in Pittsburgh; standing near the podium was Abraham Lincoln, who, four years later, would become the party's first successful presidential candidate.

holds one of North America's highest concentrations, at about 1,100.

Recreation

For land-based recreation, there may be more golf courses per capita in the Green Lake vicinity than anywhere in Wisconsin. The Scottish links-style **Golf Courses of Lawsonia** (Hwy. 23 W., 920/294-3320) have been rated as among the country's top public courses, according to *Golf Digest* magazine, which gave the elevated tees and merciless bunkers four stars. The **Tuscumbia Country Club** (680 N. Illinois Ave., 920/294-3381) is Wisconsin's oldest course; it's known as one of the best-manicured courses in the Midwest.

Food

A local favorite is **Norton's** (380 S. Lawson Dr., 920/294-6577, dinner daily, $9-28), the only supper club on the lake accessible by water. Norton's has grand alfresco dining on a lakeside deck.

Accommodations

Room rates are high in this area during summer.

A motel with a resort complex sums up **Bay View** (439 Lake St., 920/294-6504, www.bayviewgreenlake.com, $120), good value for the money. Anglers love this place—there's plenty of fishing and boat rentals. Some kitchenettes and suites are available.

Both **Miller's Daughter** (453 North St., 920/294-0717, www.millersdaughter.com, $159) and **Angel Inn** (372 S. Lawson Dr., 920/294-3087, www.angelinns.com, from $165) are both truly special superb bed-and-breakfasts.

Information

The **Green Lake Area Chamber of Commerce** (550 Mill St., 920/294-3231 or 800/253-7354, www.visitgreenlake.com) is in town.

WAUPACA AND THE CHAIN O' LAKES

The Waupaca area lies at the western edge of the east-central waters region and qualifies as hydrophilic: 22 spring-fed lakes southwest of Waupaca form one of the longest recreational stretches in the lower half of Wisconsin, with 240 lakes in the county alone. Nonnative settlement began in the region around 1848; the first flour mill went up a year after the state's birth. The city was named for an altruistic Potawatomi chief, Sam Waupaca, who collapsed and died after convincing local Native Americans not to kill the settlers.

Sights

The most popular activity in the Chain O' Lakes is to take a breezy eight-lake tour aboard the ***Chief*** (715/258-2866, 1.5 hours, departs from Clear Water Harbor 2-4 times 11:30am-4pm daily Memorial Day-Labor Day, $14), an authentic stern-wheeler and the former flagship of a brewery, or an 11-lake tour aboard the more sedate motor yacht *Lady of the Lakes* (2 hours, departs 4pm daily Memorial Day-Labor Day, call to check if there are morning departures, $13). There are less frequent departures in the weeks before Memorial Day and after Labor Day.

Just southwest of Waupaca along Highway 22 lies tiny **Rural,** a Yankee town stuck in the mid-1800s. Most buildings along the switchbacking banks of the Crystal River are on the National Register of Historic Places. The architectural renaissance is impressive; it has become so popular that Highway 22 was rerouted around the town to avoid spoiling it. You can't help but notice Rustic Roads 23 and 24, which form a V around Hartman Creek State Park; drive them. You'll pass over three stone bridges to cross the Crystal River, and you can stop and relax at a gurgling spring-fed trout stream.

Another short jaunt out of the city via Highway K takes you to **Red Mill.** The biggest waterwheel in the state, it has been converted into a hodgepodge of shops offering handicrafts, antiques, and lots of scented candles in an original interior. One of the few extant covered bridges in Wisconsin is also here (400 handcrafted oak pegs were used in its construction), along with the Chapel in the Woods. Red Mill lies along a beautiful stretch of the Crystal River with a picturesque park.

Scenic Drive

South of Waupaca along Highway E, which is fairly narrow, is Saxeville, and farther south, **26th Road,** along Highway W out of town; 26th Road stretches to Highway H along the Pine River Valley, a Class II trout stream. This drive passes several dwellings, including a log cabin, that predate the Civil War.

Recreation

A segment of the National Scenic Ice Age Trail is in **Hartman Creek State Park** (715/258-2372);

the village of Rural

the county section totals 20 miles and links on both ends with Portage County's segment. The park has a hike-in primitive cabin offered on a first-come, first-served basis. The state park also maintains off-road bike trails. Its environs are popular with canoeists and boaters, since most of the upper Chain O' Lakes are either in or adjacent to state park lands.

The lolling, tranquil Crystal River is perfect for canoeing. Organized excursions leave from **Ding's Dock** (along Hwy. Q, 715/258-2612, www.dingsdock.com), which also rents out decent cottages.

This is prime touring area for bicyclists; trails run along waterways and through some Amish farmstead areas. Northwest of the city, the topography shifts to rolls of kettles and moraines.

Food

The Clear Water Harbor (N2757 Hwy. QQ, 715/258-2866, www.clearwaterharbor.com, from 10am daily, $5), known locally as the "Har Bar," serves a menu varying from pub grub sandwiches (try its famous 'shroomburger) to salads and a Friday fish fry. It's also popular for summer entertainment, with a huge deck on the lakeside, open seasonally. From here, you can walk up the road into King to the very local **Wally's World** (N2702 Hwy. QQ, 715/258-2160), where you can get a Lunch Box shot: beer with amaretto and orange juice. It's tasty if you can down it quickly.

Waupaca suddenly has a number of fine places to eat. **T-Dub's Public House** (111 Cooper St., 715/942-0499, dinner Mon.-Sat., from $6) is an Irish pub and restaurant that is quite amazing. It boasts great beers, food ranging from shepherd's pie to Thai pasta, and really outstanding service.

Accommodations

This is another resort and cottage area, so despite the large numbers of lodgings, few are cheap.

In anachronistic Rural, *the* place for a quaint getaway, is the superb ★ **Crystal River Inn** (E1369 Rural Rd., 715/258-5333 or 800/236-5789, www.crystalriver-inn.com, $89-269), an old farmstead. The six original farmhouse guest rooms, with myriad styles and amenities, are done with antiques and brass beds. All the rooms have views of the river, a wildwood garden, or the backyard garden. You'll also find cottages and a "little house on the prairie."

CAMPING

Hartman Creek State Park is the best bet for camping. **Reservations** (888/947-2757, http://wisconsin.goingtocamp.com, reservation fee $8, nonresidents from $23, day-use $11) are advised.

Information

The **Waupaca Area Chamber of Commerce** (221 S. Main St., 715/258-7343 or 888/417-4040, www.waupacamemories.com) has all the info you need.

The Wolf River Region

MENOMINEE INDIAN RESERVATION

The Menominee nation represents the oldest established inhabitants of what is now Wisconsin. Unlike many of the diasporic Native American nations, the Menominee are strictly Wisconsin residents. The reservation lies just north of Shawano and abuts the southern perimeter of the Chequamegon-Nicolet National Forest and the northern edge of the much smaller Stockbridge Indian Reservation. Wisconsinites nod to its crown jewel, the Wolf River, one of the region's top draws.

HISTORY

Anthropologists have surmised that the Menominee, an Algonquian-speaking nation, may have been in what is now Wisconsin as far back as 10,000 years ago. The nation and its many bands once controlled regions of the Upper Great Lakes from as far south as Milwaukee to the Escanaba River in Michigan's Upper Peninsula and the entire breadth of Wisconsin.

Beginning in 1817, a series of breached federal treaties gradually eroded Menominee sovereignty until, by 1854, the nation was allowed only 12 townships on the present-day reservation; some of the ceded land was turned over to the Oneida and Stockbridge people for their own reservations. Almost 10 million acres dwindled to 200,000.

The Menominee, who had been given reservation status by a treaty signed near the Wolf River's Keshena Falls, asked for their status as Native Americans to be terminated in 1961 in an attempt at federal assimilation. It was a dismal failure, and reservation status was reinstated in 1973. The Menominee today number approximately 6,500, more than half of whom live on the reservation.

MENOMINEE INDIAN RESERVATION FOREST

The 223,500 acres of forest surrounding the reservation include some of the most pristine stands of hardwoods, hemlock, and pine in the Great Lakes region; it's regarded as an invaluable ecosystem. The Menominee people have run a lumber operation since 1908, one of the first and largest businesses owned by Native Americans in the United States; they were trading lumber with the Ho Chunk long before European contact. Their high-tech present-day plant is the largest and most modern in the region. More than two billion board feet have been removed from the forest. The Menominee have been lauded by international environmentalists for instituting a radical sustainable ecosystem model, now being examined by indigenous communities around North America. Forestry experts from as far away as Cambodia and Indonesia have come to the Menominee's new forestry institute.

★ Wolf River

Meandering through the reservation from its headwaters in Lily to the north is the nascent Wolf River, part of the Fox River system, which includes the Fox and Wolf Rivers headwaters, the lower Fox River, and Lake Winnebago. Quiet at its source, it grows in power as it crosses through Langlade and enters the reservation. This stretch of the state-designated Outstanding Water Resource and federally designated Wild and Scenic River is perhaps the most spectacular. It drops almost 1,000 feet as it crosses the reservation, from the multihued outcrops and white water of Smokey Falls to the eerie canyons of the Wolf River Dells. Water conditions range from placid, below Post Lake, to hair-raising, in sections near Smokey Falls.

The colorful toponyms describe it well: Little Slough Gundy, Sherry Rapids, Horse Race Rapids, Twenty Day Rips. The stretch of river between Gilmore's Mistake and Smokey Falls—the lower terminus for most rafters—can be rife with midrange rapids, some up to eight feet.

So pristine are these waters that the Wolf River was the inspiration for the state's most enduring environmental debate—whether or not a mine in Crandon would endanger the ecology. In terms of recreation, these waters are indeed blue-ribbon for rafters and kayakers.

The river has sections for neophytes and for hard-core river runners. During high-water periods, operators shut down trips due to the danger. Outfitters in these parts generally don't supply guides or captains, so you're on your own. White-water enthusiasts also note: The nearby Red River, especially at Gresham, is also quite good for kayaking.

Most outfitters offer camping, including **Shotgun Eddy** (715/882-4461, www.shotguneddy.com), which has been around forever and even outfitted *National Geographic* for a story.

For a cozy lodging option, try **Bear Paw Outdoor Adventure Resort** (N3494 Hwy. 55, 715/942-0499, www.bearpawoutdoors.com, $100-300) south of Langlade. "Rustic, deep-woods relaxing" best describes it. There are lodge rooms, various cabins, and camping. A full slew of water and land activities are available. Guests love this place.

Off the river and side roads, the Wolf River is worth investigating on foot. **Wolf River Dells** has a short nature trail leading to rough multicolored granite cliffs overlooking the Wolf for hundreds of yards along both the upper and lower dells. The Dells are four miles from a turnoff from Highway 55 along a road that alternates from hard-packed gravel to nerve-wracking. A footbridge crosses the 40-foot gurgling Smokey Falls to a small mid-river island. Purportedly, the mist from the waters is actually smoke from the pipe of a spirit living within the falls. **Spirit Rock,** a couple of miles above Keshena Falls, is also significant. According to legend, it's really a petrified Menominee warrior who angered the earth. This warrior, Ko-Ko-Mas-Say-Sa-Now, allegedly asked for immortality and was thrust into the earth forever. Some believe kind spirits come to offer rings of tobacco, and their willowy vapors can be observed flitting among the trees in the dusky night.

Don't forget fishing: One of Wisconsin's designated fly-fishing-only stretches of blue-ribbon trout waters is near Hollister.

Menominee Logging Camp Museum

The **Menominee Logging Camp Museum** (Hwy. VV, north of Keshena, 715/799-3757, 8am-4:30pm Mon.-Fri. May-Oct. 15, last tour at 3pm, $10 adults), at Grignon Rapids, along the Wolf River at Highway VV and Highway 47, is the largest and most comprehensive exhibit of timber heritage in the United States. Seven hand-hewn log buildings and more than 20,000 artifacts recreate an early 1900s logging camp. The rustic feel adds to the experience. Of note are the 12-to-a-bunk bunkhouse and the 1,000 pairs of oxen shoes, not to mention a 400-year-old pine log.

Next to the logging museum is the **Menominee Cultural Museum** (8am-4:30pm Mon.-Sat., $5) have opened a cultural center with artifacts and a focus on the Native American Graves Protection and Repatriation Act.

Powwows

Two powwows are held annually. On or near Memorial Day weekend, the **Veteran Powwow** honors the reservation's military veterans. Larger is the **Annual Menominee Nation Contest Powwow,** held the first weekend in August. This is one of the largest cultural events in the Upper Midwest. Both are held in the natural amphitheater, the Woodland Bowl.

STOCKBRIDGE-MUNSEE INDIAN RESERVATION

The Stockbridge-Munsee are an Algonquian-speaking band of the Mohican nations. The three groups that make up the band (along with a fourth, which eventually opted for assimilation) stretch throughout the Connecticut and Hudson River Valleys. They first appeared in Wisconsin in the early 1820s, living in the Fox River Valley, along with the Munsee, a Delaware group also forced west by European expansion. Some Stockbridge people decamped to Indian Territory in Kansas; others moved to Red Springs, Wisconsin, to live on land ceded to them in 1856 by the Menominee. The community numbers about 1,500.

Sights

The **Stockbridge Munsee Arvid E. Miller Library Museum** (Reservation Hwy. 21, Bowler, 715/793-4270, 8am-4:30pm Mon.-Fri., free) has one of the best archives of Native American material in Wisconsin, including maps dating from the 1600s (not on public display). Most exhibits are on the day-to-day life of Stockbridge and the later fur trade. Of note is the section on the missionaries—those stoic Jesuits—including a catechism written in Mohican and a 1745 Bible presented to the Stockbridge by an emissary of the Prince of Wales. The library and museum are four miles east of Bowler.

SHAWANO

Shawano lies along the Wolf River at one of its widest points and serves as the recreational heart of the Wolf. The lake bearing the name Shawano lies to the east, full of fish. The name Shawano (SHAW-no) is another mellifluous result of the Menominee term for the large lake: Sha-Wah-Nah-Pay-Sa, "Lake to the South."

It's recreation that draws most visitors—fishing on Shawano Lake and white-water rafting on the wild Wolf River. This is true-blue, mom-and-pop, family-style resort country.

Sights

Seven miles south of town, the little-known **Navarino Wildlife Area** is a restored 1,400-acre glacial lake bed, once a swamp and wetland that was drained and farmed for a century. Fifteen dikes have recreated the wetlands, from sedge meadow to cattail marsh. Prairie and oak savanna restoration work is ongoing. The marshes support a resident family of sandhill cranes; the best wildlife-viewing is along the Wolf River drainages on the western fringes, near McDonald Road. A **nature center** (715/526-4226, Mon. and Fri.) is at the site. Get to the wildlife area via Highway 156 and McDonald Road.

Scenic Drives

In the vicinity of Shawano, you'll find loads of historical markers detailing the lumber mill past. West of Shawano approximately 25 miles is tiny **Wittenburg,** the endpoint of one of Wisconsin's Rustic Roads, this one Highway M, which ends in **Tigerton.** There are lovely scenes on this route—historic round barns and stone buildings, including a gas station, and small historical museums in both Wittenburg and Tigerton.

Tigerton was also the home of Wisconsin's first antigovernment militia, the Posse Comitatus, who made some waves in the early 1980s before retreating into obscurity after several of its leaders were jailed.

Recreation

The grand **Mountain Bay State Trail** is a 65-mile multiuse trail connecting Green Bay, Shawano, and Wausau and leads to numerous other trails. The **Wiouwash State Trail** intersects with the Mountain Bay Trail in Eland.

Festivals and Events

Every August, Shawano hosts three days of fiddling and picking during the **Folk Festival** (www.shawanoarts.com) at Mielke Theater and Park. Featured in prior years have been national folk acts, along with such diverse activities as Japanese koto playing and tea ceremonies.

Food

It's hard to categorize **Classic's** (W6026 Lake Dr., 715/524-8711, dinner daily, $6-12). How many other low-key bars and restaurants with an (actual) album cover dance floor also offer wine pairings? There is nothing like this wonderful Northwoods version of the Hard Rock Café.

A nice find is **Club 22** (N3925 Hwy. 22, 715/526-3800, dinner daily, $9-22), a classic supper club. The bar is as big as the dining room, filled with antique beer detritus. Club 22 serves German and supper club fare. The folks here are very friendly.

Accommodations

Most of Shawano is classic Wisconsin rustic-lodging country—cabins and cottages that are clean but very simple. Rates vary; you can find a cabin for four as low as $600 a week. A good example of Shawano lodging is **Bamboo Shores** (W5873 Cedar Ave., 715/524-2124 or 800/969-2124, www.bambooshores.com, $1,400-2,600 weekly), which has cottages that can sleep 6 to 10.

Information

The **visitors center** (1263 S. Main St., 715/524-2139 or 800/235-8528, www.shawanocountry.com) at the chamber of commerce is well stocked.

Northeastern Wisconsin

Northeastern Wisconsin has one of the planet's highest ratios of lakes to land, with water accounting for 37 percent of the total surface. The region is more blue than green, so it's little wonder this place is such an escape.

Escape is the key: Local populations run in inverse proportion to the numbers of tourists. Two counties, Iron and Florence, are among the least-populated in the entire state; Florence County has no incorporated towns.

Somewhere among the few highways crisscrossing the region is a north-south division often discussed by Wisconsinites—a Thoreau-esque zone of tranquility rather than a Mason-Dixon line. A popular northern Wisconsin wordsmith once said, "Well, we basically consider

Highlights

Look for ★ to find recommended sights, activities, dining, and lodging.

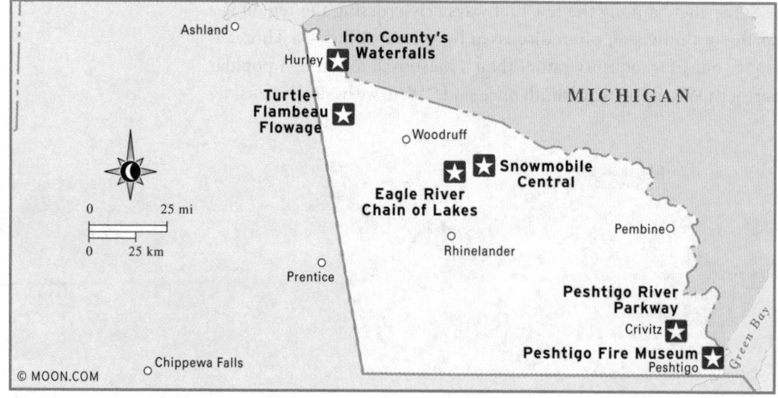

★ **Peshtigo Fire Museum:** Visit Peshtigo's old church and learn about the fire that destroyed the city in 1871 (page 237).

★ **Peshtigo River Parkway:** Marinette County has more waterfalls than any other in Wisconsin, many along Rustic Road 32 (page 237).

★ **Eagle River Chain of Lakes:** This resort area has endless recreation—boating and fishing in the summer, snowmobiling in the winter (page 251).

★ **Snowmobile Central:** Enjoy a rousing championship sled race, a museum with the world's first powered sled, and a hall of fame dedicated to the rocket riders (page 254).

★ **Turtle-Flambeau Flowage:** Canoe through "the crown jewel of the North" and experience Wisconsin's primitive paradise (page 267).

★ **Iron County's Waterfalls:** Experience the highest and most powerful waterfalls in this region of the state (page 270).

Northeastern Wisconsin

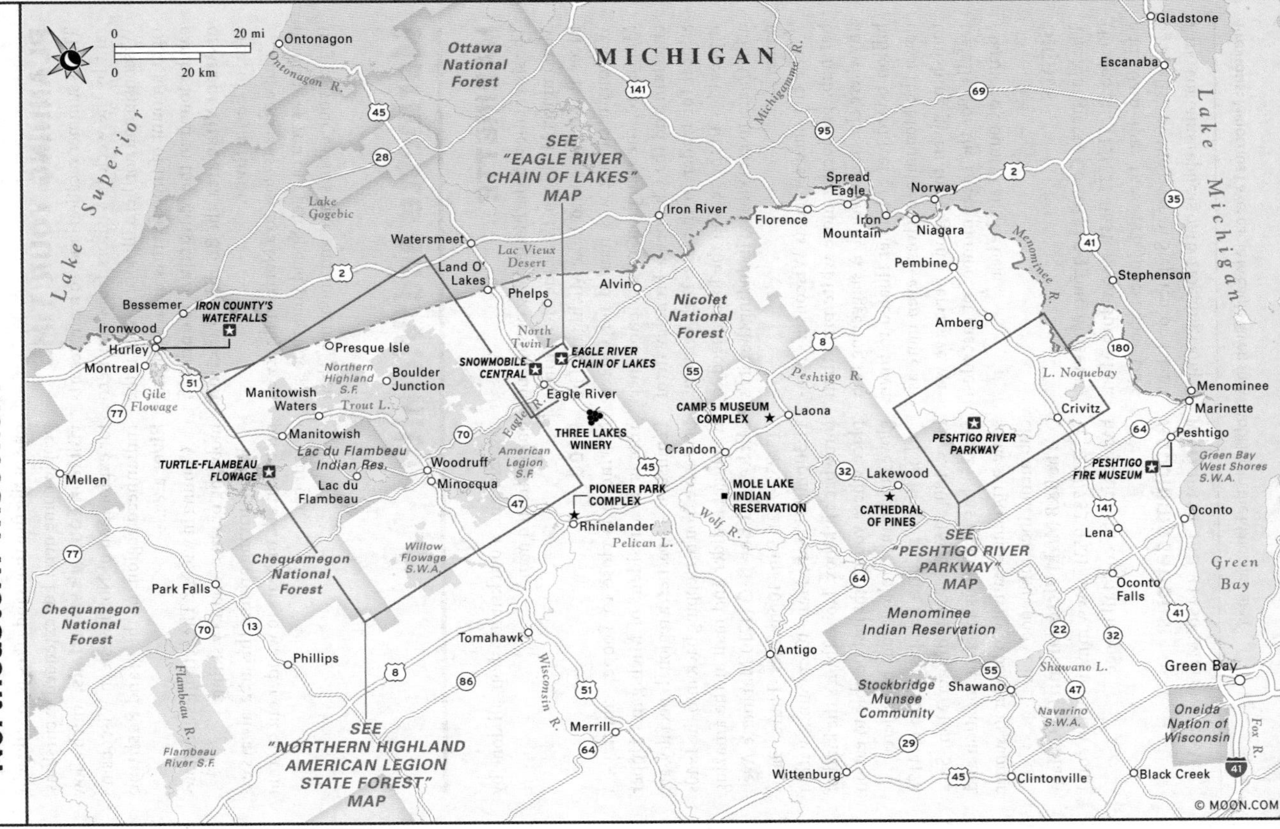

everything south of U.S. 2 to be Confederate." That's pretty far north.

PLANNING YOUR TIME

This is summer vacation land, so many resorts rent by the week to visitors from southern Wisconsin and northern Illinois. A week is the right amount of time for this area. Lodging can be found in the **Minocqua, Woodruff,** or **Arbor Vitae** area, the **Boulder Junction** area, or **Eagle River.**

This area is as close to a Norman Rockwell painting as you can get. Spend your time sitting by your cabin's lake and snoozing, then exploring a bit on a bike or a canoe. Repeat for a week. There are other options, but lolling by one of the five thousand lakes is exactly why people come here. For extended excursions, visit **Iron County's waterfalls,** which allow for exploration of Northwestern Wisconsin's Indianhead region, or the grand **Peshtigo River** area.

Coming in winter? The activities are snowmobiling or cross-country skiing.

When driving around this area, always expect deer, elk, or bears to wander out in front of your car.

Marinette and Vicinity

MARINETTE

The sister cities of Marinette, Wisconsin, and Menominee, Michigan, flank the Menominee River as it merges into Lake Michigan. The Wisconsin sibling was named for Queen Marinette, the daughter of a Menominee chieftain and the Chippewa-French wife of a local fur trader in the late 18th century. It provides all the reason the locals need to affix *Queen* to everything, including the city's name.

The city once served as Wisconsin's lumber hub, producing more white pine than anywhere else in the world. A staggering 10.6 billion board feet of timber floated to town down the Menominee River—even more astonishing given the region's pervasive waterfalls. For the sheer number of cascades, Marinette County can't be beat.

Sights

The **Marinette County Logging Museum** (Bridge St., 715/732-0831, noon-4pm Mon. and 10am-4pm Tues.-Fri. June-Labor Day, $2 adults), by the river in Stephenson Island Park, contains replicas of two logging camps, a stable, and a blacksmith shop, all done by one dedicated man.

Food

Marinette is close to Yooper country—a Yooper is a resident of Michigan's Upper Peninsula—so pasties, a regional specialty, are pervasive. You're stepping back into the 1940s if you get a slider and malt at the amazing **Mickey-Lu Bar-B-Q** (1710 Marinette Ave., 715/735-7721, 9am-10pm Tues.-Thurs., 9am-11:30pm Fri.-Sat., 11am-10pm Sun.), with a throwback jukebox. Honestly, it's the kind of place where you might just be able to eat on glove box change; follow your nose here.

The **River's Edge Supper Club** (N4178 Hwy. 180, 715/735-7344, dinner Mon.-Sat., $10-25) has a glorious riverine location and some surprising creativity to bolster its supper club menu, including good veal.

The B&B **M&M Victorian Inn** (1393 Main St., 715/732-9531, www.mmvictorian.com) has a chic little cocktail lounge.

Accommodations

Marinette Inn (1450 Marinette Ave.,

Previous: Minocqua Lake; eagle in Eagle River; snowmobiling in the Minocqua area

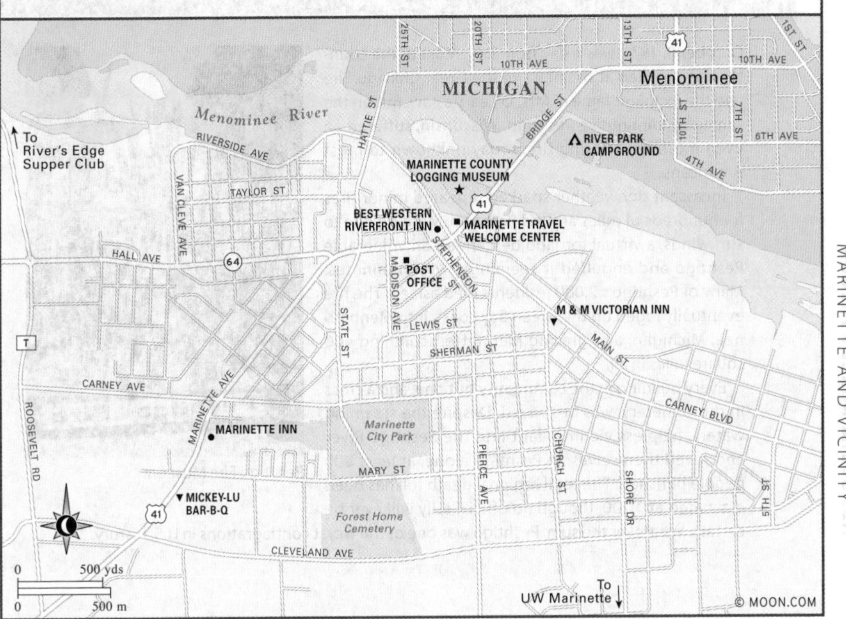

715/732-0594, www.marinetteinn.com, $65) is a solid non-chain option, with good value for the rates and friendly new proprietors.

Right in the heart of downtown, left off U.S. 41 onto Riverside Avenue along the Menominee River, the **Best Western Riverfront Inn** (1821 Riverside Ave., 715/732-0111, $99) offers rooms with river views.

Information

The **Marinette Travel Welcome Center** (1680 Bridge St., 715/732-4333) is right downtown near the logging museum. Nearby, the **Marinette County Visitor Center** (1926 Hall Ave., 715/732-7453, www.therealnorth.com) is awesome for countywide tourism information.

★ PESHTIGO FIRE MUSEUM

The highlight of Peshtigo is the old church turned into the **Peshtigo Fire Museum** (400 Oconto Ave., Peshtigo, 715/582-3244, www.peshtigofiremuseum.com, 10am-4pm daily June-Oct. 8—the fire's anniversary, free). The museum is rather spartan—few objects survived the conflagration's furnace heat—but as such is a powerful encapsulation of the grim 1871 Peshtigo fire. A few pictures in particular offer a powerful look at the tragedy. There's a somber cemetery adjacent, in which several hundred of the victims are interred.

★ PESHTIGO RIVER PARKWAY

Dropping in elevation faster than any river in the state and featuring one of the longest stretches of active white water in the Midwest, the winding Peshtigo River begins in the north-central part of Wisconsin near Crandon, bisects the Nicolet National Forest, and grows in strength as it crosses into Marinette County. The state cobbled together major chunks of privately held wild lands to create the 9,200-acre **Peshtigo River State Forest** (715/757-3979) and the contiguous

The Great Peshtigo Fire

October 8, 1871, was a day from hell. Most of the country was shocked at the news of the Great Chicago Fire and the incipient fame of Mrs. O'Leary's cow. But on the same day, diminutive Peshtigo, Wisconsin, suffered an even more devastating fire, today unknown to most Americans.

Incessant dry weather sparked repeated minor fires for hundreds of miles around Peshtigo. Merging due to stiff winds, a virtual tornado descended on vulnerable Peshtigo and engulfed it seemingly within minutes. Many of Peshtigo's 2,000 residents died asleep. The fire eventually raged up the Green Bay coast, into Menominee, Michigan, and grazing Marinette, scorching 400 square miles in all.

Peshtigo Fire Museum

Every building in the community but one, and a cross in the cemetery, was destroyed. Despite the steaming waters, helpless victims leapt into the Peshtigo River and saved themselves. In Peshtigo alone, at least 800 people perished. The total regional death toll has been estimated at 1,200, though no official tally will ever be certain. Whatever the sum, Peshtigo was one of the worst conflagrations in U.S. history.

Governor Thompson State Park (715/757-3979), locally often called Caldron Falls Park.

Private landowners in the flowage area had always kept it wild, so shoreline visual clutter is minimal. Unless you're in a kayak, there aren't opportunities to see the white water, aside from the county parks.

The area is accessible via the **Peshtigo River Parkway,** officially called Rustic Road 32. Its 26.5 miles start at Goodman Park Road in the north, thence to Parkway Road, and end at Highway W in the south. A half-dozen good county parks and campgrounds are along the road, along with the Peshtigo and Thunder Rivers and lots of established forestland. The only downside is the egregious advertising plastering the route.

The northwestern section of the county, approximately 20 miles northwest of Crivitz, combines stands of forest, acre after acre of white water, and flowages chock-full of fish. Beginning near the Athelstane County Forest Area, the white water starts at **Taylor Rapids.** The latter park has a unique stand of hemlock and, if you're up for it, a 600-foot-long beaver dam—but it's a tough, wild, hour-long hike to see the dam; ask locally how to get there.

The river then passes through Wilson Rapids and the river-runner's big-gulp, Roaring Rapids, before reaching the apex, Caldron Falls and 1,200 acres of flowage deemed Class-A1 muskie fishing. A few state records have been plucked from the area in past years.

After passing **Old Veteran's Lake Campground,** you'll come to **Twin Bridge County Park.** This is the best spot apart from the High Falls Dam to try out the blue-ribbon fishing in the High Falls Flowage.

You'll see more intimidating cascades at Veteran's Falls in **Veteran's Memorial Park,** off Parkway Road along the Thunder River. The river's roaring section ends at Johnson Falls and Sandstone Flowage, a wilderness-quality fly-fishing-only stretch along Medicine Brook.

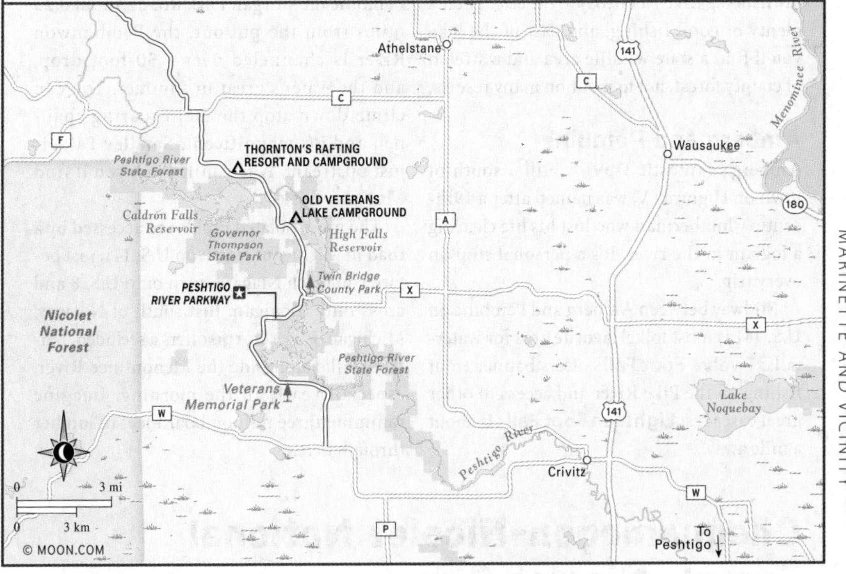

River Running

The Peshtigo is popular with kayakers and rafters. The **Peshtigo River Forest Office** (N10008 Paust Ln., Crivitz, 715/757-3965) has information, but **Marinette County** (715/732-7530, www.therealnorth.com) is really good.

Private operators rule the river. **Thornton's Rafting Resort and Campground** (Parkway Rd., Athelstane, 715/757-3311, www.thorntonsresort.com, $30) is a campground and resort offering cottages, a bar and restaurant, and a swimming beach.

Practicalities

In addition to the resort, the area between Caldron Falls Reservoir and High Falls Flowage will likely have more visitors and thus more small and unassuming resorts, meaning fewer creature comforts. Entertainment runs the gamut from basic country music and fish fry to world-famous hog wrestling at the **Caldron Falls Bar** (W12326 Parkway Rd., 715/757-3467).

THE REST OF MARINETTE COUNTY

The waterfalls and other natural areas in the rest of this gargantuan county are really the reason to visit. It's a great place to leaf through the priceless county-road *Wisconsin Atlas and Gazetteer* and nose out all the waterfalls and white-water photo ops. **Marinette County** (1926 Hall Ave., Marinette, 715/732-7453, www.therealnorth.com) has maps, which you'll need, along with tons of excellent information.

Highway signage, once woefully inadequate, has improved, but it's not perfect. Keep in mind that many of these waterfalls are on less-than-improved dirt or gravel roads. You're likely to get lost trying to find Bull Falls, Eight Foot Falls, and Horseshoe Falls, all of which are great waterfalls but tricky to find; your teeth will rattle.

Crivitz

It's hard to believe tiny Crivitz is the hub of the county. It's the center for supplies and communications in the area, and most resorts use the town as a base. Crivitz is also the main town for big Lake Noquebay to the east. There's plenty of good fishing, and east of the lake you'll find a state wildlife area and a stretch of county forest, not to mention many resorts.

Amberg and Pembine

Amberg's fantastic **Dave's Falls,** south of town on Highway V, was named after a 19th-century lumberman who lost his life clearing a logjam in the river. It's a personal stop on every trip.

Midway between Amberg and Pembine on U.S. 141 is most folks' favorite area for waterfalls. **Twelve Foot Falls** offers banner trout fishing on the Pike River and access to other great cascades; **Eighteen Foot Falls** is about a mile away.

A personal favorite, Long Slide Falls, is along a leisurely drive northeast out of Pembine on Morgan Park Road. About 0.25 miles from the pullout, the Pembonwon River is channeled over a 50-foot drop, and the water's great in summer. You can climb down atop the main roaring channel, and it's magnificent. Smalley Falls is just upstream. A few miles east you'll find **Morgan Park.**

The most isolated rapids are accessed by a road in Michigan. North on U.S. 141, just before you reach Niagara, turn onto U.S. 8 and cross into Michigan. Just south of Norway, Michigan, **Piers Gorge** offers a secluded, fantastic hike alongside the Menominee River, especially early in the morning. Imagine ramming three million board feet of lumber through here.

Chequamegon-Nicolet National Forest: Nicolet Side

The Nicolet is named for Jean Nicolet, the first European to arrive in Green Bay in 1634. This section of Wisconsin's capacious national forest is very nearly the state's perfect approximation of the "Great North Woods experience"—about 666,000 acres in all, with 1,400 miles of fishable stream and more than 1,200 lakes, many grade A1 for lunkers. The "Nick" today encompasses five primitive wilderness areas of about 44,000 acres with stands of majestic trees—some just a scant few—that somehow managed to escape logging a century ago; trees 200 to 400 years old are found in the forest.

This is one-half of the state's national forest, the other, the Chequamegon side, is in Indianhead Country. A personal observation is that the Nicolet National Forest is less cluttered than the Chequamegon. Often the backroads sectors of the forest are absolutely vacant, and even on weekends, precious few people are around. Hike into one of the admirable wilderness areas and you're guaranteed seclusion.

Francophiles will pronounce the name "neek-oh-LAY," but locally it's usually "nick-uh-LAY." Don't be surprised, though, to hear "nick-el-ETT."

Recreation

More than 820 miles of trails wind through the 666,000 acres on 32 trails (for all uses) of varying length, and there are miles of logging skid roads, old railroad grades, and abandoned truck trails to explore on your own.

The forest is known as the "Cradle of Rivers." The moniker is not a misnomer here, the forest acts as a major conduit for several of the state's renowned wilder rivers, including the Pine, Popple, Pike, Wolf, Wisconsin,

1: Peshtigo River Parkway trail **2:** Twelve Foot Falls in Pembine **3:** Dave's Falls in Amberg

and Peshtigo. This forest gave rise to the Wisconsin Wild River System.

Cradle of Rivers canoeing is sublime. Most parts of the Pine and Brule Rivers are good for beginners, as well as part of the Peshtigo segment. More advanced paddlers usually head for the Wisconsin, Deerskin, Popple, Oconto, and Wolf Rivers. The Wolf is nationally recognized for its aggressive fast waters, and thus is better suited for rafts.

Fishing? Nicolet is an angler's paradise.

Camping

Twenty-four campgrounds are established within the national forest, most in the northern half, fewer in the south around Lakewood. **Reservations** (877/444-6777, www.recreation.gov) are available at some established campgrounds. Rates range from free to $30, averaging $12 per site; an $8 reservation fee is tacked on, and it'll cost you $10 to change or cancel. Show up on the Fourth of July without a reservation and you'll be out of luck. Show up on a weekend in summer and you have a 50-50 shot and will probably have to resort to a primitive or hike-in site. Midweek you'll likely find no problems getting a space. Almost every campground is open early May through November.

A handful of primitive hike-in sites are found in the wilder regions of the wilderness areas. Less ambitious "walk-in" sites are also found at Fanny Lake in the Lakewood District and Perch and Lauterman Lakes in the Florence District. Wilderness and walk-in sites are $5, or $20 for a year pass, and no water is available. That said, wilderness areas are open year-round. Common sense and zero-impact camping rules must prevail. Contact the local ranger station if you plan to camp in the backcountry.

Fees

In addition to campsite fees, a $5 parking fee is required for boat landings, beaches, trailheads, and some remote campsites.

Information

The Nicolet National Forest section is parceled into the districts detailed below: Lakewood, Laona, and Florence-Eagle River. Florence also has the **Wild Rivers Visitors Center** (5628 Forestry Dr., 715/528-5377) to handle the whole county's tourism along with the U.S. Forest Service's office, while the main **forest headquarters** (500 Hanson Lake Rd., Rhinelander, 715/362-1300) is in Rhinelander. Other offices are in Eagle River, Glidden, Hayward, and Medford.

LAKEWOOD DISTRICT

The town of Lakewood is considered the heart of this district, perhaps because within a short radius of Lakewood are more than 60 prime fishing lakes. The only highlight besides those listed here is a restored 1881 logging camp at McCauslin Brook Golf Club. Apparently, the camp is one of the oldest of its kind in the United States, though I suspect one in Minnesota may be older. Two miles south of Lakewood are a number of gingerbread-style houses, special for their country architecture, built from local wood and stone.

Sights

Cathedral of Pines is an impressive name for some of the oldest standing wood in the Nicolet, if not Wisconsin. Even more appealing, around 100 nesting pairs of great blue herons predominate. Head south for 1.5 miles to Cathedral Drive (look for a "Watchable Wildlife" sign). It is just under a half-mile drive to get there on a very, very narrow road, and note that there are only three parking spots.

A personal favorite is the recently restored **Mountain Fire Lookout.** This is one of only a couple of the network of 20 New Deal-era fire-spotting towers throughout the region. The total height of the tower plus elevation is 880 ear-popping, possibly swaying a bit, feet. To get there, take Highway 32 east to Highway W, and then make an immediate left onto Old 32. A handful of miles later, you'll come to the access road.

The **Waupee Flowage** is east of Mountain off Highway W and Riverview Road (Forest Rd. 2309). It's serene and isolated—you'll likely be alone here—and there are painters' aesthetics and a tranquil platform designed to expedite the nesting of ospreys, also drawing bald eagles.

Recreation

Eight trails are scattered throughout the district. The 1.25-mile **Quartz Hill Trail,** south of Carter via Highway 32, takes hikers along somewhat steep McCaslin Mountain and passes a marker describing the quartz-quarrying operations of the early Ojibwa people and one of the few remaining fire-spotting towers left in the forest.

For the Thoreau in all of us, the wondrous **Jones Spring Area** is a hands-off, motors-off wild area accessible most easily from Highway T, west of Lakewood, to Fanny Lake. These 2,000 primitive acres feature three lakes, overlooks, an Adirondack shelter, pack-in hiking campsites, and wood duck boxes. The wildlife is truly puzzled by the sight of hikers.

The Wolf River technically does not flow through the Nicolet, but it skirts the far southwest boundary; with no kinetic energy yet, rafting is best here. Do not canoe beyond Markton and into the Menominee Indian Reservation without checking local regulations first.

The Oconto River flows through the area, but extended trips should be tackled only by advanced canoeists. As the rangers point out, "Many a canoe has been totaled on these stretches."

Camping

The campground at 362-acre and walleye-rich **Boulder Lake** is the Nicolet's largest and most popular. **Boot Lake** is approximately half the size and also has nice lakeside sites. A hiking trail leads across the highway to **Fanny Lake,** in tranquil, primitive Jones Spring Natural Area, with 2,000 acres of semi-wild land (with pack-in sites). **Bagley Rapids,** south of the town of Mountain along Highway 32, has 30 sites and not much else. It's primitive but great for rafting and canoeing as it's on the Oconto River.

Information

The **Lakewood Ranger Station** (15805 Hwy. 32, 715/276-6333) is on the south edge of Lakewood.

LAONA DISTRICT

The number-one highlight in the town of Laona is the Lumberjack Special at the **Camp Five Museum Complex** (715/674-3414, www.camp5museum.org, 4 departures 10am-1pm Tues.-Sat. mid-June-last Sat. in Aug., $21 adults). Getting to the museum necessitates clambering aboard a railroad buff's dream—the wheezy old Vulcan 2-6-2 steamer. The center houses a 1900s general store, rail memorabilia everywhere, a nature center, a surrey forest tour operation, and a farm corral, which is hands-on for the children. Visitors can even buzz through rice banks and a natural bird refuge on the Rat River via pontoon boats. Admission covers the museum and the train.

West of Laona near Crandon is the heart of the Forest County Potawatomi community (www.fcpotawatomi.com), or Neshnabek, "original people," as they call themselves, one of eight Potawatomi bands in the United States and Canada. A splendid cultural education comes at the **Forest County Potawatomi Cultural Center and Museum** (5460 Everybody's Rd., 715/478-7474, 9am-4pm Mon.-Thurs., $3 adults). Of particular interest is the Wall of Treaties—43 of them, more than any other Native American nation. This linguist author loves the language kiosk.

Recreation

Trails extend around Laona. Minor trails include the **Halley Creek Bird Trail,** off Highway H east of Laona via Forest Road 2136, a one-mile hike traversing four distinct habitats, and the **Knowles Creek Interpretive Trail** (Hwy. C, east of Wabeno) is less than one mile along a 200-acre wetlands impoundment with viewing platforms. The

1
2
3
4

Michigan Rapids Trail is a pretty hike along the Peshtigo River north of Laona via U.S. 8 and Forest Road 2131.

The only trail in this district for skiers and cyclists in addition to hikers is the **Ed's Lake National Recreation Trail,** via Highway W, a six-mile trail following old railroad grades.

One section on the nearby Peshtigo River is good for novice paddlers. It starts two miles northwest of Cavour off Highway 139 and ends at the Cavour Civilian Conservation Corps (CCC) bridge, a trip of about 7.5 miles. Past this point it can be downright dangerous.

West of Laona and skirting the national forest boundary, a new 37-mile **Wolf River State Trail** from Crandon to White Lake in Langlade County passes through Lake Metonga, the Bog Brook Natural Area, wetlands, the Wolf River, and plenty of rapids.

Camping

The largest and most popular of the district's five campgrounds is secluded **Laura Lake.** Along Highway 32 near Hiles, tiny **Pine Lake** lies on the sandy shore of one of the forest's largest lakes. Southwest of Wabeno, along Highway 52, isolated **Ada Lake** is a peaceful campground of 20 sites, as is **Bear Lake,** and both have good trout fishing; the latter offers good walk-in sites and great views.

Information

The **Laona Ranger Station** (4978 Hwy. 8 W., Laona, 715/674-4481) is west along Highway 8.

FLORENCE AND EAGLE RIVER DISTRICT

Phelps

The only community of any size in the Eagle River District is Phelps, which offers the best community lake view in the forest. Don't miss the **Lac Vieux Desert,** the Wisconsin River's headwaters, north on Highway E. Muskie anglers go berserk in these waters, haunted by the most ferocious of lunkers.

Florence and Spread Eagle

Spread Eagle sits at the tip of one of the most diverse ecosystems in the state—one of the few remaining plains areas. There is also a small chain of nine lakes, reportedly frequented by Al Capone and other nefarious underworld figures during Prohibition. Florence, the sparsely populated county's seat, has one of the smallest, oldest, and not-to-be-messed-with county jails in Wisconsin—a scant 24 by 30 feet—built like a tomb in 1889.

Scenic Drives

The officially designated **Wisconsin Rustic Road 34** departs Alvin and traverses parts of Lakeview Drive, Carey Dam Road, and Fishel Road. It's secluded and a nice northern forest experience on the whole, but it is unpaved and extremely narrow.

Recreation

FLORENCE AREA

A personal favorite for canoeing is the Brule River, which also forms the northern border of the **Whisker Lake Wilderness,** the district's mammoth spread of almost primeval wilderness. The tract covers about 7,500 acres, and there is a stand of virgin pine and hardwood. Whisker Lake is the place for dispersed camping.

The district's highlight, the grand **Lauterman National Recreational Trail,** offers nine miles for hikers, bikers, and skiers, connecting Lauterman Lake with Perch Lake in the north. Lauterman Lake has five walk-in campsites available and an Adirondack shelter.

The aptly named **Ridge Trail** west of Florence winds along an aspen ridge and the Pine River. **Assessor's Trail** plunges deep into hemlock stands so thick you'll notice the light fading.

Not to be confused with the Bois Brule River in far Northwestern Wisconsin is the sedate, comfy Brule River. Doubling as the Wisconsin-Michigan border, the river runs through splendid wilderness areas and offers

1: Cathedral of Pines **2:** trail in Chequamegon-Nicolet National Forest **3:** Anvil Lake **4:** campsite near Laona

great trout fishing. The Brule is decidedly lazy for most of its length and has the most dependable water levels of any in the forest, but never take a canoe past the Brule River Dam.

The Pine and Popple Rivers run through the district, and sections of both are part of Wisconsin's own Wild River System. They also traverse what might be the state's most primitive wilderness. If you can swing some sightseeing in addition to the frenetic rapids, the residuals of old logging dams are found en route.

Neither river should be explored without first checking with Florence's Wild Rivers Center (U.S. 2/141 and Hwy. 101/70, 715/528-5377, www.exploreflorencecounty.com) regarding water conditions and possible regulatory changes.

EAGLE RIVER AREA

Seven miles northeast of Eagle River is the 5,800-acre **Blackjack Springs Wilderness Area.** Highlights include four large clear springs forming the headwaters of Blackjack Creek, along with a lake and assorted streams, some of which produce Brobdingnagian trout.

The wonderful 20,000-acre **Headwaters Wilderness,** 16 miles southeast of Eagle River (producing the wild Pine River), holds some of the largest and oldest trees in the national forest and Wisconsin. The area is characterized by muskegs, bogs, and forested swamps.

The most popular trails are undoubtedly those of the **Anvil Lake National Recreation Trail,** east of Eagle River via Highway 70, 12 excellent miles of CCC trails for hikers, skiers, and mountain bikers. Dramatic plunges and tons of rutted tree roots will dismount you or snag your ski tip. Watch for the woodland warbler.

Connected to the Anvil system is the easier **Nicolet North Trail System,** 15 miles of trails that in turn connect to the **Hidden Lakes Trail.** Hard-core hikers can forge on all the way to the Anvil Trail, though the North Branch of the Pine River must be forded, as there is no bridge.

The **Franklin Nature Trail** is only one mile long, but it's impressive—some of the hardwood and hemlock spinneys are more than 400 years old. The **Sam Campbell Memorial Trail** (interpretive), off Forest Road 2178 north of Highway 32, is named for a local naturalist and writer who used nearby Vanishing Lake for inspiration and contemplation. The 0.5-mile **Scott Lake Trail** winds through 300-year-old stands of white pine and then via a short trail to Shelp Lake and outstanding bog environments. You'll be alone, except perhaps for an ornithologist or two. Finally, you can witness how the U.S. Forest Service manages timber resources on the **Argonne Experimental Forest Trail,** a so-called living laboratory of less than a mile with more than a dozen markers explaining in some detail how the forest is used. It is regularly updated to detail the history of hardwoods management. The road is east of Three Lakes via Highway 32.

The Eagle River District's **Natural History Auto Tour** is an 80-mile mélange of natural history, topographical sights, and the historical museum in Three Lakes. Maps are available at any ranger station in the district, or just follow the auto tour signs starting north of Eagle River along Highway 45. For those without much time, just take a spin through the forest nine miles east of Eagle River off Highway 70 via the old **Military Road,** Forest Road 2178, and **Butternut Lake Road,** a nice forest-in-a-nutshell trip through splendid scenery. Old Military Road, once called the Lake Superior Trail, is the modern result of a trail that's been in use for millennia—first by nomadic Native Americans, then by explorers, trappers, and miners, and, finally, of course, by the U.S. military.

Most of the Pine River is tranquil from the put-in site along Pine River Road, but there are some notable rapids after Highway 55, and a few portages are mandatory. The Eagle River District section offers a few looks at the remnants of old sawmills on the banks.

Camping

FLORENCE AREA

The carry-in **Brule River** campground, on the Wisconsin-Michigan border north of Alvin via Highway 55 and set in a lovely red pine and balsam grove, is superb. Note that high water periods, which have happened more frequently of late, have closed this.

Contiguous **Chipmunk Rapids Campground** and **Lost Lake Campground** off Highway 70 via Forest Road 2450 are 18 miles southwest of Florence. Tiny Chipmunk is adjacent to Lauterman National Recreation Trail and offers its own legendary artesian drinking well at a carry-in site along the Pine River. Lost Lake has a 150-year-old stand of hemlock and pine. No motors are allowed, so it is quiet.

EAGLE RIVER AREA

Popular but mediocre **Anvil Lake** is nine miles east of Eagle River right along Highway 70. The grand Anvil Lake trail system is here.

Franklin Lake, along the Heritage Drive Scenic Byway (Forest Rd. 2181), is huge, with tons of diversions for kids; trails also connect it to Anvil Lake Campground and to the nearby **Luna-White Deer Lake Campground,** with sites sandwiched between the motorless quiet lakes.

The largest lake in the Nicolet, Lac Vieux Desert's 2,853 acres were fished by the Ojibwa people before the Europeans found these headwaters of the Wisconsin River. You'll see lots of rustic resorts dotting the shoreline. This is one of my favorite areas for exploring and taking photos. The muskie fishing is great here.

Sister campgrounds **Spectacle Lake** and **Kentuck Lake** are 16 miles northeast of Eagle River via Highway 70. Spectacle is a family favorite for its 500-foot beach.

The eight primitive but free **Windsor Dam** campsites (free, forest fee $5) are semi-hike-in and secluded along the North Branch of the Pine River.

Information

Florence's **Wild Rivers Interpretive Center** (U.S. 2/141 and Hwy. 101/70, 715/528-5377, www.exploreflorencecounty.com) is also the best source of information in the region, shared by federal, state, and county offices. Stop by to see the albino buck display. The **Eagle River Ranger Station** (1247 Wall St., 715/479-2827) is on the north end of town.

VICINITY OF NICOLET NATIONAL FOREST

Antigo

Twenty miles west of the lower reaches of the forest, little Antigo marks your entry into ginseng country near Marathon County. It's worth a side trip for anglers, which includes most people in the area, to check out **Sheldon's Inc. Mepps Fishing Lures** (626 Center St., 715/623-2382, www.mepps.com). Tours of the lure plant are offered year-round, and anglers spend most of the time ogling the lunkers on display. Free tours (9:15am-2:30pm Mon.-Thurs. May-Dec.) are offered five times a day, less frequently January-April.

Mole Lake Indian Reservation

The Sokaogon (Mole Lake) Band of Lake Superior Chippewa occupies the smallest reservation in Wisconsin—3,000 acres west of the national forest. It's known informally as the Lost Tribe for its lengthy peregrination before arriving here and battling the Sioux for control of the area, and because the 1854 federal treaty they signed was lost in a shipwreck on Lake Superior. The name Sokaogon means "post in the lake" and refers to the appearance of a petrified tree in the midst of a nearby lake, perhaps auguring the end of the band's wandering.

A ferocious battle with the Sioux in 1806—more than 500 people died—produced a significant home for the Sokaogon. The land here is the most abundant in *manomin* (wild rice) in Wisconsin. The beds around the village of Mole Lake are among

The Legend of the Hodag

the scariest mythical creature in the state: the Hodag!

Not of the mythical proportions of big-toed Sasquatch, Rhinelander's own crafty backwoods prehistoric relic, the Hodag, has been legendary in its own right, akin to the jackalope—that hybrid of horned and long-eared fauna populating tourist towns everywhere west of the Mississippi, though, oddly enough, spotted only by the grizzled denizens of local shot-and-a-beer joints. Something monstrous and mysterious populates the Great North Woods around Rhinelander.

In 1896, local Gene Shepard showed up with a photograph of a ferocious beast that had sprung at him in the forest—it was seven feet long, half-reptilian and half-leonine, with sharpened walrus-like tusks, razor-sharp claws, a coniform row down the back worthy of a triceratops, and Brahma bull horns.

Wild rumors spread; supposedly the beast had been caught licking up the last offal of a white bulldog, its favorite meal. A lumberjack posse led by Shepard supposedly captured it, with chloroform and a long pike, yet oddly nobody but he could look at it. When the jig was about up, Shepard claimed the Hodag escaped—but ultimately, somewhat reluctantly, admitted it was a hoax.

It never quite left the psyche of the local community, however: The Hodag is everywhere. Hodag is the high school nickname and mascot. Parks and businesses are named after it. Check out the hoax and the history at the **Rhinelander Logging Museum** (Martin Lynch Dr., 715/369-5004, 10am-5pm Tues.-Sun. Memorial Day-Labor Day, donation). The coolest souvenir in the northlands is a Hodag sweatshirt. The Wisconsin Legislature once even discussed a bill that would make it the official mythical beast of Wisconsin.

the last remaining ancient stands of wild rice.

Right along Highway 55 is an 1870s **cabin** once used as a postal layover and trading post. The cabin is known as the Dinesen House and was the home of Wilhelm Dinesen, father of Isak Dinesen (the author of *Out of Africa*), who named it Frydenland or Grove of Joy. It is being refurbished to house a small cultural and visitors center.

The Lakes District: Northeast

From Tomahawk in the south, draw a line northwest to Hurley. Make another line from Tomahawk northeast to Land O' Lakes. The area outlined is one of Wisconsin's two northern lakes districts, essentially one spread of water, with seemingly a lake for every resident; many lakes remain unnamed. In terms of lakes per square mile, the region is surpassed only by areas in northern Canada and Finland's Lapland. In the three major counties in the district (Iron, Vilas, and Oneida), lakes or wetlands make up almost 40 percent of the surface area. Considering that these primeval pools of glacial hydrology are ensconced almost wholly within state and county forestland, the area is a perfectly realized Great North Woods escape.

TOMAHAWK

Somnolent Tomahawk lies on the mighty Wisconsin River and is a cheery, modest resort town, nestled near the confluence of four northern rivers. Named for an oddly configured nearby lake, Tomahawk's lumber industry at one time rivaled any town's to the north.

The **Tomahawk Chamber of Commerce** (4th St., 715/453-5334, www.gototomahawk.com) is always helpful. Most interesting are the regularly scheduled nature seminars, outdoors workshops, and scientific courses at **Treehaven** (715/453-4106, www.uwsp.edu), a natural resources education and conference center on 1,500 acres, about 15 miles east of Tomahawk via Highway A. Sporadic naturalist-guided hikes, family nature courses, and even concerts are ongoing. A $5 trail pass is required.

Harley-Davidson has a plant here, and **plant tours** (611 S. Kaphaem Rd., 877/883-1450) are possible in summer. It's easiest to call the Tomahawk Chamber of Commerce's toll-free line (800/883-1450) since they will have up-to-the-minute information on plant tours. If you're here in fall, check out the plant's sponsored Fall Ride festival and tours.

Scenic drives abound. The wondrously scenic Highway 107 hugs the Wisconsin River south to Merrill—a great stretch of eye candy. Along the way, you'll pass by the trailhead to the seven-mile multipurpose **Hiawatha Trail.** You could also depart east of town via Highways D and B and then Highway 17 to Merrill—you'll pass two nature areas, classic moraine topography, and Lookout Mountain (the highest point on the Ice Age Trail) before Gleason, aka the Trout Fishing Capital, and ending at Haymeadow County Park and the gorgeous Prairie Dells Scenic Area.

Food and Accommodations

The dining room at **Bootleggers** (Business 51 N. at Hwy. L, 715/453-7971, from 4:30pm daily in high season, shorter hours off-season, from $19) is right on Lake Nokomis, and plenty of snowmobiles pull right up at the door. It was another mob hideout in gangster days.

The pinnacle of Tomahawk lodgings is undoubtedly ★ **Palmquist Farm** (N5136 River Rd., Brantwood, 715/564-2558, www.palmquistfarm.com, from $66 B&B, $114 with meals). Generations of Finns on this 800-acre beef, deer, and tree farm have welcomed guests to their cozy North Woods cottages, and what a grand place it is. You can indulge in myriad trails, luscious breakfasts, deep hospitality, and a real-deal sauna. My faves are the winter hootenannies by the fire. It has worthy weekend package deals, a steal at the price.

RHINELANDER

Rhinelander is also a gateway to water, with the confluence of the Wisconsin and Pelican Rivers in town and all those lakes to the north, and to forests, with the Northern Highland

Eagle River Chain of Lakes

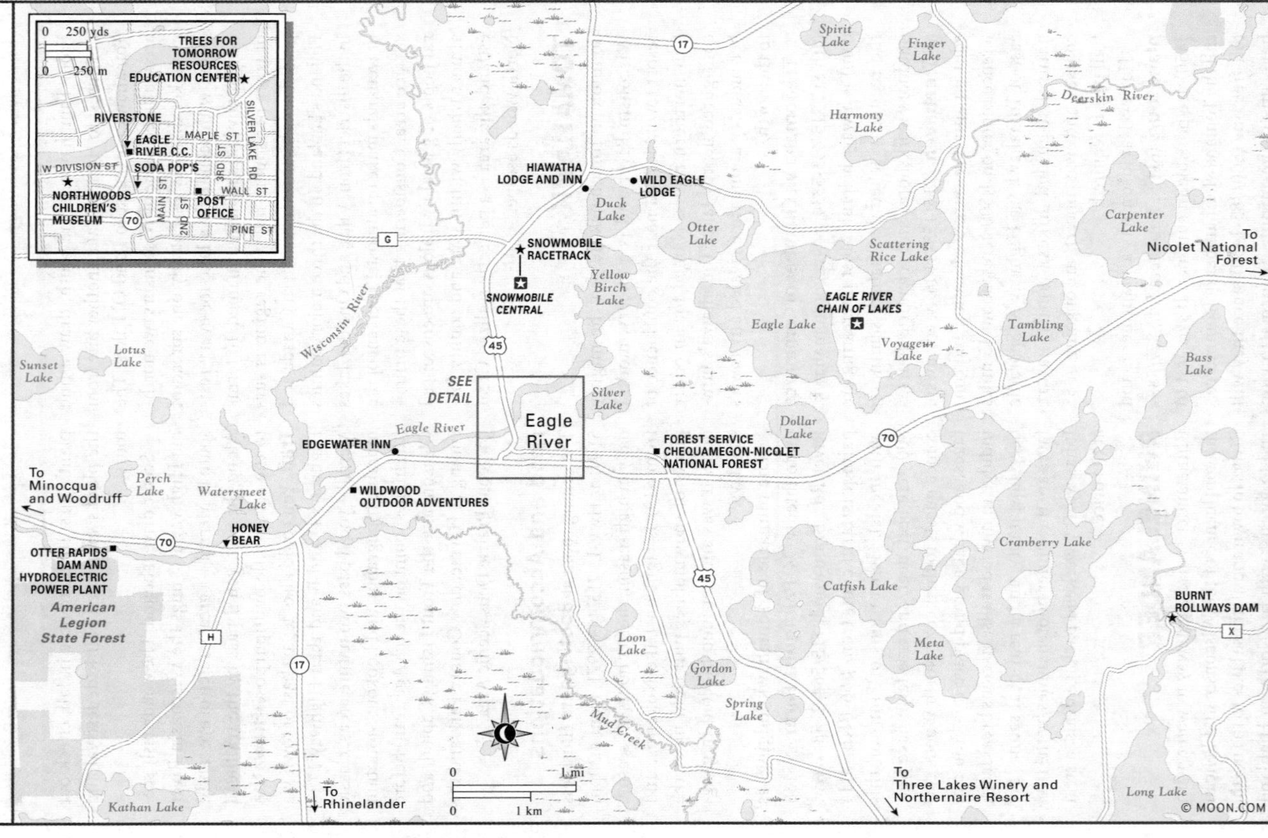

American Legion State Forest to the northwest, the Nicolet National Forest to the northeast.

Sights

The **Pioneer Park Complex** (off Business U.S. 8, 715/369-5004, 10am-5pm Tues.-Sun. summer, free) is an assemblage of lumber-era detritus exhibited in an old logging camp dining hall and the old Rhinelander depot. This is one of the larger and better-realized groupings of antiques you'll experience.

Southeast of Rhinelander about 20 miles are tiny Pelican Lake and Jennings. Jennings features the 1899 **Mecikalski Stovewood Building** (Hwy. B, Jennings). Also called cordwood or stack wall, the style of architecture refers to the short end-cut logs, which are stacked and bonded with mortar or clay. Economical and practical, it didn't require entire log lengths. The practice is decidedly American, and 19th-century Wisconsin was prime country for it; this is the best example and the only commercial building of this style.

Food

Tip of the cap to the third-generation pasty makers at **Joe's Pasty Shop** (123 Randall Ave., 715/369-1224, 11am-3pm Mon.-Thurs., 10am-1pm Fri.) downtown—they make 'em from scratch daily (no mean feat) using environmentally friendly practices.

★ **Rhinelander Cafe and Pub** (30 N. Brown St., 715/362-2918, 7am-9pm daily, $5-25) has been in business since 1911 and today is the must-see dining experience in the region. The huge hall-style dining room is buttressed by the original diner counter. Prime rib, steaks, and duck are still the specialties. Standing room only is the norm.

Holiday Acres Three Coins Dining Room (U.S. 8 E, 715/369-1500, 7am-12:30pm Mon., 5:30pm-9:30pm Tues.-Sat., brunch 8am-12:30pm Sun., $12-26) specializes in seafood and is a solid supporter of live jazz. Believe it or not, international jazz stars have tooted in little Rhinelander.

Accommodations

Just south of the chamber of commerce visitors center, the **Rodeway Inn** (667 W. Kemp St., 715/369-5880, $89) is amazingly friendly and a great deal—don't judge it by the outside.

★ **Holiday Acres** (U.S. 8 E, 715/369-1500 or 800/261-1500, www.holidayacres.com, $159-809) is a high-gear family resort well known among generations of North Woods vacationers. The more than 1,000 acres feature a motor lodge, spiffy cottages (many with fireplaces), and the Three Coins, a dining room among the most popular in the north. The resort's recreation list boggles the mind. Expect weekly-only rentals in summer.

Information

The **Rhinelander Chamber of Commerce** (450 Kemp St., 715/362-7464, www.explorerhinelander.com) is just off U.S. 8. Everyone simply must get a picture of the giant Hodag outside!

Getting There and Around

The **Rhinelander/Oneida County Airport** (3375 Airport Rd., 715/365-3416) has commuter flights to Minneapolis. Driving to Rhinelander from Eagle River (via Hwy. 17, 24 miles) takes 35 minutes. From Minocqua, Woodruff, or Arbor Vitae (via Hwy. 47, 27 miles), it takes 38 minutes. Rhinelander is small enough that you won't get lost.

★ EAGLE RIVER CHAIN OF LAKES

Eagle River's status as a tourism center was perhaps a foregone conclusion, given that it lies along a chain of 28 lakes following the Eagle River—considered the longest such interlinked chain of freshwater lakes in the world. Because there are precious few portages after linking up with the Wisconsin River, you could paddle all the way to New Orleans.

An interesting self-guided water tour is a boathouse tour; the local chamber of commerce (201 N. Railroad St., Eagle River, 715/479-8575 or 800/359-6315, www.eagleriver.org) has detailed information. Head for the **Burnt Rollways Reservoir,** made up of 20 of the lakes. At more than 7,626 acres, with 106 miles of shoreline, it's one of the region's most popular boating and fishing areas. These lakes are in turn linked to the Eagle chain of eight lakes by way of the historic Burnt Rollways boat hoist—dating from 1911—at a dam site between Long Lake and Cranberry Lake. The name Burnt Rollways comes from the revenge exacted on a work boss who couldn't pay some loggers; they torched his logs stacked on the rollway.

The **Otter Rapids Dam and Hydroelectric Power Plant** is a late-19th-century power plant still cranking out electricity. This is the beginning of the long series of dams and assorted river blocks on the Wisconsin River, which have given it the nickname "Hardest-Working River in the Country."

EAGLE RIVER

Some would say that the town Eagle River isn't properly within the lakes district—the Nicolet National Forest named one of its districts for the town, after all. I say Eagle River splits the two regions apart, so it could go either way.

Eagle River was apparently named in the 1850s by a pair of itinerant trappers camped here who marveled at the number of eagle pairs along the river. Yet another lumber town, it was a pioneer in northern Wisconsin in reshaping itself into a major tourism destination.

Winter, and specifically snowmobiling, sets Eagle River apart from the many summer retreat towns. The community's absolutely frenetic international snowmobile races in January are not to be missed.

Sights

The **Trees for Tomorrow Resources Education Center** (611 Sheridan St., 715/479-6456, www.treesfortomorrow.com) is worthwhile. On the south bank of the Eagle River, this facility, built by the Works Progress Administration (WPA), dates from the 1930s. A self-guided nature trail snakes through a demonstration forest, and Tuesday evening free lectures are popular.

The **Northwoods Children's Museum** (346 W. Division St., 715/479-4623, 10am-5pm daily in summer, $8.50) has lots of hands-on activities for kids; they can even harvest cranberries from a bog.

In Three Lakes, south of town, **Three Lakes Winery** (6971 Gogebic St., 715/388-7434, www.tlwinery.com, 9am-5pm Mon.-Sat., 10am-4pm Sun.) is in an old railroad depot. Tours and tastings are free, and there are some fantastic local cranberry wines.

Three Lakes was voted the "Single Best Town" by Disney and Kraft Foods in a contest. The little community's charming downtown and phenomenal outdoors floored the judges. There's a cute Quonset-hut arts center and two small museums, one of which features gas station memorabilia.

A historical tidbit: the **Northernaire Resort** (Hwy. 32, 715/546-2700) was among the first North Woods resorts in Wisconsin; even Bob Hope appeared here.

Recreation

For fishing, muskie, walleye, and bass predominate. Hint: The Lac du Flambeau chain of lakes has world-class muskie fishing. For guides, the chamber of commerce website (www.eagleriver.org) has a full list; doing your homework is well worth it. If you're heading out on your own, boat rentals are available from **Boat Sport Marina** (3624 Hwy. 70, 715/479-8000, www.boatsport.com). If you're not up for paddling the 28 lakes or Wisconsin River yourself, **Wildwood Outdoor Adventures** (5179 Hwy. 70, 715/477-3333, www.wildwoodoutdooradventures.com) offers an unbelievably long list of kayak/canoe/tubing tours in the area.

The excellent **Razorback Ridge** ski trails (12 miles) are a short drive west of Sayner along Highway N. These double as mountain bike trails.

It is beyond the scope of this guide to detail the massive networks of snowmobile trails to the east and west of Eagle River. **Decker**

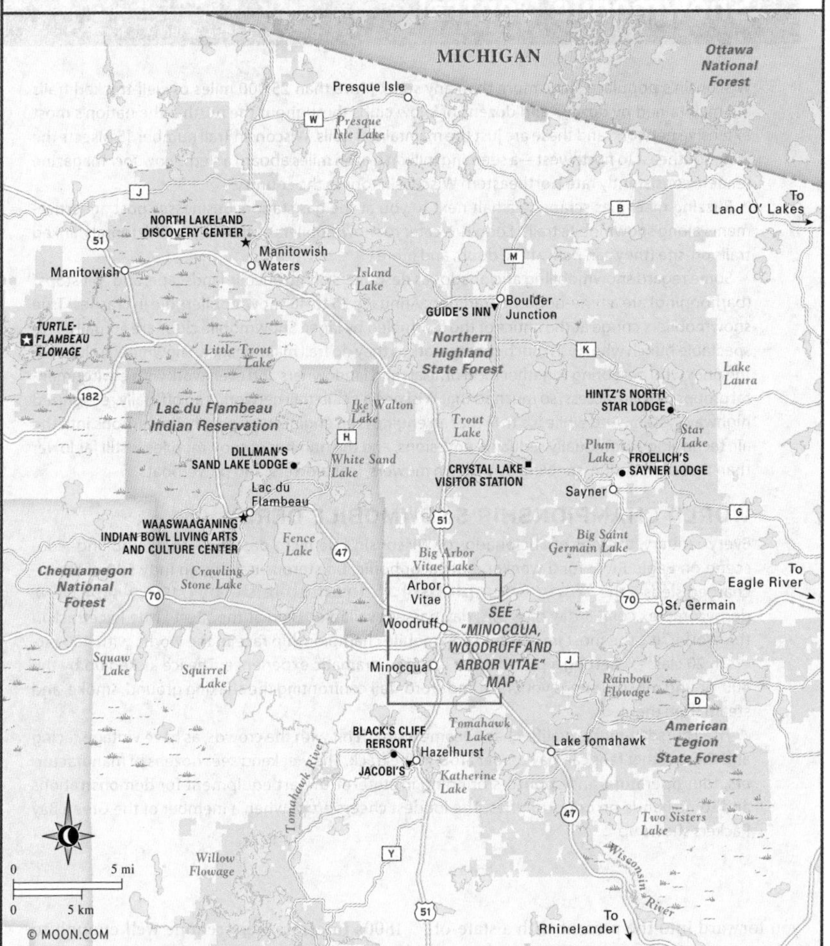

Tours (715/254-1715, www.deckerstours.com) has been leading ATV/UTV and snowmobile tours absolutely forever and is often rated number one by *Snowgoer* magazine, beating out weighty competitors from more famous national park areas.

Festivals and Events

A summertime rival to the snowmobile world championships in winter is August's **National Championship Musky Open**—the largest amateur muskie tournament anywhere.

Food

The **Riverstone** (219 N. Railroad St., 715/479-8467, dinner daily in peak season, Tues.-Sat. shoulder seasons, from $8) takes you back to logrolling days with its 1880s oak backbar and vintage ceilings and floors. Then it lurches

TOP EXPERIENCE

Snowmobile Central

Wisconsin's populace sleds more than any state. More than 25,000 miles of well-tracked trails are maintained by dozens and dozens of snow clubs throughout the north—the nation's most extensive network, and these are just the maintained trails. Wisconsin Trail number 15 bisects the state southeast to northwest—a seeming million frozen miles aboard a sled. *Snowgoer* magazine readers consistently rate Northeastern Wisconsin tops in the country.

Buzzing machines scrape to a halt next to you at the gas station. Businesses post advertisements along snowmobile trails. Lodgings cater to snowmobilers exclusively—with rentals, linked trails on-site (they can park at the door), and more.

Some regard snowmobiling aficionados as despoilers of the bucolic landscape, and "pit stops" (barhopping) are a time-honored tradition. Annually 25 to 40 snowmobilers die in crashes. True snowmobilers cringe at the antics of the few fueled by lager. Snowmobile clubs are actually a respectable bunch who do as much charity work as they do trail maintenance. Snowmobile clubs are the ones who best bring together local officials and landowners and even work with environmental groups to share access, so much so that Wisconsin's club trail network is an officially recognized highway system. And while it's true that an engine is an engine, pumping hydrocarbons into the air, technology is gradually reducing emissions, and the number of snowmobiles is still far lower than that of pollution-spewing SUVs, lawn mowers, leaf blowers, and powerboats.

WORLD CHAMPIONSHIP SNOWMOBILE DERBY

Every January, throngs of aficionados of Wisconsin's de facto pastime—snowmobiling—descend on Eagle River for a weekend of cacophonic, boisterous revelry, an Indy 500 of supercharged sleds—the **World Championship Snowmobile Derby** (715/479-4424, www.derbycomplex.com, 3-day pass $75, day passes available). Held at the "Best Little Racetrack in the World," it's the most important snowmobile championship race in the world, with 400 racers in 20 classes. Getting a pit-side seat is truly a dramatic experience: The ice kicked up by the 400-pound missiles stings your face and words fail confronting the shaking ground, smoke, and steam from the sleds.

The Thursday-night qualifier has become a smash hit with the crowds, as have vintage racing and the fact that fans can pay to roar around the track. The weekend sees dozens of manufacturers, tour operators, and sponsors bringing in state-of-the-art equipment for demonstrations and some hands-on opportunities. The loudest cheers erupt when a member of the Green Bay Packers shows up.

you forward into the present with a state-of-the-art exhibition kitchen and awards for its wine cellar and cuisine, which it precisely describes as "from comfort to creative." Their artisanal hearth baked bread is wonderful (with Wisconsin chèvre cheese, it's sublime).

Jump back in time, but in a much more lighthearted way, at the fab ★ **Soda Pop's** (125 S. Railroad St., 715/479-9424, lunch and dinner daily, $4-9), where you've never tasted such delicious bygone-days "fast food" (that's a positive, by the way) sandwiches and, better, about 200 varieties of soda pop. The original 1800s interiors were redone well enough to win an award from the state. Got kids? This is the place.

Not a supper club per se, the **Honey Bear** (5430 Hwy. 70 W., 715/479-9161, lunch and dinner daily, from $8) is darn close, with an outstanding fish fry (not all you can eat, but epic proportions—enough for a sandwich the next day), great Bloody Marys, and even house fave fried pickles. I've apparently also been remiss in not mentioning the amazing blue cheese burgers!

SNOWMOBILE RACING HALL OF FAME

West of Eagle River, St. Germain's **Snowmobile Racing Hall of Fame** (8481 W. Hwy. 70, 715/542-4463, www.snowmobilehalloffame.com, hours vary Thurs.-Sat., free) is without doubt the most essential stop in the North Woods to gain an understanding of the local ethos. The cool memorabilia includes old sleds and uniforms (in 2018 they expanded and now have some 75 sleds!). You can also watch action-packed videos of famous races, focusing logically on the Eagle River race in January. You can sled right to the entrance in winter, and in mid-January, you can ride on a trail tour with celebrity racers.

snowmobiling in Wisconsin

SAYNER

Five miles up Highway 155 is where it all began: Sayner. Snowmobilers head directly to the **Vilas County Historical Museum** (Hwy. 155, 715/542-3388, 10am-4pm daily Memorial Day-Colorama weekend in fall, $4) and the exhibit on the pride and joy of the area, local eccentric-made-good Carl Eliason, the inventor of the snowmobile in 1924. Also interesting is the look at the area's fishing guide history.

If the museum is closed for the season, more sleds are at The Carl Eliason and Company Store (2954 Main St., 715/542-3233, 8am-4:30pm Mon.-Fri.), where the first sled was assembled; old models are on display. Next door is the Sayner Pub (2962 Main St., 715/542-3647, http://sayner.pub); stop in to see the old ski hill mural on the ceiling.

One resort that people have loved for generations is Froelich's Sayner Lodge (715/542-3261, www.saynerlodge.com, late May-Sept., rooms from $112, cottages from $124) on Plum Lake. The resort has been offering snowmobilers a place to crash since the 1890s, and the Froelich family has operated the lodge since the 1950s. Note that this is absolutely nothing fancy, but it's a wonderful slice of Wisconsin tradition.

Accommodations

Resorts are everywhere, though in town there are a few basic motels, some right on the Eagle River, many with boat docks and to-the-door sled access. Many of the motels are friendly and not too pricey, including **Edgewater Inn** (5054 Hwy. 70 W., 715/479-4011, www.edgewater-inn-cottages.com, $114 rooms, $151 cottages), with charming rustic rooms and cottages overlooking the water. Dollar for dollar, this has always been a great bargain.

North along U.S. 45, the **Hiawatha Lodge and Inn** (1982 U.S. 45 N., 888/479-4442, www.hialodge.com, from $125) gets rave reviews from most folks for well-kept rooms, lots of extras (a fireplace in the main area), and super service.

North of downtown on Duck Lake, ★ **Wild Eagle Lodge** (4443 Chain O' Lakes Rd., 715/479-3151 or 877/945-3965, www.wildeaglelodge.com, from $200) is just about the loveliest rustic yet sybaritic place in the region. Guests rave about this place, its one- to three-bedroom lodge homes, and its friendliness. Their Blue Heron dining room is

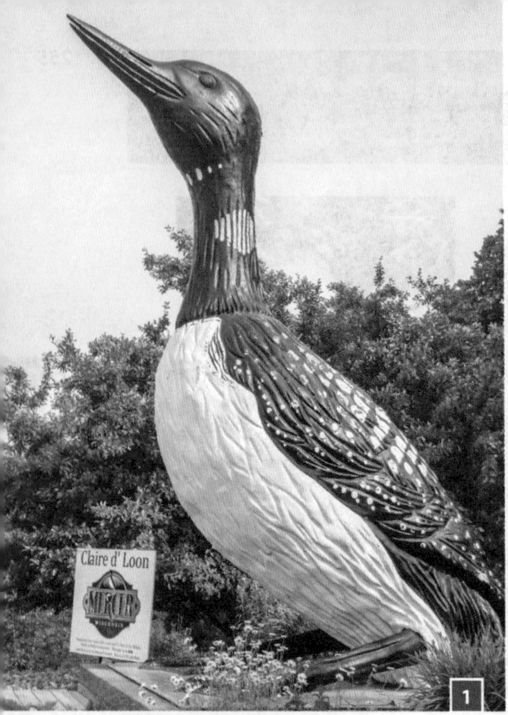

Claire d' Loon
MERCER
1
GIFTS 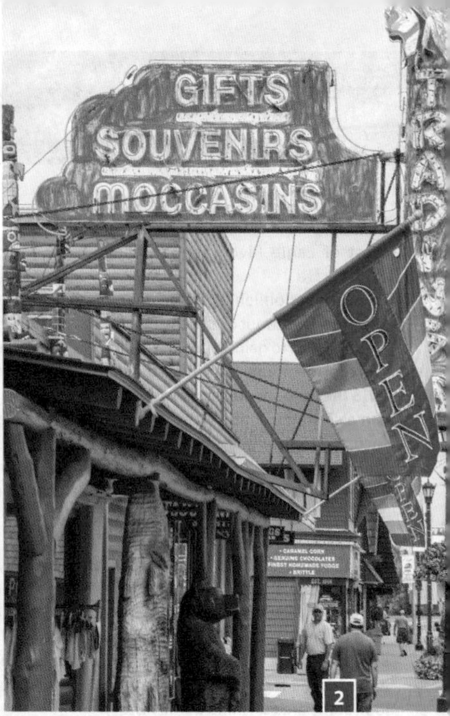
SOUVENIRS
MOCCASINS
OPEN
2
3

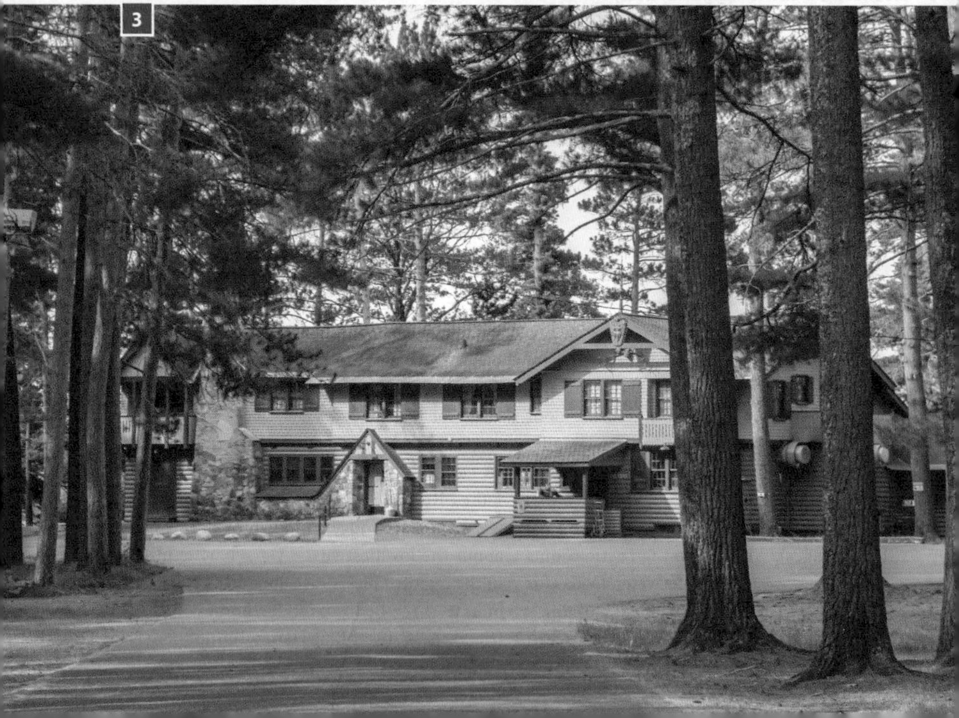

casual fine dining and well-regarded (go for the salmon).

Information

The chamber of commerce's depot **information center** (201 N. Railroad St., 715/479-8575 or 800/359-6315, www.eagleriver.org) is phenomenally well organized.

Getting There and Around

Driving to Eagle River from Minocqua, Woodruff, or Arbor Vitae (via Hwy. 70, 28 miles) takes 40 minutes. From Rhinelander (via Hwy. 17, 24 miles), it takes 35 minutes. Driving is easy given the small size of Eagle River and the excellent signage.

NORTHERN HIGHLAND AMERICAN LEGION STATE FOREST

Most of the lakes region is subsumed by the 225,000 acres of this largest of Wisconsin's state forests. Its proximity to the frenetic tourist towns of Minocqua and Woodruff bring an estimated two million visitors per year. Today, anglers rival pleasure boaters and canoeists for the 54,000 surface acres of 930 lakes and 250 miles of rivers and streams.

This is muskie country. Anglers may claim to be looking for other lunkers, but everybody knows that most are secretly lobbing and reeling, hoping for that muskie trophy. The region is in friendly competition with the Hayward area for muskie bragging rights.

Recreation

This is a canoeist's dream. Three separate lake chains lie within the forest, and the Eagle River chain of 28 lakes is to the east. Nineteen wilderness lakes in the Vilas and Oneida County sections of the forest are absolutely free of shoreline visual pollution and have no road access; 85 percent of the region is public land. A good example is Salsich Lake near Star Lake. An additional 40 lakes are development-free but have some road access; the most popular is probably Allequash.

The most popular canoe trip in the forest is doubtless on the **Manitowish River,** spanning 44 miles from High Lake, northeast of Boulder Junction, all the way to the Turtle-Flambeau Flowage through extras such as wild rice beds.

The top draw to the forest is the 18-mile **Bearskin State Trail** ($5 pass) for hikers and bikers, linking Minocqua and Harshaw in Oneida County via an old railroad grade.

Nine primary hiking and cross-country skiing trails wend their way through the forest, ranging in length from the two-mile **Schlecht** ("bad" in German—a bruising trail, with steep inclines) to 13 miles on the **Lumberjack Trail,** a wilderness track through the oldest timber in the forest as well as some recently logged areas. Many say their favorite is **Statehouse Lake,** a couple of miles of excellent riverside views along a section of the Manitowish River.

Four skiing and hiking trails do triple duty as off-road cycling options within the forest—**McNaughton, Madeline Lake, Lumberjack,** and **Shannon Lake.**

Camping

There are almost 1,100 sites at 20 campgrounds in the forest; you're sure to find one. Modern family campgrounds have reservable sites; wilderness camp areas are also available, and, unlike most places, they can also be reserved. Most impressive is the network of primitive wilderness canoe campsites—nearly 100 in all (12 can be reserved). **Reservations** (888/947-2757, http://wisconsin.goingtocamp.com, reservation fee $8, nonresidents from $25, day-use $11) are advised.

With a permit (free), dispersed camping is also allowed along the Lumberjack Trail or along any of the labyrinthine network of snowmobile trails.

1: Clare de Loon, the greeter for the Turtle-Flambeau Flowage **2:** Eagle River **3:** Little Bohemia Lodge

The Muskie: Wisconsin's White Whale

THE HUNT

Every year, the almost impossible pursuit of the muskellunge (hereafter muskie, although the entire state argues over spelling it *muskie* versus *musky*) ineluctably turns the most rational of anglers into raving Ahabs. It's more than just a fish; it's a mythical construct that life can only rarely approximate. Once hooked, these primeval behemoths can imitate the acrobatics of any marlin or play smart and lie low on the bottom, sailor-knotting your test line. Averaging an hour or more to spot from the boat when hooked, the muskie is a formidable opponent.

Boulder Junction and Hayward are locked in a friendly competition over bragging rights to the title of "Muskie Capital of the World." Wisconsin's Vilas County and its western lake groupings now make a fairly decent living on frothing anglers looking for 50-inchers.

Good luck; it takes an average of 100 hours just to get a nibble, and the average 10,000 casts required is too much for all but the most obsessed. Packer great Brett Favre purportedly hooked one on his second cast; it happened during the Packers' magical 1996-1997 Super Bowl season, so it makes sense. Once hooked, a muskie can toy with you for up to 45 minutes, tugging at but never quite taking the bait; once it does, you'd better not have anywhere else you need to be in the near future.

Information

Southeast of Woodruff off Highway 47 is the **Clear Lake Visitor Station** (8282 Woodruff Rd., Woodruff, 715/356-3668). Northeast of Woodruff east of the junction of Highways M and N is the **Crystal Lake Visitor Station** (715/542-3993). The DNR website has a PDF attachment with all possible information within.

Manitowish and Manitowish Waters

These communities lie a few miles apart via U.S. 51 at the far northwestern corner of the state forest. They were named for *manitous,* the spirits that, according to the Ojibwa people, populate the region. Set on a minor chain of 10 lakes and assorted wetlands totaling 4,265 acres, the area is a tourism center in summer.

The other economic base is cranberries, and the cranberry marshes near Alder and Little Trout Lakes outside the towns are some of the highest-producing bogs in the nation. Free one-hour **cranberry bog tours** (10am Fri. 1st week of July and 2nd week of Oct.) are available; meet at the **Manitowish Waters Chamber of Commerce** (U.S. 51 & Airport Rd., 715/543-8488). No reservations needed, and the juice provided is luscious.

The **Manitowish River Trail** is a 20-mile novice-level canoe trip from the U.S. 51 bridge in Manitowish Waters into the wild Turtle-Flambeau Flowage. Rustic campsites (no potable water) are found on the way.

On Statehouse Lake is the **North Lakeland Discovery Center** (Hwy. W, 1 mile north of U.S. 51, 715/543-2085, www.discoverycenter.net), a nonprofit ecology center with lots of trails and a wonderful array of programs and events throughout the year.

Also south of the towns, the **Powell Marsh Wildlife Refuge** (off Powell Rd.) contains native grains and grasses, luring one of the only groups of sharp-tailed grouse in northern Wisconsin.

Few people know that little Manitowish Waters was the local hideout of gangster John Dillinger. **Little Bohemia Lodge** (142 U.S. 51 S., Manitowish Waters, 715/543-8800, dinner daily, $11-23)—aka "The Hideout"—is where Dillinger, Baby Face Nelson, and two others blazed their way out of an FBI raid in 1934, killing two mobsters, an FBI agent, and

THE CREATURE

The word *muskellunge* is still of doubtful etymology. The Ojibwa people had a close cognate that essentially translates as "ugly fish." Muskies migrated eons ago from oceans to inland seas. Three basic types exist: the basic species, or Great Lakes muskie; an Eastern, or Ohio, version; and a loathed mutation of a muskie and the northern pike, the tiger muskie. The mouth contains a jaw wrapped halfway around the head and the largest canine teeth of any freshwater fish. Those teeth can be used to attack mammals and birds as large as a muskrat (or your finger); more than one puzzled fisher has pulled out a skeletal smaller fish chewed up by a muskie while on the line.

The state record is a whopping 69-pounder taken in 1949 from a dammed section of the Chippewa River near Hayward; thus began the rivalry with the Boulder Junction area, which probably has more muskie in more of its lakes.

Extreme popularity among anglers, heavily sedimented lakes, and lakeshore overdevelopment hurt muskie numbers, but catch-and-release imperatives and stocking (despite the insane cost to raise fingerling muskies) have ameliorated things somewhat. One-quarter of the current population has been raised through stocking.

If you do land a legal muskie (at least 32 inches long), consider letting it go anyway. Only 10 percent of muskies reach that legal limit, and only a small percentage live 15 years. Exact replicas can be built for show. And certainly don't eat one: Old-time muskies can be laced with PCBs.

a local constable and catching national attention. Bullet holes and assorted gangster detritus are still visible, and the lodge is still in operation. Incidentally, Dillinger wasn't the inspiration for the name of 30-30 Road in town—it was the Northland's obsession with hunting.

An anachronistic (it's low-key up-north style cabins and dated but good) lodging option with a fabulous dining room, **Voss' Birchwood Lodge** (south on U.S. 51, Manitowish Waters, 715/543-8441, www.vossbl.com, from $100) has been in the same family since 1910. The stately, rustic main lodge has a large, warm fireplace, and there are also large but not luxurious guest cottages.

The **Manitowish Waters Chamber of Commerce** (U.S. 51 N., 715/543-8488, www.manitowishwaters.org) is staffed by great people.

Presque Isle

Northeast of Manitowish Waters and technically outside the state forest, Presque Isle was dubbed "almost an island" by French explorers. The mazelike streams and lake chains gave the land a resemblance to an island within a flowage. It calls itself Wisconsin's "Last Wilderness."

The family-oriented **Lynx Lake Lodge** (Hwy. B, 715/686-2249 or 800/882-5969, www.zastrowslynxlakelodge.com, from $850 weekly) has been built up literally by hand by the same couple over 50 years and has two-bedroom cottages. There is also a three-bedroom vacation home ($260 per night).

The **Presque Isle Chamber of Commerce** (715/686-2910, www.presqueisle.com) is right on Main Street.

Boulder Junction

One word: muskie. That's pretty much the obsession around Boulder Junction, locked in competition with Hayward in Northwestern Wisconsin. The town touts itself as the "Muskie Capital of the World," as does its rival, and with nearly 200 lakes surrounding the town, you'll get the chance to meet your Pleistocene match somewhere.

In Boulder Junction, suddenly you're in a zone of chichi coffee shops (no more silty campfire cowboy coffee), boutiques, cafés, and even—gasp—a bookstore. And yet it's as North Woods as it gets. This refreshing mix impelled *Sports Afield* to dub Boulder Junction one of "America's Greatest Outdoor Sports Towns."

Something totally different: for some reason, the area's white-tailed deer herd has a recessive gene causing albinism, so don't be surprised if you see one of the local "ghost herd."

Boulder Junction, in an admirable display of civic ambition, maintains its own **Boulder Area Trail System** for mountain bikers and hikers, and more are being created all the time. The trails start right at the visitors center, including a new 13.5-mile paved route to Crystal Lake. Near Boulder Junction is the largest wilderness area donated to the Nature Conservancy in the country. At 2,189 acres with 15 wild lakes, the **Catherine Wolter Wilderness Area** is open to low-impact recreation.

A couple of miles south of town via Highway M, you'll come to Highway K, which leads east as **Rustic Road 60,** which is 11 gorgeous miles of tree canopies, lakes, an old logging site's buildings, and a sawmill at the east end in Star Lake.

Dirt-cheap mom-and-pop lodging operations and cushier condo-esque digs line the surrounding 20-odd lakes. A tip: Trout Lake, the largest and deepest in the county, is almost wholly owned by the state, so shoreline clutter is kept to a minimum. For solitude, peruse the very few options there.

The ★ **Guide's Inn** (Hwy. M and Center St., 715/385-2233, 4pm-9pm Mon.-Sat., $11-24) has long been a standard for continental cuisine. You can expect amazing supper club standards done with a twist (go for their signature dishes à la Wellington), and the owner-chef takes the time to mingle with the diners he's known for a generation.

One reason the North Woods are so precious is places like **McGann's Pub & Wine Bar** (5461 Park St., 715/385-3200), which is odd enough for having a decent wine list, but also because how many wonderful pub/wine bars are there that feel like someone's home—right down to the wondrous golden retriever welcoming you? Yup, this is the place.

Not far from the town and offering daily rates, the **Big Bear Hideaway** (10482 Main St., 715/385-2001, www.bigbearhideaway.com, $125-400) is very good for the money—a half-dozen cabins of native logs and stone made with craftsmanship—and the proprietors are lovely.

White Birch Village (8764 Hwy. K, 715/385-2182, www.whitebirchvillage.com,

camping near Boulder Junction

from $170 daily, $935-1,800 weekly), east of Boulder Junction, offers clean, modest homes with decks, and some with fireplaces—great cathedral ceilings in one. The owners have been in and around these parts for over 50 years. This place receives well-earned raves from longtime customers.

You can't miss the **information center** (Hwy. M, 715/385-2400 or 800/466-8759, www.boulderjct.org) in a renovated log cabin. Besides lots of information, the center's got a cozy living-room atmosphere, so pull up a chair and peruse the brochures.

Star Lake

Check out the **Star Lake Forestry Plantation** on the remains of an old lumber camp. The plantation, begun in 1913, was the first attempt at silviculture in northern Wisconsin, a phenomenally successful venture, considering the forest is still here. Also in the area you'll find the **Star Lake-Plum Lake Hemlock Natural Area,** one of the state forest's 14 state natural and scientific areas. It has stands of near-virgin old-growth forest.

A lodge of some repute in Wisconsin and excellent for its range of economical to extravagant lodgings, ★ **Hintz's North Star Lodge** (Hwy. K, 715/542-3600 or 800/788-5215, www.hintznorthstar.com, high-season from $600 weekly) was once a grand old logging hotel, later catering to passengers on the Chicago railroads. The lodge offers housekeeping units (from $725 weekly), villas ($1,700 weekly), and two lake homes, both with whirlpools. The lodge, however, is most popular for its creative Midwestern cuisine—a homey eatery since before the 20th century. You can get a very basic shared-bath lodge sleeping room for $30-39. I've talked to people whose families have been regulars since the 1920s!

Lake Tomahawk

The **Shamrock Pub and Eatery** (7235 Bradley St., 715/277-2544) houses what is supposedly the world's longest muskie and has decent world-view casual food like Thai curry bowls, not very common in the Way Up North! Lake Tomahawk also hosts semilegendary **snowshoe baseball** games, and it's an amazing thing to watch the little community come out and cheer/play!

Land O' Lakes

Although aptly named Land O' Lakes is technically outside the auspices of the Northern Highland American Legion State Forest, it is pulled that way by its own chains of lakes linking it with its state forest neighbors.

To the east is Lac Vieux Desert, the headwaters of the not-yet-dammed Wisconsin River. To the west are an almost incalculable number of lakes lined with resorts and summer cottages, including the 17-lake 150-mile-long Cisco Chain, the second-longest chain in Wisconsin and a historic route used by Native Americans and early explorers. West of Land O' Lakes along Highway B is the true continental divide and separation point for watersheds flowing to the Mississippi, Lake Superior, and Lake Michigan. A marker near Devils Lake shows the precise spot.

Crossing over into Michigan off Highway B via Highway Z, Highway 535 leads into the **Sylvania Wilderness Area,** an established recreation area about 21,000 acres dotted with almost 40 lakes. Camping is available. While in Watersmeet, you could check out the puzzling **mystery lights** that have been intermittently observed during the past few decades. Go north on U.S. 45 out of Watersmeet to Paulding and then west on Robbins Pond Road. Park anywhere and head for a hilltop. The freaky lights appear to wisp up and out of the woods, where they hang for up to 15 minutes; some say they resemble a star but are amber-colored.

Rohr's Tours (715/547-3639, www.rwtcanoe.com) offers guided wilderness tours heavy on canoeing. The service maintains its own primitive campground and lodge and offers complete outfitting and paddling instruction courses.

True history is at the **Gateway Lodge**

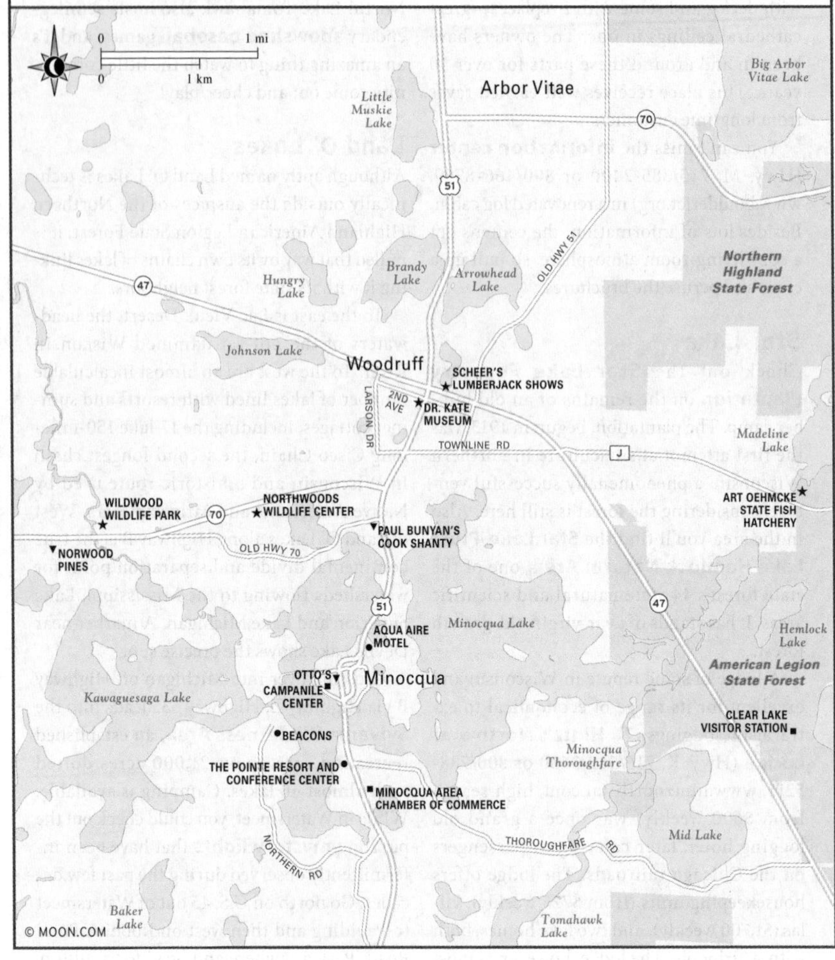

(U.S. 45 and Hwy. B, 715/547-3321 or 800/848-8058, www.gateway-lodge.com, $95 studios, $105 suites), a landmark—highlighted by a great lobby with colossal fieldstone fireplace—in the 1930s and 1940s when Hollywood big shots and presidents used to hang their hats here. A face-lift has left it comfy yet still rustic; you no longer have to worry about mice chewing holes in your bags. Modern amenities include an indoor pool, a hot tub, and a redwood sauna. It isn't the Ritz, but it's very cool, and travelers rave about it. The restaurant is worth a trip, too.

The **Sunrise Lodge** (5894 West Shore Dr., off Hwy. E, 715/547-3684 or 800/221-9689, www.sunriselodge.com, from $159), on the west shore of Lac Vieux Desert, has a fresh-scrubbed woodsy feeling in its 20 one- to seven-bedroom units, run by the same busy couple since the late 1960s. Plenty of home-cooked food is offered in the dining room and bakery. Recreation abounds, with its own exercise and nature trails in addition to the 4,600-acre lake. All-meals-included packages are required in summer. There are cabins that are accessible for people with disabilities.

You'll be hard-pressed to have a better time than at the always boisterous **Bear Trap Inn** (Hwy. B, 715/547-3422, 4pm-9pm daily summer, shorter hours fall-spring, $5-13), a couple of miles west on Highway B. It's one of the oldest eateries in Land O' Lakes, so you'll still hear expressions such as "wet your whistle" while waiting at the bar for a table. When you do sit down, go for the garlic-stuffed tenderloin. Lively big-band music may complete the effect.

MINOCQUA, WOODRUFF, AND ARBOR VITAE

Location, location, location: That sums up these contiguous communities set amid lush public lands and 3,200 lakes. Only about 8,000 people occupy the three towns, of which Minocqua is the largest, but they're drowned by a sea of southlanders every summer, with minor relief after Labor Day before the first snows and the ineluctable advance of the snowmobilers. Though it's not as well-known as Minocqua and Woodruff, the town of Arbor Vitae—literally, "tree of life," named for the plethora of white cedar all around used by French explorers to ward off scurvy—is also considered part of the trio.

Expect minivans, boat trailers, and mall-size gas stations. Although you might anticipate price-gouging or polluted gridlock, it's pretty low-stress for such a popular place.

Sights

In Woodruff, the **Dr. Kate Museum** (923 2nd Ave., Woodruff, 715/356-6896, www.drkatemuseum.org, 11am-3pm Mon.-Fri. mid-June-Labor Day, free) showcases Kate Pelham Newcomb, the "Angel on Snowshoes," a hardy country doctor early in the 20th century. Trying to raise funds for a hospital, Newcomb came up with an idea to have the township's schoolchildren solicit penny donations, initiating what became known as the Million Penny Campaign. Enter the new technology of television, and the world was galvanized—more than $20 million was raised.

Kids and parents go nuts for **Scheer's Lumberjack Shows** (Hwy. 47 and Hwy. 51, Woodruff, 715/356-4050, www.scheerslumberjackshow.com, showtimes 2pm Wed. and Fri., 7:30pm Tues., Thurs., and Sat. early June-late Aug., $15 adults), also in Woodruff. World champion lumberjacks run through the tricks of the trade in a rollicking show of logrolling, canoe jousting, ax throwing, and chopping, all with Yanko the camp cook doing his spiel of gabbing and singing.

Tucker the kiddies out at the wonderful **Wildwood Wildlife Park** (W. Hwy. 70, Minocqua, 715/356-5588, 9am-5:30pm daily summer, shorter hours spring and fall, $20 adults), a cross between a petting zoo and educational center. More than 110 species of fauna are dispersed across the spacious grounds. Boat rides, nature hikes, and educational programs are offered.

Others prefer to witness wildlife rehabilitation and wilderness return facilitation at the **Northwoods Wildlife Center** (8683 Blumstein Rd., Minocqua, off Hwy. 70 W., 715/356-7400, northwoodswildlifecenter.org, 10am-4pm Mon.-Sat., donation), designed as equal parts hospital and educational research center. Brief tours begin every half-hour.

Check out one of the planet's largest and most high-tech cool-water fish hatcheries, the **Art Oehmcke State Fish Hatchery** (Hwy. 47 and Hwy. J, Woodruff, 715/358-9213, 8am-4pm Mon.-Fri., free) in Woodruff. The hatchery raises almost 50,000 fish per year. King muskie holds court here—it ought to, since the hatchery developed methods to "farm" these fish. Guided tours (11am and 2pm Mon.-Fri.) are available.

Both the Rainbow and Willow Reservoirs offer thousands of acres of true wilderness, which is dwindling in the state. Between them lie 10,000 primeval water acres and 150 miles of unadulterated shoreline, **Rainbow Flowage** has an almost unheard-of concentration of eagles and ospreys, with up to

20 pairs of ospreys alone. **Willow Flowage** has nearly a dozen pairs of ospreys and an almost equal number of eagles; it also has the county's only waterfall—**Cedar Falls,** on the Tomahawk River. To get here, take Cedar Falls Road out of Hazelhurst. You may even see the odd wolf pack. The state of Wisconsin plunked down nearly $10 million to buy the Willow Flowage to retain its wilderness status.

Scenic Drives

West of Minocqua along Highway 70 brings you to Mercer Lake Road, one endpoint for another grand Rustic Road. It loops for almost 10 miles to U.S. 51 along innumerable lakes and hardwood spinneys before crossing the remains of the old railroad tracks that carried in the early throngs of tourists; it's now the Bearskin State Trail. Mercer Lake Road eventually links with Blue Lake Road (head east) and crosses the Tomahawk River; in the middle is an optional length of Sutton Road, which leads back to Highway 70. Along this section, look for the remains of early-20th-century cabins built by homesteaders.

Recreation

A true gem of Minocqua is the **Minocqua Winter Park and Nordic Center** (12375 Scotchman Lake Rd., Minocqua, 715/356-3309, www.minocquawinterpark.org), rated in the top 10 in the Midwest and offering 70-kilometer tracks for striding and skating, as well as three short loops for children. Some weeknights, a 1.5-mile loop is lighted. It also operates an open telemarking slope.

Guided **fishing** is a serious industry in Minocqua. In Vilas County alone, which encompasses much of the forestland and tons of the lakes, anglers registered 1,672 muskies totaling 22,000 pounds during one Muskie Marathon.

Entertainment

The **Campanile Center** (141 Milwaukee St., Minocqua, 715/356-9700, www.campanilecenter.org) is in an old Roman Catholic church building; it hosts many performances, including Broadway shows, ragtime music, and big brass bands.

Food

Best burgers in the North Woods are at **Otto's** (509 Oneida St./U.S. 51, Minocqua, 715/356-6134, from $6), a Bavarian-style lunch and dinner joint with great brats (from Sheboygan, no less) and friendly folks. This is my lunch spot.

Another fine choice is ★ **Jacobi's** (9820 Cedar Falls Rd., Hazelhurst, 715/356-5591, 5pm-9pm Fri.-Sat., $15-25), 0.25 miles from central Hazelhurst in a classic backwoods inn that looks like an upscale tavern, dating

fishing on one of hundreds of lakes in the Minocqua area

from the 1930s. The pork tenderloin with Wisconsin blue cheese is memorable.

Norwood Pines (10171 Hwy. 70, Minocqua, 715/356-3666, 5pm-10pm Mon.-Sat., $9-20) is a supper club (piano sing-alongs have been known to break out here) that has great food served on a screened deck over Patricia Lake. Expect twists like cranberry chutney on your relish tray; their wild rice chowder is excellent.

Expect friendly banter and a variety of well-made breakfasts at **Lake Placid Inn** (1520 Hwy. F, Minocqua, 715/356-4202, 7:30am-1pm Sat.-Thurs., till 8pm Fri., $7-10), northwest of Woodruff off Hwy. 47. Dry wit is part of the draw of the place, so they're always just joshing you. Follow the rules, too: write your name on the board upon arrival, and cash only.

Copious feeds and an environment great for boisterous young-uns are at **Paul Bunyan's Cook Shanty** (U.S. 51, between Minocqua and Woodruff, 715/356-6270, breakfast, lunch, and dinner until 9pm daily May-Oct., $10-12), the place with the gargantuan Paul and Babe the Blue Ox out front. Expect lumberjack-style meals and old-style cook-shack decor.

Accommodations

More than 32 lakes and a mind-boggling array of accommodations lie within the parameters of Minocqua. Do your homework and reserve early for summer.

Small and dated but clean rooms overlooking Lake Minocqua are at the **Aqua Aire Motel** (806 U.S. 51 N., Minocqua, 715/356-3433, www.aquaaire.com, from $90). Some rooms have fridges and microwaves, and it's got some extra offerings. Yours truly uses this as a home base in the North Woods.

Within the Minocqua city limits is **The Pointe Hotel and Suites** (8269 U.S. 51 S., Minocqua, 715/356-4431, www.thepointeresort.com, from $189), a first-class condo resort on a minor hillock overlooking Minocqua Lake Bay. Spacious studio and one- or two-bedroom condo suites are excellently appointed and have private lakeside balconies or patios. A full list of recreational extras is available. It's busy but gets high marks for service. Rates in low periods are a steal.

Along similar lines is the more venerable **Beacons** (8250 Northern Rd., Minocqua, 715/356-5515, www.thebeacons.com, from $135, from $750 weekly), with its landmark boathouse on Minocqua Lake. Existing in some fashion since the early 1900s, today it's a lakeside condo resort with one- to three-bedroom units, town houses, condos, and great cottages available. Nightly rates are likely not available in high season.

In nearby Hazelhurst, you can loll along a North Woods lake at the absolutely classic ★ **Black's Cliff Resort** (10223 Lower Kaubashine Rd., Hazelhurst, 715/356-3018, www.blackscliff.com, from $190 daily/$1,200 weekly). These refurbished cabins date from the 1920s and are wondrous—especially the signature swinging beds on screened porches (if napping there listening to the lake isn't classic resort downtime, I don't know what is). Some rooms have fridges and microwaves, and it's got some extra offerings. I love them because they love dogs.

Information

The **Minocqua-Woodruff-Arbor Vitae Area Chamber of Commerce** (U.S. 51, 800/446-6784, www.minocqua.org) is right on U.S. 51 and is well stocked.

Getting There and Around

Driving here from Tomahawk (via U.S. 51, 31 miles) takes 36 minutes. From Eagle River (via Hwy. 70, 28 miles), it takes 40 minutes. From Hurley (via U.S. 51, 55 miles), it takes one hour. It's easy to find your way around, but be prepared for lots of traffic.

LAC DU FLAMBEAU INDIAN RESERVATION

The Sioux nation originally controlled the current Ojibwa reservation. A strategic location at a midpoint between the Montreal River route from the Wisconsin River to Lake

Superior as well as the Chippewa River to the Mississippi, it was finally wrested away by the Ojibwa people around 1650. Lac du Flambeau ("Lake of the Torches") is what the bewildered French first said when they saw the Ojibwa spearfishing in birch-bark canoes in the inky black night, lit only by their torches. The largest Native American group never to be forcibly removed from their own land, the Ojibwa reservation status was established in 1854 with the LaPointe treaty, signed on Madeline Island. Like most, it suffered from federal mismanagement. The Depression-era WPA guide to Wisconsin took the government to task for conditions on the reservation:

> In a report published in 1934 the Land Planning Committee . . . discusses this as an outstanding example of mismanagement of Indian affairs. . . . For 25 years the reservation was held in trust by the Government, which permitted outsiders to log off the timber, thus depriving the Indian owners of the only valuable property they had. By 1914 lumbering ceased, and the Indians were left unemployed on denuded land. Eventually each Indian received a small tract, virtually worthless for farming, not large enough to be used for grazing or forestry.

Life on the reservation is better today, though certainly not perfect, judging from the events surrounding spearfishing sites. The Ojibwa population hovers around 2,500, with their enterprises including a well-respected traditional Ojibwa village, a cultural center and museum, pallet manufacturing, a mall, a fish hatchery, and a casino.

Waaswaaganing Indian Bowl Living Arts and Culture Center

An ambitious, decades-long project to focus on Ojibwa culture, **Waaswaaganing Indian Bowl Living Arts and Culture Center** (wa-SWAH-gah-ning, 603 Peace Pipe Rd., 715/588-9325, www.indianbowlproject.org) completed its first phase in 2017 with an extraordinary reconstruction of the traditional Indian Bowl for powwow, dance, and drumming performances. The complex's gorgeous design features sustainability and cultural motifs throughout. Weekly Tuesday evening **powwows** (7pm, $10) run from mid-June to mid-August and are an amazing experience; I love their invitation tagline that reads, "Don't bring a watch, a business suit, a schedule, or a rain cloud!"

The new facility also has exhibits and workshops in the arts. Part of the complex, **George W. Brown, Jr. Chippewa Museum and Cultural Center** (715/588-3333, 10am-4pm Mon.-Fri., 10am-6pm on powwow nights, Mar.-Oct., $4 adults), possesses the most comprehensive collection of Ojibwa artifacts anywhere, with exhibits including French fur trade days, traditional canoes, and ceremonial drums and clothing. A record sturgeon pulled from the Flambeau lakes is also on display. Perhaps most moving will be—when complete—the meticulous re-creation of an **Ojibwa village** that once spread over 20 acres along on the Lac du Flambeau Indian Reservation. It closed in 2017 in order to be relocated to the culture center grounds, and it could quite possibly be the most significant cultural attraction in the north when complete.

Other Sights

Lac du Flambeau Reservation operates its own **fish hatchery** (N. Hwy. 47, 715/588-3303), raising millions of walleyes, muskies, and trout. Scheduled tours are available by appointment. Trout fishing for a fee is possible daily, with no license required.

Recreation

The Lac du Flambeau **marina** has access to the 10-lake chain that Lac du Flambeau sits on. The Bear and Trout Rivers are good ways to explore most of the lakes, which are very canoe-friendly. The Lac du Flambeau chamber of commerce has a good map marking sites of historical interest along the routes, from the crucial water routes via the Bear River to sites of early trading posts, Indian camps from earliest settlement periods, battle sites, forts, Indian boarding schools, and the largest lumberyard in Wisconsin. You can also pass by Medicine Rock, on which the Ojibwa people made offerings, and the legendary "Crawling Rock," a series of rocks that were purportedly dropped as stepping-stones by a warrior fleeing a charging bear; others say it's because one rock seems to move across the water.

The mesotrophic spring-fed lakes of the Lac du Flambeau chain are also prime muskie waters—three world-class records for line fishing have been recorded here.

Lac du Flambeau

The town of Lac du Flambeau is virtually in the middle of the reservation, set amid five lakes. For information on the whole area, the chamber of commerce's website (www.lacduflambeauchamber.com) is quite useful.

Approximately 30 lodging choices are spread throughout the 10 lakes in the vicinity of the reservation. The venerable ★ **Dillman's Sand Lake Lodge** (13277 Dillman's Way, 715/588-3143, www.dillmans.com, $120-420, up to $2,900 weekly) is synonymous with North Woods Wisconsin. The lodge offers condo efficiencies in addition to comfortable cabins perfect for families; an annex has simple motel-like rooms with private baths. And there's always something to do at Dillman's—the lodge often sponsors bike tours, and the Dillman's Creative Arts Foundation sponsors wonderful arts workshops and exhibits. All the amenities would take a page to list; over its 250 acres is everything you could want to do. There's also a sports program for children in summer. Rates run $120-420 daily, up to $2,900 weekly. The gangster Baby Face Nelson once holed up here in Cabin 5.

★ TURTLE-FLAMBEAU FLOWAGE

Bookending the western side of the Northern Highland American Legion State Forest is the "Crown Jewel of the North"—also called Wisconsin's version of the Boundary Waters Canoe Area of northern Minnesota. Of all Wisconsin's numerous flowages, which are reservoirs on major river chains, the Turtle-Flambeau is perhaps the wildest and most primitive. The majority of its shoreline is state land and thus off-limits to development—in fact, many of the lakes in the flowage have only one or no resorts or cottages on them.

The area was originally dammed in 1926 by endless public and private endeavors to regulate water supply and, secondarily, supply electricity. With the Turtle backed up behind the "Hoover Dam of Iron County," the waterways of the Bear, Manitowish, Turtle, and Flambeau Rivers became enmeshed. The resulting 20,000-plus acres, one of the larger bodies of water in the state, has never had the same attention as other regions of Wisconsin—thankfully so, many people say. To keep it as close to wilderness as possible, in 1990 the state of Wisconsin bought the whole area. Nine lakes, numerous creeks, three rivers—backcountry lovers find it all intoxicating. Virtually all flora and fauna native to the state are here in spades, with the granddaddy of sport fish, the lake sturgeon, also prowling the waters. The state's highest numbers of nesting pairs of eagles, loons, and ospreys are on the property.

The flowage is broached primarily via Mercer and Manitowish Waters on the north side, Springstead in the east, and Butternut-Park Falls on the west. Note that Highway FF is a grand bicycle route stretching between Butternut and Mercer. Winding, rustic, and not too traffic-laden, it has some wearied sections of road, but overall isn't too bad.

Canoeing & Kayaking

Paddling is superlative in the flowage—as close to alone as you could hope to be. The north fork of the Flambeau River is a 26-mile trip from the flowage to Park Falls; almost two dozen rapids are traversed en route.

The **Bear River Trail** is a 25-mile trip, reasonable for novices, that leaves southwest of Lac du Flambeau on Flambeau Lake, with one easy rapid; eventually it joins with the Manitowish River and flows sedately into the town of Manitowish. The heart of the flowage is traversed by two popular trails: the **Manitowish Route** and the **Turtle River Route.** The latter is intermediate level. It goes without saying that you should do your homework before sliding a canoe into the water. Conditions and water levels vary, so check ahead.

Accommodations

Many simple North Woods-style cabins, lodges, and resorts line the southwestern section of the flowage, essentially trailing Highway FF from Butternut to Mercer. The places are no-frills, precisely the way it's supposed to be. They will also almost certainly have rentals or shared-use boats available. Included within is **Deadhorse Lodge** (4125 N. Popko Circle W., 715/476-2521, www.deadhorselodge.com, $125-260, 3-night min.). Get past the name and check out the nine newer vacation cabins of all sizes and varieties, some with whirlpools and fireplaces. They also have a new bar to relax in. Others have loved **Flambeau Vista Retreat** (Park Falls, 715/762-4612, www.flambeauvista.com, from $150, 2-night min.), which has two multiperson cabins; in summer it's weekly rentals only (from $875).

For those who would rather rough it, more than a dozen established campsites are found along the flowage, many on little islets dotting the reservoir—these are the best camping. The eastern bulbous section of the Chequamegon National Forest is also right nearby. Contact any of the area's chambers of commerce for specifics on regulations and precise locations—some of the sites are not easy to find. Sites are first-come, first-served.

Information

The Wisconsin DNR actually has little useful information; contact the **chambers of commerce** in Mercer (5150 N. U.S. 51, Mercer, 715/476-2389, www.mercerwi.com or www.mercercc.com), Hurley (316 Silver St., Hurley, 715/561-4334, www.hurleywi.com), and Park Falls (400 S. 4th Ave., Park Falls, 715/762-2703 or 877/762-2703, www.parkfalls.com). Also try a good compendium site: www.turtleflambeauflowage.com.

The Iron Range

Hurley and even smaller Montreal lie in the midst of the mighty Penokee Iron Range as well as the over-the-border Gogebic Iron Range. The range, for many Wisconsinites, has been unfairly relegated to backwater status—too many news reports in southern Wisconsin mentioned the population flight from Iron County in the bad old days of economic decline. And while it is true the county ranks low in population and thus doesn't have the tax base to pretty things up like more populous areas, Iron County has important history and even some outstanding topography. The Turtle-Flambeau Flowage is one of the most wilderness-like stretches of any northern river, and Iron County has almost as many waterfalls as Marinette County, across the state. Marinette may have more, but no falls beat Iron County's for sheer height and isolation.

The Flambeau Trail

Native Americans followed a route from Saxon Harbor, northwest of Hurley, portaging canoes and beaver pelts between their villages and Northwest Fur Company Trading Posts. The 90-mile trail from Madeline Island to Lac du Flambeau became the crucial Flambeau Trail, followed in due course by explorers, trappers, traders, and the U.S. military. The whole thing is mapped now, passing Superior Falls at the first take-out point. The trail later passes the **Continental Divide;** the northern waters above the divide were unnavigable, necessitating this 45-mile portage to southern-flowing streams.

HURLEY

Living museum Hurley was important in its headier early days. The little town arose more than a century ago on the iron riches taken from the subterranean veins of the mammoth Gogebic and Penokee Iron Ranges, the former accounting for almost 40 percent of the Upper Peninsula's economy at its zenith, when 350 mines tore through the subterranean stretches. White pine wealth followed later. "Lusty infants on a diet of lumber and iron ore," the old WPA guide noted.

What really set Hurley apart from other boomtowns was the unimaginable bacchanalia for which it became legendary. At its sybaritic zenith, more than 75 saloons lined the aptly named **Silver Street,** wooing the 7,000-odd salty miners and loggers. The WPA guide quotes the prevailing wisdom along the logger-miner transient railroad: "The four toughest places in the world are Cumberland, Hayward, Hurley, and Hell, and Hurley is the toughest of 'em all." It is against a background of such legend that Wisconsin native and Pulitzer Prize-winner Edna Ferber set the harrowing, only slightly fictionalized account of the brutal Lottie Morgan murder, *Come and Get It,* in Hurley.

Things tamed somewhat with the waning fortunes of ore and receding lines of timber—not to mention Prohibition. Many saloons and dance halls boarded up. The rest, however, went backroom or simply hibernated while the mobsters used Hurley as a haven during Prohibition. When Prohibition was repealed, the town again saw a throwback to drinking and debauchery. Even more drinking halls lined the raucous Silver Street.

Things have finally cooled off in tough Hurley, though it hasn't lost all of what made it infamous.

Sights

The grande dame hereabouts is the somewhat wearied but eminently proud **Iron County Courthouse Museum** (303 Iron St., 715/561-2244, 10am-2pm Mon., Wed., and Fri.-Sat., free). Turreted and steepled, it is a leviathan. It was built in 1893 for a then princely $40,000 and later sold to the county. A personal favorite is the mock-up of a Silver Street saloon on the top floor, using carved bars from one of those that made the town legendary. Or visit on a Saturday and you might see volunteers using original late-19th-century Scandinavian-style rag-rug weaving looms. Local artisans have also built replicas of, well, darn near everything. The basement has a morgue (seriously) with a tin casket, cooling board, altar, and requisite old Bible.

a tradition—the ice fishing shack on a northern lake

A mile west of town is the art deco **Cary Mine Building** (Ringle St., off Hwy. 77 west of town), the epicenter of mining operations for 80 years.

Finns came in waves to these regions, and their Suomi heritage is feted daily at **Little Finland** (U.S. 2, west of U.S. 51 junction, 715/561-4360, www.littlefinland.org, 10am-2pm Wed. and Sat. Apr.-Dec., free), home to a museum of Finnish immigration and homesteadings and a great opportunity to scope out traditional Finnish "fish-tail" building construction—and note that some of the timber used to build the center came from the massive Ashland ore docks. Head five miles south of Hurley to the corner of Dupont and Rein Roads, where you'll see a huge stone barn designed by a Finnish stonemason.

★ Iron County's Waterfalls

Iron County boasts more than 50 waterfalls, from the wilderness-accessible to the roadside. It's got six of the state's 10 tallest and boasts the highest concentration in the Midwest. Show up during spring snowmelt and these cascades simply roar.

Land changes hands and suddenly access roads are no longer accessible. *Do not trespass; if in doubt, stay out.* Contact the **Hurley Chamber of Commerce** (316 Silver St., 715/561-4334, www.hurleywi.com) to check on road access. Another good source is the **Iron County website** (www.ironcountywi.com), which has GPS coordinates to go with directions.

The highest waterfalls are personal favorites Potato River Falls and the hard-to-find Superior Falls, both a respectable 90 feet. To reach the **Potato River Falls,** head west; south of U.S. 2 in Gurney is a sign to Potato River Falls along a gravel road. Magnificent upper and lower falls don't see many visitors, so the trails are great for exploring. There's also rustic camping. Continuing down Highway 169 will bring you to **Wren Falls,** with great trout fishing and more primitive camping, though a meager 15-foot drop for the falls. **Superior Falls** is west of Hurley 12 miles and then north on Highway 122 for 4.2 miles. Cross the Michigan border, go 0.5 miles, and turn left on a gravel road (it's easy to miss—keep your eyes peeled). There's a parking area and signs to the great chuffing 90-foot cascade raining into Lake Superior.

The east branch of the Montreal River has **Peterson Falls** (35 feet) and **Spring Camp Falls** (20 feet). The west branch has **Kimball Park Falls,** with a series of riffles, and 15-foot **Gile Falls;** check out the large waste rock tailing piles, residual of iron ore mining, across the way.

The Turtle River in the Mercer area also has three often visited falls, including the ever-popular **Lake of the Falls,** with rustic camping. The Upson area has two cascades, **Rouse Falls** and **Little Balsam Falls,** which are accessible only with some orienteering. Easier and equally lovely falls can be found along the Black River Parkway north of Ironwood and Bessemer, Michigan, north of Hurley in the Upper Peninsula.

Recreation

This is Big Snow Country, so snowmobiling is king—bigger even than skiing. More than 350 miles of groomed trails spread throughout the vicinity, and rentals are available in Hurley.

Three cross-country trails are maintained in the vicinity, totaling about 40 miles. Contact the **Iron County Development Zone Council** (715/562-2922) for information. The trails are maintained by donations.

A magnificent trail network for bikers is the 300-mile **Pines and Mines Mountain Bike Trail System,** operated jointly by Michigan, Wisconsin, and the U.S. Forest Service and running through the carpets of forests in Iron County and the Upper Peninsula. Michigan has two good ones—the **Ehlco Tract Complex** and **Pomeroy/Henry Lake** set of gravel roads. Iron County has the third section, an amazing spiderweb of trails and roads leading along old railroad grades, logging roads, and roadways, passing historical sites (in particular the Plummer mine headframe) as well as forests, streams, and even waterfalls. If you're in good shape, you could make it all the way to Mercer or west to Upson and beyond. Thirteen of the best waterfalls are accessible via this system. For info or maps, contact the **Hurley Chamber of Commerce** (316 Silver St., 715/561-4334, www.hurleywi.com).

For type-T expert kayakers, the rare north-flowing Montreal River is a dream between Saxon Falls and the top of the dam before Superior Falls—a white-water adventure through spectacular canyons over 200 feet high.

For **camping,** the closest county park (no reservations) is **Weber Lake,** west of town on Highway 77, right on Highway E.

Entertainment and Events

Bars and taverns worth mentioning line the historic five blocks of the downtown Silver Street area, but be aware that there is a red-light district in the nether reaches.

Dawn's Never Inn (29 Silver St., 715/561-2090, 11am-close daily) was once a gangster hideout and brothel opened during Prohibition; it still has shooting slits and other reminders of its gangster heyday (Al Capone purportedly stayed here). The backbar is fascinating.

The oldest marathon in the state and second-oldest in the Midwest, dating from 1969, is August's **Paavo Nurmi Marathon,** named, appropriately, for a Finn—dubbed the "Flying Finn" for his numerous Olympic gold medals. It's a good place to feast on pasties and *mojakaa,* a beef stew.

Food and Accommodations

Here, you're so close to the Upper Peninsula of Michigan that it'd be a shame not to indulge in that epicurean delight of the Yoopers, the pasty. As a half-Yooper, I can claim that Hurley's cafés and diners make the closest approximation to a pasty as you'll find in Wisconsin.

The Bell (10381 Hwy. 51, 715/561-3753, dinner Mon.-Sat., $6-12) had been dishing up Italian and American food for nearly a century until their abrupt closure in 2018. Chaos ensued. Worry not, for it relocated a few minutes south of town and now has a lovely forest view. Most go for the pizza, but their Caesar salad is renowned.

Don't be shocked: You can get sophisticated food in a town in the middle of a mining range at **Kimball Inn** (154 Hwy. 2, 715/561-4095, dinner Tues.-Sun., from $12). I've even heard of them making special dishes off menu for people if they're not too busy.

Hurley's got a few budget motels, but it's best to head east into Ironwood, Michigan, along U.S. 2; there you'll find some good $50-60 rooms, even in summer, and many of those motels have Finnish-style saunas. For real historic lodging, head for Montreal.

Information

Visit the **Hurley Chamber of Commerce** (316 Silver St., 715/561-4334, www.hurleywi.com) for information on the area.

VICINITY OF HURLEY

Montreal

Along the way to Montreal, note exceedingly diminutive Pence, with more than 20 log structures of all sorts visible from the road. This is one of the largest concentrations of such architecture in Wisconsin.

Once peopled by company miners living in squat white shacks, Montreal today is a living microcosm of the area's heritage. Long ago it was the site of the world's deepest iron ore mine, memorialized with a marker along Highway 77. Once the only completely planned and platted company town in Wisconsin, the whole place is on the National Register of Historic Places. Mining is finished but not forgotten—west of town is the only extant mining headframe, the **Plummer Mine Headframe.** Eighty feet tall and imposing, it's a true piece of history. An interpretive park surrounds it, highlighted by the **Cary Building,** the art deco main office of the mine.

Accommodations in Montreal include **The Inn** (104 Wisconsin Ave., 715/561-5180, $85), a 1913 B&B built by the Montreal Mining Company as an administration building, which has lovely interiors. A couple of other historic dwellings are now quasi-B&Bs as well.

Indianhead Country

PLANNING YOUR TIME

One look at a map and you'll forget about a do-it-all weekend. This region is the most expansive in Wisconsin and has the greatest diversity of landscape and attractions. You won't be able to do it all in one go, so consider splitting your trips into chunks. Each part can be done in a weekend, or a week if you have the time. Many of the places in the north-central section of this region are specifically designed for week-long summer vacations—you rent a cabin and then fish, canoe, and do whatever else you feel like. The same happens in winter, except it's all about snowmobiling and cross-country skiing.

Say "cabin and a week" and most Wisconsinites imagine **Hayward** and fishing for the muskie that made it famous. Otherwise, the Chequamegon

Highlights

Look for ★ to find recommended sights, activities, dining, and lodging.

★ **The Mabel Tainter Center for the Arts:** This Romanesque sandstone edifice mimics a European opera house (page 280).

★ **Interstate State Park:** The St. Croix National Scenic Riverway is best viewed from the rugged ridges of this spectacular park (page 284).

★ **Superior Harbor:** Visit one of the deepest and farthest inland freshwater ports in the world (page 291).

★ **Pattison State Park:** See the state's most splendid cascades here (page 294).

★ **Bayfield:** This postcard-perfect town is a gateway to the Apostle Islands National Lakeshore (page 298).

★ **Highway 13 from Bayfield to Superior:** This tour passes through some of the most charming villages you'll ever see (page 303).

★ **The Apostle Islands:** These treasures are worth a week of sea kayaking and exploring (page 308).

★ **Wisconsin Concrete Park:** Find quiet, inspirational folk art at this roadside attraction in Phillips (page 317).

★ **Timm's Hill:** Wisconsin's highest point is the best place to be when the riotous colors of autumn appear (page 318).

★ **National Freshwater Fishing Hall of Fame:** Stand inside the jaws of a leviathan muskie, then learn why fishing is such a big deal in Hayward (page 323).

Indianhead Country

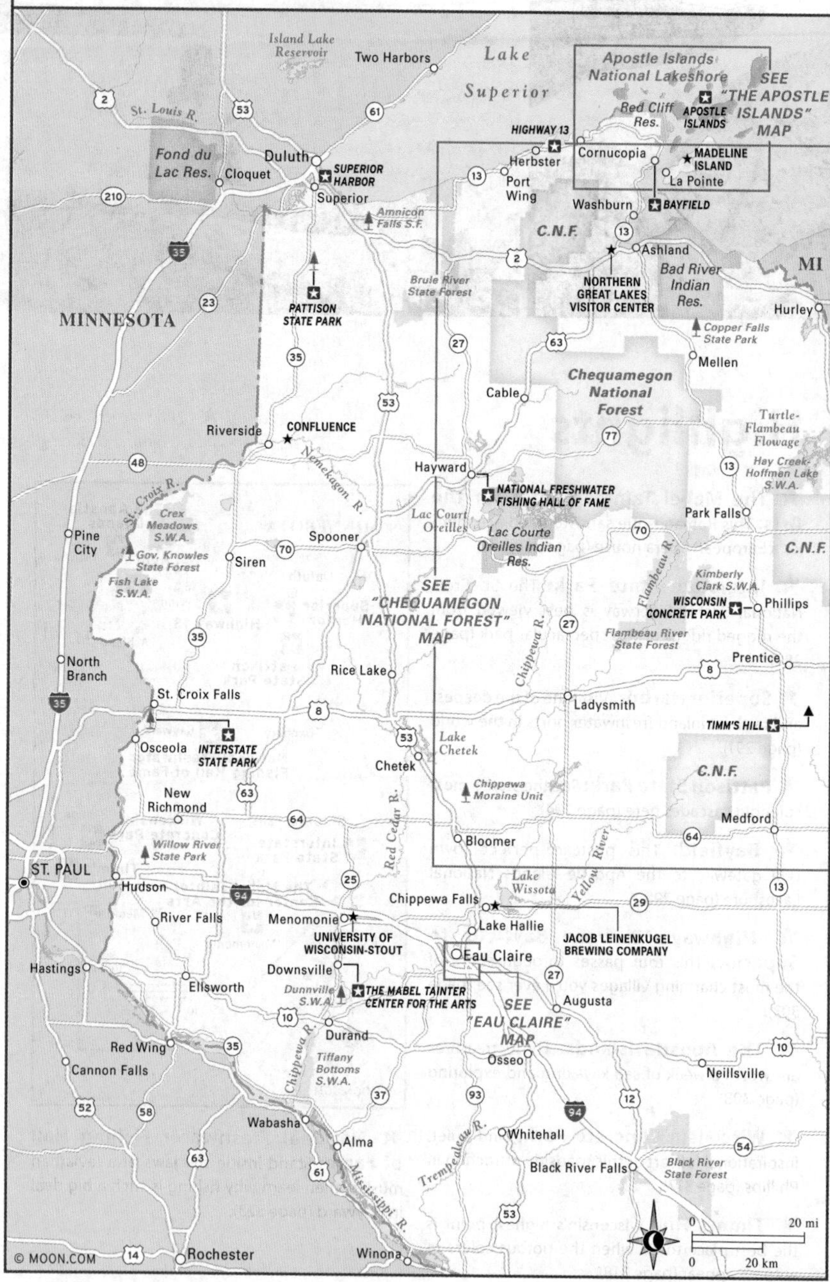

National Forest surrounding it has some of the most isolated camping in Wisconsin.

Bayfield and the Apostle Islands across the water are quite possibly the most perfectly realized weekend getaway spot in the state; some visitors spend two weeks here exploring all of the Apostle Islands by foot or kayak, then biking the mainland section. Highway 13 around Bayfield is a gorgeous drive.

If you base yourself in Hayward and need some day trips, outlying attractions can be done in a grand sweep. Cover the **Phillips** area for Wisconsin Concrete Park and Timm's Hill, and then either canoe the St. Croix National Scenic Riverway near **Trego** or do some cliff scrambling at Interstate State Park near **St. Croix Falls.** Then check out waterfalls and lake shipping in **Superior.**

Eau Claire and Vicinity

EAU CLAIRE

The city of "Clear Water" is the largest community in northern Wisconsin and lies at a strategic point in the Chippewa River Valley. Busy and pretty, the city (population 56,000) is bigger than Wisconsinites think.

Like elsewhere, timber opportunists arrived as early as 1822. In total, Eau Claire would process nearly 300 million board feet of lumber per year, which explains its nickname, "Sawdust City."

Eau Claire went through the usual lumber boomtown throes—a saloon for every five residents, internecine timber squabbles, and violent flare-ups. Industrialists had the forethought to harness the local rapids for hydroelectricity, one reason it would eventually eclipse Chippewa Falls up the river when the timber vanished.

It's not a subdued city; *Outside* magazine rated Eau Claire the number four town in the country in terms of activity.

Sights

CARSON PARK

The tourist hub is a 134-acre peninsular playground west of downtown jutting into Half Moon Lake. The primary attraction is the **Chippewa Valley Museum** (715/834-7871, www.cvmuseum.com, 10am-5pm Mon.-Sat., 1pm-5pm Sun. summer, shorter hours fall-spring, $7 adults) with award-winning displays on the valley's Ojibwa culture. Of note are the 21-room dollhouse and an anachronistic ice cream parlor.

The **Paul Bunyan Logging Camp** (715/835-6200, www.paulbunyancamp.org, 10am-4:30pm daily Apr.-Oct., shorter hours Nov.-Mar., $7 adults), a replica of an 1890s camp, features an interpretive center with unusual and wonderful logging flotsam, including a mini village of structures and Brobdingnagian heavy equipment.

The **Chippewa Valley Railroad** (www.chippewavalleyrailroad.org, noon-5pm Sun. Memorial Day-Labor Day, $3 adults, $2 children) offers rides on a 0.5-mile 16-gauge line through the park. The two coal-fired steam engines pull all-wood 1880s passenger coaches, among other beauties, some the best of their kind in the state.

Carson Park is also the home of the **Eau Claire Cavaliers** and **Eau Claire Express** baseball teams. Eau Claire has fielded semipro teams since the early 1900s and boasts a couple of Hall of Famers. Hammerin' Hank Aaron got his baseball start in Eau Claire in 1952 playing for the then-Eau Claire Bears. Burleigh Grimes, a local boy, also pitched for the Bears.

Previous: Superior's harbor; the National Freshwater Fishing Hall of Fame; sitting on the shore of Oak Island

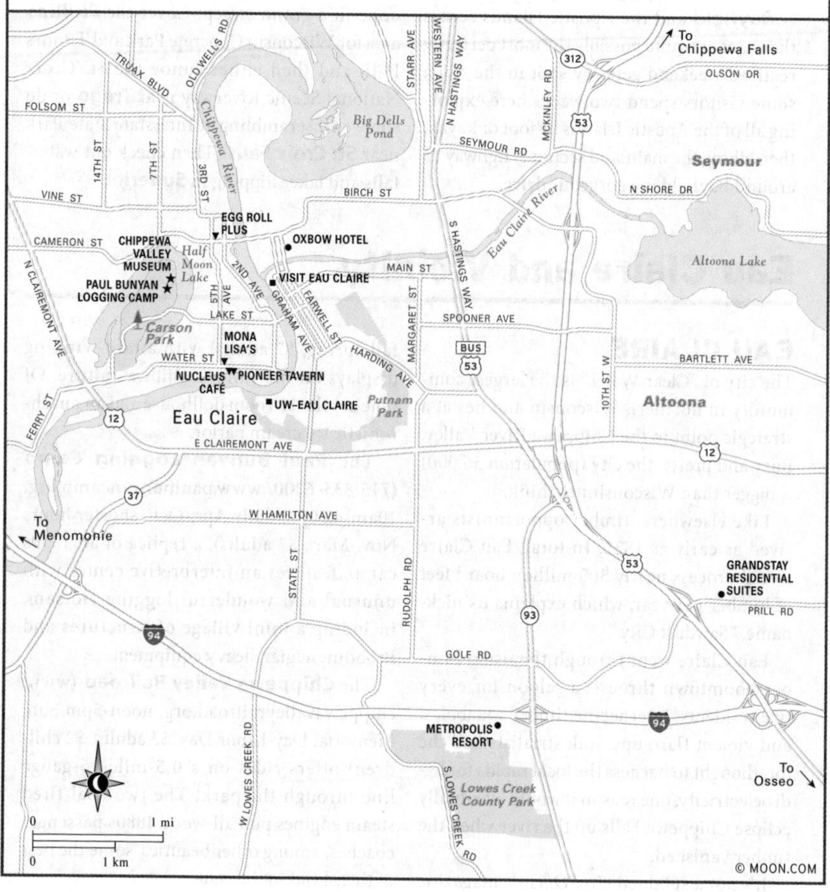

Side Trips

The most promising is to Augusta, 20 or so miles to the southeast via U.S. 12. Easily one of the most photographed gems in the state is **Dells Mill** (Hwy. V, off Hwy. 27), three miles north. This eye-catching 1864 mill is set along engaging Bridge Creek. The remarkable thing about the mill is that its five structures are constructed solely of hand-hewn timber joined only by wooden pegs. Inside you'll find more than 3,000 feet of belting and 175 water-forced pulleys. After the dedicated proprietor died, it fell into a bit of limbo, but it has recently been taken over by some gracious Amish. The bad news is it's only open/accessible on Saturday, and not exactly on a regular schedule, but if you go and get access, you'll get a much-sought after photo!

Recreation

CHIPPEWA RIVER TRAIL

This nearly three-mile-long multiuse path runs through Eau Claire's urban river corridor. The river trail in turn joins with the larger **Chippewa River Valley State Trail,** which eventually leads through prairie, mixed forest, and agrarian patchworks to Menomonie and the **Red Cedar State Trail.** You can reach the river trail at Carson Park (a spur trail) or at the University of Wisconsin-Eau Claire. No trail pass is needed in the city, but a $5-per-day pass is needed on the state trails.

Entertainment and Events

Eau Claire is not a hotbed of nightlife. **The Cabin** (715/836-4833, www.uwec.edu/uac), at the University of Wisconsin-Eau Claire, is the oldest coffeehouse in Wisconsin, with folk, blues, jazz, and occasional comedy.

The best place for a microbrew and cheddar curds in a great atmosphere is at the **Livery** (316 Wisconsin St., 715/833-7666, lunch and dinner daily), a converted stable. For a great beer garden, head for the **Pioneer Tavern** (401 Water St., 715/832-4455), in a lovely 19th-century building that once housed a pharmacy. The tavern is on Water Street, and the entire street is the epicenter of entertainment.

A vaudeville "palace" and movie house in the Roaring '20s, the **Regional Arts Center** (316 Eau Claire St., 715/832-2787, www.eauclairearts.com) is now home to regional cultural groups.

Food

The best breakfast in northern Wisconsin is at the ★ **Nucleus Café** (405 Water St., 715/834-7777, breakfast and lunch Wed.-Sun., from $5). This isn't your parents' northern Wisconsin café; everything is done with a creative twist: lemon ricotta hotcakes, pepper parmesan hash browns, and the like.

Many people don't know that Wisconsin has one of the country's largest Hmong populations, and hole-in-the-wall **Egg Roll Plus** (1611 Bellinger St., 715/832-6125, 11am-6pm Sun.-Fri., $5-10) splendidly showcases their cuisine (think Thai, Vietnamese, Laotian, even Chinese, but with a twist).

Creative Mediterranean (heavily Italian) fare comes at **Mona Lisa's** (428 Water St., 715/839-8969, dinner Tues.-Sat., $12-32), all done with seasonal influences and locally sourced ingredients. Yet this isn't what makes this place special. This is the kind of place where the staff clearly love what they do, and it shows. Balance the food, the wine/drink selections, the service, and the spirit, and it's a top-notch place.

Accommodations

Positive reviews come in for **Grandstay Residential Suites** (5310 Prill Rd., 877/388-7829, from $119), which has wonderful standard suites and fabulous service.

For families, score a room and passes to Chaos waterpark (kind of overstated) and Action City (rock climbing, bumper cars, etc.) at the intriguing **Metropolis Resort** (5150 Fairview Dr., 888/861-6001, www.metropolisresort.com, $139). With this much action going on, remember it isn't your subdued business hotel.

Chic and hip is the ★ **Oxbow Hotel** (516 Galloway St., 844/692-6932, www.theoxbowhotel.com, from $140). Owned in part by a local, a member of Wisconsin's indie music stars Bon Iver—which explains the retro turntables in the rooms—this boutique hotel has environmentally minded rooms in a hotel that smacks of a futuristic hunting lodge. A farm-to-table restaurant, outdoor relaxation areas, even an on-site outfitter for bikes and kayaks are all here. Check in to your room and get a Wisconsin-food snack tray. Wisconsin art adorns the facility.

Information and Services

The well-stocked **Visit Eau Claire** (128 Graham St., 715/831-2345, www.visiteauclaire.com) is right downtown.

Getting There

AIR

The **Chippewa Valley Regional Airport** (EAU, 3800 Starr Ave., 715/839-4900) is north of town and has daily flights to Chicago.

Eau Claire Passenger Service (715/835-0399, www.chippewavalleyairportservice.com) operates ground transportation between Eau Claire and the Minneapolis-St.

Paul Airport (hourly 2am-9pm, one-way $43). Nine trips leave daily.

BUS

There's a **Greyhound Station** (6251 Truax Ln., 715/874-6966) at a McDonald's in town.

CAR

Getting to Eau Claire from Menomonie (via U.S. 29 and I-94, 29 miles) takes 36 minutes. From Hayward (via U.S. 53, 107 miles), it takes 105 minutes. From Minneapolis (via I-94, 93 miles), it takes 100 minutes. From Madison (via I-94, 178 miles), it takes three hours.

CHIPPEWA FALLS

Eau Claire may be the city of clear water, but its chief competitor today is the "City of Pure Water," so named for the natural springs still used for the beer that made it famous, Leinenkugel's ("Leinie's").

The water in Chippewa Falls is claimed as the purest in the United States—just ask the locals. A private laboratory in Minneapolis was called in to settle a friendly dispute between Deming, New Mexico, and Chippewa Falls in 1969. The lab gave a nearly perfect quality rating to Chippewa Falls' water—and it's been boasting about it ever since. Chippewa Falls has also been noted by preservationists as one of the country's best preserved towns, and *Time* magazine rated it one of the country's top 10 small towns. The National Trust for Historic Preservation has called it one of the country's top 10 "Distinctive Destinations."

Sights

In North Woods Wisconsin taverns, the beer of choice is indisputably Leinie's (never "Leinenkugel's" if you're trying to fit in). The **Jacob Leinenkugel Brewing Company** (Hwy. 124 N., 888/534-6437, www.leinie.com, tours 10am-6pm Sun.-Wed., 10am-8pm Thurs.-Sat., $10) has been using the crystal clear waters of Chippewa Falls to brew beer since 1867. It went from 400 barrels of one brand of beer in its first year to nine premium brands, today sold throughout the region. No reservations are necessary for the tours, but it's a good idea.

You can actually view the pure gurgling springs at the phone booth-size **Chippewa Spring House** (600 Park Ave., 715/723-0872), one of the oldest landmarks in the valley and the community's first structure, built in 1836. Across the street is the **Chippewa Water Company bottling plant,** started by poet Ezra Pound's grandfather and still in operation after more than a century.

Chippewa Falls' modern history is partially chronicled at the **Chippewa Falls Museum of Industry and Technology** (21 E. Grand Ave., 715/720-9206, 10am-3pm Thurs.-Sat., $5 donation is worth it). People are fairly surprised how important Chippewa Falls has been to the computer revolution; Cray Computers, builder of the world's most powerful supercomputers, was founded in Chippewa Falls. In low season this museum is occasionally open by appointment only.

Food

The family restaurant of choice is absolutely ★ **Olson's Ice Cream Parlor and Deli** (611 N. Bridge St., 715/723-4331, 11am-8pm or 9pm daily, $2-5), a landmark since 1923 for its "Homaid" ice cream. Ice cream aficionado magazines have rated this place in the top 10 in the United States; you can observe the ice cream-making process through large windows.

OSSEO

Osseo draws scads of travelers from everywhere to an unassuming big-britches eatery, the world-renowned ★ **Norske Nook** (7th St., 715/597-3069, 6am-8pm Mon.-Sat., 8am-8pm Sun. summer, shorter hours fall-spring, from $5), which arguably bakes the world's best pies. Celebrated by road-food gourmands and feted by many, many national media appearances, the place could not be more

1: Paul Bunyan statue in Carson Park
2: Leinenkugel's beer mural **3:** Carson Park's Chippewa Valley Railroad

1 
SINCE 1867
Leinenkugel's
THE FLAVOR OF THE NORTHWOODS
2
3

underwhelming when you walk through the door, as it looks like nothing more than a classic diner. But the food is unreal. It's got the obligatory heart-stopping breakfasts and the requisite Midwestern hot beef sandwiches. Occasionally a dinner special might feature something Scandinavian such as lutefisk or *lefse*. But the pies are really the thing—a whole page of them. The strawberry pies have up to five pounds of strawberries. The Nook is *the* stop between Eau Claire and the Mississippi.

Since you're already in Osseo, stop by the **Northland Fishing Museum** (1012 Gunderson Rd., 715/597-2551, 9am-5pm daily, free), an awesome repository of classic and antique fishing equipment, featuring one of the most extensive (and kitschy and hip) fishing lure collections in the world. You want a rusted Evinrude? You got it.

MENOMONIE

One of the ubiquitous oddly spelled Wisconsin towns with the same pronunciation, Menomonie (muh-NAH-muh-nee) was a lumber town alongside a floating log highway, site of the world's largest lumber corporation at the time, processing more than five million board feet of lumber with 1,200 employees on 115,000 acres of land.

University of Wisconsin-Stout

Fantastically wealthy lumber magnate James Stout foresaw incipient timber unemployment and founded the Stout Manual Training School, today's **University of Wisconsin-Stout.** It was the first in the country to offer a curriculum designed specifically for industrial arts, helping shift local schools' emphasis toward vocational education.

★ The Mabel Tainter Center for the Arts

The enormous dark sandstone **Mabel Tainter Center for the Arts** (205 Main St., 715/235-9726, www.mabeltainter.org) was deliberately contrived by its designer and builder in 1890 to "advance American architecture, society, education, and religion." It's a lofty, if not quixotic, memorial to the builder's daughter, a local aesthete, who died at 19. In Romanesque style, it resembles a Thames-side opera house—the interior is downright eye-popping. In rare-for-Wisconsin Moorish style, the ornate auditorium has extraordinary detailing, a Steere and Turner Tracker pipe organ, and very pricey old paintings. It is open for tours by appointment only ($5), but performances and events are regularly held.

Mabel Tainter Center for the Arts

Recreation

The **Red Cedar State Trail** departs the historic depot along the west edge of Highway 29 in Menomonie and stretches nearly 15 miles south along the Red Cedar River to the **Dunville Wildlife Area.** The Menomonie depot dispenses trail passes ($5 per day) and can tell you about the dozen bridges, a "weeping" rock wall, legendary gold buried along the riverbank by fleeing French soldiers, and an old 860-foot-long railroad bridge. You can link up at the end with the Chippewa River Trail to Eau Claire. You can also canoe, kayak, or tube the Red Cedar River from Menomonie. Rentals are found at the Menomonie trailhead.

Food and Accommodations

For over two decades **Acoustic Cafe** (102 Main St. W, 715/235-1115, 8am-8pm Mon.-Fri., 9am-8pm. Sat.-Sun, $6-10) has been my stop of choice on the way through the area. Simple and unpretentious interiors (you know, mismatched everything) give a cool vibe, and the ingredients for the simple soups and sandwiches are locally sourced and made creatively. However, it's the from-scratch baking that really sets it apart—the bread alone is wondrous, but the scones are heavenly.

A large number of perfectly adequate chain motels are at the junction of I-94 and Highway 25, including the very clean and utterly friendly **Super 8** (1622 N. Broadway, 715/235-8889, $85-136), which gets the nod because bike trail access is just a couple of blocks away.

Information

You'll find local tourism information at the **Menomonie Area Chamber of Commerce** (342 E. Main St., 715/235-9087 or 800/283-1862, www.menomoniechamber.org).

Northwestern Lakes

Northwest of Eau Claire, where U.S. 53 branches north from the interstate, is another massive concentration of primeval glacial pools. Second in density only to Wisconsin's other lake district, in the northeast, but second to none in sheer numbers, the area features arguably the state's best muskie fishing and the country's first established scenic riverways.

ST. CROIX NATIONAL SCENIC RIVERWAY

The St. Croix National Scenic Riverway is one of a dozen so designated in the federal Wild and Scenic Rivers system. It was also the first, made official by Congress in 1968, and contains 252 miles of the Upper and Lower St. Croix Rivers and the entire Namekagon River. Though not technically part of the system, the Brule River was and is a de facto link in the chain. With only a short portage between the Brule and the St. Croix, this was the most crucial waterway between the Great Lakes and the Mississippi River. Though brown for most of its length in the south due to tannic acid leaching into the water from decaying pine and tamarack needles, the riverway is one of the healthiest in the United States in terms of biology and biodiversity.

The St. Croix is a schizophrenic river, split into regions at St. Croix Falls. The Upper St. Croix and Namekagon Rivers are the more challenging and isolated for canoeists, drifting and paddling through an expansive river valley streaked with creeks and dotted with thousands of glacial lakes and tracts of second-growth forest. The Lower St. Croix, by the time it departs St. Croix Falls, is somnolent and wide, full of sandbars and backwater sloughs.

The National Park Service's website (www.nps.gov) has excellent information on the entire riverway, along with local links.

Black River State Forest

Many Wisconsinites have never experienced this large forest (some 68,000 acres) since, although it's just off the interstate, it's kind of in the middle of nowhere. Black River Falls, the largest gateway town, is some 50 miles southeast of Eau Claire. In fact, that's the closest town of any size, meaning you'll often have the forest to yourself.

ELK

The forest is isolated enough that in 2016 the state transplanted 73 Kentucky **elk** here to start a herd; as of 2019 the herd numbers are strong (all the calves born in 2018 had survived to the time of writing) and trending upward toward the goal of some 400 elk. Now, your chances of seeing one are not all that high given there are fewer than 100 elk in 68,000 acres. However, locals have said North Settlement Road in the state forest is the best place to try (this also happens to be part of a state Rustic Road). Drive slowly and be hyperaware, especially at dawn and dusk. The herd has suffered no predation; the most common cause of death is vehicles. If you see one, *do not approach*. This could potentially affect their adjustment over the first few years of acclimatization, and thus breeding.

RECREATION

The Black River—named for the water's black hue, caused by a high iron content—cuts across Wisconsin's central plain and western upland regions. Most visitors come to paddle; 75 river miles are canoeable in the immediate vicinity. Trips are most commonly done out of Hatfield. One of the most popular stretches of water is the float upstream from Black River Falls between Hall's Creek to a dam. Ultracasual tubers generally take two hours to leisurely float from Irving Landing to Lost Falls. Outfitters include **Black River Express Canoe Rental** (301 S. Washington St., 608/488-7017) 17 miles south of Black River Falls in Melrose. They do shuttles and also rent kayaks.

Black River

A number of miles east of Black River Falls is icy **Wazee Lake,** a glacial lake that is 350 feet deep (the deepest inland lake in Wisconsin) with no outlets; it's also incredibly clear, so expect to see scuba flags and snorkel gear—it is among the most popular places to scuba dive in the Midwest. It is part of a 1,300-acre recreation area ($5 daily pass) with hiking and biking trails, along with a lovely large beach.

The Black River State Forest has 35 miles of mountain bike trails. Cross-country ski trails—highly rated by skiers—are five miles north of Millston. Trail passes ($5 per day) are required.

CAMPING AND BACKPACKING

Three family campgrounds are in the state forest. You'll also find canoe campsites south of Black River Falls. **Reservations** (888/947-2757, http://wisconsin.goingtocamp.com, reservation fee $8, nonresidents from $23, day-use $11) are advised.

Primitive backpacking is also available, and a permit is necessary. Camping is only in designated areas, so get the details from the forest headquarters.

INFORMATION

The **Black River State Forest Headquarters** (715/284-4103) is along Highway 12 southwest of the junction of Highway 54 and I-94. The **Black River Falls Chamber of Commerce** (120 N. Water St., Black River Falls, 800/404-4008, www.blackrivercountry.net) loves to give information.

Upper St. Croix and Namekagon Rivers: Along the Route

The St. Croix River begins as a humble creek flowing from Upper St. Croix Lake in a muskeg forest between Gordon and Solon Springs. It runs 102 miles to Prescott, but after just 20 miles the Namekagon River, its main tributary, joins it. The Namekagon starts as a chilly trout stream at a dam northeast of Cable, near the Chequamegon National Forest. Both wend through forested valleys in relatively primitive conditions. For pure backwoods isolation, the Namekagon can't be beat.

Near the St. Croix headwaters, a county park in Solon Springs contains Solon Springs' claim to fame—the **Lucius Woods Performing Arts Center** (9245 E. Main St., Solon Springs, 715/378-4272, www.lwmusic.org), a rustic outdoor amphitheater featuring established musical acts on weekends.

The Namekagon changes from an icy, extremely isolated trout stream in dense conifers to a wider channel through marshes and swamps. The river contains one hairpin turn after another, and that's why canoeists love it so much—there are no boaters.

The section from Hayward to Trego is the most developed 34 miles on the whole upper stretch. It has a few rapids, but these can be tough for novices.

Trego, at the Great South Bend of the river, was once a ready-made campsite, used by the original Ojibwa inhabitants. Jonathan Carver in 1767 and Henry Schoolcraft in 1831 also slept on sandbars here. A huge number of **river outfitters** are here, with rentals and shuttles starting at $25. The **Namekagon Visitor Center** (U.S. 63, 715/635-8346, 8am-5pm daily summer, Sat.-Sun. spring and fall) is north of town.

Below Trego, a narrow-channeled, twisty 40-mile stretch runs to Riverside. As the most backwoodsy part of the entire system, it's the most popular weekend excursion.

Confluence

Near Riverside, the two rivers join and form the Upper St. Croix National Scenic Riverway, a wider, more sedate, but no less scenic stretch leading to St. Croix Falls. Just south of Danbury, and stretching all the way past Grantsburg, is the long, sinuous **Governor Knowles State Forest,** with 33,000 acres of great canoeing, 40 miles of hiking on two 20-mile trails that trace the bluff line above the river, and some primitive campsites along the water.

East of Danbury and easily missed are the 11 communities spread through four counties of the **St. Croix Indian Reservation.** Often called the "Lost Tribe" because of its dispersion, another Native American community is across the St. Croix River in Minnesota, and the headquarters is to the southeast, near the village of Hertel. Casinos in Turtle Lake and Danbury are tourist attractions, and an annual late August or early September **Wild Rice Powwow** is a popular draw. The whole region east of Danbury along Highway 77 is dubbed the "Fishbowl" for its preponderance of glacial pools and the teeming panfish in them.

For a good side trip through the remnants of Wisconsin's Pine Barrens, an endangered ecosystem, head for the state's largest wildlife area, the thoroughly captivating **Crex Meadows Wildlife Area** east of the landing near Phantom Flowage along Highway F. This 30,000-plus-acre spread features 250 species of birds, including nesting herons, sharp-tailed grouse, sandhill cranes (13,000 are here in autumn), trumpeter swans, rare colonies of yellow-headed blackbirds, and a dozen species of duck. You may even see the Crex Pack, a pack of timber wolves that moved here from Minnesota. The prairie lands contain more than 200 of the last vestiges of pure prairie plants in the state. There is a wonderful interpretive center on-site, with a birding trail and self-guided auto tours. Visitors can also canoe, and some limited camping is allowed September-December.

Grantsburg is a pleasant one-horse town. There is an eight-foot talking wooden statue of "Big Gust," the likeness of a local historical figure; check him out at the Village Hall. The village also hosts its summertime **Snowmobile Watercross** in July, when snowmobile pilots attempt to skim their machines across a downtown lake.

Five miles east of Grantsburg in tiny Alpha is the **Burnett Dairy Cooperative** (11631 Hwy. 70, 715/689-2468, www.burnettdairy.com), a group of almost 300 local dairy farmers and the former World Cheese Championship winner. There's a cheese store-cum-bistro (8am-5:30pm Mon.-Wed., 8am-7pm Thurs.-Sat., and 9am-7pm Sun.) that serves freshly made fried cheese curds among other delicious dairy-laden sandwiches and the like.

Twenty-one miles east and north near Webster you'll find **Forts Folle Avoine** (8500 Hwy. U, 715/866-8890, www.theforts.org, 10am-4pm Wed.-Sun. summer, $10), a historical park comprising mock-ups of the 1802 fur-trading posts of XY Company and the Northwest Fur Company, along with a reconstructed Ojibwa village. Costumed docents banter in period lingo—right down to Cajun chatter. On special occasions the dining room serves up synchronous fare, from wild rice pancakes to "wilderness stew."

Fish Lake Wildlife Area is three miles south of Grantsburg; the 15,000-acre refuge covers eight flowages and one natural lake, all in a glacial lake basin, and offers walking and driving tours.

Straight Lake State Park (Hwy. 35), three miles north of Luck and midway between Grantsburg and St. Croix Falls, has great birding as you tramp around sloughs; the Ice Age Trail will eventually come through here.

St. Croix Falls

Your arrival in St. Croix Falls, the largest community along the river, is marked by the **River Headquarters Visitor Center** (401 N. Hamilton St., 715/483-2274, mid-Apr. to late Oct.). Inside you'll find maps, exhibits, restrooms, and plenty of information. There are no actual falls since the construction of the dam, by the way.

The **Polk County Information Center** (Hwy. 35, 800/222-7655, www.saintcroixriver.com) south of town on Highway 35 is the terminus for the **Gandy Dancer Trail,** named for the "Gandy dancers," or railroad workers who used Gandy tools, a multiuse trail atop an abandoned rail line stretching 98 miles to Superior, where the Saunders State Trail cuts in, crossing over the St. Croix River and into Minnesota before cutting back into Wisconsin; one trail highlight is a 350-foot bridge crossing the river. The trail passes through nine cities and villages, and a trail pass ($5) is required.

In St. Croix Falls, the **Fawn Doe Rosa Park** (Hwy. 8, 715/483-3772, www.fawndoerosa.com, 10am-5pm Mon.-Fri., 10am-6pm Sat.-Sun. and holidays mid-May-Labor Day, 10am-6pm Sat.-Sun. May and Sept.-Oct., $9.50 adults) is a rehabilitation and education center that contains a wildlife display featuring "Big Louie," a 1,200-pound Kodiak bear, a petting area, and pony rides. It's two miles east on Highway 8.

★ Interstate State Park

Interstate State Park is south of St. Croix Falls. Wisconsin's first state park, established in 1900, Interstate has perhaps the most magnificent examples of glacial topography outside Devil's Lake or Door County. Glacial runoff was so ferocious that it sluiced superb river gorges right through the area's billion-year-old basaltic lava. The parks—one each in Minnesota and Wisconsin—were set up in part to prevent extraction of the traprock in the gorge walls for roadbuilding. In the mid-19th century the gorges here saw the world's largest logjam—150 million board feet jammed together for three miles upriver, which took 200 men six weeks to disentangle.

The Dalles of St. Croix, a 200-foot gorge of basalt palisades below the falls, draws rock

1: canoeing the St. Croix National Scenic Riverway **2:** Osceola Falls **3:** riverboats near Interstate State Park

1
2
3

Bear Safety

American black bear

Wisconsin's secondary mammal is the lumbering, doe-eyed *Ursus americanus*, the black bear. In the north, chances are very good you'll spot one. No one's ever been killed by a black bear in Wisconsin, but attacks do happen; some two dozen people have been killed by black bears in the United States.

Traditionally, Wisconsin's black bears have been found roughly north of a line from St. Croix Falls along the Mississippi east to Green Bay. Numbers have exploded from 5,000 to as many as 40,000, astonishing even the Department of Natural Resources. (They were fairly confident in an estimate of nearly 29,000 in 2018.) They're migrating south again and have been spotted just a county or two from Illinois.

RUN OR CLIMB—OR NEITHER?

An old joke: The black bear will come up the tree after you; the grizzly bear will just knock it down. Seriously, knowing what to do and what not to do is paramount in bear encounters. Inquire about recent bear activity. Look for bear activity on the trail: scat, diggings, torn-up logs (they love mealy ants and worms), turned-over logs. Carry a bandanna, shirt, or hat to drop or distract the bear. Leave your backpack on for added protection. Hope that you never come between a mama bear and her cubs.

Camp in open areas away from trails, thick brush, berry patches, or spawning streams. At the campsite, food is what can kill you. Store food and all odorous items by hanging them at least 10 feet above the ground, four feet from the top and side supports, at least 100 yards from your tent. Strain all dishwater and store it with the garbage; dump water and store garbage 100 yards from your tent. Do not sleep in the same clothes you cooked in. Do not take anything odorous—such as chocolate, toothpaste, and so on—into your tent, or don't be surprised if a bear sticks his head in and asks, "Got any chocolate?"

If you meet a bear, do not run; it may incite aggression. They can run 30 miles per hour. Chances are a black bear will be more afraid of you than you are of it. Talk to the animal in a calm, low voice while slowly backing away. If it attacks, try to scare it away by shouting, making noise, or throwing small stones. Always fight back with a black bear.

climbers. The **Potholes Trail** is a funky traipse along rounded chasms formed by glacial backwash. Along other trails, oddball hoodoo formations appear; the most photographed is probably **Old Man of the Dalles,** and you'll see why. Other formations are seen from the river south of here, including what's left of 60-foot-high Devil's Chair, which crumbled in 2004; The Cross, about 15 feet high; and Angle Rock, at the sharp bend in the river. A dozen trails total eight miles through the 1,400-acre park. The final link in Wisconsin's **National Ice Age Scientific Reserve,** the park has an interpretive center (715/597-3069, 8:30am-4:30pm daily Memorial Day-Labor Day, shorter hours Labor Day-Memorial Day) with exhibits, films, displays, and even a mural or two. The family campgrounds have great isolated camping and a nice sandy beach not far away. **Reservations** (888/947-2257, http://wisconsin.goingtocamp.com, reservation fee $8, nonresidents from $25, day-use $11) are a very good idea.

Lower St. Croix River

Beginning at the St. Croix Falls Dam, this stretch runs 52 miles to Prescott, where it flows into the Mississippi River. **Osceola,** five miles downstream from St. Croix Falls, was named for a Seminole chief. The name was originally Leroy, who wouldn't allow the name change until he was paid two sheep. Downtown, a flight of wooden stairs climbs to **Cascade Falls,** or you can just wander through the charming town and stop for a look at the **ArtBarn** (1040 Oak Ridge Dr., 715/294-2787), a renovated barn housing galleries, a theater, workshops, and more. There's a statue of **Chief Osceola** and a large **state fish hatchery** (2517 93rd Ave., 715/294-2525) in town. The chugging steam engines of the **Osceola and St. Croix Railway** (114 Depot Rd., 715/755-3570, www.transportationmuseum.org) depart from the old depot just off Highway 35 downtown. The old trains steam on fantastic 90-minute round-trips to Marine-on-St.-Croix, Minnesota (11am and 3pm Sat.-Sun. and some weekdays Memorial Day-late Oct., from $20 adults).

Two miles below Osceola, a sharp left cut in the river marks the dividing line between the Sioux and Ojibwa nations under 1837 treaties. The river continues for 10 more miles, passing a Minnesota state park and great old Marine-on-St.-Croix, Minnesota, before the mouth of the Apple River appears. Canoeists should take out here or try going up the Apple River. Tons of tubers will be winding their way downstream; so many people "tube the Apple" that *Life* magazine put the event in its pages in 1941, and the press has dutifully shown up ever since. You'll pass through the **St. Croix Islands Wildlife Refuge** before entering the Apple River, and if you can make it against the current, little **Somerset** waits upstream a handful of miles. Somerset was historically known for its moonshine operations, but today the town has river tubing and pea soup. Tubing can be done at **River's Edge** (River's Edge Dr., off Hwy. 64, 715/247-3305, www.riversedgeappleriver.com), and pea soup can be sampled at the annual Pea Soup Days town festival in June.

Beyond Stillwater, Minnesota, the river widens into what is known as **Lake St. Croix**—at times up to 7,400 feet across. The next sizable Wisconsin community, **Hudson,** so named for the area's close resemblance to the Hudson River Valley of New York, started as a trading outpost and steamship supply point. This eye-catching river town, Wisconsin's fastest-growing municipality, has a relatively famous **octagon house** (1004 3rd St., 715/386-2654, tours 11am-3pm Fri.-Sun. May-Oct., $10 adults) dating from 1855. This erstwhile home of a local judge is done in period style, and a Victorian garden surrounds the outside and leads to the carriage house.

To the east, **Willow River State Park,** 2,800 modest acres along the eponymous river, offers a few waterfalls. The area was once used as an entryway to burial grounds. Three dams form three separate flowages in the park. A daily permit is $13 for out-of-state license plates.

The **San Pedro Cafe** (426 2nd St., 715/386-4003, www.sanpedrocafe.com, 11am-11pm Mon.-Fri., 8am-10pm Sat., 8am-10pm Sun., $8-17) is amazing for its Caribbean flavors, but in truth, it's pan-American in breadth. The duck nachos are worth the trip.

Or go for gut-busting Teutonic food at **Winzer Stube** (516 2nd St., 715/381-5092, lunch and dinner daily, $12-26), in a gorgeous old opera house. The Saturday sauerbraten always makes me think of my grandmother.

Cozy B&Bs are found in every direction. Dominating the historic district architecture is the huge and wonderful ★ **Phipps Inn** (1005 3rd St., 715/386-0800, www.phippsinn.com, $199-239), not far from the octagon house. Built in 1884, this bright white 1884 Italianate has more fireplaces than most B&Bs have rooms. The proprietors are amazing.

River Falls

The St. Croix River doesn't run near River Falls, but Highway 35 does, and you'll likely pass through if you're traveling the St. Croix

Riverway or the Great River Road. Ten miles southeast of Hudson along Highway 35, the town of 10,000 got its start when the first settler, a Connecticut Yankee, wrote back to the East, "I think I have found the New England of the Northwest." That assessment is debatable, but the settlers came in droves, creating yet another sawmill town, with a few brick kilns and sauerkraut factories thrown in for good measure.

It's an attractive town, and the other river in these parts, the Kinnickinnic, is blue-ribbon trout-worthy (look for all the rods). The Kinnickinnic River pathway passes historical sites and developments on its way through the town. The stone buildings—the bricks baked right here—have original features, down to glass transom windows.

The most Wisconsin-esque local lodging is found not far from town at **Kinni Creek Lodge and Outfitters** (545 N. Main St., 715/425-7378, www.kinnicreek.com, $139), a lodge with a B&B complex along the Kinnickinnic River. There's log furniture in small but clean rooms, Class I trout fishing, and even fly-tying seminars—now that's Wisconsin.

Unique is **University of Wisconsin-River Falls Falcon Foods** (410 S. 3rd St., 715/425-3702, 1pm-5pm Mon.-Fri.), a student-operated dairy and meat facility with 65 flavors of wonderful Wisconsin ice cream, fresh cheese, and delicious smoked meats.

THROUGH THE FISHBOWL: U.S. 53 TO SUPERIOR

Along the route to Superior, U.S. 53 bypasses small communities, each on its own string of lakes dotted with rustic family and fishing resorts. Veer west off the highway to pass through the "Fishbowl," an area with one of the highest concentrations of glacial lakes in Wisconsin, full to the brim with panfish.

New Auburn

Nine miles east of New Auburn on Highway M, the **Chippewa Moraine Unit** is one of the nine reserve links of the trans-state scientific reserve, a severely underappreciated gem. Nearly six miles of nature trails wend through 4,000 acres, and a blue heron rookery is visible on an easy one-hour hike. The other trails present obvious glacial topography, and a few glacial pools are canoeable. The superb **interpretive center** (715/967-2800, 8:30am-4pm Tues.-Sun., free) is perched on an ice-walled lake plain; it won a Governor's Award for design. From the deck, you can get a view of South Shattuck Lake, a kettle or ice-block lake.

To the east, the reserve is connected to **Brunet Island State Park** by a 20-mile segment of the Ice Age Trail. It's a great riverine thumb of a park, set between the confluence of two rivers, south of the Holcombe Flowage. You can hike the trails without breaking much of a sweat. Chippewa County Forest lands line the area between the state park and the Ice Age Reserve Unit, offering dozens of miles of trails, most of which are unfortunately open to noisy off-road vehicles. The canoeing is lazy and fine.

Chetek

Once a community with one of the country's largest lumber companies, Chetek is much more tranquil today. Dozens of local resorts line 128 miles of lake shoreline on a six-lake chain. There's little else unless you count the **Hydro Lites,** a local water-ski team, as an attraction, or the **ice races** across the lake, held every Sunday after the ice freezes.

Inexplicably, one of the most luxurious inns in Wisconsin is found in Chetek: ★ **Canoe Bay** (115 S. 2nd St., 715/924-4594, www.canoebay.com, from $350). The architecture of the cottages was inspired by Frank Lloyd Wright. The rooms and cottages are sprinkled through a sublime, isolated setting. They have recently added tiny homes for rent ($400/night); the views from the glass sides are magnificent. The fixed-price dinner menu ($85 pp) is superb. It's pricey, but you're paying

1: Lake Superior **2:** scenery on the Wild Rivers Trail

1
2

for peace and quiet—mobile phones are not allowed. This could be the most splendid isolation you'll find in the state.

Rice Lake

Rice Lake is named for the ancient beds of *manomin* that once lined the shores of the lake. The **Bayfield Trail,** along Lakeshore Drive, is an old Native American pipestone and wild rice trade route with a burial mounds park.

Rice Lake is the terminus of one of Wisconsin's newest multiuse trails; the **Wild Rivers Trail** stretches 96 miles through three counties. North of Rice Lake on Highway SS is the western endpoint of the **Tuscobia State Trail,** another rails-to-trails project. This one is the longest in Wisconsin, stretching 76 miles east from U.S. 53 to Park Falls. Part of the route is an official Ice Age Trail segment. Golfers might like the **Tagalong Golf Course and Resort** (2855 29th Ave., 715/354-3458), modeled after St. Andrews in Scotland.

Northeast of Rice Lake, the land is peppered with more lakes and flowages, all dotted with family resorts. Among them, legendary ★ **Stout's Island Lodge** (U.S. 53 and Hwy. V, 715/354-3646, www.stoutsislandlodge.com, $179-289) sits on an island in Red Cedar Lake. Constructed laboriously by hand in 1900 out of logs and imported four-inch-thick floor planks and carved beams, the lodge was modeled after famous Adirondack resorts. Massive boathouses, servant and guest quarters, a pistol range, a bowling alley, and a central hall were constructed. It is 26 acres of prime seclusion—so secluded that you have to be ferried out to the island property. Wander its bird sanctuary and look for eagle nests. The resort's **restaurant** is highly regarded, offering the finest dining in the area using fresh local produce and game. Keep in mind that the isolation is the draw, so you need to entertain yourself at night.

Try the newer branch of Osseo's famed ★ **Norske Nook** (2900 Pioneer Ave., 715/597-3069, www.norsenook.com, $8-15). Even an approximation of that legendary place still outpaces most others. **Lehman's** (2911 S. Main St., 715/234-2428, 11am-10pm Tues.-Sun., $8-23) has been the local supper club of choice since 1934, with good steaks and wonderful Sunday chicken dinners. *Lots* is made from scratch here!

The Blue Hills

Blue Hills Country lies due east of Rice Lake and into Rusk County. These hills are far older than either the Rockies or the Appalachians and were at one time higher than the Rockies—at least until the glaciers lumbered in and shaved them down. The best place to see them is northwest of Weyerhauser, which will also lead you to the endpoint of the Blue Hills segment of the **Ice Age National Scenic Trail.** Tracing the edge of the Chippewa Lobe, from the last glacial period, it's also part of the Tuscobia State Trail. Along the way, the oddball topography of felsenmeer (literally, "sea of rocks") can be seen, formed by excessive frost, which created steep 100-foot rocky grades. More than 12 miles of trails lie in the Blue Hills, open for biking, hiking, and cross-country skiing.

Spooner

With 350 lakes and the wild and woolly Namekagon River within shouting distance, Spooner is yet another gateway to family North Woods resorts.

Since 1953, Spooner's annual zenith has come during the second week of July, when it hosts the **Heart of the North Rodeo** (www.spoonerrodeo.com). Wisconsin isn't exactly prime rodeo country, but this august PRCA-sanctioned event is legitimate, drawing top professional rodeo champions. It is among the nation's top 100 rodeos and one of the oldest in the Mississippi Valley.

At other times of year a couple of alternative attractions exist. Downtown Spooner's **Railroad Memories Museum** (715/635-3325, spoonerrailroadmuseum.org, 10am-5pm Tues.-Sun. summer, $4) is seven rooms of memorabilia. Spooner's **Canoe Heritage Museum** (312 N. Front St., 715/635-5002, www.wisconsincanoeheritagemuseum.org, 11am-4pm Wed.-Sat., 11am-3pm Sun. summer, 11am-3pm Sat.-Sun. Sept., $4 suggested donation) is like nothing else like in the state. You'll even see workers bending ribs to make classic canoes.

Spooner is also on the 96-mile-long **Wild Rivers Trail,** which stretches through three northern counties on an old railroad bed. Long Lake is one of the largest and most popular resort zones in the area.

Side Trips

Nearby Shell Lake has the wondrous **Museum of Woodcarving** (U.S. 63 N., 715/468-7100, 9am-6pm daily May-Nov., $7 adults). This is the largest collection of wood carvings in the world, all done by one person—a local teacher—over a span of 30 years; the masterpiece is the incredibly detailed *Last Supper,* which took four years to finish. Joseph Barta, the inspired artisan, also fancied himself something of a poet. The work is not kitsch but rather wondrous folk art. Call ahead just to be sure it is actually open.

Superior

The point where Wisconsin and Minnesota share the tip of Lake Superior is home to Wisconsin's blue-collar harbor town, Superior. Superior's ultimate goal was to become the Pittsburgh of the West, an old guidebook recalls, with hopes of steel mills rising adjacent to the railroad and docks. But Duluth's direct access to larger ore ranges to the west gave it a strategic advantage. Superior's shipyards, however, would develop the first whaleback, a massive ore carrier.

Superior offers not much more than mile after mile of drab eye-level aesthetics typical of an ore town—endless coal foothills, the forlorn natural graffiti of iron oxide, a clunky patchwork of rail lines, ore docks and cranes, and too much fencing. Worse, owing to its low elevation, Superior seems to catch all of the climatic issues that slide off the bluffs and across the harbor. While the sun shines on the crown of Duluth, Superior sulks in a shroud of fog and a perceived shortage of trees.

That said, the phlegmatic port town is one of the busiest deepwater harbors in the nation. Away from the industrial straightaways, Superior reveals not only grand stretches of classic Lake Superior history but, real truth be told, tons of trees—it has the second-largest municipal forest in the United States. Don't let detractors sully Superior's image—it was nice enough for President Calvin Coolidge to move the White House here in 1928, and Arnold Schwarzenegger graduated from the University of Wisconsin-Superior as a hotel restaurant major.

SIGHTS

★ Superior Harbor

One of the farthest-inland and deepest freshwater ports anywhere, and the largest harbor on the Great Lakes, shipping up to 75 million tons of ore and grain annually, Superior is the hardest-working port on the Great Lakes.

Unreal vistas come from the frenetically busy port and the 17 miles of massive docks, grain elevators, and flotillas of monstrous ships. The **Burlington Northern Ore Docks** are the largest in the world. Not all are available for public viewing, but the docks have occasionally allowed observation. Inquire at the visitors center for access, and check online (www.duluthshippingnews.com) for lists of ship arrivals and departures.

Imagine yourself a whaleback ore sailor, drifting by 1,000-foot-long lakers and salties blowing their horns, as your ship prepares to take on unfathomable amounts—60,000 tons—of cargo. Do it via the myriad tours (2 hours, daily late May-mid-Oct., from $20 adults) by the **Vista Fleet** (218/722-6218,

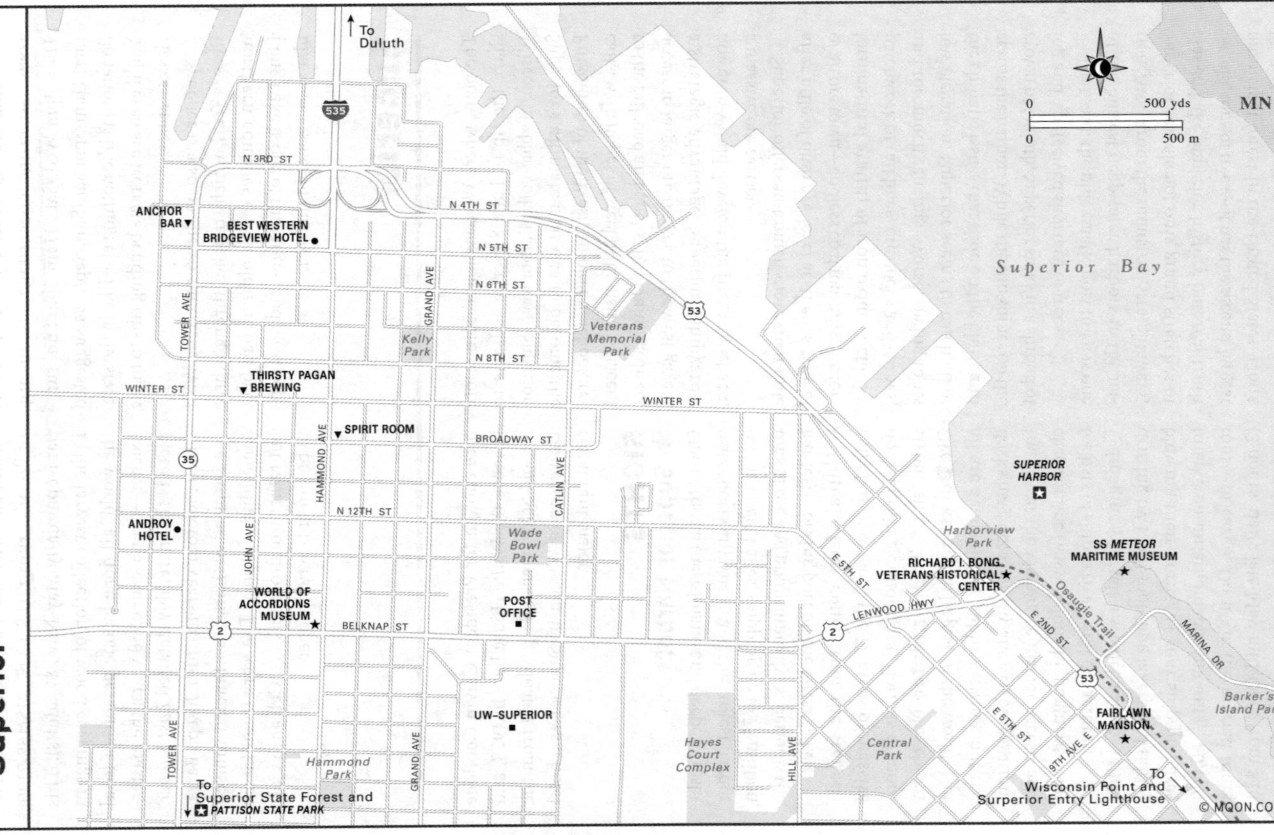

Superior
To Duluth
535
N 3RD ST
N 4TH ST
ANCHOR BAR
BEST WESTERN BRIDGEVIEW HOTEL
N 5TH ST
N 6TH ST
GRAND AVE
TOWER AVE
53
Veterans Memorial Park
Kelly Park
N 8TH ST
THIRSTY PAGAN BREWING
WINTER ST
WINTER ST
SPIRIT ROOM
BROADWAY ST
35
HAMMOND AVE
CATLIN AVE
N 12TH ST
ANDROY HOTEL
JOHN AVE
Wade Bowl Park
WORLD OF ACCORDIONS MUSEUM
POST OFFICE
BELKNAP ST
2
UW-SUPERIOR
TOWER AVE
Hammond Park
GRAND AVE
To Superior State Forest and PATTISON STATE PARK
Hayes Court Complex
HILL AVE
Superior Bay
0 500 yds
0 500 m
MN
SUPERIOR HARBOR
Harborview Park
SS METEOR MARITIME MUSEUM
E 5TH ST
RICHARD I. BONG VETERANS HISTORICAL CENTER
LENWOOD HWY
2
Osaugie Trail
E 2ND ST
MARINA DR
53
Barker's Island Park
E 5TH ST
FAIRLAWN MANSION
9TH AVE E
Central Park
To Wisconsin Point and Superior Entry Lighthouse
© MOON.COM

www.vistafleet.com), which leave from Duluth's DECC arena and take in the Duluth Aerial Lift Bridge, the Duluth Ship Canal, Port Terminal dock, all of Barker's Island, the Blatnick Bridge, and the world's largest coal docks, and then pass into the St. Louis River to watch taconite being loaded at the Mesabi Iron Ore docks.

Richard I. Bong Veterans Historical Center

From nearby Poplar, Wisconsin, Richard I. Bong became the United States' greatest World War II flying ace in his swift and deadly P-38 Lightning. After years of neglect, a P-38 is now on display at the smashing **Richard I. Bong Veterans Historical Center** (305 Harbor View Pkwy., 715/392-7151, www.bvhcenter.org, 9am-5pm Mon.-Sat., noon-5pm Sun. summer, 9am-5pm Tues.-Sat. fall-spring, $10 adults). The P-38 is the highlight, but the center does a great job of honoring all veterans.

Barker's Island and SS *Meteor*

From the Bong Veterans Historical Center, the few hundred yards to **Barker's Island,** tracing Superior Bay, are a ready-made traveler's leg stretch. The island's state-of-the-art **marina** is the largest on the Great Lakes and among the largest freshwater marinas in the world.

Moored permanently and gracefully on the west end of the island, its anchor rammed into the earth, is the crown jewel of the island. The **SS *Meteor* Maritime Museum** (715/394-5712, www.superiorpublicmuseums.org, 10:30am-4:30pm Mon.-Sat., 11:30am-4:30pm Sun. mid-May-Labor Day, limited hours Labor Day-Oct., $8 adults) is the only extant whaleback freighter on the Great Lakes of the type designed and built in Superior's early shipyards. The massive lakers that prowl the channels of the Twin Ports are direct descendants of the leviathan 1896 Superior shipyards product.

Need more exercise? From the island, Osaugie Trail continues for five miles along the harbor past some lovely natural areas, and those in good shape could walk all the way to Wisconsin Point.

Wisconsin Point

Just east of Superior, off U.S. 2 at Moccasin Mike Road, a narrow sandbar breakwater called **Wisconsin Point** acts as a protective lip to the large harbor. The formation is the largest seminatural breakwater in the world and offers a wild off-the-beaten-path look at the great harbor. It's a quiet, isolated place with innumerable forks, pull-offs, dead ends, and turnoffs. The highlight of the excursion is the **Superior Entry Lighthouse.** No tours are available, but you can get fairly close.

Fairlawn Mansion

Directly opposite Barker's Island stands what is undoubtedly one of the most opulent mansions constructed during Northwestern Wisconsin's heyday. Built in 1890, it was home to lumber and Vermilion Range iron ore magnate Martin Thayer Pattison, later Superior's second mayor. The 42-room landmark **Fairlawn Mansion** (906 E. 2nd St., 715/394-5712, www.superiorpublicmuseums.org, 9am-4pm Mon.-Sat., 11am-4pm Sun. Memorial Day-Labor Day, reduced hours Labor Day-Memorial Day, $10 adults), with a distinctive steeple worthy of any basilica, serves as the historical museum of Douglas County—and what an extraordinary cornucopia of regional history it holds.

World of Accordions Museum

Here's something you won't see anywhere but Wisconsin: the **World of Accordions Museum** (1401 Belknap St., 715/395-2787, www.museum.accordionworld.org, 3-6pm Sat., 10am-6pm Sun.-Mon., $10 adults). Inside the Harrington Arts Center, the museum is the country's only postsecondary-level certification and training program for repair and technician specialists of the accordion family. You'll find a great collection of accordions and concertinas (over 1,300!) and perhaps a delightful concert in the concert hall. This is Wisconsin, after all, where the polka is the official state dance. Call before going.

★ Pattison State Park

It wouldn't be a visit to Superior without a side trip to jewel of the state park system, **Pattison State Park.** It features the graceful, thundering 165-foot Big Manitou Falls, the highest cascade in Wisconsin—and one of the highest in the eastern United States.

Bisecting the park, the Black River actually looks like dark beer, at times even refracting reddish hues due to oxides in the area's soil. Flowing 22 miles toward Lake Superior from Black Lake along the Wisconsin-Minnesota border, it was dammed in the 1800s by the lumber companies to avoid damaging logs by tumbling them over the great falls. Though it doesn't affect the park's lake, the Department of Natural Resources dumps lampricidic chemicals above Big Manitou Falls regularly to kill sea lampreys, which infest the tributaries of Lake Superior.

Ten miles of trails lead in all directions. The must-do 0.5-mile **Big Falls Trail** is a minor traipse to get a good photo of the big waterfall. Trailing the west side of Interfalls Lake, formed by a Civilian Conservation Corps dam on the Black River, is **Little Falls Trail,** a longer trail at three miles round-trip, but to decidedly smaller 30-foot falls. The southern region has spur trails to the **backpack camping area.** Camping **reservations** (888/947-2257, http://wisconsin.goingtocamp.com, reservation fee $8, nonresidents from $27, day-use $11) are a good idea.

Of the 50-odd species of mammal in the park, the rare timber wolf and moose have been sighted, but very rarely.

Amnicon Falls State Park

Twelve miles southeast along well-traveled U.S. 2/53 is **Amnicon Falls State Park,** also on the Tri-County Recreational Trail, another prime piece of geology. The weak tea-colored Amnicon River splits around an island and flows over three impressive falls, each nearly 30 feet high; the river drops precipitously on its course through the park—180 feet in just over one mile. The river's "root beer" color is caused by tannic acid leached from decaying vegetation in the nearby bogs—great for reflecting sunlight in photos. The watershed contains the only native muskie population in far Northwestern Wisconsin, and the warm Amnicon River is a primary spawning run (the name means "place where fish spawn") for coho, chinook, rainbow trout, and smelt from Lake Superior.

Leading to the island is the park's famed bowstring covered bridge. A minor sweat-free loop trail begins here, and a **nature trail** leaves from the campground and heads toward a decaying sandstone quarry that dates from the late 1880s.

Camping **reservations** (888/947-2257, http://wisconsin.goingtocamp.com, reservation fee $8, nonresidents from $23, day-use $11) are advised.

RECREATION

Charter Fishing

You wouldn't expect anything less than a thriving business catching lake lunkers. Most guides depart Barker's Island for half- and full-day trips and return laden with walleye, lake trout, steelhead, German brown, and king and coho salmon. Many also offer guided river excursions for trout and salmon, particularly on the Brule River toward Ashland and the Root River. The St. Louis River estuary also boasts some of the best walleye takes in North America.

Superior Municipal Forest

The second-largest municipal forest in the United States, **Superior Municipal Forest** spreads across the western fringes of Superior. Easily accessible via Billings Drive, which parallels the St. Louis River, or Wyoming Avenue, off 28th Street, or even Tower Avenue heading south, the 4,500-acre spread includes 28

1: Big Falls in Pattison State Park **2:** SS *Meteor* at Barker's Island

1

2
METEOR
TOUR
The Worlds Last
WHALEBACK

kilometers of hiking, ski, and mountain bike trails.

Tri-County Corridor

The **Tri-County Corridor** is a multiuse recreational trail paralleling U.S. 2 east to Ashland. The best part of the trail is just east of Superior at Wisconsin Point. The trail is a major link to a handful of other trails in Douglas, Bayfield, and Ashland Counties.

FOOD

The **Anchor Bar** (413 Tower Ave., 715/394-9747, 11am-2am daily, $4-10) is a basic corner bar, but it has the best burgers and a huge variety—even a cashew burger.

The **Spirit Room** (1323 Broadway St., 715/817-4775, from 4pm Tues.-Sat., $6-18) defies belief—a cozy cocktail/wine bistro with tapas in Superior? Yes, and it's wonderful—especially the locally sourced smoked salmon, although the apple-jerked surf and turf is a close second.

Microbrews and fabulous deep-dish pizza are at **Thirsty Pagan Brewing** (1623 Broadway Ave., 715/394-2500, 3pm-11pm Mon.-Fri., 11am-11pm Sat.-Sun., $10-25), which most locals will point to as the place to go.

ACCOMMODATIONS

It isn't the Ritz, but the **Androy Hotel** (1213 Tower Ave., 715/394-7731, www.androyhotel.com, from $65) is a blast from the past, a 1925 cheap sleep option. Some adore its history; others shudder. It was purchased not long ago by a hospitality industry biggie, but so far, they've improved things a bit but not jacked the rates too much. Here's hoping it stays that way.

A good choice near the Bong Bridge and thus an easy drive to Duluth is the nice **Best Western Bridgeview Hotel** (415 Hammond Ave., 715/392-8174, $145). Rates are lower outside Friday- and Saturday-night stays.

Camping

The closest public camping is at **Amnicon Falls State Park** (888/947-2257, http://wisconsin.goingtocamp.com, reservation fee $8, nonresidents from $23, day-use $11), and the next closest is at **Pattison State Park** (888/947-2257, http://wisconsin.goingtocamp.com, reservation fee $8, nonresidents from $27, day-use $11).

INFORMATION

The **Superior and Douglas County Convention and Visitors Bureau** (715/392-2773 or 800/942-5313, www.superiorchamber.com) is right next to the Richard I. Bong Veterans Historical Center along U.S. 2.

GETTING THERE

Driving to Superior from Ashland (via U.S. 2, 65 miles) takes 75 minutes.

The Lake Superior Coast

Wisconsin is capped in the far north by the serpentine Lake Superior coastline. There are those who say the entire Wisconsin experience can be had in two counties: Bayfield and Ashland, whose perimeters enclose a national lakeshore (including an archipelago), two Native American communities, arguably the best concentration of waterfalls in the state, and a chunk of the massive Chequamegon National Forest.

WASHBURN

Washburn seems to get little respect from the tourism industry. The town of Washburn isn't even in Washburn County; it's in Bayfield County, and it's the county seat, though most visitors would never guess that. It's a good place to stay for budget-conscious travelers put off by Bayfield's prices or booked-out rooms.

Sights

The best thing to do is walk along the town's **lakeshore parkway walking trail,** stretching from Pump House Road in the northeast part of town to Thompson's West End Park. **Stagenorth** (123 W. Omaha, 715/373-1194, www.stagenorth.com) is a modern performing arts theater where you might get jazz or a play; even if nothing's on, stop by for a drink at the bar.

On Bayfield Street in the central part of town is an odd biological specimen—the **Lombardy Poplar.** This state-champion tree has defied odds by living—and growing—for 80 years, despite the fact that the species is generally short-lived. This one, an exotic European import, has produced a trunk 52 inches in diameter.

Food and Accommodations

A couple of bistros exist in Washburn, but simpler and better fare are the wood-fired pizzas at **DaLou's** (310 W. Bayfield St., 713/373-1125, dinner daily summer, pizzas from $10).

The cheapest lodgings and a decent deal are the aging but clean rooms, some with kitchenettes, at my road home, the **North Coast Inn and Chalets** (26 W. Hwy. 13, 715/373-5512, $79), with very friendly owners. Some rooms are more recently refurbished.

There are a couple of great U.S. Forest Service campgrounds north and south of town (no reservable sites), and the little-known **Big Rock County Campground** on the Sioux River; to get here, go three miles northwest of town on Highway C and then right on Big Rock Road.

Getting There

To Washburn from Ashland (west and north via U.S. 2 and Highway 13, 10 miles) takes 14 minutes; from here it's 13 miles and 15 minutes to Bayfield.

NORTHERN GREAT LAKES VISITOR CENTER

The grand **Northern Great Lakes Visitor Center** (U.S. 2 and Hwy. 13, 715/685-9983, www.nglvc.org, 9am-5pm daily), west of Ashland, is without question the best educational experience in Northwestern Wisconsin, and it has even better views of the big lake, and best of all, it's free. An impressive piece of architecture and construction, it's a multilevel educational center focusing on the region's ecosystem and history. A multimedia introduction produced by Bayfield's Big Top Chautauqua musically chronicles the area's cultural history. Other exhibits also examine cultural history and environmental issues. The center runs admirable educational programs, including exciting on-the-water paddle programs.

ASHLAND

Ashland became a transportation point for millions of tons of ore extracted from the Penokee-Gogebic Range of Hurley and Michigan's Upper Peninsula. Pierre-Esprit Radisson entered Chequamegon Bay as far back as 1659. The Jesuit Claude-Jean Allouez built the first mission to the Ojibwa people, abandoned in 1669. The propitious bay location engendered transport, and by the 1890s Ashland was shipping twice the tonnage of Milwaukee, Duluth, and Superior combined.

Touted as the "Garland City of the Inland Seas," it's a sedate place chock-full of old rail lines, stained wood docks, aging trestles, some superb lakeshore vistas—and great fishing.

Sights and Recreation

Northland College (715/682-1233, www.northland.edu) along Ellis Avenue (Hwy. 13) south of downtown is an inspiration for its eco-minded coursework. Locals refer to the school's students as tree huggers, a term of endearment. The **Sigurd Olson Environmental Institute** (8am-4pm Mon.-Fri. when school is in session), a think tank and educational center for environmental studies, is here, named for the pioneering ecologist who was born and raised in the Ashland area. The institute has great nature photography and other exhibits.

Along U.S. 2 in Ashland, off Bay View Park,

is **Tern Island,** producing two-thirds of the common terns in the Lake Superior region.

Ashland's **parks** spread along the lip of the lake. Most contain absolutely frigid beaches and great picnicking. Maslowski Beach on the west side offers the best views, arguably the best stretches of sand, and a bubbling artesian spring. West of town off Turner Road is Prentice Park, connecting with Superior via the **Tri-County Recreation Trail,** a 60-mile biking, hiking, and snowmobile trail that runs through Fish Creek Slough. There are more artesian wells here; the Ashland Water Utility oversees one of the largest artesian wells in North America.

Ashland and Iron Counties boast one of the highest concentrations of **waterfalls** in the state. Almost two dozen are within a quick drive of Ashland; Potato River Falls is especially worth seeing.

Food

The casual brewpub **LC Wilmarth Deepwater Grille and Southshore Brewery** (808 W. Main St., 715/682-4200, 11am-10pm daily, $6-18) is in a complex with pub grub and finer dining, both of which fully support local fisheries and produce. Peruse the menu with one of six home brews and then sample the food: walleye in particular or one of the creative takes, including Thai salmon salad although many have opined the short ribs are the real star.

The best organic java and healthy food, crafted with thought behind it, is at the ★ **Black Cat** (211 Chapple Ave., 715/682-3680, 6:30am-9pm Mon.-Fri., 8am-7pm Sat., 8am-5pm Sun.) coffeehouse. It's a wonderful place to unwind from a long drive.

Accommodations

Along U.S. 2 and you'll drive by half a dozen very clean and very good motels with rates around $70 in high season. The best is **Crest Motel** (115 Sanborn Ave., 715/682-6603, $65). For a few dollars more, the **Rock River Inn & Bait Shop** (1200 Lake Shore Dr., 715/682-3232, www.riverrockinn.net, from $89) is absolutely wonderful and has some of the nicest staff in the state. Do buy some of the fresh smoked fish!

The former grande dame **Hotel Chequamegon** (101 U.S. 2 W., 715/682-9095, www.hotelc.com, $220) was rebuilt after a 1950s fire, but you'd swear this remake is the original. You'll find rooms of various incarnations, all appointed in period detail.

Getting There

Ashland has a lot of roads running through it, so you may find yourself here. From Hurley to the east (via U.S. 2, 38 miles) it takes 43 minutes. From Mellen, the nearest gateway to the Chequamegon National Forest, to the southeast (via Highway 13, 24 miles) it takes 28 minutes. From the west Superior (via U.S. 2, 65 miles) it takes 75 minutes.

BAD RIVER INDIAN RESERVATION

The Mauvaise ("Bad") River was aptly named by the French, disgusted at its treacherous navigation. The Treaty of 1854 allowed the Loon Clan of Lake Superior Ojibwa to settle here along the river, which they renamed Mushkeezeebi, or Marsh River, along with a small contingent on Madeline Island. The 1,800 descendants of the clan live on the largest reservation (123,000 acres) in Wisconsin. It stretches for 17 miles along Lake Superior and more than 100 miles inland, including the superb Kakagon Sloughs, a 7,000-acre wetland of virginal wild rice beds, noted as a National Natural Landmark for its *manomin* (wild rice) and its waterfowl population. Some have called it "Wisconsin's Everglades."

★ BAYFIELD

This gateway village, right out of a Currier and Ives print, has sandstone bluffs offering a commanding view of the Apostle Islands. The town is gatekeeper to superlative Bayfield County, a mix of island-dotted seascapes,

1: Madeline Island Ferry **2:** Old Rittenhouse Inn **3:** Bayfield from the water

ISLAND QUEEN
ISLAND QUEEN
1
Old Rittenhouse Inn
LANDMARK
FINE DINING
WINE & SPIRITS
2
3
MADELINE ISLAND
FERRY

Great Lakes thunderheads, and pastoral dairy land. It is quite likely the most aesthetically realized village in the state; the *Chicago Tribune* has dubbed it the "Best Little Town in the Midwest." Most of the hillside mansions, virtually all on the National Register of Historic Places, were built from the earthtone and pastel brownstone underlying the Apostle Islands archipelago, and every hairpin turn on Highway 13 reveals a spectacular lake panorama.

Sights

The "Carnegie Hall of Tent Shows" is a wondrous way to relax after a day of island exploring. The **Lake Superior Big Top Chautauqua** (Ski Hill Rd. at base of Mt. Ashwabay Ski Hill, 715/373-5552 or 888/244-8368, www.bigtop.org) is equal parts vaudeville, minstrel and thespian troupe, and folkways preservation. It all takes place under Big Blue, a 60- by 150-foot tent; so revered was the original that when replaced, they sold hats made out of it. A night's slate of entertainment might feature national folk, country, or bluegrass artists; guest lectures; and dramas recounting Chequamegon Bay history. Plenty of food and drink is available on-site. Performances start at around $25 adults for reserved seats; some big-name acts command *much* higher prices.

Downtown Bayfield also has a couple of tiny museums. Better of the two is the **Bayfield Maritime Museum** (1st St. between U.S. Coast Guard Station and City Hall, 715/779-9919, www.bayfieldmaritimemuseum.com, 10am-4pm Sun.-Thurs., till 7pm Fri.-Sat., Memorial Day-Oct. 5, free) with displays on the ecosystem and species of Lake Superior, knot-tying, Native American fishing, and local history. You can also ogle an original Chequamegon Bay tug and parts from other local boats.

Recreation

Bayfield is home to the country's largest fleet of bareboat charter operations. There is also no shortage of local fishing charters. Other options include biking up and around the coastal interior behind Bayfield. A magnificent day trip on a bike wanders the uplands overlooking the town—take Washington, Rittenhouse, or Manypenny Avenues. All of these roads afford grand views and, one way or the other, lead to the golf course and Highway J; from here, Betzhold Road to the north and Highway 13 take in many of Bayfield's orchards and 500-foot lake views, providing a cool breeze the whole way.

The easiest trail is the gorgeous **Iron Bridge Trail,** winding up into the hills from the north end of Broad Street, offering a superlative view from a wooden bridge and landscaped terraces.

The coolest thing to do in Bayfield in winter is to go on a dogsled tour, either as a day trip or overnight. Check out **Wolfsong** (100 Rittenhouse Ave., http://wolfsongadventures.com, 2-hour ride from $249).

You can go wreck-diving near the islands. There are 25 established hulls littering the lake bottom; several around Sand, Long, and Stockton Islands are popular. The ***Coffinberry*** is still visible on the surface and is a popular snorkeling destination. All divers must register with the National Park Service headquarters.

Camping is a hodgepodge of public and private venues and is difficult to get on weekends, so arrive early. At Little Sand Bay of

An American First

In 2012 the Red Cliff Band of the Lake Superior Chippewa opened to the public the **Frog Bay Tribal National Park** along the Bayfield Peninsula coastline, about 15 miles north of Bayfield, with a view of several of the Apostle Islands. This is the first Native American national park in the United States. Conservancy groups, the government, and the Red Cliff Band all worked together to open this park. Small at 90 acres, it's got a lovely beach, awesome views, and a sense of achievement.

the mainland unit of the Apostle Islands National Lakeshore is a campground, and between Washburn and the Red Cliff Indian Reservation are a dozen campgrounds.

Entertainment and Events

With so much outdoor recreation, come nightfall there's not a lot to do in terms of nightclubs. The coolest event is late February's **Apostle Islands Sled Dog Race.** May brings **Bayfield in Bloom,** a monthlong celebration of the coming of blooms in natural areas and orchards. From late August through September after Labor Day is the **Apostle Islands Lighthouse Celebration** (www.lighthousecelebration.com), showcasing the area's lighthouses. The biggest local event is October's **Apple Fest,** a blowout feting apples, a fruit integral in all its forms to the local economy. It has been named a top 10 autumn festival in the United States by the Society of American Travel Writers.

Food

While in Bayfield, indulge in at least one of the area's two culinary trademarks—whitefish livers and fish boils. Eating whitefish livers started as a tradition a century ago when boats were landing millions of pounds of whitefish. The livers are generally sautéed with onions and sometimes green peppers, though individual styles vary.

The **Copper Trout** (250 Rittenhouse Ave., 715/779-0293, dinner Thurs.-Sat., $7-15) has the heart of a pizza and pasta pub, but don't underestimate it. It has locally sourced—even wild foraged—ingredients and is a strong supporter of local fisheries. Its namesake—Wild Trout Madeline—is one of the best dishes I've had.

Farm-to-table slow food can be found at the cozy and charming **Fat Radish** (200 Rittenhouse Ave., 715/779-9700, breakfast/lunch Sun.-Tues., breakfast/lunch/dinner Wed.-Sat., from $8) a major plus for foodies. The food here is eclectic and inspired. Duck confit hash and ramen might see bizarre, but it's all very well done.

An enthralling epicurean experience, the five-course all-night meals from the ★ **Old Rittenhouse Inn** (Rittenhouse Ave. and 4th St., 715/779-5111 or 800/779-2129, www.rittenhouseinn.com, 7am-10am and 5pm-9pm daily, $45) have been called the most memorable in the state. The fare spans the culinary spectrum but gives a hearty nod to creative Midwestern dishes, made with as many local ingredients as possible. The remarkably ambitious menu changes constantly.

Accommodations

Bayfield isn't cheap after April. A multiple-night minimum stay is often required in peak periods, particularly on weekends.

The **Seagull Bay Motel** (325 S. 7th St., 715/779-5558, www.seagullbay.com, from $100) is a clean and comfy place with conscientious owners; it has rates closest to $100 in these parts. Most rooms have lovely views, and a trail leads to town. Some units have kitchenettes.

Kudos to the **Pinehurst Inn** (83645 Hwy. 13, 715/779-3676, www.pinehurstinn.com, from $160) for garnering Wisconsin's highest green travel score. Don't come just for the solar panels; the refreshing updates to its 19th-century structure and a newer building make it worth the price.

Throw a rock in Bayfield and you'll hit an 1850s brownstone refurbished into a creature-comforts-outfitted B&B. The quintessential Bayfield experience is at the ★ **Old Rittenhouse Inn** (Rittenhouse Ave. and 4th St., 715/779-5111 or 800/779-2129, www.rittenhouseinn.com, from $200), an enormous old place with 20 meticulously restored rooms spread through three Victorians, all with working fireplaces. The dining here is internationally regarded.

If retro isn't your cup of tea, how about retro-upscale at the ★ **Bayfield Inn** (20 Rittenhouse Ave., 715/779-3363, www.bayfieldinn.com, from $200)? The sustainability of the design is finely detailed, down to the fixtures.

Information

The **Bayfield Chamber of Commerce** (Manypenny Ave. and Broad St., 715/779-3335 or 800/447-4094, www.bayfield.org) has lengthy lists for accommodations and assorted tours.

Getting There

Driving to Bayfield from Ashland (via Hwy. 13, 23 miles) takes 32 minutes. For the drive to Bayfield from Superior (81 miles), take U.S. 2 and Highway 13, a lovely two-hour drive.

MADELINE ISLAND

Permanently settled around 1490 by the Ojibwa people as a religious center, Madeline Island later became the most crucial island link in New France, shipping a wealth of beaver pelts. The name Moningwunakauning, "Home of the Golden Shafted Woodpecker," was replaced in 1830 when a British trader married the daughter of a local chieftain and the church renamed her Madeline.

The permanent population on Madeline Island precluded its inclusion in the National Lakeshore. Year-round numbers hover around 180, but it can swell 15-fold in summer, when residents—mostly wealthy people from Minneapolis—flock to their seasonal homes. Though it is one of the fastest-growing tourist destinations in Northwestern Wisconsin, it is not like Cape Cod or the Maine coastline, rather a humble island getaway—15 minutes from the mainland, but thoroughly rustic and with a great state park.

La Pointe

La Pointe is not much more than an assemblage of basic restaurants, a museum, taverns, accommodations, and the few island services. The **Historical Museum** (226 Colonel Woods Ave., 715/747-2415, 10am-5pm daily Memorial Day-early Oct., shorter hours in other seasons, $10 adults) holdings include actual black robes worn by Jesuits and fur baron John Jacob Astor's accounting papers.

Big Bay State Park

Two millennia ago, the land this park occupies was a shallow bay, now the canoe-worthy Big Bay Lagoon, another of the archipelago's remarkable ecosystems. The best trail is the **Bay View Trail,** which traces the eastern promontory of the park, bypassing spectacular wave-hewn sandstone formations, sea caves, and plenty of crashing Lake Superior waves. The picnic area at the apex, where the trail hooks up with the **Point Trail,** might be the most popular in Wisconsin. The beach is the most popular spot in the park, 1.5 miles of isolation.

Most **campsites** (888/947-2257, http://wisconsin.goingtocamp.com, reservation fee $8, nonresidents from $25, day-use $11) are nicely isolated from one another. Some sites are pack-in. The Madeline Island Ferry dock posts site availability notices—get there very early from July to early September. Reservations are definitely advisable and necessary for weekends.

Other Sights

Heading east out of town along the main road, turn north on Old Fort Road to Madeline Island's **Indian Burial Ground,** which is returning to its natural state. Farther east, **Memorial Park** features a warming pond and is the burial place of O-Shaka, son of legendary Chief Buffalo, who preserved Native American rights to lands on Lake Superior and Madeline Island in 1854 treaties with the federal government. Interred in the cemetery are many of the original 20,000 Ojibwa people who populated the island when the French arrived.

Recreation

Mopeds and mountain bikes are the most popular way to take in the island. To the right of the ferry landing in the large blue building are mopeds for rent. Five minutes farther along, you'll find kayaks for rent. Vans for two-hour **island tours** generally greet the Madeline Island Ferry.

The Robert Trent Jones-designed course of the **Madeline Island Golf Course** (498 Old

Fort Rd., La Pointe, 715/747-3212) is a gem, known for lake vistas and double greens; reservations are a necessity in summer.

Besides Big Bay State Park, the island has **Big Bay Town Park,** seven miles out of La Pointe and north of the state park. Campsites ($15) are available, but none are reservable.

Food

Expect simple and straightforward fare on the island. A casually comfy bistro, **Cafe Seiche** (Main St. and Middle Rd., 715/747-2033, 5pm-9pm Thurs.-Sat., 11am-4pm Sun., from $12), comes close to something special, with fresh local ingredients, a daring menu—pepito-crusted whitefish, ginger-poached tofu—and a charming, fresh atmosphere.

Out of left field but wholly appropriate for the island's laid-back ethos is ★ **Tom's Burned Down Cafe** (715/747-6100), risen from the smoldering ruins of an erstwhile island café. Walk straight from the ferry to reach this part open-air pub, part art gallery, part retreat from the real world; you never know what's available here, but don't miss it. They're open "11am-ish until whenever unless the weather sucks"—which gives you a good idea of the casual vibes here.

Accommodations

Room rates will be above $100, especially in summer. Consider a splurge for the luxury accommodations at **The Inn on Madeline Island** (715/747-6315 or 800/822-6315, www.madisland.com, $250-500). The inn is actually an island-wide assemblage of lakefront properties of all sorts: cabins in the woods, golf course cottages, and some apartments and condos downtown. Lingering in a bay-view cottage, this is one place in Wisconsin where you can say you've escaped.

Information

The **Madeline Island Chamber of Commerce** (715/747-2801 or 888/475-3386, www.madelineisland.com) operates only Memorial Day weekend to Labor Day. The ferry dock kiosk in Bayfield has information if you show up without reservations.

Getting There

In late January and usually until sometime in April, Highway 13 becomes the state's only "ice highway," an established state road plowed and maintained across the ice. During the holidays, Christmas trees mark the borders. When ice is forming or breaking up and it's too thin for vehicles, flat-bottomed air boats whiz across the short straits; what an amazing ride that is.

The **Madeline Island Ferry** (715/747-2051, www.madferry.com, round-trip $27 autos, $15 passengers) departs from Bayfield and is a landmark of the region. Ferries run from Bayfield to the island every 30 minutes 7:30am-10pm daily mid-June-Labor Day, with a 6:30am trip weekdays and an 11pm trip Thursday through Saturday. Fewer trips run in the off-season. There are no reservations.

★ HIGHWAY 13 FROM BAYFIELD TO SUPERIOR

Here's where the windshield vistas become worthy of Ansel Adams—the modest Bayfield County mosaic of orchards, multihued patches of crops, enormous rolls of hay, dilapidated one-eyed shotgun shacks weathering by the side of the road, even an abandoned truck rusting in the cattails. **Highway 13** from Bayfield hugs the coastline, coming out almost as far west as Superior—about 80 miles and totally worth the effort. These parts were settled predominantly by Finnish and other Scandinavian immigrants pushing west out of Michigan's Upper Peninsula around the middle of the 19th century. They would eventually spread through the ore docks and shipyards of Superior and into the mines of the Mesabi and Vermilion Iron Ranges in Minnesota. A number of their homesteads can still be seen poking through the weeds along the route.

West of Red Cliff and the mainland unit of the Apostle Islands National Lakeshore, lots of tiny side roads poke their way north from Highway 13, leading to assorted points and promontories. Some end at established picnic areas near beaches, others offer miles of gravel just to reach an overrated boat landing.

Red Cliff Reservation

Less than 10,000 acres in size, the **Red Cliff Reservation** (www.redcliff-nsn.gov) of the Lake Superior Chippewa people hugs the shoreline, starting three miles north of Bayfield, and wraps around the point of the peninsula, a magical stretch of lakefront property. The reservation was established by the legendary Ojibwa chief Buffalo, who stoically and respectfully resisted U.S. federal attempts to appropriate Ojibwa lands thought to contain a wealth of copper ore. At one point, this Ojibwa community and the band at Bad River belonged to the La Pointe Band, which separated in the 1840s to the present locations. The reservation has a casino as well as a **marina** and adjacent **campground** ($25-35) with resplendent views of Basswood and Madeline Islands. Another campground, privately owned but on reservation land, is at uncrowded Point Detour. The reservation's **powwow** takes place the first weekend in July.

Cornucopia

The Depression-era Works Progress Administration state guidebook described **Cornucopia** thus: "stiff gray fishing nets hang drying on big reels; weathered shacks crowd to the shore line with its old docks; thousands of gulls flash white against the sky." The northernmost community in Wisconsin, edging out Red Cliff by a scant few feet, Cornucopia features hands-down the best sunsets on Lake Superior—this is the place in Wisconsin everyone thinks is their own secret getaway. There is a marina and a public harbor. Cornucopia is also becoming something of an artists' colony. The best sight not relating to the lake is the onion dome of a Greek Orthodox church; you can also snoop around the small but fun **museum.** Get your postcards stamped here, at the northernmost post office in the state.

Stay atop Wisconsin at the gorgeous and cozy **Fo'c'sle Inn** (Hwy. 13, 715/742-3337, www.siskiwitbay.com, rooms $125) right next to the harbor on a promontory with lovely views. The owners are top-notch.

Herbster

Unincorporated Herbster, at the mouth of the Cranberry River, features a small **recreation area** right on the lake. Exit Herbster via Bark Point Road, which leads to a tall promontory overlooking Bark Bay and far into the lake. This, the **Bark Bay Slough,** is a unique conservation area, home to quite a few localized plant and animal species. There is also gorgeous scenery to the west of town. In Herbster proper, the beachfront park offers outstanding **camping** (first-come, first-served), a fishing dock, and a boat launch.

Port Wing

More cabins, camping, and boat moorings can be found at Port Wing to the west. This long-established farming town was heavily settled by Finnish immigrants expanding westward from their original bases in Michigan. The town boasts the state's first consolidated school district, a radical idea for 1903, and the first school bus, both of which are displayed in a town park as mock-ups. Today Port Wing mostly offers sportfishing charters, a couple of B&Bs and bars, and some stores and gas stations. West of Port Wing, a marked detour leads to **Brule Point,** down a pocked gravel road scratched out of rough lakeside wetland. There are lots of pull-offs along the way, and a picnic area and a great beach at the end. The place is isolated and usually less than populated, even in summer high season.

A few miles west of Port Wing, at the junction with Falls Road, the Iron River crosses Highway 13. A left turn on Falls Road leads to **Orienta Falls** of the Orienta Flowage.

Brule River State Forest

Highway 13 turns sharply south and trims

the edge of the relatively unknown 50,000-acre **Brule River State Forest,** punctuated by lowland spruce, paralleling the deep Brule River channel from its headwaters near the St. Croix Flowage into Lake Superior. It may not be unknown for long: In 2012 the Department of Natural Resources purchased more than 100 square miles of forest nearby, the largest conservation bid in state history.

The river was the most vital link in the chain of waterways between Lake Superior and the Lower Mississippi River, requiring only a short portage from the Brule to the St. Croix River. Daniel Greysolon, Sieur du Lhut, made the river known in his 1680 writings. More recently, five U.S. presidents have fished its blue-ribbon trout waters (thus the nickname "River of Presidents"). So enamored of the Brule was Calvin Coolidge that in 1928 he essentially relocated the already relocated White House to a nearby lodge.

Today canoeists and trout aficionados make up the bulk of casual users. The area between U.S. 2 and Stone's Bridge is the most popular, with proud stands of trees and lots of tranquility. Not surprisingly, this is where the presidents summered. Contact the **ranger station** (715/372-8539) in Brule, south of the U.S. 2 and Highway 27 junction, for maps and camping information.

Hikers will find one superb nature trail at the Bois Brule Campground, south of U.S. 2, and extended snowmobile and ski trails to trek almost the entire length of the river; one 26-mile trail heads to St. Croix Lake. Old logging trails branch out on myriad routes throughout Douglas County.

To Superior

There's nothing dramatic along the rest of the route until the road meets the banks of the Amnicon River. A couple of miles before the intersection with U.S. 2, you'll find a pull-off offering a great view of a traditional **Finnish windmill.** Built in 1904 and used to grind wheat, it's not in operation but hasn't been allowed to decay. The homesteader's refurbished shack stands nearby.

Apostle Islands National Lakeshore

If the Bayfield Peninsula in the north is Wisconsin's crown, then the jewels of that crown are the nearly two dozen pastel-hued sandstone islands of one of the nation's few national lakeshores. This coastal treasure, misnamed by overzealous or perhaps arithmetically overwhelmed French Jesuits, is to many the most precious region in Wisconsin. The inverse of the fierce nor'easters tearing across the lake, during the periods when Lake Superior appears placidly equable, the surface is like an extraordinary glistening mirror.

Natural History

As the last glacier retreated 10 millennia ago, the flat-topped waxy-looking islands of billion-year-old Precambrian bedrock were scraped into horizontal symmetry by ice floes, then molded further by wind and wave action.

Expect capricious weather patterns. The islands do take the brunt of legendary Superior storms, but at the same time the lake ameliorates heat. Hands-down the best summertime sleeping climate for campers anywhere in Wisconsin is found in the Apostle Islands.

Average high temperatures in summer rarely top 80°F, with nighttime lows in the 50s. Winter temperatures can plunge into the negative teens and worse with windchill, with up to 120 inches of snow. Spring and fall are variable. One day will offer halcyon warmth and azure skies, followed by pelting slush the next day with winds in excess of 30 knots and six-foot swells on the lake.

Despite how ravaged the islands were by humans for more than a century, some of the most pristine stands of old-growth northern mesic and boreal forest and more than a few

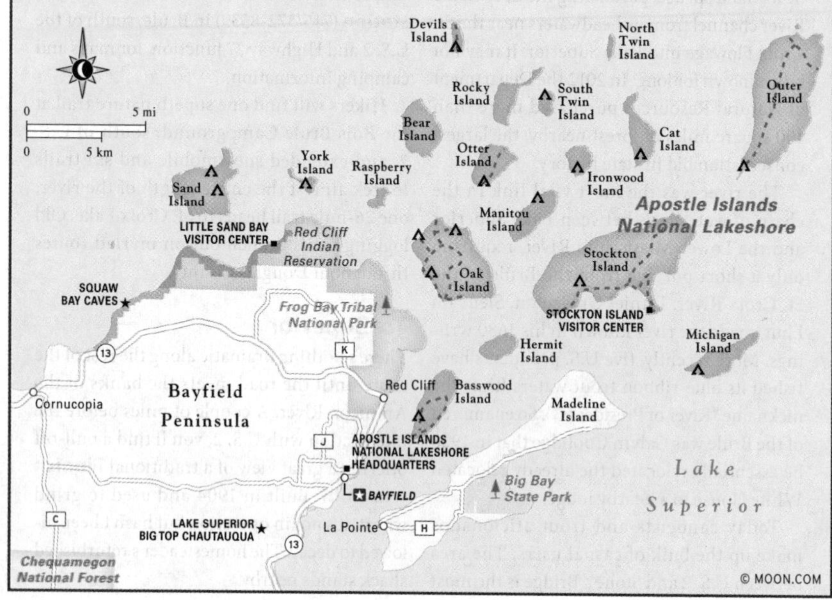

threatened or endangered plant species thrive in the unique island microclimate. In all, 16 Wisconsin State Natural Areas, officially off-limits, are interspersed through the islands. They contain myriad northern forests, bogs, lake dunes, and lagoons.

Over 100 species of bird inhabit the islands; 98 percent of Wisconsin's herring gull and tern population lives on the Lake Superior coast in and around these islands. Great blue herons and two species of cormorants are protected in two areas, and even pelicans have been introduced. Deer are managing a slow comeback; wolves are expected to follow. A delight on Stockton, Sand, and a few other islands are beaver colonies—a mammal so instrumental to the settlement and exploration of the region.

Black bears are found on a handful of the islands, including Stockton, which has one of the highest concentrations in the United States. Most of the islands have abundant blueberries, so the bears swim the straits in search of food.

Human History

Of numerous indigenous inhabitants, it was indisputably the Ojibwa people whose hegemony shaped the human history of the Apostles. Before the Jesuits named the islets, Ojibwa myths recounted their creation—a nature-creator hurled enormous sticks or stones at a fleeing animal, splashing into the glacial lakes and creating the archipelago.

Enter the French. Initially, the Quebec governor wanted to woo the indigenous people with iron goods, while the Black Robes wanted to convert them to Roman Catholicism.

However, once the wealth of beavers became known and fashionable Parisians created strong demand for fur adornments, the sway fell to busy tree-cutters. The Apostles

1: boat tour of the Apostle Islands **2:** lighthouse on Raspberry Island **3:** rock formation on Basswood Island **4:** kayaks on Basswood Island

1
ISLAND PRINCESS
2
3
4
perception

would eventually become the westernmost shipping point for beaver pelts along the fabled Voyageur's Highway on the northern Lake Superior coast.

After the beaver were wiped out, the economic linchpin to Lake Superior's south shore was commercial fishing. Despite the dearth of overland transportation, the Apostles were a mainstay in the U.S. fishing (whitefish and herring, especially) industry. An annual fishing season would net almost eight million pounds of fish. The last fishing camps withered away on the islands in the 1950s, when invasion of the Great Lakes by the parasitic sea lamprey reduced fish populations. As with Lake Michigan, sportfishing has become popular because the lake is stocked.

Interestingly, stone rejuvenated the area when fishing declined. Sandstone from the Apostles helped rebuild Chicago after the Great Fire; the ruddy brownstone can be found in virtually every Midwestern city. A visit to the Apostle Island Headquarters in Bayfield offers an up close look at the lustrous stone, dubbed second-best in the United States by architecture and construction firms.

Mention Lake Superior and associative synesthesia sets in: foghorns, hurricane-force gales, flickering ship lights, and rocks littering shoals. The Apostle Islands have the highest concentration of lighthouses in the United States, due in large part to the necessities of fish delivery to eastern and southern population centers and the treacherous nature of the lake. Twenty-five documented wrecks litter the lake bottom.

The first lighthouse went up in 1857 on Michigan Island; by 1891, six lights had been constructed on the islands, which made them the primary shipping landmark across Lake Superior. Today the Apostles are still a vital link in the North American shipping chain.

Timber is always in the conversation in the North Woods. Seemingly incongruous but bitterly ironic is the fact that the Apostle Islands today have some of Wisconsin's most breathtaking old-growth northern forest. This despite the fact that by the 1930s most islands had been depredated by the lumber saw. In 1930, when the National Park Service made research inquiries into national park status at Herbert Hoover's behest, it was told they were unrecoverable.

As in many other places, tourists played a role in "saving" the islands. Great Lakes mariners and many well-to-do shipping bigwigs became enamored of the place and its salubrious environment and began making pilgrimages here as early as the 1850s.

As far back as 1891, Northwestern Wisconsin communities had pushed for the establishment of the islands as a national park. Calvin Coolidge, who relocated the White House to Superior in the late 1920s, wholly supported the idea. In the 1960s, U.S. Senator and former Wisconsin governor Gaylord Nelson, founder of Earth Day, brought John F. Kennedy to the Apostles to trumpet federal recognition—one of the earliest environmental speeches by a U.S. politician. Richard Nixon eventually signed laws protecting the islands in 1970.

Eighty percent of the lakeshore became federally protected wilderness in April 2004. In homage to the prescient and passionate fighter for the land, it was named the Gaylord Nelson Wilderness.

★ THE APOSTLE ISLANDS

Many people land in Bayfield and head up the coast for the obligatory lakeshore experience, but how many actually see the islands? Make the effort to get on the lake, or onto one of the islands for a stroll, to see them for yourself.

Twenty-two islands make up the Apostle Islands chain. Twenty-one of them, along with a 12-mile chunk of shoreline, are within the National Lakeshore. They range in size from 3-acre Gull Island to 10,000-acre Stockton Island. Madeline Island, with year-round residents, is not included.

Two islands are off-limits as flora or fauna preserves, but the others are open for exploration. Some are primitive and wild, others are like state parks. Some are reached daily via Bayfield shuttles, while others are off the beaten- path and require a kayak, private boat, or a pricey water taxi from Bayfield.

More than 60 miles of hiking trails can be found on the islands and the mainland, mostly on old overgrown logging roads. Looking at an island map, you might assume skirting the perimeter would be a great day hike, but many shoreline areas off-limits to protect flora or fauna, and many of the islands aren't as tame as they look. Explorers and hikers have become lost in a gorge overnight.

Stockton Island

Stockton Island and its twin, Presque Isle, make up the largest landmass in the National Lakeshore. At just more than 10,000 acres, it is easily the most developed and visited island; half of the camping in the archipelago is done here. Historically it has drawn the most attention, from Native Americans 3,000 years ago to post-Civil War logging, fish camps, and sandstone quarrying. Plans to establish ranches were once considered, giving an indication of its size. Stockton Island features a beach, 15 miles of hiking, 21 campsites (primitive sites on the north side at an early-20th-century logging camp), a ranger station, and one of the superlative sights in the chain—the **Stockton Island Tombolo State Natural Area.** *Tombolo* is Italian for "mound," but it means an overgrown sandbar. A visitors center, open intermittently, is also on the island. As a protected area, it provides refuge for two threatened sedge species and the English sundew, all thriving in a diverse 680-acre ecosystem. The highest concentration of black bears in the United States is found on Stockton Island, where there are around three dozen.

A round-trip boat for campers runs four days a week from Bayfield with **Apostle Islands Cruise Service** (800/323-7619, www.apostleisland.com, 8:30am Tues. and Fri.-Sun. late June-Labor Day, $46 hikers, $60 campers). You can also travel between Stockton and Michigan Islands on the ferry for $10.

Oak Island

Oak Island is the tallest of the chain, with steep-sided 250-foot ravines etched across its surface and a maximum elevation approaching 500 feet—so tall it protruded above the postglacial lake that submerged the chain. Oak Island's 5,100 acres are the inverse of Stockton Island's development. Rustic and tough, Oak Island is isolated. There are only about 11 miles of trails, but it's a nice mix of leisurely and unforgiving, and all great fun. Before modern upgrades, hikers could be lost for days at a time wandering the gorges. Not only is off-trail trekking potentially hazardous, it may be illegal, as some areas are sporadically off-limits to protect nesting eagles.

Historically of interest are the pirates who plagued the shoreline, hiding in Oak Island's rugged topography. Frustrated loggers later followed and established five separate lumber camps. One guy took up residence on a sand spit for 25 years, becoming known affectionately as the "King of Oak Island." Their artifacts still litter the island. The cliffs are ringed by sandy spits and some superb beaches. Black bears are ubiquitous, so take care with your food supplies. Oak Island is also the best place in Wisconsin for winter camping.

Oak Island is served by a round-trip boat for campers four days a week from Bayfield with **Apostle Islands Cruise Service** (800/323-7619, www.apostleisland.com, 2:15pm Tues. and Fri.-Sun. late June-Labor Day, $60).

Raspberry Island

At only 296 acres, Raspberry is one of the most popular islands. Its 1860s **lighthouse** is the second-tallest in the region and, after reopening in 2007 after a needed face-lift, it's also one of the prettiest. The cliffs include uncommon clay-lined sandstone. Sand-spit campsites are now closed because of the establishment of the 11-acre protected Sand Spit Natural Area. This is the one tour where the National Park Service really pulls out all the stops, down to the period-costume detail and a re-creation of the lighthouse keepers' gorgeous gardens. Docents lead tours on-site constantly late May to late September.

Raspberry Island is served by a round-trip boat for campers four days a week from Bayfield with **Apostle Islands Cruise Service** (800/323-7619, www.apostleisland.com, 2:15pm Tues. and Fri.-Sun. late June-Labor Day, $46).

Michigan Island

At 1,600 acres, Michigan Island has a mile of trails and a lighthouse to explore, along with one sand-spit campsite (no water) on a small lagoon. Relatively undisturbed, this island is isolated enough to camp on a sand spit and hack through unmarked trails. It is served by a round-trip boat for campers four days a week from Bayfield with **Apostle Islands Cruise Service** (800/323-7619, www.apostleisland.com, 8:30am Tues. and Fri.-Sun. late June-Labor Day, $46); you can also take the boat between Michigan and Stockton Islands for $10.

Sand Island

On the western fringe of the chain and outside any peninsular windbreak, Sand Island's ecosystem supports thriving oddball flora. It's also got a commanding stretch of sea caves on the east side. At 3,000 acres, it was the only island besides Madeline to support a village, a community of 100 people, mostly fishing families, and big enough to have a post office. Sand Island was also home to a thriving resort, in operation 1885 to 1910; historically significant structures are still visible. One trail runs along a onetime Bayfield Highway, past a rusted auto hull to an 1881 Norman Gothic brownstone **lighthouse.** A State Natural Area is predominantly northern wet mesic forest, containing 250-year-old white pine. Black bears also live here.

Manitou Island

This 1,300-acre island is one of the flattest and least enthralling topographically. The island's fishing camp rivals the one on Little Sand Bay in its exhaustive restoration. A short trail leads from the dock past archaeological excavation sites of the Woodland people. At the time of writing, Manitou had dropped off the transport schedules, so contact the **Apostle Islands National Lakeshore Headquarters** (4th St. and Washington St., Bayfield, 715/779-3397, www.nps.gov/apis, 8am-4:30pm daily late May-early Sept., limited hours Sept.-May) to find out how to visit.

Basswood Island

From 1868, Basswood Island was the first of the archipelago's brownstone quarries, shipping stone around the country for major construction projects. The nearly 2,000-acre island was also temporarily populated by homesteaders and fishers in semipermanent camps through the late 1930s. Seven miles of trails wend through the island. Along the coast you'll see hoodoo-like rock formations.

Devils Island

The northernmost island, and as far north as Wisconsin goes, is strongly impacted in storm season. It's a crucial and tricky turning point on shipping lanes on the way to the Duluth and Superior harbors. The rough waters and merciless pounding waves are part of the prime draw of the island, the **Devils Island Cliffs State Natural Area.** There are five acres of exposed cliff, subterranean blowholes, and bluff-top boreal forest. The underground chasms of the island produce rhythmic booms and other sounds that scared off early visitors; lighthouse keepers reported ferocious foamy water during high-wave storms. Endangered plants clinging to the cliffs include butterwort and hairlike sedge. An 1891 third-order Fresnel lens lighthouse sits atop the cliffs; there was much resistance when the Coast Guard announced plans to dismantle it, and it was restored instead. The rest of the island is preserved as part of the Apostle Islands Maritime Forest Natural Area, with old-growth boreal forest in stands across the island. There is only one campsite (no water).

Outer Island

Outer Island is perhaps the one Apostle most littered with the detritus of human occupation. At 8,000 acres, it's the second-largest in the group. The south end is the best place to visit, with sand dunes and spits forming a lagoon nearly a mile long. The entire spit area is part of the protected 232-acre Apostle Islands Sandscape Natural Area, a bizarre mélange of coniferous forest, lagoon, pine barrens, and bogs containing the rare dragon's mouth orchid; migrating birds also use the spit in spring and fall. Another 200-acre spread of old-growth northern mesic hemlock may be the most extensive in the Great Lakes to survive logging.

Rocky Island

Tadpole-shaped Rocky Island is well named for the cliff-walled shoreline on the southern end. A smattering of extant structures from fish camps still lie in the weeds and along an established trail. Twenty acres of the island are protected as the Rocky Island Cuspate Unit Natural Area, juxtaposing beach dune and bog.

Rocky Island is just across the channel from South Twin Island, and the two are among the most popular islands in the archipelago.

South Twin Island

In precise topographical contrast to Rocky Island, South Twin sits across a narrow channel. The least rocky island in the chain, it's mostly flat and sandy, and diminutive at 360 acres. Despite the lack of craggy belvederes or yawning sea caves, enough people visit to warrant a small visitors center next to the dock on the west side.

Hermit Island

Hermit Island is a perennial favorite of visitors plying the waters on boat cruises. It was named for a cooper who arrived from the Michigan's Upper Peninsula named Wilson who had been severely jilted. During his spell of solitude, only one man, a Native American from Red Cliff, was allowed to visit him; all others were driven off by gunfire, including tax collectors, who had come nosing around after stories surfaced that Wilson had squirreled away a fortune on the island. Upon his death the island was swarmed with treasure hunters who dug it up en masse, but to no avail. Later, a brownstone quarry was established, and a few gargantuan blocks of stone lie on the shore. On the southern side, on calmer days, the old ribs from a loading pier can be seen in the shallow brown water.

lighthouse on Devils Island

The Untouchables

Eagle Island is an off-limits protected Critical Species Natural Area, with large numbers of sensitive nesting herring gull and double-breasted cormorant colonies. The three acres of **Gull Island** are also part of this unit, and a 500-foot buffer zone is strictly enforced for boaters May 15 to September 1 during prime nesting season. Warmly rufescent **North Twin,** an almost perfect example of northern boreal biome, inhospitable to logging and thus untouched, is also off-limits.

MAINLAND UNIT

The Apostle Islands National Lakeshore extends to the mainland—on the opposite side of the peninsula from Bayfield are 12 miles of federally protected shoreline. **Little Sand Bay** is the beginning of the shoreline, directly across from, and with nice views of, Sand Island. Here you'll find a National Park Service **visitors center** (715/779-7007, 9am-5pm daily Memorial Day-Sept.). Featuring a dock and scattered displays on fishing, shipping, and tourism, the center tells the story of the *Sevona,* a 3,100-ton steamer that was slammed to a watery grave in 1905. Adjacent to the visitors center is the restored **Hokenson Brothers Fishery;** free 45-minute ranger-led tours depart regularly.

The National Park Service is slowly forging a mainland **hiking trail** toward Bayfield. A community **campground** is cheap and has good views, although sites are close together.

Squaw Bay and Sea Caves

A trail is being blazed along the 12-mile coastline surrounding **Squaw Bay,** northeast of Cornucopia; get here by driving along Highway 13 and down one of a few roads that dead-end at or behind the waterline—none are developed.

The best way to see the two-mile-long spread of wild **sea caves** and natural arch-shaped hoodoos in the sandstone is from a kayak, paddling into the yawning chasms. Easily one of the most photographed sights on the peninsula, the caves soar to heights of 65 feet in some sections. In recent years, enough ice has formed to allow hiking onto the ice to see them, and at those times this area is crowded with visitors.

FEES

There are fees on the mainland for guided interpretive sessions (from $3) and parking ($3-20).

CAMPING

Eighteen of the archipelago's islands and one site on the mainland unit are accessible for campers. All are primitive sites, and some islands have dispersed camping. Stockton Island has one wheelchair-accessible site.

All campers must register at the **Apostle Islands Headquarters** (June-Sept. register also at the Little Sand Bay Visitor Center). Sites cost $15 ($8 reservation fee) and a few islands have group sites. **Reservations** (715/779-3398, http://recreation.gov) are necessary if you want to camp on a weekend; reservations are taken from 30 days ahead.

Most beaches, unless stated otherwise, are off-limits; if it's unclear, always ask first. Garbage and fires are also big problems. Be prepared to go without a fire and to pack out your garbage. Water is available at some, but not all, campsites.

The mainland unit of the Apostle Islands Lakeshore does not have an established campground, but one kayak-in site is available on the shoreline. Just southeast of the visitors center in Russell, you'll find a community park with campsites. There are 10 others on the peninsula.

INFORMATION

The **Apostle Islands National Lakeshore Headquarters** (4th St. and Washington St., Bayfield, 715/779-3397, www.nps.gov/apis, 8am-4:30pm daily late May-early Sept., limited hours Sept.-May) is in the huge and architecturally interesting Bayfield County Courthouse.

GETTING THERE AND AROUND

Three main ways get you to the Apostle Islands: kayak, tours, or a charter. None are inexpensive. Most hikers and campers take the boat shuttles of **Apostle Islands Cruise Service** (800/323-7619, www.apostleisland.com) to Stockton, Oak, Michigan, and Raspberry Islands, but these are the only islands served. If you're staying on or visiting another island, your options are paddling or sailing by yourself or a prohibitively expensive water taxi (from $100 one-way) from the Apostle Islands Cruise Service.

Tours and Do-It-Yourself Transportation

Kayak and equipment rentals are available in Bayfield at **Trek & Trail** (7 Washington Ave., 800/354-8735, www.trek-trail.com). All the equipment you need is here, and it offers great tours.

You could paddle the entire **Lake Superior Water Trail,** which stretches 91 miles along the coast between Port Wing and Ashland; this is part of an ambitious 3,000-mile-long trail taking in three U.S. states, Ontario, and many sovereign indigenous nations. The Wisconsin section is a tough paddle, so make sure you're up to it.

Rent sailboats and find instruction—you'll be seaworthy in three days of lessons—from **Sailboats Inc.** (800/826-7010, www.sailboats-inc.com).

Apostle Islands Cruise Service (800/323-7619, www.apostleisland.com) also offers a half-dozen tours from Bayfield. The main trip for sightseers, the Grand Tour (10am daily mid-May-mid-Oct., $46 adults) leaves Bayfield and cruises around all 22 of the islands. You'll see every sight possible without actually getting off the boat; the cost is worth it. There is a lovely sunset cruise (5:30pm daily late June-mid-Aug., 4pm or 4:30pm daily mid-Aug.-Sept.) from Bayfield.

Twenty-two wrecks lie in the shallow waters in and around the Apostles. No dive tours are organized in the archipelago; divers must register with the park's headquarters.

Warnings: Open canoes are not permitted on Lake Superior, and one would be insane to try it. Kayakers need to be experienced before they venture out. When Lake Superior looks placid, it still can hold dangerous surprises—lake levels change with barometric pressure and wind direction. In combination, a windset (caused by winds pushing water to one side of the lake) and an extreme low-pressure area will create a "saiche," a three- or four-foot drop in water level, followed by a sudden backflow. It's rare but can be deadly. Storms are severe and can crop up suddenly. Most occur in November, when the water is still warm and mixes with arctic air, but they can occur at any time.

Chequamegon-Nicolet National Forest: Chequamegon Side

The name is pronounced "shuh-WAH-muh-gun," formerly "shee-KWAM-uh-gun," Ojibwa for "land of shallow waters," and appears often across the northern tier of the state. A staggered series of four rough parallelograms stretching from the Bayfield Peninsula south 120 miles, the Chequamegon is Wisconsin's largest national forest at 850,000 acres, larger than Rhode Island. It's essentially the entire northern cap of Wisconsin.

Natural History

Chequamegon covers one-third of Wisconsin's north-south latitude; more, the geology of the central patches includes some of the oldest

Chequamegon National Forest

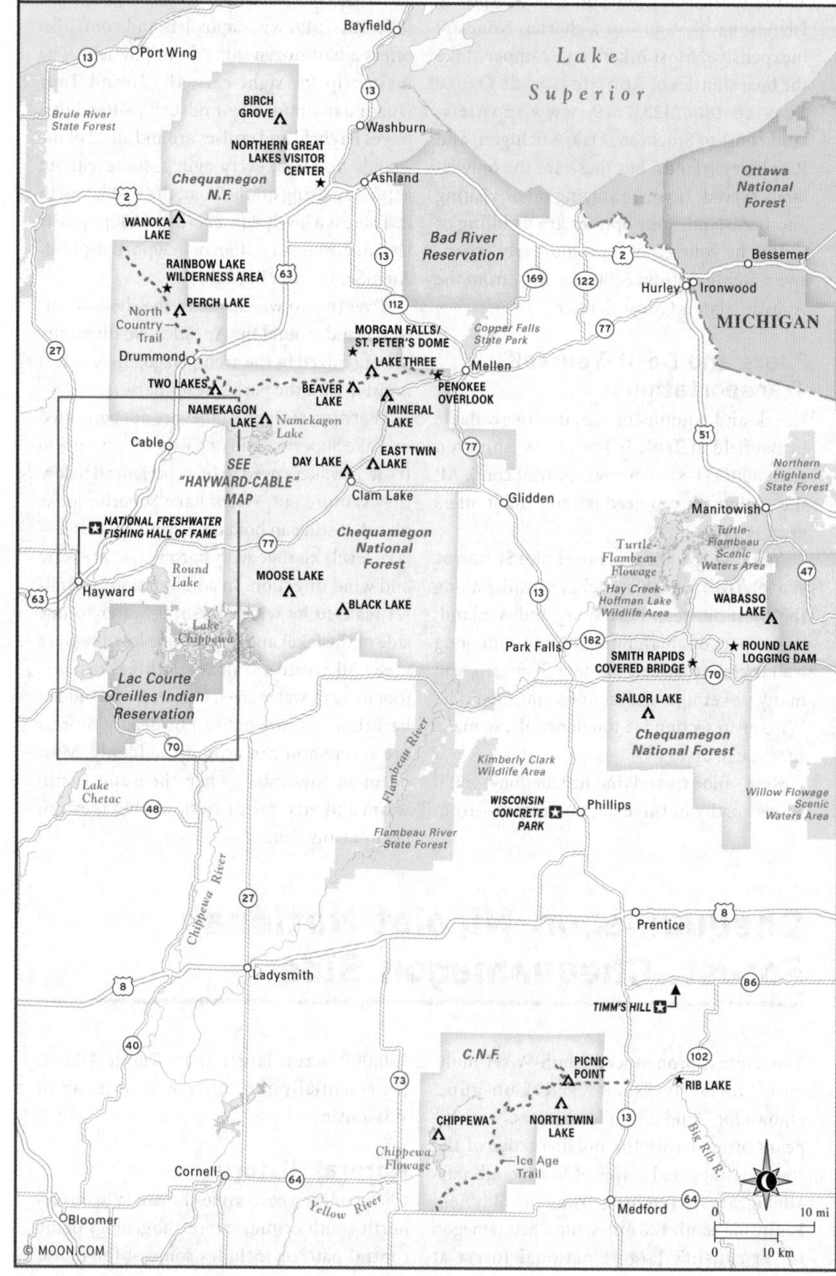

formations in the United States, forming an 80-mile ridgeline—the Great Divide, which continues into Michigan—that separates basins draining north and south. The range, at one time higher than the Alps, held one of the United States' greatest concentrations of iron ore. Subterranean chasms still hold what is believed to be the planet's most comprehensive reserves of untouched taconite ore—3.7 billion tons.

Unfortunately, early rapacious forest practices have affected the eco-diversity of the forest. Vast tracts of mixed forest have been replaced by fast-growing trees such as aspen, and cutover land is left open for bird hunting. Somehow, there are still stands of old-growth trees—some more than 200 years old—in the forest.

Flora and Fauna

Two hundred twenty-nine species of birds inhabit the national forest as planted breeders, migrants, or permanent residents; you'll incessantly hear the forest called the ruffed grouse or muskellunge capital of the world. Hundreds of mammal species also live within the forest's confines. The black bear population, particularly around Glidden, is the highest in the state. Even once-doomed species such as martens and fishers are rebounding. There are wildlife-viewing areas dotted throughout.

RECREATION

The national forest has a $5 per day ($20 annual) fee for some places inside the forest, including beaches and boat launches, but not all. Basically, if you can park there, you have to pay the fee. Campsites have this fee built in.

Trails

The forest boasts two National Scenic Hiking Trails: the **North Country** and the **Ice Age.** Other trails total more than 200 miles, all doubling as cross-country ski trails in winter; 50 miles of that total is groomed weekly.

The Chequamegon is a point of pilgrimage for mountain bikers. Most flock to the Cable and Hayward areas for the magnificent 200-mile **Chequamegon Area Mountain Bike Association (CAMBA)** trail system, most of which is not in the forest proper. More than 100 miles of trail "clusters" are maintained inside the forest, and there are hundreds of miles of service roads and logging roads.

Water Sports

The forest has 800-plus lakes, 411 larger than 10 acres. Lakes under 10 acres all go without names because there are so many. Officially, there are 632 miles of navigable river and stream inside the forest, including the best options—the Flambeau (particularly the South Fork), Chippewa, and Namekagon Rivers. The Namekagon is a federally recognized National Wild and Scenic River with Class II and III rapids. The Flambeau and Chippewa are being considered for National Scenic Riverway status for their splendid wildlife habitats.

It's no wonder that landing a lunker is the number-one recreational activity in these parts. According to statistics, the Clam Lake area offers the forest's highest concentration of lakes, containing the most consistent fish populations.

Camping

The Chequamegon side of the forest supports nearly 30 **campgrounds** of varying size and seclusion; all but two are on lakes, and those two are on fishing rivers. Rates range from free to $20 and average $15, and **reservations** (877/444-6777, www.recreation.gov, $8 reservation fee) can be made for some campgrounds. It'll cost you $10 to change or cancel a reservation. Memorial Day, the Fourth of July, and Labor Day weekends book up early. On summer weekends, reservations are advised; at other times, sites are usually available.

Backcountry camping is free and allowed anywhere within the forest, as long as you camp at least 50 feet from any trail or water source. Note that 14 percent of the lands within the forest boundaries is privately owned. Campgrounds are maintained May

Whose Forest Is It, Anyway?

The age-old battle of who controls national forests, and for what purpose, is being fought stridently here. The combatants are the usual players: hunters, environmentalists, the U.S. Forest Service, loggers, and, of course, you and I.

Environmentalists bemoan the U.S. Forest Service's Ecosystem Management practice of replacing original woods with faster-growing stands of evergreen, which are easier to recover from logging—in fact, only 15 percent of the state's public lands are reforested with original species—as well as its catering solely to hunting and timber interests at the expense of the forest's dwindling diversity. A University of Wisconsin study rated forests 0 to 5 in a Biosphere Wilderness Suitability Index, with 5 being pure wilderness. Only 6 percent of Wisconsin's forests rated a 5.

Why? The Chequamegon-Nicolet National Forest is the country's most heavily logged—120 million board feet in 2018, the sixth straight year of rising timber sales, albeit only 14,000 acres out of 868,000 available. The U.S. Forest Service says that not only do bylaws of national forests require the forest be maintained for multiuse purposes, but that the economy of northern Wisconsin demands it. Indeed, the timber industry points out that this national forest is in far better shape than it was 50 years ago and that the state's crucial timber industry—60,000 jobs and nearly $25 billion in revenues—could perish. This of course is in addition to the U.S. Forest Service having its budget cut regularly.

It is your land, after all; the U.S. Forest Service (www.fs.fed.us) is perfectly willing to hear your side, so why not participate in the discussion?

to mid-October, but you have every right to camp here at other times, though you'll need to lug your stuff in and get your own water. Leave No Trace principles are emphasized here.

SCENIC DRIVES

Highway 77 spans the 29 miles between Glidden and Lost Lake. Recognized federally as the **Great Divide Scenic Byway,** its lengths reveal systematic reforestation and an engaging mixture of natural history and immigrant settlement. The highway crosses the Great Divide, between the drainage basins to the north and south. Clam Lake is the best place to spot **elk.** In tiny Clam Lake itself is an interactive kiosk with up-to-date information on the herd along with valuable dos and don'ts; please have a look. Outside of town you can't miss the "Elk Crossing" signs and even pull-offs for viewing along Highway 77 and other roads. This also means you should drive slowly at all times and keep your head on a swivel.

INFORMATION

The **Chequamegon Forest Supervisor office** (1170 4th Ave. S., Park Falls, 715/762-2461, 8am-4:30pm Mon.-Fri.) has basic information and numerous maps on sale. Contacting individual district ranger stations is a better way to get information on the specifics.

PARK FALLS DISTRICT

The Park Falls District of the National Forest graces the western edge of the Lac du Flambeau Indian Reservation and is just a few miles to the east of the town of Park Falls. To the south is the Flambeau River State Forest.

Sights

East of Fifield are three wildlife-viewing areas, including Popple Creek, at which nests one of the only colonies of yellow-headed blackbirds in northern Wisconsin. Then there's the **Round Lake Logging Dam,** built in the 1880s on the South Fork of the Flambeau River to facilitate floating logs downstream.

At the Smith Rapids Campground, the **Smith Rapids Covered Bridge** is the only covered bridge built in the state in a century. It's a Town Lattice Truss bridge with a modern twist—its use of glue-laminated lumber, allowing continuous chords on the top and bottom of the trusses. Better, it's on the established state Rustic Road 105.

Recreation

The **Flambeau Trail System** offers 69 miles of multiuse trails. Smith Rapids bridge is found along one route, as well as ridgeline rides, a couple of impoundment flowages, and even an old log-driving dam. The Round Lake area is nonmotorized and has an old logging dam. Primitive campsites lie along the lake.

Camping

Of the half-dozen campgrounds near Park Falls, **Sailor Lake** is the closest, seven miles east of Fifield on Highway 70. Farther east on Highway 70 and then north on Forest Road 148 is **Smith Rapids,** good for canoeists, as it's on the South Fork of the Flambeau River. Still farther east is the primitive, isolated **Wabasso Lake,** so secluded that it's a walk-in-only campground (free).

BETWEEN THE DISTRICTS: PRICE COUNTY

Park Falls

Park Falls caters to shotgun-toting hunters looking for the *Bonasa umbellus* (ruffed grouse), as the U.S. Forest Service maintains more than 5,000 acres of habitat near Park Falls. A gateway community, Park Falls is not only the headquarters of the Chequamegon, but also of the wild Turtle-Flambeau Flowage.

The **Tuscobia State Trail** runs along an abandoned railroad grade for 76 miles to Rice Lake. Linked with the Flambeau River Forest trails, its western end also includes a segment of the Ice Age National Scenic Trail.

Lots of local resorts offer canoe shuttling and rentals, and a few rent mountain bikes. **AmeriVu Inn** (1212 Hwy. 13 S, 715/262-3383, $75) has always done right by me. Contact the **Park Falls Chamber of Commerce** (400 S. 4th Ave., 877/762-2703, www.parkfalls.com) for information.

★ Wisconsin Concrete Park

The town of Phillips' main claim to fame is the fabled **Wisconsin Concrete Park** (Hwy. 13). In his old age local logger, jack-of-all-trades, and folk artist gone overboard Fred

Wisconsin's most treasured folk art at Wisconsin Concrete Park

Smith began to assemble images wrought from wire, concrete, glass, mirrors, shells, beer bottles, and assorted other stuff. Painstakingly creating humanoid and animal forms, he had single-handedly created the world's largest collection—200 cowpokes, bulls, bears, farmers, beer wagons, and more—of concrete art by the time he died in 1976. The park is sort of a secular retreat from all those fervid stone religious grottoes spread across the Midwest. After Smith's death, decay and storm damage set in before the National Endowment for the Arts stepped in and began restoration. It's an eerie, personal place—and quite wonderful.

Flambeau River State Forest

This managed, multiuse 87,000-acre forest dates to a 1930 state attempt to preserve dwindling northern forests. Riparian stretches are the key to the forest—50 miles along the north and south forks of the Flambeau River. Canoeing is the primary activity besides fishing, and the South Fork has some of the most perfect white water in Wisconsin. The timber's not bad either—one stretch along Highway M is the largest virgin white pine stand in the state. The forest is so good that in 2017 and again in 2019 the state released an additional 79 **elk** here to bolster the gene pool of the original Clam Lake herd.

The North Fork's upper section is generally the tamest stretch of the river; parts of the southern section can be dangerous. A half-dozen larger lakes in the forest—a couple are designated wilderness lakes—are muskie-rich. Besides fishing, a park highlight is the **Big White Pine,** more than 130 feet tall and 300 years old, off Highway M.

Family camping is found at **Connors Lake** and **Lake of Pines,** both off Highway W, and there are a dozen or so primitive canoe campsites (permit required, free). Camping **reservations** (888/947-2257, http://wisconsin.goingtocamp.com, reservation fee $8, nonresidents from $21, day-use $11) are not usually needed, but it may be best to play it safe.

A Badger Bigfoot?

There are those who believe, passionately, that the dense forests in these parts are home to a Sasquatch, or family thereof. A hunter reported the first one in 2002 and sightings continued right up to the time of writing; in fact, a Bigfoot research organization (www.bfro.com) struck out on two expeditions in 2006 and 2007, and one researcher claimed to have heard otherworldly howls not of any canine throat from deep within the forest; I'm hoping to hear the recordings at some point. The little A-frame information kiosk in Phillips (summer only) is getting somewhat used to jokesters inquiring about it.

Eight or nine resorts and lodges are found along the river. The **Oxbo Resort** (6275 N. Oxbo Dr., 715/762-4786, www.oxboresort.com, $75-150) is legendary in these parts, and locals were aghast when it closed. Well, a wonderful trio purchased it and was in the process of lovingly refurbishing its cabins, campground, and rental/shuttle service at the time of writing. It still hadn't been fully redone, but early reports are superlative and it should be ready by the time you read this. Also, they reopened the bar/restaurant (summer hours 11am-9pm Mon.-Thurs., 10am-10pm Fri.-Sun.)—get the half-pound Oxbo burger, and if they really do it right, the famed wood tick racing (yes, that's right) will make a comeback!

Two primary trails wend through the forest. The **Oxbo** begins east of Oxbo on Highway 70 and is eight miles long. Larger **Flambeau Hills** trail is nearby and stretches for 13 miles. Trails also connect with country trails and the Tuscobia State Trail. The **forest headquarters** is at the Highway W crossing of the Flambeau River.

★ Timm's Hill

For most of its early statehood, Wisconsin's highest spot was believed to be Rib Mountain, near Wausau. Eventually, surveying work discovered that **Timm's Hill,** 25 miles south of Phillips, was actually higher. Along Highway 13 and Highway 86 and then down lovely rustic Highway RR and surrounded by a county park, the hill sports a 45-foot observation tower and, after the wobbly climb, the only truly vertiginous heights in the state. It's not the Rocky Mountains, but your spine will feel shivers. Just under 2,000 feet above sea level, the platform at the top at times attracts enough day-trippers to warrant taking numbers and waiting turns. Hiking and ski trails wend around the base of the hill. Camping is not allowed.

Rib Lake

Due south of Timm's Hill is a smattering of lakes, the nucleus of which is **Rib Lake,** a very northern European busy-as-a-beaver place. In the village you'll find a **campground** at Lakeview Park.

North of Rib Lake, between Highway 102 and Highway D, is Wisconsin's first established **Rustic Road.** This gravel ribbon stretches five miles past a handful of lakes, a beach, resorts, and a scenic overlook.

The community-maintained **Jaycee Trail** is a system of interconnected hiking and ski trails to the north and east. The Jaycee links with one of the better stretches of the **Ice Age National Scenic Trail.** Along the Ice Age Trail to the west, you'll pass glacial eskers, a county forest with a homesteader's cabin, and the **Deutsches Wiedervereinigkeits Brucke** (German Reunification Bridge), built by Ice Age Trail volunteers to commemorate the German Volksmarch tradition, which reportedly inspired the Ice Age Trail movement. Two glacially formed "mountains" are strewn with glacial boulders (erratics) and offer nice views from the top. A hike to the western end of Rib Lake's Ice Age Trail segment brings you to a great blue heron rookery. Beyond there lies East Lake, a glacial pothole lake almost totally undeveloped and open for wilderness camping.

East on the Ice Age Trail, you'll find parking for access to the local trails, north-south watershed-line markers, a trailside shelter, an enormous erratic boulder 20 feet across, and a marker pointing out an old logging sleigh road linked to the Ice Age Trail. The Jaycee Trail branches here, continuing with the Ice Age, but if you stay on the Jaycee, you'll pass an almost perfectly preserved logging camp, including a well, a bunkhouse, a cook shanty, and a root cellar. The trail along here is an old tote road, a supply route between logging villages. Eventually, the Jaycee Trail links back with the Ice Age Trail, passing scores of logging camps, bridges, farmsteads, gravel pits, and tanning bark camps. The Ice Age-Jaycee Trail then connects with the Timm's Hill National Trail leading directly to Timm's Hill.

MEDFORD DISTRICT

Sights

The Medford District is in the far southern area of the national forest, separated from the rest of the forest by the Flambeau River State Forest and an entire county. The chief draws for most travelers are the Ice Age National Scenic Trail and the **Mondeaux Flowage and Recreation Area.** The local concessionaire building has a few exhibits detailing the Civilian Conservation Corps work with the Works Progress Administration during the Great Depression. The area has been called one of the most perfect examples of New Deal works in the Midwest.

Recreation

Mondeaux Flowage and the recreation area have small boats for row fishing; four campgrounds and three boat landings line the northern half of the flowage. The **Ice Age Trail** from the east loops north around the flowage before heading west, totaling about 40 miles through the district; numerous trails branching off offer primitive camping.

Another impoundment—more than 2,700 acres along the Yellow River—is known for wildlife habitat in the Beaver and Bear Creek Waterfowl Management Areas. Of the waterfowl, tundra swans, sandhill cranes, and

Comeback Kids of the Chequamegon

In the 1990s, the state began efforts to bring back the **timber wolf,** which had been all but exterminated by the 1940s because of misinformation, fear, and rapacious bounty-hunting. As of spring 2019, an estimated 950 wolves in more than 240 packs roamed throughout virtually all of northern Wisconsin, with other packs in the west-central area of the state; one wolf was even spotted just 30 miles north of Madison, and two more were spotted in two southeastern counties. This is great news for a species down to just 15 individuals in 1985.

But things may not be so rosy for the majestic animal. The state Department of Natural Resources in 2009 announced that the wolf was no longer to be listed as "threatened," much less "endangered." The feds revoked then reinstated protected status later in 2009. Following another delisting in 2012, the state legalized wolf hunting, including using traps and dog packs. (Wisconsin is the only state to allow dogs to hunt wolves; it has been and still is being litigated.) It was then relisted as protected in 2014, and in 2016 another delisting was being considered; at the time of writing, the U.S. Fish and Wildlife Service was still taking public input. You get the picture—environmentalists are naturally, well, howling. Part of the issue is that the wolf population appears to be stabilizing, which was anticipated and which means wolves have maxed out the land's biological carrying capacity, obviating the need for hunting.

In 1995, the state launched a project to reintroduce **elk,** importing 25 from Michigan into the Chequamegon National Forest. They number around 200 at present. Some predation has occurred (resulting in relocation), and some northern highways must be closed at times, since traffic was spooking the elk away from their birthing areas. On the upside, in 2015 the state transplanted 275 more elk to diversify the gene pool, added 200 square miles to the elk's range, and moved an elk herd to the Black River State Forest area. In 2017 and 2019 nearly 80 were also released south in the Flambeau State Forest to bolster the gene pool. The herd is also well on its way to a long-term size of 1,400. It's so good that in 2018 the state had its first (very limited) elk hunt. Mellen, Clam Lake, Glidden, and points between are your best chances to spot them. Stop in Clam Lake for its interactive kiosk with up-to-date information. Paramount: do not approach the animals and do not even try to call them since it can interfere with mating. Drive slowly—vehicles are the number-one source of elk kills.

double-crested cormorants are the most interesting snag dwellers. This place is also quite popular with canoeists.

The Jump River is one of the forest's primary canoeing rivers. While not a section amateurs want to challenge, the Big Falls are worth a stop. Just north of the district boundary along Highway N, south of Kennan, **Big Falls County Park** is one of the prettier stretches of river in this district.

Medford is one endpoint to the 26-mile-long **Pine Line Recreation Trail;** the other is in Prentice. The northern tier of the trail runs through the terminal moraine of the last glacial period, through hardwood forests, cedar swamps, and rich bogland.

Out of the town of Medford and running 25 or so miles to the north is the **Pine Line,** an aptly named wilderness recreation trail.

Camping

Medford District campgrounds are quite munificent—there's free firewood at most in the district, and all but Kathryn Lake are reservable. The only warm showers in the Chequamegon National Forest are found at the **Chippewa Campground,** on the 2,174-acre Chequamegon Waters Flowage in the southwestern part of the district.

Other campgrounds are packed close together in the northeastern section, along the Mondeaux Flowage, roughly between Highways D and E. All are on or near the flowage and offer access to the Ice Age Trail; a couple are wheelchair-accessible.

Food

Simple fare predominates (although the walleye and duck are musts), but you won't get friendlier proprietors than the namesakes of ★ **Phil and Eleanor's Steakhouse** (N2319 Hwy. 13, 715/748-0700, dinner Tues.-Sat., from $11)—a true-blue North Woods-style eatery, the kind of place where Phil might sit down and chat with you while you eat if you're eating alone.

Information

The **Medford Ranger District Office** (850 N. 8th St., 715/748-4875) in Medford can offer advice.

GLIDDEN (GREAT DIVIDE) DISTRICT

Sights and Recreation

The **Penokee Overlook,** four miles west of Mellen along Highway GG, is an easy stroll up a few stairs for a top-notch view of billion-year-old hummocks. Speculators began trickling into the region—technically part of the Penokee-Gogebic Iron Range—in the 1880s to seek out profit possibilities. Before the bottom fell out at the start of the Great Depression, 300 million tons of ore were shipped from the Wisconsin-Michigan range. You can also get to the **Penokee Trail System** here.

Standing 1,710 feet above sea level, **St. Peter's Dome** is the aptly named second-highest point in the state. On a clear day, three states are visible from the crown. **Morgan Falls** drops a frothy but tame 80 feet over onyx-colored granite. A trailhead leaves the parking area at Penokee Overlook and then forks in opposite directions to the falls and the dome. Be forewarned that stream crossings and rough stretches mark the way to St. Peter's Dome.

Most popular with families, the **Day Lake Recreation Area,** now a 640-acre lake, was once marshland along the Chippewa River. A campground and short **nature trail** are found here. Northeast of Mellen a few miles, check out more grand northwest Wisconsin waterfalls at **Copper Falls State Park;** it has great hiking as well as absolutely gorgeous scenery with numerous waterfalls.

Southwest of Mellen via Highway GG is a lovely backwoods drive, along the Penokee Range past oodles of wildlife, including a chance to see one of Wisconsin's **elk herds.** Meander around this road, Highway 77, and any forest road for a chance to see them, especially in September and October. Local businesses even have maps. Drive slowly and be wary.

Camping

The largest campground in the Glidden District is **Day Lake.** This campground, accessible and with reservable sites, sits on a 600-acre muskie-laden lake. Nearby, off Highway GG, is **East Twin.** East of Clam Lake off Highway M is pack-in-only **Stockfarm Bridge,** with seven very secluded sites (no reservations) in a copse of red pine along the Chippewa River.

The remainder of the campgrounds in the district are west of Mellen via Forest Roads 187 and 198. The most popular is **Lake Three,** with its hardwood setting on the North Country National Scenic Trail; the Penokee Overlook isn't far away. The North Country Trail is also connected to the **Beaver Lake** campground, on Forest Road 198.

Information

Information on the Glidden District is available from the **Glidden District Ranger Station** (22213 N. Hwy. 13, 715/264-2511).

HAYWARD (GREAT DIVIDE) DISTRICT

Sights and Recreation

At the **Lynch Creek Habitat,** west of Clam Lake via Highway 77, four species of nesting duck are a highlight.

The Hayward District has by far the most of the forest's 550 historic sights. Many of the best preserved are the skeletal remnants of Swedish farmsteads in the forest meadows. The highlight of the Hayward District, the **North Country Scenic Trail (NCST),** passes quite a few of them, mostly in the Marengo River Valley.

Another favorite highlight is the **Porcupine Wilderness,** 4,450 acres of rolling uplands, wetland, lake, and swamp; it is totally motor-free. Porcupine Lake covers 75 acres and is rife with trout. Four established campgrounds are found along the trail, along with one primitive site on Tower Lake. Adirondack shelters can be used just west of Mellen near the Penokee Range Ski Trails.

Around **Black Lake** and leading from the campground, an interpretive trail details the lake's pine and hemlock eras, starting around 1880 and lasting until the Great Depression. The highly praised **Rock Lake Trail Cluster** is a system of six interconnecting loops for hikers, skiers, and mountain bikers.

Camping

The Hayward District has what may be the most primitive camping experience in the park: **Black Lake,** 26 miles east of Hayward. Not far from Black Lake, **Moose Lake** is accessible off Highway 77 east of Hayward. The fishing is not bad. **Namekagon,** 17 miles east of Cable on Highway M and then north on Highway D and west on Forest Road 209, offers 33 campsites and is full of RVs. Easily accessible from here are biking trails and the North Country Scenic Trail.

Information

The **Hayward District Ranger Station** (10650 Nyman Ave., 715/634-4821) is north of Hayward, off U.S. 63.

WASHBURN DISTRICT

Sights and Recreation

The stands of Norway and red pine in this district of the forest were among the purest and densest ever found during the last century. The **Drummond Rust-Owen Mill Reservoir** is the last remnant of a sawmill dating from 1883. Built from fieldstone and displaying a unique conical silo, it was used to power the mills in Drummond—one of the largest 50-odd lumber towns that sprouted in northern Wisconsin. Though the roof has fallen and weeds are encroaching, the walls for the most part are structurally sound. It's just west of town, adjacent to Forest Road 223, north of U.S. 63 via Drummond Lake Road.

The enormous 6,600-acre **Rainbow Lake Wilderness Area** is southwest of Delta along Forest Road 228. Off-limits to motorized anything, it's prime backwoods land for hikers and canoeists. The North Country Trail cuts through for six miles; Tower Lake, one of the forest's most isolated, is linked to the trail by an access route. Reynard and Wishbone Lakes are good for canoers and birders.

The **Valkyrie** multiuse trail is accessible west of Washburn off Highway C. One of the most respected trail systems in the forest, it departs near the Mt. Valhalla Winter Sports Area, an old ski-jump hill.

The **Drummond Trail** is east of Drummond along Forest Road 213. The North Country Scenic Trail intersects a Chequamegon Area Mountain Bike trail network northwest of town.

Food

You must check out the ★ **Delta Diner**

North Country Scenic Trail

The highlight of the Hayward District is the **North Country Scenic Trail.** Entering the forest a couple of miles west of Mellen, the NCST stretches for 60 miles through the forest and exits five miles southwest of Iron River. Some 150 miles of Wisconsin's projected 225 miles are done. When fully completed, it will be the longest unbroken walking path in the United States, at 3,200 miles, stretching from Crown Point, New York, to Lake Sakakawea, North Dakota, where it will link with the Lewis and Clark and then the Pacific Crest Trail to total 4,600 miles. See www.northcountrytrail.org for more information. The Chequamegon National Forest walking trail inspired the whole trail and lent its name.

(14385 Hwy. H, 715/372-6666, www.deltadiner.com, 11am "until burgers are gone" Mon., 8am-4pm Tues.-Sun., 4pm-7:30pm for fish Fri., summer, reduced hours fall-spring, from $7). A retro diner in the backwoods, it's got Wisconsin-centric fare—wild rice casserole, for example—and an utterly cheery, friendly atmosphere.

Camping

The closest campground to Washburn and definitely the most popular in the district is **Birch Grove,** 12 miles west of Washburn on Forest Road 435. There are some decently secluded sites here on a long lake, and the loons are loud. The Valhalla Trail is accessible from here for hikers and mountain biking.

East of Iron River along U.S. 2 is trout-filled **Wanoka Lake,** popular with bikers traveling the Tri-County Corridor stretching from Ashland to Superior.

Six miles north of Drummond on Forest Road 35 is the **Perch Lake** campground (no reservations), on a 75-acre bass lake; it's near the Rainbow Lake Wilderness. The **Two Lakes** campground (reservations) is five miles southeast of Drummond and among the largest campgrounds in the Chequamegon. Porcupine Lake Wilderness Area is nearby.

Information

The **Washburn District Ranger Station** (715/373-2667) is right on Highway 13 in Washburn.

Hayward-Cable

The Hayward-Cable region is probably the most visited area in the northwestern lakes region. Seventeen miles may lie between Hayward and Cable, but locally they're spoken in the same breath. Surrounded by county and federal forest, and bisected by the Namekagon River—the north fork of the St. Croix National Scenic Riverway—the area's got lakes and chains of lakes in every direction, and a decidedly recreational bent.

History

Human occupation on present-day Lac Courte Oreilles Indian Reservation dates to 5000 BC. The Namekagon River was a strategic waterway for the Ojibwa people, the French, and early settlers.

Hayward at one time was a timber big shot, its boom status starting when a lumberman named Hayward established the first lumber mills. Cable, an afterthought as a community today, actually rose first, as a railroad center and lumber headquarters. Hayward's ribaldry and raucousness when timber laborers came roaring into town to spend their pay were unrivaled and fully detailed by the national media. Timber still plays a role in the local economy, but the area has fully embraced tourism. The first resort went up on Spider Lake in 1885, and the little town today absolutely swells in summertime. Even governors have maintained a Northern Office in Hayward.

SIGHTS

★ National Freshwater Fishing Hall of Fame

Shameless kitsch or North Woods work of art? Judge for yourself the 143.5-foot-tall muskie and other assorted behemoths in the fiberglass menagerie outside the **National Freshwater Fishing Hall of Fame** (Hwy. B, 715/634-4440, www.freshwater-fishing.org, 9:30am-4pm daily June-Aug., limited hours Sept.-May, $8.50 adults). Kids will make a beeline to climb the world's only 4.5-story climbable muskie, whose innards are also a museum (snap a photo). The real museum is serious business: a four-building repository of freshwater fishing history and records, with 50,000 artifacts on display; they have 8,000 lures alone! Also find thousands of antique

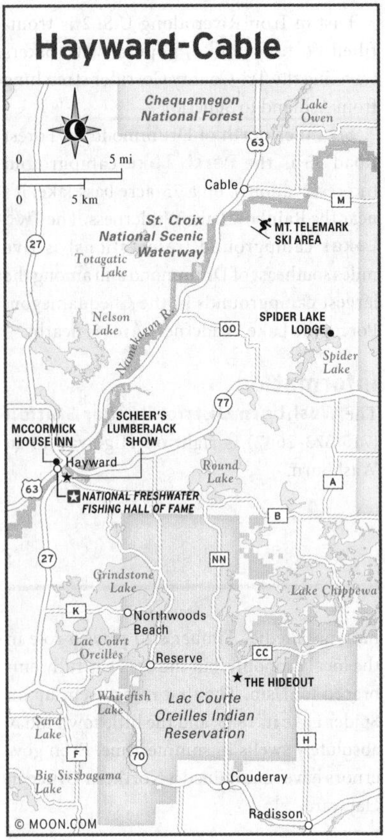

Hayward-Cable

rods and reels, outboard motors, and 400 mounted fish, including more than one world record.

Scheer's Lumberjack Shows

Scheer's Lumberjack Shows (15640 W. Hwy. B, Hayward, 715/634-6923, www.scheerslumberjackshow.com, 7:30pm Mon. and 2pm Tues., Wed., and Sat. mid-June-Aug., fewer times May-June, $15) are a hoot and a real look at timber skills. Speed climbing, team sawing, ax throwing, and canoe jousting are a perfect example of familial delight. There are also some matinee and evening shows. Scheer's shows are held in the "Bowl," an 1890s holding area for logs being floated south to mills. Now it's the site of a logrolling school—that's how big timber still is around here.

Wilderness Walk

South on Highway 27 is the family-specialty **Wilderness Walk** (9503 Hwy. 27, Hayward, 715/634-2893, www.wildernesswalkhaywardwi.com, 10am-4:30pm daily mid-May-Labor Day, $14 adults), a 35-acre wildlife menagerie and petting zoo. But they do have maze houses, panning for gold, and other draws.

The Hideout

Long a Hayward Lakes area favorite, **The Hideout,** 17 miles southeast of Hayward, was the lair of "Scarface" Al Capone. Over the years it went into foreclosure and pretty much every year it gets bandied about as possibly reopening as a tourist attraction—that held true for this edition. Fingers crossed.

The northern lakes of Wisconsin were rife with Windy City wiseguys in the 1920s and 1930s, and the Hideout is likely the best extant example of their sanctuaries. Situated within 400 acres of pines, the fieldstone buildings and their interiors were incredible works of art. The main lodge features a hand-hewn 100-ton stone fireplace. A wooden spiral staircase was crafted in Chicago and transported here. The dining room and bar were built in what was likely the most ornate garage ever constructed in the lakes region. Also still intact are the machine-gun turret, manned by thug bodyguards; a bunkhouse; and an eerie "jail." There's even a doghouse built for Capone's German shepherds.

RECREATION

CAMBA Trails

Hands-down the most comprehensive trail system for off-road bike riders in the Midwest is **CAMBA** (Chequamegon Area Mountain Bike Association, 800/533-7454, www.cambatrails.org). More than 300 total miles use old logging roads, ice-sled byways, and whatever ridgelines the glaciers left behind (and add to that about a lifetime's worth of forest roads not technically part of the system). The International Mountain Bicycle Association awarded it a bronze star. Expect varying conditions, from perfect to carpets of leaves, boggy and sandy muck, rutted dirt, and the occasional frightening python-size tree root hidden beneath top cover. The **Namekagon Trails** might be the most popular, with both the easier (Patsy Lake) and difficult (Rock Lake) trails in the forest as well as access to the semi-primitive Rock Lake Area and the remoter regions of the forest. The longest cluster, the **Delta,** has some great trails and arguably the best views, along the White River Valley, also offering access to the North Country National Scenic Trail. Dozens of operations in the area have biking supplies and rentals.

Chippewa Flowage

Abutting the Chequamegon National Forest and the Lac Courte Oreilles Indian Reservation is Wisconsin's third-largest lake (and largest wilderness lake), the 15,300-acre **Chippewa Flowage** (lovingly called the "Big Chip"). This labyrinthine waterway is surrounded by 233 miles of variegated, heavily wooded shoreline, an endless array of points, bays, sloughs, and seemingly hundreds of isolated islands. Primitive camping is permitted on the islands, but the 18 sites are first-come, first-served. There is no dispersed camping, but you will find a couple of private operations on the shoreline. Nearly every species of bird and mammal indigenous to northern Wisconsin is found within the acreage. The flowage is also a nationally known muskie lake and also hosts walleye. The world-record muskie was caught here in 1957.

Canoeing

The 98-mile-long Namekagon River is the northern tributary of the federally established St. Croix National Scenic Riverway System, and it flows through the Hayward-Cable area, its headwaters at the Namekagon Lake dam northeast of Cable. The river is no white-knuckler, though some high-water periods create medium to high hazards. For the most part, it's an exaggerated trout stream running a wide river valley and dammed into four flowages.

The **U.S. Forest Service ranger office** (10650 Nyman Ave., Hayward, 715/634-4821) in Hayward has information on water levels and rental outfitters.

Fishing

To cover all the area's fishing options would be a book in itself. Muskie and walleye are found here, first and foremost.

climbing into a muskie's mouth at the National Freshwater Fishing Hall of Fame

Skiing the Birkie

In 1973, in the depths of winter, 53 local ski aficionados headed northeast out of Hayward and skied 52 kilometers to Cable. They were attempting to recreate the famous **Norwegian Birkebeiner race,** an annual celebration of the desperation skiing of a duo of Norwegian militiamen trying to save the life of the country's infant king.

Within two decades, the Birkie, as it is affectionately known, has become the premier event of Nordic skiing. Annually in late February, around 7,500 skiers from around the world—especially Norway—turn up. The DYNO American Birkebeiner—its official name—is now the largest and most prestigious ski event in North America. They do it for the spirit, but certainly not for the money—a relatively paltry $7,500 is awarded the winner, but that's still an improvement; no prize money at all was offered until 1996. It's now a three-day blowout, featuring the main Birkie, a 25-kilometer *kortelopet,* or half-race, and a delightful children's race, the Barnebirkie, which attracts 1,500 kids. Events kick off with a 10-kilometer torch-lit race Thursday evening after the afternoon sprint races down Hayward's Main Street. Snowshoe races are part of the fun on Friday.

ENTERTAINMENT AND EVENTS

Hayward isn't the hedonistic piano-pounding saloon town it once was, but there are always a couple of joints around that have sporadic live music in summer. I adore the **Moccasin Bar** (15820 U.S. 63, Hayward, 715/634-4211), at the corner of Highway 27 and U.S. 63, where even an outsider can chew the fat with local jokesters and see the world-record muskie, a five-foot 67-pounder; all the beers on tap are made in Wisconsin.

Hayward also bills itself as a rival for Boulder Junction's claim of "Musky Capital of the World." A world-record fish was caught here, which facilitates bragging rights. The muskie is celebrated the third week of June in the **Musky Festival** (www.muskyfest.com). The largest parade in northern Wisconsin also files through Hayward's downtown.

In late July or early August, Hayward hosts the **Lumberjack World Championships** (www.lumberjackworldchampionships.com); no joke, the competition is televised on ESPN. The pro competition features chopping, sawing, tree climbing, and the perennial crowd-pleaser, logrolling—all great fun. I love the hands-on chopping booths.

Northeast of Cable is little Grand View, which hosts late August's **Firehouse Fifty** (www.firehouse50.org), the oldest and largest on-road bike race and tour in the Midwest. Spectators will find unbeatable scenery along the forest roads.

One of the largest off-road bike races in the United States goes down the second weekend after Labor Day in the area at the **Chequamegon MTB Festival** (www.cheqmtb.com)—it will always be the "Fat Tire Festival," its old name, to me. Thousands of riders gear up, ride, and party hard for this 40-mile race through the forest.

FOOD

Brewpubs

Find excellent beer, including oatmeal stout, and bistro pub grub at **Angry Minnow** (10440 Florida Ave., Hayward, 715/934-3055, 11am-9pm Mon.-Sat.), a restaurant and brewery in a wonderfully and tastefully renovated 19th-century building.

Resorts

Some resort dining rooms could be mistaken for standard family-fare eateries, a couple offer "lumberjack"-style dining, and there is, of course, the classic Wisconsin way-back supper club, still allowing resort guests to pour their own brandy Manhattans on the honor system. Most resorts and lodges in the area have well-regarded restaurants.

Supper Clubs

The **Fireside** (14451 Hwy. K, Hayward, 715/634-2710, dinner Wed.-Mon., from $8)—locals may still refer to it as Tony's Fireside in honor of the longtime owner—is, gasp, approaching fine-dining levels. Try the fried avocado appetizers or herb risotto. Go eight miles south on Highway 27, then east on Highway K.

Cafés

The breakfasts are creative and otherworldly at **Robins Nest** (11014 W. Hwy. B, Hayward, 715/462-3132, breakfast/lunch daily summer, closed winter, $6-12). They do serve lunch, but the variety of well-done breakfasts (poblano omelets or s'mores crepes?) pack them in.

ACCOMMODATIONS

I stopped counting after reaching 150 resorts, hotels, motels, and B&Bs in the area. One thing noticeably lacking is a preponderance of those condo ghettos sprouting up to make the area look like Vail.

If you show up without a reservation during summer, you will likely find some kind of lodging, but it may take lots of calls. During festivals, especially the Birkebeiner ski race (late Feb.), plan way ahead.

$50-100

The reliable (and yours truly's local home) **Riverside Motel** (10429 N. Hwy. 27, Hayward, 715/634-2661, riversidemotelhayward.com, from $85) has a variety of rooms, including standard, upgraded knotty pine, and some waterfront studios with massage tubs, not to mention a few German-style cabins. Service always gets raves.

Dun Rovin Lodge (9404 Dun Rovin Rd., off Hwy. B, Hayward, 715/462-3834, www.dunrovinlodge.com, from $795 weekly) on the Chippewa Flowage is the low-key kind of place that doesn't tout itself much but is precisely what Wisconsinites think of as an up-north vacation place that has good value at a good price. There's a fascinating taxidermy display, including the flowage's world-record 70-pound muskie. Around 20 remodeled cabins are available.

Over $150

Resorts in the Hayward-Cable area run the range of dusty old cottages that look as if they were built in the 1930s by the Civilian Conservation Corps to sybaritic digs that look suspiciously like modified condos. Surprisingly, some allow one-night rentals, although that may change on weekends.

The Chippewa Flowage southeast of Hayward has the most lodging options in the area, simply because it's so big. Organized and with-it **Treeland Resort** (9630 Treeland Rd., Hayward, 715/462-3874, www.treelandresorts.com, $180-400, $850-2,350 weekly) dates from 1928 and offers luxurious digs. Upscale cedar-lined vacation homes and newer motel suites are the lodging options. They also have other properties but somehow keep it well-run; lots of return guests here, for sure.

In the Chequamegon National Forest is **Lost Land Lake Lodge** (9436 W. Brandt Rd., 715/462-3218, www.lostlandlakelodge.com, $800-1,300 weekly), another old-timer from 1922 offering well-kept one- to three-bedroom cabins on spacious isolated grounds. The restaurant is quite good with an excellent fish fry.

Lolling at a lazy resort gets most of the travelers, but those aficionados of historic inns have an outstanding choice right in town: The ★ **McCormick House Inn** (15844 E. 4th St., Hayward, 715/934-3339, www.mccormickhouseinn.com, $165-210) was well known before it was even finished. A regional newspaper back in 1887 said: "When completed, it will be the finest house in town and one of the best on the line." After a complete renovation in the 1990s using period photos, it was later purchased by a transplanted Londoner, who did another extraordinary job of design (hence, the English gardens). The proprietor gets rave reviews.

Combine the comfort of the McCormick House Inn with the North Woods tranquility and isolation and you get the bed-and-breakfast **Spider Lake Lodge** (10472 Murphy Blvd., Hayward, 715/462-3793, www.spiderlakelodge.com, $189-289). The proprietors have done an exemplary job of refurbishing the seven rooms of the 1923 beauty.

INFORMATION

The **Hayward Visitors Information Center** (15805 U.S. 63, near Hwy. 27, Hayward, 715/634-4801, www.haywardlakes.com) is well stocked.

GETTING THERE AND AROUND

Northern Wisconsin Travel (715/634-5307, www.nwtexpressshuttle.com) operates bus shuttles to and from the Minneapolis airport, serving Spooner and Rice Lake en route.

Driving to Hayward from Ashland (via U.S. 63, 57 miles) takes one hour. From Minneapolis (via U.S. 8 and U.S. 63, 138 miles), it takes two hours and 40 minutes. From Madison (via I-94 and U.S. 53, 238 miles), it takes 4.5 hours. Driving in Hayward is easy; it's essentially one long street.

LAC COURTE OREILLES INDIAN RESERVATION

Southeast of Hayward and sandwiched between two lakes and the Chippewa Flowage, the **Lac Courte Oreilles** ("lah-koo-duh-RAY," Lake of the Short Ears) Indian Reservation (office 715/634-8934, www.lco-nsn.gov) is a 31,000-acre federal trust reservation, home to the Lac Courte Oreilles Band of Lake Superior Chippewa, who arrived at these lakes sometime in the mid-18th century. The area's human occupation dates back more than 7,000 years. The North West Company established a trading post on a nearby lake in 1800; treaties with the federal government were finally signed in 1825, 1837, and 1842, which permanently placed the band here. With a membership of 5,000, the population on the reservation itself is around 3,000. The reservation's location adjacent to the Chequamegon National Forest, the expansive Chippewa Flowage, and within the hundreds of lakes and lake chains also give it a strategic importance for outdoors lovers. The reservation's radio station, WOJB (88.9 FM), is about the only thing worth listening to in the region.

Sights

Along Highway E, the **St. Francis Solanus Indian Mission** (open daily) is a site dating from the mid-19th century. After a 1921 fire, the log buildings were rebuilt and include a rectory, a convent, and a school. Inside you'll find assorted Native American artifacts.

Festivals and Events

Lac Courte Oreilles holds an annual **Honor the Earth Traditional Powwow** the third week of July, the largest in North America; other powwows are scheduled for Veterans Day and Thanksgiving.

Great River Road

Forsake the mad swells of traffic on the interstates and major highways and give yourself at least a glimpse of one of the most precious, wonderfully undeveloped areas of the state—the Great River Road.

This famed route stretches from the source of the Mississippi River in Lake Itasca, Minnesota, and parallels the Mississippi all the way to New Orleans. Wisconsin's mileage is road-trip eye candy—the big river and nary a whiff of gentrification. This includes the best-known stretch, the 85 miles north from La Crosse; the southern half seems at times to be absolutely untouched.

There's an astonishing absence of tourist traffic on this road, but no matter where you are, freight trains roar by with alarming regularity,

Highlights

Look for ★ to find recommended sights, activities, dining, and lodging.

★ **Alma:** This sleepy river village has unique eateries and the best historic lodgings in the region (page 337).

★ **Trempealeau:** Admire the local landscape of bluffs and Mississippi floodplain at this unpretentious river town (page 340).

★ **Granddad's Bluff:** There's no doubt where the best vistas of the Mississippi are—in La Crosse (page 341).

★ **Villa Louis:** Take a tour of one of the most opulent historical homes in the Upper Midwest and you'll find authentic fur trade-era history (page 352).

★ **Wyalusing State Park:** The Mississippi joins the hardworking Wisconsin River here for excellent hikes and excellent views (page 353).

★ **Cassville:** This town is surrounded by nature preserves supporting one of the Upper Mississippi's most thriving eagle populations (page 354).

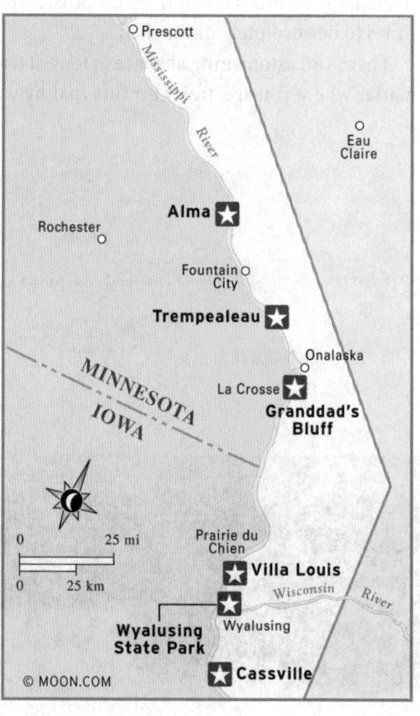

the sound clashing with the barges chugging along the river.

For further reading, start with the best website, Wisconsin Great River Road (www.wigrr.com), which even has audio tours to download, and then one from the Mississippi Valley Partners (www.mississippi-river.org), which includes some, but not all, communities in Wisconsin and Minnesota.

PLANNING YOUR TIME

Very few people see the Mississippi River north to south. They're generally crossing east-west on major highways. That's why the Great River Road is so amazing—you may even have the road to yourself. It's the perfect weekend getaway in either direction. You can't beat it, what with lovely **La Crosse** at the halfway point.

If you're coming from the Indianhead region, you'll start in **Prescott,** 10 minutes southeast of Minneapolis. Drive slowly and find some art, antiques, or coffee in the tiny town of **Stockholm,** and visit Laura Ingalls Wilder's birthplace in **Pepin** before lunching in my favorite town, **Alma,** or dine at everyone else's favorite pit stop, **Trempealeau,** famous for its anachronistic hotel-restaurant. In **La Crosse,** get a snapshot of the sunset from Granddad's Bluff and eat at one of the fine restaurants in town. Spend the night in La Crosse.

Heading toward Iowa, do some barge fishing in **Genoa,** or at least visit its fascinating fish hatchery, before picking up some snacks at Ferryville Cheese in **Ferryville.** Next stop is **Prairie du Chien** and its historically perfect Villa Louis, an examination of early Wisconsin. Picnic with some of that cheese high above the confluence of the Wisconsin and Mississippi Rivers at **Wyalusing State Park** before heading south to **Cassville,** keeping an eye out for eagles. After arriving, you'll have a decision to make: There's an awesome ferry across the Mississippi, or head east for lots of mining history.

Prescott to La Crosse

PRESCOTT

At Prescott, the westernmost community in the state, the disparately colored Mississippi and St. Croix Rivers merge into one mighty waterway. Heading north, the river roads roll on—this time tracing the St. Croix National Scenic Riverway, the top half of Wisconsin's "west coast."

The best point to view the confluence is **Mercord Park,** right downtown, which also has original 1923 bridge gear. The steely blue hues of the St. Croix, seen in the right light, seem impossibly different from the silty Mississippi; on joining, the Mississippi's waters dominate.

Freedom Park is high above the southern end of town with a lovely river walk, bike trail access, and the **Great River Road Visitor and Learning Center** (715/262-0104, http://freedomparkwi.org, 9am-5pm Mon.-Sat., noon-5pm Sun. Memorial Day-Labor Day, shorter hours Labor Day-Memorial Day).

North of town via Highway F is the superb 1,150 acres of the St. Croix and Kinnickinnic River confluence at **Kinnickinnic State Park** (715/425-1129). Canoeing should be limited to the Kinnickinnic; leviathan barges leave narrow space for tiny craft in their way on the St. Croix.

The **Welcome and Heritage Center** (233 Broad St. N., 715/262-3284, www.prescottwi.com) has travel information as well as displays of local history.

TO LAKE PEPIN

Diamond Bluff, Hager City, and Bay City

The road gets serious outside Prescott, rolling and bending, swooping and descending. Later, it gets even more ambitious, a downright roller coaster toward Diamond Bluff. The road, in fact, is bending around prominent Dry Run Coulee.

Beyond this, Highway 35 forsakes the river altogether, turning eastward in a grand curl before cutting south toward Diamond Bluff. This tiny town was the site of the state's largest river disaster in the 19th century. A plaque tells the story of the tragedy at **Sea Wing Park;** this park is also of note also as the main channel of the Mississippi is literally feet from you, offering a sobering view of the power of the river. Today, keep an eye out for clamming boats. Better, heading west on Highway E will take you along hills and small roads to grand vistas.

Once again, the river bends sharply away from straight-line Highway 35; Hager City comes and goes quickly, but pull over just east to look for rock formations called the Bow and Arrow for obvious reasons. Here is a good spot for a side trip to sample a Wisconsin culinary addiction: cheese curds. Taking U.S. 63 north brings you to Ellsworth, home of the amazing **Ellsworth Cooperative Creamery** (232 N. Wallace St., 715/273-4311, 8am-6pm daily, fresh curds at 11am), which produces 160,000 pounds of curds daily. Wow. Curds are so important here that the town was decreed officially as the state's "Cheese Curd Capital" in 1984, and they have an annual June festival to fete it.

Returning to Hager City, just south of town on U.S. 63 watch for pull-offs: This is among the first areas to thaw in spring and thus one of Wisconsin's best places to view migrant waterbirds. Eagle-eyed travelers can also spot the pullout area for a bow-and-arrow-shaped outline in the bluffs on the way to Bay City.

Take Highway EE east; there is lovely birdwatching along Isabelle Creek. At the head of Lake Pepin, Bay City was a key transit point

Previous: lovely views from the aptly named Buena Vista Park in Alma; everyone's favorite pit stop, the Trempealeau Hotel; Granddad's Bluff

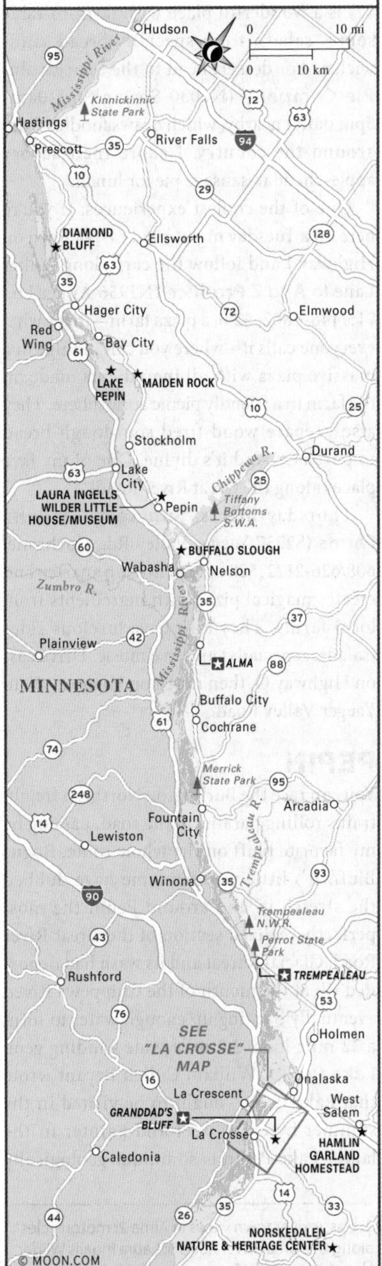

for shipping fish to Chicago. Later, it had the dubious distinction as the location of the county's first murder. Today it has an 1850s Irish immigrant **log house and history center** (1 weekend per month June-Aug.); next to it is a 19th-century church with a hand-carved altar and various items of county history.

West of Bay City in the main channel of the Mississippi River lies Trenton Island, regularly swallowed by mud floods. In the early 1990s state and county officials began to prod the 100 residents into relocation buyouts. Some will not leave—a reminder of the river's irresistible lure and the unvanquished attitude of residents descended from hardy pioneers.

Maiden Rock

On the way out of Bay City, look left—there are bluffs, coulees, and green gumdrops everywhere. The Mississippi gets so wide it is actually a lake—Lake Pepin. Between Bay City and Maiden Rock, taking Highway A east and then south to a bridge over the Rush River before heading back to Highway 35 via 385th Street is a lovely scenic drive—and one of the Midwest's top birding stretches. The name of the next village, Maiden Rock, is a visual aid. A Native American maiden preferred a plunge off the crown of the hill to an arranged marriage. Maiden Rock is another artistic enclave on Lake Pepin. North of town is a wayside with unsurpassed lake vistas and the Rush River, a stream splashing with trout.

Part winery, part pumpkin farm, part alfresco Italian eatery, **Vino in the Valley** (W3826 450th Ave., 715/639-6677, www.vinointhevalley.com, evening Thurs.-Fri., 3pm-10pm Sat. and 11am-5pm Sun.) is easy to dismiss as something of a gimmick. But there's really nothing like eating a grand plate of pasta and salad of local ingredients in a lovely rural setting. It's tough to find: from Maiden Rock, take Highway S, go west on Highway 10, and then follow the signs.

South of Maiden Rock, the road grips the river's edge; it's not quite thrilling, but you'll want to drive carefully. A mile south, for a brief side trip, take Highway AA east to 20th Street, another of Wisconsin's Rustic Roads leading on a gravel path four miles to Highway CC; from here south via Highway CC, you could check the map and head to the Laura Ingalls Wilder wayside in Pepin.

STOCKHOLM

The name of this place belies its actual size: one of the five smallest towns in Wisconsin with fewer than 100 residents. It offers artists and galleries (even Mississippi pearls, extinct since dredging in the 1930s, appear in shops), upscale eateries, and great lodging.

Scandinavian settler Eric Peterson arrived in 1851; others from his hometown of Kalskoga arrived soon after, making it one of the oldest Swedish settlements in the state. Local place-names are a loopy mishmash of river jargon and "-son" appellations.

There are a few Swedish artifacts at the **Swedish Institute** (Spring St., www.stockholmwisconsin.com, noon-5pm Sat.-Sun. Apr.-Nov., free) in the old post office, but shopping is the real lifeblood of the town. Artisans' galleries and shops galore line the few streets. The very friendly **Maiden Rock Winery & Cidery** (W12266 King Ln., 715/448-3502, www.maidenrockwinerycidery.com) has tastings and tours ($10) by appointment. Definitely try the cider.

A mile south of town is a **historic overlook** at the site of a 1686 fort built by Nicolas Perrot. From here the French laid claim to all of the Mississippi's drainage, "no matter how remote," for King Louis XIV.

The **Stockholm Village Park** has a boat ramp and swimming area. There are also a few very good grand B&Bs. Check out the village website (www.stockholmwisconsin.com) to choose one.

Eat at the **Bogus Creek Café** (N2049 Spring St., 715/442-5017, 9am-4pm Fri.-Sun., from $7), a wonderful place with soups, salads, fresh specialty-bread sandwiches, and lovely garden seating; try the Swedish pancakes. They have barbecue nights Friday and Saturday. Similar but with wine and a good beer selection, **Stockholm Village Bistro** (715/442-2056, 8am-4pm Fri.-Sun., from $7) is a wonderful place with farm-to-table soups, salads, fresh specialty-bread sandwiches. For dessert head to the **Stockholm Pie Company** (N2030 Spring St., 10am-5pm daily) nearby, which draws foodies from around the country. I adore their savory apple-cheddar-sausage pie for lunch.

One of the coolest experiences: If you're here on a Tuesday night, head east of town on Highway J and follow the cars along Anker Lane to **A to Z Produce** (N2956 Anker Ln., 715/448-4802, $25), a pizza farm—that's what everyone calls it—where you can indulge in a massive pizza with all ingredients made on the farm in a friendly picnic atmosphere. They also prepare wood-fired sourdough bread to purchase, and it's divine. One of my fave places along the Great River Road!

Thursday nights, **Suncrest Gardens Farms** (S2257 Yaeger Valley Rd., Cochrane, 608/626-2122, $20 or less) fires up an oven and creates magical pizza with ingredients from local farms. They also have luscious sides (salads, especially) and live music. Drive east on Highway O, then north on Highway 88 to Yaeger Valley Road.

PEPIN

You can race the Burlington Northern freight trains rolling parallel to the road, passing by my favorite bluff on the whole route, Bogus Bluff. It's little wonder some have dubbed the stretch in and around Pepin the most perfectly realized section of the Great River Road. Glacial retreat and its wash had deposited silt at the mouth of the Chippewa River, eventually backing up enough water to form a 22-mile-long, 2.5-mile-wide winding gem, **Lake Pepin.** William Cullen Bryant wrote that Lake Pepin "ought to be visited in the summer by every poet and painter in the land." Lake Pepin is so unique geologically

1: classic river town views in Alma **2:** motorcycles along the Great River Road **3:** Laura Ingalls Wilder House near Pepin **4:** a marina near Pepin

1
PIZZA
PUB
2
ARMY
BRAT
3
4

that for years in the early 20th century Wisconsin and Minnesota authorities quibbled as to where, exactly, the river channel—and thus the state boundary—lies.

Pepin is also cluttered with "Little House" affixations. Laura Ingalls Wilder, the author of the *Little House on the Prairie* books, was born on a homestead nearby in 1867, and the villagers are not about to let you forget it.

Sights

Seven miles northeast of Pepin via Highway CC is the **Laura Ingalls Wilder Little House,** the birth cabin and wayside picnic grounds spread over a handful of acres. In Pepin is the **Pepin Historical Museum,** better known as the **Laura Ingalls Wilder Museum** (306 3rd St./Hwy. 35, 715/600-3729, www.lauraingallspepin.com, 10am-5pm daily May-Oct., $5). It's full of displays and memorabilia pertaining to the woman in the famed books.

Why are there wineries here? The Great River Road is subsumed by one of the largest designated viticultural areas in the world due to its mix of amenable microclimates and soil nutrients.

Food

Near the marina is one of the state's best-known eateries, the ★ **Harbor View Cafe** (314 1st St., 715/442-3893, lunch and dinner Thurs.-Mon. May-late Nov., $10-20). Somewhat upscale continental and creative international cuisine is on the menu; it's the place to go for something other than eggs or beef. You'll have an hour wait for a table, but it's worth it.

PEPIN TO ALMA

Tiffany Bottoms Wildlife Area

At the confluence of the Chippewa and Mississippi Rivers spreads a magnificent marsh—an island-dotted wetland over 12,500 acres from the Mississippi and up the Chippewa River Valley, known as **Tiffany Bottoms Wildlife Area.** Paved roads did not penetrate these capacious tracts of water-pocked bottomlands until Works Progress Administration and Civilian Conservation Corps projects in the 1930s. An undeveloped network of trails—mostly old logging roads—branches out through the area, outstanding for berry-picking and inward contemplation. Amateur shutterbugs should have a field day with the ambient sunset beams playing havoc with the odd topography's colors.

Nelson

A few miles farther down the road is Nelson, crowded along a bluff so high that hang gliding and soaring above town are becoming a draw. The only other attraction is the family-owned **Nelson Cheese** (Hwy. 35, south of Nelson, 715/673-4725, www.nelsoncheese.com, 9am-7pm daily), dispensing (although not making) awesome squeaky cheese curds and a laundry list of local special cheeses since the 1850s.

South of town you'll find excellent cabins and gracious hosts at the four-acre **Cedar Ridge Resort** (Hwy. 35, south of Nelson, 608/685-4998, www.cedarridgeresort.com, $75); one enormous "loft" building is gorgeous and sleeps 11. Have grand pizza at the **Stone Barn** (Hwy. KK, 715/673-4478, www.thenelsonstonebarn.com, dinner Fri.-Sat., lunch/dinner Sun., $18-25) in a real old barn on a real farm. Go north on Highway 35, east on Highway D, then north on Highway KK. You'll dine with the chickens.

Leaving Nelson, look to the east at the bluffs. The Nature Conservancy purchased 161 acres as a habitat for dry prairie and grasslands with massive oaks. They will gradually be restored and opened to the public.

Buffalo Slough

Next, the road skirts wetlands doused by seepage from Buffalo Slough, the roadway hacked out of a bluff face or supported by concrete pylons atop mucky soil. At the mouth of the Buffalo River is what's known as **Buffalo Slough,** historically the most significant from lumber's heyday. A staggering amount of timber was floated down the Chippewa, St. Croix, and Eau Claire Rivers and stored in enclosed ponds here. "The Buffalo" virtually controlled the northern timber industry for some time, inciting Wisconsin's version of a range war between the mills of the upper Chippewa River and the Buffalo Slough mills. A single river, the Chippewa, drained one-third of northern Wisconsin and led directly to Buffalo Slough.

★ ALMA

Alma appears so gradually that it's really tough to gauge where the city starts, until you get a look at weathered Twelve Mile Bluff. Mississippi River pilots once used the bluff as a landmark and navigational aid. Aerobically inclined wanderers have a ready-made workout huffing up the steps etched into the bluffs. For scenic drives, the "dugways," what locals call roads that wind through the bluff country east of the river, can't be beat (see www.almawisconsin.com or www.explorealma.com for more). This place is my personal "secret" getaway.

Sights

Lock and Dam 4 sits across the street from the busiest part of the center of town, with an observation platform. It's also got the largest **fishing float** on the river; just hang around and they'll come fetch you.

Right above the town off Highway E is likely the best public park along the road: **Buena Vista Park,** a vantage point with amazing views of the river valley, and in particular for thousands of migrating **tundra swans,** which rest in the sloughs north of town. Alternatively, **Rieck's Lake Park,** north of Alma, has a wildlife observation deck atop the water. My favorite is the **Mossy Hollow Trail** (Cemetery Rd. between Countryside and Buffalo Electric); ask locally for specific directions.

Southeast of Alma, the proprietors of **Danzinger's Vineyards** (S2015 Grapeview Ln., 608/685-6000, www.danzingervineyard.com) may be the most charming you'll meet. Retired dairy farmers, they make a phenomenal wine from La Crescent grapes, among many others—love the currant wine.

Food

★ **Pier 4 Café & Smokehouse** (600 N. Main St., 608/685-4964, 6am-2pm Wed.-Sun., $3-7) features straight-up simple café fare—creative enough that you can avoid monotonous eggs—on a screened-in porch with river-lock views and lumbering freight trains passing just a few feet away. It's a favorite spot for its unique atmosphere. Try the potato pancakes with an omelet stuffed with luscious smoked pork.

The **Empire Room** (The Hotel De Ville, 305 N Main St., 608/685-9669, lunch/dinner daily, from $9) at the Hotel De Ville is casually upscale in a delightful patio setting. It was undergoing a makeover at the time of writing; if it is not serving, the **Afresco Pizzeria** (211 N. Main St., 608/685/3340 from $7) nearby—owned by the same proprietor—has excellent pizzas using a 40-year-old secret sauce, all in a tranquil garden setting overlooking the lock and dam.

Accommodations

Alma is home to great old lodgings, some revamped, some not so much, everywhere you look; many feature shared baths, just like the old days. The best deal of the whole trip is the sub-$50 rooms at the Italianate **Laue House B&B** (1111 S. Main St., 608/685-4923), on the south edge of town. Originally built by a German immigrant whose sawmill gave life to the city, it has been updated, but definitely not over-renovated, from a tiny one-person alcove to a huge room for four overlooking the river.

The owner of **Blue Door Inn** (331 S. Main St., 715/685-9700, www.bluedoorinnalma.com, $110) is very welcoming, and the 1850s stone walls (it was an once a blacksmith and livery) are fantastic. **Hotel De Ville** (305 N Main St., 612/423-3653, www.hoteldevillealma.com, $95-180), a lovely renovated complex of clapboard buildings with Italianate gardens, is a historic lodging that also gets many raves. The **Alma Marina** (125 Beach Harbor Rd., 608/685-3333) has houseboats for rent.

TO FOUNTAIN CITY

Buffalo City

Just off the road, Buffalo City was long the smallest incorporated city in the United States; it now has a population of 915. The only attraction is to spend time in a host of **city parks,** one of which contains the original 1861 jail, or wander riverside nature trails in a 10-acre wooded park.

Cochrane

Along the way from Buffalo City and onto Prairie Moon Road is another folk art oddity. The **Prairie Moon Museum and Sculpture Garden** (Prairie Moon Rd., 608/687-8250, dawn-dusk daily, free) is a hodgepodge of human and animal concrete figurines and a kind of folk art stone wall, all created by a local artist. It was recently recognized as a significant state cultural site by the philanthropic Kohler Foundation.

Merrick State Park

North of Fountain City, the Mississippi River widens to almost two miles because of damming. Right along the **Whitman Dam State Wildlife Area** is one of the smaller state parks in the northwestern part of the state, 320-acre **Merrick State Park** (888/947-2757, www.wisconsin.goingtocamp.com, day-use $11, camping reservation fee $8, camping from $21 nonresidents), which has prime waterfront property. Blue herons frolic on the marshy backwater islands, and there is one 1.4-mile hiking trail.

Boating is king here, with boat moorings right at the campsites, some of which are hike-in island sites. Reservations are advised.

FOUNTAIN CITY

Fountain City's **Eagle Bluff** commands the highest point on the Upper Mississippi River at 550 feet. The village seems to be carved out of the steep-walled cliffs descending into the postcard-quality town. Fountain City has a Mediterranean-island fishing village atmosphere, though there are more than a few pockets of Swiss architecture. The town was named for rivulets of spring water cascading out of the "hard heads," or sandstone bluffs. The waters at one time ran off the bluffs and through the streets, but the springs were capped and turned into fountains. You can still drink from them.

Sights

Lock and Dam 5A forms a pool north of town. The **Dam Saloon** (Hwy. 35, 608/687-8286) is a public viewing platform nearby that has the honor of being the only floating bar on the Mississippi and purportedly the whole country. (My favorite traveler quote: "It leans.") The owner is engaging; mind you, this is not a trendy place to imbibe.

For more cultured imbibing, visit one of the largest vineyards in the state, **Seven Hawks Vineyards** (17 North St., 608/687-9463, www.sevenhawksvineyards.com), with nearly 20,000 vines. They have lovely cottages with superb views, as well.

The most unusual attraction in Fountain City, the **house with a rock in it** (hours vary Mar.-Nov., $2 on the honor system), is north along Highway 35. In 1995, a 50-ton boulder fell off the majestic bluff line and smashed into a house at the base. A shrewd investor turned it into a bizarre tourist attraction. Another unique sight is **Elmer's Auto and Toy Museum** (Hwy. G, 608/687-7221, www.elmersautoandtoymuseum.com, 9am-5pm every other weekend early May-late Oct., $10), purportedly one of the largest collections of pedal cars in the world.

Food and Accommodations

Enjoy rubbing elbows with the locals? You can't go wrong in Fountain City. The **Monarch Public House** (19 N. Main St., 608/687-4231, www.monarchtavern.com, 11am-close Fri.-Sun., 5pm-close Mon. and Wed.-Thurs., from $10) downtown is a classic Wisconsin tavern with original dark wood interiors and, seemingly, the original bottles that went with it; it's also the most popular lunch and dinner restaurant in these parts. Try the home-brewed Fountain Brew.

Out of town via Highway 95 and Highway M, you can get a buffet-style chicken dinner at the **Hill Top Bar and Ballroom** (Hwy. M, 608/687-8739). Try going for the occasional polka dancing.

The tiny **Fountain Motel** (810 S. Main St., 608/687-3111, www.fountainmotelwi.com, $75) has perhaps the best location of any motel on the road. It's also got refurbished themed rooms. New owners have kept up—if not bettered—its long-standing charm.

Trempealeau National Wildlife Refuge

The superb 6,200-acre **Trempealeau National Wildlife Refuge** (608/539-2311) is a major link in the Mississippi River migratory flyway. Besides marshland, the preserve also has site-specific tracts of sand prairie and bottomland hardwood forest—lovely stands of river birch, silver maple, and swamp white oak. A five-mile auto tour offers access to two shorter nature trails open to hikers. Get off the beaten path by hiking along the spiderweb of old dikes and service roads dating from the 1930s. Be careful, though; lots of the heath now shrouds old ditches, and holes have snared more than a few. Bicyclists are not allowed off-road within the refuge, but it is linked to local bike trails along the river.

Perrot State Park

During the winter of 1685-1686, fur trader Nicolas Perrot wintered at the confluence of the Trempealeau and Mississippi Rivers; Hopewell burial mounds at what's known as **Perrot State Park** beat him by five millennia. Known as the Trempealeau Bluffs, the crown of the ridge swells to 500 feet above the bottomland of the Mississippi River.

Brady's Bluff is the crown jewel of the four primary bluffs, a towering 520-foot terrace rising steeply above the floodplain. Climbing up Brady's Bluff is a sweaty geology lesson; you'll pass 600 million years of geological stratification. Trempealeau Mountain, that landmark beckoning to Native Americans and settlers alike, is even more intriguing. A fragmented part of the bluff line, it is now a 384-foot-high island sitting in the Trempealeau River bay.

The Great River State Trail tangentially scrapes the northern park boundary.

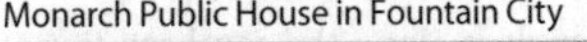

Monarch Public House in Fountain City

Canoeists can follow an established rowing trail through Trempealeau Bay. Whatever you do, do not leave the bay and head out into the river; paddling it requires superhuman strength.

Reservations (888/947-2257, www.wisconsin.goingtocamp.com, $8 reservation fee, campsites from $23 nonresidents, $11 day-use) are necessary for prime riverside campsites.

★ TREMPEALEAU

From a distance, it's impossible to miss the imposing bluffs along the Mississippi floodplain above tiny Trempealeau. So eye-catching were they that the Native Americans, French, displaced Acadians, and the odd Kentuckian referred to the "bump" at the northern end of the bluff line—now, of course, Trempealeau Mountain—either as "Soak Mountain" or "Mountain in the Water."

Even poet William Cullen Bryant was an early admirer of the local landscape. Early settlers were no less enamored; a local minister spent feverish years honestly trying to prove that Trempealeau was the site of the Garden of Eden.

Sights

Lock and Dam 6 in Trempealeau is one of the best sites to get an operations-level gander at a dam. From the tower right over the water, you could almost hop aboard a passing boat. The lock and dam, including an earth dam extending all the way to the Minnesota shore, completed in 1936, cost an astonishing $5 million.

South of Trempealeau is a chain of seven spring-fed lakes, two of them in a fish and wildlife refuge. This is the area for canoeing, and assorted private cabins on stilts over the marshy waters are available; most are decidedly low-key.

New to the scene is **Elmaro Vineyard** (N14756 Delaney Rd., 608/534-6456, www.elmarovineyard.com, closed Mon.), a winery run by a family that's been working the land for generations.

Food and Accommodations

The reason everyone should take a spin to Trempealeau is the flaxen-yellow ★ **Trempealeau Hotel** (150 Main St., 608/534-6898, www.trempeleauhotel.com, $45-70), one of Wisconsin's most endearing grande dame establishments. The proprietors thankfully resisted the generally addictive impulse to transmogrify a cool old haunt into a B&B with high rates. The eight tight upstairs rooms ($50) share a bath and are very affordable, but remember you are above a noisy bar and only one of these rooms has AC. A room with a private bath is $80, but it's about a mile away (seriously). A quaint one-bedroom riverside cottage ($140) with a private sundeck is available; newer luxury suites ($140) have whirlpool baths, fireplaces, and great views.

Wall-to-wall with locals and travelers, the hotel's equally famed restaurant (11am-9pm or 10pm daily May-Oct., 11am-9pm Wed.-Sun. Apr. and Nov.-Dec.) offers traditional fare (try the Walnut Burger) plus vegetarian-friendly entrées. A regular schedule of live entertainment is offered in the outside beer garden. The hotel rents bikes and canoes and can help arrange local river and refuge tours.

TO ONALASKA

Wildlife Areas and Midway

You can explore along the southern tier of marshy Black River and Mississippi River bottomland (a salient "terrace") in the Van Loon Wildlife Area. The Mississippi River bottomland on either side of road is part of the protected Brice and Amsterdam Prairies. Exploring the alphabet soup of Highways Z, ZB, and ZH, among others, could take most of a day—note that these roads dead-end, so you'll have to backtrack to Highway 35.

The gorgeous Rustic Road 64 starts northwest of Holmen and east of the Van Loon Wildlife Area via a short jaunt north on U.S. 53/35 and then west on Amsterdam Prairie Road and Old 93. The trip features plenty of charming river-valley views but also allows for a short walk—along McGilvray Road, also known as Seven Bridges Road. The bowstring arch construction of the bridges has earned the road a place on the National Register of Historic Places.

Getting from the GRR to Onalaska and La Crosse can be a hassle, not to mention saddening with the increase in vehicular traffic. Under the curl of the bluff line, follow Highway 35 around the edge of Lake Onalaska, an enormous pool formed above Lock and Dam 7. Acre for acre, the lake is one of the most active fishing spots on the Mississippi River.

ONALASKA

Onalaska lies north of La Crosse at the hook in the Mississippi that forms the eponymous Onalaska Lake and Spillway—much loved by anglers, who take a huge number of sunfish from the waters. The oddball name, inspired by a late-18th-century poem (spelled "Oonalaska" in that usage), is one of three in the United States. The other two are in Texas and Washington, but Wisconsin's was the first.

Sights

Onalaska is technically the southern terminus of the **Great River State Trail,** a 24-mile multipurpose rail-to-trail ($5 pass) paralleling the Mississippi River. Dozens of great partially forged iron bridges are scattered along the route, and the trail also passes through lovely Trempealeau. One frightening highlight is the active Burlington Northern railroad line, directly next to the trail. A better highlight is the Midway Prairie, a small swath of extant virgin prairie north of the trail, now maintained by the U.S. Fish and Wildlife Service. For information, check out www.discoveronalaska.com.

Food and Accommodations

★ **Mary Cody's** (205 Main St., 608/549-2200, 8am-9pm Tues.-Sat., 8am-2pm Sun., $8-30) feels like a cozy café but offers an amazing fine-dining experience. Find comfort food matched with creativity such as curry turkey burgers; vegans are also well looked after.

Mostly chain lodgings are found here. B&B aficionados adore the **Lumber Baron Inn** (421 2nd Ave. N., 608/781-8938, lumberbaroninn.com, $95-129), a mammoth 1888 B&B dream home replete with carriage house, landscaped grounds, and nice details. The owners are gracious.

La Crosse

The castellated and craggy circumference of one of Wisconsin's prettiest cities is often voted number one by Midwestern travel mavens as far as aesthetics goes. Even Mark Twain, after a visit, referred to it as "a choice town." Buffalo Bill Cody found the town so much to his liking that he brought his Wild West Show back again and again, and eventually bought part of Barrons Island.

Where the La Crosse and Black Rivers flow into the Mississippi, La Crosse is situated below one of the Mississippi's major bights, allowing heavy commercial traffic. Here the prairie, and thus all paths on it, literally march to the river's edge. The original name, "Prairie La Crosse," came when voyageurs saw the Ho Chunk people playing the fast-paced game of lattice-head sticks, permanently infusing the name of the game with cruciform symbolism.

SIGHTS

★ Granddad's Bluff

The famed rock upthrust of **Granddad's Bluff** that towers more than 550 feet above the back haunches of La Crosse is without question the number-one scenic spot in western Wisconsin. Overlooking Wisconsin, Minnesota, and even Iowa—a viewing radius of some 40 miles—and the Mississippi Valley, the bluff is a perfect representation

La Crosse

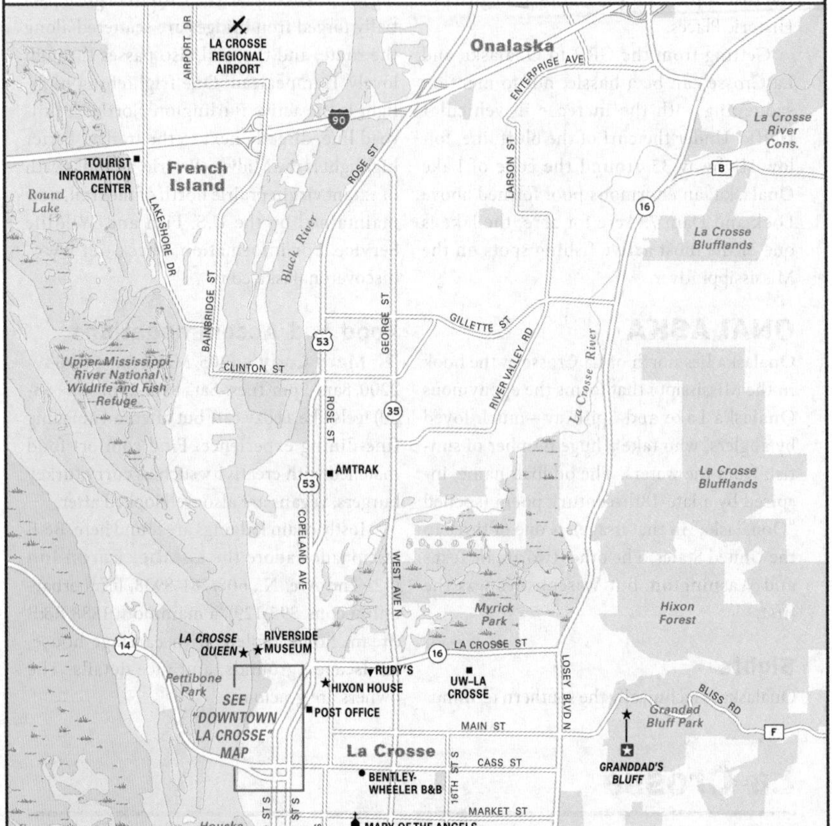

LA CROSSE REGIONAL AIRPORT
AIRPORT DR
Onalaska
ENTERPRISE AVE
90
La Crosse River Cons.
TOURIST INFORMATION CENTER
French Island
Round Lake
LAKESHORE DR
Black River
ROSE ST
LARSON ST
B
16
La Crosse Bluffland
BAINBRIDGE ST
GEORGE ST
GILLETTE ST
RIVER VALLEY RD
La Crosse River
53
Upper Mississippi River National Wildlife and Fish Refuge
CLINTON ST
ROSE ST
35
AMTRAK
53
La Crosse Blufflands
COPELAND AVE
WEST AVE N
Myrick Park
Hixon Forest
14
LA CROSSE QUEEN
RIVERSIDE MUSEUM
LA CROSSE ST
16
LOSEY BLVD N
Pettibone Park
RUDY'S
HIXON HOUSE
UW–LA CROSSE
BLISS RD
SEE "DOWNTOWN LA CROSSE" MAP
POST OFFICE
Grandad Bluff Park
MAIN ST
F
La Crosse
16TH ST S
CASS ST
GRANDDAD'S BLUFF
BENTLEY-WHEELER B&B
MARKET ST
Houska Park
3RD ST S
4TH ST S
7TH ST S
MARY OF THE ANGELS CHAPEL AT ST. ROSE CONVENT
JACKSON ST
33
Blue Lake
GREEN BAY ST
STATE RD
WEST AVE S
16TH ST S
LOSEY BLVD S
Mississippi River
SOUTH AVE
WARD AVE
14
WELCH MOTEL
MINNESOTA
0 0.5 mi
0 0.5 km
La Crosse Blufflands
Shelby
To Viroqua, Great River Road, and Wilson Schoolhouse B&B
© MOON.COM

of the 15-million-year-old geology of the Mississippi Valley. On a clear day, when the muggy August weather doesn't vaporize the whole thing into a translucent haze, the view can be superlative. To get here, follow Main Street east until it becomes Bliss Road; a hiking trail also leads here from Riverside Park.

Museums and Historic Structures

Chief among the impressive historic buildings is the **Hixon House** (429 N. 7th St., 608/782-1980, 10am-2pm Tues.-Sat. summer, $10 adults), an opulent flaxen-colored Italianate mansion. With nary a reproduction within, the place is beloved by Victorian buffs, especially for the Turkish nook, inspired by a late-1890s predilection for everything Middle Eastern and a room worthy of a sultan. Woodworkers will appreciate the variegated native Wisconsin woods.

On the grounds at Riverside Park is the **Riverside Museum** (608/782-2366, 9:30am-4:30pm Mon.-Sat., 10am-4pm Sun. summer, $4), a local historical repository for La Crosse and Mississippi River history. Expect a focus on riverboats.

Scenic Drives

Start with the **Mindoro Cut.** The southern terminus of this road (Hwy. 108) is northeast of La Crosse in West Salem, and then it stretches up to Mindoro. A massive project when undertaken around the turn of the 20th century, the road was cut into a ridge between the La Crosse and Black River Valleys. It was considered one of the most ambitious hand-carved roads in the United States when it was finished in 1906. Even with modern leviathan earthmovers and assorted belching technology, creating it would be a marvel.

In Mindoro, head for **Top Dawgs** (Hwy. 108, 608/857-3077, 4:30pm-2am daily, from $8), home of—count 'em—108 hamburger choices.

Rustic Road 31 also starts in West Salem at the I-90 exit for Highway C, running through city streets and outskirt roads and passing the Hamlin Garland Homestead, a few parks, and the local octagon house on the way to Highway 16. While in West Salem, check out the Neshonoc Dam, Mill, and Powerhouse, all examples of 19th-century residual architecture.

Otherwise, Rustic Road 26 (Hwy. MM) begins at the junction of U.S. 14 and U.S. 61 east of La Crosse and stretches along Mormon Coulee Creek Valley. The trip features eye-catching vistas of the Mississippi Valley and passes the wildlife refuge at Goose Island and the first area mill site, dating from 1854. Note that local temperature inversions can produce dense fogs.

Riverside Park

La Crosse seems to have a park for every resident, including funky river island parks. Chief among them is **Riverside Park** (100 State St.), home to a museum and the La Crosse Convention and Visitors Bureau office. Park legends say that the 25-foot 25-ton sculpture of Hiawatha here acts as a talisman against natural calamity. The park is also a departure point for riverboat cruises.

Mary of the Angels Chapel at St. Rose Convent

Since August 1, 1878, two or more Franciscan sisters from **Mary of the Angels Chapel at St. Rose Convent** (715 S. 9th St., guided tours 9am and 1pm Mon.-Sat.) have kept a continuous prayer vigil dedicated to the community and the world. Known as the "Perpetual Adoration," the vigil has been well documented in international media. The Mother House itself is quite impressive—a grand blend of Corinthian and Romanesque styles, with intricate bronze pieces and mosaics handmade by international artists.

Pump House

The local clearinghouse **Pump House Regional Center for the Arts** (119 King St., 608/785-1434, www.thepumphouse.org) is a stately 19th-century Romanesque Revival structure, La Crosse's first water-pumping

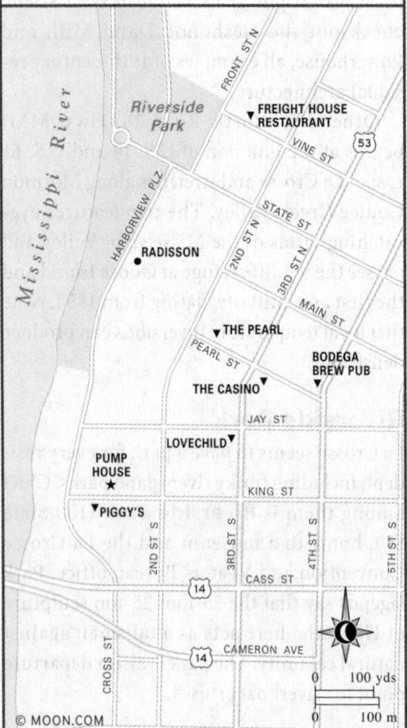

station. Art galleries within feature revolving multimedia exhibits and live, mostly folk music throughout the year.

Riverboat Tours

The ***La Crosse Queen*** (608/784-8523, www.lacrossequeen.com) is, engineering-wise, true to the past. Its propulsion is generated wholly from its split stern-wheeled design. Most contemporary re-creations of the old ships have free paddle wheels, which look nice, but the ship has modern screws underneath for real power. Fares (from $17) and schedules are complex: call or check online but generally 11am and 1:30pm daily in summer for sightseeing cruises. Boat tours depart from Riverside Park.

City Tours

Downtown La Crosse is one of the largest historic districts in Wisconsin. Well-done walking and driving tour information can be found at the visitors bureau in Riverside Park.

You can also hop aboard the **Historic Trolley Tour** (608/782-2366, www.explorelacrosse.com, $12 adults), which runs Thursday-Sunday mornings (10:30am) through the downtown area, the riverfront, and other districts.

RECREATION

Trails

The city of La Crosse has a notable network of trails following the La Crosse River through marsh and bottomland. Canoe trails also snake through these sloughs down toward the Mississippi. Easiest is to start from Riverside Park. Most hikers stay on the main trail to Granddad's Bluff.

The **La Crosse River State Trail** ($5 pass) is a 22-mile route on the packed limestone screenings spanning the abandoned grade of the Chicago and North Western Railway. The western trailhead isn't technically in La Crosse but in Medary, northeast of La Crosse along Highway 16. The eastern terminus is the Bicycle Capital of the United States, Sparta. Keep your eyes peeled for osprey nests and geese. Hard-core cyclists can connect to both the Elroy-Sparta and Great River Trails.

ENTERTAINMENT

Nightlife

La Crosse for a time had a reputation for carousing. In fact, the downtown 3rd Street district had the dubious statistical distinction of having the most bars per capita. Later on, a debauched annual festival turned violent and was canceled. More law enforcement has curtailed misbehavior, but with a University of Wisconsin school here, you're never far from a watering hole or an entertaining parade of inebriated students.

Pearl Street and environs offer pubs and a nightclub. Highly recommended by those who

1: Granddad's Bluff in La Crosse **2:** The Casino **3:** Freight House Restuarant **4:** Riverfest along the Mississippi River in La Crosse

1
2
CASINO
LOUSY
SERVICE
3
HOUSE
LA CROSSE
4

know is the jazz aficionado's dream joint, **The Casino** (304 Pearl St., 608/782-1910), an art moderne joint with a great long bar and good jazz collection, and it's easily spotted by the sign "Good Drinks, Bad Service" out front. Architecturally, the interiors represent post-Prohibition exuberance in cocktail lounge design; it's a bit flamboyant.

A number of pubs downtown offer live music on a changing schedule, including **Bodega Brew Pub** (122 S. 4th St., 608/782-0677, from $6), the longest-running; it's outstanding.

Festivals and Events

In addition to Oktoberfest, La Crosse celebrates its heritage with **Riverfest,** a July gathering mostly of music performances.

OKTOBERFEST

It's not surprising to discover that the largest (and longest-running) German heritage festival in the Midwest is held in Wisconsin. La Crosse's legendary blowout **Oktoberfest** (608/784-3378, http://oktoberfestusa.com), held the last week in September and the first week in October, features a 7:30am-midnight slate of polka, varied music, a host of family events from sports to carnivals to parades, and lots of beer. Almost half a million people attend this one, including a number of German musical acts.

FOOD

Brewpubs

Did you know La Crosse once had the world's largest six-pack? The Old Style sixer of the Heileman Brewing Co. towers no more, but La Crosse's microbreweries and brewpubs are picking up the slack. (The six-pack is now branded La Crosse Lager of the City Brewery.) A good option is **Bodega Brew Pub** (122 S. 4th St., 608/782-0677). The Bodega's bar is particularly nice, beside the brass kettles and with a nice vintage bottle collection. Beyond the 400 varieties of beer available, sandwiches such as a kimchi reuben or a classic Wisconsin braunschweiger and onion give you an idea of how eclectic the fare is.

Dessert

A treat for anyone is **The Pearl** (Pearl St., 608/782-6655, 9am-10pm Sun.-Thurs., 9am-11pm Fri.-Sat.), a 1930s-style soda fountain and confectionery along Pearl Street downtown. Besides homemade ice cream in the shakes, malts, and phosphates, there's a respectable selection of candies.

Updating that by about two decades is **Rudy's** (10th St. and La Crosse St., 608/782-2200, 10am-10pm daily Mar.-Oct., $3-5), a 1950s-era drive-in with super burgers, assorted chicken sandwiches, hot dogs, and roller-skating carhops. Best of all is the root beer, brewed daily.

Fine Dining

Renowned eatery ★ **Freight House Restaurant** (107 Vine St., 608/784-6211, www.freighthouserestaurant.com, 5:30pm-10pm daily, $10-30) is a 120-year-old Chicago, Milwaukee, and St. Paul Railroad edifice with the original old swooping beams and blond wainscoting now chock-full of railroad memorabilia, including Buffalo Bill's railroad car. Famed for its naturally aged and hand-cut steaks, it also offers a tremendous selection of seafood entrées (it brags of its Alaskan king crab) and a respectable wine list. If nothing else, perch at the bar and watch the barkeeps climb the ladder up the immense back wall.

The ineffable ★ **Piggy's** (501 Front St., 608/784-4877, www.piggys.com, 11am-2pm and from 5pm Mon.-Fri., from 4pm Sat.-Sun., $14-27) was specifically contrived for the engorgement of the carnivore—the restaurant does up hickory-smoked barbecue ribs as well as anybody. In a stunning 1871 foundry building (the suspension of the second floor is extraordinary), the restaurant has a ballroom with blues and jazz acts, a cigar room, and more.

It's rare indeed to find a new eatery that has essentially no faults. So far the experience at **Lovechild** (300 3rd St. S., 608/433-2234, www.lovechildrestaurant.com, dinner Mon.-Sat., $14-27) has been sublime. The understated but excellent food (Think chicken thighs are nothing? Wrong!), and the cool and relaxing interiors all make it well worth a trip.

ACCOMMODATIONS

Downtown

Nothing cheap exists downtown. The full-service **Radisson** (200 Harborview Plaza, 608/784-6680 or 800/333-3333, from $199) has superb river views (ask for one), a pool, a sauna, an exercise room, and decent dining. The decor is generic, but it's well taken care of and, dollar for dollar, it's better value than other riverside hotels.

Outskirts

Numerous lower-priced hotels and motels are on the north side of town along Rose Street (Hwy. 53) and on the south side, including the **Welch Motel** (3643 Mormon Coulee Rd./U.S. 14/61, 608/788-1300, www.welchmotel.com, $75), with no frills at all, but always clean and reliable.

Bed-and-Breakfasts

The ornate dwellings of ★ **Bentley-Wheeler B&B** (938-950 Cass St., 608/784-9360, www.bentley-wheeler.com, $135-175) took six years to build, and it shows. Stay in a ballroom—no kidding—or in a luxurious guesthouse. The attention to detail and service are unparalleled.

There's something charming about the restored 1917 **Wilson Schoolhouse** (W5718 U.S. 14/61, 608/787-1982, www.wilsonschoolhouseinn.com, $160). It's a real-deal school, a lovely redbrick edifice on 10 acres overlooking a valley. As it can house up to six people, it's quite economical.

Camping

La Crosse County takes its camping seriously. Nicer than some state campgrounds, the huge **Goose Island Campground** (608/788-7018) is three miles south along Highway 35. More than 400 sites—rustic to drive-through—are available here, with a sandy beach. Its location can't be beat—on the backwaters of the Mississippi River bordering a wildlife refuge full of egrets and eagles.

INFORMATION AND SERVICES

The **La Crosse Convention and Visitors Bureau** (608/782-2366 or 800/658-9424, www.explorelacrosse.com) is in Riverside Park. Additionally, the state of Wisconsin maintains a **Wisconsin Travel Information Center** one mile east of the Minnesota border.

GETTING THERE

Air

The **La Crosse Municipal Airport** (LSE, 2850 Airport Dr., 608/789-7464), northwest out of town near Onalaska, is served by flights daily from Chicago, Detroit, and Minneapolis.

Car

Getting to La Crosse from Minneapolis (via U.S. 52 and I-90, 162 miles) takes two hours and 40 minutes. From Madison (via I-90, 162 miles), it takes two hours and 20 minutes. From Wisconsin Dells (via I-90, 90 miles), it takes 90 minutes.

Bus and Train

There's an **Amtrak depot** (601 Andrew St., 608/782-6462) in town, with daily *Empire Builder* trains stopping on the route between Chicago and the Pacific Northwest. **Greyhound** (314 Jay St., 800/231-2222, www.greyhound.com) is in its own building not far away.

EAST OF LA CROSSE

Norskedalen Nature & Heritage Center

This 400-acre "Norwegian Valley" is a hodgepodge nature and heritage center in Coon Valley, approximately 16 miles southeast of La Crosse. Beginning as an outdoor arboretum laboratory, it grew to include many surrounding Norwegian and Bohemian homesteader lands. Also on-site you'll find the Skumsrud Heritage Farm. Sankt Hans Dag, an ancient Scandinavian summer solstice festival, jamborees, and classes in ecology and Norwegian language are great. Most popular are the nature trails at **Norskedalen Nature & Heritage Center** (608/452-3424, www.norskedalen.org, grounds daily May-Oct., limited hours Nov.-Apr., $6).

Hamlin Garland Homestead

Six miles east of La Crosse is **West Salem,** known for the **Hamlin Garland Homestead** (357 Garland St., 608/786-1399, tours 1pm-4:30pm daily Memorial Day weekend-Labor Day, $2), the boyhood home of Wisconsin native and Pulitzer Prize-winner Hamlin Garland. Born in 1860, Garland was among the first writers to use Midwest farm life as a central focal point, in particular creating strong female characters. Writing mostly as a social realist, he later turned to a style that pulled no punches in its grim landscapes and characters of the Midwest; he undoubtedly had a profound effect on August Derleth. Virtually unread in his lifetime, until being awarded the Pulitzer Prize in 1922, he is now remembered mostly for *A Son of the Middle Border,* a bittersweet fictionalization of growing up on a coulee-country farm.

La Crosse to Tristate Area

TO PRAIRIE DU CHIEN

Stoddard

Before the construction of Genoa's lock and dam, Stoddard wasn't even close to the Mississippi, but upon completion of the dam, almost 20,000 acres of bottomland was covered, and suddenly Stoddard could call itself a riverboat town. There's great ornithology along the Coon Creek bottoms in federal refuge land.

Stoddard has one of the best county parks in the state—**Goose Island,** with more than 1,000 acres, six miles of trails, and more than enough camping. Have a burger at **Thirsty Turtle** (102 S. Main St., 608/457-9115, 11am-1am Tues.-Sun.); they're good.

To the south, the river views turn splendid, and pull-offs pock the roadside—you can see three states. Midway between Genoa and Stoddard is an outstanding drive off the road to the east, to the Old Settlers Overlook, about 500 feet above the river.

Genoa

Here is where the mouth of the Bad Axe River opens, near Genoa, an untouched classic river town. The town grew with a decided Italian flavor as many early settlers were Italian fisherfolk who started out as lead miners in Galena, Illinois, before migrating here for the fishing. The Dairyland Power Cooperative began the first rural electric (here, hydroelectric) project in western Wisconsin. The state's first nuclear power plant was also located here, built in 1967 and taken offline in 1987. Fishing is key, with one of the upper Mississippi's best walleye runs; there's even ***Clement's Barge,*** since 1936 anchored below the lock for fishing—the oldest operation on the Mississippi. Much of the fish is stocked by the **Genoa Fish Hatchery** (S5631 Hwy. 35, 608/689-2605, 8am-3pm Mon.-Fri.), which is closer to Victory. Another of the "largest anywhere" variety of fish hatcheries the state seems to specialize in, this one is the most diverse, raising cold- and warm-water fish. Visitors can see aquariums of local aquaculture along with the areas used for raising fish. Otherwise, Genoa's **Lock and Dam 8** is one of the river's best for viewing "lock throughs" as the ships pass.

For grub, there's a decent burger pub, and then you can head for the **Old Settlers Overlook** nearby for a picnic.

Accommodations well worth the money are found at **Big River Inn** (500 Main St.,

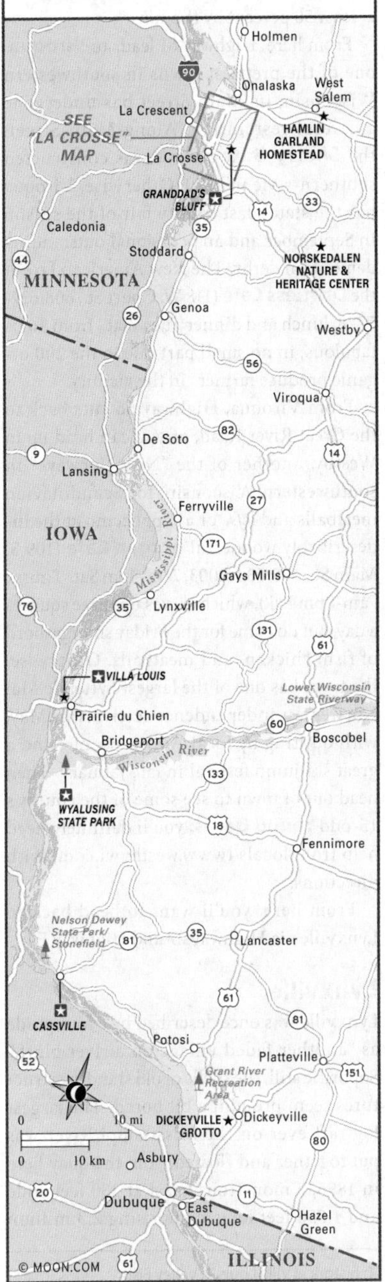

608/689-2652, www.bigriverinnwi.com, rooms from $64).

De Soto

Miles of birds hovering over the water lead to De Soto, named for the man commonly thought to be the first European to reach the Mississippi River and who eventually wound up in its watery clutches—his soldiers depositing his body there in 1541.

De Soto served as the western endpoint to one of the state's darkest moments, the pursuit of Chief Black Sparrow Hawk (immortalized erroneously as Black Hawk) and his Sauk and Fox band across the state, culminating in the Battle of Bad Axe at the mouth of the river of the same name, two miles north of De Soto. The battle had two effects: It ended serious Native American resistance to settlement, and when Black Hawk became a nationally prominent figure, a flood of settlers poured into the state. Today, the U.S. Army Corps of Engineers has established the somewhat somber **Blackhawk Park** (608/648-3314) at the battle site, with riverfront camping, a sandy beach, and a slew of historical sites. Ironically, two miles to the north, the town of Victory was named for Black Hawk's defeat.

Ferryville

Just north of Ferryville are the wonderful 3,000 acres of the **Rush Creek State Natural Area** (https://dnr.wi.gov), with incredible views from its trails; there are rattlesnakes here, however, so be careful. This is also an amazing spot to view eagles and hawks. Ferryville has a fairly long main street—recognized as the longest in any town or village with only one street. Apocryphal or not, the more colorful stories tell it that local laws allowed for the dispensation of liquor only every mile; saloonkeepers dutifully measured exactly one mile between venues.

Ferryville has cheese pickings at **Ferryville Cheese** (Hwy. 35, 608/734-3121, 5am-9pm Mon.-Fri., till 10pm Sat., 6am-9pm Sun.), with more than 100 varieties. It's also a good spot to pick up Amish or country-style quilts, and stop by the **Swing Inn** (106 Main St., 608/734-9916) to get a peek at the four-foot-plus rattlesnake skin, taken from surrounding hills, which are rumored to be rife with rattlers; the tavern is also purportedly haunted.

Note that visitors say Ferryville has strict enforcement of road rules and many traffic citations for its small size.

After Ferryville, Highway 35 is accompanied by the railroad for nine miles through a historical recreation area and more old river towns. You can take county roads east to loop through rolling hills for some S-curve routes to classic southwestern Wisconsin river villages. This is the area to pull out the county road maps and explore atop the bluff lines; lots of grand river vistas are apparent north of Lynxville.

Side Trips

Not quite halfway to Lynxville, head east 13 miles along Highway 171 through Mt. Sterling into the topography of green gumdrops that the region is known for. Mount Sterling has little other than a cheese factory specializing in award-winning goat cheese. Wisconsin writer Ben Logan grew up in the surrounding coulees and wrote a touching memoir titled *The Land Remembers.* Eventually you'll come to **Gays Mills,** legendary for its apple orchards. Just after the turn of the 20th century, the state scoured the southern tier of Wisconsin for promising orchards in which to plant experimental apple trees. The coulee valleys between the Wisconsin and Mississippi Rivers turned out to be perfect for the hardy fruit. Come spring and fall, roadtrippers flock for the blossoms or the harvesting. Along Highway 131 (which you'll need to take to the next stop) is **Log Cabin Village,** a grouping of original structures from the region.

North from Gays Mills along Highway 131 is the cutting-edge community of **Soldier's Grove,** notable as the only solar-powered town you may ever see. Picking up the pieces and moving to higher ground after a flood, the town had the commendable foresight to plan its current ecofriendliness—all of the buildings of **Solar Town Center** are heated at least 50 percent by the sun.

From here, Highway 61 leads to **Viroqua,** one of the prettiest towns in southwestern Wisconsin; its Main Street has undergone a careful restoration. Along Main Street, the **Sherry-Butt House** was constructed southern-style in 1870. Otherwise, Viroqua has the state's last county fair of the season in September and an occasional outstanding demolition derby. The New American fare at the **Driftless Cafe** (118 W. Court St., 608/637-7778, lunch and dinner Tues.-Sat., from $6) is fabulous, in no small part due to the 200 organic produce farmers in the vicinity.

From Viroqua, Highway 56 cuts back to the Great River Road, or you can head up to Westby, another of the "New Norways" in southwestern Wisconsin, for Scandinavian meatballs and *lefse* or a cappuccino at the indescribably wonderful **Borgen Cafe** (109 S. Main St., 608/634-4003, 7am-4pm Sat.-Thurs., 7am-8pm Fri.), which serves up three squares a day, but do come for the Friday smorgasbord of fish, chicken, and meatballs. Otherwise, the town has one of the largest Syttende Mai Norwegian independence festivals in May, with quilting by local Amish people, and a great ski-jump festival in late January. Then head out of town to see some of the county's 15-odd **round barns;** you'll definitely need help from locals (www.westbywi.com) with directions.

From here, you'll want to head back to Lynxville via Highway 27 and Highway E.

Lynxville

Lynxville was once described by a tour guide as "another faded village on a river bluff." Soporific still, the shells of old standing structures seem proud if a bit bored. The largest log raft ever on the Mississippi River was put together and floated from the quay here in 1896, a monstrous beast at 250 feet wide and 1,550 feet long, comprising 2.3 million

1: historical Villa Louis **2:** Valley Fish

1
2
VALLEY
FISH & CHEESE
SEAFOOD TURTLE GATOR
SAUSAGE JERKY BOLOGNA
APPROVED BY
"The STURGEON GENERAL"
GATOR JERKY
CATFISH BOLOGNA
VALLEY
FISH
CHEESE
VALLEY
FISH SHO
FRESH SMOKED PICKL
TURTLE MEAT
OPEN
FISH &
GATOR
BURGERS

board feet, rivaling the barges of today. The town back then was eight times as large as it is today, with many residents living on then-extant islets dotting the river before locks and dams flooded them out. The village sits at the southern cusp of a 17-mile-long lake created by the dams.

Lynxville offers few services—a tavern, a gas station, an antiques shop, and very basic sustenance dining—but there's some decent river scenery along **Lock and Dam 9.** (Actually, just south of town you can head up to Larson Bluff for a bird's-eye view.) Don't be shocked to see eateries labeled as "fishing float and diner" here. When you arrive at Gordon's Bay boat landing, just raise the flag and the float boat will come down on the hour to get you.

PRAIRIE DU CHIEN

To secure the strategic viability of the Fox and Wisconsin River corridors, the U.S. military started hacking a road and stringing forts through the wilderness to deter the Native Americans and the British and French interlopers. Prairie du Chien, chronologically the second-oldest settlement after Green Bay, would become the westernmost point of that chain of forts.

Native Americans originally inhabited the islands in the Mississippi River channels—up to several thousand on this site. Nicolas Perrot showed up not long after Marquette and Joliet and may or may not have erected a fort on one of the islands, by then a main node in the fur trade. The name comes not from prairie rodents but from a respected Indian chief who was honored by French settlers. It was at one time a major clamming center—clams were all the rage as buttons, and the oysters could command high prices in Eastern markets.

★ Villa Louis

One of the state's most respected historical sites is **Villa Louis,** in its time likely the most ostentatious and opulent home in the Upper Midwest. Fort Shelby was originally constructed on this island site immediately after the War of 1812 to protect the lucrative trade routes from the British. Native Americans had used the island for numerous burial mounds, and the structures were built right on top of some of them. In 1840, Hercules Dousman, a phenomenally wealthy fur trader, known as Wisconsin's first millionaire, originally built a home here—the House on the Mound, a slap in the face of Native Americans. His son, H. Louis Dousman, decided to raise a palatial estate here. Like many such acts, this one went broke. The estate underwent extensive and expensive ($2 million) restoration work, begun in an attempt to correct earlier historical renovations. Renovators used the original designs and implements, some kept in vaults in London. Even better, curators have managed to relocate original artwork and furniture. Its collections are now unparalleled in the country. The **Villa Louis Museum** (521 N. Villa Louis Rd., 608/326-2721, www.villalouis.wisconsinhistory.org, 9:30am-4:30pm daily mid-May-late Oct., $13.50) conducts tours on the hour 10am-4pm. The grounds are always open, and nearby on the same island is a Victorian historical education walk.

Other Sights

Somewhat less known is the **Prairie du Chien Museum at Fort Crawford** (717 S. Beaumont Rd., 608/326-6960, 9am-4pm daily May-Oct., $5 adults), the remainder of the fort where Black Hawk surrendered. On the site of the second Fort Crawford, both Zachary Taylor and Jefferson Davis spent military service time. The more intriguing segment of the museum, "Medical Progress," features Dr. William Beaumont's experiments on the human digestive system (on an Acadian fur trader with an untreatable belly wound) in the 1830s, in which he tied bits of food to surgical string to time the digestive process of the willing patient—200 times. Among the results: the first recorded temperature of the human stomach. The look at Mississippi clamming is fascinating.

The **Old Rock School,** on the edge of

downtown, is considered the oldest surviving school structure in Wisconsin.

Festivals and Events

Over Father's Day weekend in June, Prairie du Chien hosts one of the Midwest's largest **Rendezvous,** where buckskin-clad and beaver hat-adorned trapper, trader, and soldier reenactors congregate. The biggest of them all, the **Villa Louis Carriage Classic** (www.carriageclassic.com) with competitive carriage-driving events, is the weekend after Labor Day in September.

Food

You'll note the numerous places dishing up or selling the local specialty—Mississippi catfish, smoked or fresh—and even the odd purveyor of turtle meat.

A Sunday institution of sorts in the area is a leisurely drive to Prairie du Chien to sample the sliders at ★ **Pete's** (118 S. Blackhawk Ave., 11am-8pm Fri.-Sun.), a dainty burger-only joint built out of a caboose right downtown. It's been there over a century! A couple of dollars will fill you up. The unassuming **Spring Lake** (608/326-6907, lunch and dinner Tues.-Sun., from $6), 10 miles north of town, looks like tavern from outside, but inside the fare is a lovely mélange of supper club, old-style café, and darn near gastropub. The drinks are phenomenal. You can just pick up some cheese and fish (if not turtle jerky) at **Valley Fish** (304 S. Prairie St., 608/326-4719, 9am-5pm Mon.-Thurs. and Sun., 9am-6pm Fri.-Sat. Mar.-Dec.) and set off on a picnic.

Accommodations

Nothing sub-$100 in high season is all that great. That said, in a pinch, the best bet is the **Prairie Motel** (1616 S. Marquette St., 608/326-6461), which does have a friendly proprietor and acceptable rooms. Somewhat astonishing in little Prairie du Chien is the new and superb ★ **River District Hotel** (130 S. Main St., 608/326-7878, www.riverdistricthotel.com, from $175). Beyond the posh rooms, you will be amazed by the meals and snacks included, not to mention the made-to-order omelets for you in the morning. Yes, service is outstanding.

Information and Services

Visit the **Prairie du Chien Chamber** (211 S. Main St., 608/326-8555, www.prairieduchien.org) for more information.

★ WYALUSING STATE PARK

At **Wyalusing State Park** (https://dnr.wi.gov), high above the confluence of the Wisconsin and Mississippi Rivers, the Jesuit missionary Jacques Marquette and Louis Joliet discovered the upper Mississippi in 1673. The most popular spot in the park is Point Lookout, 300 feet above the rich blue waters of the two rivers. Sixteen impeccable miles of trails branch and twist through variegated topography. **Sentinel Ridge Trail** passes amazingly well-preserved effigy mounds—and wild turkeys. Along the Wisconsin River, a trail follows segments of a real-life immigrant path; another wagon trail loops back to the main trails and goes past a settler's semipermanent pit-stop point. Canoeists have marked routes totaling 20 miles along the backwater sloughs of the Mississippi; fishing is excellent. Local legend has it that there's gold treasure buried somewhere in the bluffs.

Here you can find superlative hiking but not-too-special **camping.** The sites are large but not very secluded. **Reservations** (888/947-2257, http://wisconsin.goingtocamp.com, reservation fee $8, from $23 nonresidents, day-use $11) are available.

Highways X, A, and then VV lead to Cassville through deep, winding valleys—a pretty drive via Wyalusing village and Bagley. Highway X features some of the best river views along the route, and Highway VV offers a sandy swimming beach. Wyalusing, once a rousing 600 people, now counts a dozen permanent residents. In comparison, Bagley looks absolutely worldly: A bar in town has a large world map full of pushpins left by international visitors.

Eagle-Watching

a bald eagle in flight

One of the primary U.S. bald eagle habitats is the Lower Wisconsin State Riverway, starting in Sauk City in south-central Wisconsin and stretching to the confluence of the Mississippi River. South of here to the state line, the Upper Mississippi Wildlife Refuge is another, and the Cassville area is one of the best to view eagles within that region. Having rebounded from perilously small populations, Wisconsin as of 2018 had approximately 1,700 eagle nesting sites, up from 108 in 1972, when it garnered federal endangered status. Statewide, 71 of 72 counties have active nests. Only Minnesota and Florida have more. Though eagles are still getting pushed out by development, poached by knuckleheads, electrocuted by power lines, and poisoned by toxic fish, the future isn't quite so grim; nearly every county in the state now has nesting pairs. The Wisconsin Department of Natural Resources even transplanted four eagle chicks to New York City parks.

Bald eagles really aren't bald; that word came from the Middle English *balled* ("white spot"). The much more impressive scientific name, *Haliaetus leucocephalus,* roughly translates as "white-headed sea bird." The white head doesn't fully appear until the bird is four or five years old.

Some incidental data: Eagles travel 30 to 40 mph in flight but in dives can eclipse 100 mph, and their vision is six times more acute than a human's. Eagles generally live 30 to 50 years, though in the wild that number has slowly dropped. Generally, nesting pairs mate for life; and both birds incubate the eggs. One nest weighed in at two tons.

HABITAT AND VIEWING

Situated near Lock and Dam 10 along the Mississippi River, and with two riverside power plants, Cassville has open water year-round. Furthermore, the craggy variations in southwestern Wisconsin's topography allow nests maximum isolation. Prey fish are attracted to the warm waters of the power plant discharge.

In the winter, Cassville can have as many as 200 eagles in one location; as many as 10 will stay in the region for the summer, with the rest moving back to northern Wisconsin or Michigan's Upper Peninsula. They do not migrate per se; they simply move south in winter for food and stop when they find it. The best sites around town to view the eagles are the Wisconsin Power and Light Company generating station along Highway VV northwest of Cassville (look for the road marked "Boat Landing"), and the bluffs of Nelson Dewey State Park, also accessible from Highway VV. The other power plant is on the south side of town, via Highway 133.

One obscure spot is six miles north of Nelson Dewey State Park along Highway VV and then west on Duncan Road. The Eagle Valley Nature Habitat-Glen Haven is a grouping point for up to 1,000 birds in winter. Don't expect a sparkling visitors center; it's nothing but tranquil Mississippi River banks and lots of eagles on 1,500 acres.

★ CASSVILLE

Majestic eagles and their migratory journeys up and down the Mississippi River draw most folks here—one of the top spots in the region to witness them.

With a solitary general store after its founding in 1831, locals nonetheless championed Cassville to become the capital. The California gold rush and silting on the Grant River doomed once-booming Potosi; Cassville took over the crucial river traffic control and soon eclipsed its neighbor.

River transportation began with a ferry as far back as 1836, and today the **Cassville Car Ferry** (608/725-5180, 10am-8pm daily Memorial Day weekend-Labor Day, Fri.-Sun. May and Sept.-Oct., $15 per car) still plows across the Mississippi to Iowa. This is one of the few remaining river ferries in the United States (another is in Merrimac, Wisconsin); the paddle wheel and horse-and-treadmill versions have finally been retired, but it's still a tristate tradition. Keep in mind, though, that river levels determine whether the ferry runs. At different times, water levels can be too low or too high.

The big draws for Cassville are **Stonefield** (12195 Hwy. VV, 608/725-5210, http://stonefield.wisconsinhistory.org, 10am-4pm daily late May-early Oct., shorter hours July-Aug., $12 adults), the agricultural heritage and village life museum, and, across the road, Nelson Dewey State Park, both of which are a mile north of town. Docents lead tours of a contiguous 1900 farmstead and the innovations (antique equipment and designs) of the time. Farther along across Dewey Creek, through a covered bridge, are the 30 reconstructed buildings done up as a showcase of turn-of-the-20th-century Midwest village life. Proudly overlooking all is the home site of Wisconsin's first governor, Nelson Dewey. It's a particularly rare architectural specimen—a Southern plantation amid pastoral dairy land, fitting the mold of rural Gothic, a leading design of the time, though not in Wisconsin. Dewey meticulously planned his rustic retreat also to give local masons jobs.

Nelson Dewey State Park (Hwy. VV, 608/725-5374, 6am-11pm daily) is a 750-acre plot hewn from the original 2,000 acres of the Dewey family spread along Dewey Creek, one of the only large plantations in the Upper Midwest. Most visitors head up to the majestic belvedere bluffs for miles-long vistas of the Mississippi River valley. Along the bluffs you'll see groupings of prehistoric **Native American mounds,** the two most prominent at the cliff top. These are not effigy mounds, such as those found up the road in Wyalusing State Park. A seven-acre bluff facing southwest above the river encompasses the Dewey Heights Prairie, a dry limy prairie set aside by the state as a scientific reserve. Reservations for **camping** (888/947-2257, http://wisconsin.goingtocamp.com, reservation fee $8, sites from $21 nonresidents, day-use $11) are available.

One little-known place is the sublime **Cassville Bluffs-Roe Unit,** 2.5 miles southeast along Highway 133 and a right turn onto Sand Lake Lane. This State Natural Area has rare flora such as goat prairie, Kentucky coffee tree, and honey locust. Trails bypass an eagle effigy mound. Even if you're not interested in the trees, go for the great views.

One of the largest assemblages of bald eagles along this stretch of the Mississippi River, part of a massive national wildlife refuge, is on display in January during **Bald Eagle Days.**

LANCASTER

You can take a side trip on your way from Cassville, since you won't see the river anyway. Lancaster, known as the "City of the Dome," is 15 miles up the road. Once you see the glass-and-copper-topped dome of the courthouse, modeled after St. Peter's Basilica, you'll understand the nickname. There is a Civil War Monument and Grand Army of the Republic (GAR) display on the grounds, the first such memorial in the United States.

From Lancaster, take the scenic country route along Highways N and U to Potosi.

POTOSI

The state's self-proclaimed "Catfish Capital," the town proudly boasts the longest main street in the world without an intersection. That's three miles without a stop or a cross street. Potosi was the earliest in the state to open a mine, and the last to close one; the town name even means "mineral wealth." "Badger huts," the hastily constructed sleeping quarters that lead miners burrowed into hillsides, inspiring the state's nickname, can

The Mighty Mississippi

The Mississippi River takes the bronze medal at 2,350 miles, though some say the Missouri River headwaters raise that number to 3,890 miles. It's impressive either way, its wildly tornado-shaped drainage basin spreading across 30 U.S. states and into two Canadian provinces, draining 41 percent of the United States' water.

The Wisconsin-Minnesota Mississippi trench runs for more than 200 miles from Prescott, Wisconsin, to East Dubuque, Iowa, with average widths of one to six miles and bluff lines rising to nearly 600 feet above the floodplain. The Upper Mississippi's bluffs are the most salient features and distinguish the Mississippi from other major rivers, which lack a vertiginous backdrop. The Wisconsin bluffs, facing west and thus drier, are grassier and rockier, and the surrounding prairie can resemble regions of the West.

EUROPEAN DISCOVERY

The Ojibwa people called it Messippi—appropriately, "Big River." Lookout Point in Wyalusing State Park, overlooking the confluence of the Wisconsin and Mississippi Rivers, was purportedly the first vantage point over the Mississippi for Marquette and Joliet, who wrote on July 17, 1673, of their "joy that cannot be expressed" at finally seeing the rumored great river. After exploring as far south as Arkansas, the pair realized they had found the route to the Gulf of Mexico and thus proved a waterway existed between Acadia and the Gulf. Nicolas Perrot laid claim to all the lands drained by the Mississippi for France in 1686 with the establishment of a fur trade outpost and fort near Pepin.

The first permanent settlement came near Prairie du Chien. Larger boats displaced Native American canoes for transporting beaver pelts and iron goods. The Chippewa, Buffalo, and St. Croix Rivers and their tributaries drain most of northern Wisconsin via the Mississippi, and, for a time, Wisconsin sawmills and log transportation villages controlled the vast industry. Between 1837 and 1901, more than 40 million board feet were floated down the Mississippi from Wisconsin.

MODERN MISSISSIPPI

Mark Twain would hardly recognize the river of his mind's eye, where barefooted boys mucked around on mudflats. During the Civil War, the river, in particular at La Crosse, Wisconsin, was invaluable to Union transportation networks; up to 1,000 boats per day traveled to and from La Crosse. Thereafter, river traffic for commercial purposes soared.

Natural history changed significantly in 1930, with the first locks and dams built by U.S. Army Corps of Engineers. Ten locks and dams form the western boundary of Wisconsin between Prescott and Dubuque, Iowa. Instead of a free-flowing body of water with a mind of its own, a mocha-colored chain of reservoirs, each 15 to 30 miles long, formed above dam lines, with sloughs and tidepools below. The sludgy backwater regions are amazing swamp-like groupings of lake and pond, with up to 200 in a given 20-square-mile area.

still be seen in the bluffs above the town. The largest port on the upper Mississippi, predating statehood, and the lead mines supplying Union forces (as well as, some say, the Confederates) solidified the local economy to the extent that Potosi real estate was the most valuable in the state by 1850.

Potosi even has the **National Brewery Museum** (209 S. Main St., 608/763-4002, 10:30am-9pm daily, $5). Little Potosi beat out St. Louis and Milwaukee for it due to the history of the town but also the extraordinary passion of the citizenry. It's actually within the old complex of the Potosi Brewing Co., which started in 1852 and brewed millions of gallons of beer until 1972. The complex was to be demolished, but the community rallied, raised $7 million, and transformed it into an amazing place, which also has a free transportation museum and, if that weren't

ENVIRONMENTAL ISSUES

the Mighty Mississippi

As the waters were corralled and ebbed into sluggish lakes and pools, sediment dropped and gradually squeezed out the riparian aquatic life. Factories and sewer lines discharged effluents directly into tributaries, and agricultural pesticides and fertilizer seeped in. Biologists fret that the five-decades-old reservoirs are gradually exhausting their livability and becoming inhospitable to aquatic life. Sedimentation—mostly due to agricultural runoff—remains a vexing part of the problem.

More worrisome is flooding (2018 and 2019 had some of the longest periods of above-flood stage in history). The dams ensure commercial traffic year-round, but that's only for the dry season; they do nothing to control flooding, and as the massive Midwestern floods of the mid-1990s proved, dikes and levees have severe limitations. American Rivers has put the Mississippi on its endangered rivers list. Environmentalists have heard it before; the Corps of Engineers is one of the densest layers of bureaucracy and is often criticized. River lovers say the Wisconsin stretch of the Mississippi, already the most dammed section of the whole river, should be allowed to return to its presettlement natural state by ripping the locks out and shipping things by rail—which would be cheaper, by most estimates. Some backwater areas would be allowed to dry out, preserving the ecosystem for the following floods.

RECREATION

Most of Wisconsin's segment of the Mississippi is protected as part of the Upper Mississippi National Wildlife Refuge, stretching 261 miles south of the mouth of Wisconsin's Chippewa River, the longest refuge in the United States. Some say this happened just in time, as Wisconsin had lost 32 percent of its wetlands by its establishment. This refuge is a crucial link in a migratory flyway, including points south to the Gulf of Mexico and the Atlantic Seaboard.

And while recreation brings in more than $1 billion a year to regional coffers, some claim the personal watercraft and wake-inducing pleasure craft are abrading the shoreline and causing untold damage to the aquatic ecosystem.

For anglers, walleye and sauger are most common, but the waters are also rife with catfish, and a catfish fish fry is a Great River Road classic. The area around Genoa has one of the best walleye runs on the Mississippi. Oddball creatures include the paddlefish and the infrequent snapping turtle.

enough, a Great River Road interpretive center and a restaurant-pub. Many travelers on the Great River Road stop here for a breather or a burger.

South of Potosi along Highway 133 is the **Grant River Recreation Area** (608/763-2140), a U.S. Army Corps of Engineers-maintained riverside campground. The managers can give good advice on **canoeing** in the area.

North of Potosi a mile and then east on Hippy Hollow Road brings you to the **British Hollow Smelter,** the last of its kind in this region. With a 200-foot underground chimney thrust deep into the hillside, the smelter was once one of the largest around.

Restaurants abound in the Potosi area, but wherever you eat, sample the Mississippi catfish, which is hard to avoid. The main street features a bunch of supper clubs, and you'll find more places to eat in Tennyson.

Triangular brown and yellow signs, marking an **auto tour** that takes in all the regional points of historical significance, line the roads around Potosi and Tennyson.

TRISTATE AREA

South of Potosi you have no choice but to get on U.S. 63, with little to see till you cross the Platte River. The road runs away from the Mississippi as the river rolls toward it. One more must-see before you hit the corner of three states is Dickeyville.

An over-the-top marriage of jingoism and religious reverence, the **Dickeyville Grotto** (305 W. Main St., grounds always open, tours 11am-4pm daily June-Aug., 11am-4pm Sat.-Sun. Sept., donation) is one of innumerable Midwest grottoes constructed around the turn of the 20th century, when a papal blessing allowed many religious people to become inspired and build what became serious tourist attractions. Constructed around an Italian-carved statue of the Virgin Mary cradling Jesus, the Dickeyville Grotto was the 10-year devotional labor of a priest named Mathias Wernerus. Like other grottoes, it is an odd, aesthetically challenging assemblage of broken glass, tile, stone, gravel, petrified wood, shells, and even gems affixed to virtually every nook and cranny. Linings are even done in onyx. And this just begins to describe the visuals.

Some view religious grottoes as an embarrassment to the devout; others will road-trip through two states to pick up a souvenir; and still others find them truly inspirational. Whatever the case, this is one of the best.

Beyond Dickeyville, there's nothing to see until the Illinois and Iowa borders. One intriguing idea is to head east on Highway 11 and link up with southwestern Wisconsin's Lead Zone.

the Dickeyville Grotto, a masterpiece of folk grotto art

The Driftless Region

Wisconsin's Driftless Region encompasses

nearly one-quarter of the state's geography—four times the square mileage of Connecticut—and the world's only pocket of land completely surrounded by glacial drift.

Ten thousand years ago, as the icy bulldozers of the ultimate glacial epoch gouged their way across the hemisphere, two adjacent thrusting lobes were rerouted by the declensions of natural valleys and immovable quartzite. The forks twisted around the natural borders of southwestern Wisconsin but never encroached on the interior—as had none of the previous mantles of glaciers.

Early geologists remarked on the region's similarities to the Cumberland Plateau in the Appalachians. An oddball topographical

Highlights

Look for ★ to find recommended sights, activities, dining, and lodging.

★ **Lower Wisconsin State Riverway:** Nothing's lovelier than a drive or a paddle along this beauty (page 362).

★ **Taliesin:** Frank Lloyd Wright's inspiring Taliesin was named a UNESCO World Heritage Site in 2019; come see it and you'll know why (page 366).

★ **The House on the Rock:** Equal parts kitsch and pack rat's dream, this house comes from one man with a singular vision (page 369).

★ **Mineral Point:** It feels like the 1850s in this place that gave us the name "Badger" (page 375).

★ **New Glarus:** Find a little slice of Switzerland in the United States (page 380).

★ **Elroy-Sparta State Recreational Trail:** This is the granddaddy of all U.S. rail-to-trail efforts, with grand tunnels and gregarious small towns (page 388).

★ **Kickapoo Valley Reserve:** Enjoy lazy canoeing past gumdrop topography along the country's crookedest river (page 390).

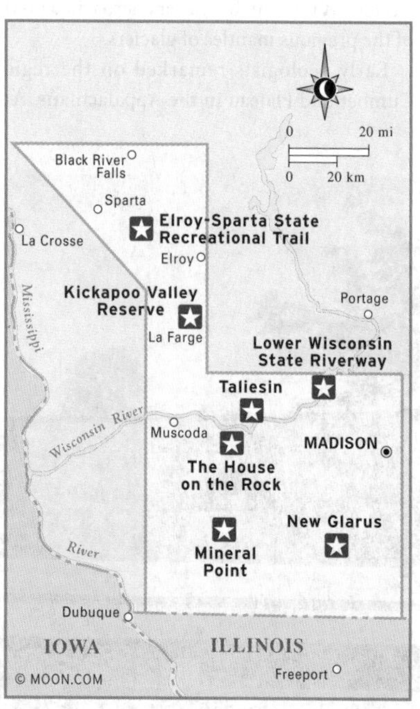

The Driftless Region

94
54
Sandhill S.W.A.
54
Black River Falls
Black River State Forest
Black River
73
Plainfield
22
54
173
13
Yellow River
80
Petenwell Lake
Wautoma
FORT McCOY
27
Lemonweir River
21
21
Necedah
Adams
Tomah
Mill Bluff State Park
Sparta
90
La Crosse R.
ELROY-SPARTA STATE TRAIL
Castle Rock Lake
Westfield
New Lisbon
39
Norwalk
Wilton
Kendall
Mauston
82
Montello
33
Ontario
Elroy
12
90
Wildcat Mountain State Park
14
Westby
Wisconsin Dells
KICKAPOO VALLEY RESERVE
16
33
Viroqua
La Farge
Kickapoo River
82
Reedsburg
Portage
22
58
Baraboo
Baraboo River
51
23
Devils Lake State Park
Poynette
27
14
Richland Center
Natural Bridge State Park
Sauk Prairie S.R.A.
Lake Wisconsin
171
60
35
61
Prairie du Sac
WOLLERSHEIM WINERY
Ferry Bluff S.N.A.
Sauk City
LOWER WISCONSIN STATE RIVERWAY
90
12
Wisconsin River
133
Muscoda
Spring Green
Waunakee
TALIESIN
14
Lake Mendota
Boscobel
THE HOUSE ON THE ROCK
Middleton
MADISON
SEE "THE OLD MILITARY ROAD" MAP
Blue Mound State Park
60
Governor Dodge State Park
Mount Horeb
L. Monona
L. Waubesa
Blue Mounds
18
18
Verona
51
Dodgeville
78
Paoli
East Branch
Lancaster
39
NEW GLARUS
Belleville
MINING AND ROLLO JAMISON MUSEUMS
133
MINERAL POINT
14
Belmont Mound State Park
New Glarus Woods State Park
81
Evansville
61
Yellowstone S.W.A.
23
Platteville
Belmont
Monticello
Cassville
Pecatonica R.
Potosi
81
Darlington
213
151
69
Mississippi River
59
80
Pecatonica R.
Benton
Shullsburg
Monroe
11
52
BADGER MINE
81
11
Hazel Green
IOWA
Dubuque
East Dubuque
ILLINOIS
20
26
0 10 mi
0 10 km
Galena

hodgepodge, the swooping coulees in the upper quarter are the uplands' most salient feature, marked by ambitious valleys so imposing and eye-catching that early Wisconsinites could find no English-language equivalent. In the north, northern and southern biotic regions intermingle. The rolling variegated terrain of red barns and roads slowed by chugging tractors is likely the most quintessentially rural in America's Dairyland.

This topography makes for awful cell phone reception and Internet access—this is absolutely true, by the way—but tourism officials are now touting this as a draw—a place where you can truly get away.

PLANNING YOUR TIME

You should spend more time here than you'd have otherwise planned—you won't regret it. Virtually every small area of southwestern Wisconsin is a ready-made day or weekend trip, each with a distinct flavor—ethnic heritage, recreation, or another draw. Most people stay in centrally located **Spring Green** for Frank Lloyd Wright's school, an amazing piece of folk art architecture at House on the Rock, and possibly some hiking and waterfalls at Governor Dodge State Park.

From here, head to the **Kickapoo Valley Reserve** near La Farge, part of this region's unglaciated coulee region, for lazy canoeing on a lovely river or a slow drive or bike ride through Amish country. This is my favorite getaway spot. Or take a jaunt down the road to see the picturesque and Swiss-style **New Glarus** and then go on to **Monroe** to bike a recreation trail and eat a limburger-and-onion sandwich for lunch. The Lead Zone doesn't sound like much, but hordes of people go to **Mineral Point** for its early mining-town architecture, art galleries, historical sites, and traditional Cornish fare like figgy hobbin and pasty for dinner. Recreation buffs will want to bike the first rail-to-trail state trail in the country, the **Elroy-Sparta State Recreational Trail.**

Along the Wisconsin River

★ LOWER WISCONSIN STATE RIVERWAY

From Sauk Prairie, in south-central Wisconsin just north of Madison, to its confluence with the Mississippi River, the 92.5 miles of officially sanctioned casual wilderness make up the **Lower Wisconsin State Riverway.** It's the longest remaining never-dammed stretch of river in Wisconsin.

A grand achievement of civic middle-ground cooperation—after seven years of hard fighting and horse-trading—these miles couldn't have been better chosen: Precious little development had ever taken place. Ultimately the state hopes to own up to 80,000 acres of riverfront property; slightly more than half that is now under state control.

The Riverway subsumes 19 official Natural Areas as diverse as Bakken's Pond near Spring Green and the haunting park of the Battle of Wisconsin Heights. It has been called one of the most amazing collections of natural history, ecology, pioneer and Native American history, recreation, flora and fauna, and topography in the Midwest. Shoreline incursion is barred, keeping the bluffs and greenery intact, and timber extraction has to first pass muster with a tough advisory board review. Among the flora and fauna inside the Riverway's parameters are 60 threatened or endangered species and 35 species of flora specific to the unglaciated Driftless Region. In some years, 500 eagles have been reported on this stretch of the river.

Previous: view from Ferry Bluff State Natural Area near Sauk Prairie; a surprising find on a trail in New Glarus Woods State Park; High Street in Mineral Point

The Riverway is also a work in progress. Development of new campgrounds, rustic or otherwise, are planned, as are a few new boat landings. Most are to be concentrated on the Sauk City-Spring Green upper third and gradually diminish farther along toward Wyalusing State Park. The stretch south and west of Boscobel will retain primitive status.

Sights

Four-plus miles southwest of Sauk City is the inspiring **Ferry Bluff State Natural Area,** just off Highway 60. From the 300-foot-high bluff, which is actually Cactus Bluff (go figure), the gorgeous vista includes the Baraboo Range to the east and Blue Mound to the south. Many disembark in Spring Green for an extended stay. Near the Lone Rock Boat Landing is a protruding cliff called **Devil's Elbow** for its hazardous navigation and numerous wrecks. The **Avoca Prairie,** seven miles west of the Highway 133 Lone Rock bridge, is almost 1,000 acres of wet mesic prairie, the largest tallgrass prairie remnant east of the Mississippi River. Turn north from Highway 133 onto Hay Lane Road, past Marsh Creek to the parking area; be aware of wet conditions or you will get stuck. You'll pass two of the last hand-operated draw-span bridges built by the railroads before reaching Bear Creek. After passing Richland City, **Bogus Bluff** comes into view, rich with apocryphal tales of subterranean riches, as well as splendid views. **Muscoda** is the only town of any size before Boscobel, and to the west is the **Blue River Sand Barrens,** a genuine desert—cacti, snakes, and a species of lizard all live here.

Recreation

CANOEING

Spring Green marks the southern end of the most populated canoe segment of the 92-mile Riverway; Sauk Prairie, 25 miles away, is the northern terminus.

The whole of the Riverway can be canoed, as there are no dams, cascades, rapids, or portages; it is among the longest unimpeded stretches of river in the Midwest. Many Spring Green-area travelers pitch a tent at **Tower Hill State Park** (5808 Hwy. C, Spring Green, 608/588-2116, http://dnr.wi.gov). Other popular access points include Peck's Landing, beneath the Highway 23 bridge, and the Lone Rock Landing, just east of the Highway 130 bridge.

A number of canoe outfitters offering trips

canoeing the Wisconsin River

on the Wisconsin can be found in Sauk Prairie and Spring Green.

HIKING

Hiking is grand, with trail networks along the Black Hawk Unit between Mazomanie and Sauk City and more between Muscoda and Blue River. These 40 acres have the wonderful challenge of no established trails. Know where you are, as private land borders the area.

SWIMMING

No matter what you see the locals doing, respect the river. Drownings are not uncommon. The sandbars make for enticing beach-the-canoe-and-frolic spots, but the current is misleadingly slow; the layered currents can drag you under. Worse, river fluctuations create deep sinkholes, which can be neither seen nor predicted by observing the current—stepping into one could be dangerous.

FISHING

Game fish are present in the Wisconsin River's main channel, but panfish predominate on poles and are especially pervasive in the sloughs and bayous off the river channel. For serious anglers, it might be worth a 17-mile drive east along U.S. 14 to Black Earth Creek, one of the top 100 trout streams in the country, with more than 1,500 brownies per mile.

Camping

Free dispersed camping is allowed on all state-owned lands, both the inner-stream islands and the banks. It isn't always easy to know what land is public; check locally before setting up camp. In certain areas, only the sandbars are not privately owned. They're a grand Huck Finnish way to experience the river, but water levels fluctuate and sandbars disappear, so be wary. Glass containers and fireworks are absolutely not allowed, and DNR wardens do check ($750 fine).

Information

Start with the **Lower Wisconsin State Riverway Commission** (800/221-3792, www.lwr.state.wi.us).

SAUK PRAIRIE

Sauk Prairie is both Sauk City and Prairie du Sac. In the 1840s, Upper and Lower Sauk were founded by Hungarian immigrant and dandy Agoston Haraszthy before he lit out for California to become the "father of the California wine industry." Sauk City managed to one-up Prairie du Sac by incorporating first, becoming Wisconsin's oldest incorporated village. It also gained fame throughout Europe as one of the country's last bastions of Freethinkers.

The cities were inspiration for native son August Derleth, the verbose wordsmith who championed the common Wisconsinite; his "Sac Prairie" stories were modeled on this area.

The ice-free and calm free-flowing waters (thanks to power plants) of the lower Wisconsin River and notched sandstone bluffs for roosts have also given rise to the reappearance of endangered bald eagles. Of the state's 1,400 nesting pairs of eagles, up to 10 percent are on the Sauk Prairie stretch of river.

Sights and Recreation

In January, **eagle-watching** is possible at several venues. Prairie du Sac has an information kiosk and viewing scopes. Veterans Park only allows viewing from inside cars. Another viewing site is one mile north of Prairie du Sac and then onto Dam Road to the hydroelectric plant. If you're feeling ambitious, drive out of town on Highway PF, where you might see eagles feeding on farmland.

Wollersheim Winery (Hwy. 188, 608/643-6515, www.wollersheim.com, 10am-5pm daily) has been producing wines since before the Civil War and now accounts for over half the wine produced in Wisconsin. The antebellum buildings, limestone aging caverns, and vineyards are an official National Historic Landmark. They have also opened a distillery. The winery offers hourly tours (10:15am-4pm daily May-Sept., guided tour $10).

Approximately 10 miles northwest of Sauk Prairie is a day-use and seasonal state park ($11 day for out-of-state license plates) focused on the only natural bridge in Wisconsin, **Natural Bridge State Park,** with crags and battlement outcroppings like those found throughout the state's Driftless Area. This wind-eroded hole in a sandstone promontory measures 25 by 35 feet and is one of the oldest sandstone natural features on the planet. Stratigraphic dating has also revealed Paleo-Indian encampments as far back as 12,000 years—among the oldest sites in the Upper Midwest. A couple of trails lead to a natural area. North of the park you'll find **Orchard Drive** and parts of Schara and Ruff Roads, one of Wisconsin's official Rustic Roads. This six-mile drive winds through grand glacial topography and plenty of wildflowers. This is as off the beaten path as it gets.

Approximately eight miles northwest of town via U.S. 12 and Highway C is the amazing **Baxter's Hollow,** a 4,950-acre parcel of the extraordinary Baraboo Hills, itself a vast tract of 144,000 acres and one of the last vestiges of contiguous upland hardwood forest in the United States. So rich with flora and fauna are these regions that Baxter's Hollow has been listed by the Nature Conservancy as one of the 75 Last Great Places in the Western Hemisphere. It has also been cited as the state's second official Important Birding Area.

The most humbling site in central Wisconsin is the **Black Hawk Unit** of the Lower Wisconsin State Riverway, of archaeological note for the rare and mysterious linear effigy mounds from the Late Woodland period (AD 600-1300), found only in the quad states region, including southwestern Wisconsin. The splendid and cryptic history is overshadowed by the massacre that occurred along the park's northern perimeter, the **Battle of Wisconsin Heights,** a skirmish was between Fox-Sauk warriors and a U.S. militia that had pursued them across the state. To get here, take U.S. 12 south to Highway Y and west to Highway 78, and head south.

Sauk Prairie is a popular spot to indulge in a favorite pastime on the lower Wisconsin: **canoeing.** The float from around Highway 60 and back to town is easiest; it's possible to go all the way to Spring Green. Canoe rental and shuttle service for a 2.5-hour trip costs $40-45; multiple-night trips are also possible. Among the half-dozen outfitters is **Bender's Bluff View Canoe Rentals** (608/544-2906, www.canoelady.com), run by responsible and

classic rural scene near Sauk Prairie

helpful people who have been in the business for generations.

Festivals and Events

Sauk Prairie proudly hosts the annual **Wisconsin State Cow Chip Throw** (www.wiscowchip.com), held Labor Day weekend.

Food

The dense German food at the ★ **Dorf Haus** (Hwy. Y, Roxbury, 608/643-3980, 5pm-9pm Wed.-Sat., 11:30am-8:30pm Sun., $8-22) includes real-deal Teutonic specialties—even *leberkaese* (pork and beef loaf)—one of the few spots in the state you'll see it. (Anyone else love chicken gizzards? They have them.) Special Bavarian smorgasbords are offered the first Monday of every month year-round, and also the third Monday in summer. Polka predominates, and they've started up dinner theater.

SPRING GREEN

Famed Wisconsin curmudgeon Frank Lloyd Wright found the area's lush beauty, nestled into the crook on the north side of a Wisconsin River bight, to fit his architectural visions so well that he founded a groundbreaking design school and lived here for five decades.

The prime geography on the edge of the Wyoming Valley has given Spring Green an edge. From an afterthought livestock shipping point, Spring Green has become a serious tourism town for canoeists, artisans, and Wright devotees viewing his works. Yet there is still a sense of pastoral simplicity; farmers still roll tractors down the roads and through town. Expansion of village roadwork coincided with projects to build ponds, wetlands, and a wildlife area. Spring Green didn't get a stoplight along busy U.S. 14 until 1995.

Sights

★ TALIESIN

Throw a dart in the Spring Green area and it'll hit the word "Wright." In 1911, three miles south of Spring Green's village center in the Jones Valley, Frank Lloyd Wright began work on **Taliesin** (Welsh for "Shining Brow") on the homestead of his Welsh ancestors. He had already made a name for himself in Wisconsin and in architectural circles. An unabashed monumental egoist, Wright had a profound artistic and architectural influence on the Badger State. He also enraged proper society with his audacity and uncanny ability to indulge his own notorious devil-may-care predilections no matter how offended others were. When he wasn't creating preternaturally radical designs, he was a deadbeat dad, browbeater, and megalomaniac who cut a figure with his ever-present cape and porkpie hat. As he said, "I had to choose between hypocritical humility and hated arrogance." His most famous exchange occurred over a client's phoning Wright to inform him that rainwater was dripping on his table in his new Wright home. Wright purportedly replied, "Move your table."

Wright stressed the organic in everything, and his devotion to the natural world predated environmental consciousness by generations, although this was intrinsic in Japanese culture centuries before Wright visited Tokyo and adopted the idea. Taliesin is a perfect example, gradually pulling itself along the crown of a hill, not dominating the peak.

As a preeminent architectural design school, today thousands of acolytes study here on the Taliesin Fellowship. The 600-acre grounds consist of his residence, Taliesin; Hillside Home School, a boardinghouse for a school run by an aunt; a home built for his sister, Yan-Y-Deri, Welsh for "under the oaks"; a windmill, his first commissioned project; and Midway Farm, all built between 1902 and 1930 while Wright and his associates operated his studio and workshop from the main building. Locally quarried sandstone is the predominant rock, and everywhere are those unmistakable Frank Lloyd Wright roofs. Wright would shudder to see how time has

1: the House on the Rock **2:** Frank Lloyd Wright's home, Taliesin

1

2

begun to ravage his estate—herculean efforts are under way to restore aging and nature-damaged structures.

The **Frank Lloyd Wright Visitor Center** (877/588-7900, www.taliesinpreservation.org or www.wrightinwisconsin.org, 9am-5:30pm daily May 1-Oct. 31, shorter hours Apr. and Nov.-mid-Dec.), more like a huge gift shop, offers myriad tours. The basic Hillside Studio Tour ($22 adults) is an hour long; the longest is the Estate Tour (4 hours, $92), a traipse around the entire grounds. There are lots of other options besides these. Advance reservations are not a bad idea.

OTHER SIGHTS

An alternative to the Wright sites is **American Players Theatre** (608/588-2361, www.americanplayers.org), which has created a following for its broad offerings and for its accessible direction. Carved into a hillside, it's a personal favorite: a steamy evening with nighthawks swooping and actors literally crashing through the underbrush. Or visit the new indoor theater. Performances generally run daily except Monday, with matinees on weekends, mid-June-early October; tickets average $50.

In the mid-1800s, as cannonballs started to fly across the Mason-Dixon line, what is today **Tower Hill State Park** (5808 Hwy. C, 608/588-2116, http://dnr.wi.gov, day use $11 out-of-state license plates) was the site of a major lead-shot production operation, but it went belly up in competition with farther-flung and cheaper facilities, all made possible by the railroad. The old shot tower and smelter have been refurbished, and it's a cool (literally and figuratively) traipse down into the cooling tank, where the lead pellets fell 180 feet to the bottom, becoming spheres and cooling off as they went.

Shopping

The **Wisconsin Artists Showcase** (143 S. Washington St.) in a 1900 cheese warehouse was being renovated at the time of writing to include studio space. Contact the local chamber of commerce to follow its progress, as it was always worth a trip.

From the other side of the planet, the wares at **Global View** (608/583-5311, hours vary), off Highway C along Clyde Road in a converted barn, are not the usual mass-produced Asian crafts; each item from Indonesia and India comes directly from the artisan. Global View maintains a reference library and location photographs of the source of each item, if not of the artists themselves, and tours to meet the artists are also organized here.

The whole of the Wisconsin River Valley is like one big farmers market. Summertime vegetable stands crop up every half mile. In autumn go for huge pumpkins.

Food

The area features classic road food-quality eats, greasy eggs diners, hard-core Midwest supper clubs, and wannabe chichi restaurants.

The ★ **Riverview Spring Green Restaurant** (5607 Hwy. C, 877/588-7900, 11am-3pm daily May-Oct., 11am-3pm Fri.-Sun. Apr., $5-11) in the **Frank Lloyd Wright Visitor Center** is the planet's only Frank Lloyd Wright-designed restaurant, constructed out of a popular 1940s local diner and a World War II aircraft carrier. Expect grand river views. It's staffed by culinary apprentices overseen by Odessa Piper, a farm-to-table pioneer and founder of the legendary L'Etoile in Madison.

A friendly family-run natural foods café and grocery in an old cheese warehouse, the inimitable ★ **General Store** (137 S. Albany St., 608/588-7070, kitchen open 8am-2pm daily, $4-9) serves healthful yet creative lighter fare—absolutely everything made from scratch—keeping vegetarians squarely in mind. They have the best espresso and are always on my itinerary.

At **Freddie Valentine's Public House** (134 E. Jefferson St., 608/588-0220, www.freddievalentines.com, lunch/dinner Wed.-Sun., $11-20) the menu is English classics (shepherd's pie) but also heartland classics (roasted apple grilled cheese), or maybe a curveball (their signature brisket), all in the cozy confines of an erstwhile local neoclassical bank.

Accommodations

Don't bet on finding budget lodgings in Spring Green, at least not between Memorial Day and Labor Day. The best bet for finding something worthwhile even close to $100 comes at the remarkably well-kept local **Spring Green Motel** (E U.S. 14, 888/647-4410, $125), in a countryside setting with comfortable rooms and attentive owners. Rates are far lower outside weekends.

Appealing for Wright aficionados is the **Spring Valley Inn** (U.S. 14 and Hwy. C, 608/588-7828, www.springvalleyinn.com, from $135), designed by Taliesin Associates. You can't miss its steepled upthrust, and its location is secluded but still prime. There are large rooms, an indoor pool, a whirlpool, a sauna, a rec room, and 28 kilometers of cross-country ski trails for guests. The restaurant features alfresco dining by a huge stone fireplace.

The most all-encompassing resort around is **The Springs Golf Club and House on the Rock Resort** (400 Springs Dr., 608/588-7000 or 800/822-7774, www.thehouseontherock.com, $185-285), a spread with a Robert Trent Jones Jr. championship course out the window as well as hiking, biking, and tennis. An inn has more family-style rooms, and lots of package deals—too many to process, really—are offered. It's a bit dated and some opine the resort tries to do too much at once, but it's clean, and the staff get high marks.

You'll find an artistic air at the oversize log building ★ **Silver Star** (3852 Limmex Hill Rd., 608/935-7297, www.silverstarinn.com, $149-175), displaying professional regional photographers' works within its chic café-coffeehouse and in all the rooms—minor museums of historical photographic figures. It's spread out over 300 acres of farmland (with chickens, which are awesome); sticklers for tradition are happy to find a cozy main room with a large fieldstone fireplace. The owners are lovely.

CAMPING

Good camping is at **Tower Hill State Park** (888/947-2757, www.wisconsin.goingtocamp.com, $8 reservation fee, campsites $21 out-of-state license plates, $11 day-use), but it is very limited—only 10 sites, so don't expect to show up and get a spot. Tenters in Spring Green also have **Wisconsin Riverside Resort** (S13220 Shifflet Rd., 608/588-2826, www.wiriverside.com), offering canoe rentals but little shade and at times noise; the restaurant gets good marks.

Information and Services

Contact the **Spring Green Chamber of Commerce** (608/588-2054 or 800/588-2042, www.springgreen.com).

★ THE HOUSE ON THE ROCK

The House on the Rock (Hwy. 23, south of Spring Green, 608/935-3639, www.thehouseontherock.com, mid-Mar.-early Nov., full package $30) defies description. Novella-length magazine articles have gushed about the left-handed grandeur and spectacle of its true-blue American anything-can-happen overkill. Cynical scribes paint this Shangri-La as contrived solely to assault visitors aesthetically. This is the grandest shakedown of them all in Dairyland, mere miles from the Wisconsin Dells. Best of all, it is less than 10 miles from that enclave of natural architecture, that altar to an ego, that house that Wright built—Taliesin, in Spring Green.

Back in the 1940s, Alex Jordan stumbled over a 60-foot candle-like outcropping in the Wyoming Valley. Intending to construct a weekend retreat and artists haven, Jordan somehow wrestled the original structure into completion atop the chimney. Bit by bit, this architectural gem began to morph into what it is today—the original house atop the rock, plus several other mind-blowing rooms and add-ons, all stuffed with the detritus that

Jordan accumulated through a lifetime, much of it museum-worthy in quality or scope.

Included are the Mill House, Streets of Yesterday, Heritage of the Sea, the Largest Carousel (20,000 lights and 275 handcrafted wooden animals, not one of which is a horse), the Organ Room (with three of the world's largest), and more. The best is the loopy Infinity Room, a glassed-in room that spikes 218 feet over the valley floor.

Is it art? Is it a giant Rorschach test of the mental wilds of an inspired eccentric? A feeling of visionary honesty pervades the place, never a feeling that it's all a sham or simple overindulgence. Many visitors overlook what a remarkable artistic and design achievement it was. Jordan never failed to think of how the visitor would see it all, from the 30-mile-panorama observation decks to the floral displays. Those devoted to tackiness have found their mecca; even the most jaded will shake their heads and grin.

WEST TO THE MISSISSIPPI

Muscoda

The story goes that the Fox and Sauk people who lived in encampments on this site lent the descriptive moniker *mash-ko-deng,* or "meadow of prairie" to their home. Henry Wadsworth Longfellow's "Hiawatha" includes the line "Muscoday, the meadow." At least he got the pronunciation to fit the spelling; Muscoda is pronounced "MUS-cuh-day."

Sleepy little Muscoda gets its kicks as the "Morel Mushroom Capital of the World." Tough to find but worth the hunt, the morel is feted annually with a festival in May. You might also stop by relic-quality **Tanner Drug Store** (N. Wisconsin Ave., 608/739-3218), a working drugstore with original oak and pine counters and some antiques. Right on the river at **Victoria Park** outside town sits the Muscoda Prairie, a lovingly restored stretch of prairie. In June the Sand Barrens section has cacti.

Boscobel

Back on the south side of the river, charming little Boscobel's location was pegged as *bosquet belle,* or "beautiful woods," by Marquette and Joliet as they passed through in 1673. There's great turkey hunting and canoeing, but another claim to fame is the Christian Commercial Travelers Association, known as the Gideons, founded in downtown's stone Hotel Boscobel in 1899. The story goes that two devout Christian salesmen were forced to double up in the hotel and got to discussing how tough it was to be God-fearing traveling men, especially in hellish river towns, and hatched the idea of an interdenominational fraternity for travelers. By 1914 almost 250,000 Bibles had been placed in hotel rooms nationwide. The old stone hotel still stands today, having reopened in the early 1990s.

In one of the oldest buildings in town, the aptly named ★ **Unique Cafe** (1100 Wisconsin Ave., 608/375-4465, 6:30am-2pm Sun.-Mon. and Wed., 6:30am-4pm Thurs., 6:30am-8pm Fri., 6:30am-3pm Sat., $3-6) features great pies, from-scratch café food, and an amazing assortment of "memorabilia" gathered by the proprietor. It's a genuinely interesting place.

Fennimore, 10 miles south of Boscobel, was once a major player in the lead trade. People generally stop by to see the **Fennimore Doll and Toy Museum** (1135 6th St., 608/822-4100, 10am-4pm daily Memorial Day-Labor Day, $3). The displays of tractors, trucks, cars, and more from various museums are ever-increasing.

Then there's the **Fennimore Railroad Museum** (610 Lincoln Ave., 608/822-6319, 10am-4pm daily Memorial Day-Labor Day, $3 suggested) down the street. Small steam engines ply a 15-inch track, and children can ride for a buck. The claim to fame here is the Dinky, significant as part of a 16-mile rail line in the Green River Valley, famed for its horseshoe curve, necessitated by the grade of the valley.

The Old Military Road

Essentially a cobbling together with lots of ancient Native American trails south of the Wisconsin River, the historic Old Military Road, the first overland link east to west in the state, was constructed in 1835-1836 by soldier labor. It used to stretch as far as Prairie du Chien. Today you're as likely to see bicyclists as you are cattle on the Fitchburg-Dodgeville Military Ridge State Trail.

MOUNT HOREB

The "Trollway," as the main drag in predominantly Norwegian Mount Horeb is known, is reminiscent of a northern European mountain village. Predating statehood, Norwegian, Swiss, and a few Irish farmers staked out the rolling ridges and valleys here. The whole area boasts a thoroughly northern European brick-and-frame architecture and several log structures and octagonal barns.

A significant number of visitors come to cycle the **Military Ridge State Trail,** since the access is central and well implemented; a $5 daily pass is required.

Otherwise, the **Mount Horeb Driftless Historium** (100 S. 2nd St., 608/457-6486, 10am-4pm daily, $7) is new for this edition and smashing (award-winning, in fact). Over 4,000 square feet document the land and every group that has called the region home since the Ice Age.

Wallet-wise, there are more Scandinavian gift huts than trolls in this town. All the information you need is at www.trollway.com.

Food and Accommodations

Housed in an old cheese factory, the **Grumpy Troll Brewpub** (105 S. 2nd St., 608/437-2739, lunch and dinner daily, $6-14) is the perfect spot to unwind after a long bicycle ride. Their food, beer, and service really are excellent.

But the mainstay for about a century has been the Scandinavian and Midwestern cuisine at **Schubert's** (128 E. Main St., 608/437-3393, breakfast/lunch daily, $6-10), a café and bakery that one simply must visit to appreciate the local ethos.

For something special, drive north to Mazomanie, via Highway F and U.S. 14, to the ★ **Old Feed Mill** (114 Cramer St., 608/795-4909, lunch Fri.-Sat., dinner Tues.-Sun., brunch Sun., $11-25). The eclectic heartland fare is luscious (signatures are meat loaf and pot roast, natch), but there's so much more. The exquisitely well-renovated 1857 mill and period detailing are equally fine—garnering nods from the state's historical society.

The **Clarence Gonstead Guest Cottage** (602 S. 2nd St., 608/437-4374, www.vrbo.com/139397, $130) was designed as a retreat for famed chiropractor Clarence Gonstead in the Prairie style by an acolyte of Frank Lloyd Wright. It's a one-bedroom gem that sleeps four and is worth the splurge. Two-night minimums sometimes apply.

BLUE MOUNDS AREA

Three miles west of Mount Horeb, the town of Blue Mounds, now centered between three highlights on the Old Military Road, began as a tiny mining encampment, and a huge amount of lead was extracted from its grounds.

Blue Mound State Park

In his notes of his Wisconsin River explorations in 1776, Jonathan Carver detailed extensively the "mountains" due south of the river. The highest point in southern Wisconsin at 1,719 feet the salient upthrust, now **Blue Mound State Park** (608/437-5711, camping reservations 888/947-2757, wisconsin.goingtocamp.com, 6am-11pm, from $23 nonresidents, daily fee $11 nonresidents), is rumored to hold Native American treasure.

Note the singular Blue Mound park and the plural Blue Mounds town. It's not a historical mistake, there are in fact two mounds—the

The Old Military Road

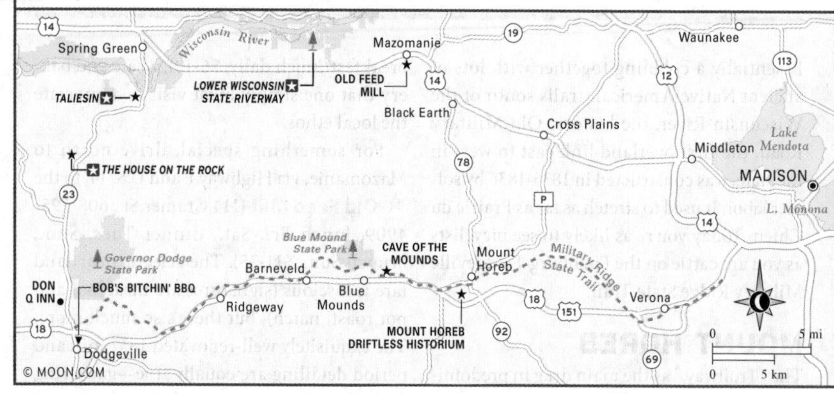

shorter eastern twin is now Brigham County Park in Dane County. Both have multilayered geology.

A number of trails wind throughout the area. Mountain bikers actually have a dedicated trail, unsurprisingly, as it is in close proximity to the Military Ridge State Trail.

Cave of the Mounds

Cave of the Mounds (2795 Cave of the Mounds Rd., 608/437-3038, www.caveofthemounds.com, 9am-6pm daily summer, shorter hours mid-Mar.-Apr. and Sept.-mid-Nov., $19) is a residual of the eons-old limestone cementation process; another cave, Lost River Cave, exists near Blue Mound State Park.

Although the area above the subterranean caverns was settled, mined, plowed, and grazed as far back as 1828, making the homestead the oldest in the county, the caves weren't discovered until 1939. It took until the 1980s for geologists of the U.S. Department of the Interior to declare it a National Natural Landmark. It's better known as the jewel box of large caverns, neither as large nor as famous as others, but, as the Chicago Academy of Sciences called it, "the significant cave of the upper Midwest."

The grounds of the farm up top, with a few assorted gardens, also make for great walking and picnicking.

DODGEVILLE

The name "Dodge" is big in this area thanks to Henry Dodge, a miner who became a leading figure in the Black Hawk War, which thrust him to regional prominence. Capitalizing on his fame, he was elected Wisconsin's first territorial governor. Dodgeville today is a bit somnolent but not forlorn—the downtown district has been touted for its careful balance of historic preservation.

Sights

The second-largest state park in Wisconsin and definitely worth the time, massive 5,000-acre **Governor Dodge State Park** (888/947-2757, http://wisconsin.goingtocamp.com, day-use $11) has just about everything a visitor could want, including some notable examples of Driftless Area terrain in the form of awesome bluffs. Naturalist-led hikes are held in summer. Almost 35 miles of multipurpose trails wind throughout the woodlands, open meadows, and around the two lakes; one short trail leads to a pretty waterfall.

1: the Military Ridge State Trail **2:** waterfall at Governor Dodge State Park **3:** Don Q Inn near Dodgeville

3

Two trails, totaling 10 miles, are also open to mountain biking. The shorter three-mile **Mill Creek Trail** is more popular, owing to the fact that it connects with the popular **Military Ridge State Trail.** There are 39 trail miles in total from Dodgeville east to Fitchburg, which in turn has lovely trails to Madison. The trail is wide and easy, passing primarily through bucolic cattle ranges. But there're plenty of woods, prairies, wetlands, and the Sugar River Valley—and almost 50 bridges. There's little camping along the way, and the park as a whole has over 250 campsites.

Take a gander at the residue of Dodgeville's lead-mining days at the first **slag furnace,** along East Spring Street next to the lumberyard. Extra lead was extracted from molten waste rock, and according to period reports, the glow could be seen for miles.

The Greek Revival limestone courthouse, the oldest in the state, is open to self-guided walking tours during business hours.

Food and Accommodations

Locals will definitely point you toward **Bob's Bitchin' BBQ** (107 N. Iowa St., 608/930-2227, lunch/dinner Tues.-Sun., from $7), which has outstanding meats but also a nice layout and friendly staff. For dessert, head up the street to the only old-fashioned soda fountain in the county at the **Corner Drug Store** (206 N. Iowa St., 608/935-3661, 8am-6pm Mon.-Fri., 8am-1pm Sat.).

It would be nearly impossible to miss the regionally famous **Don Q Inn** (Hwy. 23 N., 608/935-2321 or 800/666-7848, www.donqinn.net, $90-225), one of Wisconsin's most distinctive lodging options. You can't miss the landmark C-97 Boeing Stratocruiser parked out front. How about the trademarked FantaSuites? Jungle Safari and Sherwood Forest are good examples. Some rooms are the real thing—the original, the Steeple, is an 1872 church steeple; the erstwhile Dodgeville Station of the Chicago and North Western Railway also houses several rooms. It's kitschy, sure, but it is well run and almost everyone loves it.

Governor Dodge State Park (888/947-2757, http://wisconsin.goingtocamp.com, reservation fee $8, campsites from $23 nonresidents, day-use $11) has 250 campsites; six backpack sites are also available. Reservations are advised.

The Lead Zone

The hills in this area were the first reason nonnative interlopers who weren't soldiers stayed around. Native Americans had long scavenged the lead deposits, so rife that lead littered the topsoil. The first European to cash in on the ready-made ore, Nicolas Perrot, started bartering with the indigenous people around 1690. A century later, homesteaders quickly became mining opportunists and wound up as the first "Badgers." Mines were hewn into the sides of hills everywhere; accidentally forming the first cohesive region in the territory, these early pioneers solidified the economy that launched the state.

The results were staggering: The region generated 500,000 pounds of lead. Only 200 intrepid miners populated the region when the federal government first confronted the Fox, Sauk, and Miami people. By 1830 that number had grown to almost 10,000. Unsurprisingly the resident Native Americans felt they had been cheated and no longer agreed to cooperate. The resulting Black Hawk War flared on and off until the U.S. Army slaughtered Black Hawk's band at the Battle of Bad Axe near Prairie du Chien.

Settlers then poured in and made the region the country's largest lead producer. By the mid-1840s railroads had stretched far enough to transport cheaper lead from other areas, however, and the mining petered out. The Swiss and Germans, along with Irish and

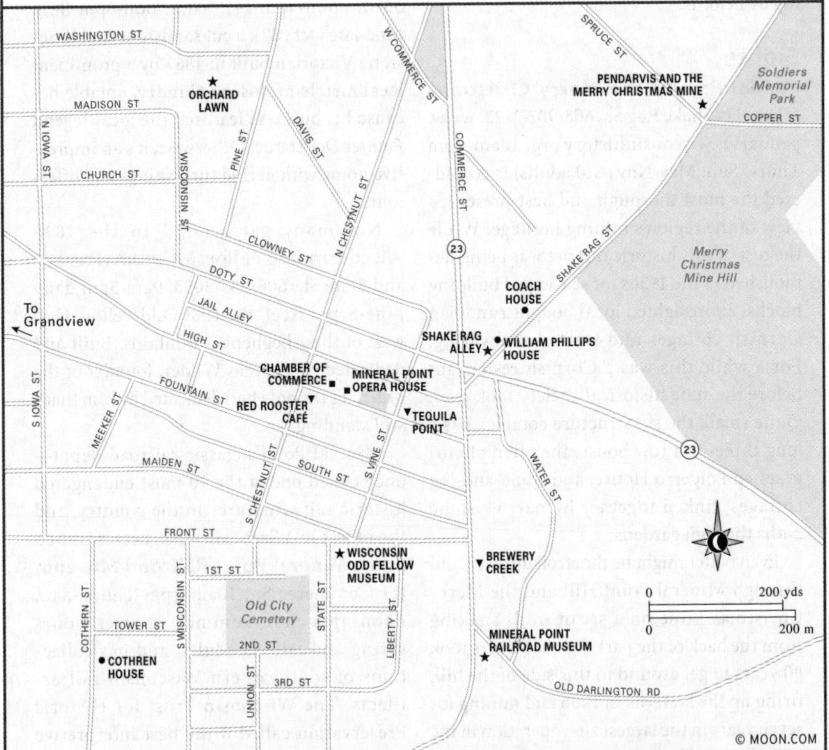

Yankee settlers, helped the area bounce back with the dairy industry.

★ MINERAL POINT

Despite its population of 2,500, Mineral Point's significance is huge; in many ways it is the heart and soul of the state's heritage. So important was it that the National Trust for Historic Preservation called it one of America's Dozen Distinctive Destinations.

The name was no fluke: Ore fever ran through the region when a prospector discovered huge deposits under Mineral Point Hill. Cornish immigrants took to the hillsides, tirelessly scratching gouges into the bluffs where they could rest and escape the elements. Many thus believe Mineral Point to be the origin of the nickname "Badger," as these ubiquitous holes and the miners in them were dubbed.

The territory of Wisconsin was established in Mineral Point on July 4, 1836. The railroads rolled through, and Mineral Point soon had the largest zinc operation in the United States; it persisted through 1979, when the last mine closed after 150 years.

More than 500 structures in this small town still stand on the 1837 platting. Most buildings contain locally quarried limestone and feature Cornish designs, and all date from the century after 1830. The town's gem-like status has impelled artisans to move to Mineral Point and set up studios, shops, and galleries.

The pervasive term *shake rag* stems from a

Cornish tradition: At noon, wives summoned their husbands home from the mines by waving dishcloths.

Sights

Pendarvis and the Merry Christmas Mine (114 Shake Rag St., 608/987-2122, www.pendarvis.wisconsinhistory.org, 10am-4pm Thurs.-Sun. May-Nov., $10 adults) is considered the most thorough and best-preserved view of the region's mining heritage. While the rest of this historic district was being demolished in the 1930s for scavenged building blocks, a foresighted local bought rundown Cornish cottages and started renovating. For a while this was a Cornish restaurant before the state historical society took over. Quite small, the six-structure complex has a long three-unit row house, the often photographed Polperro House, and stone-and-log cottages, linked together by narrow stone paths through gardens.

Even better might be the stroll up, over, and through Mineral Point Hill and the Merry Christmas Mine on a set of trails snaking from the back of the parking lot. Miners took 80 years to get around to this side of the hill, firing up the lanterns in 1906 and mining for seven years in the largest zinc operation in the area. Assorted hulks of rusting equipment and more than 100 abandoned crevice shafts dot the 43 acres. Native prairie restoration is ongoing, and big bluestem is already blooming again.

Guided tours led by garbed docents depart regularly; the last tour leaves at 3pm.

Up Shake Rag Street from Pendarvis, you can see other stone and stone-and-log dwellings originally built in the 1830s by Cornish potters, weavers, and other artisans, including Wisconsin's first pottery. This is **Shake Rag Alley** (www.shakeragalley.com), with nine historic structures, including one of the oldest log cabins in the state, surrounded by tailored gardens. Here you'll find artisans' workshops, galleries, inns, a café, and other worthy sights. Just looking at the classic structures is worth a few minutes.

North of the Chamber of Commerce is the **Orchard Lawn** (234 Madison St., 608/987-3670, noon-4pm Fri.-Sat., noon-3pm Sun. June-late Oct., $7), a cut sandstone and limestone Victorian built in 1867 by a prominent local merchant, Joseph Gundry, notable because his business featured the local-legend *Pointer Dog* statue. Otherwise, it's an impressive home with period furnishings and offers tours.

Not many get around to the 1838 **Wisconsin Odd Fellow Museum** (Front St. and State St., 608/987-3093, 9am-3pm daily June-Sept., free), the first Odd Fellow Hall west of the Allegheny Mountains. Built and dedicated by Thomas Wildey, founder of the order, it's the only hall dedicated by him that's still standing.

Mineral Point's classic railroad depot—once called one of the 10 most endangered historic rail structures in the country, and the oldest in Wisconsin—has been restored as the **Mineral Point Railroad Museum** (11 Commerce St., 10am-4pm Thurs.-Sat., noon-4pm Sun. summer, shorter hours spring and fall, $3 adults) and has collections of southwestern Wisconsin rail artifacts. The Wisconsin Trust for Historic Preservation called it the best interpretive site in Wisconsin.

If you're up for a road trip, 13 miles east of town is Hollandale, and a mile west of Hollandale, along Highway 39, is **Grandview,** the erstwhile home of folk artist Nick Engelbert, an immigrant dairy farmer turned self-taught artist. In the 1930s he began to transform his artistic visions into concrete, glass, and stone and scattered them throughout the gardens around his farm. It's a great experience and a splendid look at rural folk art.

Mineral Point is not known as an exercise destination, but locals are trying to change that. There is a dandy **hike-bike trail** to Dodgeville, connecting to the Military Ridge State Trail.

The **Chamber of Commerce** (225 High St., 888/764-6894, www.mineralpoint.com)

has information on **historic walking and driving tours.**

Entertainment

The **Mineral Point Opera House** (139 High St., 608/987-3501, www.mineralpointoperahouse.org) has undergone a long and painstaking renovation of its erstwhile grandeur. It features a slate of live performances during its May-October season. Once a major stop on the Midwest theater tour, it now also shows movies (daily in summer) as well as occasional theatrical presentations by the local Shake Rag Players and some traveling shows.

Shopping

Get ready to unshackle the calf hide. Ever since some pioneering artisans discovered the tasteful architecture and low-key small-town tranquility here in the 1940s, Mineral Point has been a hotbed for Wisconsin artisans. More than 40 galleries and studios populate the town, and more seem to open annually. One weekend each October, southern Wisconsin artisans open their studio doors for back-room views of the artistic process; Spring Green and Baraboo participate, but Mineral Point is the place to start any tour. The three-day festival is a great combination of art and halcyon autumn. They also hold the open house the first Saturday of April, June, August, and December.

Food

Better get used to hearing figgy hobbin, because you'll see the phrase incessantly. It is a Cornish dish, a pastry of raisins and walnuts, and it's quite rich. Other Cornish food includes saffron cakes, Mawgan meatballs, and pasties.

Once a county bank, the ★ **Red Rooster Cafe** (158 High St., 608/987-9936, 5am-5pm daily, $5-10) is a one-of-a-kind road food-quality eatery where diners sit at a horseshoe-shaped counter on old red vinyl and chrome swivel chairs beneath a coffered ceiling. The café serves pasty and figgy hobbin in a classic diner atmosphere.

Mexican filtered through the Southwest but spiced with an awful lot of open-minded creativity makes **Tequila Point** (43 High St., 608/987-6556, lunch/dinner Tues.-Sat., from $8) a great choice. In addition to what you expect, you might get muenster cheese curds with a Thai chicken taco; better, they love to update the menu regularly. The drinks are on point, too—the passion fruit margaritas are unreal.

Century-old limestone walls from its previous incarnation as a brewery storehouse have new ambience at **Brewery Creek** (23 Commerce St., 608/987-4747, 5-8pm Wed.-Thurs., 11:30am-8pm Fri.-Sat., 11am-3pm Sun., $7-15), a B&B and restaurant. The fare is gets high marks not just for home-brewed beer; they are wholly behind locally sourced ingredients. While you wait, notice the meticulous woodworking and imported tables. The B&B also has historic 1830s cottages for rent (from $110).

Accommodations

This is the town that time forgot, so take your pick from lodging in a dozen or more authentic historic structures. A caveat: Mineral Point's historic dwellings are legendary for having paranormal guests.

Laying your head on Mineral Point's Shake Rag Street, near Pendarvis, is the way to go. Choose between **William Phillips House** (14 Shake Rag St., 608/509-3940, www.williamphillipshouse.com, $179), an 1839 cottage which you may hear referred to as its erstwhile name The Mousehole, or rooms and suites in the **Coach House** (18 Shake Rag St., 608/987-3292, www.mineralpointlodging.com, $99), an 1840s structure, among others. It doesn't get much more historic than these. More information can be had from **Shake Rag Alley** (608/987-3292, www.shakeragalley.com).

Stay at the ★ **Cothren House** (320 Tower St., 608/987-1522, www.cothrenhouse.com, $139-159); you'll swear you're in Cornwall, such is the architecture and landscaping, modeled on the Cornish town of Redruth. Choose from a stone cottage or rustic log cabin, both with two bedrooms, and relax in the secluded gardens. The cabin, a pioneer dwelling from 1835, might be the most perfectly realized historic lodging experience in southwestern Wisconsin.

East and south along Highways D and F is **Yellowstone Lake State Park** (888/947-2257, http://wisconsin.goingtocamp.com, reservation fee $8, nonresidents from $25, day-use $11), a modest state park with 128 campsites, showers, a good fishing lake, and eight miles of hiking trails. A wildlife reserve is also part of this 2,600-acre park. Reservations are advised.

Information and Services

The **Mineral Point Chamber of Commerce** (225 High St., 888/764-6894, www.mineralpoint.com) is friendly and helpful.

PLATTEVILLE

The name doesn't exactly flow like honey, but Platteville it is as pleasant as any hilly agrarian burg you'll find.

The town was configured after the founder's home in Yorkshire. The name Platteville was inspired by the long gray bowls left by the lead-smelting process practiced by the Native Americans. While the lead lasted, it turned Platteville into "the present metropolis of the lead industry," as the old guidebooks referred to it. As the nucleus for the tristate mining industry, it became home to the country's first mining college—immortalized by a large M east of town atop Platteville Mound.

Sights

An exhaustive examination of the lead industry is at the **Mining and Rollo Jamison Museums** (385 E. Main St., 608/348-3301, www.mining.jamison.museum, 10am-5pm daily May-Oct., shorter hours Nov.-Apr., both museums $10 adults). The local Bevans mine was the region's best producer, pushing out two million pounds per year. Guided tours include clammy shaft walks replete with simulated mining. Top it all off with a hop aboard a genuine 1931 mine locomotive for a chug around the grounds, perhaps to the contiguous **Rollo Jamison Museum,** best described as a world-class junk collection with a keen eye on history. Keep in mind that the detailed exhibits of carriages and tools, and the general store, kitchen, and parlor mock-ups, are the work of a single collector.

Mitchell-Rountree Stone Cottage (Lancaster St. and Ann St., 608/348-2287, guided tours Sat.-Sun. Memorial Day-Labor Day, free) is the oldest surviving homestead in Platteville, and one of the oldest in the state. Built in 1837 by a local veteran of the Revolutionary War, it's distinctively built in the Tidewater Virginia style, and its two-foot-thick dolomite limestone construction is heralded as some of the finest in the U.S.

Food and Accommodations

Plenty of restaurants offer Midwestern comfort food. Get the soup (there's always one vegetarian and one vegan on offer) and a hunk of fresh bread to go at the **Driftless Market** (95 W. Main St., 608/348-2696, lunch Mon.-Sat.), a natural foods store.

A true slice of history is found at Platteville's **Walnut Ridge** (2238 Hwy. A, 608/732-1116, www.walnutridgewi.com, from $165). These three meticulously restored buildings date from the very beginnings of the lead era, including an 1839 miners' bunkhouse relocated from British Hollow, now a bungalow, and an immigrant family's house-barn for a kitchen. Note you'll likely have limited cell phone reception.

BELMONT

Don't blink or you'll miss what is likely Wisconsin's smallest state park—**First Capitol Historic Park** (608/987-2122, 10am-4pm weekends summer, free), seven miles east of Platteville at Highways B and G. Gladhanding politics were standard in Wisconsin long before it was even a state when the powers that be finagled microscopic Belmont into accepting territorial capital status. The hogs, chickens, and cows that stunk up the overhead gallery in the original building are long gone (legislators would stir up the piggies below with long poles when things weren't going their way), as is the legislative building. Two structures remain, now restored and featuring small exhibits on early-19th-century Wisconsin and a diorama of the first capitol.

Up North County Road G 0.5 miles is the day-use **Belmont Mound State Park,** with some trails leading to the mound, used by the first legislators as a landmark to find Belmont when traversing the prairies, no doubt wondering the entire way what they were doing here in the first place.

SHULLSBURG

This tiny town with the inspirational street names of Charity, Friendship, Justice, Mercy, Hope, and Judgment (and the less explicable Cyclops) was founded by a trader and platted by a priest. The city still has a 19th-century feel, with four dozen museum-quality buildings along its Water Street Commercial Historic District, built mostly between 1840 and the turn of the 20th century and devoid of modern fakeries.

A walk-through museum of mining life known as the **Badger Mine** (279 W. Estey St., 608/965-4860, http://badgermineandmuseum.com, 11:30am-4pm Wed.-Sun. summer, $7 adults) showcases the erstwhile Badger Lot Diggings, dating from the 1820s. Tours descend the same 51 steps the miners took into the ore shafts, extending 1,300 feet into the hillsides. Other lead mines exist and are open to the public, but none are this extensive. Among the aging artifacts, watch for Jefferson Davis's signature on the old Brewster Hotel register.

Outside town to the south is **Gravity Hill,** a supernaturally charged summit where cars drift backward up a hill, or so it appears. Ask for directions in town.

A number of historic structures line downtown Water Street, including the historic **Water Street Place** (202 W. Water St., 608/965-3226, 8am-8pm Tues. and Sat., 11am-8m Wed.-Fri., 8am-2pm Sun., from $9) restaurant, originally a bank. You never know what they'll come up with day to day, but pasty is always a good option.

BENTON

In this former mining hub, once named Cottonwood Hill, all that's left are the tailing piles. Benton is the final resting place of Friar Samuel Mazzuchelli, the intrepid priest and architectural maven who designed two dozen of the regional buildings and communities and gave Shullsburg its sweet street names. He is buried in St. Patrick Church cemetery; the church itself was the first stone structure in the area, and Mazzuchelli's restored home is on the church grounds. Ask at the new rectory for tour details. Mazzuchelli's 1844 masterpiece, the **Church of St. Augustine,** is in New Diggings, about five miles southeast via County Highways J and W. It's the priest's last still-intact wooden structure, although an expensive restoration has given it a new sheen. Only one mass a year is held here, at 2:30pm on the last Sunday of September. You may find someone around on weekends in summer to let you look inside; otherwise, it's a lovely stroll around the grounds to see the buildings.

Learn about the ugly shenanigans that went along with the mining at the truthfully named **Swindler's Ridge Museum** (25 W. Main St., 10am-4pm Fri.-Mon. summer, free) so called after a nearby bluff notorious for thievery. Friar Mazzuchelli's original rectory was recently moved from here down the street.

HAZEL GREEN

They should have called this place Point of Beginning: In 1831 a U.S. land commissioner sank a post here along the 4th Meridian, and every single piece of surveyed land in the state of Wisconsin is referenced from it. It's marked along Highway 80, south of town, but the actual site is a sweaty half-hour trudge. Wisconsin's only disputed non-natural border was the segment near Hazel

Green separating Illinois from what was then Michigan Territory.

In Hazel Green, head down to the **Opera House and Old Town Hall** (2130 N. Main St.). Stroll through the auditorium, which was the original stage and has a new hand-painted curtain. Believe it or not, it's now a fully realized puppetry house with amazing classes, demonstrations, and performances ($5). There are no official hours, but you may find it open.

West of Hazel Green along Highway 11 and Highway Z, Mazzuchelli also founded a men's college, now home to **Motherhouse of Sinsinawa Dominica** (608/748-4411), high upon Sinsinawa Mound (a sheer rise of Niagara dolomite), with awesome vistas. Some buildings date from the 1840s; the complex also has an exhibit on Friar Mazzuchelli, a sustainable agricultural farm, and best of all, a great bakery.

DARLINGTON

This impeccably preserved anachronism along the Pecatonica River features wide streets and a host of preserved architecture. The **Lafayette County Courthouse** (627 Washington St.) is the only courthouse in the United States built using the funds of a solitary individual; note the lovely rotunda with Tiffany glass. Foot for foot, there is arguably more mural space in this courthouse than any other in the state. Alexander Hamilton's son staked a claim in Darlington in 1828; later, Fort Hamilton became one of the oldest permanent settlements in the state, indicated by a marker on Highway 78.

Nine miles north of Darlington on WI-23 is the **Prairie Springs Hotel,** one of the earliest buildings in the region. It's one of the most unusual, well built in the southern vernacular style by an early miner turned soldier and local leader.

Swiss Valley

Green County might as well be called "Little Switzerland." The Swiss culture shows itself most prominently in New Glarus, an amazing Alpine-esque village. In Monroe, farther south, world-famous swiss cheese is produced thanks to a substrata of limestone soil, allowing a certain digestive process by which cows produce creamy milk.

In the 1930s, Monroe cheese-making had grown so prodigious that a postmaster in Iowa grew weary of the waftings of ripe Monroe limburger passing through his tiny post office. The Depression-era Works Progress Administration (WPA) guide captured the moment:

> Cheese was stoutly defended when Monroe's postmaster engaged in a sniffing duel with a postmaster in Iowa to determine whether or not the odor of Limburger in transit was a fragrance or a stench. Well publicized by the press of the Nation, the duel ended when a decision was reached which held that Limburger merely exercised its constitutional right to hold its own against all comers.

PAOLI

Before reaching Green County, you pass through some ready-made Sunday drive country and charming towns, including the quaintest of them all, Paoli. This lovely place is known mostly for its somnolent waterside small-town appeal, and now, due to its renovated grand 1864 **Paoli Mill,** one of a dozen Civil War-era structures in this village full of shops, galleries, and relaxed cafés where the food may even be grown by the people serving it.

★ NEW GLARUS

In 1845, a group of 190 Swiss left the canton of Glarus during an economically devastating period. Scouts dispatched earlier had stumbled onto southwestern Wisconsin and

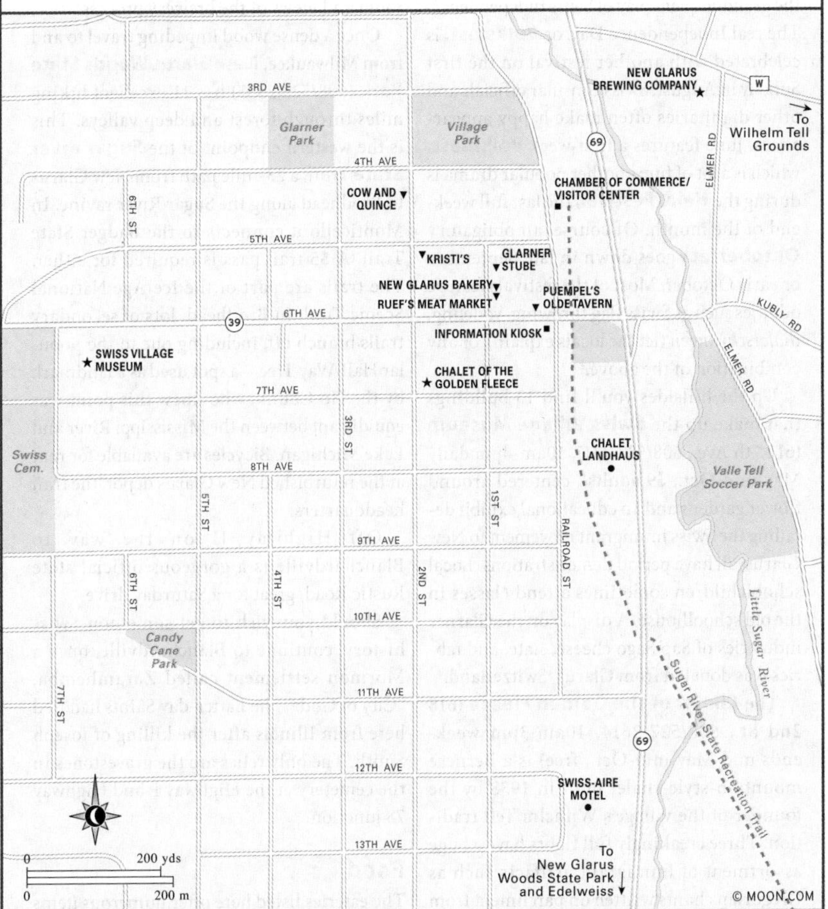

marveled at its similarities to Switzerland—nestled in the crook of a short but steep valley. Only 100 made it this far. After toughing out a rough winter, the farmers attempted to grow wheat, but they were unaccustomed to it. Returning to dairy, they soon began to gain interest in the East for their trademark cheeses.

New Glarus is full of white-and-brown architecture, umlauts, and scrolled Swiss-German sayings, many gift shops, frequent Swiss festivals, and Swiss music piped throughout the village. It may sound tacky, but it's done with class. The Swiss ambassador stopped by once to drop off a $4 million check for the establishment of a North American Swiss Heritage Center (www.theswisscenter.org) in New Glarus.

Sights

One word can fully encapsulate this town: festivals. Celebratory shindigs feting the Swiss heritage are held continually. The big draw is the **Wilhelm Tell Pageant,** held on Labor

Day annually since 1938. Virtually the whole town puts on the lederhosen and half perform the grandiloquent play of Swiss independence. The real Independence Day, or **Volksfest,** is celebrated with another festival on the first Sunday in August. Swiss consular officials and other dignitaries often make happy appearances. June features a first-week **Polkafest,** which is a lot of fun; another popular drama is during the **Heidi Festival,** the last full weekend of the month. Of course, an obligatory **Oktoberfest** goes down in late September or early October. Most of the festivals feature oddities such as Swiss flag throwing, yodeling, *thalerschwingen* (let the locals explain), or any combination of the above.

Up the hillsides you'll find 13 buildings that make up the **Swiss Village Museum** (612 7th Ave., 608/527-2317, 10am-4pm daily May-mid-Oct., $9 adults), centered around flower gardens and an educational exhibit detailing the Swiss immigrant movement to New Glarus; all have period demonstrations. Local schoolchildren sometimes attend classes in the old schoolhouse. A display on the Glarner industries of Sap Sago cheese, slate, and fabrics was donated from Glarus, Switzerland.

The **Chalet of the Golden Fleece** (618 2nd St., 608/527-2614, 10am-3pm weekends mid-May-mid-Oct., free) is a Bernese mountain-style chalet built in 1938 by the founder of the village's Wilhelm Tell tradition. Three creakingly full floors have a huge assortment of immigrant artifacts such as Gregorian chants written on parchment from the 15th century, Etruscan earrings, and a host of folk art.

New Glarus has, in my humble opinion, the best of the state's small-town breweries, the eponymous **New Glarus Brewing Company** (Hwy. W at Hwy. 69, 608/527-5850, www.newglarusbrewing.com, tours and tastings 10am-5pm Mon.-Sat., noon-5pm Sun., $8). The *braumeister,* trained in Europe, reaps accolades and ribbons at every World Beer Championship. This beer is so good that one Minneapolis bar was busted by the feds for illegally transporting it across state lines. Stop by the brewery's Hilltop site, south of town (the original is north of town), for its tasting room and views of the brewery process.

Once a dense wood impeding travel to and from Milwaukee, **New Glarus Woods State Park** (608/527-2335) has 11 excellent hiking miles through forest and deep valleys. This is the western endpoint of the **Sugar River State Trail,** a 23-mile path from New Glarus to Brodhead along the Sugar River ravine. In Monticello it connects to the Badger State Trail. A $5 trail pass is required for either. The trails are part of the Ice Age National Scenic Trail. In Brodhead, lots of secondary trails branch off, including one to the popular Half-Way Tree—a spot used as a landmark by the Ho Chunk, who knew this point was equidistant between the Mississippi River and Lake Michigan. Bicycles are available for rent at the refurbished New Glarus depot, the trail headquarters.

Off Highway H on the way to Blanchardville is a gorgeous official state Rustic Road, great for a Saturday drive.

Should you wish to get some non-Swiss history, continue to Blanchardville, once a Mormon settlement called Zaramhemba, "City of God." The Latter-day Saints had fled here from Illinois after the killing of Joseph Smith. The only relics are the gravestones in the cemetery at the Highway F and Highway 78 junction.

Food

The eateries listed here offer numerous items of Swiss cuisine. One unique drink is *rivela,* a malted, milky, alcohol-free sweet drink popular in Switzerland.

Ruef's Meat Market (538 1st St., 608/527-2554, www.ruefsmeatmarket.com, 9am-4pm Mon.-Thurs., 9am-5pm Fri., 10am-5pm Sat., noon-3pm Sun.) offers real-deal Swiss food. Ruef's smokes its own meats and makes *kalberwurst* and *landjaegers.* The best for cheese variety might be **Edelweiss Creamery**

1: view from the New Glarus Brewing Company gardens **2:** Badger State Trail east of New Glarus

1
2

(W6117 Hwy. C, Monticello, 608/938-4094), a cheese maker just 10 minutes away in Monticello and among the United States' only makers of wheel (180 pounds!); they also have a heavenly line of grass-fed only cheese.

For delectable Swiss-style baked goods, the ★ **New Glarus Bakery** (534 1st St., 608/527-2916, 7am-5pm daily, $4-10) is the only stop necessary. The Swiss-trained bakers turn out the house specialty, Alpenbread, but you might also find stollen, a dense, *two-pound* bread concoction of raisins, spices, marzipan, and almonds, often served at the end of meals or as the centerpiece at brunches.

The freshest options for breakfast or lunch, hands-down, are at the specialty market of local farm fare **Cow and Quince** (407 2nd St., 608/257-2900, breakfast/brunch/lunch Thurs.-Mon., from $6). The eggs and produce are extraordinarily fresh.

Along the main drag, **Glarner Stube** (518 1st St., 608/527-2216, lunch and dinner Wed.-Sun., $13-22), on a restaurant site dating from 1901, specializes in fondue (cheese cooked in wine), and *Genschnitzelettes* (tender veal sautéed in white wine sauce). This place is immensely popular, and no reservations are taken—get here early, especially since they close at 8pm Tuesday-Thursday.

★ **Kristi's** (119 5th Ave., 608/527-2012, lunch/dinner Tues.-Sat., shorter hours in winter, $7-22) seems to have an overreaching menu, with Mexican food next to seared ahi tuna. Don't worry—it's done fabulously, and the outdoor seating has lovely views. The service has always been excellent.

The requisite watering hole in New Glarus is a classic 1893 tavern, **Puempel's Old Tavern** (608/527-2045, www.puempels.com). This is the real thing, with the original backbar, dark woods, high ceilings, and the real draw, patriotic folk art murals painted in 1913 by Andrea Hofer. Run as a hobby by its owner, it's the kind of place where people stop by to play Swiss dice games.

Accommodations

The cheapest lodging in New Glarus is the **Swiss-Aire Motel** (Hwy. 69 S., 608/527-2138, www.swissaire.com, from $85), a basic motel right on the Sugar River Trail. The reviews are mixed, but most find it decent.

The **Chalet Landhaus** (801 Hwy. 69, 608/527-5234 or 800/944-1716, www.chaletlandhaus.com, $170) is built in rustic traditional Swiss style. The main room features a bent staircase, Swiss detailing, and a fireplace. Rooms have balconies strewn with geraniums, and there are a few suites available with whirlpools.

You'll find loads of quaint farmhouses, B&Bs and cottages in the surrounding countryside, most around $150 and up per night, but remember that means you're not in walking distance to the village center. The local **chamber of commerce** (608/527-2095, www.swisstown.com) has a full list.

CAMPING

Once a dense wood impeding travel to and from Milwaukee, **New Glarus Woods State Park** (888/947-2257, http://wisconsin.goingtocamp.com, reservation fee $8, nonresidents from $23, day-use $11) has arguably the best state park campsites, some of them bike-in, in this part of Wisconsin. Reservations are strongly advised.

Information and Services

The exceedingly tiny New Glarus **information kiosk** (608/527-2095 or 800/527-6838, www.swisstown.com) is run by the New Glarus Chamber of Commerce.

MONROE

An official from the National Trust for Historic Preservation once said it best: "If you put up a fence around Monroe, you could charge admission to get in." Swiss settlers in the area took cheese-making from a home industry to a gold mine just before the demise of the state's wheat industry. It was fabulous timing: By the 1880s, about 75 area cheese factories were producing swiss, limburger, gruyère, and other odoriferous varieties.

How serious is cheese in Monroe? Besides

"Swiss Cheese Capital of America" posted everywhere, the biannual Cheese Days draws in more than 100,000 people for equal parts revelry and education. Monroe has one of the country's only limburger cheese factories, and the only swiss and gruyère factory still using traditional copper vats is in Monroe. Appropriately, the local high school team name is the Cheesemakers—how's a Monroe Cheesemakers sweatshirt for an ineffably kitschy souvenir?

Be sure to listen to the **Swiss Program,** still heard on local radio station WEKZ (1260 AM) at 1pm Monday-Saturday.

Sights

The nucleus of town is the stately, almost baroque **Green County Courthouse,** with a quad-faced clock on the Yankee-style square. The architecture of Monroe displays an intriguing blend of subtle Swiss, common worker bungalow, and gingerbread Victorian, plus the odd octagon house or two.

The countryside no longer reeks of cheese, but no maker receives more attention than **Alp and Dell** (657 2nd St., 608/328-3355, www.alpanddellcheese.com). Carpeted walkways with large viewing windows overlook the famed copper vats, this being the only remaining cheese factory still using traditional copper. It's open during business hours, but it recommends arriving between 9am and 1pm for optimal cheese-viewing.

An aside: Diminutive operation **Franklin Cheese** (7256 Franklin Rd., 608/325-3725, Mon.-Sat., tours by appointment) is one of the few remaining true cooperatives in the United States and still offers tours if you call first.

Tours are offered at the brewery of the college student's staple beer, the eminently rich and tasty yet undervalued Huber. **Minhas Brewing** (1208 14th Ave., 608/325-3191, www.minhasbrewery.com, daily summer, Mon.-Sat. winter, museum free, tour $12) is the oldest continually operating brewery in Wisconsin and the second-oldest in the United States. Tours are daily in summer but complicated—expect at least 11am and/or 1pm.

Passing through Monroe, the **Badger State Trail** is a 40-mile former railroad bed/multipurpose trail running from Madison to Illinois; a $5 daily sticker is required.

See rare old-world Swiss alpine cabinetry and folk painting at the studio of **Gottlieb Brandli** (508 17th Ave., 608/325-6681, www.swisscabinetry.com, 8am-5pm Mon.-Fri.). Gottlieb, a former *Bauernmalerei,* or Swiss-German folk artist immigrant, has lectured on the stylistics of alpine design at the Smithsonian. Their custom design work can be viewed at the shop, or drive up to New Glarus to see more of it.

West of Monroe, **Argyle** is a lovely little community on the Pecatonica River. Check out the old gristmill on the river and then head for the old Partridge Hall-Star Theatre and gaze at the lovely trim work (it's a restaurant, so perhaps have a bite to eat). Argyle was the boyhood home of Fightin' Bob La Follette, a legendary Badger progressive politico, and local communities are pitching in to preserve and restore his family's home.

Festivals and Events

Cheese Days (www.cheesedays.com), held the third weekend of September in even-numbered years, has feted "Cheese Country" since 1914 with celebratory fairs, Swiss musicians, fun runs, a street dance, a carnival, exhibitions, an absolutely enormous cheese-flavored parade, and tons and tons of swiss and limburger, including a 200-pound wheel produced on the square over the weekend.

Food

A prerequisite while in Monroe is the local delicacy, the swiss cheese sandwich, at ★ **Baumgartner's** (1023 16th Ave., 608/325-6157, 8am-11pm Sun.-Thurs., till midnight Fri.-Sat., from $1), a southwestern Wisconsin institution since 1931. It's a cheese shop and locally favorite tavern, though you'd hardly know it was a supersize cheese operation by looking at the front door. Through the swinging saloon doors you'll enter a six-decade-old Shangri-La of small-town life—a long polished bar, wooden flat ceiling, horn racks, and mural maps of Wisconsin. Be daring and go native—try limburger and braunschweiger, just like the locals.

Equally precious local flavor is at the wonderful ★ **Turner Hall** (1217 17th Ave., 608/325-3461, www.turnerhallofmonroe.org, lunch Tues.-Fri., dinner Tues.-Sat., $4-7), which also offers a Friday-night fish fry. There's great basic Midwestern fare along with some creative Swiss-style food. There's even a great bowling alley. Show up for polka dances on Sunday.

Accommodations

Cheap and good describe the **Gasthaus Motel** (685 Hwy. 69 S., 608/328-8395, www.gasthausmotel.com, $70-85), a well-spruced little place; new owners did a good job.

West of town, ★ **Inn Serendipity** (7843 Hwy. P, 608/329-7056, www.innserendipity.com, $125-150) is in a heavenly bucolic location, but it's so much more. The innkeepers—corporate refugees from Chicago—show us all what could be done. It's an admirable exercise in purely sustainable living—100 percent powered by renewable sources, organic gardens (the greenhouse even has papayas year-round), and more; it has won multiple accolades for its efforts. This is a pure escape.

Information and Services

The **Monroe Depot** (2108 7th Ave., 608/328-1838, www.greencounty.org) is a county tourist information center as well as the trail headquarters of the Cheese Country Recreational Trail and a museum and heritage center to cheese-making.

Cranberry Country

In southwestern Wisconsin, "Cranberry" essentially means Monroe County and its primary community, Tomah, although 20 counties in the state produce the fruit as well. The county is one of the top sources of cranberries in the nation—4.3 million barrels annually, 57 percent of the nation's total.

TOMAH

Forty percent of the state's cranberries are produced within a 15-mile radius of Tomah. Cranberry heritage is best viewed 12 miles north in Warrens at the **Cranberry Discovery Center** (Hwy. E, Warrens, 608/378-4878, www.discovercranberries.com, 10am-4pm Tues.-Sat., 10am-3pm Sun. Apr.-Oct., shorter hours Nov.-Mar., $5 adults). A hands-on museum devoted to the cranberry, this is a fun place with a businesslike approach to a vital local industry. Seeing the old-time harvesting equipment is worth the admission cost. Cranberry ice cream can be sampled in the gift shop.

Warrens's September **Cranberry Festival** (www.cranfest.com) is one of the most popular in the state. A red explosion with cranberry products as far as the eye can see, it's a good time to take a bog tour. Organized tours on bike are offered over Memorial Day; 20- to 30-mile tours roll through cranberry marshes, sphagnum moss drying beds, great blue heron nesting sites, and old European (and one Mormon) homesteading enclaves.

Back in Tomah proper, head to Milwaukee Street and Superior Avenue—better known as "Gasoline Alley," after local Frank King's comic strip, which used Superior Avenue as its inspiration.

SPARTA

Bike trail capital Sparta—it's on the La Crosse River and Elroy-Sparta State Recreational Trail—is great for a trail-end cooldown. Canoeing is also pleasant along the La Crosse River all the way to the Mississippi. Sparta also has the **Deke Slayton Memorial Space**

Rural Wisconsin's African American Heritage

Today the majority of Wisconsin's African American population is concentrated in southeastern counties, particularly Milwaukee, Racine, and Kenosha.

Few realize that the state's African American history goes back to the initial presettlement voyageur exploration, and fewer still realize that the state once had thriving African American rural communities. Of these, perhaps best known is Pleasant Ridge in rural Grant County.

Pleasant Ridge started in 1850 with the arrival of a former slave owner who relocated to the rolling hills of southwestern Wisconsin from Virginia along with two of his erstwhile slaves and some of their family members. Whites and blacks settled in the agriculturally fecund and affordable region together; settlement grew with a hodgepodge of freed and escaped enslaved people and other migrants drawn to the new territory. Within five years there were more than 100 African Americans farming in the county.

This was certainly not utopia—there were two racially motivated murders—but the community achieved remarkable results in cross-racial tolerance for the time. Blacks and whites intermarried, attended schools together (blacks also went on to college), and farmed land side by side. But the growth of urban economies shrank the town, and by the 1920s Pleasant Ridge was nearly gone.

Another interesting African American community was found in the Cheyenne Valley area near Hillsboro in Vernon County. Founders followed a trail similar to that of the early settlers of Pleasant Ridge, making their way from North Carolina and Virginia. By 1880, more than 150 African American residents had settled the area. Their legacy remains in both the population and in the new Cheyenne Settlers' Heritage Park in Hillsboro, the starting point of a regional heritage driving tour detailing the lives of Wisconsin's early African American settlers. For information and a downloadable map, check www.hillsborowi.com.

and Bike Museum (208 Main St., 608/269-0033, www.dekeslaytonmuseum.org, 10am-4:30pm Mon.-Sat. summer, shorter hours in winter, $5), devoted to the local man turned NASA astronaut as well as bicycling, since it is a hub of Wisconsin biking. More eye-catching is the amazing **FAST Corporation** (14177 Hwy. Q, 608/269-7110, www.fastkorp.com), northeast of Sparta in Angelo, along Highway 21; the name stands for "fiberglass animals, shapes, and trademarks." Chances are you've spotted one of their 20-foot fiberglass sculptures of animals or logos at a business somewhere. The grounds are often liberally strewn with the product, which is why locals refer to it as the "Sparta Zoo."

Even farther north along Highway 27/71 is a roadside attraction in the **Paul and Matilda Wegner Grotto** (608/269-8680, dawn-dusk daily summer, free), 2 miles south of Cataract, 0.5 miles west of the Highway 71/27 split, another in southwestern Wisconsin's lengthy list of folk art mini masterpieces—concrete sculptures with broken glass and crockery facades, imbued with equal parts patriotism and religious fervor. The philanthropic Kohler Foundation rehabilitated the site and donated it to the county.

Even the town library, built to resemble a Roman temple with an open Palladian portico and short Ionic support columns, is worth a look.

Recreation and Accommodations

Perhaps that perfect synthesis of bucolic relaxation and recreation is at the super ★ **Justin Trails** (7452 Kathryn Ave., 608/567-3113, www.justintrails.com, $135-325), combining a country B&B, a Nordic ski area, and even a pro disc golf course. Day passes ($5) are available for nonguests.

FORT MCCOY

The only U.S. Army installation in Wisconsin sprawls for 60,000 acres around the community of Fort McCoy. While this isn't noteworthy for travelers, there are two recreation areas on the base. **Whitetail Ridge Recreation Area** has ski areas and **Pine View Recreation Area** has a beach, boat rentals, minigolf, and a large campground. A rather comprehensive **historical center and equipment park** is also on the base. The historical center is open sporadically; the equipment park is generally open 8am-4pm daily. Contact the public affairs office (608/388-2407, www.mccoy.army.mil) for information and to request a great driving tour guide of the base.

For more military history, head east along I-90/94 to Camp Douglas and the **Volk Field Air National Guard Training Site Museum** (608/427-1280, call for hours), an 1890s-era log cabin housing a full history of the National Guard, from the Civil War to the present.

Mill Bluff State Park

Along U.S. 12/Highway 16 near Camp Douglas and Volk Field is the underappreciated **Mill Bluff State Park** (608/427-6692). A geologist's palette, Mill Bluff is one of the region's only true mesas; most others are a hodgepodge of buttes, or the rarer pinnacle, such as Mill Bluff's Devil's Needle. Inspiring Mill Bluff was so high that when glacial Lake Wisconsin covered all of the central part of the state, this mesa and the assorted buttes around it were rocky islands. The geology is so diverse in this park that it was chosen as one of the nine units of the Ice Age National Scenic Trail. Petroglyphs have been found on bluff faces.

★ ELROY-SPARTA STATE RECREATIONAL TRAIL

In a state that popularized rail-to-trail conversions, the one that pioneered them all, finished in 1967, is the nationally regarded **Elroy-Sparta State Recreational Trail** (http://dnr.wi.gov). The 32-mile trail, virtually surrounded by wildlife refuge lands, roughly parallels Highway 71 and passes the headwaters of the Kickapoo River, along with the Baraboo River and numerous trout-laden creeks.

There are three otherworldly railroad tunnels, hand-carved into massive limestone rises for the railroad. Two tunnels are 0.25 miles long, but the other—the terrifying Norwalk Tunnel—is a full 0.75 miles of drippy spelunkers-delight darkness. There are no lights, so bring a flashlight—and a jacket.

a rustic farm in Sparta

It's an incredible experience—the light at the end of the tunnel disappears, and all you can hear is the overhead natural springs cascading through the faults worn in the cement. The tunnels took two or three years each to bore in the 19th century, and at present it can feel as if it takes that long to get through them. The Norwalk Tunnel still has the old "keeper's shack" in which a solitary watchman kept vigil on the thunderous doors, clapped shut between trains during winter to protect the tunnels from heaving and cracking from winter cold.

My favorite part is one mile from Sparta, where the path crosses over I-90; take a break and wave at the truckers to honk.

Trail Passes and Services

Trail passes ($5 daily), available in Kendall, are required; hiking is always free. Rentals and repairs are available at all communities along the route. Of note is Kendall, offering an electric vehicle for people with disabilities and a drop service for a nominal fee.

Small Towns

The historic railroad depot in **Kendall** is now the headquarters for the state trail; it serves as a repository for trail information, as well as being a small museum. Camping is available at the village park, and Kendall, the most "cosmopolitan" along the route, also has a B&B, a motel, and a restaurant, not to mention a great horse- and pony-pull festival on Memorial Day weekend.

Wilton serves a copious farmhand-size pancake breakfast every Sunday morning Memorial Day-Labor Day; the village park also offers a public campground. (Another campground, directly on the trail, is the Tunnel Campground.) Wilton offers bike rentals and has a habitat for rare wood turtles, one mile south.

In addition to the epic tunnel, **Norwalk** also offers easy access to Tunnel 2 for those just looking for photos. North of town, a flood-control dam has created an additional recreation area. Right on the trail you'll find the Norwalk Cheese Factory.

Elroy

Elroy is the hub of two additional trails—the **400 State Trail,** stretching to Reedsburg, and the **Omaha Trail,** a 12.5-mile seal-coated trail to Camp Douglas. The coolest accommodations along the trail are the domed units at Union Center's **Garden City Motel** (326 Bridge St., Wonewoc, 608/462-5409). Wonewoc also has an interpretive nature trail as well as a camp hall of the **Modern Woodmen of America** (Hwy. EE and Hwy. G, 608/983-2352, generally afternoon weekends. summer). The visually intriguing century-old landscape murals—called "The Painted Forest"—covering the entire interior were restored by the Kohler Foundation. La Valle's **Hemlock Park,** west of town, has great sandstone bluffs for hiking as well as lakes on either side. The Omaha Trail features another long tunnel, about 875 creepy feet long. Both trails require trail passes.

The lovely common area of central Elroy links all three trails and features an old depot chock-full of rentals and information for cyclists, along with public restrooms.

The **Elroy City Park,** on Highway 80/82 on the edge of town, offers a swimming pool and is a good place for a shower. **Waarvik's Century Farm** (N4621 Hwy. H, 608/462-8595, $125) is a fourth-generation family bed-and-breakfast with a separate house and a log cabin, offering bike shuttle service.

Coulee Range

Best representing what southwestern Wisconsin is all about is part of Monroe and all of Vernon and Richland Counties. Well within the topography of the challenging coulee country, the area also features excellent state parks, interesting architecture, glimpses of Amish life, and even classic pastoral grazing land.

Scenic Drives

Pick any country road and it will roll, dip, turn back on itself, and then seemingly forget itself in gravel and dissipate into something else—but always run along or over a creek or past a dilapidated homesteader's cabin, a rusted wreck, an Amish home-bakery, a bent-stick furniture maker, or a black horse buggy, and through fields of trillium.

The Ontario-La Farge area, north of Richland Center around Wildcat Mountain State Park, is a perfect encapsulation of everything the region offers. Two state-designated Rustic Roads run within these parameters. The shorter **Tunnelville Road** begins along Highway 131 south of La Farge and twists for almost three miles to Highway SS. Spectacular countryside wildflowers line Tunnelville, and there are few people here. More popular is the nine-mile trail, including Lower Ridge, Sand Hill, and Dutch Hollow Roads, all off Highway 131. Dutch Hollow Road is right at the southern tip of Ontario Amish country. Fantastic old-style architecture—a couple of Vernon County's 15 round barns—can be seen all along this road, as well as some contour farming. Highway D, east of Cashton, has the **Old Country Cheese Factory** (S510 Hwy. D, 608/654-5411, www.oldcountrycheese.com), a cooperative of hundreds of Amish farmers.

KICKAPOO RIVER WATERSHED

Highway 131 runs the course of the Kickapoo River watershed south from Tomah through Wilton, past the river's headwaters north of Ontario and Wildcat Mountain State Park, and into federal wild lands before hitting its southern half around Soldiers Grove, a total of 65 miles. The Kickapoo River, which doesn't stretch even as far north as Tomah when you total the serpentine bights and watery switchbacks, tops out at 120 miles. Thus it has become known as "the crookedest river in the nation," as one soon discovers when canoeing.

The original inhabitants of most stretches were the Algonquian Kikapu people. The word *ki-ka-pu* translates roughly as "one who travels there, then here," describing quite well both the rolling river as well as the peripatetic Native American people, who wound up in the Texas-Mexico region.

Note that the area has seen road improvements along Highway 131, making it safer to drive.

★ Kickapoo Valley Reserve

Many hydrophiles would name the Kickapoo River as best in the state for paddlers. The water is always low, challenging canoeists only during springtime melt-offs or summer deluges, and the scenery is superb—craggy, striated bluffs with pockets of goat prairie, oak savanna, and pine. The Ocooch Mountains along the west fork are legendarily gorgeous.

Escape the madding crowd and head south to La Farge and beyond to almost 9,000 acres of the **Kickapoo Valley Reserve.** For two decades, the feds had hemmed and hawed and vacillated over whether to dam the Kickapoo near La Farge, hoping to put a damper on spring floods and create a lake and recreation area. Opposed by some environmentalists, the project never got far off the ground; 1,100 acres were returned to the Ho Chunk Nation and the rest back to nature. Pockets of private land exist everywhere, so check first if you're hoping to leave the river. Another option is

Amish Countryside

In the mid-1960s, pioneering Amish began escaping stratospheric Eastern land prices, urban encroachment on their pastoral way of life, and droves of camera-toting tourists.

With a verdant landscape resembling the eastern Appalachians, southwestern Wisconsin—Vernon, Trempealeau, and Taylor Counties, along with some in Monroe County—was initially welcoming. The region was in an economic depression, and the hard work and spending by the newcomers was appreciated. But welcome soon turned to uneasiness when the Amish started to "pester" (as locals said) folks incessantly for rides or to use the phone, and when it was discovered that these ardent homeschoolers might be costing the townships state educational aid.

Amish carriage

LIFE AND ETHICS

There are approximately 100,000 Amish spread across North America today, and many more Mennonites, who are often mistaken for Amish. The crux of Amish life is a strong community based on two central tenets: separation and obedience. Separation (from the outer community) is necessary as the outside is inherently distracting. The Amish live by an ethereal concept called *gelassenheit,* roughly translated as "yielding" or "submission to an authority." This is part of the *Ordnung* ("order"), the unwritten collection of social mores to which each member must subscribe.

There are many kinds of Amish. Old Order Amish are more conservative, but more progressive communities are taking hold. For example, some will ride in automobiles, although they still won't drive them; some will use electricity, if it isn't theirs; some own property, and so on. All Amish still cultivate the ethic of hard work, thrift, and community support.

Though most people recognize the Amish by their black horse-drawn carriages, more widely discussed are the dictums regarding electricity. Most, but not all, electricity is banned in Wisconsin Amish communities. Electricity plays a significant role in Wisconsin Amish history for one big reason: milk. America's Dairyland understandably has rather stringent rules pertaining to milk storage and transport. The Amish, if they wanted to conduct commercial operations, had to be up to code, which is impossible without electricity. After years of negotiations, agreements were reached.

WISCONSIN AMISH TODAY

Population estimates are tough to fix precisely, but it's close to 8,000 statewide. Most are still concentrated in Vernon County; La Farge and Ontario are the largest centers for Amish agriculture in the state.

The Amish are particularly well known for their old-world artisanal work. Bent-hickory furniture is a staple of regional shops, as are the meticulously handcrafted quilts. Home-based bakeries and other cottage industries are found along every country road.

to head for the depths of the Kickapoo River Impoundment area at Rockton.

The west fork draws lots of serious anglers, and the main fork is almost perfect for lolling rolls. If you do want to start in Ontario—easiest for novices, as the outfitters are all right here—plan on 12 hours, or more if you like to take your time, to get to La Farge; most operations take you halfway, to Rockton.

The reserve has 50 miles of hiking, biking,

1
2

and horse trails along with 21 primitive campsites, about half reachable by car. It's first-come, first-served, and you must have a permit ($5 daily, camping $10-15) to use the reserve. Information is found at the **Reserve Office** (S3661 Hwy. 131 N., La Farge, 608/625-2960, www.kvr.state.wi.us). Another great source of information is the website of the **Kickapoo Valley Association** (www.driftlesswisconsin.com).

Food and Accommodations

Some fine burgers and steaks are in Cashton at the **Badger Crossing Pub and Eatery** (909 Front St., Cashton, 608/654-5706, 11am-8pm Sun.-Thurs., 11am-9pm Fri.-Sat.); it's in a cool old 19th-century general store.

I love both the **Driftwood Inn** (608/337-4660, 203 N. Garden St., $75) in Ontario and, even more, the **Hotel Hillsboro** (608/489-3000, 1235 Water Ave., $89) for their basic but clean and very friendly budget lodging.

A lovely drive to the northeast near Hillsboro, you'll find the equally admirable ★ **Inn Serendipity Woods** (S3580 St. Patrick's Rd., 608/329-7056, www.innserendipity.com, $395 weekend, $795 weekly), an A-frame retreat cabin by a pond surrounded by a 30-acre wildlife conservation area. It's run by the same earth-conscious folks who operate the top-pick Inn Serendipity in Monroe in southwestern Wisconsin.

If the primitive Kickapoo Reserve sites are full, most campers go to Wildcat Mountain State Park. La Farge's Village Park has primitive sites and charges a few dollars.

WILDCAT MOUNTAIN STATE PARK

Wildcat Mountain State Park (http://dnr.wi.gov) is the best untrammeled state park in Wisconsin. The state's Department of Natural Resources has called this little park one of its "undiscovered gems." It isn't exactly empty, but it's amazing how often it's not full.

The topography is splendid. Canoe the languid Kickapoo River, a stone's throw from Amish enclaves and some of the southern region's most unusual ecosystems. This is the only state park that caters to equestrians.

Much of the park's interior is established as a wildlife refuge. Along the line of demarcation separating biotic zones, the natural areas include plantlife and trees from northern and southern Wisconsin, some of them rare stands.

Canoeing

The Kickapoo River parallels the far northwestern perimeter of the state park and then bends away and doubles back into the park's interior.

Hiking

The shortest of three exceedingly short hikes is the **Ice Cave Trail,** south off Highway 33 onto Highway F. You could almost jump to the end of this trail. The **Hemlock Nature Trail** leads into the Mt. Pisgah Hemlock Hardwoods Natural Landmark Area and ascends to the 1,220-foot summit of the mini mountain, offering the best views in the park. Look for wild ginseng and trillium, as well as shaggy mane and puffball fungi, not found in many other places. The longest trail, **Old Settler's,** incorporates pathways foot-hewn by homesteaders.

Camping

The main campground offers 30 basic sites. Not far beyond the park's canoe landing, and east of Highway 131, is a primitive campsite. Reservations (888/947-2257, http://wisconsin.goingtocamp.com, reservation fee $8, nonresidents $20, $11 day-use) are advised in summer.

RICHLAND CENTER

Frank Lloyd Wright was born in Richland Center in 1869, and several of the community's buildings were designed by the famed

1: lovely Kickapoo River 2: bluffs of Wildcat Mountain State Park

Suffragette City

Richland Center, Frank Lloyd Wright's birthplace, was also arguably the birthplace of women's suffrage. Many women, recently successful in the Temperance movement, turned their sights onto the egregious American predisposition toward sexism. The town was one of the few to allow women to work in the newsrooms of the local papers. Richland Center fiercely debated the inclusion of a suffrage clause in its charter when the city finally incorporated in 1887; it didn't pass, but that galvanized the movement even more.

ADA JAMES

A pioneer of U.S. women's suffrage, Ada James was born in Richland Center, the daughter of a founding member of one of the original Women's Clubs in the state. James was a political progressive from the start, destined by a familial predilection for activism. In 1910 she founded the Political Equality Club and instituted an unheard-of notion for the time—grassroots campaigning.

James's father and uncle were the first politicians to introduce Wisconsin legislation for suffrage. Both failed, but James was ultimately successful in dispatching her father to Washington to present Wisconsin's 19th Amendment ratification papers, giving women the right to vote. Most had assumed Wyoming would be the first state to force the issue; many believed Wisconsin's progressives only paid lip service to the issue.

As a direct result, four decades later, in 1960, Dena Smith was elected state treasurer, the first woman elected to a statewide office in Wisconsin. James herself never held elected office.

architect. Ada James, a pioneer in U.S. women's suffrage, was also born in Richland Center; she led a second wave of women's rights campaigners to the passage of the 19th Amendment.

Sights

Architect Frank Lloyd Wright dubbed it his "Mayan House," and the redbrick **A. D. German Warehouse,** with its flat roof and concrete frieze, does show some temple overtones. Designed and built in 1915, during what many experts have called the zenith of his artistry, it is one of few surviving structures of this period. Renovations to transform it into a public space are currently underway.

Rockbridge is a well-named spot five miles north of town. Right off Highway 80 is legendary **Natural Bridge Park,** in the Pine River Valley. The site is of historic significance, as it was one of the shelters for Black Hawk and his band in their doomed flight from the U.S. Army in 1832.

In addition to the famed natural bridge, along Highway SR you'll find another oddity, **Steamboat Rock,** as they say around here, "dry-docked above the Pine River." A final whittled rock in the regional menagerie is **Elephant Rock,** viewed along Highway 58.

Central Wisconsin Sands

Meander a mere mile off the I-39 and you'll find a variegated and challenging topography—multicolored striations in mammoth sandstone cliffs, wetlands, residual prairie and woodland, superb major rivers, and that famous but underappreciated gritty soil.

Gazing at a map, it's hard not to notice the Wisconsin River, the Sand Country's most salient feature, slicing through the heart of the region. This "hardest-working river in the nation" and its valley have given residents sustenance and sculpted an amazing topographical diversity. Within the region is Wisconsin's third-highest point, flatlands, and some chocolate-drop undulation.

Eons of primeval lakes and oceans washing in and out of the central region have produced a mishmash of predominantly bog and

Highlights

Look for ★ to find recommended sights, activities, dining, and lodging.

★ **The Dells:** Do not miss a river cruise through the otherworldly Upper and Lower Dells of the Wisconsin River (page 402).

★ **Water Parks:** The Dells are home to the biggest water parks, the most slides, and the wildest rides in the state (page 402).

★ **Circus World Museum:** This museum is a favorite spot for kids, but everyone will get a laugh at the jugglers and clowns here (page 408).

★ **Merrimac Scenic Drive:** Roll through glacial terrain on your way to one of the last free river ferries in the country (page 411).

★ **Parfrey's Glen Natural Area:** Devil's Lake State Park's most precious area features bluff trails and obsidian waters (page 415).

★ **Central Necedah Wildlife Preserve:** This is a splendid locale for hiking and spotting cranes (page 418).

★ **The Highground:** The drive here runs through charming farming communities and stops at an inspiring memorial devoted to peace (page 425).

★ **Leigh Yawkey Woodson Museum:** This museum draws visitors for its amazing ornithological art collections (page 427).

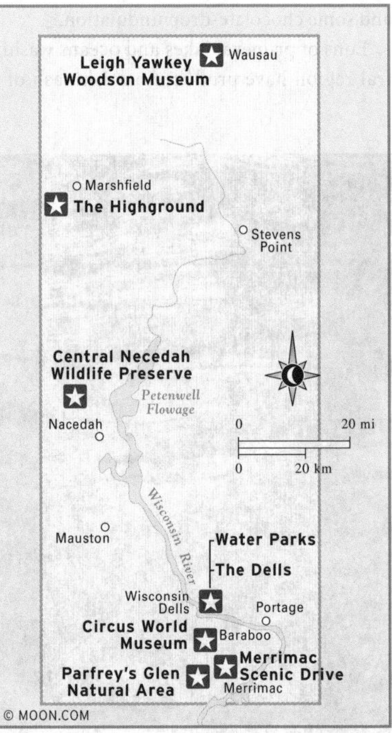

Central Wisconsin Sands

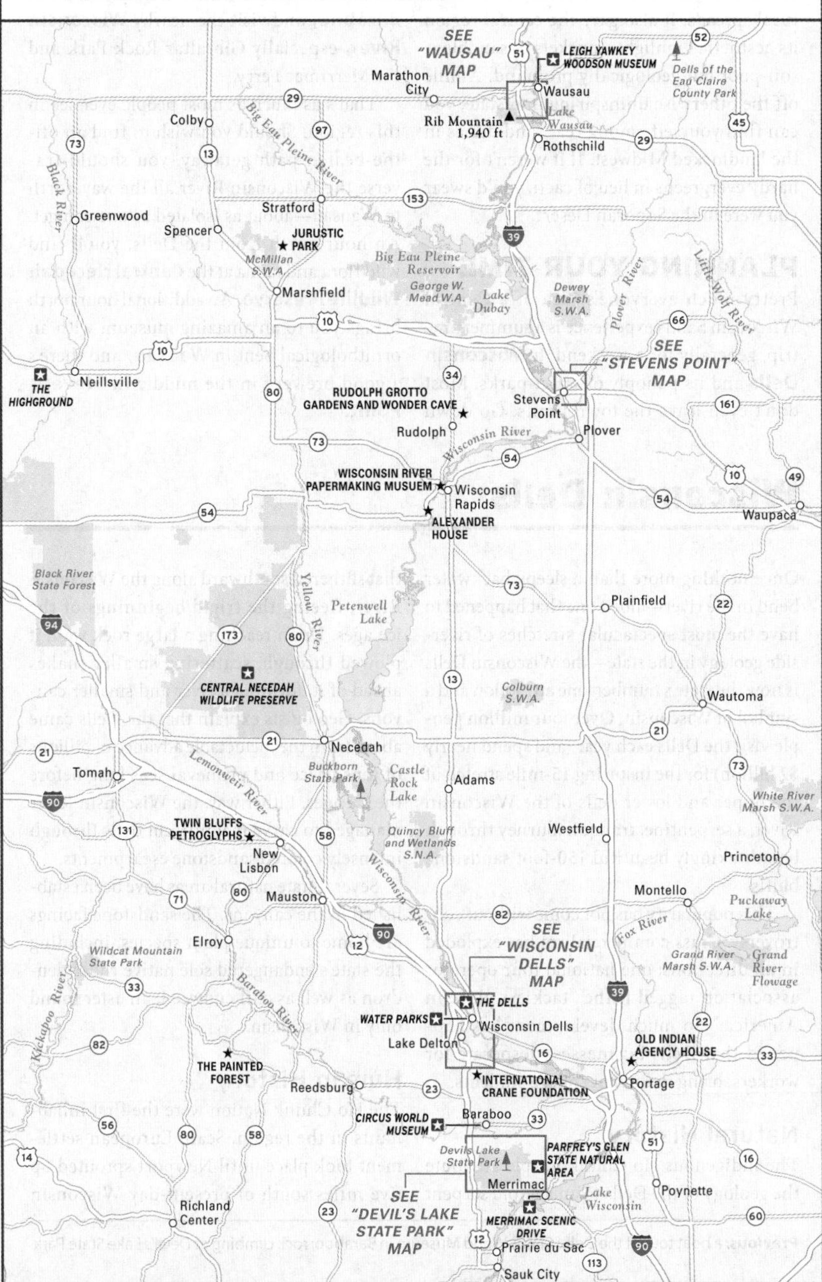

marshland interspersed with spinneys of forest, bits of grassland, and plenty of agricultural spreads. It also gave the central region its aesthetic highlight—pockets of sandblow, soil-poor but geologically profound. A mile off the otherwise uninspiring interstate, you can find yourself among real sand dunes in the landlocked Midwest. If it weren't for the hardy evergreens in lieu of cacti, you'd swear you were in the Sonoran Desert.

PLANNING YOUR TIME

Pretty much everyone's idea of a Central Wisconsin Sands experience is a summertime trip, generally for a weekend, to **Wisconsin Dells** and its panoply of water parks. Most don't even leave the town limits. Go down the road and spend at least one day hiking in **Devil's Lake,** see the circus clowns in **Baraboo,** and visit the nearby **Wisconsin River,** especially Gibraltar Rock Park and the Merrimac Ferry.

That's as much as most people ever see in this region. Should you wish to find an off-the-beaten-path getaway, you should traverse the Wisconsin River all the way north to Wausau—about as isolated as one can get. An hour north from the Dells, you'll find wild flora and fauna at the **Central Necedah Wildlife Preserve.** An additional hour north brings you to an amazing museum with an ornithological bent in **Wausau,** and there's a good brewery in the middle in **Stevens Point.**

Wisconsin Dells

Once nothing more than a sleepy backwater bend in the river—albeit one that happened to have the most spectacular stretches of riverside geology in the state—the Wisconsin Dells is now the state's number-one attraction and a symbol of Wisconsin. Over four million people visit the Dells each year (and spend nearly $2 billion) for the inspiring 15-mile stretch of the upper and lower dells of the Wisconsin River, a serpentine, tranquil journey through breathtakingly beautiful 150-foot sandstone bluffs.

This popularity has not come without controversy. Crass commercialism has exploded in all directions; one national tour operator association tagged it the "tackiest place in America." So much development has happened that Dells businesses, desperate for workers, bring in foreign college students.

Natural History

The indigenous Ho Chunk people attribute the geology of the Dells to an age-old serpent that slithered southward along the Wisconsin River, fleeing the frigid beginnings of the ice ages. Upon reaching a large rock wall, it plowed through, scattering smaller snakes ahead of it, forming a river and smaller canyons. Geologists explain that the Dells came about from the ineluctable advance of billions of tons of ice and primeval seas long before the ice ages. Either way, the Wisconsin River managed to carve magnificent dells through intensely colored sandstone escarpments.

Several state natural areas have been established in the canyons. The sandstone facings are home to unique plant species, including the state's endangered sole native rhododendron as well as cliff cudweed, an aster found only in Wisconsin.

Human History

The Ho Chunk Nation were the first inhabitants in the region. Scant European settlement took place until Newport sprouted up five miles south of present-day Wisconsin

Previous: a boat tour of the Dells; Circus World Museum in Baraboo; rock climbing at Devil's Lake State Park

Wisconsin Dells

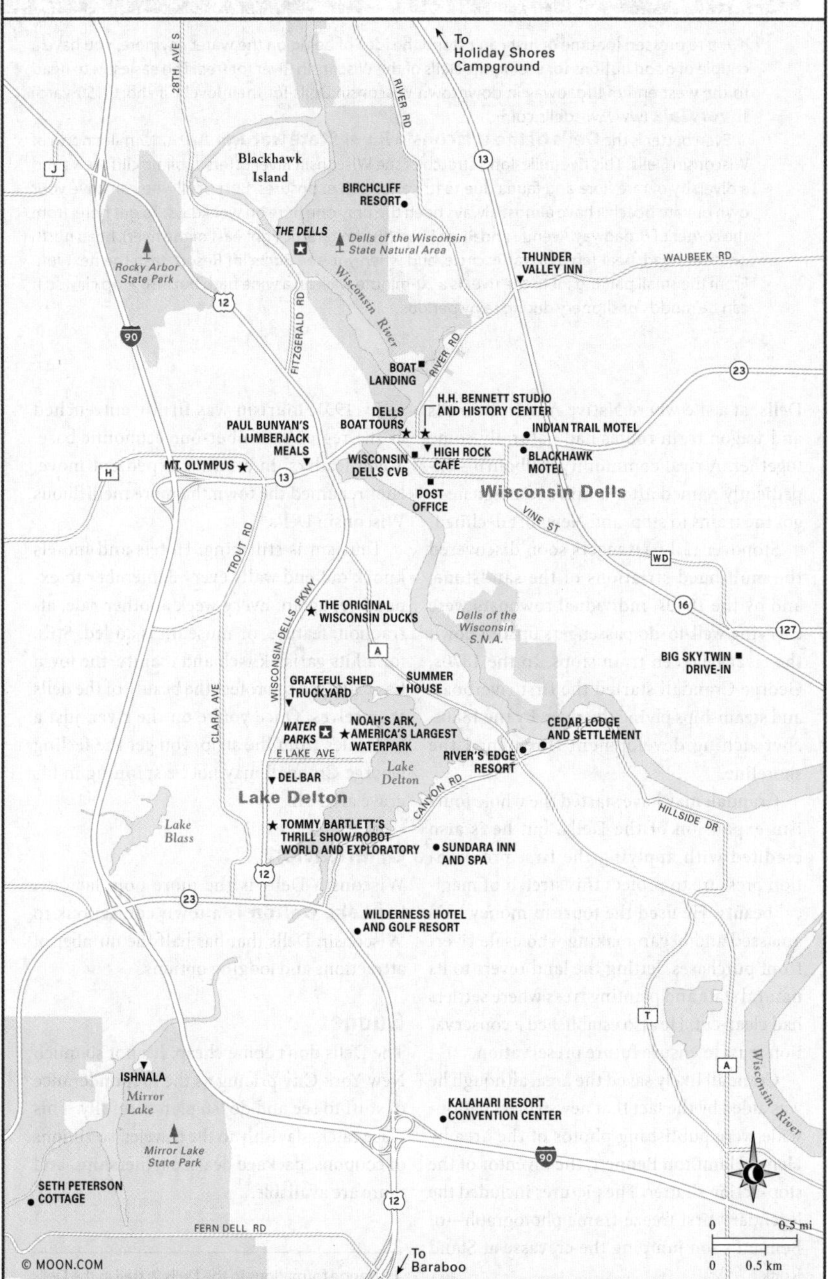

The Dells for Free

If you're pressed for time or just can't stand the idea of being on the water anymore, you have a couple of good options for seeing the Dells of the Wisconsin River for free. The easiest is to head to the west end of Broadway in downtown Wisconsin Dells for their lovely, if short (150-yard) **RiverWalk** (www.wisdells.com).

Even better is the **Dells of the Wisconsin River State Natural Area,** 1.7 miles north of Wisconsin Dells. This five-mile-long stretch of the Wisconsin River offers sublime cliff views and a diversity of rare flora and fauna due to its varied sun exposures. Best of all, you can have your own private beach; I have almost always been the only one here on weekdays. To get here, from the corner of Broadway Avenue and River Road (the first traffic light east of the river), head north on River Road, bear left at a traffic circle, and when you see Birchcliff Resort, take the next left. From the small parking lot to the river is a 20-minute walk on a wide path but also atop clay, so it can be muddy or slippery during rainy periods.

Dells, at a site where Native American trails and wagon train routes had naturally come together. A rival community, Kilbourn—expediently named after a railroad magnate—got the trains to stop, and Newport declined.

Stopover rail passengers soon discovered the multihued striations of the sandstone, and by the 1850s, individual rowboats were carrying well-to-do passengers up and down the river between train stops. In the 1870s, George Crandall started the first riverboats and steamships plying the river. By the 1880s, encroaching development threatened the shoreline.

Crandall may have started the whole tourism expansion of the Dells, but he is also credited with applying the first preservation pressure to protect this stretch of magical beauty. He used the tourism money he'd amassed and began making wholesale riverfront purchases, letting the land revert to its natural state and planting trees where settlers had clear-cut. He also established a conservation trust to ensure future preservation.

Crandall likely saved the area, although he was aided by the fact that newspapers nationwide were publishing photos of the area by Henry Hamilton Bennett, the inventor of the stop-action shutter. The pictures included the legendary first freeze-frame photograph—of Bennett's son jumping the crevasse at Stand Rock.

By 1931, tourism was firmly entrenched as the region's number-one economic base. Town leaders, in another expedient move, later renamed the town the more mellifluous Wisconsin Dells.

Tourism is still king. Hotels and motels knock out end walls every September to expand yet again. Every week another ride, attraction, feature, or museum is added. Still, for all its garish kitsch and inanity, the town has managed to protect the beauty of the dells themselves. Once you're on the river, just a few miles from the strip, you get the feeling George Crandall may not be spinning in his grave after all.

Orientation

Wisconsin Dells is the more popular city, but **Lake Delton** is a town contiguous to Wisconsin Dells that has half the number of attractions and lodging options.

Budget

The Dells don't come cheap. It's not so much New York City pricing as the preponderance of stuff to see and do, so plan carefully. This place caters slavishly to the traveler, so zillions of coupons, package deals, partnerships, and more are available.

1: strange formations in the Dells **2:** trail in the Dells

1
2

★ THE DELLS

What exactly is all the fuss about? These rock formations are freaks of nature, with oddball names such as Devil's Elbow, Fat Man's Misery, Witches Gulch, Cold Water Canyon, and so on. They can be found along 15 miles of upper and lower dells, and everywhere you see craggy palisades and soft-hued sandstone. The trademark of the Wisconsin Dells is **Stand Rock,** a mushroom-shaped sandstone protuberance made famous in 19th-century first-of-its-kind stop-action photography. Stand Rock is accessible via Highway A and Stand Rock Road, to the north of town.

The Original Wisconsin Ducks

Some swear by the Ducks. The **Original Wisconsin Ducks** (608/254-8751, www.wisconsinducktours.com, tours 8am-7pm daily Apr.-Oct., $32 adults) are the real thing: green-and-white, 14,000-pound behemoth amphibious World War II landing craft. These slowly roar along the main drag of the Dells, picking up passengers for a one-hour, eight-mile trip that includes jaunts through restored prairie lands and access to wilderness trails. You won't have any trouble finding a Ducks info kiosk. Tours depart whenever enough passengers show up.

Dells Army Ducks

Not to be confused with the Original Wisconsin Ducks, the **Dells Army Ducks** (608/254-6080, www.dellsducks.com, tours 9am-6pm daily summer, 10am-4pm daily May and Sept., $30 adults) also tours the Lower Dells Islands. Tours depart the main dock along U.S. 12 every 15 to 20 minutes. The company also runs a zip line, jet boats, and a faux-World War II PT boat.

Dells Boat Tours

The **Dells Boat Tours** (608/254-8555, www.dellsboats.com, mid-Apr.-Oct., Upper Dells $32 and Lower Dells $24 adults) uses modern cabin cruisers and offers separate Upper Dells tours (two hours), the only boat tour that offers a stop at the Dells trademark Stand Rock. The Lower Dells tour takes half as long. Tours operate every 20 to 30 minutes, 10am-6pm daily in high season, less frequently in spring and fall seasons. How about tours on 700-horsepower jet boats? There's nothing like the tranquility of the Dells at 40 mph.

TOP EXPERIENCE

★ WATER PARKS

Mere minutes in the Dells and your eyeballs begin to wrinkle just from looking at all the water. There are more big-draw water parks than at any other U.S. tourist destination. Find over 200 waterslides and some 16 million gallons of water sloshing around at any one time! Consider this thumbnail sketch of the highlights a mere overview. Always check online; you are almost guaranteed to find great discounts on ticket prices for any water park.

The oldest is the Brobdingnagian **Noah's Ark, America's Largest Waterpark** (S. U.S. 12/Hwy. 23, 608/254-6351, www.noahsarkwaterpark.com, 9am-8pm daily Memorial Day-Labor Day, $40 adults). This place is housed on 70 acres with more than 60 separate activities. On-site are three dozen waterslides, two wave pools, a kiddie pool, minigolf, bumper boats, go-karts, a surf pool, a white-water raft adventure, and much more. Its legendary Big Kahuna is one of the largest wave pools in the country—big enough to offer surfing. The Incredible Adventure is a water ride with the effects of a roller coaster (a 10-story, five-second drop). And there's the Time Warp, on which you race down at 30 miles per hour into the nation's largest bowl. There's also the Scorpion's Tail, a 10-story drop at 50 feet per second with a nearly vertical loop (by the way, this is the ride the most people chicken out on). To top that, they built Raja, the World's Largest King Cobra; a side-by-side tube drops from six stories to 30 miles per hour. The Quadzilla, a family mat racer that gets you up to 20 mph, is an amazing ride. All told, nearly five million gallons of water gush through the place.

Mt. Olympus (S. U.S. 12, 608/254-2490,

www.mtolympuspark.com, $45 adults) is another original city-state-size park à la Noah's Ark—1.3 million square feet indoors and out, which makes it the world's largest water resort. Technically it's several parks and properties combined that have become a megalopolis of fun. More than three dozen waterslides are the highlight of Mt. Olympus, but on its crown jewel, Poseidon's Rage, two million gallons of water create a nine-foot wave. Among the insane number of non-water rides, Hades 360 is a roller coaster with the world's longest underground tunnel. The Zeus coaster will rattle you like nothing else, as will the Cyclops coaster, although the latter has two cool big drops. I can personally vouch for its go-karts—again, on the largest course in the world—including racing underwater and through the colossal wooden Trojan horse that has become a landmark in town. A new attraction is 140-foot-tall circular swing, which is scarier than it sounds.

The **Kalahari Resort Convention Center** (1305 Kalahari Dr., 608/254-5466, www.kalahariresort.com, day pass $45) is the largest indoor water park in the United States, a whopping 125,000 square feet. Highlights include a 920-foot-long indoor river, numerous two- to four-person raft and tube rides, the country's only uphill waterslide, water walks, body flume rides, and even a zoo. Kalahari also boasts the world's largest indoor wave pool, beating out even the Ark's Big Kahuna. The park also has a terrifying side-by-side Sahara Sidewinder waterslide (they had to cut open the roof to get it in), the nation's only indoor looping waterslide. All of this is in a funky African-themed style. Most recently, Kalahari worked with Disney animators on its new 100,000-square-foot indoor park featuring, among a dozen other things, a zombie apocalypse. Parents will love the spa to unwind after all the family craziness.

OTHER SIGHTS

Tommy Bartlett's Thrill Show

For more than 45 years, **Tommy Bartlett's Thrill Show** (560 Wisconsin Dells Pkwy., 608/254-2525, www.tommybartlett.com, adults $21.50, reserved seating $24.50) has defined the Dells, though it's no longer run by Tommy Bartlett. It's a two-hour grand mélange of vaudeville, three-ring circus, laser light show, and sheer daredevil gonzo on the stunt boats or, perhaps, contortionists and frenetic juggling acts. One of the best acts is the Sky Flyers Aerial Helicopter Trapeze. It

Mt. Olympus

runs two times daily, rain or shine, through Labor Day.

Adjacent to the show is **Tommy Bartlett's Robot World and Exploratory** (9am-9pm daily Memorial Day-Labor Day, 10am-4pm daily Labor Day-Memorial Day, $15 adults), a surreal mix of high-tech and kitsch aboard an intergalactic cruiser and house of the future. For this edition, they underwent a half-million dollar expansion to add on to the hundreds of hands-on activities to explore gravity, energy, light, and motion. Robots actually guide the tours. The original *Mir* space station is here too.

Broadway

The Dells' main drag is **Broadway,** the netherworld of Americana, commercialism, and souvenir T-shirts. Duck into a couple of haunted houses, have your picture taken Wild West style, or perhaps engage in laser tag or some sort of wizard quest. Top it all off with a sarsaparilla at an old-timey saloon.

H. H. BENNETT STUDIO AND HISTORY CENTER

The **H. H. Bennett Studio and History Center** (215 Broadway, 608/253-3523, www.hhbennettstudio.wisconsinhistory.org, 10am-4pm daily May-Oct., later hours in summer, $10 adults), the yin cultural spirit to Broadway's yang weirdness, is the historic former studio of renowned photographer H. H. Bennett, the man who literally put the Dells on the map a century ago with his glass negative prints of the sandstone escarpments, developed in the oldest darkroom and photographic studio in the United States. There are interactive exhibits, with the overall theme of the evolution of the Dells region from prehistory to the 21st century. Lots of photography is featured—vintage prints adorn the walls—and the Ho Chunk Nation isn't overlooked.

ENTERTAINMENT AND EVENTS

Big Sky Twin Drive-In

Catch this nearly dead American tradition while you can: At the **Big Sky Twin Drive-In** (N9199 Winnebago Rd., 608/254-8025, www.bigskydrivein.com, $8), two huge screens show four shows nightly—all first-run Hollywood stuff. The snack bar is huge. Cash only, by the way. Big Sky is one mile south of Wisconsin Dells via U.S. 16E.

Festivals and Events

It's not technically a festival or event, but unofficially the Dells is pushing for March and April to be **Spring Break** season—for travelers it means outstanding discounts on indoor water parks!

The newest festival, May's **Automotion,** is a showcase of nearly 1,000 cars—antiques, street machines, and classics—that includes swap meets, a car corral, cruises, and motorcycle classes.

Fall is feted with not one but two events: the **Wo-Zha-Wa** autumn welcome in mid-September, followed by the **Fall Festival** in mid-October, both with lots of scarecrow stuffing, pumpkin carving, food, and very scenic boat, train, and Duck tours.

FOOD

Many but not all restaurants in the Dells area are open seasonally. These usually shut for the winter between late October and December, reopening in May.

Family-Style Dining

Paul Bunyan's Lumberjack Meals (near I-90/94 and Hwy. 13 junction, 608/254-8717, 7am-9pm daily) is every kid's favorite place to eat. All-you-can-eat meals are served, specializing in breakfast and chicken-and-ribs. Seriously, for $40, a family of four gets all they can eat. Not bad.

Farm Restaurants

Take a wondrous step back in time just north of town in a pocket of old-country dwellings at the ★ **Thunder Valley Inn** (W15344 Waubeek Rd., 608/254-4145, www.thundervalleyinn.com, hours vary, from $36). You can get an all-you-can-eat farm breakfast

Kitsch on the Dells

The first road signs—huge and color-splashed and screamingly designed—crop up somewhere around Madison if you're coming from the south. With each mile, the traveler becomes more fully informed as to the delights that the distant oasis offers. It's a numbing onslaught of visual pollution.

There are those who believe—stridently—that the Wisconsin experience necessitates a descent into the kitschy, cacophonic purgatory of the Strip in the Dells and Lake Delton, that multiple-mile Middle America meander clogged by 10am with belching RVs and minivans disgorging sunburned consumers like Marines wading ashore. It's a giant, corny shakedown.

Obscenity or pure Americana? It's got the classic symptoms of Niagara Falls: magnificent aesthetics and geological history mashed with the dizzying clatter of tourism run amok. There are seemingly endless miles of water parks, knickknack and curio shops, miniature golf courses, a Statue of Liberty-size Trojan horse, go-karts, bungee jumping, helicopter rides, the odd casino or two, otherwise rational people with arrows sticking out of their heads, and a ticket tout on every corner. The entire design of this Wisconsin city is aimed at the hedonistic delight of the child, real and inner. And it's wonderful—every frightening, wearying second of it.

experience, though à la carte menus are also provided. It's a working farm with goats and chickens running around; chores are optional. The food is in the grand old-world style, from German potato salad to roast chicken, and the inn does a superb fish fry. Many ingredients are grown on-site; the restaurant even grinds its own wheat and rye berries. Each bite of the family-style breakfast is a bit of Wisconsin culinary heritage, such as unbeatable Norwegian pancakes with lingonberries. Even better are the old-timey music performances, with storytelling and Midwestern farm jokes, that occur some evenings. Hours vary widely, depending on the shows, so call ahead. You'll need a reservation for the dinner shows. The restaurant is open in summer, the inn year-round.

New American

Broadway's strip is generally about fried food or raucous bars. How wonderful, then, is **High Rock Café** (232 Broadway, 608/254-5677, lunch and dinner daily, $7-13)? It has creative but not trendy cuisine, cool but not chic, and it's healthy. (Well, except maybe for the fried cheese curds in truffle oil, which you absolutely must try.) They have tapas until 2am daily.

Eclectic

Absolutely brilliant is **Grateful Shed Truckyard** (1470 Wisconsin Dells Pkwy., 608/253-0588, 7am-2am daily, $7-13), which takes the cool food truck idea and Wisconsinifies it. Indeed, several Madison mainstay food trucks along with a plethora of others are gathered under one roof (winter, of course). Oh, you can get your sushi and Mexican, but you can also find a grilled cheese truck (Wisconsin, natch). And a bar (Wisconsin, natch).

On the Water

Summer House (1280 E. Hiawatha Dr., Lake Delton, 608/253-0207, lunch and dinner daily, $8-13) has creative locally sourced cuisine with lovely unexpected items such as beet hummus—of course, the perch standard is outstanding (the service is excellent, as well). The decor is Wisconsin summer home, and the views of Lake Delton are wondrous.

Supper Clubs

The ★ **Del-Bar** (800 Wisconsin Dells Pkwy. S., 608/253-1861, 4:30pm-9pm Mon.-Fri., 4:30pm-9:30pm Sat., 4:30pm-8:30pm Sun., $17-39) is has been an institution in the Dells since the 1940s. A bistro-cum-supper club, it has the most exquisite custom dry-aged Angus steaks and prime rib as well as some excellent seafood. Even better is the ambience—the building was designed by a protégé of Frank Lloyd Wright, and the dining rooms feature fireplaces. The third generation recently took over and was told (in Midwestern polite ways) not to mess with anything (such as the beloved pork schnitzel) after minor changes to the salads were made.

Ishnala (Ishnala Rd., 608/253-1171, 4pm-10pm Mon.-Fri., dinner daily, $12-30) offers superlative vistas on a 100-acre spread of meadow overlooking Mirror Lake, as well as 40 years of experience serving steaks, prime rib (literally tons of it), seafood, ribs, and a house-special roast duck and baby-back pork ribs. Before-dinner cruises are available. Check out the Norway pines growing right through the roof. It has regularly received honors for the state's best supper club, trading off with the Del-Bar above.

ACCOMMODATIONS

It's hard to believe that with nearly 7,000 guest rooms, at times finding a place to stay in peak season without a reservation can be a chore. Excluding major holidays, you'll likely come up with something. And what a bizarre and entertaining range of accommodations there is.

There are nearly two dozen water park resorts of 5,000 square feet or more, but every place has somewhere to splash. Unless otherwise stated, all these options are open year-round; plenty of others are seasonal. Single-night stays on weekends in summer are not allowed at many places.

During the high summer months, you'll pay no less than $80 a night for one person, and as much as $250 in a swankier place. Weekly rentals cost less, and securing a multiperson cabin and splitting the cost is a great way to save. The usual rule: If you can stay Monday through Thursday, you save a bundle on lodging. Off-season, rates can dip as low as $50 for a single. All prices listed are the lowest high-season rates.

Basic motels are losing out seriously to water-themed resorts, and in recent years several were offering doubles for as low as $60, even during Memorial Day and Labor Day weekends. These motels, desperate for business, also often have connections for discounted tickets to water parks.

Under $50

Camping is always an option. Public camping is at **Mirror Lake** and **Rocky Arbor State Parks.** Mirror Lake (from $27 nonresidents) is just south of Lake Delton along U.S. 12 and the more populated of the two. Considering it's a large-capacity campground (145 sites), privacy is fairly decent. Rocky Arbor (from $25 nonresidents) is closer to the Dells and not as well known. For both, absolutely try to make reservations (888/947-2757, http://wisconsin.goingtocamp.com, $8 reservation fee) as early as possible—up to 11 months ahead. An $11 entrance fee is also required for nonresidents.

Eighteen private campgrounds are in and around the Dells. In summer they will be chock-full and boisterous, not an isolated bucolic experience. A large and popular operation is the **Holiday Shores Campground** (3900 River Rd., 608/254-2717, www.holidayshores.com, from $46), a resort operation along the Wisconsin River with camping available in a separate tenting area, along with a whole catalog of extras.

$50-100

From June to August, you'll be lucky to find anything near $70. That said, if you check for specials online, it's sometimes possible to get a motel room for $60 Monday to Thursday.

The **River's Edge Resort** (20 River's Edge Rd., 608/254-7707, www.riversedgeresort.com, from $80). Think "log cabin" and you get the decor at this decent option with motel rooms, apartments, and one- to four-bed cottages. There's a sandy beach, boat rental, and a heated pool.

Absolutely outstanding for many, many years and somehow still doing a fantastic job is the ★ **Blackhawk Motel** (720 Race St., 608/254-7770, www.blackhawkmotel.com, $99), which is well-liked, clean, and reasonably priced; the owners are friendly. Dollar for dollar, it's the best around. Oh, and they just renovated their indoor pool.

The **Indian Trail Motel** (1013 Broadway, 608/253-2641, www.indiantrailmotel.com, $99) is always a good budget option. A motel on 15 acres, it remains within walking distance to downtown—for that, it created nature trails. All rooms have fridges and microwaves; amenities include a whirlpool and sauna, laundry, and a restaurant.

There is simply nothing like one of the most classic B&Bs in the Midwest, the isolated Scandinavian-style 130-year-old *farmhus,* the ★ **Thunder Valley Inn** (W15344 Waubeek Rd., 608/254-4145, www.thundervalleyinn.com, $79-145), also a sublime eatery. Original farm rooms have Franklin stoves; some feature balconies overlooking the woods. Even little cabins tucked into trees are available. Entertainment includes fiddling hoedowns and some weekend chautauquas (outdoor cultural education assemblies) and threshing suppers.

$100-150

A secluded option for families, in a lovely setting, is the cottage colony **Birchcliff Resort** (4149 River Rd., 608/254-7515, www.birchcliff.com, $149-420), featuring myriad log cabins. Worry not—they're not holdovers from the 1950s; these are grand. They do, however, have a couple old-time cabins for cheap. Amenities include a couple of pools, hiking access to the Wisconsin River, and plenty of recreation. Best of all, the management earns very positive reviews.

Over $150

A wonderful find is **Cedar Lodge and Settlement** (E11232 Hillside Dr., 608/253-6080, www.cedarlodgedells.com, $220-400), with gorgeous huge log lodge rooms in infinite varieties; they also have log cabins. They have a heated outdoor pool, but there's also 400 feet of sandy beach along the Wisconsin River. Management is attentive and never seems to be in a bad mood. If you want to escape the over-the-top cacophony of the Dells, this is the spot.

The **Kalahari Resort Convention Center** (1305 Kalahari Dr., 608/254-5466, www.kalahariresort.com, $240-429) is a whopping 125,000 square feet of fun that is the largest indoor water park in the United States. Highlights of the park include an indoor river, numerous raft/tube rides, the country's only uphill waterslide, water walks, body flume rides, and even a zoo. The most recent addition is a terrifying side-by-side Super Loop waterslide. Parents will love the new spa. Rooms have satellite TV, blow dryers, fridges, microwaves, hot tubs, and fireplaces.

Another massive operation (America's largest resort, with four indoor and four outdoor waterparks) with endless additions is the ★ **Wilderness Hotel and Golf Resort** (511 E. Adams St., 800/867-9453, www.wildernessresort.com, $240-429). All 135,000 square feet of water fun are exclusively for guests. It's all family stuff all the time here, so don't plan on a romantic getaway. The absolute draw is the $150 million high-tech foil dome that lets in sunlight—January tanning in Wisconsin. The recently added virtual reality area is absolutely mind-blowing and can engage even the most jaded preteen. Otherwise, there's a championship golf course and the well-regarded Field's at the Wilderness restaurant. Luxury condo rooms and cabins in the woods are also available.

Inside tranquil Mirror Lake State Park in Lake Delton is the ★ **Seth Peterson Cottage** (608/254-6551, www.sethpeterson.org, $325), a Frank Lloyd Wright-designed cottage and the only one available for overnighting. It's been described as having "more architecture per square foot than any other building Wright designed." The one-room cottage with a splendid view is fully furnished with a complete kitchen, an enormous stone fireplace, a flagstone terrace, floor-to-ceiling

French doors and windows, and complete seclusion. Reservations are necessary far in advance. Tours (1pm-4pm 2nd Sun. of every month, $2) are also available.

The most sybaritic choice in the Dells is without question **Sundara Inn and Spa** (920 Canyon Rd., 888/735-8181, www.sundaraspa.com, $398-800), the only freestanding spa devoted exclusively to luxury pampering. It has won major awards in the industry for its devotion to luxury and eco-mindedness and has been absolutely gushed over by the media. It offers simply otherworldly comfort and serenity, especially in the amazing villas. The organic cuisine is divine too. It is doubling in size with another pool, a rooftop greenhouse, and miles of trails. A few have opined that the service doesn't always match the $400 price tag.

INFORMATION AND SERVICES

The **Wisconsin Dells Visitors and Convention Bureau** (701 Superior St., 608/254-4636 or 800/223-3557, www.wisdells.com) is a gem of professionalism and helpfulness. It's open dawn to dark (no exaggeration) from June to August, with shorter hours thereafter.

GETTING THERE

Car

Getting to the Dells from Minneapolis (via I-90/94, 216 miles) takes 3.5 hours. From Madison (via I-90/94, 56 miles), it takes one hour. From Chicago (I-90/94, 195 miles), it takes 3.25 hours. If you're heading south from Stevens Point (via I-39 and Hwy. 13, 79 miles), it takes 90 minutes.

Bus

Wisconsin Dells has no central bus station. **Greyhound** (800/231-2222, www.greyhound.com) buses arrive and depart from the **McDonald's** (30 Commerce St.), which has no ability to sell tickets.

Train

Amtrak (800/872-7245, www.amtrak.com) stops at the junction of Superior and Lacrosse Streets north of downtown; this stop has no quick ticket machine, so you'll have to use the Internet or a travel agent.

Vicinity of the Dells

BARABOO

This could be the model for Tinytown USA, where life still revolves around the courthouse square. Baraboo consistently earns top 10 listings in national media rankings of livability quotients.

And then there's the circus. Though Baraboo has always been an important regional cog in dairy distribution, the local circus museum is what really draws visitors. In 1882, a family of enterprising local German farmers named Ringling, much enamored of a traveling troupe's performance in Iowa, organized the Ringling Brothers' Classic and Comic Concert Company. Thus began that "greatest show." Wisconsin would become the Mother of Circuses—more than 100 circuses had their origins and based their operations here. Baraboo was home to the Greatest Show on Earth until 1918, and the Ringling legacy remains its biggest draw.

★ Circus World Museum

The site of the **Circus World Museum** (426 Water St., 608/356-8341, www.circusworldbaraboo.org, 9am-5pm daily mid-June-late Aug., 10am-5pm daily mid-late May to Labor Day, less spring/fall, $20 adults, spring and fall $10) was the original headquarters of the Ringling Brothers circus in an attractive setting along the Baraboo River. Summer is the best time to visit, when the capacious 51-acre grounds are open and the three-ring circus and sideshows reappear. Under the big top is a dazzling, frenetic, fun mélange of jugglers, aerialists, clowns, bands, magic, circus nuts and bolts, steam-driven calliope concerts, and animal shows. Another hall has memorabilia and displays from long-gone U.S. circuses and an exhaustive historical rundown of the Ringlings. Also in the hall is the world's most complete collection of circus vehicles (214 and counting) and circus posters (8,000 and counting). It is so comprehensive that Disney designers consulted here for the 2019 movie *Dumbo.* Hey, you can ride a pachyderm (or a pony). Great family entertainment includes clown shows for kids, in which ecstatic urchins can slap on face paint and go wild, and circus music demonstrations, which feature hands-on access to rare circus musical instruments. A $2.5 million expansion has added a state-of-the-art facility for restoring circus wagons.

International Crane Foundation

The most inspiring attraction is the respected ornithological preservation ongoing northeast of Baraboo at the **International Crane Foundation** (E11376 Shady Lane Rd., 608/356-9462, www.savingcranes.com). The world-renowned institution is dedicated to saving the world's largest flying birds, all 15 species of which are endangered or threatened; this is the only place in the world that houses all species. The whooping crane population, from a nadir of 15 birds in 1940, has rebounded to more than 200 birds. So respected is this place that the crown princess of Japan came as a researcher, and Indira Gandhi later founded the Keoladeo Ghana National Park in India to protect the Siberian crane after a visit. At the time of writing it was also in the midst of a $10 million upgrade with a new state-of-the-art facility but should be open by the time you read this.

The center sponsors a spring sandhill crane volunteer count, the largest such endeavor in the country. Wisconsin, a Mississippi Flyway hot spot, hosts almost 13,500 sandhill cranes, with more than 1,000 in Marquette County alone. It's quite a change from six decades ago, when hunters and agricultural expansion had pared sandhill numbers to less than 100.

Other Sights and Recreation

Modeled on European opera houses, in particular the Great Opera Hall at the Palace of Versailles, the **Al Ringling Theatre** (136 4th Ave., 608/356-8864) is a fetching local gem of architecture. Tours ($15) are given Tuesday through Saturday in summer at 1:30pm (or if someone is around), or come for one of the movies or live music events held regularly. A multimillion-dollar renovation brought back the resplendence.

In nearby North Freedom is another favorite: the chugging iron roosters at **Mid-Continent Railway and Museum** (608/522-4261, midcontinent.org, museum 9:30am-5pm daily mid-May-Labor Day, 9:30am-5pm Sat.-Sun. Labor Day-Oct., free), west of Baraboo on Highway 136 and Highway PF. The last operating steam engine of the Chicago and North Western Railway is the largest. All of these trains are refurbished originals; many worked the area's quartzite mines. Most visitors come, however, for the nine-mile train ride (11am, 1pm, and 3pm, $20-55 adults) through the Baraboo River Valley; the highest-priced tickets get you a ride in the engine. Special seasonal trips also run.

Totally cool is a one-of-a-kind sculpture collection just south of town via U.S. 12. Dr. Evermor, better known as Tom Every, has placed an assemblage of scrap-metal sculptures created from what could best be described as the detritus of the Cold War and its belching factories; it is, in fact, directly opposite the hulking remains of the dormant Badger Munitions Depot. This menagerie of machines has the **Forevertron** (http://worldofdrevermor.com/) as its nucleus: a 400-ton monstrosity—and the largest scrap-metal sculpture in the world, according to *Guinness World Records.* This author was

3

43

amazed that it contained the decontamination chamber from the Apollo 11 moon landing. The creator would like to use the erstwhile armaments factory as a sculpture garden dedicated to the munitions industry of the United States throughout history. This is an amazing place and well worth a donation to keep going.

Baraboo has also become intriguing for paddlers. With the removal of the Glenville Dam in 2002, the Baraboo River became the United States' longest restored free-flowing river, at 115 miles from Elroy to the confluence of the Wisconsin River near Portage.

★ Merrimac Scenic Drive

A great side trip from Baraboo is a spin through Devil's Lake State Park and then a trip across the Wisconsin River via the *Colsac III,* one of the last free ferries in the country, operated by the state Department of Transportation. This site has had a ferry in some form since 1844. Every year beginning in mid-April until late fall, the only way to get from the town of Merrimac to Okee is on this chugger. It goes 0.5 miles in 10 minutes or so all day and night. On summer weekends, you might wait an hour or two to cross. If you see flashing lights on the highway approaches, however, drive on; it means the ferry's not operating.

From here, you can head in to the scenic Lake Wisconsin resort area, which stretches 53 miles from Farmer's Bay, south of Portage, to Prairie du Sac. Every species of fish native to Wisconsin is found in the lake, so anglers flock here. Blue highways stretch the length of the river, offering splendid vistas and access to trim Wisconsin towns. Little **Lodi** is the sleeper of southern Wisconsin, a picturesque off-river town of winding streets, cheery old buildings, and not much tourist traffic. From here, head northwest to **Gibraltar Rock Park** via Highway J, then Highway JV, then Highway V, then Highway VA to get a bird's-eye view of the Wisconsin River Valley. It's slightly less inspiring than Devil's Lake but has a *much* smaller crowd, if any. Lodi also contains a three-mile segment of the **Ice Age National Scenic Trail,** which passes through bluff-view topography (you can see Devil's Lake), a grand overlook, and oak savannas.

Food and Accommodations

Every corner seems to have a classic small-town eatery with pressed-tin ceilings reminiscent of the pages of *Roadfood.* But then, just a few steps from the Al Ringling Theatre, the hip Southwestern (and Caribbean, and Latin American) flavors of the **Little Village Cafe** (146 4th Ave., 608/356-2800, 11am-8pm or 9pm Mon.-Sat., 11am-3pm Sun., $5-12) are a lovely find. Vegetarians are generally able to get something great here.

The ★ **Cheeze Factory** (618 Oak St., 608/448-4804, 11:30am-3pm Sun.-Wed., 11:30am-7pm Thurs.-Sat., $5-13) is one of the best vegetarian restaurants in the state. It relocated here from Wisconsin Dells and has lost none of its legendary skill in preparing vegan cuisine. It's so good that its cookbook is an online best seller. They are deservedly famed for their cranberry-orange cupcakes.

Everyday lodgings are found at the junction of Highway 33 and U.S. 12. A good bet is the mom-and-pop-style **Willowood Inn** (S. Hwy. 123, 888/356-5474, www.willowoodinn.com, from $80), friendly, cheap, clean, and in an excellent location; it also has a cottage for six.

An interesting B&B is **Pinehaven** (E13083 Hwy. 33, 608/356-3489, from $159), an enormous dwelling atop a rise out of town and near a spring-fed lake. There's also a private guest cottage.

Absolutely fantastic is the sybaritic B&B ★ **Inn at Wawanissee Point** (E13609 Tower Rd., 608/305-2258, http://innatwawanisseepoint.com, from $299), 10 minutes south of town. It's stunning, from its rooms

1: Al Ringling Theatre in Baraboo **2:** a unicycle act at Circus World Museum in Baraboo **3:** classic steam train at the Mid-Continent Railway and Museum

to its service to its 36-mile views high above the Wisconsin River Valley.

Information

The **Baraboo Chamber of Commerce** (600 W. Chestnut St., 608/356-8333 or 800/227-2266, www.baraboo.com) is near the U.S. 12 and Highway 33 junction.

DEVIL'S LAKE STATE PARK

The diamond-hard, 1.5-billion-year-old quartzite bluffs of the Baraboo Range tower above a primeval icy lake of abysmal depth. The lake reflects the earthy rainbow colors of the rises—steel gray and blood red—and mixes them with its own obsidian for dramatic results. It's Wisconsin's number-one state park, at more than 8,000 acres larger than Door County's Peninsula State Park, and draws more visitors annually than Yellowstone National Park.

Devil's Lake State Park lies at the junction of three imposing ranges of impenetrable geology constituting the magnificent Baraboo Range.

Glaciers gouged out the eastern half of the range of hills, stopping just short of the western edge, where a terminal moraine lies today. The Wisconsin Glacier rerouted glacial rivers and gapped the endpoints of the north and south ranges, forming a lake bed now fed by subterranean springs. The result is one of the most topographically diverse areas of Wisconsin—challenging bluffs adjacent to pastoral dairy land, both next to a tranquil river valley. The natural areas of Devil's Lake are among the most scrutinized by scientists in the state.

Or maybe, as the Ho Chunks' story of the area's formation has it, giant thunderbirds warred with the spirits in the depths of the lake, hurling thunderbolts and dodging the water gods' boulders and water spouts. The battle raged for eons, until the thunderbirds flew away victorious, leaving the rocks and bluffs scarred from battle and the spirits in the depths licking their wounds and waiting.

HUMAN HISTORY

The Ho Chunk people were the first known inhabitants of the area, fishing in the lake and hunting on nearby lowlands; several burial and effigy mounds are still within the park. Steam trains opened the Devil's Lake region, but development was slow since the Baraboo Range made access difficult. After hacking and blasting through, a minor golden age of hotel building began after the Civil War. While not as extensive as in the Lake Geneva resort area of southeastern Wisconsin, it was no less upscale. Four grand hotels were raised, but because of inefficient train service and unmanageable vagaries of early summer weather, by 1910 resort owners gave up, leaving the lodging business to the more mundane mom-and-pop cottages and minor resorts. In 1911, the land became public and was made into a state park.

BADGER MUNITIONS

In a major coup for environmentalists and locals, in 2007 the enormous 7,500-acre-plus plot once home to the defunct Badger Munitions plant was officially handed off to be shared by the Wisconsin DNR, the Ho Chunk Nation, and a couple of federal agencies, and a new fallow area destined to return to its natural state was created. As it abuts the south end of Devil's Lake and links to the Wisconsin River, it's a huge boost to an already important park. Scientists are interested in the chance to watch how, exactly, industrial practices through the decades might affect an attempt to reclaim the land.

CLIMATE

One revealing aspect of Devil's Lake is how the ranges affect temperatures. It's more than 500 feet from the top of the bluff to the lake; the quartzite traps the air and inverts it—warmer air above and cooler air below. Even the flora is affected: More climatically hardened plantlife flourishes at the base of the

Devil's Lake State Park

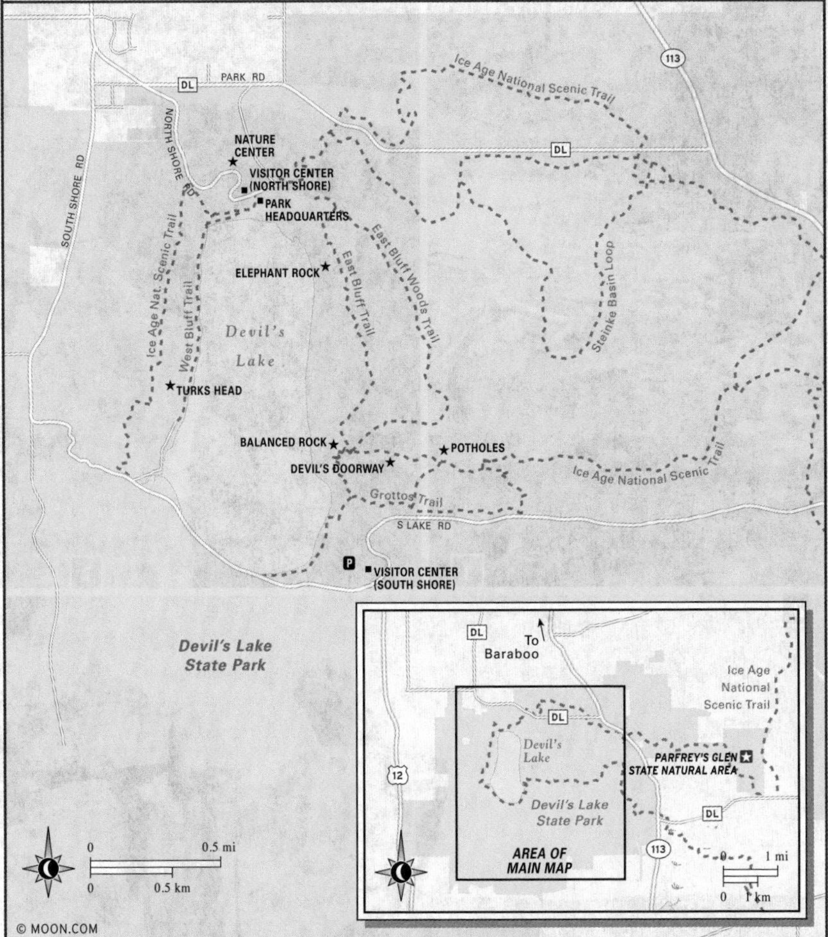

rises, while easygoing oak and hickory are scattered across the top reaches.

Hiking

The hiking cannot be beat. Nearly 30 miles encompass both the east and west bluffs. The west has only two trails and is a bit easier in grade.

On the east bluff, the best trails are the **Grottos Trail** and the **Potholes Trail.** The first is an easy one-mile skirt of the bottom of the south end of the bluffs; from here, you can connect to the heart-stopping, knee-bending, straight-uphill Potholes, one-third of it tortuous and not for the faint of heart. Two more trails follow the woodland topography off the bluff (you can combine these). Another good route is to connect them and then take a leg of the **Ice Age National Scenic Trail** loop, which you will encounter; this in turn runs into the **Parfrey's Glen Ice Age Trail.**

Many of these trails are used in winter for

1
2
3

cross-country skiing, and eight miles are also available for mountain biking; be sure you know if you're on a bike-friendly trail. The **Naturalist Program** leads lots of hikes to the rock highlights as well as Elephant Rock and Cave.

Other Recreation

The hard quartzite bluffs of the park are ready-made for excellent rock climbing. It is, in fact, the only state park permitting rock climbing in Wisconsin. At one time it maintained rock-climbing routes, but numerous falls led to it being shut down. Climb at your own risk.

The name Devil's Lake was applied since no one knew just how deep the foreboding icy lake was. If you're interested in plumbing those depths, **3 Little Devils** (S5780 Hwy. 123, 608/356-5866) is a full-service scuba operation with equipment, training, repair, rental, and air fills.

Ice Age Reserve

Devil's Lake is one of nine official reserve segments of the **Ice Age National Scenic Trail.** The nature center has exhibits on the geology of the surrounding area and on the trail itself, a moderately difficult four-miler, wooded and grassy, between Parfrey's Glen and the park's 16 miles of trails.

★ Parfrey's Glen Natural Area

It's astonishing how many people come through Devil's Lake and completely miss this place, not far from the Devil's Lake campgrounds. Thick, moss-covered ridge walls; hushed, damp silence; a creaking boardwalk; gurgling waters—it's all in the state's oldest natural area, four short miles from the perimeter of the park. A 0.25-mile trek through a minor canyon, cool and dripping, is all that's required. The area is meticulously studied by research scientists for its dramatic microclimates and oddball geology. Hundred-foot canyon walls are studded with enormous quartzite boulders, having ridden here four miles on glacial wash; the flora consists of hardy northern-climate plants and ferns not found elsewhere in the state.

1: hiking along Parfrey's Glen Ice Age Trail **2:** bluffs at Gibraltar Rock Park **3:** Devil's Doorway at Devil's Lake State Park

Camping

Wisconsin's largest state park has three campgrounds with 425 well-used sites ($27-42 nonresidents, $16 day-use) in total, but they're little more than open-air sites spread over large expanses of grass with little seclusion. Seventy sites stay open in winter. Most are reservable, and given the popularity of the place, for weekends, **reservations** (888/947-2757, http://wisconsin.goingtocamp.com, reservation fee $8) well in advance are advised.

Information

The **park office** (608/356-8301) has the required Wisconsin park admission stickers. The park is also a part of the Ice Age National Scientific Reserve; thus, federal Golden Eagle, Golden Age, and Golden Access passes are honored.

REEDSBURG

Slightly off the beaten track, 15 or so miles southwest of the Dells, is Reedsburg, the southern terminus of the grand 22-mile **400 State Trail,** a multipurpose resurfaced railroad-bed trail running from here along the Baraboo River to Elroy, where you can connect with the Elroy-Sparta State Recreational Trail. A $5 daily pass is required for both trails.

For a great side trip, head northwest of town via Highway 33 and Woolever Road to tiny Valton, where you'll find **The Painted Forest,** a venerable 1890s camp hall. The name comes from the lovely folk art murals painted from 1897 to 1899 by an itinerant landscape painter, Ernst Hupeden. Along the way you'll pass La Valle, home to Bundy Hollow Road. In 2012 Bundy Hollow Road became the state's newest Rustic Road. It's only three miles long, but it's worth driving.

Link-Up: The Portage Canal

In the early 1800s, travel by water from Green Bay to the Mississippi River was still impossible; goods were hauled by ox team along a rickety plank road. A canal was proposed at *le portage,* the half-mile gap between the Fox and Wisconsin Rivers.

Machinations were under way by 1829, and by 1848 the state legislature got involved and with federal help got a makeshift canal dug. The project was nearly out of money when a financial scandal struck. The state, mired in debt and fearful of not completing the canal, handed the project to a private investor, whose mysterious golden touch with federal regulators and legislators aroused suspicions. Somehow, by 1851, the canal was nearly finished, though most river traffic still couldn't get through until major costly riverside adjustments were made.

During Wisconsin's financial panic of 1857, the project once again ran out of money. The canal was there, but there was still no river traffic. Another consortium of interests wrested control of the project but couldn't finish the task on the Wisconsin River side. Enter again the federal government, whose engineers frittered away three years and all of the funding while not one commercial boat passed through the canal.

This pattern persisted until the late 1870s, when enough rough work was done on the Wisconsin side to allow for large transport barges and ferries. Unfortunately, the railroad had already arrived. For 75 years large pleasure boats mostly used the canal, until the locks were filled in to create an earthen dam.

From La Valle and Highway 33, drive south on Highway 58, then north on Highway G.

PORTAGE

The name says it all. In June of 1673, intrepid Jesuit missionary Jacques Marquette, along with Louis Joliet, happened upon the 0.5-mile gap between the Fox River and the Wisconsin River, which empties into the Mississippi in Southwestern Wisconsin. The Ho Chunk people had been well aware of the site for centuries, calling it Wa-U-Na, "Carry-on-Shoulder." When trappers and traders began filtering through the new territory, *le portage* became a crucial point in the land-and-water trade routes. Jefferson Davis even found himself here, fresh from West Point, in 1829, hacking logs to help raise Fort Winnebago, upon which much of the region depended.

Sights

Head 0.25 miles east of town and follow a tight turn off Highway 33 onto what must be the state's shortest Rustic Road at less than one mile. Along the way, you'll see sandhill cranes, blue herons, and even a link to the Ice Age National Scenic Trail.

Also along the road stands the **Old Indian Agency House** (off Hwy. 33, 608/742-6362, 10am-4pm Wed.-Sun. mid-May-mid-Oct., $7.50 adults), opposite the site of Fort Winnebago. The house, extraordinarily plush for the period, was built in 1832 for John Kinzie, the federal government's Indian agent with the Ho Chunk people. An enigmatic man, Kinzie spoke the Native American languages used in the Indiana Territory. Juliette Kinzie later wrote a book of modest fame titled *Wau-Bun,* recounting their time in the state.

Two miles farther east along Highway 33 is the **Surgeon's Quarters** (608/742-2949, 10am-4pm Wed.-Sun. mid-May-mid-Oct., $7.50 adults), built during the 1820s and the only extant building from Fort Winnebago. It once housed the medical officers of the garrison. Noteworthy among the rooms of artifacts and antiques are the original plans for the fort and some papers of Jefferson Davis.

Downtown is **Zona Gale's Home** (506 W. Edgewater St., 608/742-7744), built by Gale for her parents after her first novel was a success in 1906; she did most of her writing here until she won the Pulitzer Prize in 1928. There are a few antiques and pieces of Gale memorabilia. It's open by appointment and charges only a nominal fee.

Getting There

The **Amtrak** (www.amtrak.com) *Empire Builder* train makes a stop in Portage (401 Oneida St.) on its Chicago-Seattle run, but you'll need to make reservations online.

Mackenzie Environmental Center

In Poynette, 12 miles southeast of Portage, is the **Mackenzie Environmental Center** (along Hwy. CS/Q, 608/635-8105, 10am-4pm daily, grounds and trails dawn-dusk, free) and state game farm, specializing in pheasant introduction. Wildlife highlights are bison, wolves, and eagles. A trail network runs past a sugar bush of maple trees and an observation tower. Museum exhibits include the oft-overlooked world of game wardens, who are on the front line of environmental management.

Wisconsin Rapids

The nucleus of the nation's top cranberry-producing region, Wisconsin Rapids is also a leading reason for Wisconsin's status as the nation's number-one paper-producing state. Visit in autumn for glorious photo opportunities in the surrounding cranberry bogs.

History

The first sawmills went up more than half a century before the town appeared, as early as 1831. In June 1880 forest fires raged through the area. No sooner had the beleaguered citizenry gone to bed after extinguishing one threatening fire than the Wisconsin River's rapids turned ugly, rising 100 feet after midnight and sweeping away much of the downtown area.

SIGHTS

Wisconsin River Papermaking Museum

The major industrial force in Wisconsin Rapids is shown briefly at the **Wisconsin River Papermaking Museum** (730 1st Ave. S., 715/424-3037, 1pm-4pm Tues. and Thurs., free), which shows not just the local but also world history of paper; the Japanese exhibits are amazing.

Cranberries

Wisconsin Rapids' chamber of commerce can provide a map for the lovely **Cranberry Highway Tour,** a 60-mile route for bikes and cars taking in sights and farms crucial to the local agricultural linchpin product. September and October are basically a nonstop cranberry festival. You may see trumpeter swans along the route as well.

Alexander House

The **Alexander House** (1131 Wisconsin River Dr., 715/887-3442, 1pm-4pm Sun., Tues., and Thurs., free) is the former residence of a Nekoosa Edwards Paper Company executive. Boasting original furnishings, it houses a ground-floor exhibit area displaying the work of local, regional, and national artists to buttress local history holdings.

Side Trips

Eight miles north of Wisconsin Rapids along Highway 34 is the **Rudolph Grotto Gardens and Wonder Cave** (Hwy. 34, 715/435-3120, 10am-5pm daily summer, gardens free, cave $2.50 adults). Inspired by the grotto at Lourdes, founder Father Philip Wagner vowed to construct one if he recovered from an illness. Father Wagner worked diligently for

40 years until his death to create his dream. The gardens are a hodgepodge of flora and assorted rocks, including a boulder the size of a barn the priest somehow moved here; the Wonder Cave is a representational collection of kitschy shrines and statues.

FOOD

Lake Aire Supper Club (6510 Hwy. 13 S., 715/325-5147, dinner Tues.-Sat., brunch Sun., $10-30) is an archetypal supper club—steaks and seafood. The solicitous service is oft-mentioned.

Grandma's USA Cafe (1920 Wylie St., 715/424-3843, breakfast/lunch daily) is a greasy spoon in a World War II-era Quonset hut. The food is cheap and good.

ACCOMMODATIONS

During cranberry season, some decent packages are available at the many chain options.

Undoubtedly the best in town is **Hotel Mead** (451 Grand Ave., 715/423-1500 or 800/843-6323, www.hotelmead.com, $109-204), in the heart of downtown along the river. Full-service amenities include a health club, a lounge, an indoor pool, a sauna, and a whirlpool.

INFORMATION AND SERVICES

The **Wisconsin Rapids Chamber of Commerce** (2507 8th St. S., 715/423-1830 or 800/554-4484, www.visitwisrapids.com) has visitor information.

CASTLE ROCK-PETENWELL FLOWAGES

The Castle Rock and Petenwell Dams are consummate examples of why the upper Wisconsin River has been called the "hardest-working river in the nation." These two dams—east and southeast of Necedah—created the fourth- and second-largest bodies of water in the state at 23,300 and 32,300 acres.

Surrounding the two lakes are numerous county parks and **Roche-A-Cri State Park** (https://dnr.wi.gov), west 10 miles on Highway 21. You can't miss this park, dominated by a towering 300-foot-tall crag jutting from a hill at the base, resulting in a height of more than 1,200 feet. A trail leads to the top of the spire, where outstanding views of the surrounding countryside unfold.

Parts of the Castle Rock dike system are being used as a trout fishery, and the local power company has constructed osprey nesting stands. Petenwell Dam sloughs are a great place to spot bald eagles. East of the Petenwell Dam is the **Van Kuren Trail,** a short multipurpose trail with excellent vistas; to the southwest is the **Petenwell Wildlife Area Hiking Trail,** skirting the shallow southern rim of Petenwell Lake through Strongs Prairie. These and other county parks are accessible along Highway 21 and Highway Z.

Also check out **Petenwell Rock** on the west bank of the river, the largest rock formation in the region. Apocryphal tales tell of a man who showed up and fell in love with an already betrothed woman. They both leaped to their deaths rather than lose each other, and the woman, Clinging Vine, had her spirit returned to this rock, which was named after her lover.

★ CENTRAL NECEDAH WILDLIFE PRESERVE

Sprawling north and west of Necedah and bordered by Highway 80 and Highway 21 is the stark, moving **Central Necedah Wildlife Preserve** (https://fws.gov), almost 44,000 acres that allow up close glimpses at isolated wildlife and awesome scenery. Once in the preserve, you'll soon understand why Native Americans dubbed the area Necedah, "Land of Yellow Waters."

The preserve makes national news annually for its ambitious whooping crane recovery program—ultralight planes launched here guided the birds all the way to Florida, marking the first whooping crane migrations since 1878.

The preserve is essentially what remains of an enormous peat bog—residual glacial

Lake Wisconsin—called the Great Central Wisconsin Swamp. It's now one-quarter wetlands, home to 20,000 ducks and Canada and snow geese, all introduced beginning in the 1950s.

A total of 35 miles of hiking and skiing trails wind throughout the Necedah refuge. The 11-mile auto tours outlined in maps obtained from the **nature center office** (9am-4pm Mon.-Sat.) at the south end of the refuge are good. There's even great berry-picking. Be careful while hiking, though; the state has reintroduced the eastern massasauga rattlesnake.

Contiguous to the refuge are three national wildlife areas: To the west is **Meadow Valley Wildlife Area,** bisected by Highway 173; north is the **Wood County Wildlife Area;** and farther north along Highway X and bordered to its north by Highway 54 is the **Sandhill Wildlife Demonstration Area** (Sandhill WDA), which houses a fenced-in bison herd, tons of eagles, a 12-mile loop trail, and a 20-mile hiking trail. Native prairie oak savanna restoration is ongoing. The Sandhill WDA has an outdoor skills center devoted to instruction in game-tracking skills using firearms, bows, or cameras. Both the Sandhill and Necedah confines are home to more than 700 majestic sandhill cranes and trumpeter swans, the latter transplanted from Alaskan nesting pairs.

BUCKHORN STATE PARK

This diverse 2,500-acre promontory southeast of Necedah juts into the Castle Rock-Petenwell Flowages. A short boardwalk trail leads to what could be the dunes and sandblow of the Sonoran Desert, if it weren't for the evergreens. A wide array of ecosystems native to the state is protected here, from oak forests to restored grasslands. Rare species of turtle can be found along a wonderful interpretive canoe trail in the backwaters; the canoeing is very isolated and a good look at how the land appeared 100 years ago.

The **camping** is even better because there isn't much of it. Forty-two primitive sites and just 11 drive-in ("family") sites mean a good chance of solitude. Reservations (888/947-2757, http://wisconsin.goingtocamp.com, $8 reservation fee, $25-37 nonresidents, $11 day-use) are not always necessary.

NEW LISBON

Due south of the Central Necedah Wildlife Preserve is this pleasant town of 1,491 folks. One of the Upper Midwest's largest groups of **effigy mounds** is south of town off Highway 12/16. Even rarer are the **Twin Bluff petroglyphs,** done by early Woodland people, west along Highway A; hardy hikers can make it up Twin Bluff and to the caverns to check out the Thunderbird etchings. West of town five miles you can pick up the multiuse

Sandhill Cranes at Central Necedah Wildlife Preserve

Omaha Recreational Trail as it passes through Hustler. Much of the area's history is on display at the **New Lisbon Public Library** (115 W. Park St., 608/562-3213, 9am-6pm weekdays, 9am-noon Sat.) representing part of the state's largest private prehistoric Native American artifact collection.

Stevens Point

At approximately the north-south halfway point in Wisconsin, Stevens Point is a picturesque city spread out along the Wisconsin and Plover Rivers within the fecund Golden Sands region. Travelers note an inordinate amount of green space and parkland—perhaps one reason why the University of Wisconsin-Stevens Point (UWSP) is so renowned for its environmental science disciplines.

City settlement happened almost accidentally. Starting in 1830, enterprising lumber speculators had been pushing northward from the forts of the lower Fox and Wisconsin Rivers. Lumberman George Stevens temporarily deposited supplies at this spot, later called "the Point," and unwittingly founded the town.

The city wasn't close enough to the timber tracts to experience overnight growth or sustained boomtown status. By 1850, three years after the first platting of the town, there were only 200 citizens.

Later, sawmills became paper mills, and with the surrounding prime agricultural fields, the local economy drew more settlers—mainly Polish immigrants.

SIGHTS

Point Brewery

The third-oldest continuously operated (from 1857) brewery in the country, **Point Brewery** (2617 Water St., 715/344-9310, www.pointbeer.com, $5) concocts the beers of choice for many North Woods residents and college students. A personal favorite is the Spring Bock and their excellent root beer. One Chicago newspaper called Point the best beer in America; it won a gold medal for its Horizon Wheat Beer at the 2010 World Beer Cup. The brewery gives tours (hourly 11am-2pm Mon.-Sat., noon-2pm Sun. summer, fewer rest of year).

UW-Stevens Point

WISCONSIN FORESTRY HALL OF FAME

One of Wisconsin's best environmental resources programs, the College of Natural Resources is housed at the UWSP—fitting, since these are the lands immortalized by naturalist Aldo Leopold, honored in a corner of the building's **Wisconsin Forestry Hall of Fame** (800 Reserve St., hours vary). In addition to the shrine to Leopold, there are exhibits on mammals, fish, turtles, and more. It's in the east lobby of the first floor of the Natural Resources building.

SCHMEEKLE RESERVE

On the northern edge of the university campus, the diminutive 200-acre tract known as **Schmeekle Reserve** (2419 Northpoint Dr., dawn-dusk daily) could be the city's crown jewel, an amalgam of pristine ecology with a 0.25-mile interpretive trail and other walking trails through the interspersed wetland, prairie, and woodland topography; the woodland features an imposing stand of tall pines. The **visitors center** (8am-5pm daily) houses the **Wisconsin Conservation Hall of Fame**—UWSP initiated the country's first natural resources degree program.

George W. Meade Wildlife Area

Fourteen miles west of town via Highway 10 in Milladore is the **George W. Meade Wildlife Area** (Hwy. S., free), with 28,000 acres of wildlife, marsh, and farmland. There are nesting eagles in parts of the preserve, a

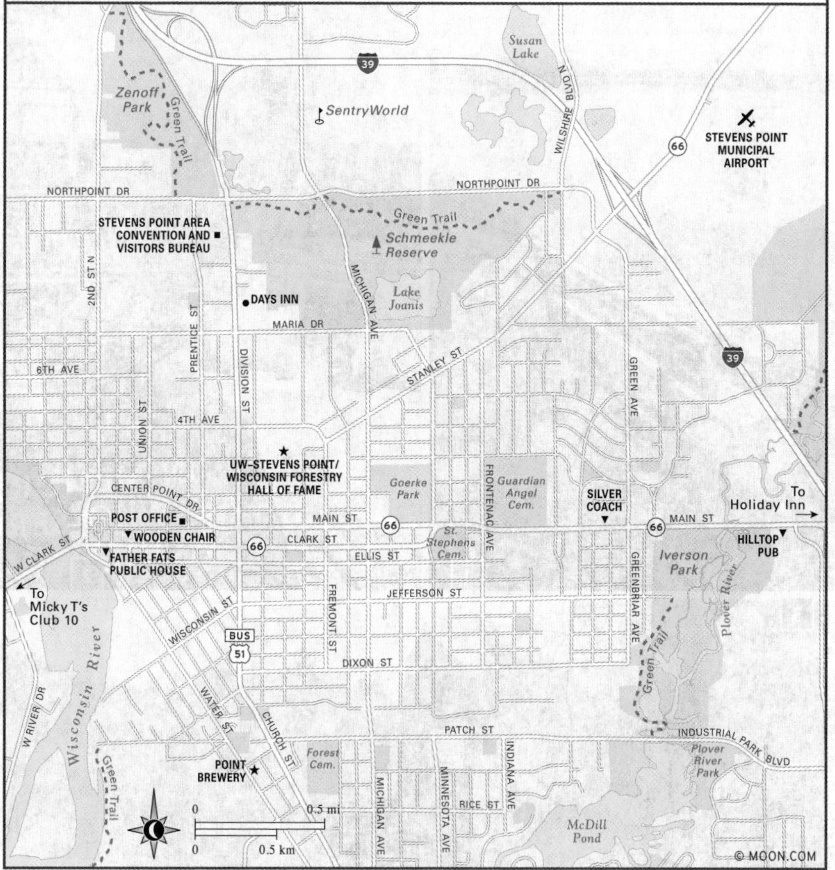

plethora of mammals, and a few prairie chickens. Rough and not-so-rough trails are constantly being expanded.

RECREATION

SentryWorld

SentryWorld (601 N. Michigan Ave., 715/345-1600, www.sentryworld.com, from $155 for nonresidents) is highly rated by a variety of golf media outlets as one of the best golf courses in the country, including the legendary flower hole, with 33,000 individual plants.

Green Trail

The **Green Trail** is a fantastic 24-mile multipurpose loop trail that skirts the Wisconsin and Plover Rivers. There's lots of wildlife- and bird-watching. Ten parking areas are interspersed along the trail's length; the easiest to reach is downtown along Main and 1st Streets.

ENTERTAINMENT AND EVENTS

Nightlife

Mickey T's Club 10 (1602 Hwy. HH W., 715/344-7128) is a classic old roadhouse bar

1
2
IN MEMORY
ALL WHO
WORLD
3
CAUTION
Boardwalks
may be
slippery

taken over by the scion of a famous local pizza restaurateur. It's perfect—awesome pizza, homemade potato salad, a roadhouse, and live music.

Festivals and Events

On a decidedly weird note is UWSP's **Trivia Weekend,** held each April. The largest of its kind in the world, this event is an excruciating 54-hour brain-tease hosted by the university radio station, WWSP (90 FM), and broadcast throughout central Wisconsin. It's great fun and extremely difficult.

FOOD

Bistro

New to the Point dining scene, **Father Fats Public House** (945 Clark St., 715/544-4054, dinner Tues.-Sat., lunch Fri.-Sat., brunch Sun., $11-18), says its small-plate menu deliberately has tastes of Asia, New York, Spain, and the Deep South. It may sound odd, but it works—the food is excellent.

Cafés

Very cozy and aesthetically pleasing is the ★ **Wooden Chair** (1059 Main St., 715/341-1133, 7am-2pm daily, $3-9), a warm and spacious eatery with hardwood-floor areas, bookshelves, brick walls, fireplaces, and wide tables with elbow room. The specials change monthly, and the eggs selection is as diverse as it gets. There are good healthy options too.

Fish Fries

A great fish fry is off U.S. 51 at the **Hilltop Pub** (4901 Hwy. 10 E., 715/341-3037, lunch and dinner daily, $5-15), with outdoor seating in the summer and great burgers. This old pub—now a microbrewery—is chock-full of Point memorabilia, including photos and an antique bottle collection. Diners eat in a comfy screened porch.

Supper Club and American Dining

An excellent creative eatery with a wide range of regional dishes is local institution ★ **Silver Coach** (38 Park Ridge Dr., 715/341-6588, 4pm-10pm Mon.-Sat., $7-19), serving from a turn-of-the-20th-century railcar since World War II. The ribs are excellent, as are the blackened steaks and the seafood. Wisconsin-themed artwork is displayed on the walls.

ACCOMMODATIONS

The lowest price option worth the money is the **Days Inn** (159 N. Division St., 715/254-8685, $109 s or d), with the usual amenities and clean rooms. It is perfectly located near hiking in the Schmeekle Reserve.

Still higher in price is the nearby **Holiday Inn** (1001 Amber Ave., 715/344-0200, $179), one of the Midwest's largest facilities and sporting a new water park, great for the little ones. You can often get great deals.

Camping

The nearest public parks for camping are **Lake DuBay** (715/346-1433), northwest off Highway 10 onto Highway E, and **Jordan Park** (715/345-0520), six miles northeast on Highway 66.

INFORMATION AND SERVICES

The **Stevens Point Area Convention and Visitors Bureau** (340 Division St., 715/344-2556, www.stevenspointarea.com) is next to the Holiday Inn.

GETTING THERE

The **Central Wisconsin Airport** (CWA, 100 CWA Dr., Mosinee, 715/693-2147, www.flycwa.org) is in nearby Mosinee and has flights from Chicago, Minneapolis, and Detroit.

Getting to Stevens Point from Madison (via I-39, 111 miles) by car takes 90 minutes. From Wausau (via I-39, 34 miles), it takes 40 minutes.

1: the Green Trail follows the Wisconsin River
2: The Highground, a somber memorial
3: Schmeekle Reserve, Stevens Point

Sand County Sage

> There are some who can live without wild things, and some who cannot. . . . Like winds and sunsets, wild things were taken for granted until progress began to do away with them.
> —Aldo Leopold, from the foreword to *A Sand County Almanac and Sketches Here and There*

Leading experts on environmentalism were once asked to name the most influential work in raising ecological consciousness. The hands-down winner was Aldo Leopold's *A Sand County Almanac and Sketches Here and There.*

Aldo Leopold was a seminal naturalist, a pioneering figure in ecology and especially conservation. He introduced the idea of setting aside protected forestland and later devised the concept of wildlife management. Not a native Badger, Leopold nonetheless lived the better part of his life not far from where John Muir grew up. Above all, he was a polished writer with a lucid, engaging, eloquent style celebrating life and its connection to the land.

EARLY YEARS

After attending Yale—its graduate forestry program was very progressive, controversial, and the first of its kind—in 1909, Leopold went to work for the U.S. Forest Service (USFS). In Arizona, when he looked into the dying eyes of a wolf that had been shot—eradication was the norm—his passion for educating people on the need to coexist germinated.

He accepted a fortuitous transfer to a new USFS lab in Madison in 1924 and within a few years had revolutionized how we view the natural world. His belief in a cause-and-effect relationship

Marshfield

The Depression-era Works Progress Administration (WPA) guide summed up Marshfield with the line, "The city is sprinkled out on a flat green prairie . . . patterned rigidly as a chessboard, and industries are as diverse as pawns, knights, bishops, queens, and kings." As far as overnight stops go, one could do far worse than this attractive city. State residents associate the city mainly with its cutting-edge Marshfield Clinic, a major medical group practice of some national repute. But Marshfield's livability quotient is also always tops in the state and among the top five in the Midwest.

The city is now one of the state's leading dairy research areas and hosts a dairy festival and regional fair. At the fairgrounds, check out the world's largest round barn—a lovely 1916 edifice still used to house purebred animals.

SIGHTS

Marshfield Clinic and New Visions Gallery

Not a tour spot per se, **Marshfield Clinic** does sport some impressive credentials. One of the leading private group practice medical facilities in the United States, with 21 regional Wisconsin satellites (and 5,000 employees), the Marshfield Clinic began in 1916 as a dedicated group of six physicians trying to give the rural communities a higher standard of medical care. It now comprises three massive facilities—Marshfield Clinic, Saint Joseph's Hospital (with 19,000 patients per year), and the Marshfield Medical Research Foundation, a consortium of more than 100 research projects.

Adjacent to the clinic, in a space it donated, **New Visions Gallery** (1000 N. Oak Ave., 715/387-5562, 9am-4pm Mon.-Fri., free)

with the land led him to a two-year survey of game in North America and his founding of game management theory.

By 1933 he was named the chair of UW's new game management department. Part of his job was to examine and essentially restore central Wisconsin, which had been laid waste during previous generations of misinformed agricultural exploitation. Leopold's tenure oversaw reforestation, wetland restoration, and the establishment of state and county forests, game preserves, and parks.

A SAND COUNTY ALMANAC

While covering the central region for his work, Leopold found the perfect retreat. He spent most of the rest of his life in examination of this land. The result is his evenhanded and scientifically pragmatic masterpiece for which he is justly famous, setting down what is now referred to as land ethic, the origin of modern-day land-use management.

A Sand County Almanac was in essence a florid, cheerful way of describing the symbiotic nature of humans and the land. What we today couch in multisyllabic jargon (biodiversity or eco-awareness), Leopold recognized intuitively.

One fantastic way to get a glimpse of the lands he so adored is to travel approximately 15 miles northeast of Baraboo to **Rustic Road 49,** Levee Road—10 miles stretching along the Wisconsin River between Highway 33 and Highway T and passing through the Aldo Leopold Reserve. You can also take tours of the grounds (Mon.-Sat. Apr.-Oct., Sat. only off-season, $15; self-guided $7) which include the original **shack** and the wondrous new **Aldo Leopold Legacy Center** (608/355-0279, free) a mile away via a trail. See www.aldoleopold.org for information.

is an educational gallery; permanent holdings include Marc Chagall prints, West African sculptures and masks, Australian aboriginal art, Haitian paintings, and world folk arts. Temporary exhibits change every few weeks. St. Joseph's Hospital also has a corridor of Wisconsin artists; about 50 are displayed.

Jurustic Park

Cheeky and fun is **Jurustic Park** (M222 Sugar Bush Ln., 715/387-1653, www.jurustic.com, grounds until 4:30pm daily, free), north of town a handful of miles via Highway E, a collection of "dinosaur" sculptures that, rumor has it, once inhabited this marsh. In all seriousness, the 250 metal sculptures, ranging from less-than-a-foot spiders to massive 45-foot-long beasts, are fantastic pieces of art from a local couple. Local bike trails are being built out this way, so it will be a lovely ride. Call ahead to confirm that the park is open.

Stierle Bird Exhibit

The subdued **Stierle Bird Exhibit** (211 E. 2nd St., 715/387-8495, 9am-8pm Mon.-Fri., 9am-5pm Sat., 1pm-5pm Sun. Labor Day-Memorial Day, limited hours Memorial Day-Labor Day, free), in the Marshfield Public Library, is one of the country's most complete and diverse collections of bird eggs (110 species and 1,900 eggs). It also features 140 species of birds in 380 specimens in total, all collected by a local taxidermist and photographer.

Wildlife-Viewing

South of town via Highway 13 and then north on Highway X leads to the 9,500-acre **Sandhill Wildlife Area,** a marshland dedicated to the restoration of sandhill cranes; there are also even a few bison herds.

★ The Highground

Eerie silence pervades **The Highground** (W7031 Ridge Rd., Neillsville), Wisconsin's Veterans Memorial Park on 100 acres surrounded by one of the largest glacial moraines in the state. A most somber memorial, dominating a central rise, is the Vietnam

Veterans Memorial statue, while a nearby grove of trees forms a five-star pattern, dedicated to sacrifices of families in wartime. Most compelling is the Effigy Mound, an enormous dove-shaped earthen mound for POWs and MIAs and all those "prisoners of their own experience." (A similar mound is gradually being constructed in Vietnam by Vietnamese veterans, with the cooperation of Wisconsin vets.) An admirable mixture of flora and sculpture, the park is designed for the sound of wind chimes (many constructed from military hardware) to pervade the entire expanse. Lighted at night, the park is open 24 hours daily. Memorials also honor Native Americans and vets of the Persian Gulf War and the Korean War. Some picnic tables are available, and walking trails are constantly being developed. The whole experience is quite moving, particularly at night. Various festivals, including emotional powwows, take place throughout the year. It's 37 miles south and west of Marshfield, via U.S. 10; follow Highway 13 south out of town to reach U.S. 10. Just west of Highground is a lovely Wisconsin **Rustic Road** drive through a decaying settlers' village.

Other Sights

Near The Highground is charming little **Neillsville,** famed for a huge statue of Annabelle the cow on the east side of town. In town is an 1897 reconstructed jail listed on the National Register of Historic Places. U.S. 10 west of town brings you first to a lovely arboretum adjacent to the Black River and then, after five miles, to the fetching Silver Dome Ballroom, a Great Depression WPA project with original decorations and fixtures.

North of Neillsville, just east of Withee, is another fantastic **Rustic Road** through classic Amish country; this one also rolls across an old wooden bridge to herds of bison and elk.

FOOD

This is another city of cafés. You'll find an emphasis on local ingredients in the food and handcrafted beers (all very much above-average) at **Blue Heron Brewpub** (108 W. 9th St., 715/389-1868, 11am-late daily, $5-15).

For something completely different, Marshfield's old train depot has been achingly well restored and now houses **Royal Tokyo** (112 E. 1st St., 715/486-8868, dinner Tues.-Sat., $7-23). The sushi is enhanced by the slice-and-dice teppanyaki chefs preparing food before your eyes.

ACCOMMODATIONS

Marshfield's most centrally located lodging is the **Park Motel** (1806 Roddis Ave., 715/387-1741, $60) which is perfectly adequate.

The best option is the **Hotel Marshfield** (2700 S. Central Ave., 715/387-2700, www.hotelmarshfield.com, from $139), a classic hotel gutted and transformed into comfort (they call it urban chic) not seen in many places in central Wisconsin. There are full amenities, and the place is highly regarded. It is dog-friendly as well.

INFORMATION

The **Marshfield Chamber of Commerce** (700 S. Central Ave., 715/384-3454, www.marshfieldchamber.com) is friendly.

Wausau

Wausau is the last city of any size all the way to Superior in the northwest. Underrated and unseen by many, it features the mighty Wisconsin waterway and hourglass-shaped Lake Wausau. Just south of town, Rib Mountain—for centuries erroneously assumed to be Wisconsin's highest—dominates the topography.

The heart of Marathon County, Wausau has become legendary since the late 1980s for something decidedly unexpected from north-central Wisconsin: ginseng. The county is now the nation's number-one producer of high-quality ginseng, second worldwide only to Korea in exports. Dairying hasn't completely been replaced, however; Marathon County is still number-one in milk and cheese output (colby cheese got its name from a town in this county).

SIGHTS

★ Leigh Yawkey Woodson Museum

Ornithological mavens rub elbows with ginseng buyers during the internationally regarded early autumn **Birds in Art** exhibition at the **Leigh Yawkey Woodson Museum** (700 N. 12th St., 715/845-7010, www.lywam.org, 9am-4pm Tues.-Fri., noon-5pm Sat.-Sun., free), when the museum rolls out its exquisite and astonishing menagerie of birds in all media. The little museum in a grand Cotswolds-style mansion has holdings that draw artists and birders worldwide. The 8-12 exhibitions each year, plus a steadily growing permanent collection, include rare Royal Worcester porcelain, Victorian glass baskets, and complete multimedia artist collections with birds as the focus.

Rib Mountain

Dominating the terrain and the local psyche is **Rib Mountain,** for most of the state's history presumed to be its highest point. Technically not a mountain, Rib is a 70-billion-year-old quartzite monadnock rising 1,940 feet above sea level and 800 feet above the surrounding peneplain. Though not exactly imposing in height, its slopes are steep, with a 1,200-foot rise per mile. As a state park, there is an $11 daily entrance fee for out-of-state license plates.

ArtsBlock

Wausau is to be commended for its devotion to cultural affairs. The city block bounded by Scott, Fourth, Jefferson, and 5th Streets is now an arts district, unrivaled in Wisconsin, known as **ArtsBlock.** The cornerstone 1927 Greek Revival **Grand Theater** (427 4th St., 715/842-0988, www.grandtheater.org) was recently given a multimillion-dollar face-lift to bring back its original shine and allow space for national and international acts. Studios and galleries of **Center for the Visual Arts** (427 4th St., 715/842-4545, www.cvawausau.com, 10am-5pm Tues.-Fri., noon-4pm Sat., free) and performances by the **Performing Arts Foundation** are also right here.

Historic District

The lumber wealth of the area went to superlative use. More than 60 structures of many architectural styles are showcased in a well-planned **walking tour** through part of downtown. The maps are available at the information center (219 Jefferson St., 888/948-4748, www.visitwausau.com).

The Center

Take Highway 29 west to Poniatowski (follow the signs), and at some point you might start feeling some odd twinges. It could be because you're approaching 45 degrees longitude and 90 degrees latitude—the exact midpoint between the Greenwich prime meridian and the international date line as well as the midpoint between the North Pole and the equator. It's well marked with a little park.

Ginseng

This trim, solidly Wisconsin city turns into an ersatz Asian nation come autumn, when buyers from Hong Kong, Korea, China, and American Chinese communities converge en masse to begin the cryptic ritual of sorting through the ginseng harvest.

If you're serious about ginseng, contact the **Ginseng Board of Wisconsin** (715/443-2444, www.ginsengboard.com) for details on regional growers and crops. Some offer tours of operations, sometimes for a fee.

Dells of the Eau Claire County Park

A gem by any standard is the **Dells of the**

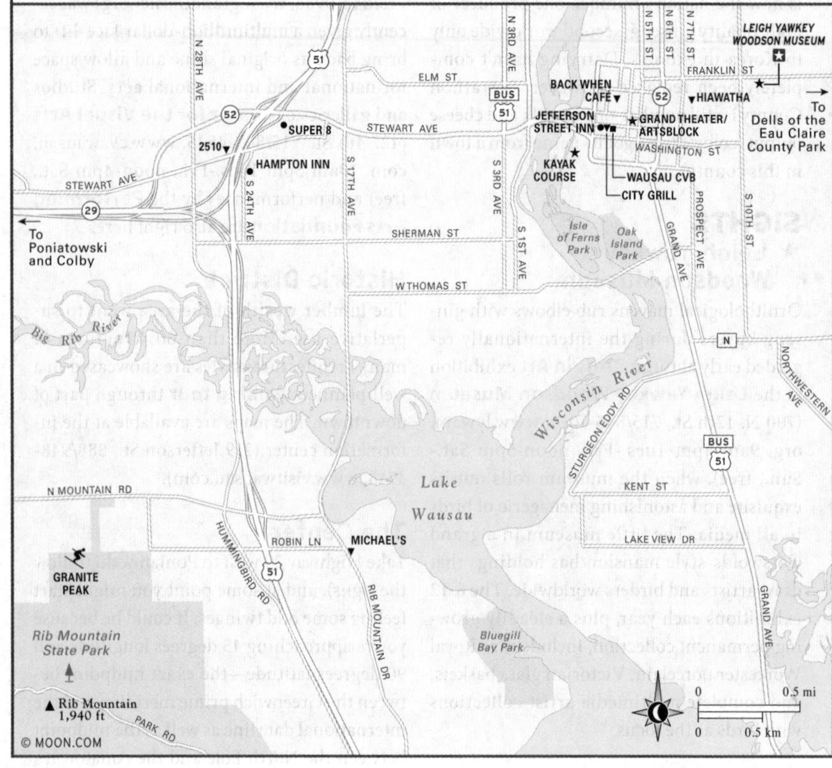

Eau Claire County Park. Officially a state Scientific Area, it's a freak of geology, with striated rock outcroppings and, as the name implies, recessed water valleys with bluffs up to 70 feet high. In parts, the surrealistic rocky surfaces look like hardened cottage cheese. The park has superlative scenery and a segment of the Ice Age National Scenic Trail to supplement the grand hiking. To get here, head 15 miles east on Highway 29 to Highway Y.

Side Trips

Head out of town west along Highway 29 about 30 miles and you'll come to little **Colby,** the birthplace of the eponymous cheese. Also of interest here is the **Rural Arts Museum** (715/223-2264, Sun. Memorial Day-Labor Day), a country museum with an old box factory, a depot, cabins, and more.

RECREATION

Skiing

The highest ski hill in the state, Rib Mountain's **Granite Peak** (715/845-2846, www.skigranitepeak.com) has the second-longest vertical drop in the Midwest at just under 700 feet. There are 74 runs (bunnies, steep chutes, and even forest glades) plus an enormous original chalet. It does a great job on kid-centric activities too. Prices vary wildly according to season and time of day.

For cross-country skiing, a personal

1: the phenomenal Leigh Yawkey Woodson Museum **2:** Rib Mountain **3:** downtown Wausau

Leigh Yawkey Woodson Art Museum
1
QUEEN'S CHAIR
2
3

Ginseng: Wisconsin's Golden Root

Wisconsin may be America's Dairyland, but in the Wausau area, the revered root ginseng is the economic mainstay. Between 90 and 95 percent of the United States' ginseng crop comes directly from the secretive farmers of Marathon County, now the world's fourth-largest ginseng producer, at 500,000 to 1.5 million pounds annually. It's among the top agricultural cash crop exports for the state.

THE IMAGE OF MAN

Ginseng means the "root in the image of man," and in Asian cultures is considered a cure-all for any ailment. Ginseng preserves the crucial balance of yin (cool, dark, feminine) and yang (warm, light, masculine). It is most highly revered in China and Korea, where legends tell of mountain ginseng being a gift from the gods, caught in a mountain stream through lightning. Koreans say that if a fortunate event occurs in your dreams, you'll find wild ginseng—and maybe save someone's life. Some Chinese will pay a month's wages for prime ginseng.

Western scientists remain divided on its efficacy, and there has been a lack of research despite the boom in its popularity in supplements. A stimulant-like effect has been observed on the nervous and endocrine systems, and it has also been shown to affect hormones and decrease blood sugar.

THE PLANT

All ginseng species are members of the Aralinceae family, relatives of celery and carrots, but all are not the same. Ginseng has always grown wild across the eastern half of the United States from

favorite is the hidden, classical-style three-mile **Ringle Trail,** for beginners, in isolated hardwood stands; it's east along Highway 29, then north on Highway Q, and east on Poplar Lane.

Kayaking

Lumber boomtowns on the Fox and Wisconsin Rivers notwithstanding, Wausau lays claim to the most persistent set of rapids. No longer powering the mills, the water now attracts thousands of white-water aficionados and pro kayakers to make use of its downtown, dam-controlled white-water course in national and international competitions. Not many other cities have a course right through the city, complete with bankside seating. The city's program garnered kudos from the U.S. Canoe and Kayak Team, which has made Wausau one of its top training sites. Contact **Whitewater Park** (www.wausauwhitewater.org) for information. The Wisconsin River and Lake Wausau are part of a popular water trail; portaging is required.

Biking

Wausau's segment of the **Mountain-Bay Trail** is an 83-miler constructed along the former Chicago and North Western Railway railbed and stretching from Weston to Green Bay. The trailhead begins by the Weston Community Center (5500 Schofield Ave.). A daily pass ($5) is required and can be obtained at the trailhead.

The city **Convention and Visitors Bureau** (219 Jefferson St., 888/948-4748, www.visitwausau.com) has excellent maps of other area trails.

Snowshoeing

Rib Mountain State Park is one of the few in Wisconsin to offer trails specifically designed for snowshoeing—five miles in total. The sport is popular in the Wausau area, and

as far south as Mississippi. Daniel Boone traded it, and John Jacob Astor got his legendary fur company started by dealing it to the Chinese.

It is tremendously difficult to cultivate: Cash- and labor-intensive, the root is extraordinarily sensitive to temperatures and susceptible to rot and many pests and blights. One acre can yield 2,000 pounds, but it takes four years to reach maturity, and once a field has grown ginseng, it won't grow other crops for at least a century.

WISCONSIN SHANG

Known locally as "shang" or "sang," Wisconsin's ginseng *(Panax quinquefolius)* is among the most valuable—economically and pharmacologically—in the world. First cultivated by German farmers, it was first commercially raised by a pair of Marathon County brothers around the turn of the 20th century.

Problems have arisen. Local overproduction, newer competition from British Columbia, and—worst of all—piracy (putting the Wisconsin seal on cheap Chinese shang in retail settings) caused prices to plummet from highs of $80 a pound to $22. The state also had just 200 ginseng farmers, down from 1,600 in the 1990s. Prices rebounded to $50 per pound in 2012. The state organized a Ginseng Board to coordinate efforts and protect the Wisconsin product.

Worst of all are wild ginseng poachers, who devastate the wild plant, since it can command more than 10 times the price of its cultivated version. Despite the seeming impossibility of actually catching someone in the act, the state has had some 36 convictions in high years. One poacher was actually shot and killed in Ohio, for which the landowner was prosecuted.

you'll find rentals at downtown sporting goods stores.

FESTIVALS AND EVENTS

Grab a sandwich and head to the popular **Concerts on the Square** (6pm-8pm Wed.) across from the Great Hall of the ArtsBlock.

FOOD

Fish Fries

The fish fry at the **Hiawatha** (713 Grant St., 715/848-5166, dinner weekdays, brunch weekends, $6-15) is where locals will tell you to eat. It's got great fish, but also find creativity—mac and cheese to citrus salmon.

Quick and Casual

"Upscale family-style" best describes **2510** (2510 Stewart Ave., 715/845-2510, lunch/dinner daily, $7-20), west on Stewart Avenue. The place also has its own bakery and deli and a great fish fry.

Right near the ArtsBlock district, the farm-to-table New American **Back When Cafe** (606 N. 3rd St., 715/848-5668, dinner Tues.-Sat., from $5) has healthful sandwiches on homemade breads and slightly more gourmet options in the evening. It is also the best local option for vegetarians.

Supper Clubs and Fine Dining

Downtown in the Jefferson Street Inn, the ★ **City Grill** (203 Jefferson St., 715/848-2900, lunch/dinner Mon.-Sat., dinner Sun., $7-20) and its casual contemporary American fare has been raved about by more than one reader and local residents. It has a comfortably chic atmosphere and, often, live entertainment.

Michael's (2901 Rib Mountain Dr., 715/842-9856, 4pm-10pm Mon.-Sat., $12-45) may give the City Grill a run for its money. Find fine European and straightforward supper club fare in a comfortably old-world atmosphere.

ACCOMMODATIONS

Under $100

The junction of Stewart and South 17th Avenues, on the west side of town, essentially the interchange of U.S. 51 and Highway 52, has the largest grouping of accommodations, with rooms around $50. You can expect generic rooms but you'll get solicitous service at the local **Super 8** (2006 W. Stewart Ave., 715/203-4876, from $72). The complex was refreshed not long ago, and the service is above expectations.

$100-150

Midrange, the best hotel close to downtown is the **Hampton Inn** (615 S. 24th Ave., 715/848-9700, hamptoninn.hilton.com, $150), a chain that—gasp—doesn't feel generic either.

Over $150

The same amenities along with rooms filled with cool modernity mesh with historicism at the ★ **Jefferson Street Inn** (201 Jefferson St., 715/845-6500, www.jeffersonstreetinn.com, $170-225). Best of all, it's in the heart of downtown.

Camping

Council Grounds State Park, 15 miles north, has 55 isolated sites ($25-35 nonresidents, $11 day-use) are in a heavily wooded park along the Wisconsin River. The camping is private in some fairly impressive stands of proud pines. Reservations (888/947-2757, http://wisconsin.goingtocamp.com, $8 reservation fee) are advised.

INFORMATION AND SERVICES

The **Wausau Convention and Visitors Bureau** (219 Jefferson St., 888/948-4748, www.visitwausau.org) is right downtown.

GETTING THERE

Air

The Wausau area is served by the **Central Wisconsin Airport** (CWA, 100 CWA Dr., Mosinee, 715/693-2147, www.fly-cwa.org) in nearby Mosinee, with flights from Chicago, Minneapolis, and Detroit.

Car

Getting to Wausau from Stevens Point (via I-39, 34 miles) takes 40 minutes. From Eau Claire (via Hwy. 29, 102 miles), it takes one hour and 45 minutes. From Minocqua (via U.S. 51, 68 miles), it takes 70 minutes. From Green Bay (via Hwy. 20, 97 miles), it takes one hour and 40 minutes.

Background

The Landscape

Topographically, Wisconsin may lack the jaw-dropping majesty of other states' vaulting crags or shimmering desert palettes. But it possesses an equable slice of physicality, with fascinating geographical and geological highlights—many of them found nowhere outside Wisconsin.

Where is the state? Sticklers call this area "eastern north-central United States." One outlander classified it simply as "north," which makes sense only if you look at a map. Wisconsinites themselves most often consider their state a part of the Midwest—more specifically, the

upper Midwest. And some even prefer you call it a Great Lakes State.

One-third of the U.S. population lives within a day's drive of the state. Its surface area of 56,514 square miles ranks it the 26th largest in the nation. Wisconsin is by no means high, yet this is a state of rolling topography, chock-full of hills and glacial undulation. The highest point is Timm's Hill in north-central Wisconsin; at 1,953 feet, it's significant for the Midwest.

Hydrophiles love it here. Even excluding all the access to the Great Lakes, approximately 4 percent of the state's surface is water—including more than 16,000 ancient glacial lakes, 40 percent of which have yet to be named.

Most of Wisconsin's perimeter sidesteps surveyors' plotting. The grandest borders—Lakes Michigan and Superior—are unique to Wisconsin and Michigan. Superior occupies the far-north cap of the state, ensconcing the Bayfield County promontory and its Apostle Islands. More subdued Lake Michigan runs for an enormous stretch down the state, interrupted only by the magnificent Door County peninsula.

GEOGRAPHY

Wisconsin was once at the earth's equator. Plate shifting created the Canadian Shield, which includes about two-thirds of eastern Canada along with Wisconsin, Minnesota, Michigan, and New York. Five hundred million years ago, a glacial lake flooded the Wisconsin range—the northern section of present-day Wisconsin.

Glaciation during the two million years of the four glacial periods—geologically, a blink of an eye—is responsible for Wisconsin's one-of-a-kind topography. The final advance, occurring 70,000-10,000 years ago, was even named the Wisconsin period. Wisconsin endured five glacial "lobes" penetrating the state, reducing the state's previous heights to knobs and slate flatlands and establishing rivers and streambeds. Only the southwestern lower third of the state escaped the glaciers' penetration, resulting in the world's largest area surrounded completely by glacial drift.

Northern Highland

Covering 15,000 square miles, the Canadian Shield is the most salient geographical feature of northern Wisconsin. Underlain by crystalline rock on a peneplain, the bedrock and glacial soils are particularly suited to growing timber.

This area's high concentration of lakes is what separates the region from the rest of the Midwest—and, in fact, distinguishes it in the world, since only the remotest parts of Quebec and Finland have more lakes per square mile.

Lake Superior Lowlands

Wisconsin's northern cap along Lake Superior displays a geological oddity, unique in the Great Lakes—a fallen trench of Lake Superior, flanked by palisades. Before the glaciers arrived to finish carving, shifting lowered this 10- to 20-mile-wide belt, now 0.5 miles lower than the surrounding land. This wedge-shaped red-clay plain consists mainly of copper-hued outcroppings and numerous streams and rivers as well as waterfalls.

Eastern Ridges and Lowlands

Bordered by Lake Michigan on the east and north, this 14,000-square-mile region was much richer in glacial deposits, and the fecund soils attracted the first immigrant farmers. The impeded waterways were ideal conduits for floating timber to mills.

The Kettle Moraine region southeast of Lake Winnebago is a physical textbook of glacial geology.

Central (Sand) Plain

Bisected by the mighty Wisconsin River, the crescent-shaped Central Plain region spreads for 13,000 square miles. Once the bottom of

Previous: Alp & Dell Cheese cheddar cow, Monroe

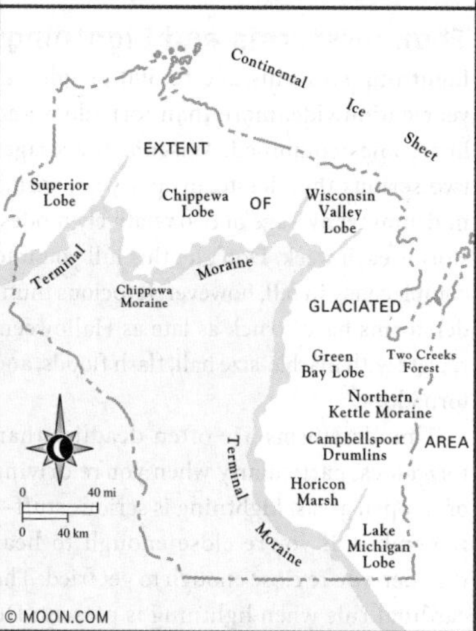

enormous glacial Lake Wisconsin, the region is most noted for its oddball topography of sand dune-esque stretches mingled with peat bog, cranberry marsh, buttes and outliers (younger hoodoo-shaped oddities), and jack pine and scrub oak—all made famous by Aldo Leopold's *A Sand County Almanac.* The central section of this region is relatively flat, but the lower third contains buttes and outliers. And all this at the Wisconsin Dells.

Western Uplands

The Western Uplands region subsumes the radical Driftless Area. Geologically the roughest and wildest sector of Wisconsin, it contains rises up to 400 feet higher than the contiguous Central Plain. The unglaciated plateau experienced much stream erosion, and the result is an amazing chocolate-drop topography of rolling hillock and valley—with the odd plateau and ridges not unlike West Virginia—capped by hard rock and sluiced by the lower Wisconsin and Mississippi Rivers.

CLIMATE

Contrary to what you may have heard, Wisconsin weather isn't all that bad. Temperatures ranging from 105°F to -30°F degrees spice things up a bit, and by late February, most people are psychotically ready for the snow to go, but overall it isn't terrible.

Wisconsin is near the path of the jet stream, and it lacks any declivity large enough to impede precipitation or climatic patterns. Its northerly latitude produces seasonal shifts in the zenith angle, which result in drastic temperature fluctuations. It's not unusual for farmers near Lake Geneva to be plowing while ice fishers near the Apostle Islands are still drilling holes in the ice.

Temperatures and Precipitation

The state's mean temperature is 43°F, though this is not a terribly useful statistic. You'll find 100°F in the shade come August, -40°F or colder with windchill in winter, and everything in between.

The average precipitation (that is, all water) amount is 38.6 inches annually. Northern counties experience more snowfall than southern ones, and anyplace near the Great Lakes can see some sort of precipitation when the rest of the state is dry. Snow cover ranges from 140 days per annum in the north to 85 days in the south. Snowfall ranges from 30 inches in the extreme south to 120 inches or more in Bayfield County and the Lake Superior cap.

"Cooler Near the Lake"

Wisconsin has two contiguous sea-size bodies of water that give rise to their own littoral microclimates. Get used to hearing "cooler near the lake" in summer and "warmer near the lake" in winter. This moderating influence is particularly helpful for the orchards and gardens in Door County on Lake Michigan and Bayfield County on Lake Superior. On the other hand, it also means more precipitation: One freaky day, this author experienced it—Milwaukee's south side had 14.8 inches of snow, while 30 miles to the west it was sunny all day.

Physiographic Regions

Tornadoes

Generally, not much here in Wisconsin can kill you—no hurricanes or grizzlies. But the state does endure the eye-popping experience of tornadoes, generally averaging six serious twisters and many more near-misses or unsubstantiated touchdowns each year.

Tornado season begins in March and peaks from late May to July, with June the riskiest month. A secondary spike occurs during September and occasionally into mid-October. Many of the midsummer tornadoes are smaller and less intense than the ones in April-June or in September.

A **tornado watch** means conditions are favorable for the development of a tornado. A **tornado warning** means one has been sighted in the vicinity. In either case, emergency sirens sound almost everywhere in Wisconsin; you might want to get an emergency weather radio and keep it with you.

Seek shelter in a basement and under a table if possible. Avoid windows. If there is no basement, find an interior room, such as a bathroom, that has no windows. If you are driving, position your vehicle at a right angle to the tornado's apparent path. If it overtakes you, you have a dilemma; experts disagree about whether to stay in the car with your seatbelt on or to get out and lie flat in a ditch.

Thunderstorms and Lightning

Lightning still kills 200 to 300 people per year nationwide, more than tornadoes and hurricanes combined. Wisconsin averages two serious thunderstorms per year, with a midsummer average of two relatively modest storms each week. Don't let this lull you into complacency in fall, however; ferocious thunderstorms have struck as late as Halloween, replete with marble-size hail, flash floods, and tornadoes.

Thunderstorms are often deadlier than tornadoes, particularly when you're driving or in open areas. Lightning is serious stuff—remember, if you're close enough to hear thunder, you're close enough to get fried. The cardinal rule when lightning is present: Do the opposite of what your gut instincts tell you. Avoid anything outside—especially trees. If you cannot get indoors, squat on the balls of your feet, hugging your knees in a balled position, reducing your contact with the ground and your apparent size. If indoors, stay away from anything that has a channel to the outside: telephones, TVs, radios, even plumbing.

Snowstorms

Technically, four inches of snow in a 24-hour period qualifies as heavy snowfall, but a Wisconsinite would laugh off such a paltry amount. Six inches of snow in 8-12 hours will cause serious transportation disruptions and definitely close airports for a while. The snow generally begins to stay in mid-late October in northern Wisconsin, and in early December in southern Wisconsin, although snow has fallen as early as September and as late as May on occasion.

If you're in Wisconsin in the winter, you'll probably be driving in the stuff. Even the hardiest winter drivers need to practice caution, and if you're a novice at winter driving, don't learn it on the road, especially on a crowded highway at dawn or dusk.

Most importantly, slow down. Be cautious

Average Temperatures

All temperatures are listed in degrees Fahrenheit.

Location	July (high/low)	January (high/low)
Ashland	79/54	22/0
St. Croix Falls	82/58	20/-1
Eau Claire	81/58	20/0
Eagle River	78/52	19/1
Wausau	80/57	20/1
Stevens Point	81/58	23/4
Green Bay	80/58	23/6
Sturgeon Bay	76/56	26/11
La Crosse	83/62	23/5
Wisconsin Dells	82/59	25/6
Prairie du Chien	85/62	27/8
Madison	81/57	27/9
Milwaukee	81/59	28/12
Kenosha	81/60	29/13

on bridges, even when the rest of the pavement is OK; bridges are always slippery. In controlled skids on ice and snow, take your foot off the accelerator and steer into the direction of the skid. Follow the owner's manual advice if your car is equipped with an anti-lock braking system (ABS). Most cars come equipped with all-season radials, so snow tires aren't usually necessary (even though they are outstanding), and tire chains are illegal in Wisconsin.

During nighttime snowstorms, keep your lights on low beam. If you get stuck, check your owner's manual for the advisability of "rocking" the car; be sure to keep the front wheels clear and pointed straight ahead. Don't race the engine; you'll just spin your wheels into icy ruts. Winterize your vehicle, and carry an emergency kit that includes anything you may need to spend the night in a snowbank; many people have learned this the hard way while trapped in a blizzard on an interstate highway for 10 hours. And if you see someone stuck in a snowbank, do stop and help push them out.

The **Department of Transportation's website** (www.wisconsindot.gov) updates winter driving conditions four times daily November-late March. You can also call the state's toll-free roads hotline; dial 511 on your mobile phone or go to www.511wi.gov. It's a brilliant service that many surrounding states also participate in.

Windchill and Frostbite

The most dangerous part of winter in Wisconsin is the windchill factor—the biting effect of the wind that makes the air colder and more lethal. For example, when the temperature is 30°F and the wind is blowing at 40 mph, the temperature with windchill is actually -6°F; at a temperature of 0°F, a 40 mph wind makes it -54°F.

When the windchill sends temperatures low enough, exposed skin is in immediate danger. Lots of Badgers can recount tales of serious cases of frostbite that they swear they can still feel today when the weather changes. The most serious cases of frostbite—you may have seen photos of mountain climbers with black ears and fingers—can require amputation. Worse, without proper clothing, you're at risk for hypothermia.

ENVIRONMENTAL ISSUES

A state that produced both John Muir and Aldo Leopold must have a fairly good record of being green. If you overlook the first century of statehood, when the area, like much of the world at the time, was pillaged at full bore for its natural resources, Wisconsin has in fact been ahead of its time environmentally. The state government initiated exceptionally farsighted environmental laws beginning in the 1950s, when tourism was seen as a burgeoning major industry. The state was the first to meet the requirements of the 1972 Clean Water Act; it had enacted similar legislation at the state level half a decade earlier. Former Wisconsin governor and U.S. senator Gaylord Nelson founded Earth Day in 1970.

Superfund Sites and Dirty Water

Still, things could be better. Wisconsin has more than three dozen sites designated by the federal Environmental Protection Agency (EPA) as Superfund sites, areas so contaminated that large amounts of money are allotted to clean them up. The Wisconsin Department of Natural Resources (DNR) has found that about 900 miles of rivers in the state have failed environmental standards since the mid-1990s, and another 50 or so lakes were questionable or worse. Twenty-two percent of rivers and streams fail, in one way or another, to meet the state's clean-water goals. Fish-consumption advisories have been in effect since 2000 for well over 300 lakes and rivers. Although these problems involve less than 5 percent of rivers and an even smaller percentage of lakes, they are still major issues of concern.

Wisconsin has some of the country's strictest groundwater laws and is cited by the EPA as one of three exemplary states, but not enough local water sources pass muster. Land use, particularly agriculture, forestry, and construction, often creates eroded soils and runoff polluted with fertilizers and toxins. But agriculture isn't the only source of contaminants; urban runoff causes up to 50 times as much soil erosion, and whatever is dumped on the street can wind up in the groundwater.

autumn in Wisconsin

Contaminated sedimentation from decades of abuse remains a secondary problem. Pulp and paper mills discharged almost 300 million gallons of wastewater, most of it untreated, into surface water. In East-Central Wisconsin, the EPA was asked to declare 39 miles of the Fox River—the heart of the paper industry—a Superfund site because 40 tons of an original 125 tons of toxic polychlorinated biphenyls (PCBs) that were dumped remained in the river from factory waste discharge.

As a result of other pollution, the Wisconsin DNR issues almost 200 "boil water" notices annually; one Wisconsin county found half of its 376 wells to be seriously contaminated by pollutants such as atrazine and nitrates. More than 90 percent of state lakes have been affected one way or another, including sedimentation, contamination, and, the most common and difficult to handle, eutrophication—when increased nutrients in the water lead to algae blooms and nuisance weeds, which eventually kill off aquatic life. Visit Madison, the city on four lakes, in July, and you'll see the evidence; worse, with heavier and increasing frequency of rain amounts, more runoff equals setbacks to progress in this.

Mercury and Other Toxins

Toxic environmental pollutants are among the most pernicious silent crises in the health of forests today. Government statistics estimate that 1,200 Wisconsin children are exposed to elevated levels of mercury each year. The federal Centers for Disease Control and Prevention say 1 woman in 10 in the United States already has dangerous levels of mercury in her blood.

Mercury pollution isn't a problem in Lake Superior or Lake Michigan, but fish consumption advisories exist for the lakes because of PCBs, toxins that can cause cancer. And a recent shocking discovery is that dioxin is the likely culprit of crashing lake trout populations rather than invasive species or overfishing. In bottom-feeders such as carp and Mississippi River channel catfish, contamination levels are at 0.11 and 0.09 ppm, respectively. Contrast this with predators such as bass and walleye, both with much higher levels, the latter at a whopping 0.52 ppm. Northwestern Wisconsin, despite all those lush tracts of trees, has a high level of mercury contamination compared to the rest of the state, mostly because of airborne contaminants.

This is in part why recommended daily intake of fish for women of childbearing years, nursing mothers, and children under 15 is one meal per week of bluegill, sunfish, yellow perch, and bullheads, among panfish; and one meal per month of walleye, northern pike, bass, channel catfish, and flathead catfish, among predators and bottom-feeders. Do not eat walleye longer than 20 inches, northern pike longer than 30 inches, or muskellunge.

For men and women beyond childbearing years, consumption of panfish isn't limited, while predators and bottom-feeders are recommended at most one meal per week. If you eat fish only during vacation or sporadically otherwise, you can double these amounts. To increase your chances of eating a healthy fish, eat smaller fish and panfish such as sunfish, and crappies rather than predators such as walleye and northern pike, and trim off the skin and fat.

Mall Sprawl

With 90.1 people per square mile, Wisconsin ranks in the middle among American states for population density. Two-thirds of the residents live in the 12 southeastern counties, however, creating a serious land-use and urban-sprawl issue. In Southeastern Wisconsin, agricultural land is being converted to urban use at a rate of 10 square miles per year. All of southern Wisconsin may be in danger—Scenic America declared three sites (Vernon County's Kickapoo River Valley, Washington County around Erin, and the Mississippi River bluffs) as some of the worst examples of rural landscape degradation; then again, things are not as bad as in Colorado, where the entire state made the list.

The northern forests are being encroached

on as flight from burgeoning urban areas continues. This sprawl results in diminished air quality from use of commuter automobiles, loss of farmland and wildlife habitat, more toxic runoff, and continued soil erosion.

Air Quality

At one point in the 1970s, half of Wisconsin counties failed standards for ozone, total suspended particulates, and sulfur dioxide. All have gotten better, save for ground-level ozone—the main ingredient of smog—still found in 11 southeastern counties. The problem is so severe that southeast Wisconsin was forced by federal law to begin using expensive reformulated gasoline in the mid-1990s; Wisconsinites naturally blamed Chicago for the pollution.

Once a grave crisis for northern lakes and forests, acid deposition, known as acid rain when it falls from the sky, has slowed, largely as a result of strict national legislation enacted in the mid-1980s. It's still a problem, however; 90 percent of the pollutants in Lake Superior come from the air.

Invasive Species

One culprit in the decline of Lake Michigan's yellow perch population could be the pesky **zebra mollusk,** the species that best represents what can happen when a nonnative species is introduced into an ecosystem. Most likely transplanted by a visiting freighter from the Caspian Sea in the mid-1980s, the zebra mollusk is a ferocious and tough little Eurasian mollusk that loves the warmer waters and phytoplankton of the Great Lakes. It loves to breed in warm areas, such as at the discharge pipes around power plants. They breed so rapidly that they create unbelievably dense barnacle-like crusts that do serious damage. Worse, they are being blamed for the decline and decimation of native species as they literally suck all the nutrients out of an area. Great Lakes states are frantically fighting to keep them from spreading into inland lakes and streams.

The tough-nut **Asian carp** is poised to, quite literally, invade Lake Michigan via Illinois, which is doing everything but poisoning rivers to keep it out. If it gets into Lake Michigan, it could mean doom for fish species present here.

PLANTS AND ANIMALS

Plants

The Eastern Transition and Great Lakes Forest Zones cover most of Wisconsin. Both are primarily mixed meadow and woodland, a far cry from the time before the Europeans arrived, when 85 percent of the state was covered by forest and the rest by tallgrass. By the mid-19th century, those numbers had dipped to 63 percent forest, 28 percent savanna, and 9 percent grassland. Today, the state's forest cover is 37 percent, and precious little of that is original. Of the two million acres of prairie that once covered the state, only 2,000 scattered acres survive. In all, Wisconsin has more than 2,100 species of plants, approximately a tenth of which are classified as rare, and some of them are threatened.

Four major vegetation types cover the state: **boreal forest,** a subarctic coniferous spread near Lake Superior; **deciduous forest,** the second-largest swath of Wisconsin woodlands; **mixed forest,** consisting of species of both, throughout the state; and **nonforest and grasslands,** found throughout the southern third of the state into west-central Wisconsin along the Mississippi River.

Before the Europeans arrived, Wisconsin had a huge expanse of wetlands, including more than 10,000 acres along Green Bay alone. Today, that amount has dwindled by more than half, a sad indicator of rapacious development and overuse, but it still constitutes the largest amount of wetlands remaining on the Great Lakes.

Animals

Wisconsin lies within three well-defined life zones conducive to species diversity: the Canadian, the transition, and the upper

Loons

The shrill call of a loon across placid lake waters: unforgettable. Yet these gorgeous birds are threatened by shoreline development, pollution, and even unknowing harassment by recreational lake users. The Wisconsin counties of Vilas and Oneida have close to 2,000 loons, half the statewide estimated total. The Turtle-Flambeau Flowage has the largest number of common loon nesting sites anywhere. The common loon, found on Wisconsin waters, is one of four species and the only one outside of northern Canada and Alaska. It is their head that is most striking—obsidian green with a narrow pointed beak. The neck is ringed in a thick band of white. Usually black and white, with a wingspan of about five feet, its streamlined but oddly configured body is decidedly not for land—loons often have to remain half-in, half-out of the water, resting their chests on the shore.

A loon can dive as deep as 200 feet for a full 10 minutes searching for aquatic delicacies. When it wants air, it sprints across the water surface for almost 0.25 miles, gathering speed for flight. Ferociously territorial, only one nesting pair of loons will occupy a lake, except for large lakes, which might have two.

Scientists have classified loon calls into four categories: wails, hoots, tremolos, and yodels. The former two are what you'll probably hear at your campsite. The wails and hoots both indicate either concern or interest; the latter two are defensive cries.

austral or Carolinian. The Canadian, not surprisingly the coldest, features small mammals such as the snowshoe hare but also the state's primary large mammals, the deer and the black bear. The warmest zone, the Carolinian, falls in the southern tier of the state and lacks big-game mammals. In total, Wisconsin has 73 species of mammals, 339 native bird species, and more than 200 species of amphibians, reptiles, frogs, bats, butterflies, and insects.

Of Wisconsin's two large mammals, the ubiquitous **white-tailed deer** is a traffic and garden nightmare. The other resident big mammal, the **black bear,** is still relatively common in the northern woods and has also been seen farther south, but you won't likely see a bear in Door County.

Wisconsin lies in the middle of several migratory waterfowl flyways, so birding is a big activity. **Tundra swans, sandhill cranes,** and **Canada geese** are three of the most conspicuous species. The last are so predominant at the Horicon Marsh National Wildlife Refuge in Southeastern Wisconsin that ornithologists make pilgrimages here each spring and fall.

Threatened, Endangered, Exterminated

The last plains buffalo was shot five years before Wisconsin even became a territory. Next to become extinct here were the Richardson's caribou, the American elk, the cougar, the Carolina parakeet, the passenger pigeon (the world's last one was shot in Wisconsin), the peregrine falcon, the pine marten, the trumpeter swan, the whooping crane, the wild turkey, the moose, the fisher, and, in 1922, the common wolverine.

Jump forward to today. First, the bad news: Wisconsin has more than 200 species of flora or fauna listed by state or federal agencies as either endangered or threatened. The state ranks in the middle for species diversity and at-risk status—0 percent of mammals are at risk, but 6.2 percent of fish are at serious risk; the rest are in the middle. But all is not lost. Wisconsin instituted preservation measures long before the federal government did and is consistently recognized by environmental groups for at least trying to stem the carnage. The fisher, falcon, pine marten, trumpeter swan, and wild turkey have been reintroduced to varying degrees of success.

Cranes are making a comeback. The regal

French horn-sounding trumpeter swans, once nearly extinct, are well on the way to the target of 51 breeding pairs by 2020; they have exploded in numbers to over 5,000 in 14 counties, up from just 300 in 2000. The **International Crane Foundation** (E11376 Shady Lane Rd., 608/356-9462, www.savingcranes.com) has information on wonderful volunteer opportunities to tramp through central Wisconsin counting the birds; it's great fun. In 2000 the state also established nesting sites for whooping cranes on 100,000 acres in central Wisconsin; eventually nests will be found at the Sandhill State Wildlife Area, Necedah National Wildlife Refuge, and two other sites. In 2002, witnessed by the national media, the first eight whooping cranes made their migration to Florida behind an ultralight plane; most returned. By 2019, 100 cranes were migrating back and forth between Wisconsin and the southeastern U.S., though most of these birds were transplanted—the ultimate goal is a self-sustaining population.

Most amazing was the return of a nesting pair of **piping plovers** to the shores of the Apostle Islands National Lakeshore in 1999. In the entire Great Lakes, only 30 nesting pairs exist, all of them in Michigan. As a result, the U.S. Fish and Wildlife Service has proposed setting aside nearly 200 miles of Lake Superior and Lake Michigan shoreline, including 20 miles of Door County shoreline, for critical habitats, and possibly to establish a colony.

One of the most visually arresting birds—the **white pelican**—has also made a recent comeback. You might spot one in the Horicon Marsh National Wildlife Refuge.

Though never extinct, the **bald eagle,** once perilously close to vanishing, may have had the most successful recovery of all. The state now harbors about 1,400 breeding pairs, and the birds are so prevalent along the Wisconsin and Mississippi Rivers that certain communities make much of their tourism income because of them. The state is also acquiring riverine land near Prairie du Sac to continue the comeback.

Wisconsin does take forceful steps to preserve wildlife through its Department of Natural Resources. It was the first in the country to designate natural areas throughout the state. These vigilantly protected areas harbor fragile geology, archaeology, or plant and animal life; some are even being nudged toward a return to their presettlement ecology.

The most intriguing question now is whether **cougars** are hunting prey in the woods. Since 1994 more than 300 sightings have been reported, some in Door County and environs, and many have been confirmed, even though the last cougar supposedly perished in 1908; today's cats are most likely migrants from the Black Hills of South Dakota.

If there is one endangered fish all Badgers worry about, it's the **perch,** especially the yellow perch. In a state that considers the fish fry to be almost a religious experience—and there is no better fish than perch for a fish fry—plummeting lake perch stocks in the early 1990s freaked out the fish-loving population; the state banned commercial perch fishing in 1996 and it hasn't been allowed since, except in Green Bay. Sport anglers once caught 900,000 perch annually; now it's as low as 17,000. The main culprit is likely invasive species, but if the state spent half as much on perch as it did stocking trout and salmon in Lake Michigan, things would be better. Perch counts in 2015 began to rise, but by 2019 had plummeted again. **Trout** lovers, however, can rejoice—blue-ribbon status streams have increased 1,000 percent in 20 years.

Still, the picture could be much better. Even as many species are rebounding, other native species are added to the threatened and endangered lists every year. Just under 3 percent of native plants are now threatened or endangered, and 25 percent of the state's species are nonnative.

History

EARLY ARRIVALS

The Siberia-to-Alaska Beringia theory, which posits that the progenitors of North America's first human residents arrived over a land bridge that rose and submerged in the Bering Strait beginning as long as 20,000 years ago, was seriously challenged in the late 1990s. Provocative new anthropological discoveries in North and South America have led some scientists to reconsider it. A Wisconsin archaeologist was one of the first to present new evidence from finds at digs in Kenosha County. The last of the glacial interludes in the Pleistocene epoch, called the Two Rivers, probably saw the first movement into the state of early Paleo-Indians about 11,500 years ago. That time frame is based on examinations of fluted points as well as a rare mastodon kill site, the Boaz Mastodon, which revealed the hunting techniques of the Paleo-Indians in Wisconsin. Glacial retreat helps explain why the Paleo-Indian people entered the area from the south and southwest rather than from the north. Nomadic clans followed the mastodon and other large mammals northward as the glaciers receded.

Solid archaeological evidence establishes definite stages in Wisconsin's earliest settlement. The **Archaic** period lasted approximately 8000-750 BC. People still lived transiently, pursuing small game and fish in the newly formed lakes. Around 2000 BC, these Native Americans became the first in North America to fashion copper.

The later **Woodland** people, with semi-permanent dwellings, are generally regarded as the first Native Americans in the region to make use of ceramics, elaborate mound burials (especially in southern Wisconsin), and, to a lesser extent, domesticated plants such as squash, corn, pumpkins, beans, and tobacco. From around 750 BC until European exploration, the Woodland period was a minor golden age of dramatic change for indigenous people. Around 100 BC, the Middle Woodland people experienced cultural and technological proliferation simultaneous with the period of Ohio's and Illinois's Hopewell societies, when villages formed and expanded greatly along waterways.

The people who lived at the end of the Woodland period have been classified into two additional groups: the **Mississippian** and the **Oneota.** The former's impressive sites can be found from New Orleans all the way to Wisconsin and parts of Minnesota. Mississippian culture showed high levels of civic planning and complex social hierarchies, and it lasted at least until the Spanish arrived.

EUROPEAN CONTACT

The Spanish, Portuguese, and English all blazed westward in an effort to circumvent the Arabs, reach the courts of the Great Khan of the Silk Route, and establish ways to appropriate the riches of new lands. Along the way, indigenous people were to be "pacified" under papal hegemony. After England's naval power grew under the Tudor monarchs and began conflicting with the French, North America became a battleground for the European powers.

New France: Black Robes and the Fur Trade

Thanks to the Reformation, the French, relative latecomers to maritime and expansionist endeavors, were conveniently freed of papal dicta for divvying up the new continent and its inherent wealth. With the Spanish in the Caribbean and along the Gulf Coast and the up-and-coming English having a foothold in the mid-Atlantic colonies, France was effectively forced to attempt to penetrate the new land via the northern frontier.

Jacques Cartier first opened the door to the Great Lakes region with his "discovery" of the Gulf of the St. Lawrence River in

1534. The insular French monarchy left the scattered outposts to languish for another 40 years, except the fur traders, who found some success.

The French did establish sparse settlements in the early 16th century, but they were dismayed by the lack of ready riches, the roughness of the land, and the bitter weather. The original fur traders had one superlative talent: forging relationships with the Native Americans, who became enamored of French metal implements, especially firearms. Eventually, the French found their coveted mother lode in beaver pelts.

Paris hatmakers discovered that beaver pelts—especially those softened for a year worn around the waists of Native Americans—made a superior grade of felt for hats, and these soon became the rage in Paris and other parts of Europe, becoming the lifeblood of the colonies and sustaining the region through the mismanagement and vagaries of both British and French rule.

Facilitating both the fur trade and French control over the colonies were the missionaries of the Society of Jesus—the Jesuits. These "Black Robes," as the Huron and Ottawa people called them, first arrived during a time of religious fervor in France. The Franciscans had originally come to North America as missionaries, but they found the task of conversion too daunting for their small order. The Jesuits became the foundation on which New France operated. The traders needed them to foster harmony with Native American traders, and more importantly, the often complicated French systems of operation required that all day-to-day affairs be carried out at the local level. By 1632 all missionary work in French Canada was under the auspices of the Jesuits.

The Jesuits also accompanied voyageurs (explorers) as New France attempted to widen its sphere of influence westward. Eventually, the Black Robes themselves, along with renegade fur traders, were responsible for the initial exploration and settlement of present-day Wisconsin.

THE FRENCH IN WISCONSIN

Samuel de Champlain, who first arrived in Quebec in 1603, was the province's most famous and effective leader, despite his obsession with finding the legendary route to the Great Khan. After arriving and hearing of the "People of the Stinking Waters" (the Winnebago people), which he surmised to mean an ocean-dwelling people, he dispatched the first Europeans from Acadia to explore the wild western frontier.

Although there is speculative evidence that Étienne Brûlé, Champlain's first explorer, may have poked around Wisconsin as early as 1620—the same year many assume the Pilgrims founded the new colonies—most historians credit Jean Nicolet as the first European to turn up in Green Bay, landing at Red Banks in 1634. Garbed in Chinese damask and using thunder-stick histrionics to impress the indigenous people—the Potawatomi people he met immediately dubbed him "Thunder Beaver"—Nicolet efficiently and diplomatically forged immediate ties with the locals, who guided him throughout the region to meet other communities.

As before, Nicolet couldn't rouse the wilted interest of the French royalty—all it wanted was bags of Chinese silk—and France once again neglected their part of North America. Legitimate French fur traders were scooped by Pierre-Esprit Radisson and Médard Chouart des Groseilliers, two pesky *coureurs-de-bois* (renegade trappers) who couldn't be bothered to get licensed by the crown. They delved farther into Wisconsin than any had before but had nowhere to trade their furs after being blacklisted by the ruling powers in New France. This led them to England, which gave them a charter to establish the Hudson's Bay Company north of New France—one reason for the later conflict between France and Britain. In 1666 these two were followed by Nicolas Perrot, who extended Nicolet's explorations and consequently opened the French fur trade with Native Americans in Wisconsin.

The seasoned priest Claude Allouez simultaneously founded the first mission at La Pointe in the Apostle Islands and founded St. Francois Xavier, Wisconsin's first permanent European settlement, at De Pere, south of Green Bay.

The most famous Jesuit explorer was the priest Jacques Marquette, who, along with Louis Joliet, was sent by La Salle in 1673 to discern whether the Mississippi River emptied into the Gulf of Mexico. The first Europeans to cross Wisconsin, they made it to the Mississippi on June 17, 1673, and went as far south as Arkansas, where they saw Indians with European goods, confirming both a route to the gulf and the presence of the Spanish. The French hesitated in buttressing their western frontier—and it wound up costing them dearly.

Conflict with the British and British Rule

The fate of New France and thus Wisconsin was determined not in North America but in Europe, as Louis XIV, who had reigned during the zenith of French power, frittered away French influence bit by bit in frivolous distracting battles.

The French never fully used the western edges of the Great Lakes, and James II's rise to the throne in England marked the end of France's never exactly halcyon days in the region. James II forced Louis XIV into wild strategies to protect French colonial interests—strategies that led to further exploration of the hinterlands but also drove France to overextend itself and, eventually, collapse in the region.

At the behest of the Jesuits, who hoped to corral some recalcitrant Native American communities, the French crown closed trade completely in the Great Lakes interiors, cutting off possible ties to the English or the Spanish. Louis XIV correctly reckoned that whomever the Native Americans sided with would end up controlling the new lands. This naturally drained royal coffers, and he decided instead to keep the Native Americans, the English, and the Spanish in check by exploring as far inland as possible and trying to establish a line of garrisons from Montreal all the way to New Orleans.

France succeeded in this second plan but in the process alienated the uneasy Native Americans that had sworn loyalty to France and, worse, aroused the ire of France's bitterest enemies—the Iroquois and the Fox people. Wars with the Fox, which raged 1701-1738, temporarily sapped the determination of the French, but they had enough pluck and military might to string forts along the Mississippi River to look for inroads into territories already held by the British in the Ohio River Valley. By 1750, British colonists in the western Great Lakes outnumbered the French 20 to 1, and many Native Americans, discovering that the British made higher-quality goods more cheaply, switched to the British side. The French and Indian War (1755-1763) was a thorough thrashing of the French by the British and greatly determined European spheres of influence in North America.

Under the British, little changed in daily life; the English never even had an official presence in what is now Wisconsin. One Englishman of note, however, was Jonathan Carver, a roguish explorer who roamed the state 1766-1768 and returned to England to publish fanciful, lively, and mostly untrue accounts of the new lands west of the inland seas.

The French had been content simply to trade and had never made overtures for the land itself. But the British who did come—many barely able to conceal their scorn for the indigenous people—began parceling up property and immediately incited unrest. Pontiac, an Ottawa chieftain, led a revolt against the British at Muscoda.

Additionally, the British monarchy's finances were in disarray from the lengthy conflicts with the French in North America and with other enemies in European theaters. And then the monarchy decreed that the colonies could foot their own bill for these new lands and instituted the Stamp Act.

THE AMERICAN REVOLUTION

British settlers in Wisconsin who remained after the area was made part of Britain's Quebec Province under the Quebec Act of 1774 remained resolutely loyal to the British crown but kept out of the American Revolution, apart from scattered attempts by both sides to enlist the Native Americans. The 1781 surrender of Cornwallis at Yorktown cost Britain a great part of its holdings, including the Northwest Territory, which included Wisconsin, but practical British influence remained in the state until after the War of 1812.

British commercial interests had little desire to abandon the still-lucrative beaver trade, and the Native Americans had grown tolerant, if not loyal to, the British. When hostilities broke out in 1812, the British, aiming to create a buffer zone of Native American alliances in Indiana and Illinois, quickly befriended the local indigenous nations—an easy venture, as they were already inflamed over the first of many U.S. government snake-oil land treaties.

The Northwest, including Wisconsin, played a much larger role in this new bellicosity than it had in the Revolution; British loyalists and American frontiersman fought for control of the Native Americans as well as of the water-route forts of the French and British. British forts, now occupied and understaffed by U.S. troops, were easily overwhelmed by English and Indian confederates. Commodore Perry's victory on Lake Erie in 1813, however, swung the momentum to the American side. Treaties signed upon reaching a stalemate in 1814 allowed the United States to regain the previous national boundaries. Almost immediately, John Jacob Astor's American Fur Company set up operations in Wisconsin, but by this time, the golden age of the beaver trade in the area was already over.

Though not yet even a territory and despite both the intractability of the Native Americans and the large populations of British and French, Wisconsin was fully part of the United States by 1815. In 1822 the first wave of immigration began, with thousands of Cornish and other miners burrowing into the hillsides of Southwestern Wisconsin to search for lead; their burrowing was the origin of the Badger State moniker. As miners poured into Wisconsin to scavenge lead, speculators multiplied, land offices sprang up, and the first banks opened; everyone was eager to make money off the new immigrants. Before the area achieved territorial status in 1836, more than 10,000 settlers had inundated the southern part of the state.

NATIVE AMERICAN RELATIONS

Unfortunately, none of the foreign settlers had consulted the indigenous residents before carving up the land. The United States practiced a heavy-handed patriarchal policy toward the Native Americans, insisting that they be relocated west—away from settlers on the Eastern Seaboard—for the betterment of both sides. Simultaneously, the new government instituted a loony system designed to reprogram Native Americans to become happy Christian farmers. Land cessions, begun around the turn of the 19th century, continued regularly until the first general concourse of most western Native Americans took place, in 1825, at Prairie du Chien, Wisconsin, at which time the first of the more draconian treaties was drawn up. The first Native Americans from New York—the Oneida, Stockbridge, Munsee, and Brothertown people—were moved to Wisconsin beginning in 1823. The cocktail of misguided U.S. patronization and helplessly naive Native American negotiations turned lethal when many came to realize what had been done to them.

The first skirmish, the so-called Winnebago War of 1827, was nothing more than a frustrated attempt at vengeance by a Winnebago chieftain, Red Bird, who killed two settlers before being convinced to surrender to avert a war. The second was more serious—and more legendary.

The Black Hawk War

In 1804, William Henry Harrison, a ruthless

longtime foe of indigenous people in the west, rammed through a treaty with Native Americans in St. Louis that effectively extinguished the nations' title to most of their land. Part of this land was in Southwestern Wisconsin, newly dubbed the "lead region." Mining operations—mostly wildcatters—proliferated but ebbed when the miners began to fear the Native Americans. The ire and paranoia of the federal government, which had assumed carte blanche in the region, was piqued in 1832, when a militant band of Fox-Sauk people refused to recognize treaties, including the one that had forcibly moved them out of the southern part of Wisconsin. Their leader was Black Sparrow Hawk, better known as Black Hawk, a warrior who was not so much pro-British as fiercely anti-American. With blind faith in the British, obdurate pride, and urging from other Native American nations (who would later double-cross him), Black Hawk initiated a quixotic stand against the United States, which culminated in tragic battles in Wisconsin.

Black Hawk and his group of about 1,000 fighters, dubbed "the British Band," balked at U.S. demands that they relocate across the Mississippi River. Insisting that they were exempt because Black Hawk had been blacklisted from treaty negotiations, in April 1832 they began moving up the Rock River to what they deemed their rightful lands. Other nations had promised support along the way in both provisions and firepower. Instead, Black Hawk found his erstwhile supporters—the Potawatomi, Sioux, and Winnebago people—turning on him. Worse, news of Black Hawk's actions was sweeping the region with grotesque frontier embellishment, and the U.S. military, private militias, and frontiersmen were all itching for a fight.

His people lacked provisions (one reason for the band's initial decampment was a lack of corn in the area after the settlers squeezed in) and soon grew tired. Black Hawk wisely realized his folly, and in May sent a truce contingent. Jumpy soldiers under Major Isaiah Stillman instead overreacted and attacked. Black Hawk counterattacked and, although seriously outnumbered, his warriors chased the Americans away—an event that became known as Stillman's Run. Nevertheless, the fuse was lit.

The band then crossed into Wisconsin near Lake Koshkonong and began a slow, difficult journey west, back toward the Mississippi River. Two commanders led their forces in pursuit of the hapless Native Americans, engaging in a war of attrition along the way. They cornered Black Hawk and fought the quick but furious Battle of Wisconsin Heights along the Wisconsin River. The warriors escaped in the darkness, with the soldiers in hungry pursuit. One large group of mostly women, children, and old men tried to float down the Wisconsin toward the Mississippi but were intercepted by soldiers and other indigenous people; most were drowned or otherwise killed.

What followed is perhaps the most tragic chapter in Wisconsin history, the Battle of Bad Axe, an episode that garnered shocked national attention and made Black Hawk as well known as the president. On August 1, 1832, Black Hawk made it to the Mississippi River. Hastily throwing together rafts, the group tried to cross but was intercepted by a U.S. gunboat. The U.S. forces mercilessly opened fire for two hours, despite the display of a white flag from the Native Americans. Black Hawk and a group of 50 escaped, assuming the other group—300 women, children, and elderly people—would be left alone. Instead, this group was butchered by General Henry Atkinson's men and their Sioux cohorts when they reached the opposite shore.

Black Hawk and the 50 warriors were pursued by legions of soldiers and Native American accomplices. Black Hawk was eventually brought alive to St. Louis, guarded by Jefferson Davis, and later imprisoned on the East Coast, where he found himself in the media spotlight. He later wrote a compelling autobiography, one of the first documents offering a glimpse of the baffled, frustrated

Native American point of view. Black Hawk was eventually sent back to Wisconsin.

In truth, Black Hawk was likely never half as belligerent as he's been characterized. By the 1830s he was well into his 60s and weary of protracted and unbalanced negotiations and battles with the Americans. The Black Hawk War marked a watershed of Native American presence in Wisconsin: By 1833, the few cessions the United States had gained to indigenous lands below the Fox and Wisconsin Rivers had been extracted. However, in 1837 the northern Wisconsin nations signed away for a pittance more than half of the land north of the Fox River, giving free rein to the rapacious lumber industry. Perhaps as a direct result of Black Hawk's doomed grasp for legitimacy, the U.S. government began playing hardball with the Native Americans.

THE WISCONSIN TERRITORY

The Northwest Ordinance of 1787 established many of the borders of present-day Wisconsin; Thomas Jefferson had initially envisioned dividing the region into 10 states. Later, before the War of 1812, Wisconsin became part of first the Indiana Territory and then the Illinois Territory as the Northwest was chiseled down. In 1818 the Illinois Territory was further divided to create the Michigan Territory. Finally, in 1836, the Wisconsin Territory was established, taking in all of modern Wisconsin, the Upper Peninsula of Michigan, Iowa, Minnesota, and parts of North and South Dakota.

Despite the loss, the Black Hawk fiasco had another effect contrary to the Sauk leader's intentions: The well-publicized battles put Wisconsin on the map. This, combined with the wild mining operations in the southwestern part of the state, burgeoning lumber operations along the Great Lake coast, and discovery of fertile soils outside Milwaukee, ensured Wisconsin's status as the Next Big Thing. The new Erie Canal provided immigrants a direct route to this new land. By 1835 there were 60,000 eager settlers pushing through the Erie Canal each year, and most were aiming for what became, the following year, the Wisconsin Territory. Two years later, when the chunk of Wisconsin Territory west of the Mississippi was lopped off, more than half of the 225,000 settlers were in Wisconsin. With the enforcement of Indian land cessions, up to three billion acres became available for government surveyors; the first land title sales had started in 1834. Wisconsin had fully arrived—and it still wasn't even a state.

STATEHOOD: GROWING PAINS

Wisconsin's entry into the Union as the flag's 30th star was a bit anticlimactic; there wasn't even a skirmish with the British over it. In fact, the populace voted on the issue of statehood in 1841, and every year for nearly the entire decade, but distinctly disinterested voters rejected the idea until 1848, when stratospheric levels of immigration impelled the legislature to more animated attempts, and the first measures passed.

Incessant immigration continued after statehood. Most newcomers arrived from New England or Europe—Ireland, England, Germany, and Scandinavia. The influx of Poles was still decades away. Milwaukee, a diminutive village of 1,500 at the time of territorial status, burgeoned into a rollicking town of 46,000 by the start of the Civil War, by which time the population of the state as a whole was up to 706,000 people.

During the period leading up to the Civil War, Wisconsin was dominated by political and some social wrangling over what, exactly, the state was to be. With the influence of Yankee immigrants and the Erie Canal access, much of Wisconsin's cultural, political, and social makeup finally resembled New England. In fact, New York legislation was the model for many early Wisconsin laws. The first university was incorporated almost immediately after statehood, and school codes for primary and secondary education soon followed—a bit ahead of the Union as a whole.

Abolition was a hot issue in Wisconsin's

early years. It reached top-level status after the annexation of Texas and the Mexican-American War. As a result of this and many other contentious issues, Ripon, Wisconsin, became the founding spot of the Republican Party, which soon took hold of the legislature and held fast until the Civil War.

During the Civil War, despite being among the first states to near enlistment quotas, Wisconsin suffered some of the fiercest draft rioting in the nation. Many new immigrants had decamped from their European homelands for precisely the reasons for which the government was now pursuing them. Eventually, 96,000 Wisconsinites would serve.

Post-Civil War: Immigrants, Dairy, and Industry

After the Civil War and through the turn of the 20th century, Wisconsin began getting its economic bearings while politicians wrestled over issues as disparate as temperance, railroads, and immigrants' rights. This last hot potato galvanized enormous enclaves of German Americans into action; they mobilized against anti-immigration laws sweeping through the legislature. Despite the mandates, such as one banning the German language in schools, successive waves of immigrants poured into the state.

The first sawmills had gone up in Wisconsin at the start of the 19th century. Yankee and British settlers built them to use the timber they were felling in clearing farmland. One area of the Chippewa River possessed one-sixth of all the pine west of the Adirondacks—and Wisconsin pine was larger and harder than that in surrounding states. Easily floated down streams and rivers, pine became an enormous commodity on the expanding plains. In Wisconsin, even the roads were fashioned from pine and hardwood planks. By 1870, more than one billion board feet of lumber were being churned out of the state's 1,000-plus mills each year, easily making Wisconsin the country's largest timber producer, which paid one-fourth of all state wages. In time, more than 20 billion board feet were taken from the shores of Green Bay alone; one year, 425 million board feet were shipped through the port of Superior. Wisconsin wood was used in other parts of the expanding country to make homes, wagons, fences, barns, and plank roads. As a result, by the turn of the 20th century, more than 50 million acres of Wisconsin and Minnesota forest had been ravaged—most of it unrecoverable. By 1920 most of the state was a cutover wasteland.

Land eroded, tracts of forest disappeared and weren't replaced, and riparian areas were destroyed with dams for "float flooding." Worse, the average size of pine trees was shrinking rapidly, and the lumber barons expressed little interest in preparing for the ultimate eradication of the forests. The small settlement of Peshtigo and more than 1,000 of its people perished in a furious conflagration made worse by logging cutover in 1871, and in the 1890s vast fires swept other central and northern counties.

Badgers began to diversify. A handful of years after the Civil War, the state kicked its wheat habit (by 1860, Wisconsin had been producing more wheat than any other state in the United States) and began looking for economic diversity. Wheat was sapping soil fertility in southern Wisconsin, forcing many early settlers to pick up stakes once again and shift to the enormous golden tracts of the western plains states. Later, when railroads and their seemingly arbitrary pricing systems began affecting potential income from wheat, farmers in Wisconsin began seriously reviewing their options. Farmers diversified into corn, cranberries, sorghum, and hops, among other crops. Sheep and some hogs constituted the spectrum of livestock, but within two decades, the milk cow would surpass everything else on four hooves.

Myriad factors influenced the early trend toward dairy. Most of the European immigrant farmers, many of them dairy farmers in the old country, found the topography and climate in Wisconsin similar to those of their homelands. Transplanted Yankees had seen

The Dairy Industry

Dairying was not the first gear in the state's agricultural machine; wheat was. Wisconsin was a leading world wheat producer and exporter through the 1870s. The initial forays in the state into home butter and cheese production were derisively called "western grease." Wisconsin cattle were initially hybrids of hardier species, and milk production was hardly a necessity.

THE BIRTH OF A STEREOTYPE

In the 1850s, transplanted New York farmers organized the first commercial cheese-making factory systems, and the first experiments in modern herd management and marketing were undertaken. One New Yorker, Chester Hazen, opened a cheese factory in Ladoga in 1864; in its first year, it produced 200,000 pounds of cheese. Within a few years the state had nearly 50 factories, and in some places the demand for milk outstripped the supply.

Subsequent immigrants found the topography reminiscent of Europe and the glacial till profoundly fertile. Old-world pride mixed with Yankee ingenuity created an explosion in Wisconsin dairying. The first dairy organizations were founded after the Civil War, and a dairy board of trade was set up in Watertown in 1872. The state's dairies shrewdly diversified the cheese-making and took the Western markets by storm. By the 20th century, a stereotype was born: Jefferson County, Wisconsin, was home to 40,000 cows and 34,000 people.

W. D. HOARD

A seminal figure in Wisconsin's rise to dairy prominence was the previously unknown W. D. Hoard. In 1870, Hoard began publishing *The Jefferson County Union*, which became the mouthpiece of Wisconsin farmers. The only central source for disseminating information, the paper's dairy columns became *Hoard's Dairyman*. It was the most influential publication in Wisconsin's dairy industry.

Hoard had never farmed, but he pushed tirelessly for previously unheard-of progressive farming techniques. Through his publications, farmers learned to be not so conservative, to keep records, and to compare trends. Most significantly, Hoard almost single-handedly invented the specialized milk-only cow. He became such a legend in the industry he was elected governor in 1889.

The University of Wisconsin followed Hoard's lead and established its College of Agriculture's experimental stations in 1883. The renowned department would invent the butterfat test, dairy courses, cold-curing processes, and winter feeding.

KEEPING THEM ON THE FARM

Dairying in Wisconsin is a $43.5 billion industry, accounting for 10 percent of the state's total economic output and half its agricultural output. (Nearly one quarter of all dairy herds in the country can be found in Wisconsin.) It is more crucial to the state's economy than citrus is to Florida or potatoes are to Idaho.

Nearly 30 percent of all the butter and cheese consumed in the United States is produced in Wisconsin. It produces 30.6 billion pounds of milk per year on average; if it were a country, it would

it before in New York and Vermont and knew a dairy revolution was coming. Led by foresighted dairying advocate William Hoard and his germinal journal, *Hoard's Dairyman*, and by the new Wisconsin Dairymen's Association, farmers began adding dairy cattle to their other crops and livestock until, by 1899, fully 90 percent of Wisconsin's farmers were predominantly keeping cows.

Butter production initially led the new industry, since it was easier to keep than milk. But technology and industrialization, thanks in large part to the University of Wisconsin Scientific Agriculture Institute, propelled Wisconsin into milk, cheese, and other dairy-product prominence. The institute was responsible for extending the dairy season, introducing several highly productive new methods, and the groundbreaking 1890 Babcock butterfat test, a simple test of

have the world's fourth-largest production. Wisconsin cheese makers have won 33 percent of World Cheese Championship first prizes; California, less than 5 percent. At the 2018 World Cheese Championship, Wisconsin won more awards than any other state or country. Wisconsin is the only U.S. entrant to win Best Overall in the past 30 years, and it has done so twice. At the 2019 U.S. Championship Cheese Contest, it won more awards than any other state, including 57 best in class.

Wisconsin is the only state to require a master's license to make cheese, and 90 percent of milk produced in the state is used for cheese. Wisconsin has more than 26 percent of the U.S. cheese market today, while California has 20 percent, and while experts have long predicted California production would eclipse Wisconsin's, Wisconsin maintains its lead in specialty cheeses with 650 varietals, double the number made in California. (In fact, 99 out of 118 cheese plants in the state produce specialty cheese.)

And yet, things have been far from easy. In 1993 California surpassed Wisconsin in whole-milk output. The number of family dairy farms has dwindled from a post-World War II figure of 150,000 to less than 13,000 in 2018; at one point the state was losing an average of 1,000 dairy farms per year. (As of 2019 this was around 500 per year.) Milk production is rising; however, consolidation means farms are getting larger, though they are still technically family-owned. What this means is cultural—the quaint red barns with a family milking their cows, many worry, could be a thing of the past.

Badger State politicians blame the dairy industry's problems on byzantine federal milk-pricing guidelines, which inadvertently help corporate farms, resulting in overproduction and, thus, lower prices. International competition—not helped by federal international tariffs and resulting retaliation—exacerbate the problem.

Although it's in decline, Wisconsin is in little danger of losing its cultural underpinnings of rural Americana. Supplying so much of the cheese in the United States still means it has a huge market—and predicted rises in U.S. cheese consumption will help. Badger farmers are also finding ways to slow the rate of farm loss. One innovative program involves rural villages banding together, pooling resources, and buying family farms to keep them operational. Also, experts have rated the state first in diversity in farming practices. The results? The number of cows in the state has again begun to rise, and cheese production has increased at a steady 2 percent per year. Once again in 2018, Wisconsin produced 3.4 billion pounds of cheese—as always more than a quarter of U.S. production.

Economists also say that competitor's dairy industries can be dangerously linked to the stock market or government control—which can help in the short term but make them vulnerable.

Finally, Wisconsin agriculture will never have to worry about its water, unlike California agriculture, where climate projections paint a dire picture in terms of water availability for the enormous farm operations of the Golden State. So even though it may not be able to compete in whole numbers, Wisconsin is still America's Dairyland.

chemically separating and centrifuging milk samples to determine their quality, thereby ensuring farmers were paid based on the quality and not just the weight of the milk.

By 1880, despite less-fertile land and a shorter growing season than other agricultural states, Wisconsin ranked fourth in dairy production, thanks to university efficiency, progressive quality control, herculean efforts in the fields, and the later organization of powerful trade exchanges. The southern half of the state, with its minerals in the southwest and rich loamy soils in the southeast, attracted European agrarian and dairy farming immigrants and speculators. "America's Dairyland" made it onto state license plates in the 1930s.

THE PROGRESSIVE ERA

Wisconsinites have a fickle political history. Democrats held sway in the territorial days;

then, in 1854, the newly formed Republican Party took the reins. The two monoliths—challenged only occasionally by upstarts such as the Grangers, the Socialists (Milwaukee consistently voted for Socialist representatives), Populists, and the Temperance movement—jockeyed for power until the end of the century.

The Progressive Party movement, formed of equal parts reformed Democrats and Republicans, was the original third-party ticket, molted from the frustrated moderates of the Wisconsin Republican Party keen on challenging the status quo. As progressivism gained steam, the citizenry of Wisconsin—tireless and shrewd salt-of-the-earth workers—eventually embraced the movement with open arms, even if the rest of the country didn't always. The Progressive movement was the first serious challenge in the U.S. political machine.

Fightin' Bob: Legacy of Progressivism

One thing about the Wisconsin political mosaic that warrants kudos is its inveterate inability to follow categorization. Whether politically prescient or simply lacking patience, the state has always ridden the cutting edge. These qualities are best represented physically by the original Progressive, Robert La Follette, aka "Menace to the Machine." One political writer in the early 20th century said of La Follette: "The story of Wisconsin is the story of Governor La Follette. He's the head of the state. Not many governors are that." The seminal force in Wisconsin, La Follette eschewed the pork-barrel status quo to form the Progressive Party. The La Follette family dominated state politics for two generations, fighting for social rights most people had never heard of.

Robert M. La Follette was born on a Dane County farm in 1855, where the typically hardscrabble life prepared him for the rigors of the University of Wisconsin, which he entered in 1875. He discovered a passion and talent for oratory but, too short for theater, gravitated to politics, a subject befitting the ambitious young man. He was elected Dane County district attorney in 1880. Well-liked by the masses, he gave them resonance with his hand-pumping and off-the-cuff speeches about hard work and personal responsibility in government. An entrenched Republican, he was more or less ignored by the party brass, so in 1884 he brashly ran for U.S. Congress on his own—and won. He was the youngest state representative in U.S. history.

Initially, La Follette toed the party line fairly well, though he did use his position to crow elegantly against the well-oiled political infrastructure. After the Republicans were voted out en masse in 1890, La Follette returned to Wisconsin and formed the Progressive Party. He ran for governor, and after two tries, landed the nomination. A tireless circuit and chautauqua lecturer, he relied on a salt-of-the-earth theme and left audiences mesmerized. This marked the birth of the "Fightin' Bob" image, which persists to this day. He was elected governor three times, returned to the Senate for a tempestuous career, and made serious runs at the presidency.

La Follette's critics found him as self-righteous and passionately tactless as he was brilliant, forthcoming, and gregarious. This driven man of the people was no more enigmatically contradictory than many other public figures, but historians have noted that even his most vehement opponents respected his ethics. Under him, Wisconsin instituted the nation's first direct primary and watershed civil service systems, passed anticorruption legislation and railroad monopoly reforms, and most importantly, formed the Wisconsin Idea.

Progressivism and the Wisconsin Idea

Progressivism represented a careful balance of honest-to-goodness idealism and what may today be termed Libertarian tenets. La Follette saw it as an attempt to overcome, on a grassroots level, the dehumanizing aspect of corporate greed and political corruption. *The*

The Other La Follette

While Robert La Follette dominated Wisconsin politics for most of three decades, he didn't do it alone: He and his wife, Belle, were an inseparable team, both passionate crusaders for social justice.

Belle La Follette (1859-1931) was behind Bob in every way, and in many cases, it could be said, was Bob. Her grandmother inculcated in her a fierce determination to obtain the education she herself had been denied. It was at the University of Wisconsin that this very independent woman caught the eye of her soul mate, Bob La Follette. The two flaunted many of society's constricting traditions. They were the first couple in Wisconsin to delete the word *obey* from their marriage vows. Belle later became the first woman to graduate from the University of Wisconsin law school.

Her postcollege life was supporting Bob and maintaining her own crusading career as a journalist, editor, and suffrage leader. She marched in the state's first major suffrage parade and became a leading researcher and writer on practices of segregation, welfare, and other social issues. In addition to all that, she lectured, acted as her husband's attorney, and raised the La Follette brood.

She knew Bob would need an enlightened insider, so she chose to study law. She immersed herself in the issues and became his most trusted adviser. When Bob La Follette died, she rejected public life; instead, she devoted herself to *The Progressive* magazine, which Bob had founded. Her own activism may be best remembered in her moving, eloquent 1913 speech to a transfixed U.S. Senate Committee on Woman's Suffrage, during which she quoted Abraham Lincoln in asking, "Are women not people?"

Progressive, the Madison-based periodical he founded, remains one of the country's leading media outlets for social justice.

Fightin' Bob's most radical creation was the Wisconsin Idea. Officially a system whereby the state used careful research and empirical evidence in governing, in reality it meant that La Follette kept a close-knit core of advisers as de facto aides. His was the first state or federal government to maintain expert panels and commissions, a controversial idea at the time. Some criticized it as elitist, but he argued that it was necessary to combat well-funded industry cronyism.

EARLY 20TH CENTURY

La Follette's most infamous personal crusade was his strident opposition to U.S. participation in World War I, due equally to Wisconsin's heavily German population and La Follette's vehement pacifism. He suffered tremendous regional and national scorn and was booted to the lower echelons of politics. Interestingly, when the United States officially entered the war, Wisconsin was the first state to meet enlistment requirements. Eventually, La Follette enjoyed something of a vindication with a triumphant return to the Senate in 1924, followed by a final presidential run.

Also a political activist, Bob's wife, Belle La Follette, mounted a long-standing crusade for women's suffrage that helped the 19th Amendment get ratified; Wisconsin was the first state to ratify it. In other political trends starting around the turn of the 20th century, Milwaukee began electing Socialist administrations. Buoyed by nascent labor organizations in the huge factory towns along Lake Michigan, the movement was infused with an immigrant European populace not averse to social radicalism. Milwaukee was the country's most heavily unionized city, and it voted Socialist—at least in part—right through the 1960s. The Progressive banner was picked up by La Follette's sons, Phil and Robert Jr., and the Wisconsin Progressive Party was formed in 1934. Robert Jr. took over for his father in the U.S. Senate, and Phil dominated Wisconsin politics during the 1930s. Despite these efforts, the movement waned. Anemic and ineffective from internal splits and World

War II, it melded with the Republican Party in 1946.

Dairying became Wisconsin's economic leader by 1920 and gained national prominence as well. The industry brought in nearly $210 million to the state, wholly eclipsing timber and lumber. This turned out to be a savior for the state's fortunes during the Depression; dairy products were less threatened by economic collapse than either forest appropriation or manufacturing, though farmers' management and methodology costs skyrocketed. Papermaking, in which Wisconsin is still a world leader, ameliorated the blow in the jobless cutover north- and east-central parts of the state. Concentrated fully in Southeastern Wisconsin, heavy industry—leather, meatpacking, foundries, fabrication, and machine shops—suffered more acutely during the Depression. Sales receipts plummeted by two-thirds and the number of jobs fell by nearly half in five years. Brewing was as yet nonexistent.

SINCE WORLD WAR II

Wisconsin's heavy-manufacturing cities drew waves of economic migrants to its factories after World War II, and agribusiness receipts grew despite a steady reduction in the number of farms. The state's economic fortunes were generally positive right through the mid-1980s, when the state endured its greatest recession since the catastrophic days of the Depression. Wisconsin companies were bought out by competitors in other states. In the early 1990s, agribusiness, still one of the top three Wisconsin industries, became vulnerable for the first time to California milk production.

The one industry that blossomed like no other after the war was tourism. Wisconsin politicians with foresight enacted the first sweeping environmental legislation, and resort owners instituted effective PR campaigns. By the late 1950s Wisconsin had become a full-fledged four-season vacation destination, and by the early 1990s tourism had become a $6 billion industry in the state; a cabinet-level Department of Tourism was established and regional travel centers were set up in other states.

People and Culture

THE PEOPLE

Wisconsin's population is just over six million. With 90.1 people per square mile, the state ranks 24th nationally in population density. General population growth in the state is 3.9 percent annually, unusual because the upper Great Lakes area as a whole shows steadily declining numbers, though this decline is slowing. At the turn of the 20th century, it was the most ethnically diverse state in the Union, and most residents had family ties to Germany.

While still predominantly European American, the state has a fast-growing nonwhite population—12 percent and growing fast.

Native Americans

Wisconsin has one of the most diverse Native American populations of any state, taking into account the number of cultures, settlement history, linguistic stock, and affiliations. The state is home to six sovereign Native American nations on 11 reservations, not all of which are demarcated by boundaries. In addition to the six nations, Wisconsin historically has been the home of the Illinois, Fox, Sauk, Miami, Kickapoo, Satee, Ottawa, and Mascouten people. The total Native American population is around 40,000, or 1 percent of the population.

The largest native group is the **Ojibwa,** also rendered historically as Chippewa and now

Ojibway, Ojibwe, and Ojibwa. Ethnologists, historians, linguists, and even community members themselves disagree on the spelling. *Ojib* means "to pucker up" and *ub-way* is "to roast," and the words together denote the nation's unique style of moccasin stitching. Wisconsin has five Ojibwa communities. The Ojibwa inhabited the northern woodlands of the upper Great Lakes, especially along Lakes Huron and Superior. They were allied with the Ottawa and Potawatomi but branched off in the 16th century and moved to Michigan's Mackinac Island. The Ojibwa said that their migration westward was to fulfill the prophecy to find "food that grows on water"—wild rice. The **Bad River** group today lives on a 123,000-acre reservation along Lake Superior in Ashland County. It's the largest reservation in the state and is famed for its wild rice beds on the Kakagon Sloughs. The **Red Cliff** band, the nucleus of the Ojibwa nation, has been organized along the Bayfield Peninsula's shore since 1854. The **St. Croix** band ("homeless" communities scattered over four counties with no boundaries) lives in northwest Wisconsin. The **Lac du Flambeau** band is the most visited and recognizable because of its proximity to Minocqua and state and federal forests and for exercising its spearfishing rights. **Lac Courte Oreilles** is originally of the *Betonukeengainubejib* Ojibwa division. The **Sokaogan** (Mole Lake) band of Lake Superior Ojibwa is known as the Lost Tribe because its original legal treaty title was lost in an 1854 shipwreck. Originally from Canada, the band moved along to Madeline Island before defeating the Sioux near Mole Lake in 1806.

The Algonquian **Menominee** have been in Wisconsin longer than any other people. The Menominee once held sway south to Illinois, north into Michigan, and west to the Mississippi River, with a total of 10 million acres. Known as the "Wild Rice People"—the early French explorers called them "Lords of Trade"—the Menominee were divided into sky and earth groups and then subdivided into clans. Although the hegemony of the Menominee people lasted up to 10,000 years in Wisconsin, they were almost exterminated by eastern Canadian indigenous people fleeing Iroquois persecution and by pestilence imported by the Europeans. Today, the population has rebounded to around 3,500, and the Menominee reservation constitutes an entire Wisconsin county.

The Forest County **Potawatomi,** also Algonquians, are the legacy of the Native Americans that were most successful moving into Wisconsin, beginning in the 1640s. Originally inhabitants of the shores of Lake Huron, the Potawatomi people later moved to Michigan, Indiana, and places along the St. Joseph's River. The name means "People of the Fire," or, more accurately, "Keeper of the Fire," after their confederacy with the Ojibwa and Ottawa people. Potawatomi lands stretched from Chicago to Door County, and they were among the people who greeted explorer Jean Nicolet when he arrived in 1634. Wisconsin's band of Potawatomi was one of the few to survive forced relocation to Oklahoma in 1838.

Wisconsin's only Mohicans, the **Stockbridge-Munsee** people, live on a reservation bordering the Menominee. The Stockbridge (also called Mahican, meaning "wolf") originally occupied the Hudson River Valley and Massachusetts all the way to Lake Champlain. The Munsee are a branch of the Delaware people and lived near the headwaters of the Delaware River in New York, New Jersey, and Pennsylvania.

The **Oneida** belonged to the Iroquois Five Nations Confederacy, comprising the Mohawk, Oneida, Onondaga, Cayuga, and Seneca people. The Oneida, originally from New York, supported the colonists in the American Revolution but were forced out by the Mohawk and land-grabbing settlers along the Erie Canal after the war. Beginning in the 1820s, the Iroquois-speaking Oneida people merged with the Mahican, Mohegan, Pequot, Narragansett, Montauk, and other groups in Wisconsin. The Green Bay area is where most reside in Wisconsin today.

The Winnebago Nation has reverted to

Wisconsin Linguistic Primer

The source of the majority of Wisconsin place-names is illiterate and occasionally innumerate trappers and traders struggling to filter non-European words and speech through Romance and Germanic languages. Place-names generally fall into several categories: corrupted Native American words, whose origins are the most difficult to identify; practical monikers pertaining to local landforms or natural wonders; and memorials to European American "founding" fathers.

Even the origins of the word *Wisconsin* are difficult; a historical linguist has called Wisconsin's name the most cryptic of all 27 states with Native American names. As early as 1673, the missionary priest Jacques Marquette named the river, from which some say the state's name derived, Meskousing ("red stones"), perhaps because of a red coloration of the banks. "Ouisconsin" appeared on a Jesuit missionary map in 1688. But most widely accepted is the Ojibwa word for the state, *wees-kon-san,* meaning "gathering place of waters."

WISCONSINISMS

Perhaps the most famous example of a Wisconsinism is "bubbler," for a drinking fountain. The *Dictionary of American Regional English* from the University of Wisconsin-Madison, says that the other truly Wisconsin term is "golden birthday," when your age matches the date of the month you were born: for example, if you were born on January 13, your 13th birthday is your golden birthday. Other words and phrases in common Midwestern or national usage that started in Wisconsin include "flowage" (water backed up behind a dam), "hot dish" (casserole), and "ishy" (icky).

Milwaukee colloquialisms—though some vociferously deny it—include "bumbershoot," for umbrella, and "ainah hey?" for "Isn't that so?" In other parts of the state the same phrase is rendered "inso?" You'll also hear "down by"—everything is "down by" something. "Grease yourself a piece of bread and I'll put you on a hamburger" is a Milwaukeeism if ever there was one. Wisconsinites also seem somewhat averse to liquid consonants, like the *l* in Milwaukee; it's "M'waukee" as often as not.

HOWZAT AGAIN?

The phonology of Wisconsin English contains only one dramatic sound: the "ah," seriously emphasized and strongly run though the nasal cavity, as in "wis-KHAN-sin." Note that it's never, ever pronounced "WES-khan-sin." Check MissPronouncer.com (www.misspronouncer.com) to learn the pronunciation of the state's town names:

- **Algoma**—al-GO-muh
- **Chequamegon National Forest**—shuh-WAHM-uh-gun

its original name, **Ho Chunk,** or, more accurately, **Ho Cak** (meaning "big voice" or "mother voice"), in an attempt to restore the rightful cultural and linguistic heritage to the nation. Also known as Otchangara, the group is related to the Chiwere-Siouxan Iowa, Oto, and Missouri people, although their precise origin is unknown. Extremely powerful militarily, they were nonetheless relatively peaceful with the Menominee and Potawatomi, with whom they witnessed Jean Nicolet's 1634 arrival. French scourges and encroaching tribes fleeing Iroquois hostilities in New York devastated Ho Chunk numbers; later, forced relocation nearly killed off the rest. The nation pulled up stakes in Oklahoma and walked back to Wisconsin, following its chief, Yellow Thunder, who bought them a tract of land, deftly circumventing relocation and leaving the federal government no way to force them out of Wisconsin.

An excellent resource about Native Americans is the website of the **Great Lakes Intertribal Council** (www.glitc.org).

- **Fond du Lac**—FAHN-duh-lack
- **Green Bay**—green-BAY, not GREEN-bay
- **Kenosha**—kuh-NO-shuh
- **Lac Courte Oreilles**—la COO-der-ray
- **Manitowoc**—MAN-ih-tuh-wock or MAN-uh-tuh-wock
- **Menominee/Menomonie**—muh-NAH-muh-nee
- **Minocqua**—min-AHK-wah
- **Muscoda**—MUSS-kuh-day
- **New Berlin/Berlin**—new BER-lin
- **Nicolet National Forest**—nick-oh-LAY (sometimes nick-ul-ETT)
- **Oconomowoc**—oh-KAHN-uh-muh-wahk (sometimes uh-KAHN-uh-muh-wahk)
- **Oshkosh**—AHSH-kahsh
- **Prairie du Chien**—prairie du SHEEN
- **Racine**—ruh-SEEN
- **Ripon**—RIP-pin
- **Shawano**—SHAW-no (sometimes SHAH-no)
- **Sheboygan**—shuh-BOY-gun
- **Trempealeau**—TREM-puh-low
- **Waukesha**—WALK uh-shaw
- **Waupun**—wau-PAHN
- **Wausau**—WAW-saw (There's no "r.")

European Americans

At statehood, only 10 nationalities were represented in Wisconsin; by 1950, more than 50 could be counted. The vast majority of these were European, and Wisconsin is still 88 percent Caucasian.

A decidedly **German** state, Wisconsin boasts more residents claiming Teutonic roots (54 percent) than anywhere else in the country. So thick is the German milieu of Milwaukee (34 percent) that German chancellors visit the city when they're in the United States for presidential summits. Wisconsin has more than 50,000 native speakers of German—quite remarkable for a century-old ethnic group. Germans came in three waves. The first arrived 1820-1835 from both Pennsylvania and southwestern Germany. The second wave, 1840-1860, came mostly from northwest Germany and included the legendary "48ers"—enlightened intellectuals fleeing political persecution. During this wave, as many as 215,000 Germans moved to Wisconsin each year; by 1855, fully one-third of Wisconsin's Germans had arrived. The third wave occurred after 1880 and drew emigrants mainly from Germany's northeastern region to Southeastern Wisconsin, where they worked in the burgeoning factories.

The state's **French** roots can be traced back to the voyageurs, trappers, and Jesuit missionaries. They started the first settlements along the Fox and Wisconsin River Valleys. Although Wisconsin shows no strong French presence in anything other than place-names, the Two Rivers area still has an Acadian influence.

As the **British** and the French haggled and warred over all of the Wisconsin territory, many crown-friendly British Yankees did move here, populating virtually every community. The **Irish** began arriving in the late 19th century in numbers second only to the Germans. Irish influence is found in every community, especially Milwaukee's Bay View, Erin in Washington County, Ozaukee County, Adell and Parnell in Sheboygan County, and Manitowoc County.

Pockets of **Welsh** and **Cornish** are found throughout the state, the latter especially in the southwestern lead-mining region of the state. A distinct **Belgian** influence exists in Kewaunee County, where Walloon can still be heard in local taverns.

Poles represent the primary Eastern European ethnic group. The largest contingent is in Milwaukee, where kielbasa is as common a dietary mainstay as bratwurst. Most Poles arrived 1870-1910. At that time, Poland was not recognized as a country, so Ellis Island officials erroneously categorized many of the immigrants as Prussian, Austrian, or Russian. While 90 percent of Wisconsin's Polish immigrants moved into the cities, about 30 percent of those who arrived farmed, mostly in Portage and Trempealeau Counties; the latter is the oldest Polish settlement in the United States. **Czechs,** another large Eastern European group, live mostly in north and East-Central Wisconsin, especially Kewaunee and Manitowoc Counties.

Many **Norwegians** also emigrated to the Upper Midwest, primarily Minnesota and Wisconsin. Most were economic emigrants trying to escape Norway's chronic overpopulation. Most Norwegians in Wisconsin wound up in Dane and Rock Counties. **Finnish** immigrants to the United States totaled 300,000 between 1864 and 1920, and many of these settled in the Upper Peninsula of Michigan and northern Wisconsin. **Swedes** were the smallest Scandinavian contingent, the original settlement comprising a dozen families near Waukesha.

By the turn of the 20th century, Wisconsin was home to almost 10 percent of all the **Danes** in the United States—the second-largest national contingent. Most originally settled in the northeast (the city of Denmark lies just southeast of Green Bay), but later immigrants wound up farther south. To this day, Racine is nicknamed "Kringleville" for its flaky Danish pastry.

The **Dutch** settled primarily in Milwaukee and Florence Counties beginning in the 1840s, when potato crops failed and protests flared over the Reformed Church. These southeastern counties today sport towns such as Oostburg, New Amsterdam, and Holland.

In 1846, a large contingent of **Swiss** from the Glarus canton sent emissaries to North America to search out a suitable immigration site. Eventually, the two scouts stumbled upon the gorgeous, lush valleys of Southwestern Wisconsin. A great deal of Swiss heritage remains in Green County.

Italians began arriving in the 1830s—many Genoese migrated north from Illinois lead camps to fish and scavenge lead along the Mississippi River—but didn't arrive in substantial numbers until the early 1900s. Most settled in the southeast, specifically Milwaukee, Racine, and especially Kenosha.

Perhaps unique to Wisconsin is the large population of **Icelandic** immigrants, who settled on far-flung Washington Island, northeast of the Door Peninsula. It was the largest single Icelandic settlement in the United States when they arrived in 1870 to work as fishers.

African Americans

Some theories hold African Americans first arrived in Wisconsin in 1835, in the entourage of Solomon Juneau, the founder of Milwaukee. But records from the early part of the 18th century detail black trappers, guides, and explorers. In 1791-1792, in fact, black fur traders established an encampment estimated to be near present-day Marinette. Although the Michigan Territory was ostensibly free, slavery was not uncommon. Henry Dodge, Wisconsin's first territorial governor, had slaves but freed them two years after leaving office. Other slave owners were transplanted Southerners living in the new lead-mining district of the southwest. Other early African Americans were French African immigrants who settled near Prairie du Chien in the early 19th century. Wisconsin's first African American settlement was Pleasant Spring, outside Lancaster in Southwestern Wisconsin; the State Historical Society's Old World Wisconsin in Eagle has an exhibit on it.

After passage of the Fugitive Slave Act in 1850, which allowed slave catchers to cross state lines in pursuit, many freed and escaped slaves flocked to the outer fringes of the country. Wisconsin's opposition to the act was strident. One celebrated case involved Joshua Glover, an enslaved person who had escaped and had been living free and working in Racine for years. He was caught and imprisoned by his erstwhile master but was later broken out by mobs from Ripon, Milwaukee, and Southeastern Wisconsin. The state Supreme Court ruled the act unconstitutional.

After the Civil War, the African American population increased, and most chose to live in rural, agricultural settings. Large-scale African American migration to Milwaukee, Racine, and Kenosha took place after World War II, as northern factories revved up for the Korean War and, later, the Cold War. Today, the vast majority of Wisconsin's nearly 300,000 African Americans, around 6 percent of the state population, live in these urbanized southeastern counties. The African American population is one of the fastest growing, increasing by 25 percent per decade.

Latinos

Wisconsin's Latino population has doubled in the last two censuses. **Puerto Ricans** began arriving in Milwaukee after World War II as blue-collar laborers. **Mexicans** represent one of the more recent immigration waves, many of them having arrived in the mid-1960s, though Mexican immigrants have been in the state since as far back as 1850. Mexicans today live mostly in Southeastern Wisconsin—Milwaukee, Madison, and especially Racine.

Asians

Wisconsin has upward of 77,000 residents of Asian descent, about 2 percent of the population. One of the fastest-growing elements, **Laotian Hmong,** began arriving during the Vietnam War and settled mostly in Appleton, Green Bay, the Fox River Valley, Manitowoc, Eau Claire, La Crosse, and pockets in Southeastern Wisconsin. The state also has substantial **Chinese** and **Korean** populations.

CULTURE

Handicrafts

There are dozens of types of handicrafts in Wisconsin, and every community has artisans specializing in various ethnic styles: Norwegian rosemaling, for example, is flowery, colorful, painted-trim artwork. Unique are the creations of the Amish and the Hmong. A large contingent of Amish families, famed for their quilting, crafts, bent-hickory furniture, and outstanding bakeries, live in southwestern and west-central Wisconsin.

Hmong crafts include story cloths, which recount narratives visually, and exquisite decorative *paj ntaub,* a 2,000-year-old hybrid of needlework and appliqué, usually featuring geometric designs and often animals. These quilts and wall hangings require more than 100 hours of work. Some young Amish and Hmong women are synthesizing their quilt styles into wonderful bicultural mélanges.

Festivals and Events

JANUARY

- In mid- to late January is Eagle River's wild **World Championship Snowmobile Derby,** the world's best snowmobile drivers competing on a 0.5-mile iced oval track.

FEBRUARY

- In late February, the largest cross-country ski race in North America, the **Birkebeiner,** is held in Hayward and Cable. Six thousand competitors from around the world race on the grueling 55-kilometer course. The four-day event features tons of smaller races.

APRIL

- Late April to mid-May heralds the beginning of the festival season, which runs through fall. An amazing way to start it is with Door County's monthlong cherry and flower **blossoms,** a riot of color rivaled perhaps only by Holland's tulips.

JUNE

- One apt nickname for Milwaukee is the "City of Festivals." Milwaukee's **Polish Fest** is one of the larger ethnic festivals in the country.
- The city really gets into high gear the last week of June, when it hosts the mammoth **Summerfest,** billed as the largest music festival in the United States. In the 11-day extravaganza, more than 2,500 national acts perform everything from big band to heavy metal.

JULY

- July brings cars and parades. The largest automotive festival in the Midwest, the **Iola Old Car Show and Swap Meet** takes place in the southeastern town of Iola. Milwaukee's major ethnic festival of July is **German Fest.**
- In late July Wisconsin's Lac Courte Oreilles people hold the **Honor the Earth Traditional Powwow** of ceremonial dancing, drumming, food, games, workshops, and speakers.
- The most prestigious event outside of Summerfest is likely Oshkosh's **EAA AirVenture Oshkosh** fly-in convention in July, the world's most significant aviation event. As part of the Experimental Aircraft Association's yearly gathering, 15,000 experimental and historic aircraft—including NASA-designed craft—descend on the city and surrounding area for a week.

Hmong artisans are often found at craft fairs and farmers markets. Amish wares are found in home shops throughout Southwestern Wisconsin and in a few stores.

Food

Midwestern cuisine. An oxymoron? Hardly. Banish those visions of tuna casserole dancing in your head. Midwestern cuisine—real, original fare handed down generationally—is more eclectic and more representative of American heritage than better-known and better-marketed cooking styles.

If you search out the latent Americana in Wisconsin cooking, you'll be amazed. Wisconsin's best cooking is a thoughtful mélange of ethnicities, stemming from the diverse populace and prairie-cooking fare that reflects a heritage of living off the land. Midwest regional cuisine is a blend of originally wild food such as cranberries, wild rice, pumpkins, blueberries, whitefish livers,

AUGUST

- In August, Milwaukee hosts the **Wisconsin State Fair,** the state's largest annual event, with more than a million visitors over 11 days. In late August, Milwaukee features **Irish Fest,** the world's largest Irish cultural event outside of the Emerald Isle.

SEPTEMBER

- New Glarus shows itself as North America's most Swiss village during its **Wilhelm Tell Pageant** in early September. The famous Tell drama is presented in both English and Swiss German. And, of course, there's plenty of yodeling, log throwing, and the like.
- Mid-September brings the nation's premier off-road bike race, the **Chequamegon MTB Festival** in Hayward and Cable—three days of off-road fat-tire racing, orienteering, 16- and 40-mile events, and criterium lap racing.
- Believe it or not, up to 80,000 people crowd west-central Wisconsin, near Warrens, for late September's **Cranberry Festival,** which celebrates the tart little fruit.

OCTOBER

- Nature's autumn majesty is a big deal in Wisconsin, drawing thousands of visitors annually. Local news reports even feature nightly **leaf color watches.** The state Department of Tourism maintains 24/7 color updates via phone and website.
- One of October's major festivals is **Oktoberfest** in La Crosse, fashioned after Munich's celebrations. There is a Maple Leaf Parade, music, rides, and a lot of beer.
- Being America's Dairyland, it seems appropriate for Wisconsin to hold the world's largest dairying trade show, the **World Dairy Expo.** More than 50 countries participate in the event, held yearly in Madison.
- Bayfield closes out the season of warm-weather festivals with its early October **Apple Fest,** featuring food booths, parades, arts and crafts, carnivals, and music. It's worth going just to see the Apostle Islands.

NOVEMBER

- In mid-November, more than 50 ethnic groups participate in the Milwaukee **Holiday Folk Fair.** The largest annual multiethnic festival in the country, it's a great place to shop for folk art, and the ethnic dancing is popular.

catfish cheeks, and morel mushrooms incorporated into standard old-country recipes. Added to the mix are game animals such as deer, pheasant, and goose. Many Midwesterners simply shoot their own rather than raising them or buying them from a grocery wholesaler. It's a home-based culinary style, perfected from house to house through generations of adaptation.

While the state features a panorama of European fare, the rest of the culinary spectrum is also represented. Milwaukee's got real-deal soul food and a fantastic array of Puerto Rican and Mexican restaurants, and in Madison you'll find Asian eateries rivaling any city's. Despite the preponderance of hot beef and meat loaf, it's quite possible to find good imaginative food in Wisconsin.

CHEESE

Wisconsin produces more than 500 varieties and more than one-third of the nation's cheese, leading in cheddar, colby, brick, muenster, limburger, and many Italian varieties. And yes, people here really do eat a great deal of it; Wisconsinites are loyal dairy eaters, and laws prohibiting the use of margarine remained on the books until 1967.

The most common cheese is the ever-versatile **cheddar.** For something different, eat it with fruit (apples are best) or melt it on hot apple pie. **Colby** cheese was invented in the northern Wisconsin town of the same name. It has a very mild, mellow flavor and a firm, open texture. It's most often eaten breaded and deep-fried, but try cubing it in fruit or vegetable salads. Firmer, with a smooth body, **colby jack** cheese is marbled white and yellow—a mixture of the mellow colby cheese along with the distinctive broad taste of **monterey jack,** a semisoft, creamy white cheese.

Wisconsin effectively brought **swiss** cheese to prominence in the United States more than a century ago. Swiss cheese fans should head for the town of Monroe in Southwestern Wisconsin, where you'll find the greatest swiss you've ever tasted, as well as a milder **baby swiss.** While there, slip into a tavern or sandwich shop and really experience Wisconsin culture by sampling a **limburger** sandwich—the pungent, oft-misunderstood swiss on pumpernickel with onions and radishes. Wisconsin may be the last place on earth where it's couth to munch limburger in polite company; it is definitely the last place in the world making the cheese.

Another Wisconsin original is **brick cheese,** a semisoft cheese with a waxy, open texture. Creamy white, young brick has a mild flavor; when aged, it becomes sharp. It's perfect for grilled cheese sandwiches or with mustard on pumpernickel bread.

Two transplants the state produces to near perfection are **gouda** and **edam,** imported by Western Europeans. They're semisoft to firm and creamy in texture, with small holes and mild, slightly nutty flavor.

Finally, for the most authentic cheese-eating cultural experience, go to a bar and order **cheese curds,** commonly breaded and deep-fried. When bought at a dairy or a farmers market, cheese curds leave a distinctive squeaky feeling on the teeth and are a perfect snack food. Another unique cheese dish, especially in Green Bay, is beer cheese soup.

The **Wisconsin Milk Marketing Board** (www.wisconsincheese.com) is a wonderful place to peruse each cheese factory, dairy, or store that offers tours. The foodie sections are superb.

FROZEN CUSTARD

You will of course find loads of delicious ice cream here, but Wisconsinites have a predilection for **frozen custard.** Take a lick and be wowed. The difference is slight—egg yolk—but what a difference it makes! An emulsifier, the yolk's lecithin gives it a dense yet creamy goodness, and you may never go back to ice cream.

SUPPER CLUBS

What, exactly, is a supper club? What the zocalo is to Latin Americans, the sidewalk café to Parisians, the beer garden to Bavarians, so is the supper club to Wisconsinites. Every Badger State community has one, and it's the social and culinary underpinning of Wisconsin. Indeed, although supper clubs exist in many Midwestern states, Wisconsin has far more.

Equal parts homey, casual meat-and-potatoes restaurant and local kaffeeklatsch, supper clubs traditionally have three obligatory specialties: prime rib, always on Saturday, although some serve it every day; home-style chicken; and most importantly, a Friday-night fish fry. No fish fry, no business. Most menus feature steaks in one column, seafood in the other. Regional variations buttress these basics with anything from Teutonic carnivore fare to Turkish food. This being Wisconsin, venison occasionally makes an appearance. One side dish will always be a choice of potato. If it's a true supper club, a relish tray comes out with the dinner rolls. On it you'll find everything from sliced vegetable sticks to pickles

The Butter Battle

To demonstrate the importance of the dairy industry in Wisconsin, consider the Butter Battle, also called the Oleo Wars. Oleomargarine, or margarine, was developed in 1895, but it wasn't until 1967 that selling or buying it in Wisconsin was decriminalized. Dairy farmers initially feared that the buttery nondairy spread would ruin them; later they would march and protest for a ban on anything resembling butter that wasn't a dairy product. Of course, margarine smuggling started, and diet-conscious consumers would cross the state line into Illinois to the "margarine villages" that sprouted alongside border service stations. Butter's most partisan supporter was Gordon Roseleip, a Republican U.S. senator from Darlington, whose rantings against margarine could occasionally overshadow Joseph McCarthy's anticommunist paranoia. But the good senator doomed the butter industry in 1965 when he agreed to take a blind taste test between butter and margarine—and chose the margarine. His family later admitted that he had been unknowingly consuming margarine for years; he was obese and his family had switched to margarine, hoping to reduce his weight.

to coleslaw—and sometimes an indescribably weird "salad" concoction such as green Jell-O with shaved carrots inside.

No two supper clubs look alike (the only prerequisites are an attached bar and perhaps faux wood paneling somewhere), but all can be partially covered by clichés such as "rustic," "cozy," and "like someone's dining room." Nicer supper clubs will have crackling fireplaces; low-end joints feel more like run-down family restaurants in both decor and menu. The coolest ones have animal heads dangling above the diners; the tackiest ones feature overdone nautical decor. Wear a suit and you'll be conspicuous; jeans are perfectly acceptable. In many places—especially Madison—Badger red is de rigueur on football Saturday. Beware impostors: In recent years, "supper club" has been adopted by fancy restaurants on both coasts, but a coopted supper club is not the real thing. If you ever see a dress code posted, you're not at a real supper club.

One book I love is *Wisconsin Supper Clubs* by Ron Faiola (Agate, 2013); I've never read a book that gets it as right as his.

Alcohol

I'm from Wisconsin, and the rumors are true: Badgers drink a *lot*. Alcohol is the social lubricant of the state, and many out-of-staters are a bit wide-eyed when they move here. Almost 70 percent of the drinking-age population report participation in legal imbibing. Madison and surrounding Dane County have one of the highest percentages of binge drinkers in the United States, but Milwaukee actually took that crown in 2009. Wisconsin is also number one in driving under the influence. At last count, the state had more than 13,000 taverns, by far the most per capita in the country. One town of 69,000, for example, has more bars than all of Memphis.

Note that "brown mumbler" means any brown drink made with whiskey or brandy. You'll hear it in northern Wisconsin.

BEER

Wisconsinites do not drink more beer per capita than residents of any other state in the country; that's Nevada, and alas, the days of quaffing a brew with breakfast and finding a beer garden on every street corner are long gone.

Wisconsin beer-drinking began with the hordes of European immigrants. The earliest brewery has been traced back to an 1835 operation in Mineral Point, but there may have been one a few years before that, although what most early Southwestern Wisconsin brewers were making was actually top-fermented malt liquor. Surprisingly, Germans did not initiate Milwaukee's legendary beer-making industry; it was a couple of upstarts from the British Isles. But massive German settlement did set the state's beer standard, which no other state could hope to match. By 1850, Milwaukee alone had almost 200 breweries, elevating beer-making to the city's number-one industry. Throughout the state, every town, once it had been platted and while waiting for incorporation, would build three things—a church, a town hall, and a brewery, not necessarily in that order.

The exact number of breweries in the state in the 19th century isn't known, but it is easily in the thousands; up to 50 years ago, local brew was still common. At that time, beer-making went through a decline; industry giants effectively killed off the regional breweries. But by the 1970s, a backlash against the swill that big brewers passed off as beer sent profits plummeting. In stepped microbreweries and brewpubs. The nation is going through a renaissance of beer crafting, and Wisconsin is no different; Madison and Milwaukee have numerous brewpubs and a few microbreweries. In other parts of the state, anachronistic old breweries are coming back to the fore, usually with the addition of a restaurant and lots of young professional patrons. Time will tell if this trend marks a permanent national shift toward traditional brews, made according to four-century-old purity laws, or if it's simply a fad.

Some local standards still exist. **Leinenkugel's,** or Leinie's, is the preferred choice of North Woods denizens, closely rivaled by **Point,** which is brewed in Stevens Point. Tourists rave about New Glarus Brewery's **Spotted Cow**, and you can only enjoy it here since it isn't exported out of the state.

BRANDY

What traditionally has made a Badger a Badger, drink-wise? Brandy, of any kind. When the Wisconsin Badgers play a football game on the road, the 30,000-plus Cheeseheads who follow generally get newspaper articles written about their bratwurst, postgame polka dancing, and prodigious brandy drinking. In 1993, when the rowdy Badger faithful descended on the Rose Bowl in a friendly invasion, Los Angeles hotels ran out of brandy; by the time the Badgers returned in 1999 and again in 2000, local hoteliers had figured it out. The state has slipped to second place behind Washington DC, of all places, in per capita consumption, but Korbel still sells just under half its brandy here.

Wisconsinites are decidedly not connoisseurs of brandy; you'll never hear discussions of "smoky" versus "plump" varieties or vintages. Try to chat somebody up about cognac versus brandy in a bar and you'll probably be met with an empty stare. (Cognac is a spirit distilled from the white wine grapes of Cognac in France; brandy is a more general term for a spirit distilled from wine.)

Here's how to make Wisconsin's fave drink: Put ice cubes in a glass. Add two ounces of brandy (any kind you want), one lump of sugar, and one dash of cocktail bitters. Fill the rest of the glass with water or white soda. Top off with fruit or mushrooms.

Essentials

Transportation

GETTING THERE

Air

The major U.S. airlines have direct domestic flights into Wisconsin, but you often have to stop first in Chicago, Minneapolis, or another major hub. Ticket prices vary wildly depending on when you travel and, more important, when you buy the ticket. The best way to find deals is through a travel agent or digging around on the Internet; dealing directly with the airline can, in fact, lead to a better overall experience.

Milwaukee's **Mitchell International Airport** (MKE, www.

mitchellairport.com) is the only international airport in the state and has the most direct flights around the country. Madison has a few cross-country flights as well, and Madison, Green Bay, Stevens Point/Wausau, La Crosse, Oshkosh, Eau Claire, Marinette, Rhinelander, Appleton, and a few other small airports are served by regional flights feeding hub airports.

Bus

Greyhound (800/231-2222, www.greyhound.com) operates in major Wisconsin cities, but only along the interstate highways. **Van Galder** (800/747-0994, www.coachusa.com) operates between Chicago (O'Hare Airport and downtown) and Madison, making stops at Wisconsin communities along the way.

Wisconsin Coach Lines' **Airport Express** runs from Milwaukee to Chicago via Racine and Kenosha. **NWT Express Shuttle** (715/634-5307, nwtexpressshuttle.com) operates between the Minneapolis Airport (MSP) and Hayward in Northwestern Wisconsin.

Train

Amtrak (800/872-7245, www.amtrak.com) operates trains through Wisconsin. The long-distance ***Empire Builder*** originates in Chicago and runs through Milwaukee, Columbus, Portage, Wisconsin Dells, Sturtevant, Tomah, and La Crosse on its way to Seattle/Portland.

Metra (312/322-6777, www.metrarail.com) commuter trains run between Kenosha and Chicago's Madison Street Station.

Water

The **SS *Badger*** (www.ssbadger.com), the only active passenger and car steamship left on the Great Lakes, runs daily in season between Manitowoc, Wisconsin, and Ludington, Michigan.

Milwaukee has the high-speed **Lake Express** ferry (866/914-1010, www.lake-express.com) to Muskegon, Michigan, a nice way to avoid the congestion and white-knuckle driving on outer Chicago's interstate arteries.

On a much smaller scale, one of the few remaining interstate ferries left in the country, the **Cassville Car Ferry,** operates seasonally in Southwestern Wisconsin. It shuttles passengers across the Mississippi River between Cassville, Wisconsin, and Iowa.

Car

The largest number of visitors to Wisconsin come from Chicago via I-94 to Milwaukee via Kenosha and Racine, and via I-90 to Madison via Beloit and Janesville. From Chicago to Milwaukee (I-94, 92 miles) takes around 90 minutes. From Chicago to Madison (I-90, 148 miles) takes 2.5 hours. If you're planning to visit Door County from the Chicago area, from Milwaukee, take I-43 to Green Bay and then Highway 57 to Sturgeon Bay in Door County. The trip is 155 miles and takes 2.5 hours.

Many visitors come from Minneapolis via I-90 and I-94. From Minneapolis to Madison (I-94, 273 miles) takes 4.5 hours; add another 80 miles from Madison to Milwaukee. If you're coming from Minneapolis to Door County, take I-94 E to Highway 29, which is four lanes all the way to Green Bay, and then take Highway 57 to Sturgeon Bay; the trip is 327 miles and takes 5.5 hours.

Many people from Minneapolis prefer to visit the Bayfield and Apostle Islands National Lakeshore, since it's closer to home. The route is I-35 to U.S. 2; it's 234 miles and takes 4 hours.

GETTING AROUND

Highways

An interesting tidbit: Wisconsin was the first state to use numbers for their highways! (Interesting also because later, after

Previous: ATVs in summer and snowmobiles in winter have equal rights with cars here.

international adoption, the state changed to letters for county highways.)

For years, the state's 110,300 miles of roads were all in pretty good shape and consistently highly rated by travel media outlets. The experts, however, have begun to quibble, resulting in the 2015 report by the U.S. Department of Transportation calling the state's roads the nation's fourth worst. In truth the bad roads are mostly far from the places tourists visit. Best of all for drivers, Wisconsin has no toll roads.

Urban interstate highways around Milwaukee and to a lesser extent Madison can be awful for congestion. The stretch of I-94 running through Milwaukee is one of the nation's 10 most congested. A stretch of I-43 between Milwaukee and Green Bay has been a rough road for some time. The next-worst roads are Madison's Beltline Highway and I-90 interchange, both of which, along with Milwaukee's interstates, are inhospitable during rush hours.

Theoretically, the state Department of Transportation is now operating under a 20-year plan to improve existing multilane highways and expand certain two-lane highways. These two-lane roads are crucial, as they constitute only 4 percent of the state's highways but carry 42 percent of the traffic, and they have been sorely neglected.

County highways are designated by letters. You can determine the size and condition of the road in advance by the letters designating it. The roads are less important if they have more letters. So Highway RR will be narrower than Highway R, and possibly in worse repair. County roads are generally paved, but don't be surprised if they're not.

MAJOR ROUTES

I-94 from Chicago and its siblings, I-794 and I-894, carve up Milwaukee and always seem to be polar opposites: either terrifyingly busy and fast or maddeningly congested. There are no alternative routes. To head north to Green Bay and Door County, I-43 is in terrible condition; it's in better shape southwest from Milwaukee to the Lake Geneva resort area.

I-94 leads from Milwaukee to Madison, where it joins I-90 also from Chicago, at which point they lead west toward Minnesota. Traffic is always heavy for the first hour out of Madison. An hour northwest of Madison, I-39/U.S. 51 splits from the interstate and heads up the middle of the state 200 miles before becoming two lanes in the Great North Woods on the way to Michigan's Upper Peninsula.

I-90 and I-94 split in western Wisconsin. I-90 continues west to La Crosse before crossing the Mississippi River and entering Minnesota. I-94 swoops northwest toward Minneapolis. Halfway to Minneapolis, U.S. 53 is a four-lane major highway that serves Northwestern Wisconsin.

In the southern half of the state, two other four-lane arteries exist. U.S. 151 runs from Dubuque, Iowa, through Madison and all the way to Fond du Lac at the southern tip of Lake Winnebago, where it joins U.S. 41 running from the Lake Winnebago region (up to Green Bay) southeast to Milwaukee.

Only one four-lane road bisects Wisconsin east-to-west in the northern half of the state. If you look at a map, you'll notice a preponderance of north-south highways. In Eau Claire, approximately 90 miles east of Minneapolis, Highway 29 joins I-94 and crosses the state all the way to Green Bay. North of this road, there are only two-lane highways, and you're guaranteed to encounter many, many boat trailers as well as the odd farm tractor.

REGULATIONS AND ETIQUETTE

Wisconsin permits radar detectors in cars. There is a mandatory motorcycle helmet law for people under age 18. All vehicle passengers are required by law to wear seat belts. Car seats are mandatory for children under age four.

The speed limit on Wisconsin interstate highways is 70 mph, reduced to 55 mph in metropolitan areas. Milwaukee's fringes are

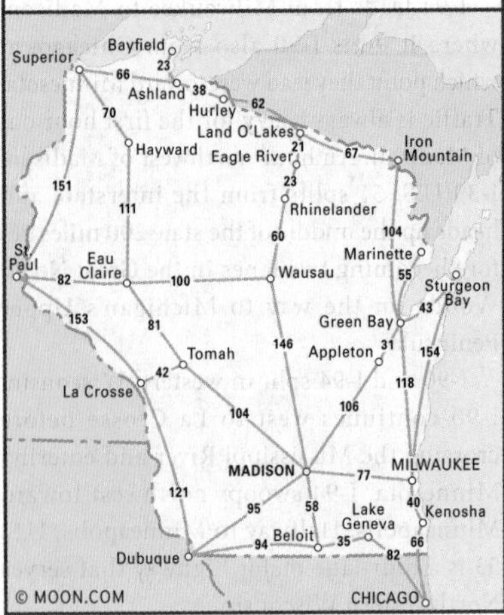

well patrolled for speeding, so be forewarned. You can travel 65 or 70 mph on some four-lane highways in the northern part of the state.

Drivers in Wisconsin tend to be very courteous, to the point that some grumble about the "methodical" pace of Wisconsin traffic. The interstate arteries surrounding larger cities, especially Milwaukee, are the only places conducive to speed.

ROAD CONDITIONS

The state Department of Transportation maintains a **road condition hotline** (866/511-9472, https://511wi.gov) detailing the conditions of all major roads across the state; it also lists construction delays. Dial 511 on your mobile phone to access it.

It's important to winterize your vehicle while driving in Wisconsin. Always keep your antifreeze level prepared for temperatures of -35°F (half water, half fluid usually suffices). Most important: Keep a full tank of gas—it helps prevent freeze-ups in the line and lets you run your car if you're stuck in a ditch.

Bus

You can always hop aboard **Greyhound** (800/231-2222, www.greyhound.com), but only as long as you're traveling to communities along the large main highways.

The communities of Janesville, Beloit, Racine, Kenosha, Milwaukee, and Bayfield Peninsula have bus systems linking nearby communities. Madison and Milwaukee are linked by the frequently running **Badger Bus** (877/292-8259, www.badgerbus.com).

Outdoor Recreation

STATE PARKS AND TRAILS

"Work hard, play hard" is the ethic in Wisconsin. There's always a trail, a lake, or an activity within shouting distance. Wisconsin contains 95 state parks, forests, and trails, varying in size from Green Bay's 50-acre living museum **Heritage Hill** to the 225,000-acre **Northern Highland American Legion State Forest** near Woodruff and Minocqua. A state park lies within an hour of every Wisconsin resident, a deliberate feature of the state park system; they've been dubbed the most diverse in the Midwest. A few of them, like **Devil's Lake State Park, Peninsula State Park,** and the **Kettle Moraine State Forest,** for example, rival other major state parks in the nation. Since 2000, the Wisconsin's state park system has been a finalist in the national Gold Medal Parks award for the best in the country.

State parks and forests require a vehicle access sticker, which you can buy daily ($8 resident, $11 nonresident) or annually ($28 resident, $38 nonresident). Several more popular parks—Devil's Lake and Peninsula, for example—charge extra money for a daily pass.

Wisconsin's massive multiuse trail system

Roadkill

Driving in Wisconsin, you will see a large number of deer as well as deer carcasses on the roadside that have been hit by cars; we are sixth in the United States for the number of deer-car collisions. In one report, State Farm Insurance released data showing that the odds for hitting a deer are 1 in 164 nationwide but 1 in 77 in Wisconsin.

DEER DISPLACEMENT

The fertile croplands and suburban gardens that replaced the state's original meadows and forests have also brought huge numbers of deer, to the point that some suburban areas ringed with rural lands have higher deer concentrations than public parklands. Some wildlife biologists now worry that the social capacity of the land, meaning the number of deer that humans can tolerate, has been maxed out in some areas. The primary cause is a lethal modern combination of an abundance of crops available for the deer to eat and refusal to allow hunting on private land, which results in no thinning of the herd. And it's not the same old divisions in this debate—some environmentalists are pro-deer hunting, as enormous deer populations destroy fragile and rare flora when feeding in winter.

THE NUMBERS

Wisconsin has the sixth-highest number of car-deer crashes in the United States—it averages 56 per day, and every day in one year had multiple deer-car crashes. The Department of Natural Resources estimates the deer population statewide at 1.4 to 1.9 million. Annually, nearly 20,500 car-deer crashes are reported, causing 6 to 12 deaths and 400 to 700 injuries among humans; many more collisions go unreported. Statewide, deer account for more than 15 percent of car crashes since 1978, but the numbers have fallen since the mid-1990s, when deer populations exploded. In 1999, the worst year, half of all crashes involved deer. A conservative estimate of total damage, including cars and agricultural losses, is over $100 million per year. Thankfully, less than 2 percent of car-deer crashes result in human fatalities.

AVOIDING COLLISIONS

Driving in Wisconsin, at some point you're going to meet a deer on a highway. October and November are statistically the worst months for collisions, along with high numbers in May and June as well. Crashes happen mostly after 8pm April to August; the rest of the year, they typically occur 5pm-7pm. Deer, like much wildlife, are most active around dawn and dusk, but they are active day and night. Most crashes occur on dry roads on clear days. And the old adage about them freezing in the headlights is absolutely true. The best thing you can do is pay close attention, don't speed, and keep an intelligent stopping distance between you and the next car. Use your peripheral vision, and if you see one deer, expect there to be more. If one appears, do not swerve or slam on the brakes, even if this means hitting the deer. Experts agree that braking or swerving only creates more danger for you and other motorists.

is also run by the Department of Natural Resources, and a **trail pass** ($5 daily, $25 annually) is required; note that some trails are not state trails but county trails, and you'll need a different pass. Also note that hikers do not need to buy a pass; only those using bicycles, horses, skis, or ATVs do.

The Wisconsin **Department of Natural Resources** (DNR, 608/266-2181, www.dnr.wi.gov) is an invaluable source of information on state lands and environmental issues.

NATIONAL FORESTS, RESERVES, AND LAKESHORE

The state also boasts a mammoth national forest, the **Chequamegon-Nicolet,** totaling 1.5 million acres and home to two national scenic trails. The final jewel is the **Apostle Islands**

Badger State Parks and Forests

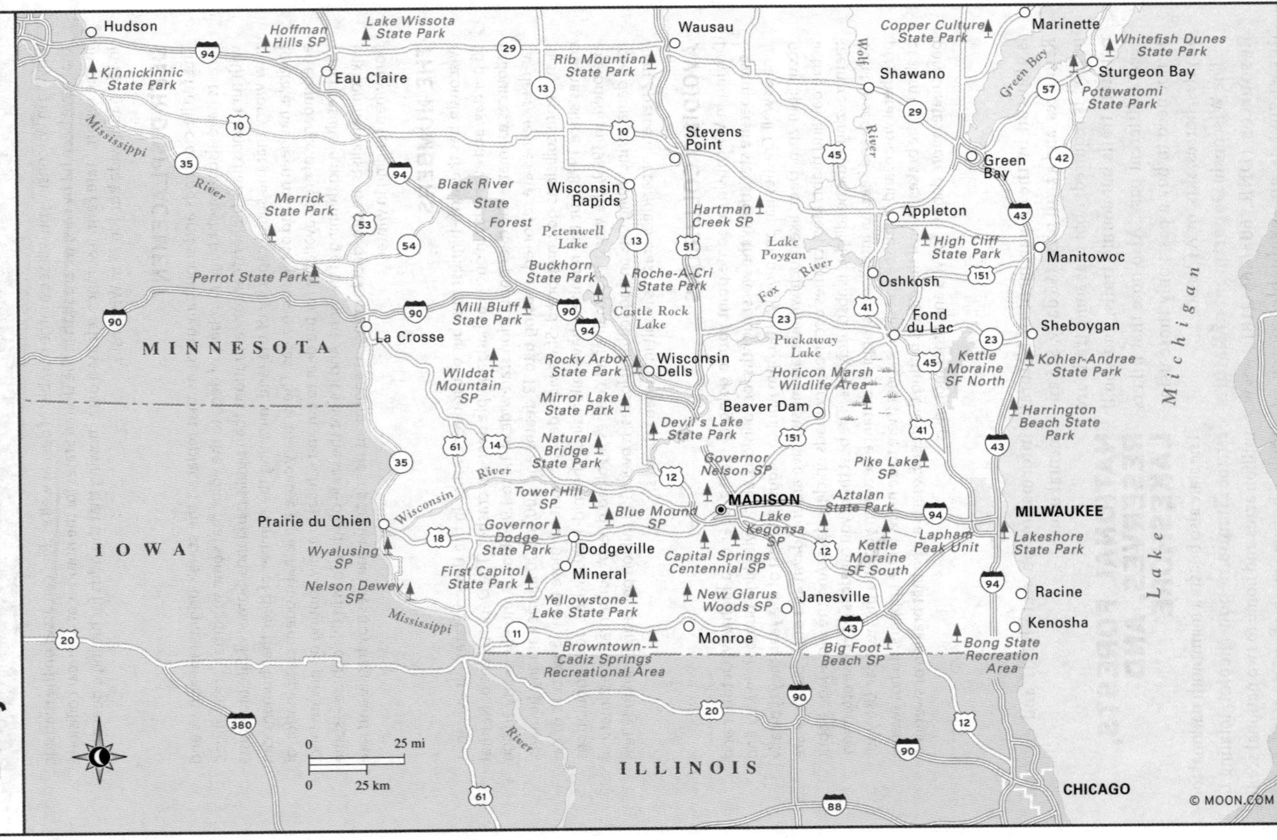

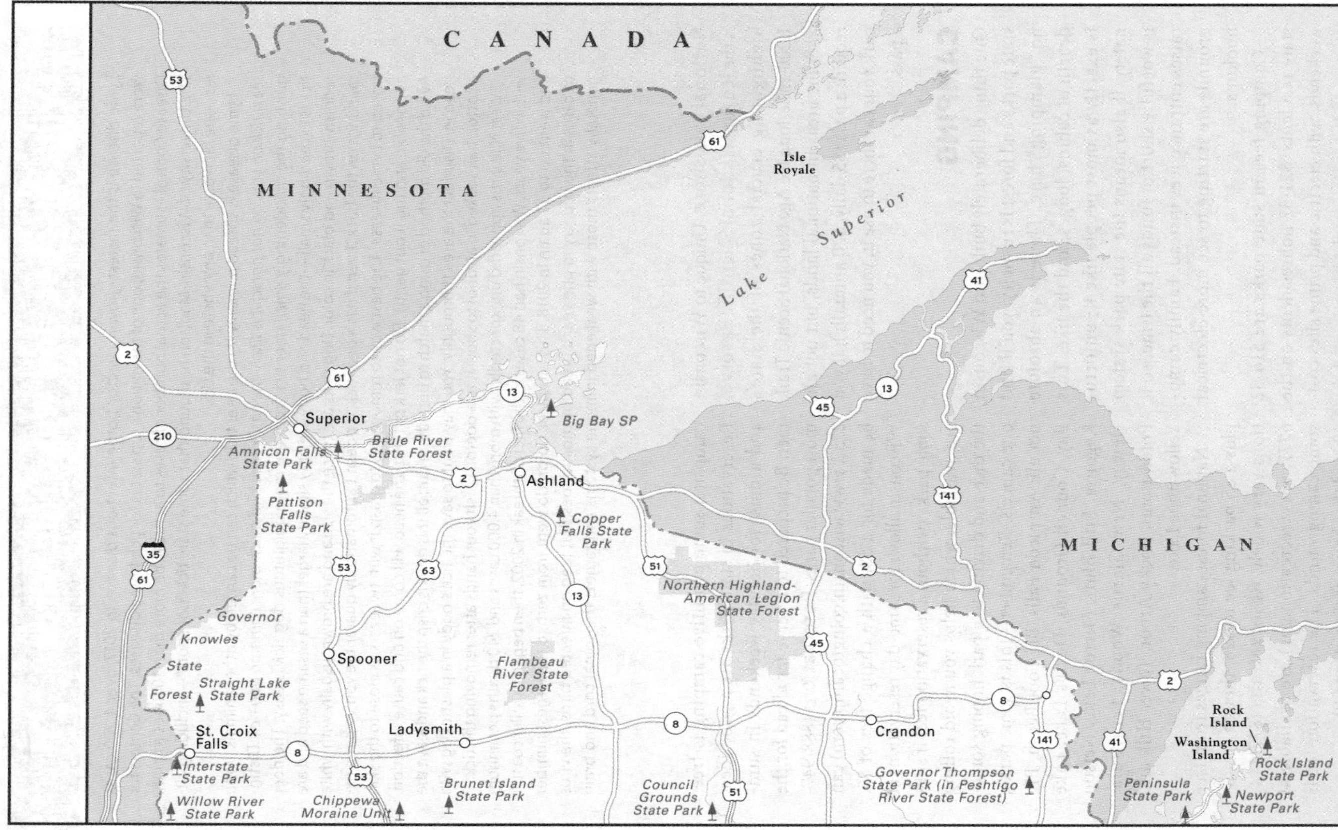
CANADA
MINNESOTA
Isle Royale
Lake Superior
MICHIGAN
Superior
Amnicon Falls State Park
Brule River State Forest
Pattison Falls State Park
Big Bay SP
Ashland
Copper Falls State Park
Northern Highland-American Legion State Forest
Governor Knowles State Forest
Straight Lake State Park
Spooner
Flambeau River State Forest
St. Croix Falls
Ladysmith
Crandon
Interstate State Park
Willow River State Park
Chippewa Moraine Unit
Brunet Island State Park
Council Grounds State Park
Governor Thompson State Park (in Peshtigo River State Forest)
Peninsula State Park
Rock Island
Washington Island
Rock Island State Park
Newport State Park
53
61
2
210
35
13
63
51
45
141
41
8

Lyme Disease and West Nile Virus

Lyme disease is the fastest-growing vector-borne infectious disease. In 2017, over 4.200 cases were reported in Wisconsin, one of the nation's top states for tick-borne diseases. The Centers for Disease Control estimates the actual number of cases to actually be more than 10 times as high. The University of Wisconsin-Madison has found that some state tick "hot spots"—including cities—are far worse than anywhere in the U.S.

Lyme disease is spread *primarily* by the deer tick, which can be carried by other animals. *If you see a tick on you, do not panic; it is likely the easily seen and much more common dog tick.* Distinguishing the maddeningly small deer tick from the more ubiquitous dog tick is easy. The deer tick is exceedingly small—the head and body are only slightly larger than a sesame seed and are reddish-brown and black in color. Dog ticks are twice the size and are brown, usually with white markings on the back. Even if it is a deer tick, it doesn't automatically guarantee you've been exposed to Lyme disease. The best way to remove it is to grasp it with tweezers as close to the skin as possible and tug it out gently. Do not jerk or twist; the head will come off and cause infection. Avoid the old method of using a match to burn them out; all this does is crisp the tick and leave the head in. Disinfect the area thoroughly. You may want to save the tick's body in a plastic bag with a cotton ball soaked in alcohol to show it to a doctor. Wash your hands after removing the tick.

West Nile virus appeared unexpectedly, with more than 4,000 cases and 240 deaths per annum within five years. Wisconsin had 48 cases in the first outbreak in 2002, then began to roller coaster and went up to 33 again in 2018. This is typical; Colorado went from zero to the largest number of cases in the country in one year. Spread by mosquitoes that feed on infected birds, the virus generally affects those with weakened immune systems and targets the spinal cord and brain

National Lakeshore. Unique to Wisconsin is the **Ice Age National Scientific Reserve,** highlighting crucial zones of the state's 1,200-mile-long Ice Age National Scenic Trail.

Some areas in national lands, but not all, require a pass ($5 daily, $20 annually); if you park your car there to use it, you need to have a pass.

CAMPING

One thing deliberately built into Wisconsin state parks and forest is rusticity; you'll find no "glamping" here. There is an absolute dearth of cabins, lodges, and the like. This is exactly as most people like it; unfortunately, it also means the state park system is woefully short of funds all the time, so it raises entrance fees instead. Family campgrounds are starting to see more electrical hookups.

Camping fees in state parks are $16-32 state residents, $21-37 nonresidents on the weekends, with electric and prime sites costing more, depending on the location and the campsite; some primitive camping is free. Reservations in state parks are a good idea, and a must for holiday weekends in summer. Be prepared to reserve far ahead for the most popular parks. **Reservations** (888/947-2757, www.wisconsin.goingtocamp.com) can be made for a $8, with a change fees of $5. Wisconsin allows for same-day reservations at *some* parks (without a reservation fee) if sites are available, which helps you avoid rolling the dice and driving to a park hoping someone cancels. Remember—this is some parks, not all: Amnicon Falls, Big Foot Beach, Big Bay, Council Grounds, Devil's Lake, Lake Kegonsa, Mill Bluff, Mirror Lake, Nelson Dewey, New Glarus Woods, Peninsula, Potawatomi, Rocky Arbor, Tower Hill, and Yellowstone Lake.

National forest camping ranges from free plus a $5 parking fee to $28, though conditions vary widely. **Reservations** (877/444-6777, www.recreation.gov) are available at some campgrounds. The reservation fee is $8, and the change fee is a steep $10.

membranes, causing encephalitic symptoms. The virus is not transmitted by person-to-person contact. No vaccine exists.

PREVENTION

Lyme disease is highly preventable. Deer ticks are active year-round, so you always have to be wary. Deer ticks cannot fly or jump; they cling to vegetation and attach themselves to objects pushing past. Always wear light-colored clothing, long sleeves, and long pants, and tuck the cuffs into your boots. A hat is always a good idea. Walk in the center of trails and avoid branches and grasses whenever possible. Check your skin and that of others thoroughly, paying particular attention to the hair. Children are always candidates for tick attachment. Check everybody every 24 hours, even if you haven't been in the deep woods. Studies have indicated that the deer tick must be attached to your skin for 24 to 72 hours before the bacterium is spread. Pet owners beware: Domestic animals can develop Lyme disease, so check them as well.

West Nile virus is spread by common mosquitoes, so it's imperative you don't walk around at night in shorts and flip-flops without insect repellent. People swear by insect repellents containing DEET, but DEET is toxic, and long exposure may damage your nervous system. If you use DEET, buy it in concentrations of no higher than 20 percent for kids, 30 percent for adults. Do your research on natural repellents; they've never worked for me, but they have been improving and many hard-core DEET users have switched.

In 2019 the University of Wisconsin released a tick app (iOS devices only for the moment); it may be a good idea. It has a quick tick ID system as well as surveys to report all pertinent data for research.

BIKING

Bicycling magazine rates Wisconsin one of the top three states for cyclists. The League of American Bicyclists says Wisconsin is tops in the Midwest and second in the United States for its quality and diversity of biking. Madison is second only to Seattle among the nation's most bike-friendly cities. The **Elroy-Sparta State Recreational Trail** was the country's first rail-to-trail system and is regarded as the progenitor of all multipurpose state recreational trails, and the **Chequamegon Area Mountain Bike Association** (CAMBA) trail system is among the most respected outside Colorado and Utah. All this, combined with the immense concatenate labyrinth of rural farm-to-market roads, makes it obvious why Wisconsinites leave bike racks on their cars year-round. In total, the state maintains more than 10,000 miles of established, mapped, and recommended bike routes.

Since the completion of the Elroy-Sparta State Recreational Trail, the state has added 41 other railbeds, logging roads, and state park trails to its **State Trail System,** for a total of nearly 1,700 miles. It's impossible to keep up with how many more miles are added annually, since cities and counties are establishing their own networks to link with state trails. **Trail passes** ($5 daily, $25 annually) are required for all cyclists over age 15.

HIKING

With more than two million acres of state and federal land open for public use, along with 34 state recreation trails, hiking opportunities are endless. Two trails of interest to serious backpackers are the **Ice Age National Scenic Trail** and the **North Country National Scenic Trail.** The ultimate goal is to link Wisconsin's network of 42 rails-to-trails via city-county-state plans. This would double the state's trail mileage.

FISHING

Given that Wisconsin has more than 16,000 lakes, 27,000 miles of fishable river and stream, and more than 1,000 miles of Lake Superior, Lake Michigan, and Mississippi River coastline, and that most of the state's 135 native species of fish are fair game, it's no surprise that the number-one activity is angling. Wisconsin ranks in the top five states nationwide for the number of fishing licenses dispensed and is first in number of nonresident licenses sold annually. Most of the North Woods resorts cater to muskie anglers and tagalong families. Boulder Junction and Hayward both claim to be the Muskie Capital of the World. Though the **muskellunge** is revered as king of the waters, in sheer numbers the most popular sport fish is the **walleye.** Wisconsin's only native stream trout is the **brook trout,** closely related to the lake trout. Good news: hundreds of blue-ribbon streams are chock-full of them.

Great Lakes fishing has grown to become an enormous industry, with entire fleets devoted to working the well-stocked waters. Not all the fish in the Great Lakes are native species. Much of the restocking took place in response to early-century overfishing and the decline of fish stocks due to exotic species. In terms of fish taken per angler hour, Kenosha, Racine, and the Kewaunee-Algoma area rate extremely highly. The entire Door Peninsula is also hugely popular. In all, the state Department of Natural Resources stocks more than 2.1 million **coho** and **chinook salmon,** 1 million **lake trout,** and 2 million brook, **brown,** and **steelhead trout.** Invasive species like the zebra mussel suck up much of the food in the lake, leading average salmon weights, for example, to drop from nearly 20 pounds at the turn of the millennium to less than 14 pounds presently.

A time-honored tradition of Wisconsin winters is driving the truck out on a frozen lake to a village of shanties erected over holes drilled in the ice, sitting on an overturned five-gallon pail, stamping your feet quite a bit, and drinking a lot of schnapps. **Ice fishing** is serious business: Up to two million angler-days are spent on the ice each year, and ice

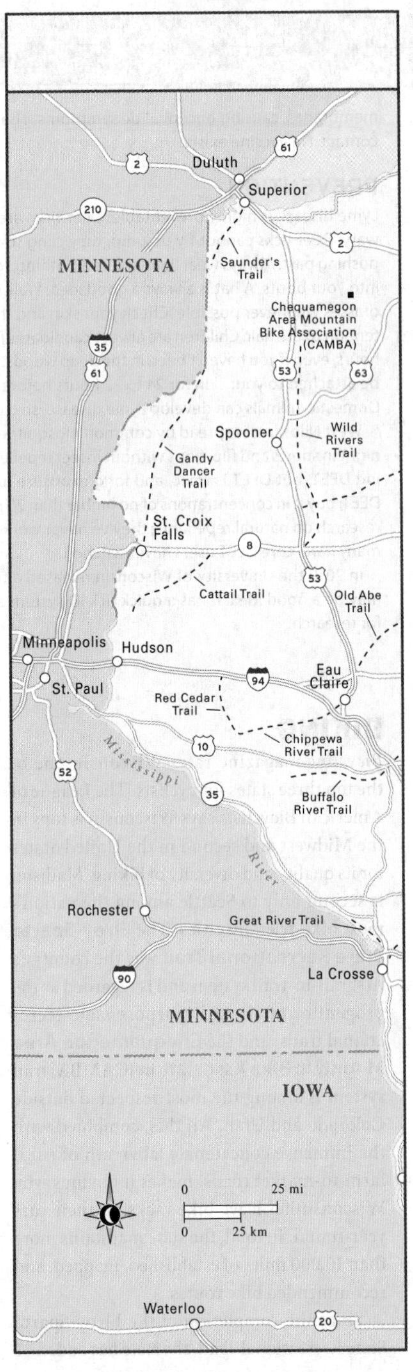

Badger State Recreation Trails

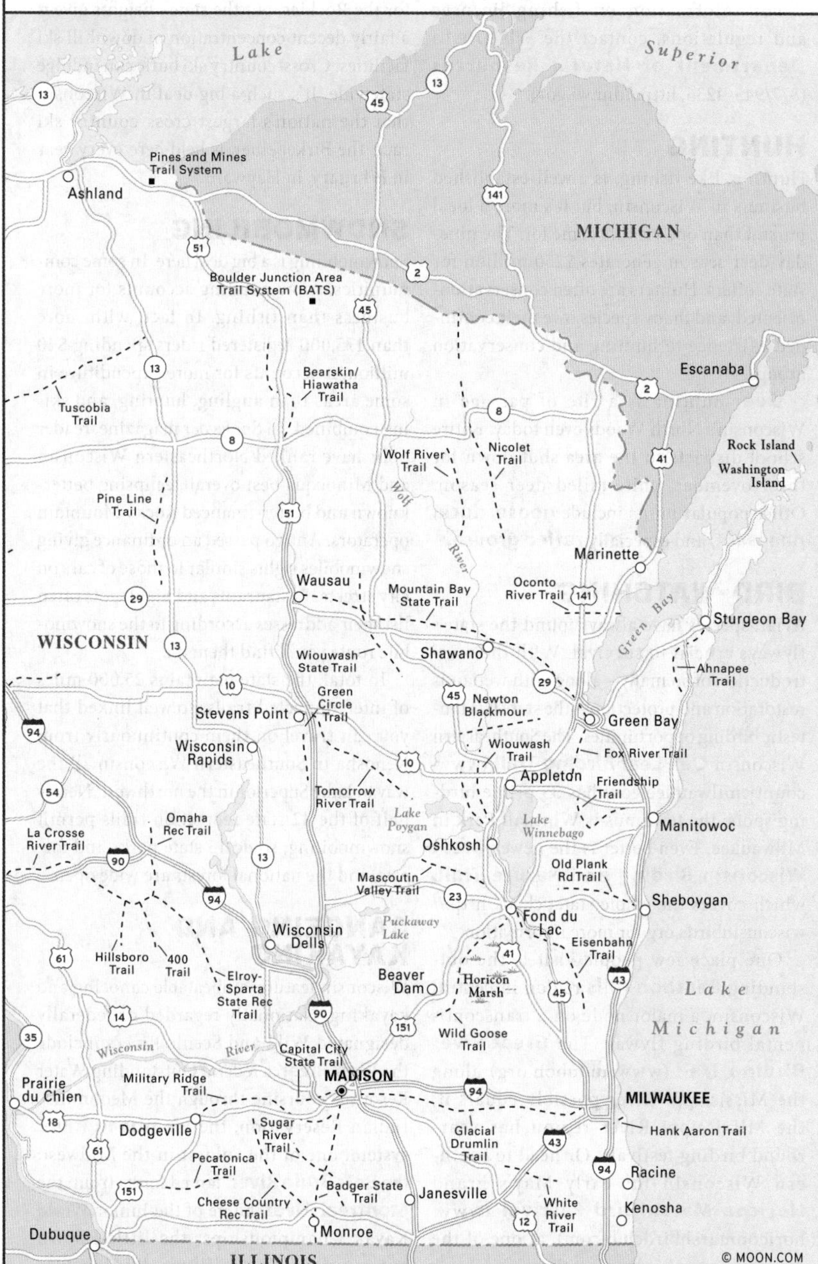

fishing accounts for up to one-fifth of the state's annual catch.

For information on fishing licenses and regulations, contact the **Wisconsin Department of Natural Resources** (877/945-4236, http://dnr.wi.gov).

HUNTING

Hunting, like fishing, is a well-established business in Wisconsin, but it's more a local pursuit than one visitors come for. The nine-day deer season generates $250 million for state coffers. Hunters are often conservation-oriented, and many species owe their continued existence to hunting and conservation groups.

Deer hunting is a rite of passage in Wisconsin's North Woods even today. Entire school districts in the area shut down for the November white-tailed deer season. Other popular hunts include **goose, duck, pheasant,** and especially **ruffed grouse.**

BIRD-WATCHING

Avian species have always found the state's flyways crucial to survival. With the reintroduction of so many—along with wetlands restoration and protection—the state has fantastic birding opportunities. The Southeastern Wisconsin **Oak Leaf Birding Trail** (www.county.milwaukee.gov) has 35 prime birding spots; the terminus is Whitnall Park in Milwaukee. Even better is the newer **Great Wisconsin Birding and Nature Trail,** which covers the whole state; check http://wisconsinbirds.org for more information.

One place few people visit is the outstanding **Baraboo Hills** region in central Wisconsin, a major node on a transcontinental birding flyway. The **Great River Birding Trail** (www.audubon.org) along the Mississippi River possibly equals it; the Mississippi River region has year-round birding festivals. Or head to southern Wisconsin for early May's grand **Horicon Marsh Bird Festival** (www.horiconmarshbirdclub.com), at one of the country's great birding locations.

SKIING

Wisconsin mountains will never be mistaken for the Rockies, but the state's heights give it a fairly decent concentration of downhill ski facilities. Cross-country ski buffs can indulge statewide. It's such a big deal in Wisconsin that the nation's largest cross-country ski race, the Birkebeiner, is held here every year in February, in Hayward.

SNOWMOBILING

Snowmobiling is a big deal here. In some communities, snowmobiling accounts for more business than fishing. In fact, with more than 175,000 registered riders spending $40 million, it accounts for more expenditure in some areas than angling, hunting, and skiing combined. In *Snowgoer* magazine, reader polls have ranked Northeastern Wisconsin and Minocqua best overall, eclipsing better-known and better-financed Rocky Mountain operators. Antigo passed an ordinance giving snowmobiles rights similar to those of cars on city streets. Restaurants and nightspots often list their addresses according to the snowmobile route you'll find them on.

In total, the state maintains 25,000 miles of interconnected trails, so well linked that you can travel on them continuously from Kenosha in Southeastern Wisconsin all the way to Lake Superior in the northwest. Nearly half of the 42 state recreation trails permit snowmobiling; so do 15 state parks and forests, and the national forests are wide open.

CANOEING AND KAYAKING

Wisconsin features unbeatable canoeing and kayaking. Nationally regarded or federally designated Wild and Scenic Rivers include the **Wolf River,** a federal Outstanding Water Resource coursing through the Menominee Indian Reservation; the **Flambeau River** system, one of the wildest in the Midwest; the **Bois Brule River,** famed for its trout; the **Montreal River,** home of the Junior World Kayak Championships; the little-known but exquisite **Turtle River,** leading into

Wisconsin's Turtle-Flambeau Flowage in the most unspoiled section of the state; the **Pine** and **Popple Rivers** in the Nicolet National Forest; the wild **Peshtigo River;** the lazy classic **Lower Wisconsin State Riverway;** the **La Crosse River;** the **Kickapoo River** (the "crookedest in the world"); the **Yahara River,** one reason *Canoeist* magazine calls Madison a canoeing mecca; and perhaps the most popular, the **Manitowish River,** in the Northern Highland American Legion State Forest, in one of the planet's densest concentrations of lakes.

The **Namekagon-St. Croix National Scenic Riverway** stretches west from northeast of Cable, joins the St. Croix River and its scenic geology, and eventually flows to the confluence with the Mississippi River. Kayakers enjoy the superb **Apostle Islands National Lakeshore** along Lake Superior and, to a lesser extent, the magnificence of Door County on the Lake Michigan side.

GOLF

Believe it or not, forlorn, wintry Wisconsin has one of the nation's highest concentrations of golf courses per capita. Nearly 430 courses are listed in the state's *Wisconsin Golf Guide.* Among the courses most often pursued are **Blackwolf Run** in Kohler, **Lawsonia** in Green Lake, **Sentryworld** in Stevens Point, **University Ridge** in Madison, and **Brown Deer Golf Course** near Milwaukee.

Information and Services

WHAT TO PACK

You can buy anything you need in the state, even in the village outposts of the North Woods (not including computer parts), but one thing you don't want to be caught without is **mosquito repellent.** A face net for blackflies and mosquitoes is a good idea if you plan on going into the woods or camping.

Wisconsin is a place where most consider L. L. Bean dressy clothing. Heels, ties, and fancy skirts are fine for clubbing in Milwaukee or Madison—although even in these places it's not necessary—but you'll be conspicuous in all but the most chichi restaurants anywhere else A sweatshirt is perfectly fine even in the most famous supper clubs.

Weather is often the deciding factor. Dress appropriately for it at all times—that includes wearing a hat. Do not come to Wisconsin in winter without a good pair of **gloves or mittens.** Arctic-worthy mittens are something you'll be grateful for on a sleigh ride or while you await a tow truck. A good pair of **boots** is also a necessity; some people carry a heavy-duty pair in the car at all times in case of an emergency.

Given the state's variable weather, it's paramount to prepare your car for any possibility by **winterizing your vehicle.** Carry an emergency kit with booster cables, sand or gravel (in a pinch, try sandpaper strips or kitty litter), flares, candles, matches, a shovel and scraper, a flashlight and extra batteries, blankets (space blankets are excellent), extra heavy clothing, high-calorie nonperishable food, and anything else you might need if you have to spend the night in a snowbank. I cannot emphasize how important it is if you have to spend a winter night in the car.

INFORMATION

For information on anything and everything in the state, contact the **Wisconsin Department of Tourism** (800/432-8747, www.travelwisconsin.com), which has a decent website and offers fantastic printed guides.

Media

The only publication that covers Wisconsin on a wide scale travel-wise is the travel section of the newspaper *Milwaukee Journal*

Sentinel (www.jsonline.com). *Midwest Living* magazine (www.midwestliving.com), another monthly, features Wisconsin regularly. More for the conservation-minded, ***Wisconsin Natural Resources*** (www.wnrmag.com) is published by the state Department of Natural Resources. The well-put-together periodical features detailed natural history and is very well written and photographed.

The ***Journal Sentinel*** (www.jsonline.com), the largest of Wisconsin's newspapers, is a daily morning paper out of Milwaukee. Madison has two traditional papers (www.host.madison.com): the conservative morning ***Wisconsin State Journal*** and the more liberal weekly ***Capital Times.***

LGBT Resources

Madison has a large, active gay community. One great resource is **OutReach** (www.lgbtoutreach.org) along with **Our Lives** (www.ourlivesmadison.com). Milwaukee's **LGBT Community Center** (www.mkelgbt.org) can also help.

MAPS

You can get a decent Department of Transportation state road map free by calling the state Department of Tourism hotline (800/432-8747, www.travelwisconsin.com). The best maps for snooping around the state are those contained in the ***Wisconsin Atlas and Gazetteer,*** available from any outdoors store or direct from the DeLorme Publishing Company (www.garmin.com). On a somewhat smaller scale than topo maps, the maps in this 100-page, large-format book are absolutely indispensable for exploring the back roads.

MONEY

Wisconsinites are highly taxed, but in general travelers don't have to share the burden; the state doesn't even have toll roads. Prices in general are lower in Wisconsin than in the rest of the country, and gasoline is usually cheaper than anywhere else in the Midwest except Iowa. Once you get out into rural areas, prices for goods and services are absolutely cheap. Wisconsin's sales tax is 5 percent. Some counties and cities tack on an additional 0.5 percent. There are also additional hotel room taxes.

Exchanging foreign currency can be problematic. Banks in Madison and Milwaukee will often have just one branch that deals with money-changing. In smaller cities, such as Green Bay, La Crosse, and Appleton, it is advisable to arrive with U.S. currency.

Travel Green in Wisconsin

In 2007, in a U.S. first, Wisconsin launched its **Travel Green** (www.travelgreenwisconsin.com) program, designed to highlight businesses, lodgings, and attractions for their efforts to reduce the environmental impact of tourism and to highlight the fact that this can be done. Find hybrid car rentals, restaurants that follow sustainability protocols, and more.

COMMUNICATIONS

Telephone

Wisconsin has six area codes, and it may soon have seven. Milwaukee, along with most of Southeastern Wisconsin, is covered by the 414 area code. Areas immediately outside of Milwaukee are 262. Madison and the southwestern and south-central regions have the 608 area code, and most of the northwest has area codes 715 and 534. All else is area code 920.

TIME ZONE

All of Wisconsin is on central time (CT), which is six hours earlier than Greenwich mean time. Wisconsin observes daylight saving time from March to November. Driving into Michigan, the counties bordering Wisconsin are also on central time, but most of the Upper Peninsula is in the eastern time zone, one hour later than central time.

Resources

Suggested Reading

If you're in Madison, head to the State Historical Society Museum, whose gift shop bookstore has better holdings than the library.

CUISINE

More and more cookbooks detail Midwestern cuisine. Most bookstores will have great selections on regional cooking.

Allen, Terese, and Harva Hachten. *The Flavor of Wisconsin.* Madison: State Historical Society of Wisconsin, 2009. A dense volume cataloging all the ethnic groups of the state and their contributions to cuisine. Terese Allen is one of Wisconsin's most noted food writers, so look for her name; she updated Harva Hachten's legendary book.

Apps, Jerry. *Breweries of Wisconsin.* Madison: University of Wisconsin Press, 2004. This amazing book came out and surprised everyone. It's a thorough examination of the culture of beer in Wisconsin as had never been done before. It's not just a guidebook, but a cultural journey. Apps has written other great Wisconsin books.

Boyer, D. *Great Wisconsin Taverns.* Black Earth, WI: Trails Book Guides, 2002. The author is a professional folklorist and storyteller.

Draeger, J., and M. Speltz. *Bottoms Up.* Madison: Wisconsin Historical Society Press, 2012. Two Badgers take a loving tour of

rustic roadside in Ellison Bay

traditional taverns around Wisconsin; the photos alone are worth the price, as are the stories within.

Faiola, Ron. *Wisconsin Supper Clubs: An Old-Fashioned Experience.* Chicago, IL. Agate Publishing, 2004. Never have I read a book that nailed the topic so dear to a Badgers' heart as this book does.

Revolinski, Kevin. *Wisconsin's Best Beer Guide.* Holt, MI: Thunder Bay Press, 2010. It's informative but also fun, from the kind of guy you'd like to have in the shotgun seat on a long trip.

DESCRIPTION AND TRAVEL

Lyons, John J., ed. *Wisconsin. A Guide to the Badger State.* American Guide Series, Work Projects Administration, 1941. From the mother of all guidebook series, the Wisconsin edition, nearly seven decades old, is still the standard for anyone interested in the history, natural history, and culture of the state.

Ostergren, Robert C., and Thomas R. Vale, eds. *Wisconsin Land and Life.* Madison: University of Wisconsin Press, 1997. This amazing, heavy, but eminently readable book may be the most perfect synthesis of natural history and cultural geography.

FOLKLORE

Leary, J. *Wisconsin Folklore.* Madison: University of Wisconsin Press, 1998. Linguistics, storytelling, music, song, dance, folk crafts, and material traditions. The chapter on Milwaukeeisms is worth the price of the book. Even the Smithsonian has recognized the uniqueness of this work.

HISTORY

McAnn, D. *The Wisconsin Story: 150 Years, 150 Stories.* Milwaukee: *Milwaukee Journal Sentinel,* 1998. Most articles are about historical minutiae most folks have never heard about but are fascinating addenda to general history. It's engaging and a good bet for an easy vacation read.

Nesbit, Robert. *Wisconsin: A History.* Madison: University of Wisconsin Press, 1989. A standard reading of the state's history.

Old World Wisconsin

LITERATURE

Boudreau, Richard, ed. *The Literary Heritage of Wisconsin: An Anthology of Wisconsin Literature from Beginnings to 1925.* La Crosse, WI: Juniper Press, 1986. This is a condensed version of the state's literary canon.

Perry, Michael. *Population: 485.* New York: Harper Perennial, 2002; *Truck: A Love Story.* New York: Harper Perennial, 2006; and *Coop.* New York: HarperCollins, 2009. Wisconsin has had a few luminaries of literature—Jane Hamilton, Kelly Cherry, Lorrie Moore—but Perry describes small-town Wisconsin in a wonderfully low-key, hilarious way.

Stephens, Jim, ed. *The Journey Home: The Literature of Wisconsin through Four Centuries.* Madison: North Country Press, 1989. A remarkable multivolume set of Wisconsin literature, tracing back as far as the trickster cycles of the first inhabitants.

NATURAL HISTORY

Martin, Lawrence. *The Physical Geography of Wisconsin.* Madison: University of Wisconsin Press, 1965. The granddaddy of all Wisconsin geography books, first published in 1916 and updated in subsequent editions.

Reuss, Henry S. *On the Trail of the Ice Age.* Sheboygan, WI: Ice Age Park and Trail Foundation, 1990. A good compendium of the oddball geology of the state and the effort to establish the Ice Age National Scenic Trail.

OUTDOORS AND ENVIRONMENT

Leopold, Aldo. *A Sand County Almanac.* New York: Oxford University Press, 1949. A must-read for anyone who is attuned to the land. Also an education for those who think Wisconsin is a vast nothingness.

Olson, Sigurd. *Collected Works of Sigurd Olson.* Stillwater, MN: 1990. Wisconsin's seminal ecologist along with Aldo Leopold, Olson had as much influence as his more famous contemporary. This excellent overview of his life's work shows an incredible depth of ecological awareness in an approachable format for a layperson.

PEOPLE

The state historical society has produced brief booklets profiling every immigrant group in Wisconsin. They're available from the State Historical Society Museum in Madison.

Bieder, Robert E. *Native American Communities in Wisconsin, 1600-1960.* Madison: University of Wisconsin Press, 1995. The first and, really, only comprehensive in-depth look at Native Americans in the state.

Maxwell, R. S. *La Follette and the Rise of the Progressives in Wisconsin.* Madison: State Historical Society, 1956. A fine account of Robert La Follette, the much-beloved Progressive Party politician of the late 1800s and early 1900s.

McBride, G. *On Wisconsin Women.* Madison: University of Wisconsin Press, 1993. An excellent book and one of few sources about many of the important women in the state's history.

Meine, C. *Aldo Leopold: His Life and Work.* Madison: University of Wisconsin Press, 1988. The best book on ecologist Aldo Leopold.

Internet Resources

ACCOMMODATIONS

Wisconsin Bed-and-Breakfast Association

www.wbba.org

This association has a reputation for having one of the more stringent membership policies, even offering help for those interested in starting a B&B from the ground up; thus, you can trust their referrals.

Wisconsin Lodging

www.wisconsinlodging.org

Visit this site to view photos and information of lodging options around the state.

ARTS AND CULTURE

Portal Wisconsin

www.portalwisconsin.org

A fantastic resource for all visual and performance arts in the state.

FOOD

Farm Fresh Atlas

www.farmfreshatlas.org

Find out where you can purchase and eat Wisconsin-sourced products.

Wisconsin Agricultural Marketing Board

www.eatwisconsincheese.com

This is a great place to find resources on seeing, tasting, and buying cheese or dairy products.

Wisconsin Public Television

www.wpt.org

Click on "Wisconsin Foodie" and enjoy the episodes about the state's cuisine, past and present.

HISTORY

State Historical Society of Wisconsin

www.wisconsinhistory.org

This is the best starting place for state history.

RECREATION

Wisconsin Bicycling Federation

www.bfw.org

An educational and advocacy group working strenuously for cyclist rights, more trails, and bike lanes in the cities. They have excellent cycling maps for sale.

STATE PARKS

Wisconsin Department of Natural Resources

https://dnr.wi.gov

A good resource from the Department of Natural Resources; it also covers state trails.

TRANSPORTATION AND ROAD TRIPS

Wisconsin Department of Transportation

www.wisconsindot.gov

The state's Department of Transportation website has all the necessary information on construction, road conditions, and more. Check out its "Rustic Roads" section for fantastic country drives.

TRAVEL

Travel Wisconsin

www.travelwisconsin.com

From the state's Department of Tourism, it's very useful and worth a look.

Wisconsin Association of Convention and Visitors Bureaus (WACVB)

www.escapetowisconsin.com

A good starting point for local information sources.

Index

C

D

E

F

I

J

K

L

M

N

O

P

QR

S

T

U

V

WXYZ

INDEX

List of Maps

Photo Credits

All photos by Thomas Huhti except: page 12 © (bottom) Jhansen2, Dreamstime.com; page 13 © Kristen Prahl, Dreamstime.com; page 15 © (top) Jim Roberts, Dreamstime.com; (bottom) Walter Arce, Dreamstime.com; page 16 © (top) Travel Wisconsin; (bottom) Jacob Boomsma, Dreamstime.com; page 31 © Travel Wisconsin; page 32 © Anthony Aneese Totah Jr., Dreamstime.com; page 43 © Rhbabiak13, Dreamstime.com; page 97 © (bottom) Rhbabiak13, Dreamstime.com; page 255 © Jeffrey Holcombe, Dreamstime.com; page 286 © Randall Pease, Dreamstime.com; page 354 © Brian Kushner, Dreamstime.com; page 358 © Rhbabiak13, Dreamstime.com; page 367 © (bottom) Jhansen2, Dreamstime.com; page 388 © Baluzek, Dreamstime.com; page 401 © (top) Lorraine Swanson, Dreamstime.com; (bottom) Jacob Boomsma, Dreamstime.com; page 410 © (top right) Rhbabiak13, Dreamstime.com

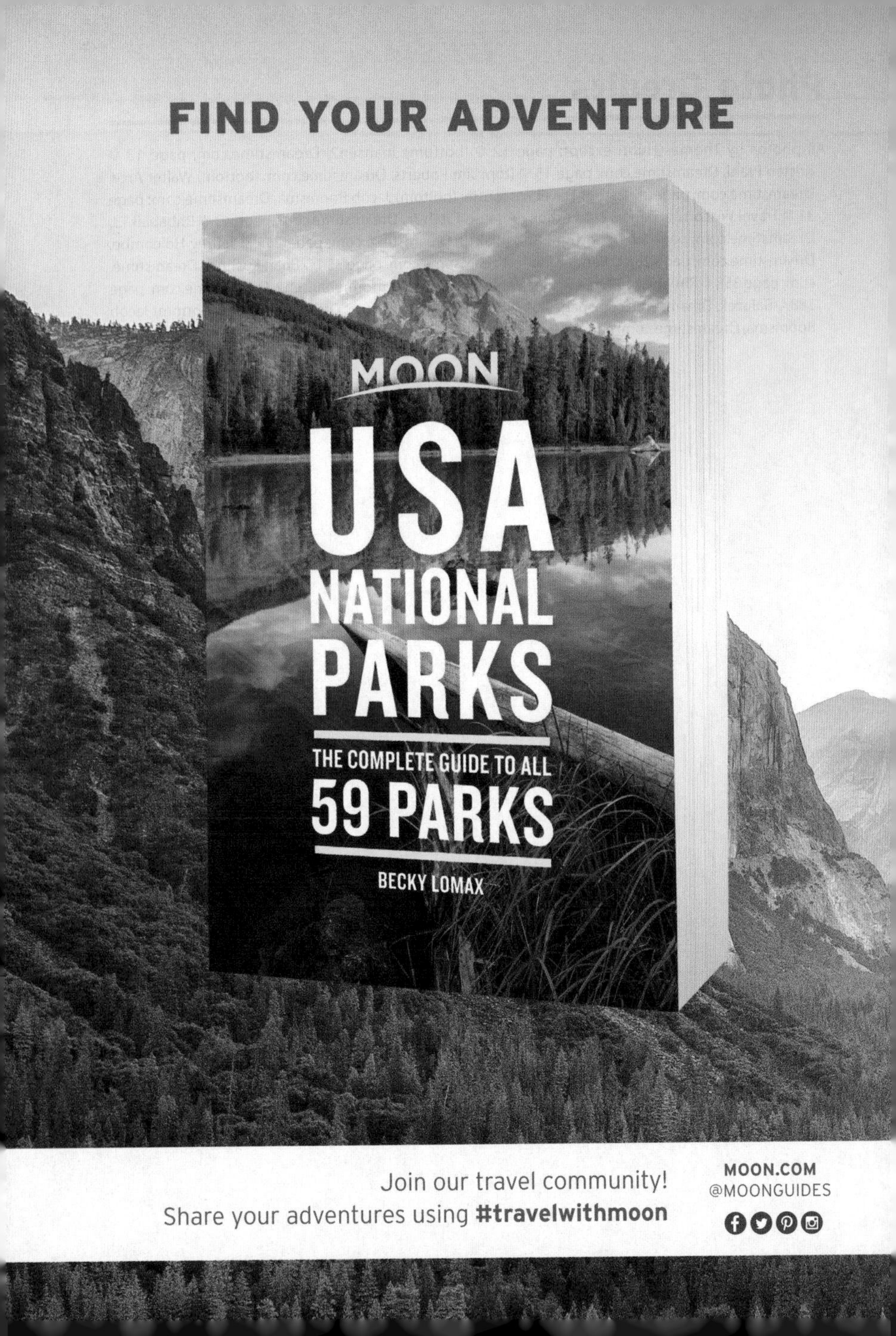
FIND YOUR ADVENTURE
MOON
USA NATIONAL PARKS
THE COMPLETE GUIDE TO ALL
59 PARKS
BECKY LOMAX
Join our travel community!
Share your adventures using #travelwithmoon
MOON.COM
@MOONGUIDES

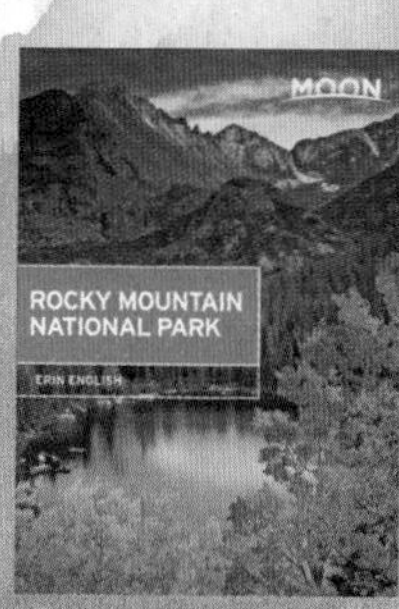

In these books:

- Full coverage of gateway cities and towns
- Itineraries from one day to multiple weeks
- Advice on where to stay (or camp) in and around the parks

MOON
ROUTE 66
Road Trip
JESSICA DUNHAM
MOON
SOUTHWEST
Road Trip
LAS VEGAS, ZION & BRYCE, MONUMENT VALLEY, SANTA FE & TAOS, AND THE GRAND CANYON
TIM HULL

MOON
SOUTH FLORIDA & THE KEYS
Road Trip
WITH MIAMI, WALT DISNEY WORLD, TAMPA & THE EVERGLADES
JASON FERGUSON
MOON
VANCOUVER & CANADIAN ROCKIES
Road Trip
VICTORIA, BANFF, JASPER, CALGARY, THE OKANAGAN, WHISTLER & THE SEA-TO-SKY HIGHWAY
CAROLYN B. HELLER

MOON
SOUTHERN CALIFORNIA
Road Trips
DRIVES ALONG THE BEACHES, MOUNTAINS, AND DESERTS WITH THE BEST STOPS ALONG THE WAY
IAN ANDERSON
MOON
YELLOWSTONE TO GLACIER NATIONAL PARK
Road Trip
JACKSON HOLE, CODY, THE GRAND TETONS & THE ROCKY MOUNTAIN FRONT
CARTER G. WALKER

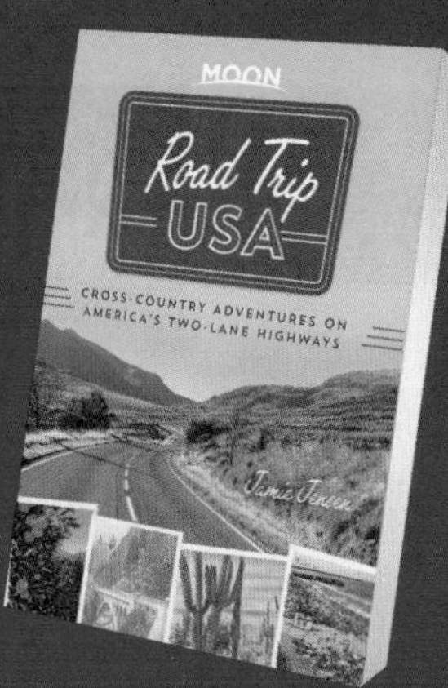
MOON
Road Trip USA
CROSS-COUNTRY ADVENTURES ON AMERICA'S TWO-LANE HIGHWAYS
Jamie Jensen

MAP SYMBOLS

- Expressway
- Primary Road
- Secondary Road
- Unpaved Road
- Feature Trail
- Other Trail
- Ferry
- Pedestrian Walkway
- Stairs

- ○ City/Town
- ◉ State Capital
- ⊛ National Capital
- ★ Point of Interest
- • Accommodation
- ▼ Restaurant/Bar
- ■ Other Location
- Λ Campground

- Airport
- Airfield
- ▲ Mountain
- ✦ Unique Natural Feature
- Waterfall
- Park
- Trailhead
- Skiing Area

- Golf Course
- Parking Area
- Archaeological Site
- Church
- Gas Station
- Glacier
- Mangrove
- Reef
- Swamp

CONVERSION TABLES

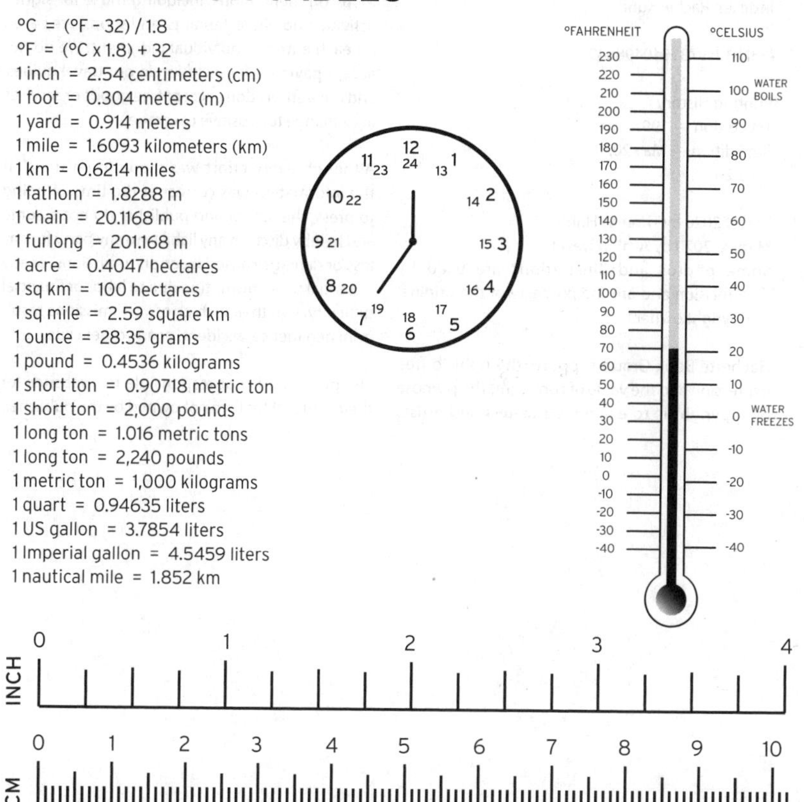

°C = (°F - 32) / 1.8
°F = (°C x 1.8) + 32
1 inch = 2.54 centimeters (cm)
1 foot = 0.304 meters (m)
1 yard = 0.914 meters
1 mile = 1.6093 kilometers (km)
1 km = 0.6214 miles
1 fathom = 1.8288 m
1 chain = 20.1168 m
1 furlong = 201.168 m
1 acre = 0.4047 hectares
1 sq km = 100 hectares
1 sq mile = 2.59 square km
1 ounce = 28.35 grams
1 pound = 0.4536 kilograms
1 short ton = 0.90718 metric ton
1 short ton = 2,000 pounds
1 long ton = 1.016 metric tons
1 long ton = 2,240 pounds
1 metric ton = 1,000 kilograms
1 quart = 0.94635 liters
1 US gallon = 3.7854 liters
1 Imperial gallon = 4.5459 liters
1 nautical mile = 1.852 km

MOON WISCONSIN
Avalon Travel
Hachette Book Group
1700 Fourth Street
Berkeley, CA 94710, USA
www.moon.com

Editor: Rachael Sablik
Acquiring Editor: Nikki Ioakimedes
Series Manager: Kathryn Ettinger
Copy Editor: Ashley Benning
Graphics Coordinator: Scott Kimball
Production Coordinator: Scott Kimball
Cover Design: Chaseout Studios, Charles Brock
Interior Design: Domino Dragoone
Moon Logo: Tim McGrath
Map Editor: Kat Bennet
Cartographers: Karin Dahl, Andrew Dolan
Proofreader: Samia Abbasi
Indexer: Rachel Kuhn

ISBN-13: 9781640498549

Printing History
1st Edition — 1997
8th Edition — May 2020
5 4 3 2 1

Front cover photo: © Kenneth Keifer | Shutterstock
Back cover photo: © Thomas Huhti

Printed in China by RR Donnelley.

All recommendations, including those for sights, activities, hotels, restaurants, and shops, are based on each author's individual judgment. We do not accept payment for inclusion in our travel guides, and our authors don't accept free goods or services in exchange for positive coverage.